PARALLEL SCIENTIFIC COMPUTATION

Parallel Scientific Computation

A Structured Approach Using BSP

SECOND EDITION

ROB H. BISSELING

Utrecht University

OXFORD
UNIVERSITY PRESS

OXFORD
UNIVERSITY PRESS

Great Clarendon Street, Oxford, OX2 6DP,
United Kingdom

Oxford University Press is a department of the University of Oxford.
It furthers the University's objective of excellence in research, scholarship,
and education by publishing worldwide. Oxford is a registered trade mark of
Oxford University Press in the UK and in certain other countries

First Edition published in 2004

Impression: 1

Published in the United States of America by Oxford University Press
198 Madison Avenue, New York, NY 10016, United States of America

British Library Cataloguing in Publication Data
Data available

Library of Congress Control Number: 2020932793

ISBN 978–0–19–878834–8 (hbk.)
ISBN 978–0–19–878835–5 (pbk.)

DOI: 10.1093/oso/9780198788348.001.0001

Printed and bound by
CPI Group (UK) Ltd, Croydon, CR0 4YY

PREFACE

Why this book on parallel scientific computation? The first edition of this book appeared in 2004, and the time was ripe for learning how to design and analyse portable parallel algorithms and to write portable parallel programs. Parallel computing became a lot easier and there was no need anymore to suffer from highly esoteric hardware or software systems. The second edition is motivated by the multicore revolution that took place around 2007. Suddenly, CPU clock speeds stopped increasing and, after a while, we found our laptop and desktop computers equipped with several processor cores. Great news for parallelism: parallel computers are everywhere. My yearly poll of the students in my parallel algorithms class reveals: the best equipped student has 12 cores in his personal computer (class of 2018). This is an opportunity for teaching, since students can now run parallel programs on their own computer, and I exploit this in the second edition. At the other end of the spectrum, massively parallel supercomputers now reach up to millions of cores.

The continuing growth in computing power due to increased parallelism and the availability of huge amounts of data has led to the emergence of Big Data as a new application area. Often, the data is irregular and possesses a network structure, which is mathematically modelled by a graph. This motivated the inclusion of a whole new chapter on graph matching in the second edition.

Today's state of affairs in parallel programming is that one can theoretically develop a parallel algorithm, analyse its performance on various architectures, implement the algorithm, and run the resulting program with high and predictable efficiency on a shared-memory personal computer or departmental compute server. Unfortunately, to run the same program efficiently on a massively parallel computer, with both shared and distributed memory, requires a lot more work these days. Programmers often employ two systems such as MPI+X, where X stands for either OpenMP or POSIX threads, or even three systems such as MPI+X+Y, where Y could be CUDA or OpenCL, in case graphics processing units (GPUs) are involved as well. Often, these systems themselves are large and unwieldy. This complicates matters, and our aim in this book is to simplify parallel programming again, by providing a single system that unifies the shared and distributed memory systems. With this book, I hope to convince you that parallel programming is not much harder than sequential programming and need not be left only to the experts. GPUs are outside the scope of this book, as their architecture is very specific and hard to capture in a single system together with the other two types of parallelism. Still, many lessons learned from this book directly apply to GPUs and other manycore accelerators.

Improvements in parallel hardware and software, together with major advances in the theory of parallel programming led to the first edition of this book. An important theoretical development was the advent of the Bulk Synchronous Parallel (BSP) programming model proposed by Valiant in 1989 [289, 290], which provides a useful and elegant theoretical framework for bridging the gap between parallel hardware and software. For this reason, I have adopted the BSP model as the target model for my parallel algorithms. In my experience, the simplicity of the BSP model makes it suitable for teaching parallel algorithms: the model itself is easy to explain and it provides a powerful tool for expressing and analysing algorithms.

For massively parallel supercomputers with $p = 10^6$ processors (i.e., cores), the total number p^2 of interacting processor pairs becomes huge and as a consequence we may have to rethink our algorithms to make them scalable up to such high values of p. To address this scalability problem, we need to model the architecture as a hierarchy consisting of many nodes, each with many cores. Our approach is to use a flat BSP model as the basis of this book, but to extend it by an additional level, where needed, to represent a hybrid abstract architecture with two levels, consisting of nodes and cores. This approach is simple enough to still benefit from the flat BSP model, but realistic enough also in postrevolutionary times. Modelling a thousand nodes, each with a thousand cores, in a two-level model, is far more realistic than modelling one million processors in a single-level model. For this purpose, hierarchical variants of the BSP model have emerged, including multi-BSP [292] by Valiant himself, decomposable BSP [81], and the simple two-level variant proposed in this book, which I call hybrid-BSP. In practice, one hardly ever obtains access to a whole supercomputer, but only to a smaller part, so that two levels of hierarchy usually suffice, and the number of interacting node pairs stays within reasonable bounds.

An important goal in designing parallel algorithms is to obtain a good algorithmic structure. One way of achieving this is by designing an algorithm as a sequence of large steps, called supersteps in BSP language, each containing many basic computation or communication operations and a global synchronization at the end, where all processors wait for each other to finish their work before they proceed to the next superstep. Within a superstep, the work is done in parallel, but the global structure of the algorithm is sequential. This simple structure has proven its worth in practice in many parallel applications, within the BSP world and beyond.

Many efficient implementations of the BSP model are publicly available. The first implementation that could be run on many different parallel computers, the Oxford BSP library, was developed by Miller and Reed [223, 224] in 1993. The BSP Worldwide organization was founded in 1995 to promote collaboration between developers and users of BSP. It is a loose organization that mainly runs a mailing list and a website http://www.bsp-worldwide. org where one can find pointers to BSP software and BSP research groups. One of the goals of BSP Worldwide was to provide a standard library for BSP programming. After extensive discussions in the BSP community, a standard called BSPlib [153] was proposed in May 1997 and an implementation by Hill and coworkers [151], the Oxford BSP toolset, was made available in the public domain. The standard was modernized by Yzelman and coworkers (including the author) in 2014 [318], and a shared-memory implementation was released as MulticoreBSP for C. The programs in this book make use of the modernized standard. I suggest you install the latest version of MulticoreBSP for C on your laptop or desktop computer if you want to run the programs of this book; version 2.0.4 was released in March 2019.

I wrote this book for students and researchers who are interested in scientific computation. The book has a dual purpose: first, it is a textbook for a graduate course on parallel scientific computation. The material of the book is suitable for a one-semester course at a mathematics or computer science department. I tested all the material in class at Utrecht University during the period 1993–2019, in an introductory course on parallel scientific computation given every year (by now, 27 times), called 'Parallel Algorithms', see the course page https://www.staff.science.uu.nl/~bisse101/Education/PA/pa.html. The course is taken by students from mathematics, computer science, physics, and, more recently, also artificial intelligence. Second, the book is a source of example parallel algorithms and programs for computational scientists from many different disciplines who are eager to get a quick start in parallel computing and want to learn a structured approach to writing parallel programs. Prerequisites are knowledge about linear algebra and sequential programming in a modern language such as C, C++, Java, or Python. The program texts assume basic knowledge of the programming language C, but this should not scare anyone away.

The scope of this book is the area of scientific computation in a broad sense. The book treats numerical scientific computation by presenting a detailed study of several important numerical problems. Through these problems, techniques are taught for designing and implementing efficient, well-structured parallel algorithms. I selected these particular problems because they are important for applications and because they give rise to a variety of important parallelization techniques. This book treats well-known subjects such as dense LU decomposition, fast Fourier transform (FFT), and sparse matrix–vector multiplication. The second edition also includes several nonnumerical computations such as sorting and graph matching, which are important in computer science.

Since this book should serve as a textbook, it covers a limited but carefully chosen amount of material; I did not strive for completeness in covering the area of scientific computation. A vast number of sequential algorithms can be found in *Matrix Computations* by Golub and Van Loan [124] and *Numerical Recipes: The Art of Scientific Computing* by Press, Teukolsky, Vetterling, and Flannery [253]. In my course on parallel algorithms, I have the habit of assigning sequential algorithms from these books to my students and asking them to develop parallel versions. Often, the students go out and perform an excellent job. Some of these assignments became exercises in the present book.

The organization of the book is as follows. Chapter 1 introduces the BSP model and BSPlib, and as an example it presents a simple complete parallel program for inner product computation. This two-page program alone already teaches half the primitives of BSPlib. The chapter then continues to teach the remaining important primitives in an example on sorting. The first chapter is a concise and self-contained tutorial, which tells you how to get started with writing BSP programs, and how to benchmark your computer as a BSP computer.

Chapters 2–5 present parallel algorithms for problems with increasing irregularity. Chapter 2 on dense LU decomposition presents a regular computation with communication patterns that are common in matrix computations. It also treats optimization to achieve high performance close to the peak performance of the parallel computer. Chapter 3 on the FFT also treats a regular computation but one with a more complex flow of data.

The execution-time requirements of the LU decomposition and FFT algorithms can be analysed exactly and the performance of an implementation can be predicted quite accurately. Chapter 4 presents the multiplication of a sparse matrix and a dense vector. The computation involves only those matrix elements that are nonzero, so that in general it is irregular. The communication involves the components of dense input and output vectors. Although these vectors can be stored in a regular data structure, the communication pattern becomes irregular because efficient communication must exploit the sparsity of the matrix. This chapter also connects to the area of machine learning: employing a deep artificial neural network can be viewed as performing many matrix–vector multiplications, one for each hidden layer or output layer of the network. Chapter 5 presents an algorithm for matching vertices in a sparse graph. This computation is highly irregular because the graph is sparse and because it changes by the removal of matched vertices and their edges.

The order in which the chapters can be read is given by the following directed acyclic graph (with chapters as vertices and prerequisites as directed edges):

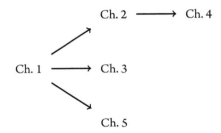

Major changes in the second edition compared to the first are:

- New Sections 1.8–1.10 on sorting.
- New Section 2.5 on high-performance LU decomposition.
- Simplified Section 3.5 on weights for the FFT.
- New Section 4.6 on fine-grain and medium-grain partitioning.
- New Section 4.10 on hybrid-BSP.
- New Chapter 5 on graph matching.
- Bibliographic Section 1.11.3 instead of appendix on MPI.

All sections of the book have been brought up to date.

Chapter 1 can stand on its own and serve as the basis for a short course on parallel programming (3–4 ECTS points, in the European Credit Transfer System where 60 ECTS comprise a full year of study). For a full semester course of eight ECTS in Parallel Algorithms, one could choose to treat Chapters 1, 2, and 4, and possibly Chapter 3 for a mathematics audience, or Chapter 5 for a computer science audience.

Each chapter contains: an abstract; a brief discussion of a sequential algorithm, included to make the material self-contained; the design and analysis of a parallel algorithm; ideas for possible optimization; an annotated program text; illustrative experimental results of an implementation on a particular parallel computer; bibliographic notes, giving historical background and pointers for further reading; theoretical and practical exercises.

My approach in presenting algorithms and program texts has been to give priority to clarity, simplicity, and brevity, even if this comes at the expense of a slight decrease in efficiency. In this book, algorithms and programs are only optimized if this teaches an important technique, or improves efficiency by an order of magnitude, or if this can be done without much harm to clarity. Hints for further optimization are given in exercises. The reader should view the programs as a starting point for achieving fast implementations.

One goal of this book is to ease the transition from theory to practice. For this purpose, each chapter includes an example program, which presents a possible implementation of the central algorithm in that chapter. The program texts form a small but integral part of this book. They are meant to be read by humans, besides being compiled and executed by computers. Studying the program texts is the best way of understanding what parallel programming is really about. Using and modifying the programs gives you valuable hands-on experience.

The aim of the section on experimental results is to illustrate the theoretical analysis. Often, one aspect is highlighted; I made no attempt to perform an exhaustive set of experiments. A real danger in trying to explain experimental results for an algorithm is that a full explanation may lead to a discussion of nitty-gritty implementation details or hardware quirks. This is hardly illuminating for the algorithm, and therefore I have chosen to keep such explanations to a minimum. For my experiments, I have used several different parallel machines, older ones as well as newer ones: parallel computers come and go quickly.

The bibliographic notes of this book are lengthier than usual in a textbook, since I have tried to summarize the contents of the cited work and relate them to the topic discussed in the current chapter. Often, I could not resist the temptation to write a few sentences about a subject not fully discussed in the main text, but still worth mentioning.

Most exercises of this book have the form of programming projects, which are suitable for use in an accompanying computer-laboratory class. I have graded the exercises according to difficulty/amount of work involved, marking an exercise by an asterisk ($*$) if it requires more work than a basic exercise and by two asterisks ($**$) if it requires a lot of work, meaning that it would be suitable as a final assignment or small research project. Inevitably, such a grading is subjective, but it may be helpful for a teacher in assigning problems to students. The main text of the book treats a few central topics from parallel scientific computation in depth; the exercises are meant to give the book breadth. At the end of my Parallel Algorithms course, I ask the students to give a 15–20 minute presentation on their final project. This exposes their fellow students to the breadth of parallel scientific computation.

The source files of the printed program texts, together with a set of test programs that demonstrate their use, form a package called BSPedupack, available at https://www. staff.science.uu.nl/~bisse101/Software/software. The package is copyrighted, but freely available under the GNU General Public License, meaning that its programs can be used and modified freely, provided the source and all modifications are mentioned, and every modification is again made freely available under the same license. As the name says, the programs in BSPedupack are primarily intended for teaching. They are definitely not meant to be used as a black box. Only rudimentary error handling has been built into the programs.

Other software available from my software site is the Mondriaan sparse matrix partitioning package [304], which is used extensively in Chapter 4. This is actual production software, available under the GNU Lesser General Public License.

To use BSPedupack, a modernized BSPlib implementation such as MulticoreBSP for C [318] must have been installed on your shared-memory parallel computer. The programs of this book have been tested extensively for MulticoreBSP for C. As an alternative, you can use C++ versions of several BSPedupack programs written for the Bulk library [52], which are available from https://jwbuurlage.github.com/Bulk. Currently, all programs of Chapters 1–3 are available in C++/Bulk. Bulk can handle hybrid-BSP programs. Finally, another possibility is to use BSPonMPI [281], which provides the distributed-memory portability offered by MPI also to BSP programmers.

Another communication library, which can be used for writing parallel programs and which has had a major impact on the field of parallel computing is the Message-Passing Interface (MPI), formulated in 1994 as MPI-1, and extended in 1997 by MPI-2 and in 2012 by MPI-3. The MPI standard has promoted the portability of parallel programs and one might say that its advent has effectively ended the era of architecture-dependent communication interfaces. We presented MPI versions of the BSPedupack programs in the first edition of this book, showing that it is possible to program in BSP style while using MPI, but we have removed these MPI programs to save space and also because the MPI standard has expanded and a brief treatment would not do justice to the many new developments. Still, we include a more extensive discussion of MPI in the bibliographic notes of Chapter 1.

The programming language used in this book is C99, the 1999 ISO standard for C. The reason for this choice is that historically many students learned C as their first programming language (nowadays, this is Python) and that efficient C compilers are available for many different sequential and parallel computers. On massively parallel supercomputers, the languages used are mainly C, C++, and Fortran.

Finally, let me express my hope and expectation that this book will transform your barriers: your own activation barrier for parallel programming will disappear; instead, synchronization barriers will appear in your parallel programs and you will know how to use them as an effective way of designing well-structured parallel programs.

Rob H. Bisseling
Utrecht University
December 2019

ACKNOWLEDGEMENTS

Many people helped me shape this book, from the inception of the first edition in 1993 until the completion of the second edition in 2019. Here, I would like to express my gratitude to all of them. I apologize if I forgot anyone.

First of all, I would like to thank Bill McColl for introducing the BSP model to me in 1992 and convincing me to abandon my previous habit of developing special-purpose algorithms for mesh-based parallel computers. Thanks to him, I turned to designing general-purpose algorithms that can run on every parallel computer. Without Bill's encouragement, I would not have written this book. Also for the second edition, Bill's strong stands on BSP have had an impact.

Special mention should be made of Jon Hill, co-designer and main implementor of BSPlib. The BSPlib standard gives the programs in the main text of this book a solid foundation. Many discussions with Jon, in particular during the course on BSP we gave together in Jerusalem in 1997, were extremely helpful in writing this book. Sadly, Jon passed away at a far too young age.

Several visits abroad gave me feedback and exposure to constructive criticism. For visits during the writing of the first edition, I would like to thank my hosts Michael Berman of Silicon Graphics Biomedical in Jerusalem, Richard Brent and Bill McColl of Oxford University, Iain Duff of CERFACS in Toulouse, Jacko Koster and Fredrik Manne of the University of Bergen, Satish Rao of NEC Research at Princeton, Pilar de la Torre of the University of New Hampshire, and Leslie Valiant of Harvard University, inventor of the BSP model. I appreciate their hospitality. I also thank the Engineering and Physical Sciences Research Council in the UK for funding my stay in Oxford in 2000, which enabled me to make much progress with the first edition of this book.

For visits after the publication of the first edition, I am grateful to colleagues who invited me to give talks on the book and who provided me feedback that eventually led to this expanded and updated second edition. I would like to thank Erik Boman, Karen Devine, and Bruce Hendrickson of Sandia National Laboratories for their hospitality in 2004 and for inspiring me to improve my software engineering skills. Alex Pothen has been a generous host at Old Dominion University; I had many fruitful discussions with him on combinatorial scientific computing. Fredrik Manne introduced me to the topic of parallel graph matching, and our joint work from 2007 became the basis for the algorithms of Chapter 5. Fredrik also tested Chapter 1 of the new edition in class at the Computer Science department in Bergen. Luc Giraud invited me to CERFACS in Toulouse in 2010, where I could work on a new release of the Mondriaan package, discussed in Chapter 4.

By 2010, I had sufficiently recovered from the efforts of writing a first edition to imagine writing a new edition. Visits to KU Leuven in the years 2012–14, hosted by Albert-Jan Yzelman and Dirk Roose, helped me define the desired content of the new edition, in particular the addition of parallel sorting and graph algorithms. I thank Albert-Jan and Dirk for their feedback on the use of the first edition in their course in Leuven. A guest professorship at the University of Orléans in May 2014 became the start of the actual writing of the new edition. I thank Hélène Coullon, Sébastien Limet, Frédéric Loulergue, and Sophie Robert for their great hospitality. Assaf Schuster hosted numerous visits to the Technion in Haifa, where parts of the first edition were used as course material. A visit to Sherry Li at Lawrence Berkeley National Laboratory in 2016 provided helpful new insights into high-performance LU decomposition. Sherry also helped me obtain access to the Cori supercomputer, which I happily used in the numerical experiments of Chapter 2; this chapter used resources of Cori at the National Energy Research Scientific Computing Center (NERSC), a US Department of Energy, Office of Science, User Facility operated under Contract No. DE-AC02-05CH11231.

Finally, visits in 2018 to Sivan Toledo at Tel Aviv University and Oded Schwartz at the Hebrew University of Jerusalem helped me in the final stages of this second edition. Looking back on all these travels, I realize that this book could not have been written on a desert island, however beautiful and isolated it might have been.

The BSPedupack software accompanying this book has been tested on many different parallel computers, of different generations for the two editions. I thank all the people from the supercomputer centres who have assisted me and the institutes and companies that gave me access and computer time. For the first edition, I would like to thank Jeremy Martin and Bob McLatchie of Oxford University, the Oxford Supercomputer Centre, and Sychron Ltd in Oxford. In the Netherlands, I gained assistance from Jana Vasiljev, Willem Vermin, Aad van der Steen, and for the second edition from Valeriu Codreanu. For both editions, I benefited from yearly grants of computer time from NCF (National Computer Facilities), now part of the Dutch Science Organization NWO. My students and I enjoyed all the work we could do on generations of national supercomputers, from Vermeer in Delft to Teras, Aster, Huygens, and Cartesius at SURFsara in Amsterdam. The final runs in the second edition on Cartesius were carried out under grant SH-349-15 from NWO.

The Mathematics Institute of Utrecht University provided me with a stimulating environment for writing this book. Henk van der Vorst started the Computational Science education programme in Utrecht in 1993. Later it became the Scientific Computing programme, which gave me the opportunity to develop and test the material of the book. Since 2012, I have also regularly spent time at CWI in Amsterdam, where I participated in the computational life sciences group led by Gunnar Klau and the scientific computing group led by Daan Crommelin, and where I currently participate in the computational imaging group led by Joost Batenburg. I thank all of my colleagues at CWI for many inspiring ideas and for providing a sanctuary where I could work steadily on the second edition.

Over the years, hundreds of students have graduated from my parallel scientific computation courses. Many have contributed, occasionally by being guinea-pigs (my apologies!), but more often as partners in a genuine dialogue. These students have helped me to improve the exposition of the material and they have forced me to be as clear and brief as I can (except in this acknowledgement). I thank all of them, with special mention of Tammo Jan Dijkema, Stefan Korenberg, Maarten Löffler, Angelo Mekenkamp, and Katharina Klein, who were champion proofreaders, and Jan-Willem Buurlage, Mick van Duijn, Mitchell Faas, Wijnand

Suijlen, Dik Takken, Paul Visscher, Abe Wits, and Albert-Jan Yzelman, who developed their own BSP libraries while taking my course, or soon afterwards.

During the period of writing this book, I was joined in my parallel computing research by MSc students, PhD students, and postdocs. Discussions with them often yielded new insights, and I enjoyed many working and off-working hours spent together. For the first edition, I would like to mention here: Márcia Alves de Inda, Ildikó Flesch, Jeroen van Grondelle, Alexander van Heukelum, Neal Hegeman, Guy Horvitz, Frank van Lingen, Jacko Koster, Joris Koster, Wouter Meesen, Bruce Stephens, Frank van der Stappen, Mark Stijnman, Dik Takken, Patrick Timmers, and Brendan Vastenhouw. For the second edition, I would like to mention: Sarita de Berg, Folkert Bleichrodt, Jan-Willem Buurlage, Bas Fagginger Auer, Timon Knigge, Tristan van Leeuwen, Marco van Oort, Daniël Pelt, Raoul Schram, Davide Taviani, Nick Verheul, and Albert-Jan Yzelman. A comment by Raoul Schram led to the faster bit-reversal algorithm in the second edition, Algorithm 3.3. An industrial contribution came from Pascal Ramaekers, Daniel Sevilla Sánchez, and Hans van der Voort from Scientific Volume Imaging in Hilversum, the Netherlands, who posed a real-life parallelization problem for a 3D fluorescence microscopy application to the students in my Mathematics for Industry course in 2018, which led to Exercise 4.6.

Much of my pre-BSP work has contributed to this book as well. In particular, research I carried out in 1987–93 at the Koninklijke/Shell-Laboratory in Amsterdam has taught me much about parallel computing and sparse matrix computations. Ideas from the prototype library PARPACK, developed in those years at Shell, profoundly influenced the present work. The importance of a structured approach was already apparent then; good structure was obtained in PARPACK by writing programs with communication-closed layers, the predecessor of the BSP superstep. I would like to express my debt to the enlightened management by Arie Langeveld and Theo Verheggen at Shell and to my close colleagues Daniël Loyens and Hans van de Vorst from the parallel computing group.

Going back even further, to my years 1981–6 at the Hebrew University of Jerusalem, my PhD supervisor Ronnie Kosloff aroused my interest in fast Fourier transforms, which has become the subject of Chapter 3. Ronnie seriously influenced my way of working, by injecting me with a large dose of (quantum molecular) dynamics. In Jerusalem, Larry Rudolph introduced me to the field of parallel computing. His enthusiasm and juggling acts left an imprint forever.

Comments on draft chapters of the first edition have been given by Márcia Alves de Inda, Richard Brent, Olivier Dulieu, Jon Hill, Slava Kokoouline, Jacko Koster, Frank van Lingen, Ronald Meester, Adina Milston, John Reid, Dan Stefanescu, Pilar de la Torre, Leslie Valiant, and Yael Weinbach. Comments for the second edition have been given by Fatima Abu Salem, Ariful Azad, Sarai Bisseling, Aydın Buluç, Jan-Willem Buurlage, Mick van Duijn, Robert van de Geijn, Fredrik Manne, Joshua Maynard, Daniël Pelt, Wijnand Suijlen, and Albert-Jan Yzelman. Aesthetic advice for the first edition was given by Ron Bertels, Lidy Bisseling, Gerda Dekker, and Gila and Joel Kantor. Thanks to all of them. Disclaimer: if you find typing errors, small flaws, serious flaws, unintended Dutch, or worse, do not blame them, just flame me! All comments are welcome at: `r.h.bisseling@uu.nl`. I thank my editors of the first edition at Oxford University Press, Elizabeth Johnston, Alison Jones, and Mahua Nandi, for accepting my vision of this book and for their ideas, good judgement, help, and patience.

I thank my editors for the second edition, Keith Mansfield, Dan Taber, and Katherine Ward, for their enthusiasm, their infinite patience, and their suggestions which made this book project a finite effort.

Finally, in the writing of this book, I owe much to my family. My wife Rona showed love and sympathy, and gave support whenever needed. Our daughter Sarai, born in 1994, had already acquired quite some mathematical and computer skills when I completed the manuscript of the first edition in 2003. At the time, I tested a few exercises on her (admittedly, unmarked ones), and I was amazed how much a nine-year-old can understand about parallel computing. If she could do it then, you can now. Today, she is a skilled programmer herself, and she encounters parallel computing everywhere. Without knowing it, I wrote the book for her.

ABOUT THE AUTHOR

Rob H. Bisseling is a full professor in Scientific Computing at the Mathematics Institute of Utrecht University, the Netherlands, where he has held a position since 1993. Previously, he worked as a research mathematician at the Koninklijke/Shell-Laboratorium, Amsterdam, the Netherlands, where he investigated the application of parallel computing in oil refinery optimization and polymer modelling. He received a BSc degree cum laude in mathematics in 1977, with minors in physics and astronomy, and an MSc degree cum laude in mathematics in 1981, both from the Catholic University of Nijmegen, the Netherlands, and a PhD degree in theoretical chemistry in 1987 from the Hebrew University of Jerusalem, Israel. He is a member of the Society for Industrial and Applied Mathematics and the Royal Dutch Mathematical Society.

The author has spent periods as a visiting scientist at Silicon Graphics Biomedical, Jerusalem (1997); at the Programming Research Group of Oxford University, UK (2000); at Sandia National Laboratories, Albuquerque, NM (2004); at CERFACS and INRIA, Toulouse, France (2010); and as a visiting professor at the University of Orléans, France (2014). He is co-author of the BSPlib standard (1997) and of several open-source packages: Mondriaan for partitioning sparse matrices (2002); SAWdoubler for counting self-avoiding walks on a lattice (2012); and the BSP libraries MulticoreBSP for Java (2012), MulticoreBSP for C (2014), and Bulk (2018). Since 2000, he has maintained the website of the BSP Worldwide organization. He was co-chair of the SIAM conference on Parallel Processing for Scientific Computing in Seattle, WA, in 2010. He was local chair of the Dutch Mathematical Congress 2017 in Utrecht. He is a member of the steering committee of the SIAM Workshop on Combinatorial Scientific Computing since 2011. At Utrecht University, he has taught the MSc course Parallel Algorithms, every year since 1993; he has also taught courses on Networks, Scientific Computing, and Mathematics for Industry.

The author's research interests are numerical and combinatorial scientific computing in general, and parallel algorithms, sparse matrix computations, graph algorithms, and their application in Big Data in particular. His research goal is to design algorithms and develop software tools that are useful in a wide range of applications in scientific computation and beyond. Despite his professional interest in parallel computing, he finds it hard to do two things at the same time.

CONTENTS

1 Introduction 1
  1.1 Parallel computing is everywhere 1
  1.2 The BSP model 2
  1.3 BSP algorithm for inner product computation 9
  1.4 Starting with BSPlib: example program `bspinprod` 13
  1.5 BSP benchmarking 24
  1.6 Example program `bspbench` 27
  1.7 Benchmark results 32
  1.8 Sorting 38
  1.9 Example function `bspsort` 44
  1.10 Experimental results for samplesort on a Cartesius node 53
  1.11 Bibliographic notes 57
    1.11.1 BSP-related models of parallel computation 57
    1.11.2 BSP libraries 58
    1.11.3 The non-BSP world: message passing and threads 62
    1.11.4 Benchmarking 66
    1.11.5 Sorting 67
  1.12 Exercises 69

2 LU decomposition 74
  2.1 The problem 74
  2.2 Sequential LU decomposition 75
  2.3 Basic parallel algorithm 82
  2.4 Two-phase broadcasting and other improvements 89
  2.5 High-performance LU decomposition 96
  2.6 Example function `bsplu` 100
  2.7 Experimental results on the Cori supercomputer 113
  2.8 Bibliographic notes 119
    2.8.1 Matrix distributions 119
    2.8.2 Collective communication 120
    2.8.3 Parallel matrix computations 121
  2.9 Exercises 122

3 The fast Fourier transform 134
  3.1 The problem 134
  3.2 Sequential recursive fast Fourier transform 136

3.3	Sequential nonrecursive algorithm	139
3.4	Parallel algorithm	148
3.5	Weight reduction	155
3.6	Example function `bspfft`	158
3.7	Experimental results on the Cartesius supercomputer	166
3.8	Bibliographic notes	173
	3.8.1 Sequential FFT algorithms	173
	3.8.2 Parallel FFT algorithms	176
	3.8.3 Applications	179
3.9	Exercises	180
4	**Sparse matrix–vector multiplication**	**190**
4.1	The problem	190
4.2	Sparse matrices and their data structures	195
4.3	Parallel algorithm	201
4.4	Cartesian matrix distribution	208
4.5	Mondriaan distribution for general sparse matrices	215
4.6	Fine-grain and medium-grain matrix distribution	225
4.7	Vector distribution	231
4.8	Random sparse matrices	237
4.9	Laplacian matrices	244
4.10	Parallel algorithm for hybrid-BSP	255
4.11	Example function `bspmv`	261
4.12	Experimental results on the Cartesius supercomputer	269
4.13	Bibliographic notes	275
	4.13.1 Sparse matrix computations	275
	4.13.2 Parallel sparse matrix–vector multiplication algorithms	277
	4.13.3 Partitioning methods	279
4.14	Exercises	283
5	**Graph matching**	**291**
5.1	The problem	291
5.2	Sequential algorithm	293
5.3	Suitors and sorting	298
5.4	Parallel algorithm	305
5.5	Correctness	310
5.6	Tie-breaking	314
5.7	Load balancing	316
5.8	Further improvements	318
5.9	Example function `bspmatch`	325
5.10	Experimental results on the Cartesius supercomputer	340
5.11	Bibliographic notes	346
	5.11.1 Sequential graph matching	346
	5.11.2 Parallel graph matching	348
	5.11.3 GraphBLAS	349
5.12	Exercises	351

Appendix A   Auxiliary BSPedupack functions **359**

A.1   Header file bspedupack.h   359

A.2   Utility file bspedupack.c   360

Appendix B   A quick reference guide to BSPlib **363**

References   365

Index   383

1

. . • . .

Introduction

1.1 Parallel computing is everywhere

Today's personal computers are almost without exception parallel computers. At the time of writing, it is actually becoming hard to buy a computer with fewer than four processor cores. Some smartphones already have eight cores, happily computing away at their often dumb but increasingly smarter little tasks. In the area of scientific computing, developers of scientific application software must pay attention not only to the use of computer time and memory, and to the accuracy of their results, but also to **parallelism**, the use of more than one processor to solve a problem. Nowadays, parallel algorithms are routinely being developed and used by many computational scientists in fields such as astronomy, biology, chemistry, and physics. In industry, engineers are trying to accelerate their simulations by using parallel computers, and data analysts are trying to create new knowledge by running machine learning algorithms on huge amounts of data, employing computers with thousands of processor cores. The main motivation of all these brave people developing and using parallel algorithms is the tremendous computing power promised by parallel computers.

The potential of parallel computers could be realized if the practice of parallel programming were just as easy and natural as that of sequential programming. In the past decades, much progress has been made in this direction. Parallel computing started off as a very specialized area where exotic parallel algorithms were developed for even more exotic parallel architectures, where software could not be reused, and many person-years of effort were wasted in developing software of limited applicability. Automatic parallelization by compilers could have been a solution for this problem, but this has not been achieved yet, nor is it likely to be achieved in the near future. Our only hope for harnessing the power of parallel computing lies in actively engaging ourselves in parallel programming. Therefore, we might as well try to make parallel programming easy and effective, turning it into a natural activity for everyone who writes computer programs.

An important step forwards in making parallel programming easier has been the development of **portability layers**, i.e., application programming interfaces (APIs) such as MPI (Message-Passing Interface) [218] and OpenMP (Open Multi-Processing) [62] that enable us to run the same parallel program on many different parallel computers without changing

Parallel Scientific Computation: A Structured Approach Using BSP. Second Edition. Rob H. Bisseling, Oxford University Press (2020). © Rob H. Bisseling.
DOI: 10.1093/oso/9780198788348.001.0001

a single line of program text. Still, the resulting execution time behaviour of the program on a new machine is unpredictable (and can indeed be rather erratic), due to the lack of an underlying parallel programming model with a suitable cost function.

To achieve the noble goal of easy parallel programming, we need a model that is simple, efficiently implementable, and acceptable to all parties involved: hardware designers, software developers, and end users. This model should not interfere with the process of designing and implementing algorithms. It should exist mainly in the background, being tacitly understood by everybody. Such a model would encourage the use of parallel computers in the same way as the Von Neumann model did for the sequential computer.

The bulk synchronous parallel (BSP) model was proposed by Valiant in 1989 [289, 290]. The BSP model satisfies all the requirements of a useful parallel programming model: it is simple enough to allow easy development and analysis of algorithms, but on the other hand it is realistic enough to allow reasonably accurate modelling of real-life parallel computing. The original BSP model was extended by Valiant in 2011 [292] to the multi-BSP model, with an architecture consisting of several BSP subcomputers, to account for evolving parallel machines with deep memory hierarchies and increasing numbers of cores, up to millions.

A portability layer has been defined for the BSP model in the form of BSPlib [153]. This standard has been implemented efficiently in several libraries: the pioneering Oxford BSP toolset [151]; the Paderborn University BSP library [40]; the recently modernized BSPonMPI library [281] which provides a BSPlib interface on top of MPI; and the recent MulticoreBSP for C library [318] with a modernized interface which is targeted towards multicore computers. Another portability layer suitable for BSP programming is the one-sided communications part of MPI [218], which was inspired by BSP; it has been included in version 2 and improved in version 3 of the MPI standard.

Today, the BSP model is being used as the framework for algorithm design and implementation on a range of parallel computers with completely different architectures from small embedded manycore processors on a single chip, to multicore PCs with memory shared by the processor cores, to huge massively parallel supercomputers with distributed memory. Furthermore, the BSP model has influenced the design of Big Data software for processing large graphs such as Google's Pregel [205] and Apache's open-source package Giraph [211], which is used at Facebook to handle graphs of up to 10^{12} edges [65]. The BSP model is explained in the next section.

1.2 The BSP model

The BSP model proposed by Valiant [290] comprises a computer architecture, a class of algorithms, and a function for charging costs to algorithms. In this book, we use a variant of the BSP model; the differences with the original model are discussed at the end of this section.

A **BSP computer** consists of a collection of processors, each with private memory, and a communication network that allows processors to access memories of other processors. The architecture of a BSP computer is shown in Fig. 1.1. Each processor can read from or write to every memory cell in the entire machine. If the cell is local, the read or write operation

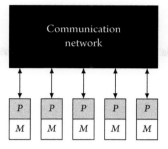

Figure 1.1 Architecture of a BSP computer. Here, 'P' denotes a processor and 'M' a memory.

is relatively fast. If the cell belongs to another processor, a message must be sent through the communication network, and this operation is slower. The access time for all nonlocal memories is the same. This ensures that the communication network can be viewed as a black box, where the connectivity of the network is hidden in the interior. As users of a BSP computer, we need not be concerned with the details of the communication network. We only care about the remote access time delivered by the network, which should be uniform. By concentrating on this single property, we are able to develop **portable** algorithms, that is, algorithms that can be used for a wide range of parallel computers.

A **BSP algorithm** consists of a sequence of supersteps. A **superstep** contains either a number of computation steps or a number of communication steps, or in certain cases both, followed by a global barrier synchronization. In a **computation superstep**, each processor performs a sequence of operations on local data. In scientific computations, these are typically floating-point operations, also called flops. (A **flop** is a multiplication, addition, subtraction, or division of two floating-point numbers. For simplicity, we assume that all these operations take the same amount of time.) In nonnumerical computations, such as sorting or graph computations, more often other types of basic operations are performed, not involving floating-point numbers, and in that case we rather call a basic operation an **op**.

In a **communication superstep**, each processor sends and receives a number of messages. In a **mixed superstep**, both computation and communication take place. We will use separate computation supersteps and communication supersteps as much as possible, as this simplifies cost analysis, but for certain irregular computations, such as those treated in Chapter 5, it is more convenient to allow mixing of computation and communication.

At the end of a superstep, all processors synchronize, as follows. Each processor checks whether it has finished all its obligations of that superstep. In the case of a computation superstep, it checks whether the computations are finished. In the case of a communication superstep, it checks whether it has sent all messages that it had to send, and whether it has received all messages that it had to receive. Processors wait until all others have finished. When this has happened, they all proceed to the next superstep. This form of synchronization is called **bulk synchronization**, because usually many computation or communication operations take place between successive synchronizations. (This is in contrast to pairwise synchronization, used in most message-passing systems, where each

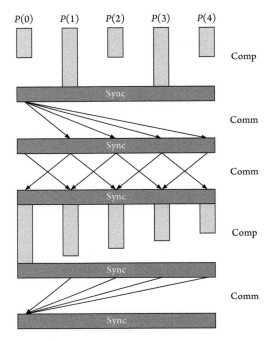

Figure 1.2 BSP algorithm with five supersteps executed on five processors. The time direction is downwards. A vertical bar denotes local computation; an arrow denotes communication of one or more data words to another processor. The first superstep is a computation superstep. The second one is a communication superstep, where processor $P(0)$ sends data to all other processors. Each superstep is terminated by a global synchronization denoted by a horizontal bar.

message causes a pair of sending and receiving processors to wait until the message has been transferred.) Figure 1.2 gives an example of a BSP algorithm.

The **BSP cost function** is defined as follows. An **h-relation** is a communication superstep where each processor sends at most h data words to other processors and receives at most h data words, and where at least one processor sends or receives h words. A data word is a real or an integer. We denote the maximum number of words sent by any processor by h_s and the maximum number received by h_r. Therefore,

$$h = \max\{h_s, h_r\}. \tag{1.1}$$

This equation reflects the assumption that a processor can send and receive data simultaneously. The cost of the superstep depends solely on h. Note that two different communication patterns may have the same h, so that the cost function of the BSP model does not distinguish between them. An example is given in Fig. 1.3. Charging the costs on the basis of h is motivated by the assumption that the bottleneck of communication lies at the entry or exit of the communication network, so that simply counting the maximum number of sends and

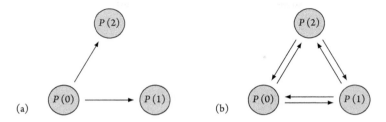

Figure 1.3 Two different h-relations with the same h. Each arrow represents the communication of one data word. (a) A 2-relation with $h_s = 2$ and $h_r = 1$; (b) a 2-relation with $h_s = h_r = 2$.

receives gives a good indication of communication time. Note that for the cost function it does not matter whether the data are sent together or as separate words.

The time, or **cost**, of an h-relation is

$$T_{comm}(h) = hg + l, \qquad (1.2)$$

where g and l are machine-dependent parameters and the time unit is the time of one flop. This cost is charged because of the expected linear increase of communication time with h. Since $g = \lim_{h \to \infty} T_{comm}(h)/h$, the parameter g can be viewed as the time needed to send one data word into the communication network, or to receive one word, in the asymptotic situation of continuous message traffic. The choice of the letter g comes from the **gap** in time between sending two subsequent data words. The linear cost function includes a nonzero constant l because executing an h-relation incurs a fixed overhead, which includes the cost of global synchronization, but also the fixed cost components of ensuring that all data have arrived at destination and of starting up the communication. We lump all such fixed costs together into one parameter l. The choice of the letter l comes from the **latency** of communicating data (the delay between sending data at a source and receiving data at their destination).

Approximate values for g and l of a particular parallel computer can be obtained by measuring the execution time for a range of **full** h-relations, that is, h-relations where each processor sends and receives exactly h data words. Figure 1.3(b) gives an example of a full 2-relation. (Can you find another full 2-relation?) In practice, the measured cost of a full h-relation will be an upper bound on the measured cost of an arbitrary h-relation. For our measurements, we usually take 64-bit reals or integers as data words.

The cost of a computation superstep is

$$T_{comp}(w) = w + l, \qquad (1.3)$$

where the amount of work w is defined as the maximum number of flops performed in the superstep by any processor. For reasons of simplicity, the value of l is taken to be the same as that of a communication superstep, even though it may be less in practice.

The cost of a mixed superstep is

$$T_{mixed}(w, h) = w + hg + l. \qquad (1.4)$$

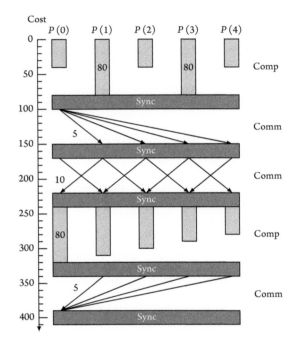

Figure 1.4 Cost of the BSP algorithm from Fig. 1.2 on a BSP computer with $p = 5$, $g = 2.5$, and $l = 20$. Communication costs are shown for only one source/destination pair of processors in each communication superstep, because we assume in this example that the amount of data happens to be the same for every pair, denoted by an arrow. The cost of the first superstep is determined by processors $P(1)$ and $P(3)$, which perform 80 flops each. Therefore, the cost is $80 + l = 100$ flop time units. In the second superstep, $P(0)$ sends five data words to each of the four other processors. This superstep has $h_s = 20$ and $h_r = 5$, so that it is a 20-relation and hence its cost is $20g + l = 70$ flops. The cost of the other supersteps is obtained in a similar fashion. The total cost of the algorithm is 410 flops.

As a result, the total synchronization cost of an algorithm can be determined simply by counting its supersteps. Because of (1.2), (1.3), and (1.4), the total cost of a BSP algorithm becomes an expression of the form $a + bg + cl$. Figure 1.4 displays the cost of the BSP algorithm from Fig. 1.2.

A BSP computer can be characterized by four parameters: p, r, g, and l. Here, p is the **number of processors**. The parameter r is the **single-processor computing rate** measured in flop/s (floating-point operations per second). This parameter is irrelevant for cost analysis and algorithm design, because it just normalizes the time. (But if you are having to wait for the result of your program, you may find it highly relevant!) From a global, architectural point of view, the parameter g, which is measured in flop time units, can be seen as the ratio between the computation throughput and the communication throughput of the computer. This is because, in the time period of an h-relation, phg flops can be performed by all

Table 1.1 The BSP parameters.

p	number of processors
r	single-processor computing rate (in flop/s)
g	communication cost per data word (in time units of 1 flop)
l	global synchronization cost (in time units of 1 flop)

processors together and ph data words can be communicated through the network. Finally, l is called the **global synchronization cost**, and it is also measured in flop time units. Here, we slightly abuse the language, because l includes fixed costs other than the cost of synchronization as well. Measuring the characteristic parameters of a computer is called **computer benchmarking**. In the BSP case, we do this by measuring r, g, and l. (For p, we can rely on the value advertised by the computer vendor.) Table 1.1 summarizes the BSP parameters.

We can predict the execution time of an implementation of a BSP algorithm on a parallel computer by theoretically analysing the cost of the algorithm and, independently, benchmarking the computer for its BSP performance. The predicted time (in seconds) of an algorithm with cost $a + bg + cl$ on a computer with measured parameters r, g, and l equals $(a + bg + cl)/r$, because the time (in seconds) of one flop equals $t_{flop} = 1/r$.

One aim of the BSP model is to guarantee a certain performance of an implementation. Because of this, the model states costs in terms of upper bounds. For example, the cost function of an h-relation assumes a worst-case communication pattern. This implies that the predicted time is an upper bound on the measured time. Of course, the accuracy of the prediction depends on how the BSP cost function reflects reality, and this may differ from machine to machine.

Separation of concerns is a basic principle of good engineering. The BSP model enforces this principle by separating the hardware concerns from the software concerns. (Because the software for routing messages in the communication network influences g and l, we consider such routing software to be part of the hardware system.) On the one hand, the hardware designer can concentrate on increasing p, r and decreasing g, l. For example, she could aim at designing a $BSP(p, r, g, l)$ computer with $p \geq 100\,000$ and $r \geq 1\,Gflop/s$ (the prefix G denotes Giga $= 10^9$), and with $g \leq 10$ and $l \leq 1000$. To stay within a budget, she may have to trade off these objectives. Obviously, the larger the number of processors p and the computing rate r, the more powerful the communication network must be to keep g and l low. These days, when it is almost impossible to increase clock speeds further beyond a few GHz (gigahertz), it is wiser to spend more money on a better communication network than on faster processors. The BSP parameters help in quantifying these design issues. On the other hand, the software designer can concentrate on decreasing the algorithmic parameters a, b, and c in the cost expression $a + bg + cl$; in general, these parameters depend on p and the problem size n. The aim of the software designer is to obtain good scaling behaviour of the cost expression. For example, he could realistically aim at a decrease in a as $1/p$, a decrease in b as $1/\sqrt{p}$, and a constant c.

The BSP model is a distributed-memory model. This implies that both the computational work and the data are distributed. The work should be distributed evenly over the processors, to achieve a good load balance. The data should be distributed in such a way that the total communication cost is limited. Often, the data distribution determines the work distribution in a natural manner, so that the choice of data distribution must be based on two objectives: good load balance and low communication cost. In all our algorithms, choosing a data distribution is an important decision. By designing algorithms for a distributed-memory model, we do not limit ourselves to this model. Distributed-memory algorithms can be used efficiently on shared-memory parallel computers, simply by partitioning the shared memory among the processors. (The reverse is not true: shared-memory algorithms do not take data locality into account, so that straightforward distribution leads to inefficient algorithms.) We just develop a distributed-memory program; the BSP system does the rest, also for shared-memory architectures. This even holds for **hybrid architectures**, which consist of a set of processor nodes with distributed memory where every node in turn contains a number of processor cores that share its memory. Therefore, BSP algorithms can be implemented efficiently on every type of parallel computer. In our BSP terminology, we will call the basic processing unit a **processor**, irrespective of whether it is a central processing unit (CPU), a core, or a thread.

The main differences between our variant of the BSP model and the original BSP model [290] are:

1. The original cost function for a mixed superstep with an h-relation and a maximum amount of work w is $\max(w, hg, L)$, where L is the **latency**, that is, the minimum number of time units between successive supersteps. In our variant, we charge $w + hg + l$ for the corresponding superstep. We use the synchronization cost l instead of the (related) latency L because it facilitates the analysis of algorithms. For example, the total cost in the original model of a 2-relation followed by a 3-relation equals $\max(2g, L) + \max(3g, L)$, which may have any of the outcomes $5g$, $3g + L$, and $2L$, whereas in our variant we simply charge $5g + 2l$. If g and l (or L) are known, we can substitute their values into these expressions and obtain one scalar value, so that both variants are equally useful. However, we also would like to analyse algorithms without knowing g and l (or L), and in that case our cost function leads to simpler expressions. (Valiant [290] already mentions the sum of the cost terms as a possible alternative cost function for a superstep with both computation and communication, but he uses the maximum in his analysis.)

2. The data distribution in the original model is controlled either directly by the user, or, through a randomizing hash function, by the system. The latter approach effectively randomizes the allocation of memory cells, and thereby it provides a shared-memory view to the user. Since this approach is only efficient in the rare case that g is very low, $g \approx 1$, we use the direct approach instead. Moreover, we use the data distribution as our main means of making computations more efficient.

3. The original model allowed for synchronization of a subset of all processors instead of all processors. This option may be useful in certain cases, and it is available in several BSPlib implementations (the first being the Paderborn University BSP library [40]), but for reasons of simplicity we disallow it in our BSP variant.

1.3 BSP algorithm for inner product computation

A simple example of a BSP algorithm is the following computation of the inner product α of two vectors $\mathbf{x} = (x_0, \dots, x_{n-1})^{\mathrm{T}}$ and $\mathbf{y} = (y_0, \dots, y_{n-1})^{\mathrm{T}}$,

$$\alpha = \sum_{i=0}^{n-1} x_i y_i. \tag{1.5}$$

In our terminology, vectors are column vectors; to save space we write them as $\mathbf{x} = (x_0, \dots, x_{n-1})^{\mathrm{T}}$, where the superscript 'T' denotes transposition. The vector $\mathbf{x}$ can also be viewed as an $n \times 1$ matrix. The inner product of $\mathbf{x}$ and $\mathbf{y}$ can concisely be expressed as $\mathbf{x}^{\mathrm{T}}\mathbf{y}$.

The inner product is computed by the processors $P(0), \dots, P(p-1)$ of a BSP computer with p processors. We assume that the result is needed by all processors, which is usually the case if the inner product computation is part of a larger computation, such as in iterative linear system solvers.

The data distribution of the vectors $\mathbf{x}$ and $\mathbf{y}$ should be the same, because in that case the components x_i and y_i reside on the same processor and they can be multiplied immediately without any communication. The data distribution then determines the work distribution in a natural manner. To balance the work load of the algorithm, we must assign the same number of vector components to each processor. Card players know how to do this blindly, even without counting and in the harshest of circumstances. They always deal out their cards in a cyclic fashion. For the same reason, an optimal work distribution is obtained by the **cyclic distribution** defined by the mapping

$$x_i \longmapsto P(i \bmod p), \quad \text{for } 0 \le i < n. \tag{1.6}$$

Here, the mod operator stands for taking the remainder after division by p, that is, computing modulo p. Similarly, the div operator stands for integer division rounding down. Figure 1.5(a) illustrates the cyclic distribution for $n = 10$ and $p = 4$. The maximum number of components per processor is $\lceil n/p \rceil$, that is, n/p rounded up to the nearest integer value, and the minimum is $\lfloor n/p \rfloor = n$ div p, that is, n/p rounded down. The maximum and the minimum differ at most by one. If p divides n, every processor receives exactly n/p components. Of course, many other data distributions also lead to the best possible load balance. An example is the **block distribution**, defined by the mapping

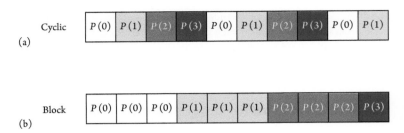

Figure 1.5 Distribution of a vector **x** of size ten over four processors. Each cell represents a vector component x_i; the number in the cell and the colour denote the processor that owns the cell. The processors are numbered 0, 1, 2, 3. (a) Cyclic distribution; (b) block distribution.

$$x_i \longmapsto P(i \text{ div } b), \quad \text{for } 0 \leq i < n, \tag{1.7}$$

with block size $b = \lceil n/p \rceil$. Figure 1.5(b) illustrates the block distribution for $n = 10$ and $p = 4$. This distribution has the same maximum number of components $\lceil n/p \rceil$ per processor (attained by $P(0)$), but the minimum can take every integer value between zero and the maximum. In Fig. 1.5(b) the minimum is one. The minimum can even be zero: if $n = 9$ and $p = 4$, then the block size is $b = 3$, and the processors receive 3, 3, 3, 0 components, respectively. Since the computation cost is determined by the maximum amount of work, this is just as good as the cyclic distribution, which assigns 3, 2, 2, 2 components. Intuitively, you may object to the idling processor in the block distribution, but the work distribution is still optimal!

Algorithm 1.1 computes an inner product in parallel. It consists of three supersteps, numbered (0), (1), and (2). The synchronizations at the end of the supersteps are not written explicitly. All the processors follow the same program text, but their actual execution paths differ. The path of processor $P(s)$ depends on the processor identity s, with $0 \leq s < p$. This style of programming is called **single program multiple data** (SPMD), and we shall use it throughout the book. The resulting value α is replicated such that all processors possess a copy at the end of the algorithm. This is expressed by the notation $\text{repl}(\alpha) = P(*)$, where $P(*)$ is the set of all processors.

In superstep (0), processor $P(s)$ computes the local partial inner product

$$\alpha_s = \sum_{\substack{0 \leq i < n \\ i \bmod p = s}} x_i y_i, \tag{1.8}$$

multiplying x_s by y_s, x_{s+p} by y_{s+p}, x_{s+2p} by y_{s+2p}, and so on, and adding the results. The data for this superstep are locally available. Note that we use global indices so that we can refer uniquely to variables without regard to the processors that own them. We access the local components of a vector by stepping through the arrays with a **stride**, or step size, p. In the program texts of our algorithms, we denote an assignment by ':=', e.g. $\alpha := 0$ meaning that α becomes 0. This differs from the equality sign '=', e.g. $\alpha = 0$ meaning that α already equals 0. (In program texts in the C language, however, assignments are written as '=' in typewriter font.)

Algorithm 1.1 Inner product algorithm for processor $P(s)$, with $0 \leq s < p$.

---

input: $\mathbf{x}, \mathbf{y}$: vector of length n, $\text{distr}(\mathbf{x}) = \text{distr}(\mathbf{y}) = \phi$, with $\phi(i) = i \bmod p$, for $0 \leq i < n$.
output: $\alpha = \mathbf{x}^{\mathrm{T}}\mathbf{y}$, $\text{repl}(\alpha) = P(*)$.

$\alpha_s := 0;$ $\qquad\qquad\qquad\qquad\qquad\qquad\qquad\qquad\qquad$ ▷ Superstep (0)
for $i := s$ **to** $n - 1$ **step** p **do**
$\qquad \alpha_s := \alpha_s + x_i y_i;$

for $t := 0$ **to** $p - 1$ **do** $\qquad\qquad\qquad\qquad\qquad\qquad$ ▷ Superstep (1)
$\qquad$ put α_s in $P(t);$

$\alpha := 0;$ $\qquad\qquad\qquad\qquad\qquad\qquad\qquad\qquad\qquad\quad$ ▷ Superstep (2)
for $t := 0$ **to** $p - 1$ **do**
$\qquad \alpha := \alpha + \alpha_t;$

In superstep (1), each processor **broadcasts** its result α_s, that is, it sends α_s to all processors. We use the communication primitive 'put x in $P(t)$' in the program text of $P(s)$ to denote the one-sided action by processor $P(s)$ of storing a data element x at target processor $P(t)$. This completely determines the communication: both the source processor and the destination processor of the data element are specified. The 'put' primitive assumes that the source processor knows the memory location on the destination processor where the data must be put. The source processor is the initiator of the action, whereas the destination processor is passive. Thus, we assume implicitly that each processor allows all others to put data into its memory. Note that the program includes a put by processor $P(s)$ into itself. This operation is simply skipped or becomes a local memory-copy, but it does not involve communication. It is convenient to include such puts in program texts, to avoid having to specify exceptions.

Sometimes, it may be necessary to let the destination processor initiate the communication. This may happen in irregular computations, where the destination processor knows that it needs data, but the source processor is unaware of this need. In that case, the destination processor must fetch the data from the source processor. This is done by a statement of the form 'get x from $P(t)$' in the program text of $P(s)$. In most cases, however, we use the 'put' primitive. Note that using a 'put' is much simpler than using a matching 'send'/'receive' pair, as is done in message-passing parallel algorithms. The program text of such an algorithm must contain additional if-statements to distinguish between sends and receives. Careful checking is needed to make sure that pairs match in all possible executions of the program. Even if every send has a matching receive, this does not guarantee correct communication as intended by the algorithm designer. If the send/receive is done by the handshake (or kissing) protocol, where both participants can only continue their way after the handshake has finished, then it can easily happen that the sends and receives occur in the wrong order. A classic case is when two processors both want to send first and receive afterwards; this situation is called **deadlock**. Problems such as deadlock cannot happen when using puts.

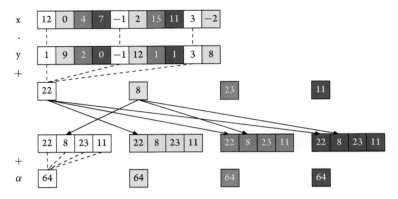

Figure 1.6 Parallel inner product computation. Two vectors **x**, **y** of size ten are distributed by the cyclic distribution over four processors. The processors are shown by colours. First, each processor computes its local inner product. For example, processor $P(0)$ computes $12 \cdot 1 + (-1) \cdot (-1) + 3 \cdot 3 = 22$. Then the local result is sent to all other processors. Finally, the local inner products are summed redundantly to give the result $\alpha = 64$ in every processor. For clarity, some local computations and some communications are not shown.

In superstep (2), all processors compute the final result. This is done **redundantly**, that is, the computation is replicated so that all processors perform exactly the same operations on the same data. The complete algorithm is illustrated in Fig. 1.6.

The cost analysis of the algorithm is as follows. Superstep (0) requires a floating-point multiplication and an addition for each component. Therefore, the cost of (0) is $2\lceil n/p \rceil + l$. Superstep (1) is a $(p-1)$-relation, because each processor sends and receives $p-1$ data. (Communication between a processor and itself is not really communication and hence is not counted in determining h.) The cost of (1) is $(p-1)g + l$. The cost of (2) is $p + l$. (With clever initialization of α to α_s, we could shave off one flop, but the resulting program text would be ugly, so we refrain ourselves from doing this.) The total cost of the inner product algorithm is

$$T_{\text{inprod}} = 2\left\lceil \frac{n}{p} \right\rceil + p + (p-1)g + 3l. \tag{1.9}$$

An alternative approach would be to send all partial inner products to one processor, $P(0)$, and let this processor compute the result and broadcast it. This requires four supersteps. Sending the partial inner products to $P(0)$ is a $(p-1)$-relation and therefore is just as expensive as broadcasting them. While $P(0)$ adds partial inner products, the other processors are idle and hence the cost of the addition is the same as for the redundant computation. The total cost of the alternative algorithm would be $2\lceil n/p \rceil + p + 2(p-1)g + 4l$, which is higher than that of Algorithm 1.1. The lesson to be learned: if you have to perform an h-relation with a particular h, you might as well perform as much useful communication as possible in that h-relation; other supersteps may benefit from this.

1.4 Starting with BSPlib: example program bspinprod

BSPlib is a standard library interface, which defines a set of primitives for writing bulk synchronous parallel programs. The original BSPlib standard by Hill *et al.* [153] contains 20 primitives and was published in 1998; it unified and extended its two predecessors, the Oxford BSP library designed by Miller and Reed [223, 224] and the Green BSP library by Goudreau *et al.* [126, 127]. The BSPlib standard was modernized in 2014 in the API of the MulticoreBSP for C library [318], with updates of type definitions and an extension by two new primitives.

MulticoreBSP for C is the implementation of choice for shared-memory architectures and we will use it throughout the book for all our program texts. If you have a laptop or desktop computer with multiple cores, MulticoreBSP for C is the easiest option for running the programs of this book, and also for getting started with writing programs yourself. MulticoreBSP for C has a compatibility mode for running programs written for the original BSPlib interface, such as the programs from the first edition of this book (packaged as BSPedupack, version 1.02).

For distributed-memory architectures, we employ the BSPonMPI library [281], making use of the MPI system that is almost universally available on these architectures, thus running BSPlib on top of MPI, with hardly any loss in efficiency and sometimes even a gain. (Note that this software has recently been updated to the new interface.) As a result, we can run implementations of BSPlib across a whole range of computers, from laptops with shared memory to massively parallel supercomputers with distributed memory. In addition, the library can also be used on an ordinary sequential computer to run a parallel program with $p = 1$ as a sequential program; an efficient BSP system would even strip off the parallel overhead (a nice feature of the early Oxford BSP toolset [151]). This is advantageous because it allows us to develop and maintain only one version of the source program, namely the parallel version. It is also possible to simulate a parallel computer by running p processes in parallel on fewer processors, or even on one processor, sharing the time of the common CPU. MulticoreBSP for C has this option, giving us a useful environment for developing and testing, for instance, a 1000-core parallel program for correctness on a much smaller multicore machine.

The BSPlib library contains a set of primitive functions, which can be called from a program written in a conventional programming language such as C, C++, Java, or Fortran 90. At present, the most developed implementations are for C and C++. The MulticoreBSP for Java implementation from 2012 [317] has inspired the MulticoreBSP for C version we use here, and is an alternative for those already familiar with Java. The Fortran implementation available in the Oxford toolset from 1998 has become obsolete; there have been additions to newer versions of the Fortran language facilitating parallel programming.

BSPlib was designed following the motto 'small is beautiful'. The primitives of BSPlib were carefully crafted, and particular attention was paid to the question of what to exclude from the library. As a result, BSPlib in its present version contains only 22 primitive functions. A complete list is given in Appendix B. In this section, we present a small C program, which uses 12 different primitives. The aim of this tutorial program is to get you started using the library and to expose the main principles of writing a BSPlib program. The remainder of this book gives further examples of how the library can be used. Two primitives for high-performance communication ('hpput' and 'hpget') are primarily meant for programmers who want the ultimate in performance, in terms of memory and computing speed, and who are prepared to live on the edge and be responsible for the safety of their programs, instead of relying on the BSP system to provide this safety. Six primitives for so-called bulk synchronous message passing will be explained in Section 1.9, where they are first needed. Furthermore, a new high-performance send primitive for bulk synchronous message passing is now available, as well as a new primitive that enables exploitation of the shared memory of a computer, by directly reading data from that shared memory. We will discuss these new primitives further on in this book.

A quick reference guide to the BSPlib primitives is given as Appendix B. For a full explanation of the BSPlib standard, see the definitive source by Hill *et al.* [153]. For full details of the updated primitives, see the appendix of the MulticoreBSP for C paper by Yzelman *et al.* [318]. In the following, we assume that the latest version of the MulticoreBSP for C implementation has already been installed; see the online quick-start guide [315] for a useful guide to installing the software. Installation is indeed quick, and should not take you more than 15 minutes.

The parallel part of a BSPlib program starts with the statement

```
bsp_begin ( reqprocs );
```

where `unsigned int reqprocs` is the number of processors requested. The function `bsp_begin` starts several executions of the same subprogram, where each execution takes place on a different processor and handles a different stream of data, in true SPMD style. The parallel part is terminated by

```
bsp_end ();
```

Two possible modes of operation can be used. In the first mode, the whole computation is SPMD; here, the call to `bsp_begin` must be the first executable statement in the program and the call to `bsp_end` the last. Sometimes, however, one desires to perform some sequential part of the program before and after the parallel part, for example, to handle input and output. For instance, if the optimal number of processors to be used depends on the input, we want to compute it before the actual parallel computation starts. The second mode enables this: processor $P(0)$ executes the sequential parts and all processors together perform the parallel part. Processor $P(0)$ preserves the values of its variables on moving from one part to the next. The other processors do not inherit values; they can only obtain desired data values by communication.

To allow the second mode of operation and to circumvent the restriction of `bsp_begin` and `bsp_end` being the first and last statement, the actual parallel part is made into a separate function `spmd`, and an initializer

```
bsp_init (spmd, argc, argv );
```

is called as the first executable statement of the `main` function. Here, `int argc` and `char **argv` are the standard arguments of `main` in a C program, and these can be used to transfer parameters from a command line interface. The variable `argc` is the argument count, and `argv` is an array of `argc` arguments, which are character strings. Funny things can happen if `bsp_init` is not the first executable statement. Do not even think of trying it! The initializing statement is followed by: a sequential part, which may handle some input or ask for the desired number of processors (depending on the input size it may be better to use only some of the available processors); the parallel part, which is executed by `spmd`; and finally another sequential part, which may handle output. The sequential parts are optional.

The rules for I/O are simple: processor $P(0)$ is the only processor that can read from standard input or can access the file system, but all processors can write to standard output. Be aware that this may mix the output streams; use an `fflush(stdout)` statement to empty the output buffer immediately and increase the chance of obtaining ordered output. Sorry, no guarantees here. The only way to ensure proper ordering is first transferring all output data to $P(0)$ and then letting this processor write the data to output in the desired order.

At every point in the parallel part of the program, one can enquire about the total number of processors. This unsigned integer is returned by

`bsp_nprocs ();`

In our algorithms and programs, we usually call this value p. The function `bsp_nprocs` also serves a second purpose: when it is used in the sequential part at the start, or in the `bsp_begin` statement, it returns the available number of processors, that is, the size of the BSP machine used. Any desired number of processors not exceeding the machine size can be assigned to the program by `bsp_begin`. (On installation, certain implementations may enable the machine size to be exceeded by a small factor, e.g. to allow the exploitation of **hyperthreading** or the use of **virtual processors**. Do not expect full speedups in that case.) The local processor identity, or processor number, is returned by

`bsp_pid ();`

It is an unsigned integer with value between 0 and `bsp_nprocs()` -1. This function can only be called from within the parallel part. One can also enquire about the time elapsed in seconds (or ms or μs) on the local processor since `bsp_begin`; this time is given as a double-precision value by

`bsp_time ();`

Note that in the parallel context the **elapsed time**, or wall-clock time, is often the desired metric and not the CPU time. In parallel programs, processors are often idling because they have to wait for others to finish their part of a computation; a measurement of elapsed time includes idle time, whereas a CPU time measurement does not.

Each superstep of the SPMD part, or **program superstep**, is terminated by a global synchronization statement

`bsp_sync ();`

except the final program superstep, which is terminated by `bsp_end`. The structure of a BSPlib program is illustrated in Fig. 1.7. Program supersteps may be contained in loops

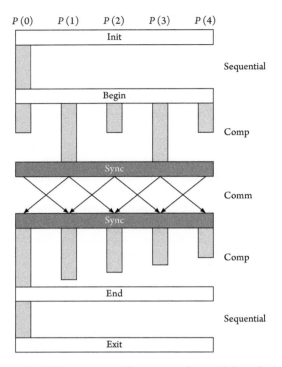

Figure 1.7 Structure of a BSPlib program. The program first initializes the BSP machine to be used and then it performs a sequential computation on $P(0)$, followed by a parallel computation (between 'Begin' and 'End') on five processors, and a sequential computation on $P(0)$.

and if-statements, but the condition evaluations of these loops and if-statements must be such that all processors pace through the same sequence of program supersteps. The rules imposed by BSPlib may seem restrictive, but following them makes parallel programming easier, because they guarantee that all processors are always in the same superstep. This allows us to assume full data integrity at the start of each superstep.

The variant of the BSP model presented in Section 1.2 allows mixing computation and communication in the same superstep of a BSP algorithm. The BSPlib system automatically separates computation and communication in BSP programs, since it delays communication until all computation is finished. The main benefit of this separation is that it enables the system to optimize the communication. This benefit is automatic: the user does not have to perform the separation herself and she also does not have to include a bsp_sync in the program for this purpose; furthermore, communication often involves address calculations and it would be awkward for a user to separate these computations from the corresponding communication operations. In practice, this means that BSPlib programs can freely mix computation and communication.

As a consequence of the automatic separation just described, we can view a program superstep as a sequence of computation, implicit synchronization, communication, and explicit synchronization. The computation part or the communication part may be empty. Therefore, a program superstep may correspond to one or two algorithmic supersteps as defined in the BSP model, either to a mixed superstep, or to a computation superstep and a communication superstep. From now on, we use the shorter term 'superstep' to denote program supersteps as well, except when this would lead to confusion.

Wouldn't it be nice if we could compute and communicate at the same time? This tempting thought may have occurred to you by now. Indeed, processors could in principle compute while messages travel through the communication network. Exploiting this form of parallelism would reduce the total computation/communication cost $a + bg$ of the algorithm, but at most by a factor of two. The largest reduction would occur if every superstep were mixed and the computation cost of a superstep were always equal to its communication cost, and if computation and communication could always be overlapped completely. In most cases, however, either computation or communication dominates a superstep, and the cost reduction obtained by overlapping is not worth the trouble. Surprisingly, BSPlib guarantees *not* to exploit potential overlap (except in case of the high-performance primitives). Instead, it delays all communication to create more scope for optimization, since this allows the system to combine different messages from the same source to the same destination and to reorder the messages with the aim of balancing the communication traffic and avoiding congestion. As a result, the cost may be reduced by much more than a factor of two.

Processors can communicate with each other by using the bsp_put and bsp_get functions (or their high-performance equivalents bsp_hpput and bsp_hpget, or the bsp_send function, see Section 1.9). A processor that calls bsp_put reads data from its own memory and writes them into the memory of another processor. The function bsp_put corresponds to the put operation in our algorithms. The syntax is

bsp_put (pid , source , dest , offset , nbytes);

Here, unsigned int pid is the identity of the remote processor; void *source is a pointer to the source memory in the local processor from which the data are read; void *dest is a pointer to the destination memory in the remote processor into which the data will be written; size_t offset is the number of bytes to be added to the address dest to obtain the address where writing starts; and size_t nbytes is the number of bytes to be written. In C, size_t is an unsigned integer type used to represent object sizes. It is sufficiently large to hold any array index. The dest variable must have been registered previously; the registration mechanism will be explained soon. If pid equals bsp_pid, the put is done locally by a memory copy, and no data are communicated. The offset is determined by the local processor, but the destination address is part of the address space of the remote processor. The use of an offset separates the concerns of the local processor, which knows where in an array a data element should be placed, from the concerns of the remote processor, which knows the address of the array in its own address space. The bsp_put operation is illustrated in Fig. 1.8.

The bsp_put operation is safe in every sense, since the value to be put is first written into a local out-buffer, and only at the end of the superstep (when all computations in all processors are finished) is it transferred into a remote in-buffer, from which it is finally copied into the destination memory. The user can manipulate both the source and destination

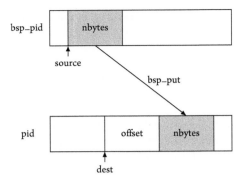

Figure 1.8 Put operation from BSPlib. The bsp_put operation copies nbytes of data from the local processor bsp_pid into the specified destination processor pid. The pointer source points to the start of the data to be copied, whereas the pointer dest specifies the start of the memory area where the data will be written. The data will be written at offset bytes from the start.

value without worrying about possible interference between data manipulation and transfer. Once the bsp_put is initiated, the user has got rid of the source data and can reuse the variable that holds them. The destination variable can be used until the end of the superstep, when it will be overwritten. It is possible to put several values into the same memory cell, but of course only one value survives and reaches the next superstep. The user cannot know which value, and he bears the responsibility for ensuring correct program behaviour. Put and get operations do not block progress within their superstep: after a put or get is initiated, the program proceeds immediately.

Although a remote variable may have the same name as a local variable, it may still have a different physical memory address because each processor could have its own memory allocation procedure. To enable a processor to write into a remote variable, there must be a way to link the local name to the correct remote address. Linking is done by the registration primitive

bsp_push_reg (variable , nbytes);

where void *variable is a pointer to the variable being registered. All processors must simultaneously register a variable, or the NULL pointer if opting out; they must also deregister simultaneously. This ensures that they go through the same sequence of registrations and deregistrations. Registration takes effect at the start of the next superstep. From that moment, all simultaneously registered variables are linked to each other. Usually, the name of each variable linked in a registration is the same, in the right SPMD spirit. Still, it is allowed to link variables with different names.

If a processor wants to put a value into a remote address, it can do this by using the local name that is linked to the remote name and hence to the desired remote address. The second registration parameter, size_t nbytes, is an upper bound on the number of bytes that can be written starting from variable. Its sole purpose is sanity checking: our hope is to detect insane programs in their youth.

A variable is deregistered by a call to

bsp_pop_reg(variable);

This takes effect at the start of the next superstep, as in the case of registration. Within a superstep, the variables can be registered and deregistered in arbitrary order. The same variable may be registered several times, but with different sizes. (This may happen for instance as a result of registration of the same variable inside different functions.) A deregistration cancels the last registration of the variable concerned. The last surviving registration of a variable is the one valid in the next superstep. For each variable, a stack of registrations is maintained: a variable is pushed onto the stack when it is registered; and it is popped off the stack when it is deregistered. A **stack** is the computer science equivalent of a physical stack of books where you can put a new book only on top of the others and where you can only remove the top book, thereby following the Last In, First Out (LIFO) principle. In a sensible program, the number of registrations is kept limited. Preferably, a registered variable is reused many times, to amortize the overhead costs associated with registration; registration requires a broadcast of the registered local variable to the other processors and possibly an additional synchronization. Deregistering a variable after its use is not strictly necessary, but it is a good habit, which helps keep the stack small, with possible efficiency benefits.

A processor that calls the bsp_get function reads data from the memory of another processor and writes them into its own memory. The syntax is

bsp_get(pid, source, offset, dest, nbytes);

The parameters of bsp_get have the same meaning as those of bsp_put, except that the source memory is in the remote processor and the destination memory in the local processor and that the offset is in the source memory. The offset is again computed by the local processor. The source variable must have been registered previously. The value obtained by the bsp_get operation is the source value immediately *after* the computations of the present superstep have terminated, but *before* it can be modified by other communication operations.

If a processor detects an error, it can take action and bring down all other processors in a graceful manner by a call to

bsp_abort(error_message, ...);

Here, char *error_message is a format string such as used by the printf function in C; it is followed by a corresponding number of parameters. Proper use of the abort facility makes it unnecessary to check periodically whether all processors are still alive and computing.

BSPlib contains only the essential primitive operations. By keeping the library small, the BSPlib designers hoped to enable quick and efficient implementation of BSPlib on every parallel computer that appears on the market. This has indeed happened for a number of architectures and often such an implementation started as a student project. A very interesting example is the Epiphany BSP library [53] developed for the crowdfunded Parallella board of credit-card size, promoted as 'a supercomputer for everyone', the 16-core version running at 32 Gflop/s with only 5 watt power consumption.

Higher-level functions such as broadcasting or global summing, generally called **collective communication**, are useful but not really necessary. Of course, users can write their own higher-level functions on top of the primitive functions, giving them exactly the desired functionality, or use predefined ones available in libraries built by others, such as the Oxford BSP toolset [151]. Section 2.6 gives an example of a collective-communication function, the broadcast of a vector.

The best way of learning to use BSPlib is to study an example and then try to write your own program. Below, we present the function bspip, which is an implementation of Algorithm 1.1 in C using BSPlib, and the test program bspinprod, which handles input and output for a test problem. Now, try to compile the program by the UNIX command

```
bspcc −std=c99 −Wall −O3 −o inprod bspinprod.c\
bspedupack.c −lm
```

which uses the C compiler chosen by BSP for the C99 standard, produces all warnings, and optimizes the code to the highest (third) level. In many cases, the gcc compiler will be chosen, and sometimes a vendor-specific compiler. Furthermore, the compilation with -lm links to the C mathematics library. The bspcc command hides some of the system-specific choices to be made and it should be available on good BSP systems. The given compilation command works on my Linux and MacOS X computers, but you may have to change it to get it working on yours. Then, run the resulting executable program inprod on the maximum available number of processors by the command

```
bsprun ./inprod
```

and see what happens for this particular test problem, defined by $x_i = y_i = i + 1$, for $0 \le i < n$. (If you are not running a UNIX variant, you may have to follow a different procedure.) A listing of the file bspedupack.c can be found in Appendix A. It contains functions for allocation and deallocation of vectors and matrices.

The relation between Algorithm 1.1 and the function bspip is as follows. The variables p, s, t, n, α of the algorithm correspond to the variables p, s, t, n, alpha of the function.[1] The local inner product α_s of $P(s)$ is denoted by inprod in the program text of $P(s)$, and it is also put into Inprod[s] in all processors. The global index i in the algorithm equals i * p + s, where i is a local index in the program. The vector component x_i corresponds to the variable x[i] on the processor that owns x_i, that is, on processor $P(i \bmod p)$. The number of local indices on $P(s)$ is nloc(p,s,n); the function nloc is part of bspedupack.c, see Appendix A. The first $n \bmod p$ processors have $\lceil n/p \rceil$ such indices, while the others have $\lfloor n/p \rfloor$. Note the efficient way in which nloc is computed, and check that this method is correct, by writing $n = ap + b$ with $0 \le b < p$ and expanding the expression returned by the function.

---

[1] Here, a mathematician's preference for short variable names becomes apparent: in this book I tend to use them wherever possible. Don't do this at home! You may want to use longer, more meaningful names for your variables, especially in programs larger than the short example programs of this book.

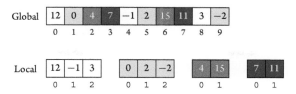

Figure 1.9 Two different views of the same vector. The vector of size ten is distributed by the cyclic distribution over four processors. The numbers in the square cells are the numerical values of the vector components. The processors are shown by colours. The global view is used in algorithms, where vector components are numbered using global indices j. The local view is used in implementations, where each processor has its own part of the vector and uses its own local indices j.

It is convenient to describe algorithms such as Algorithm 1.1 unambiguously in global variables, but to implement them using local variables. This avoids addressing by a stride and its worse alternative, the superfluous test '**if** i mod $p = s$' in a loop over the global index i. Using local consecutive indices is most natural in an implementation because only a subarray of the original global array is stored locally. The difference between the global and local view is illustrated in Fig. 1.9. For all our distributions, we store the local vector components in order of increasing global index. This gives rise to a natural mapping between local and global indices.

The program printed below largely explains itself; a few additional explanations are given in the following. The included file bspedupack.h can be found in Appendix A. It contains inclusion statements for standard header files and also constants such as the value of π in 20 decimals. All our floating-point variables will be in double precision (i.e., double) so we do not have to worry too much about round-off errors in arithmetic operations, and all our integers will be of type long, so the size of integers is sufficient for most uses. We do not bother saving a bit of memory by using shorter types. The desired number of processors is first stored as a global variable P (global in the C sense, that is, accessible to all functions in its file), so that we are able to transfer the value of P from the main program to the SPMD part. Values cannot be transferred other than by using global variables, because the SPMD function is not allowed to have parameters. The function vecallocd from bspedupack.c is used to allocate an array of doubles of length p dynamically and vecfreed is used to free the array afterwards.

The offset in the first bsp_put is s times the size of a double in bytes, since the local inner product of processor s is put into Inprod[s] on every processor t. The processors synchronize before the time measurements by bsp_time, so that the measurements start and finish simultaneously. The program text of bspinprod is:

```
#include "bspedupack.h"

/*   This program computes the sum of the first n squares,
        sum = 1*1 + 2*2 + ... + n*n
     by computing the inner product of x=(1,2,...,n)^T and
```

```
    itself, for n>=0.
    The output should equal n*(n+1)*(2n+1)/6.
    The distribution of x is cyclic.
*/

long P; // number of processors requested

double bspip(long n, double *x, double *y){
    /* Compute inner product of vectors x and y
       of length n>=0 */

    long p= bsp_nprocs(); // p = number of processors
                          //     obtained
    long s= bsp_pid();    // s = processor number

    double *Inprod= vecallocd(p);
    bsp_push_reg(Inprod,p*sizeof(double));
    bsp_sync();

    double inprod= 0.0;
    for (long i=0; i<nloc(p,s,n); i++)
        inprod += x[i]*y[i];

    for (long t=0; t<p; t++)
        bsp_put(t,&inprod,Inprod,s*sizeof(double),
                sizeof(double));

    bsp_sync();

    double alpha= 0.0;
    for (long t=0; t<p; t++)
        alpha += Inprod[t];

    bsp_pop_reg(Inprod);
    vecfreed(Inprod);

    return alpha;

} /* end bspip */

void bspinprod(){

    bsp_begin(P);
    long p= bsp_nprocs();
```

```
long s= bsp_pid ();
long n;
if (s==0){
    printf("Please enter n:\n"); fflush(stdout);
    scanf("%ld",&n);
    if(n<0)
        bsp_abort("Error in input: n is negative");
}
bsp_push_reg(&n, sizeof(long));
bsp_sync ();

bsp_get(0,&n,0,&n, sizeof(long));
bsp_sync ();
bsp_pop_reg(&n);

long nl= nloc(p,s,n);
double *x= vecallocd(nl);
for (long i=0; i<nl; i++){
    long iglob= i*p+s;
    x[i]= iglob+1;
}
bsp_sync ();
double time0= bsp_time ();

double alpha= bspip(n,x,x);
bsp_sync ();
double time1= bsp_time ();

printf("Proc %ld: sum of squares up to %ld*%ld"
        "is %.1f\n", s,n,n,alpha); fflush(stdout);
if (s==0){
    printf("This took only %.6lf seconds.\n",
            time1-time0);

    /* Compute exact output (number can become
       large) */
    long long sum= (n*(n+1)*(2*n+1)) / (long long)6;
    printf("n(n+1)(2n+1)/6 = %lld\n", sum);
    fflush(stdout);
}

vecfreed(x);
bsp_end ();
```

```
} /* end bspinprod */

int main(int argc, char **argv){

    bsp_init(bspinprod, argc, argv);

    /* Sequential part */
    printf("How many processors do you want to use?\n");
    fflush(stdout);

    scanf("%ld",&P);
    if (P > bsp_nprocs()){
        printf("Sorry, only %u processors available.\n",
               bsp_nprocs());
        fflush(stdout);
        exit(EXIT_FAILURE);
    }

    /* SPMD part */
    bspinprod();

    /* Sequential part */
    exit(EXIT_SUCCESS);

} /* end main */
```

1.5 BSP benchmarking

Computer benchmarking is the activity of measuring computer performance by running a representative set of test programs. The performance results for a particular sequential computer are often reduced in some ruthless way to one number, the computing rate in flop/s. This allows us to rank different computers according to their computing rate and to make informed decisions on what machines to buy or use. The performance of parallel computers must be expressed in more than a single number because communication and synchronization are just as important for these computers as computation. The BSP model represents machine performance by a parameter set of minimal size: for a given number of processors p, the parameters r, g, and l represent the performance for computation, communication, and synchronization. Every parallel computer can be viewed as a BSP computer, with good or bad BSP parameters, and hence can also be benchmarked as a BSP computer. In this section, we present a method for BSP benchmarking. The aim of the method is to find out what the BSP computer looks like to an average user, perhaps you or me, who writes parallel programs but does not really want to spend much time optimizing programs, preferring instead to let the compiler and the BSP system do the job. (The benchmark method for optimization enthusiasts would be very different.)

The sequential computing rate r is determined by measuring the time of a so-called DAXPY operation ('Double precision A times X Plus Y'), which has the form $\mathbf{y} := \alpha\mathbf{x} + \mathbf{y}$, where $\mathbf{x}$ and $\mathbf{y}$ are vectors and α is a scalar. The name DAXPY comes from the level-1 Basic Linear Algebra Subprograms (BLAS) library [193], which was designed to help users benefit from vectorization of their programs, without having to optimize their code themselves. A DAXPY with vectors of length n contains n additions and n multiplications and some overhead in the form of $\mathcal{O}(n)$ address calculations. We also measure the time of a DAXPY operation with the addition replaced by subtraction. We use 64-bit arithmetic throughout; on most machines this is called **double-precision arithmetic**. This mixture of operations is representative for the majority of scientific computations. We measure the time for a vector length that on the one hand is large enough to ignore the startup costs of vector operations, but on the other hand is small enough for the vectors to fit into the smallest cache of the computer; a choice of $n = 1024$ is often adequate. A **cache** is a small but fast intermediate memory that allows immediate reuse of recently accessed data. Proper use of the cache considerably increases the computing rate on most modern computers. The existence of a cache makes the life of a benchmarker harder, because it leads to two different computing rates: a flop rate for in-cache computations and a rate for out-of-cache computations. Even worse, modern computers have increasingly deep memory architectures, with a small primary cache (also called an L1 cache), a larger but slower secondary cache (L2 cache), and an even larger tertiary cache (L3 cache). Therefore, intelligent choices should be made if the performance results are to be reduced to a single meaningful figure that still reflects the actual performance in the desired application area.

The DAXPY measurement is repeated a number of times, both to obtain a more accurate clock reading and to amortize the cost of bringing the vector into the cache. The number of repetitions may have to be increased with an increase in computer speed over the years, to maintain accuracy, in case the resolution of the timer stays the same. We measure the sequential computing rate of each processor of the parallel computer, and report the minimum, average, and maximum rate. The difference between the minimum and the maximum indicates the accuracy of the measurement, except when the processors genuinely differ in speed. (One processor that is slower than the others can have a remarkable effect on the overall time of a parallel computation!) We take the average computing rate of the processors as the final value of r. Note that our measurement is representative for user programs that contain mostly hand-coded vector operations. If we want to realize top performance, then system-provided matrix–matrix operations should be used wherever possible (in BLAS terms, level-3 operations such as DGEMM [93], Double precision GEneral Matrix–Matrix multiplication), because these are often efficiently coded in assembler language and tailored for the machine used, and because matrix–matrix operations have a high cache-reuse intensity. Our benchmark method is simpler and does not reflect that situation.

The communication parameter g and the synchronization parameter l are obtained by measuring the time of full h-relations, where each processor sends and receives exactly h data words. To be consistent with the measurement of r, we use double-precision reals as data words. We choose a particularly demanding test pattern from the many possible patterns with the same h, which reflects the typical way most users would handle communication in their programs. The destination processors of the values to be sent are determined in a cyclic fashion: $P(s)$ puts h values in remote processors $P(s+1), P(s+2), \ldots, P(p-1)$, $P(0), \ldots, P(s-1), P(s+1), \ldots$, wrapping around at processor number p and skipping the

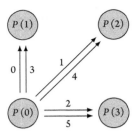

Figure 1.10 Communication pattern of the 6-relation in the BSP benchmark. Processors send data to the other processors in a cyclic manner. Only the data words sent by processor $P(0)$ are shown; other processors send data in a similar way. Each arrow represents the communication of one data word; the number shown is the index of the data word.

source processor to exclude local puts that do not require communication, see Fig. 1.10. In this communication pattern, all processors receive the same number, h, of data words (this can easily be proven by using a symmetry argument). The destination processor of each communicated value is computed before the actual h-relation is performed, to prevent possibly expensive modulo operations from influencing the timing results of the h-relation. The data is sent out as separate words, to simulate the typical situation in an application program where the user does not worry about the size of the data packets. This is the task of the BSP system, after all! Note that our way of benchmarking h-relations is a test of both the machine and the BSP library for that machine. Library software can combine several data words into one packet, if they are sent in one superstep from the same source processor to the same destination processor. An efficient library will package such data automatically and choose an optimal packet size for the particular machine used. This results in a lower benchmark value of g, because the communication startup cost of a packet is amortized over several words of data.

Our variant of the BSP model assumes that the measured time $T_{comm}(h)$ of an h-relation is linear in h, see (1.2). In principle, it would be possible to measure $T_{comm}(h)$ for two values of h and then determine g and l. Of course, the results would then be highly sensitive to measurement error. A better way of doing this is by measuring $T_{comm}(h)$ for all integer values in an interval $[h_0, h_1]$, and then finding the best least-squares approximation, given by the values of g and l that minimize the error

$$E_{LSQ} = \sum_{h=h_0}^{h_1} (T_{comm}(h) - (hg + l))^2. \qquad (1.10)$$

The values g and l are obtained by setting the partial derivatives of eqn (1.10) with respect to g and l to zero, and solving the resulting 2×2 linear system of equations. We choose $h_0 = p$, because packet optimization becomes worthwhile for $h \geq p$; we would like to capture the behaviour of the machine and the BSP system for such values of h. A value of $h_1 = 2048$ will often be adequate, except if $p \geq 2048$ or if the asymptotic communication speed is attained only for very large h.

Timing parallel programs requires caution since ultimately it often relies on a system timer, which may be hidden from the user and may have a low resolution. Always take a critical look at your timing results and your personal watch and, in case of suspicion, plot the output data on a graph! This may save you from potential embarrassment: on one occasion, I was surprised to find that according to an erroneous timer the computer had exceeded its true performance by a factor of four. On another occasion, I found that g was negative. The reason was that the particular computer had a small g but a huge l, so that for $h \leq h_1$ the measurement error in $gh + l$ was much larger than gh, thereby rendering the value of g meaningless. In this case, h_1 had to be increased to obtain an accurate measurement of g.

1.6 Example program bspbench

The program bspbench is a simple benchmarking program that measures the BSP parameters of a particular computer. It is an implementation of the benchmarking method described in Section 1.5. In the following, we present and explain the program. The least-squares function of bspbench solves a 2×2 linear system by subtracting a multiple of one equation from the other. Dividing by zero or by a small number is avoided by subtracting the equation with the largest leading coefficient. (Solving a 2×2 linear system is a prelude to Chapter 2, where large linear systems are solved by LU decomposition.)

The computing rate r of each processor is measured by using the bsp_time function, which gives the elapsed time in seconds for the processor that calls it. The measurements of r are independent, and hence they do not require timer synchronization. In contrast, the measurements of the h-relations involve all processors, so that we have to synchronize and let processor $P(0)$ determine the resulting time. The number of iterations NITERS is set such that each DAXPY pair (and each h-relation) is executed 1000 times. You may decrease the number if you run out of patience while waiting for the results. On the other hand, you may have to increase NITERS if the timer resolution is too low, so that timings round down to 0. To fool some aggressively optimizing compilers (especially if they fly the maximum optimization flag -O3), we generate some superfluous foolish output. We may fool some computers some of the time, but alas ...

The h-relation of our benchmarking method is implemented as follows. The data to be sent is put into the array dest of the destination processors. The destination processor destproc[i] is determined by starting with the next processor $s + 1$ and allocating the indices i to the $p - 1$ remote processors in a cyclic fashion, that is, by adding i mod $(p - 1)$ to the processor number $s + 1$. Taking the resulting value modulo p then gives a valid processor number unequal to s. The destination index destindex[i] is chosen such that each source processor fills its own part in the dest arrays on the other processors: $P(s)$ fills locations $s, s + p, s + 2p$, and so on. The locations are defined by destindex[i] = $s + (i \text{ div } (p - 1))p$, because we return to the same processor after each round of $p - 1$ puts into different destination processors. The largest destination index used in a processor is at most $p - 1 + ((h - 1) \text{ div } (p - 1))p < p + 2 \cdot \text{MAXH}$, which guarantees that the array dest is sufficiently large.

The special case $p = 1$ is handled well by the program, which then actually measures g for a memory copy with parallel overhead; the value of l should be close to that of g but it may be hard to retrieve accurately. The program text of bspbench is:

```
#include "bspedupack.h"

/*  This program measures p, r, g, and l of a BSP
    computer using bsp_put for communication.
*/

#define NITERS 1000      // number of iterations
#define MAXN 1024        // maximum length of DAXPY
#define MAXH 2048        // maximum h in h-relation,
                         // must be >> p
#define MEGA 1000000.0

long P;  // number of processors requested

void leastsquares(long h0, long h1, double *t,
                  double *g, double *l){
    /*  This function computes the parameters g and l
        of the linear function T(h)= g*h+l that best fits
        the data points (h,t[h]) with h0 <= h <= h1. */

    /*  Compute sums:
        sumt  =  sum of t[h] over h0 <= h <= h1
        sumth =       t[h]*h
        nh    =       1
        sumh  =       h
        sumhh =       h*h      */

    double sumt= 0.0;
    double sumth= 0.0;
    for (long h=h0; h<=h1; h++){
        sumt  += t[h];
        sumth += t[h]*h;
    }
    long nh= h1-h0+1;
    double h00 = (double)h0*(h0-1);
    double h11 = (double)h1*(h1+1);
    double sumh= (h11 - h00)/2;
    double sumhh= (h11*(2*h1+1) - h00*(2*h0-1))/6;

    /*  Solve    nh*l +  sumh*g  =  sumt
             sumh*l + sumhh*g  =  sumth */
```

```
double a= nh/sumh;      // nh <= sumh

/* Subtract a times second eqn from first eqn
   to obtain g */
*g= (sumt−a*sumth)/(sumh−a*sumhh);

/* Use second eqn to obtain l */
*l= (sumth−sumhh* *g)/sumh;

} /* end leastsquares */

void bspbench(){

    /**** Determine p ****/
    bsp_begin(P);
    long p= bsp_nprocs();  // p = number of processors
    long s= bsp_pid();     // s = processor number

    double *Time= vecallocd(p);
    bsp_push_reg(Time,p*sizeof(double));
    double *dest= vecallocd(2*MAXH+p);
    bsp_push_reg(dest,(2*MAXH+p)*sizeof(double));
    bsp_sync();

    /**** Determine r ****/
    double x[MAXN], y[MAXN], z[MAXN];
    double r= 0.0;
    for (long n=1; n <= MAXN; n *= 2){
        /* Initialize scalars and vectors */
        double alpha= 1.0/3.0;
        double beta= 4.0/9.0;
        for (long i=0; i<n; i++){
            z[i]= y[i]= x[i]= (double)i;
        }
        /* Measure time of 2*NITERS DAXPY operations of
           length n */
        double time0= bsp_time();
        for (long iter=0; iter<NITERS; iter++){
            for (long i=0; i<n; i++)
                y[i] += alpha*x[i];
            for (long i=0; i<n; i++)
                z[i] −= beta*x[i];
        }
```

```
double time1= bsp_time ();
double time= time1-time0;
bsp_put(0,&time,Time,s*sizeof(double),
        sizeof(double));
bsp_sync ();

/* Processor 0 determines minimum, maximum,
   average computing rate */
if (s==0){
    double mintime= Time[0];
    double maxtime= Time[0];
    for (long s1=1; s1<p; s1++){
        if (Time[s1] < mintime)
            mintime= Time[s1];
        if (Time[s1] > maxtime)
            maxtime= Time[s1];
    }
    if (mintime>0.0){
        /* Compute r = average computing rate in
           flop/s */
        long nflops= 4*NITERS*n;
        r= 0.0;
        for (long s1=0; s1<p; s1++)
            r += nflops/Time[s1];
        r /= p;
        printf("n= %5ld min= %7.3lf ",
                n, nflops/(maxtime*MEGA));
        printf("max= %7.3lf av= %7.3lf Mflop/s ",
                nflops/(mintime*MEGA), r/MEGA);
        /* Output for fooling too clever
           compilers */
        printf(" fool=%7.1lf\n",y[n-1]+z[n-1]);
    } else
        printf("minimum time is 0\n");
    fflush(stdout);
}
}
/* r is taken as the value at length MAXN */

/**** Determine g and l ****/
long destproc[MAXH], destindex[MAXH];
double src[MAXH], t[MAXH+1]; // t[h] = time of
                            // h-relation
```

```
for (long h=0; h<=MAXH; h++){
    /* Initialize communication pattern */
    for (long i=0; i<h; i++){
        src[i]= (double)i;
        if (p==1){
            destproc[i]= 0;
            destindex[i]= i;
        } else {
            /* destination proc is one of the p-1
            others */ destproc[i]= (s+1 + i%(p-1)) %p;
            /* destination index is in my own part
            of dest */ destindex[i]= s + (i/(p-1))*p;
        }
    }

    /* Measure time of NITERS h-relations */
    bsp_sync();
    double time0= bsp_time();
    for (long iter=0; iter<NITERS; iter++){
        for (long i=0; i<h; i++)
            bsp_put(destproc[i],&src[i],dest,
                    destindex[i]*sizeof(double),
                    sizeof(double));
        bsp_sync();
    }
    double time1= bsp_time();
    double time= time1-time0;

    /* Compute time of one h-relation */
    if (s==0){
        t[h]= (time*r)/NITERS; // time in flop units
        printf("Time of %5ld-relation = %.2lf"
               " microsec = %8.0lf flops\n",
               h, (time*MEGA)/NITERS, t[h]);
        fflush(stdout);
    }
}

if (s==0){
    double g0, 10, g, 1;
    printf("size double = %ld bytes\n",
           (long)sizeof(double));
    leastsquares(0,p,t,&g0,&10);
    printf("Range h=0 to p    : g= %.1lf,"
```

```
                  "l= %.1lf\n" ,g0 , l0 );
         leastsquares (p ,MAXH, t ,&g,& l );
         printf("Range h=p to %ld : g= %.1lf , l= %.1lf\n" ,
                  (long )MAXH,  g , l );

         printf("The bottom line for this BSP computer"
                  " is :\n" );
         printf("p= %ld , r= %.3lf Mflop/s , g= %.1lf ,"
                  "l= %.1lf\n" , p , r /MEGA, g , l );
         fflush (stdout );
    }
    bsp_pop_reg (dest );
    vecfreed (dest );
    bsp_pop_reg (Time );
    vecfreed (Time );

    bsp_end ();

} /* end bspbench */

int main(int argc , char **argv ){

    bsp_init (bspbench , argc , argv );
    printf("How many processors do you want to use?\n" );
    fflush (stdout );
    scanf ("%ld" ,&P );
    if (P > bsp_nprocs ()){
         printf("Sorry , only %u processors available .\n" ,
                  bsp_nprocs ());
         fflush (stdout );
         exit (EXIT_FAILURE );
    }
    bspbench ();
    exit (EXIT_SUCCESS );

} /* end main */
```

1.7 Benchmark results

What is the cheapest parallel computer you can buy? A dualcore or quadcore personal computer. At the start of my course Parallel Algorithms, many of my students tell me that they possess such a computer, usually with four cores, sometimes more. So in May 2016, following my students, I decided to buy a quadcore desktop for my home, an Apple iMac i5-5675R with a 3.1 GHz Intel Core i5 quadcore processor, an L1 data cache per core of 32 kB,

Table 1.2 Benchmarked BSP parameters p, g, l and the time of a 0-relation for a 4-core Apple iMac desktop computer with 3.1 GHz Intel i5 processor. All times are in flop units and they are normalized to the same computing rate ($r = 8.44$ Gflop/s).

p	g	l	$T_{\text{comm}}(0)$
1	250	4 300	402
2	254	4 969	3 249
3	263	7 090	4 712
4	311	16 087	5 179

an L2 cache per core of 256 kB, a shared L3 cache of 4 MB and a RAM (random access memory) of 8 GB, now running the MacOS 10.14.3 operating system. The Intel processor of this computer belongs to the Broadwell family, which is based on 14 nm lithography.

I installed MulticoreBSP for C [318], version 2.0.4β, and benchmarked my computer by using the program bspbench. I turned the computer into a single-user machine by asking my lovely wife and daughter not to use it for a while. The possibility of a single-user mode is an advantage of a personal computer over shared systems such as the other two computers that will be tested in this section.

Table 1.2 shows the results of benchmarking my home computer. Noteworthy is the high floating-point computing rate of 8.44 Gflop/s, which almost seems too good to be true with 2.72 flops per core per clock cycle, but still is reasonably close to the performance obtained by using another benchmark, Geekbench 3 [254], which reaches 5.03 Gflop/s on double-precision matrix multiplication (DGEMM). This high performance can be explained by the fact that a modern processor core can perform several flops within a clock cycle by exploiting **vectorization**, for instance by creating a pipeline that performs an addition $x_i + y_i$ while computing a multiplication $\alpha \cdot x_j$. In the table, the communication parameter g grows only slowly, but the synchronization parameter l grows superlinearly. To provide a sanity check, we also give the time of a 0-relation (i.e., an empty communication superstep), which is a lower bound on l, since it represents only part of the fixed cost of a superstep. Indeed, $T_{\text{comm}}(0)$ is always observed to be less than l and it has the same order of magnitude, except for $p = 1$, where it is much less.

To investigate the communication behaviour in more detail, we should plot the time of an h-relation as a function of h. Figure 1.11 does this for $p = 4$. Overall, the figure displays a nice linear increase in time with increasing h, with a few outliers. The outlier of about 500 000 flops at $h = 851$ is equivalent to a time of 60 μs for an h-relation. The straight line of the least-squares fit is hidden in the cloud of data points. Each data point represents the average of NITERS=1000 h-relations, so that fluctuations are reasonably smoothed out.

Out of curiosity, I decided also to measure the power usage of my home computer during the benchmarking of h-relations. It turned out that my computer consumes about 35 watt when idling, uses 50 watt for $p = 1$, 60 for $p = 2$, 70 for $p = 3$, and 80 watt for $p = 4$. Furthermore, for $p = 3, 4$, I heard that the fan of my computer started running and my computer became noisy. Performing benchmarks comes at a price!

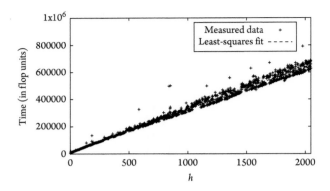

Figure 1.11 Time of an h-relation for a 4-core Apple iMac desktop computer with 3.1 GHz Intel i5 processor. The time is normalized to the measured computing rate of 8.44 Gflop/s.

Table 1.3 presents benchmark results obtained by the program `bspbench` on the compute server Gemini of the Faculty of Science of Utrecht University. This server is used for large computations by staff members and students, but also for other purposes such as gatekeeping for remote logins, providing web services, and so on. The machine runs Scientific Linux, version 7.6, and it has two Intel Xeon E5-2683 v4 CPUs with a total of 32 processor cores running at 2.1 GHz clock speed. The clock speed may increase to 3.0 GHz when the Turbo Booster switches on. The CPUs belong to the Intel Broadwell family. We installed MulticoreBSP for C, version 2.0.4, for $p = 32$ and ran our benchmark program `bspbench` for $p \leq 24$, leaving some cores idle to be nice to other users. We carried out our experiments on a rainy Wednesday afternoon in April 2019. We normalized all results to the same single processor rate of 2.3 Gflop/s, measured in the $p = 1$ experiment, but we observed a large variability in this rate within a range 2.2–3.6 Gflop/s. Each measured rate is already an average over all cores involved and over 1000 iterations, pointing towards even larger variability for single cores and single iterations. More reliable results could perhaps have been obtained by repeating the benchmark experiment at night, preferably after a system reboot, or by organizing a party for colleagues and students (and sneaking out in the middle) in the hope of encountering a user-free period. Even then, if we use all the cores of the computer, occasionally system chores carried out at the same time will compete with our benchmarking program and hence will slow it down. This makes it sometimes hard to reproduce experimental results.

The BSP parameters presented in Table 1.3 show that g remains more or less constant for $p \leq 8$, and then grows linearly for $p > 8$. The measurements of l show a more erratic growth with p, where we would expect monotonic growth. This erratic behaviour must be due to interference by other processes running on the system that are unrelated to our benchmark but may cause delays in synchronization. Such interference may also happen in actual parallel application programs, causing once in a while a problematic superstep, which is especially bad if the supersteps are small, as in our benchmark, with little computation

Table 1.3 Benchmarked BSP parameters p, g, l and the time of a 0-relation for a 32-core 2.1 GHz Intel Xeon multi-user compute server. All times are in flop units and they are normalized to the same computing rate ($r = 2.300$ Gflop/s).

p	g	l	$T_{comm}(0)$
1	92	2 767	286
2	95	3 970	1 623
3	105	10 095	5 426
4	113	3 905	3 593
5	120	14 086	8 622
6	138	13 957	10 273
7	124	28 166	11 706
8	106	12 011	7 185
12	145	39 109	20 251
16	222	11 501	16 433
20	192	54 440	35 615
24	309	46 224	49 337

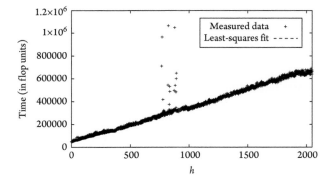

Figure 1.12 Time of an h-relation on 24 cores of a 32-core 2.1 GHz Intel Xeon multi-user compute server. The time is normalized to the measured computing rate of 2.3 Gflop/s.

and communication. For large supersteps with more bulk, this type of interference will be negligible.

Figure 1.12 shows benchmark results obtained on Gemini for $p = 24$. The least-squares fit is nicely hidden in the cloud of measurement points, and we observe near-linear behaviour that fits well with the asymptotic value of g as given by the least-squares line, with some interferences noticeable in the range $h = 750$–900.

What is the most expensive parallel computer you can buy? A supercomputer, by definition. Commonly, a **supercomputer** is defined as one of today's top performers in terms of computing rate, communication/synchronization rate, and memory size. Most likely, the cost of a supercomputer will exceed a million US dollars.

The Dutch national supercomputer Cartesius, named after the French philosopher and mathematician René Descartes (1596–1650), is located at the SURFsara supercomputer centre in Amsterdam. This is the computer that my students and I regularly use. Cartesius is a Bullx cluster of symmetric multiprocessors constructed by Atos/Bull. A **symmetric multiprocessor** (SMP) is a tightly coupled system of identical processors that share the same memory and operating system instance. Cartesius has four types of CPU nodes and two types of accelerator nodes, graphics processing units (GPUs) and Intel Xeon Phi accelerators. The CPU nodes each possess either 24 or 32 cores, and a memory of 64 GB (for thin nodes) or 256 GB (for fat nodes). Each node of the machine can be considered an SMP. The total number of CPU cores of the machine at the time of writing is 47 776. The top measured speed using only the thin nodes (38 880 cores in total) on the High-Performance LINPACK (HPL) benchmark [92], which solves a large dense linear system by LU decomposition, is 1.088 Pflop/s at a power consumption of 706 kwatt, where 1 Pflop = 1 petaflop = 10^{15} flop. In June 2019, this machine was placed at position 456 on the TOP500 list [279] of the fastest supercomputers on earth; in November 2019, it dropped out of the list. (It is scheduled to be replaced sometime in the next few years.)

Here, we will examine the performance of a single Broadwell node of Cartesius, as a shared-memory architecture. This node belongs to the BullSequana X1000 cell with 177 thin nodes that was added to Cartesius in 2016. The node consists of two 16-core 2.6 GHz Intel Xeon E5-2697A v4 (Broadwell) CPUs and a memory of 64 GB. The clock speed of a core can be increased from 2.6 to 3.6 GHz when the Turbo Booster is switched on. We installed MulticoreBSP for C [318], version 2.0.4, and ran our benchmark program bspbench for up to 32 cores. Table 1.4 presents the BSP parameters measured for this node, showing a small steady growth rate of g as a function of p, and a near-linear growth of l with p. The benchmark gave a negative l-value for $p = 1$, so here it is better to take $l = T_{\text{comm}}(0)$ instead. BSP parameters obviously cannot be negative, and the explanation for such an unphysical measurement value is that l is of the same order as g, so that the fit over the long range $h = 0$–2048 is more influenced by g than by l.

The best way to gain insight into what is happening in a benchmark measurement is to plot the data, see Fig. 1.13, where we display only part of the whole range $h = 0$–2048. The plot shows a good fit to a straight line, but the line is below the measurements for $h \leq 170$. Around $h = 170$, a switch point is visible, most likely caused by a different data transfer mechanism being used for larger amounts of data.

Figure 1.14 shows the least-squares fit for $p = 32$, again displaying only part of the whole range $h = 0$–2048. Here, the l-value of the fit is meaningful and there are no big outliers.

A lesson to be learned from these benchmarks is that the BSP cost model is valid and especially that it describes the linear cost of an h-relation well, but also that we should be prepared for all kinds of surprises on actual hardware and hence should not get carried away about the predictive power of the model. The BSP parameters are useful indicators of performance, but they may be off occasionally. The single-processor computing rate r may be the most evasive parameter here, as it depends very much on the type of computation measured. It is

Table 1.4 Benchmarked BSP parameters p, g, l and the time of a 0-relation for a 32-core 2.6 GHz Intel Xeon E5-2697A (Broadwell) node of the Bullx supercomputer Cartesius. All times are in flop units and they are normalized to the same computing rate ($r = 5.711$ Gflop/s).

p	g	l	$T_{\text{comm}}(0)$
1	197	—	294
2	199	18 408	6 759
3	215	24 438	8 932
4	225	38 275	14 291
5	247	30 783	17 970
6	262	38 670	20 322
7	242	56 010	24 781
8	274	49 655	27 609
12	300	82 374	40 879
16	330	93 365	52 653
20	403	103 090	70 562
24	409	107 769	88 262
28	451	124 240	106 754
32	455	132 618	111 267

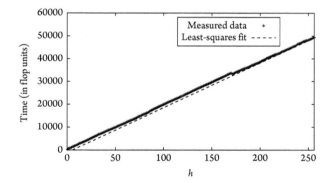

Figure 1.13 Time of an h-relation on one core of a 32-core 2.6 GHz Intel Xeon E5-2697A (Broadwell) node of the Bullx supercomputer Cartesius. The time is normalized to the measured computing rate of 5.711 Gflop/s.

beyond our scope and ability to explain every peculiarity of every benchmarked machine. We feel free to leave some surprises unexplained.

Another lesson we learned when benchmarking many different computers is that sometimes we have to adjust the input parameters MAXN, MAXH, and NITERS of the benchmark program bspbench, which may require trial and error; plotting the data is helpful in this

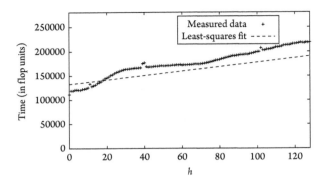

Figure 1.14 Time of an h-relation on all cores of a 32-core 2.6 GHz Intel Xeon E5-2697A (Broadwell) node of the Bullx supercomputer Cartesius. The time is normalized to the measured computing rate of 5.711 Gflop/s.

process. For instance, reducing the range of h by reducing MAXH for $p = 1$ on Cartesius would yield a better, more meaningful value for l. It is unlikely that one set of default parameters will yield sensible measurements for every imaginable parallel computer.

1.8 Sorting

Sorting a set of items is a fundamental operation in daily life, as we experience when arranging the books on our bookshelves in alphabetical order by author, colour, or size. For computer scientists, sorting methods are part of their basic toolbox, appearing in many variations, each applicable in a particular situation. The classic work by Donald Knuth, *The Art of Computer Programming*, devotes a whole volume to sorting (and searching) [187]. Here, we will present a **Parallel Sort by Regular Sampling** (PSRS) [266] of an array of reals, based on splitting the array at regular intervals.

The **quicksort** algorithm [157], invented by Tony Hoare in 1961, is a very fast sorting algorithm that sorts an array in increasing order by splitting it into a lower and upper part according to a randomly chosen splitter, and then repeating the procedure on the separate parts. This can most elegantly be expressed by a **recursive function**, i.e., a function that calls itself on smaller problem instances. Algorithm 1.2 displays the quicksort algorithm. The recursion continues as long as the problem size is two or more. The split operation is often called 'partition' in computer science following Hoare's terminology, see for example the extensive treatment by Cormen *et al.* [72, Chapter 7], but we will avoid that term because of possible confusion with data partitioning for the purpose of parallelism. The cost of a full quicksort is about $n \log_2 n$ comparison operations for an array of length n: the first split requires comparing all the n data values to the splitter value, and after that there are two splits of subarrays of length $n/2$, costing another n operations, and so on, during $\lceil \log_2 n \rceil$ splitting phases. Here, we assume that the splitters are perfect, so that each split is right in the middle. In practice, ratios such as $n/3$ vs. $2n/3$ may occur, but overall the expected time complexity is still of order $\mathcal{O}(n \log n)$, and we will simply consider the cost of quicksort to be $n \log_2 n$. Note that in complexity expressions such as $\mathcal{O}(\log n)$, we drop the base (subscript) from the logarithm, because the $\mathcal{O}$ ('big-Oh') absorbs all constants.

Algorithm 1.2 Recursive function Quicksort.

input: **x** : vector of length n, interval $[lo, hi]$ with $0 \le lo \le hi < n$.
output: **x** is sorted with $x_i \le x_j$ for all i, j with $lo \le i \le j \le hi$.

    function QUICKSORT$(\mathbf{x}, lo, hi)$

        $i := \mathrm{Split}(\mathbf{x}, lo, hi)$;
        if $i - 1 > lo$ **then**
            Quicksort$(\mathbf{x}, lo, i - 1)$;
        if $i + 1 < hi$ **then**
            Quicksort$(\mathbf{x}, i + 1, hi)$;

Let us examine the basic splitting operation in more detail. For a vector[2] **x** of length n, we call index r, with $0 \le r < n$, a **splitter**, or **splitting index**, if

$$x_i \le x_r \text{ for } i < r,$$
$$x_i \ge x_r \text{ for } i > r. \tag{1.11}$$

We call x_r the corresponding **splitting value**.

Example 1.1   The vector **x** of length $n = 10$ has one splitter, $i = 5$, with value $x_5 = 8$, given in bold:

$x_i =$	3	6	2	7	5	**8**	13	14	10	11
$i =$	0	1	2	3	4	**5**	6	7	8	9

Splitting the upper part of the array **x** based on a splitting value of 11 leads to an array with two marked splitters, $i = 5, 7$ with values 8 and 11, respectively:

$x_i =$	3	6	2	7	5	**8**	10	**11**	13	14
$i =$	0	1	2	3	4	**5**	6	**7**	8	9

Note that $i = 6, 8, 9$ also turn out to be splitters, but they have not been marked because they were not used as splitters in the splitting process. A full quicksort would now continue by splitting the lower part, and so on.

---

[2] A **vector** in mathematics can be viewed as an **array** in computer science, and we will take both views on different occasions. Sometimes we talk of vector components x_i, sometimes of array elements $x[i]$. Thus, we can 'sort a vector', meaning that we sort its components, or the elements of the corresponding array.

The splitting operation is presented by Algorithm 1.3, which splits a nonempty interval $[lo, hi]$ into two parts, the lower part representing values below that of a randomly chosen splitter, and the upper part representing the values that are equal or above; we have decided rather arbitrarily to assign the equal values to the upper part. The splitter is also commonly called the **pivot**. (This kind of pivot should not be confused with the pivot of LU decomposition that we will encounter in Chapter 2. The world revolves around many different pivots.) The pivot value is first parked in the end position hi, and then the **for**-loop swaps all lower values from their present position j into the first available position i.

Algorithm 1.3 Splitting a vector based on a random pivot.

---

input: $\mathbf{x}$: vector of length n, interval $[lo, hi]$ with $0 \le lo \le hi < n$.
output: $\mathbf{x}$ is split in the interval such that $x_j < x_i$ for all j with $lo \le j < i$, and $x_j \ge x_i$ for all j
  with $i < j \le hi$. The splitter i is returned, with $lo \le i \le hi$.

> **function** SPLIT$(\mathbf{x}, lo, hi)$
>
>   pick piv, with $lo \le piv \le hi$;
> $val := x_{piv}$;
>   swap(x_{piv}, x_{hi});
> $i := lo$;
>   **for** $j := lo$ **to** $hi - 1$ **do**
>   **if** $x_j < val$ **then**
>   swap(x_i, x_j);
> $i := i + 1$;
>   swap(x_i, x_{hi});
>   **return** i;

We can express the progress made in the **for**-loop by the following statement: at the start of iteration j, the values in the interval $[lo, i - 1]$ are less than the pivot value, those in $[i, j - 1]$ are equal or larger, and those in $[j, hi - 1]$ have not been processed yet. Such a statement is called a **loop invariant**, a statement maintained during the execution of the loop that leads to the desired outcome at the end of the loop. (A loop invariant can be seen as the computer-science equivalent of mathematical induction.) After the loop has finished, and the pivot value has been swapped into its proper position, the splitter is returned for further use.

We will use the quicksort algorithm as our reference algorithm, aiming to speed it up by adapting it to a parallel context. It turns out that the PSRS algorithm proposed by Shi and Schaeffer in 1992 [266] is such an adaptation that is very efficient, provided p is not too large, and that is also suitable as a BSP algorithm. The resulting algorithm, with five supersteps and based on a block distribution, is given as Algorithm 1.4. We make two assumptions to simplify the explanation of the basic ideas: (i) we assume that $n \bmod p^2 = 0$, so that, on input, all processors have the same block size n/p, which furthermore is a multiple of p; (ii) we assume that all values to be sorted are distinct, so that we do not have to break **ties**.

In superstep (0) of Algorithm 1.4, the local block is sorted by using the quicksort algorithm since it is our reference algorithm; this costs $\frac{n}{p} \log_2 \frac{n}{p}$ flops. (We assume that the input vector consists of reals, and thus we do not hesitate to call a comparison operation a flop.) The algorithm then takes p samples at regular distance n/p^2, which costs p copy operations; we neglect their cost. (We could avoid them by performing some extra bookkeeping, or by merging them with the next operation.) The samples divide the block of length n/p into p **subblocks**, each of length n/p^2. The values within each subblock are in increasing order, and so are the subblocks themselves. Figure 1.15 illustrates the algorithm. In particular, superstep (0) transforms the vector of panel (a) into that of (b).

In superstep (1), the samples are broadcast to all processors, instead of being sent only to $P(0)$, for the same reason as in the inner product algorithm, Algorithm 1.1, namely to save a communication superstep. This also saves a computation superstep. The cost is $p(p-1)g + l$, because each sample set *sample$_s$* consists of p values, and these are sent to $p - 1$ other processors.

In superstep (2), all processors redundantly determine the same set of p splitter values from the p^2 samples they possess. This is done by first sorting the samples, and then taking a subset at regular distance p, which yields the splitter values. Because of our assumption that all values of the input **x** are distinct, we only need the value of the splitters and not their index. This choice of splitters has provable quality, as we will discuss later on.

We use a mergesort instead of a quicksort to benefit from the fact that the p^2 samples are already arranged as p sorted parts. This mergesort repeatedly merges a pair of sorted parts, in $\lceil \log_2 p \rceil$ phases, each costing p^2 flops. Mergesort(**x**, $start, p$) sorts the vector **x** in the interval $[start[0], start[p] - 1]$ using the fact that the intervals $[start[t], start[t+1] - 1]$ are already sorted, for $t = 0, \ldots, p - 1$. The total cost of the mergesort is $p^2 \lceil \log_2 p \rceil$. In an implementation, a pair of input vectors can be merged by repeatedly comparing their current

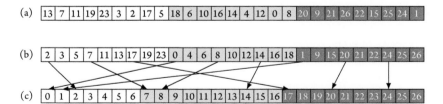

Figure 1.15 Parallel regular samplesort of a vector of size $n = 27$ distributed by the block distribution over $p = 3$ processors, shown by colours. (a) The unsorted vector; (b) the vector after local sorting, with the $p^2 = 9$ samples shown as the start of an arrow; (c) the sorted vector obtained by using the splitters 0, 7, and 17. The movement of the samples is shown by the arrows.

Algorithm 1.4 Regular samplesort for processor $P(s)$, with $0 \leq s < p$.

---

input: $\mathbf{x}$: vector of length n, $n \bmod p^2 = 0$, $x_i \neq x_j$ for all $i \neq j$.
         distr($\mathbf{x}$) = ϕ, with $\phi(i) = i$ div b, for $0 \leq i < n$, where $b = n/p$.
output: $\mathbf{x}$ is sorted with $x_i \leq x_j$ for all i,j with $0 \leq i \leq j < n$.
         The vector $\mathbf{x}$ is block distributed with variable block size $b_s \leq 2b$.

     { Sort the local block and create samples }   ▷ Superstep (0)
     Quicksort($\mathbf{x}, sb, (s+1)b - 1$);
     for $i := 0$ **to** $p - 1$ **do**
         $sample_s[i] := x[sb + i \cdot \frac{n}{p^2}]$;

     { Broadcast the samples }   ▷ Superstep (1)
     for $t := 0$ **to** $p - 1$ **do**
         put $sample_s$ in $P(t)$;

     { Concatenate and sort the samples }   ▷ Superstep (2)
     for $t := 0$ **to** $p - 1$ **do**
         for $i := 0$ **to** $p - 1$ **do**
             $sample[tp + i] := sample_t[i]$;
         $start[t] := tp$;
     $start[p] := p^2$;
     Mergesort($sample, start, p$);

     { Determine splitter values }
     for $t := 0$ **to** $p - 1$ **do**
         $splitval[t] := sample[tp]$;
     $splitval[p] := \infty$;

     { Split the local block and send the resulting parts }   ▷ Superstep (3)
     for $t := 0$ **to** $p - 1$ **do**
         { Contribution from $P(s)$ to $P(t)$ }
         $X_{st} := \{x_i : sb \leq i < (s+1)b \wedge splitval[t] \leq x_i < splitval[t+1]\}$;
         put X_{st} in $P(t)$;

     { Concatenate the received parts }   ▷ Superstep (4)
     $X_s := \cup_{t=0}^{p-1} X_{ts}$;

     { Sort the local block }
     $start_s[0] := 0$;
     for $t := 1$ **to** p **do**
         $start_s[t] := start_s[t-1] + |X_{t-1,s}|$;
     $b_s := start_s[p]$;
     Mergesort($X_s, start_s, p$);

---

minima, writing the smallest minimum to the output vector, and removing the smallest minimum from its input vector.

In superstep (3), the same set of p splitter values is used by all the processors to split the local block into p parts of varying size, where some parts might even be empty. These parts X_{st} are sent from processor $P(s)$ to their destination processor $P(t)$, which concatenates them in superstep (4) into a set

$$X_s = \{x_i \; : \; splitval[s] \le x_i < splitval[s+1]\}. \tag{1.12}$$

Note the different points of view in supersteps (3) and (4): today's sender will be tomorrow's receiver, explaining the switch from X_{st} to X_{ts}. Superstep (3) costs at most $2ng/p + l$, because every processor sends at most n/p data words and receives at most $b_s \le 2n/p$ data words, where b_s is the local output block size. The upper bound on b_s was first proven by Shi and Schaeffer [266], in a slightly different variant, and it is the basis for a well-balanced final sort in superstep (4) as well as well-balanced memory usage. The communication of superstep (3) is illustrated by the arrows from panel (b) to panel (c) in Fig. 1.15.

Let $P(s)$ be a given processor, with $0 \le s < p$. The proof of the upper bound on b_s for processor $P(s)$ is obtained by considering two types of subblock, namely those that contribute a sample to the local output block of size b_s, and those that do not. Each subblock starts with a sample and has length n/p^2. There are exactly p subblocks that contribute a sample, because the output block contains exactly p samples. The total number of data words in these subblocks is at most $p \cdot n/p^2 = n/p$. In Fig. 1.15(c), $P(2)$ has obtained contributions from subblocks (17,19,23), (20,21,22), and (24,25,26) with contributed samples 17, 20, and 24, respectively. A subblock that does not contribute a sample is for instance subblock (14,16,18), which only contributes the value 18 to $P(2)$. At most one subblock per processor $P(t)$ can contribute in this way to $P(s)$, because the sample must be less than the splitter value starting the block of $P(s)$ (here, 17), and the subblock must also contain a value (here, 18) larger than or equal to the splitter value. Therefore, at most p such subblocks exist, with a total size of at most $p \cdot (n/p^2 - 1) = n/p - p$. Note that excluding the sample from the subblock causes the subtraction of p. Adding the two sizes together proves that $b_s \le 2n/p - p$, which is even a bit better than the bound $2n/p$ stated above.

Superstep (4) merges the received sets of data words by a mergesort, with $\lceil \log_2 p \rceil$ phases, each accessing at most b_s local data, with a total cost $b_s \lceil \log_2 p \rceil \le \frac{2n}{p} \cdot \lceil \log_2 p \rceil$.

The total cost of Algorithm 1.4 is obtained by adding the costs of the five supersteps, giving

$$
\begin{aligned}
T_{\text{samplesort}} &= \frac{n}{p} \log_2 \frac{n}{p} + p^2 \lceil \log_2 p \rceil + \frac{2n}{p} \cdot \lceil \log_2 p \rceil + \left(p(p-1) + 2\frac{n}{p} \right) g + 5l \\
&\approx \frac{n}{p} (\log_2 n + \log_2 p) + p^2 \log_2 p + \left(p^2 + 2\frac{n}{p} \right) g + 5l, \tag{1.13}
\end{aligned}
$$

where we removed the ceiling symbols in our approximation and ignored lower-order terms. Applying Richard Hamming's famous motto [140]

'The purpose of computing is insight, not numbers.'

to the computation of BSP cost, we try to obtain insight by asking ourselves what the terms mean in our approximated cost formula. The first term, $\frac{n}{p} \cdot \log_2 n$, represents the time of perfect parallelization. The second term, $\frac{n}{p} \cdot \log_2 p$, represents load imbalance in superstep (4). In the example of Fig. 1.15, $P(0)$ has only seven values, whereas $P(1)$ and $P(2)$ have ten, so the final superstep takes more time than would happen in the balanced case, with each processor having nine values. Shi and Schaeffer [266] demonstrate experimentally that for a random input vector, this imbalance is much smaller than the given upper bound. The third term, $p^2 \log_2 p$, is caused by the redundant computation of the splitter values. If $p \le n^{1/3}$, then $p^2 \le n/p$ and $\log_2 p \le \log_2 n$, so that the term $p^2 \log_2 p$ is dominated by the main computation term, $\frac{n}{p} \cdot \log_2 n$, meaning that the computation part is efficient. We call a computation already **efficient** if the main computation time dominates the time of each of the three possible overheads separately; these overheads are load imbalance, communication, and synchronization. In the range $p \le n^{1/3}$, the communication cost will be dominated by the fifth term, $2ng/p$. This means that to run the algorithm efficiently, it must hold that $2g \le \log_2 n$. For $n = 10^{10}$, we require $g \le 16.6$, which is quite a strong restriction, caused by the fact that the $n \log_2 n$ time needed for sorting is close to the linear time n, so that communicating all n data only once is already costly: we need a large problem size to recover the communication cost and actually gain something.

To end this section on a positive note, my view on the limited expected speedup is that sorting is all about moving data, and that the cost of communicating data is just part of its inevitable expense. Parallel sorting on distributed-memory computers allows us to solve much larger problems than sequential sorting, which is a great achievement even if this happens at only modest speedups.

1.9 Example function `bspsort`

To implement the samplesort and make it practical to use, we need to relax the assumptions we made in explaining the algorithm. First of all, the relation between n and p should be less restrictive than $n \bmod p^2 = 0$, as we cannot expect n to be a multiple of p^2 for every possible input. One solution would be to pad the input array with zeros until the next multiple of p^2, but we choose to adjust the block sizes to make them fit exactly to the input. We still require $n \ge p^2$ for the program to work correctly, since otherwise we cannot have p^2 samples, which is the basis of samplesort. If n is smaller, we simply use fewer processors. Note that for the program to work efficiently, we even require $n \ge p^3$, as analysed in the previous section.

To guarantee that we locally have at least p samples, we cannot use the (otherwise perfectly fine) block distribution given by eqn (1.7), because the last processor may have fewer than p items. For example, with $n = 17$ and $p = 4$, we would have local blocks of size $5, 5, 5, 2$, respectively, so that $P(3)$ has too few items. The constraint $n \ge p^2$ implies $p \le n/p$ and hence also $p \le \lfloor n/p \rfloor$, so if we change the distribution such that every processor has at least $\lfloor n/p \rfloor$ values, we obtain our guarantee.

An alternative variant of the block distribution that achieves a minimum block size $b = \lfloor n/p \rfloor$ is defined by the mapping

$$
x_i \longmapsto \begin{cases} P(i \text{ div } (b+1)) & \text{if } i < (n \bmod p)(b+1) \\ P((i - (n \bmod p)) \text{ div } b) & \text{otherwise,} \end{cases} \qquad \text{for } 0 \leq i < n.
$$

$$(1.14)$$

For $n = 17$ and $p = 4$, where $n \bmod p = 1$, this gives local blocks of size 5, 4, 4, 4, which is the same as for a cyclic distribution.

The division of blocks into subblocks can also be carried out using the alternative variant of the block distribution, with n replaced by the local block size. The maximum size of a subblock is then $\lceil \lceil n/p \rceil /p \rceil = \lceil n/p^2 \rceil$, where we have used the following lemma.

Lemma 1.2 *Let k, q, r be integers with $k \geq 0$ and $q, r \geq 1$. Then*

$$
\left\lceil \frac{\left\lceil \frac{k}{q} \right\rceil}{r} \right\rceil = \left\lceil \frac{k}{qr} \right\rceil.
$$

Proof Write $k = \alpha qr + \beta q + \gamma$, with α, β, γ nonnegative integers satisfying $\beta < r$ and $\gamma < q$. If $\beta = \gamma = 0$, both sides of the equation equal α. Otherwise, they equal $\alpha + 1$, as can easily be verified. □

For those interested in other properties of floors and ceilings, see the book by Graham, Knuth, and Patashnik [128, Chapter 3].

For the alternative distribution into blocks and subblocks, every output block contains at most $p \cdot \lceil n/p^2 \rceil$ values from subblocks that contribute a sample and at most $p(\lceil n/p^2 \rceil - 1)$ from other subblocks. The output block size thus satisfies

$$
b_s \leq p \left(2 \left\lceil \frac{n}{p^2} \right\rceil - 1 \right) \leq p \left(2\frac{n}{p^2} + 1 \right) \leq 2\frac{n}{p} + p. \qquad (1.15)
$$

The extra term p in the upper bound is small (and bounded by n/p), so that superstep (4) and the memory usage are still well-balanced.

Another assumption we made, that all values are distinct, is unrealistic and needs to be relaxed as well. In fact, all values might be the same, and we still would like to run samplesort in a balanced fashion. The solution to this problem is to break ties using some other property than the numerical value, and thus make the items to be sorted unique. A good choice would be the global index where the value is stored, and in particular the index after the local sort of superstep (0), depicted in Fig. 1.15(b). Using the index after the local sort, rather than the index before, has the advantage that we can break ties arbitrarily during the local sort, which is faster. We can add this index information to the samples and splitter values and use it when we compare the value x_i in superstep (3) with a splitter value to see whether $splitval[t] \leq x_i < splitval[t+1]$. In case of equality, we also need to check whether the index i is less than the splitter (which is an index).

An efficient implementation of tie-breaking tries as much as possible to avoid communicating extra information such as global indices. A global index i is determined by the processor number in the block distribution and the local index. For item x_i on $P(s)$, both are known. For a sample, we know the processor that sent it in superstep (1), and we can compute its local index on the sending processor because all samples are regularly spaced. Thus, no communication of index information is needed. If we had chosen to let $P(0)$ select the splitter values and then broadcast them, this would also require communication of indices.

As a result of tie-breaking, we need to sort the sample values together with their indices and select the splitters from these samples in superstep (2), and then use the splitter values and their indices in superstep (3) to send the items to their final destination.

A convenient way of sending the items is by using the bsp_send primitive, which is the most important primitive of **bulk synchronous message passing**, a new style of communication introduced in this section. The function bspsort is the first occasion where we see the five important bulk synchronous message passing primitives of BSPlib in action. (For the moment, we ignore the high-performance versions of these primitives.) The bsp_send primitive allows us to send data to a given processor without specifying the location where the data should be stored. One can view bsp_send as a bsp_put with a wildcard for the destination address. In all other aspects, bsp_send acts like bsp_put; in particular, it performs a one-sided communication since it does not require any activity by the receiver in the same superstep. (In the next superstep, however, the receiver must do something if it wants to use the received data, see below.) The bsp_send primitive is quite unlike traditional (two-sided) message passing primitives, which require coordinated action between a sender and a receiver.

The reason for the existence of bsp_send is nicely illustrated by superstep (2)/(3) of bspsort, which employs bsp_send to send count $= |X_{st}|$ data words to processor $P(t)$. The information about how many words have to be sent is only available at the sender. As a consequence, a sending processor does not know what the other processors send. Furthermore, processors do not know what they will receive. If we were to use bsp_put statements, we would have to specify a destination address. One method of doing this is by having each receiving processor reserve memory space to store p times the maximum number of data words that can be received from a single processor, which is n/p. If this is done, the processor that sends X_{st} can write it directly into the memory cell reserved for it on $P(t)$. Unfortunately, the amount of reserved local memory, $p \cdot n/p = n$ cells, is $p/2$ times larger than the memory actually needed because of the upper bound $b_s \leq 2n/p + p$, and a large part of this memory may never be used for writing data. Thus, this method is **nonscalable** in memory. An alternative is a rather clumsy method that may be termed the 'three-superstep' approach. In the first superstep, each processor tells each of the other processors how many items it is going to send. In the second superstep, each receiving processor reserves exactly the required amount of space for each of the senders, and tells them the address from which they can start writing. Finally, in the third superstep, the items themselves are put.

Fortunately, we can organize the communication in a more efficient and more elegant way by using the bsp_send primitive instead of bsp_put. This is how it is done in the function bspsort. Anyone writing programs with irregular communication patterns will be grateful for the existence of bsp_send! Note that the irregularity here occurs at the end of the algorithm where an unknown number of data items are sent to their destination. This irregularity is despite the name 'regular sampling', which refers to the regular intervals between the samples at the start of the algorithm.

The bsp_send primitive sends a message which consists of a **tag** and a **payload**. The tag is used to identify the message; the payload contains the actual data. The use of the bsp_send primitive is illustrated by the top part of Fig. 1.16. In our example program, we use the tag to convey a data count and we use the payload to communicate the actual data set X_{st}. The syntax is

bsp_send (pid , tag , source , nbytes);

Here, unsigned int pid is the identity of the destination processor; void *tag is a pointer to the tag; void *source is a pointer to the source memory from which the data to be sent are read; size_t nbytes is the number of bytes to be sent. In our example program, the identity of the destination processor is simply t. It is important to choose a tag that enables the receiver to handle the payload easily. Here, the receiver is told the message length as the number of doubles sent.

The message to be sent using the bsp_send primitive is first stored by the system in a local send buffer. (This ensures that the tag and source variable can be reused immediately.) The message is then sent and stored in a buffer on the receiving processor. The send and receive buffers are invisible to the user (but there is a way of emptying the receive buffer, as you may guess).

Some time after the message has been sent, it becomes available on the receiving processor. In line with the philosophy of the BSP model, this happens at the end of the current superstep. In the next superstep, the messages can be read; reading messages means moving

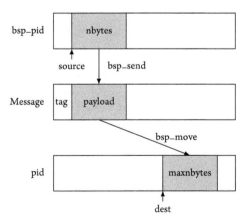

Figure 1.16 Send operation from BSPlib. The bsp_send operation copies nbytes of data from the local processor bsp_pid into a message, adds a tag, and sends this message to the specified destination processor pid. Here, the pointer source points to the start of the data to be copied. In the next superstep, the bsp_move operation writes at most maxnbytes from the message into the memory area specified by the pointer dest.

them from the receive buffer into the desired destination memory. We cannot make any assumptions about the order of the received messages because they may have arrived in any arbitrary order. At the end of the next superstep, all remaining unmoved messages will be lost. This is to save buffer memory and to force the user into the right habit of cleaning his desk at the end of the day. (As already mentioned, the BSP model and its implementation BSPlib are quite paternalistic. They often force you to do the right thing, for lack of alternatives.) The syntax of the move primitive is

```
bsp_move ( dest , maxnbytes ) ;
```

Here, `void *dest` is a pointer to the destination memory where the data will be written; `size_t maxnbytes` is an upper bound on the number of bytes of the payload that are to be written. This is useful if only part of the payload needs to be retrieved. The use of the `bsp_move` primitive is illustrated by the bottom part of Fig. 1.16. In our example program, the payload of a message is written in its entirety into x, so that `maxnbytes` equals the number of bytes of the payload.

The header information of a message consists of the tag and the length of the payload. This information can be retrieved by the statement

```
bsp_get_tag ( status , tag ) ;
```

Here, `size_t *status` is a pointer to the status, which equals the length of the payload of the currently read message in bytes, except if the buffer is empty; in that case its value is set to the maximum value `size_t` can take. (This is almost like setting it to infinity!) Furthermore, `void *tag` is a pointer to the memory where the tag has been written. The status information can be used to decide whether there is an unread message, and if so, how much space to allocate for it.

We could use the status in the termination criterion of the loop in superstep (4), to determine whether we have handled all incoming messages. Instead, we choose to use the enquiry primitive

```
bsp_qsize ( nmessages , nbytes ) ;
```

Here, `unsigned int *nmessages` is a pointer to the total number of messages received in the preceding superstep, and `size_t *nbytes` is a pointer to the total number of bytes received. In our program, we use `bsp_qsize` only to determine the number of iterations of the loop, that is, the number of parts received. In general, the `bsp_qsize` primitive is useful for allocating the right amount of memory for storing the received messages. Here, we do not need to allocate memory, because we move the data into x, which has already been allocated and has sufficient room. The name `bsp_qsize` derives from the fact that we can view the receive buffer as a queue: messages wait patiently in line until they are processed.

In our program, the tag is a long integer, but in general it can be of any type. The size of the tag in bytes is set by

```
bsp_set_tagsize ( tagsize ) ;
```

On input, `size_t *tagsize` points to the desired tag size. As a result, the system uses the desired tag size for all messages to be sent by `bsp_send`. The function `bsp_set_tagsize` takes effect at the start of the next superstep. All processors must call the function with the same tag size. As a side effect, the contents of `tagsize` will be modified, so that on output it contains the previous tag size of the system. This is a way of preserving the old value, which can be useful if an initial global state of the system must be restored later.

We use a wrapper `bsp_size_t` instead of `size_t` for the parameters of type `size_t *` (pointer to `size_t`) in the primitives `bsp_get_tag`, `bsp_qsize`, and `bsp_set_tagsize`. For the modern version of BSPlib [318], this wrapper is simply defined as `size_t` in the file `bsp.h`, which is included in the file `bspedupack.h`, see Appendix A. For the previous version [153], `bsp_size_t` is defined as `int`. This is a way to maintain backwards compatibility if desired. Similarly, we use a wrapper `bsp_nprocs_t` defined as `unsigned int` for the `nmessages` parameter in the primitive `bsp_qsize`. The wrapper `bsp_nprocs_t` is defined as `int` in compatibility mode.

In one superstep, an arbitrary number of communication operations can be performed, using either `bsp_put`, `bsp_get`, or `bsp_send` primitives, and they can be mixed freely. The only practical limitation is imposed by the amount of buffer memory available. The BSP model and BSPlib do not favour any particular type of communication, so that here it is up to the user to choose the most convenient primitive in a given situation.

Some additional explanations of the program `bspsort` are as follows. The function `compare_doubles` compares two doubles a and b and returns -1 if $a < b$, 0 if $a = b$, and 1 if $a > b$. The function `compare_items` does the same for items consisting of a double (called the 'weight') and an index, where the weight is used as a primary comparison and the index as a secondary one. The supersteps of the program are numbered in the same way as in Algorithm 1.4, but they are sometimes combined. Determining the local samples requires some thought, because the subblocks may differ slightly in size. This also complicates the computation of the global index of the nonlocal samples received. Still, all processors possess the necessary distribution information to compute the global index of every sample.

The samples are sorted by a specialized mergesort function, `mergeparts`, which exploits already ordered parts of the array. In superstep $(2)/(3)$, p messages or fewer are sent by $P(s)$, and these are received in arbitrary order. The increasing order of the values within a message is preserved, however. The final sort in superstep (4) is again done by using `mergeparts`, this time only sorting the weights. The program text of `bspsort` is:

```
#include "bspedupack.h"

void bspsort(double *x, long n, long *nlout){

    /* Sorts an array x of n doubles by samplesort,
       without keeping track of the original indices.
       On input, x is distributed by a block distribution
       over p processors, where p^2 <= n; x must have
       been registered already.
       On output, x is distributed by a block distribution
       with variable block size. The local output block
```

```
    size  satisfies  1 <= nlout <= 2n/p + p.
*/

int compare_doubles (const void *a, const void *b);
int compare_items (const void *a, const void *b);
void merge(char *x, char *tmp, long a, long b,
           long c, size_t size,
           int (*compare)(const void *,const void *));
void mergeparts(char *x, long *start, long p,
                size_t size, int (*compare)
                (const void *,const void *));

long p= bsp_nprocs (); // p = number of processors
                       //     obtained
long s= bsp_pid ();    // s = processor number
if (p*p > n)
    bsp_abort("Error: bspsort only works if"
              "p*p <= n \n");

/* Allocate and register */
double *Sample= vecallocd (p*p);
bsp_push_reg (Sample,p*p*sizeof(double));

/* Set tag size, where tag will store
   the length of the message */
bsp_size_t tag_size= sizeof(long);
bsp_set_tagsize(&tag_size);
bsp_sync ();

/****** Superstep (0)/(1) ******/

/* Sort local block using system quicksort */
long nl= nloc(p,s,n); // number of local elements
qsort (x,nl,sizeof(double),compare_doubles);

/* Determine p (nearly) equally spaced samples */
long nlp= nl/p;                     // nlp >= 1
                                    // because nl >= p
for (long i=0; i <= nl%p; i++)
    Sample[i]= x[i*(nlp+1)];        // subblocks of size
                                    // nlp+1
for (long i= nl%p+1; i<p; i++)
    Sample[i]= x[i*nlp + nl%p];     // subblocks of
                                    // size nlp
```

```
/* Put samples in P(*) */
for (long t=0; t<p; t++)
    bsp_put (t , Sample , Sample , s*p*sizeof (double ) ,
            p*sizeof(double ));
bsp_sync ();


/****** Superstep (2)/(3) ******/

/* Copy weight of samples */
Item *SampleItem= vecallocitem (p*p);
for (long i=0; i < p*p; i++)
    SampleItem [ i ] . weight= Sample [ i ];


/* Add global index to samples */
long blocktotal_s=0; // size of all blocks
                     // processors < s
for (long t=0; t<p; t++){
    long blocktotal_t; // size of all blocks of
                       // processors < t
    long nt= nloc (p,t ,n); // number of local
                           // elements of P(t)
    if (t <= n%p)
        blocktotal_t= t *(n/p+1);
    else
        blocktotal_t= t *(n/p) + n%p;
    if (t==s)
        blocktotal_s= blocktotal_t; // keep for
                                    // later use

    /* Determine global index of samples of P(t) */
    long ntp= nt/p;
    for (long i=0; i <= nt%p; i++)
        SampleItem [ t *p+i ] . index= blocktotal_t
                                    + i *(ntp +1);
    for (long i= nt%p+1; i<p; i++)
        SampleItem [ t *p+i ] . index= blocktotal_t
                                    + i *ntp + nt%p;
}


/* Sort samples with their indices */
long *start= vecalloci (p+1);
for (long t=0; t<p; t++)
    start [t]= t *p;
```

```
start[p]= p*p;
mergeparts ((void *)SampleItem,start,p,sizeof(Item),
             compare_items);

/* Choose p equidistant splitters from the samples */
Item *Splitter= vecallocitem(p);
for (long t=0; t<p; t++)
    Splitter[t]= SampleItem[t*p];

/* Send the values */
long i= 0;
for (long t=0; t<p; t++){
    /* Send the values for P(t) */
    long i0= i;      // index of first value to be sent
    long count= 0;  // number of values to be sent
    while (i < nl &&
            (t==p-1 || (x[i] < Splitter[t+1].weight)
                    || (x[i] == Splitter[t+1].weight
                        && blocktotal_s + i <
                        Splitter[t+1].index)
            )){
        count++;
        i++;
    }


    if (count > 0)
        bsp_send(t,&count,&x[i0],count*sizeof(double));
}
bsp_sync();

/****** Superstep (4) ******/

/* Concatenate the received parts, in arbitrary
   order */
bsp_nprocs_t nparts_recvd;  // <= p
bsp_size_t nbytes_recvd;
bsp_qsize(&nparts_recvd,&nbytes_recvd);

start[0]= 0;
for (long j=0; j<nparts_recvd; j++){
    bsp_size_t payload_size; // payload size in bytes
    long count; // number of doubles in the message
    bsp_get_tag(&payload_size,&count);
```

```
        bsp_move(&x[start[j]], count*sizeof(double));
        start[j+1]= start[j] + count;
}

/* Determine the total number of doubles received,
    which is the output local block size */
*nlout = start[nparts_recvd];

/* Sort the local values for final output */
mergeparts((void *)x, start, nparts_recvd, sizeof(double),
                compare_doubles);

vecfreei(start);
vecfreeitem(Splitter);
vecfreeitem(SampleItem);
bsp_pop_reg(Sample);
vecfreed(Sample);

return;

} /* end bspsort */
```

1.10 Experimental results for samplesort on a Cartesius node

To study the performance of our parallel regular samplesort program, we ran `bspsort` on a single Broadwell node with $p = 32$ cores of the Bullx supercomputer Cartesius, which was benchmarked in Section 1.7 using MulticoreBSP for C; see Table 1.4 for the BSP parameters of the node. Table 1.5 presents timings for array lengths ranging from $n = 10^4$ (the smallest power of 10 exceeding $p^2 = 1024$) up to $n = 10^8$ (the largest power of 10 for which the problem fits in memory). The table shows that the sequential computation time grows slightly faster than linearly with n, which corresponds well with the expected $\mathcal{O}(n \log n)$ time complexity of quicksort. The table also shows that parallel speedups are indeed achieved when increasing p, especially for large n.

The **speedup** $S_p(n)$ of a parallel program is defined as the increase in speed of the program running on p processors compared with the speed of a sequential program (with the same level of optimization),

$$S_p(n) = \frac{T_{\text{seq}}(n)}{T_p(n)}. \tag{1.16}$$

Note that we do not take the time of the parallel program with $p = 1$ as reference time, since this may be too flattering; obtaining a good speedup with such a reference for comparison may be reason for great pride, but it is an achievement of the same order as becoming the Dutch national champion in alpine skiing. The latter achievement is put into the right

Table 1.5 Time (in s) of a parallel regular samplesort on a 32-core 2.6 GHz Intel Xeon E5-2697A (Broadwell) node of the Bullx supercomputer Cartesius. The array length is n and the number of cores used is p.

p		Length n				
		10^4	10^5	10^6	10^7	10^8
1	(seq)	0.0011	0.0124	0.146	1.714	19.51
1	(par)	0.0012	0.0136	0.156	1.836	20.83
2		0.0009	0.0075	0.087	0.948	10.69
4		0.0008	0.0046	0.046	0.501	5.56
8		0.0009	0.0032	0.027	0.271	2.88
16		0.0015	0.0040	0.019	0.166	1.59
32		0.0032	0.0047	0.022	0.129	0.99

perspective if you know that the Netherlands is a very flat country, which does not have skiers of international fame. (Surprisingly, for snowboarding the situation is different, since the 2010 Winter Olympics in Vancouver, Canada). Similarly, the speedup achieved on a parallel computer can only be put into the right perspective if you know the time of a good sequential program, which here is quicksort. A parallel program run on one processor will always execute superfluous operations, and for $n = 10^8$ this parallel overhead amounts to about 7%. Sometimes, it may be unavoidable to measure speedup vs. the parallel program with $p = 1$, for instance if it is too much work to develop a sequential version, or if one adheres to the purist principle of maintaining a single program source: 'a sequential program is a parallel program run on one processor'. In such a situation, speedups should be reported with a clear warning about the reference version.

Figure 1.17 displays the speedups for $n = 10^7, 10^8$. The largest speedup obtained is about 19.7 for $p = 32$ and $n = 10^8$. Presenting timings of parallel programs through such a speedup plot gives much insight: it exposes good, as well as bad, scaling behaviour and it also allows easy comparison between measurements for different lengths. Keeping the problem size fixed while increasing the number of processors, as we do here, is a test of **strong scalability**. We observe that the speedup for $n = 10^8$ is larger than that of $n = 10^7$. Indeed, eqn (1.13) predicts a monotonic increase of $S_p(n)$ with n, as the main computation term $(n \log_2 n)/p$ grows faster than the main communication term $2ng/p$.

In principle, $0 < S_p(n) \leq p$ should hold, because p processors cannot be more than p times faster than one processor. This is indeed true for our measured speedups. Practice, however, may have its surprises: in certain situations, a **superlinear speedup** of more than p can be observed. This phenomenon is often the result of cache effects, owing to the fact that in the parallel case each processor has less data to handle than in the sequential case, so that a larger part of the computation can be carried out using data that is already in cache, thus yielding fewer cache misses and a higher computing rate. A speedup $S_p < 1$ may sometimes occur, owing to overheads, and in fact this means a **slowdown**. For $p = 1$, a slight slowdown is quite common.

The **efficiency** $E_p(n)$ gives the fraction of the total computing power that is usefully employed. It is defined by

$$E_p(n) = \frac{S_p(n)}{p} = \frac{T_{\text{seq}}(n)}{pT_p(n)}. \tag{1.17}$$

In general, $0 < E_p(n) \leq 1$, with the same caveats as before, and ideally $E_p(n) = 1$. This definition of efficiency is based on keeping the problem size fixed, and hence is a measure of strong scalability. In contrast, we can also argue for using the **weak scalability** metric, which is measured by keeping the problem size *per processor* fixed, thus reflecting the situation where we solve larger problems when more processors (and possibly more memory) become available; this was suggested by Gustafson and Barsis of Sandia National Laboratories [134]. For a problem with linear sequential time complexity, one should then measure the ratio $T_{\text{seq}}(n)/T_p(pn)$, and view it as the **weak-scalability efficiency**. (For problems with nonlinear time complexity, the situation becomes more complicated because we need to redefine the fixed problem size in a suitable manner.) We will stick, however, to using strong scalability in our experiments.

Figure 1.17 shows that we reach over 60% efficiency for $n = 10^8$ for all $p \leq 32$, comparing to a sequential system quicksort. The question of interest is then, where do we lose the other 40%, in the case $p = 32$? The answer to this question can be found by using the cost formula eqn (1.13) together with the benchmark values of Table 1.4 to predict the costs of the supersteps of the sorting algorithm.

Table 1.6 presents predictions of the different superstep contributions to the total cost. The table helps us, for instance, in identifying operations with negligible cost, such as broadcasting samples (with $p(p - 1)g$ cost), sorting samples ($p^2 \log_2 p$), and synchronizing ($5l$); these operations all take far less than a millisecond and hence can be ignored. The dominant predicted cost is the cost $2ng/p$ of communicating the data values to their final destination.

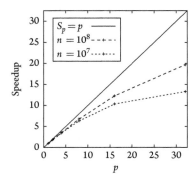

Figure 1.17 Speedup $S_p(n)$ of parallel regular samplesort.

Table 1.6 Breakdown of predicted execution time (in s) of a parallel regular samplesort on p cores of a 32-core 2.6 GHz Intel Xeon E5-2697A (Broadwell) node of the Bullx supercomputer Cartesius. The array length is $n = 10^8$. For comparison, we also give the average measured time obtained in ten runs of the `bspsort` program on 32 cores.

p		$\frac{n}{p} \log_2 \frac{n}{p}$	$p^2 \log_2 p$	$\frac{2n}{p} \log_2 p$	$p(p-1)g$	$\frac{2n}{p}g$	$5l$	T_p
1		0.465	0	0	0	6.899	0	7.364
2		0.224	0	0.018	0	3.485	0.000016	3.726
4		0.108	0	0.018	0	1.970	0.000034	2.095
8		0.052	0	0.013	0.000003	1.199	0.000043	1.264
16		0.025	0	0.009	0.000014	0.722	0.000082	0.756
32	(pred)	0.012	0.000001	0.005	0.000079	0.498	0.000116	0.515
32	(meas)	0.537	0.000124	0.247	0.000183	0.213	0.000102	0.998

We can also compare our predictions with actual measurements obtained by adding `bsp_time` calls to the program `bspsort`. Measurements for $p = 32$ are given on the last line of Table 1.6. Well, we have to explain a few discrepancies between the measured and predicted times for $p = 32$. First of all, for the computation cost, it is clear that sorting operations such as comparisons that randomly access a large array are much slower than in-cache floating-point operations that are part of a DAXPY vector operation (our chosen benchmark). A better prediction can of course be obtained by using the sequential sorting time to obtain the basic computing rate r. The predictions of the communication cost are reasonably accurate, and the factor of 2.34 between prediction and measurement for the cost term $2ng/p$ is mostly due to the fact that the theoretical prediction is a worst-case upper bound, whereas in practice (for random array values) the load balance is almost perfect, each processor possessing about n/p data words at the end of the sort. Therefore, we have to send only half the data predicted by the bound.

To answer the question above, the 40% loss of efficiency is partly attributable to communication of the data to the final destination, and partly to merging the data by a slower, educational mergesort (part of BSPedupack) instead of by a system sort. On some systems, the standard C library `stdlib.h` contains a mergesort and using this will considerably reduce the efficiency loss.

A crude and simple explanation for the discrepancy between prediction and experiment is that there are lies, damned lies, and benchmarks. Substituting benchmark results into a theoretical time formula gives an **ab initio** prediction, that is, a prediction from basic principles, and though this may be useful as an indication of expected performance, it will hardly ever be an accurate estimate. There are just too many possibilities for quirks in the hardware and the system software, ranging from obscure cache behaviour to inadequate implementation of certain communication primitives. Therefore, we can benefit a lot from having a parallel computation model, but as said before we should not get carried away and have unrealistic quantitative expectations of such a model.

1.11 Bibliographic notes

1.11.1 BSP-related models of parallel computation

Historically, the Parallel Random Access Machine (PRAM) [111] has been the most widely studied general-purpose model of parallel computation. In this model, processors can read from and write to a shared memory. Several variants of the PRAM model can be distinguished, based on the way concurrent memory access is treated: the concurrent read, concurrent write (CRCW) variant allows full concurrent access, whereas the exclusive read, exclusive write (EREW) variant allows only one processor to access the memory at a time. The PRAM model ignores communication costs and is therefore mostly of theoretical interest; it is useful in establishing lower bounds for the cost of parallel algorithms. The PRAM model has stimulated the development of many other models, including the BSP model. The BSP variant with automatic memory management by randomization in fact reduces to the PRAM model in the asymptotic case $g = l = \mathcal{O}(1)$. For an introduction to the PRAM model, see the survey by Vishkin [305]. For PRAM algorithms, see the books by JáJá [167] and Keller, Keßler, and Träff [175]. To bring theory to practice, Vishkin [306] and coworkers developed the Immediate Concurrent Execution (ICE) language for easy PRAM programming and at the same time they built the XMT architecture as a prototype of PRAM-on-Chip hardware.

The BSP model has been proposed by Valiant in 1989 [289]. The full description of this 'bridging model for parallel computation' is given in [290]. This article describes the two basic variants of the model (automatic memory management and direct user control) and it gives a complexity analysis of algorithms for fast Fourier transform, matrix–matrix multiplication, and sorting. In another article [291], Valiant proves that a hypercube or butterfly architecture can simulate a BSP computer with optimal efficiency. (Here, the model is called XPRAM.) The BSP model as it is commonly used today has been shaped by various authors since the original work by Valiant. The survey by McColl [212] argues that the BSP model is a promising approach to general-purpose parallel computing and that it can deliver both scalable performance and architecture independence. Bisseling and McColl [32] propose a variant of the model with pure computation supersteps of cost $w + l$ and pure communication supersteps of cost $hg + l$. They show how a variety of scientific computations can be analysed in a simple manner by using their BSP variant. McColl [213] analyses and classifies several important BSP algorithms, including dense and sparse matrix–vector multiplication, matrix–matrix multiplication, LU decomposition, and triangular system solution.

The LogP model by Culler et al. [73, 74] is an offspring of the BSP model, which uses four parameters to describe relative machine performance: the latency L, the overhead o, the gap g, and the number of processors P, instead of the three parameters L, g, and p of the original BSP model. The LogP model treats messages individually, not in bulk, and hence it does not provide the notion of a superstep. The LogP model attempts to reflect the actual machine architecture more closely than the BSP model, but the price to be paid is an increase in the complexity of algorithm design and analysis. Bilardi et al. [27] show that the LogP and BSP model can simulate each other efficiently so that they are, in principle, equally powerful.

The decomposable BSP (D-BSP) model [81] is a **hierarchical** model which decomposes a parallel computer into submachines, each with its own parameters g and l; their values will in general be lower than those of the complete machine. The scaling behaviour of the submachines with p is described by functions $g(p)$ and $l(p)$.

The BSPRAM model by Tiskin [286] replaces the communication network by a shared memory. At the start of a superstep, processors read data from the shared memory into their own local memory; then, they compute independently using locally held data; and finally they write local data into the shared memory. Access to the shared memory is in bulk fashion, and the cost function of such access is expressed in g and l. The main aim of the BSPRAM model is to allow programming in shared-memory style while keeping the benefits of data locality.

The multi-BSP model was proposed by Valiant [292] in 2011 to capture the shared-memory style of programming used on emerging multicore processors within a BSP framework. The new model adds a parameter m that expresses the **memory size** in data words, for any form of memory, whether cache or RAM. Furthermore, the multi-BSP model is hierarchical as it views a parallel computer as a tree with depth d, where each node at level i has p_i children, for $i = 1, \ldots, d$. The root (at level d) represents the whole machine. A node at level i represents a submachine which contains a memory of size m_i and p_i submachines of level $i - 1$, and which communicates at cost g_i with the memory of its parent node and also synchronizes its children at cost l_i. The additional complexity created by generalizing the BSP model is restricted to some extent by allowing only a single set of parameters for each level. A leaf node (at level 0) is defined as a single raw processor core without memory, which performs computations on data residing in level-1 memory in unit time ($g_0 = 1$). The leaf nodes are synchronized by their parent at zero cost ($l_1 = 0$). By convention, $g_d = \infty$. If furthermore we choose $d = 2$, $p_1 = 1$, $p_2 = p$, $g_1 = g$, and $l_2 = l$, we retrieve the original BSP model. If we choose $d = 3$, we can model a hybrid shared/distributed-memory architecture in its simplest form. This instance is a good candidate for application of multi-BSP in practice, as it is relatively simple and many of today's parallel computers are of the hybrid type. We will present a related BSP-based model for hybrid architectures called hybrid-BSP in Section 4.10.

1.11.2 BSP libraries

The first portable BSP library was the Oxford BSP library by Miller and Reed [223, 224]. This library contains six primitives: put, get, start of superstep, end of superstep, start of program, and end of program. Reed, Parrot, and Lanfear [259] describe the use of this library in parallelizing a large-scale industrial application code for solving Maxwell's equations. The Cray SHMEM library, first introduced in 1993 for the Cray T3D parallel computer, can be considered as a nonportable BSP library. It contains among others: put, strided put, get, strided get, and synchronization. OpenSHMEM [249] is an ongoing project that aims at unifying the many existing variants of SHMEM into a common standard API. The Oxford BSP library is similar to the Cray SHMEM library, but it was available for many different architectures. Neither of these libraries allows communication into dynamically allocated memory. The Green BSP library by Goudreau *et al.* [126, 127] is a small experimental BSP library of seven primitives. The main difference with the Oxford BSP library is that the

Green BSP library communicates by bulk synchronous message passing, using send and move primitives. Goudreau *et al.* [126] present results of numerical experiments using the Green BSP library in ocean eddy simulation, computation of minimum spanning trees and shortest paths in graphs, *n*-body simulation, and matrix–matrix multiplication.

BSPlib, used in this book, combines the capabilities of the Oxford BSP and the Green BSP libraries. It has grown into a *de facto* standard, which is fully defined by Hill *et al.* [153]. These authors also present results for fast Fourier transformation, randomized sample sorting, and *n*-body simulation using BSPlib. The Oxford BSP toolset [151] is the implementation that accompanied the initial definition of the BSPlib API. It contains C and Fortran 90 versions, as well as profiling tools that can be used to measure and visualize the amount of computation and communication of each processor during a sequence of supersteps. Frequently asked questions about BSP and BSPlib, such as 'Aren't barrier synchronizations expensive?' are answered by Skillicorn, Hill, and McColl [270]. A modernization of the BSPlib API for C incorporating recent changes to the C language has been implemented in the MulticoreBSP for C library by Yzelman *et al.* [318] from 2014; this update has been adopted in this book.

Hill and Skillicorn [154] discuss how to implement BSPlib efficiently. They demonstrate that postponing communication is worthwhile, since this allows messages to be reordered (to avoid congestion) and combined (to reduce startup costs). If the natural ordering of the communication in a superstep requires every processor to put data first into $P(0)$, then into $P(1)$, and so on, this creates congestion at the destination processors, even if the total h-relation is well-balanced. To solve this problem, Hill and Skillicorn use a $p \times p$ Latin square, that is, a matrix with permutations of $\{0, \ldots, p-1\}$ in the rows and columns, as a schedule for the communication. An example is the 4×4 Latin square

$$R = \begin{bmatrix} 0 & 1 & 2 & 3 \\ 1 & 2 & 3 & 0 \\ 2 & 3 & 0 & 1 \\ 3 & 0 & 1 & 2 \end{bmatrix}. \tag{1.18}$$

The communication of the superstep is done in p rounds. In round j, processor $P(i)$ sends all data destined for $P(r_{ij})$. In particular, in round 0 processors talk to themselves, which is a cheap memory copy. In another article [155], Hill and Skillicorn discuss the practical issues of implementing a global synchronization on different machines. In particular, they show how to abuse the cache-coherence mechanism of a shared-memory parallel computer to obtain an extremely cheap global synchronization. (In one case, 13.4 times faster than the vendor-provided synchronization.)

Suijlen [281] developed the open-source BSPonMPI library in 2006, which provides a BSPlib interface on top of MPI; it has proven to be very useful on many different architectures. The latest version (v1.1) was released in 2019. Suijlen also presented Mock BSPlib [280] which enables testing and debugging of BSPlib programs for very large p on a computer with a single processor. This should help software developers to gain more confidence in correctness of parallel programs. As an example, Suijlen mocks the `bspip` inner-product program of this book. The superstep structure provided by BSP, with a single point of synchronization at the end of every superstep, greatly simplifies the mocking process. Suijlen presents timing results for the `bsplu` program of this book, which show that mocking is much faster than simulating p processes on a single processor.

Zefiros BSPLib [300] is a recent C++ implementation of BSPlib for a shared-memory parallel computer. It is a header-only library, based exclusively on C++11 without any external dependencies, and it runs on top of threads. It can also execute classic BSPlib programs in C and BSPlib programs with the updated API from MulticoreBSP for C, such as the programs from this book. The library works on Windows, Linux, and MacOs X operating systems. Recently, Zefiros SyncLib [301] has appeared which can also handle distributed-memory programming and hybrid programming.

The Paderborn University BSP (PUB) library [40] is an implementation of the C version of the BSPlib standard with extensions. One extension of PUB is **zero-cost synchronization** [6], also called **oblivious synchronization**, which exploits the fact that for certain regular computations each receiving processor $P(s)$ knows the number of data words $h_r(s)$ it will receive. Processor $P(s)$ performs a `bsp_oblsync(`$h_r(s)$`)` operation at the end of the superstep, instead of a `bsp_sync`. This type of synchronization is cheap because no communication is needed to determine that processors can move on to the next superstep. Another extension is decomposing a BSP machine into submachines, each of them again a BSP machine, which can also be decomposed. The submachines must be rejoined later. The processors of a submachine must be numbered consecutively. This decomposition mechanism provides a disciplined form of subset synchronization. The PUB library also includes a large set of collective-communication functions.

Apache Hama [269] is an open-source framework founded by Edward Yoon in 2010 for Big Data computations based on the BSP model. It provides BSP primitives similar to those of BSPlib and also higher-level functionality for graph computations and machine learning. It is primarily written in Java. The data distribution of Hama is based on hashing (automatic memory management) using the Hadoop Distributed File System (HDFS); it does not exploit any available specific data locality.

The one-sided communications added in MPI-2 to the original MPI standard and improved in MPI-3 [218] can also be viewed as comprising a BSP library. The MPI-3 primitives for one-sided communications are put, get, and accumulate, which perform an atomic operation such as adding a value to a remote variable. Hoefler *et al.* [160] describe the one-sided communications of MPI-3, called Remote Memory Access (RMA, which we call DRMA, Direct RMA). They discuss their formal semantics, which were used for consistency proving, and present several application examples, including stencil computations from solving partial differential equations on a physical domain and 3D fast Fourier transforms. MPI-3 RMA offers many different ways of performing one-sided communications and synchronizing the processors (either pairwise, in groups, or globally). To use this large functionality, an RMA programmer needs to have advanced knowledge of the API; RMA is primarily targeted at experts such as the builders of high-performance parallel libraries. In common with BSP, RMA separates communication from synchronization. The sequence of local communication operations between different synchronization events is called an **epoch** in RMA, and a global sychronization is called a **fence**. Thus, if we only use fences, in so-called active target synchronization mode, the epochs become supersteps in the way we know from BSP. The authors recommend this mode for bulk synchronous applications with a relatively static communication pattern. For a tutorial introduction on RMA, see the book by Gropp, Hoefler, Thakur, and Lusk [131].

Bulk [52] is a BSP library based on C++17 which tries to make programming in bulk synchronous parallel style as easy as possible by exploiting modern C++ features such as smart pointers, range-based for-loops, and anonymous functions. It removes some of the tedium of standard BSPlib programs; for example, it registers variables automatically upon their creation, and in general it makes program texts shorter. For convenience, Bulk provides a short-hand assignment syntax to express puts and gets. Furthermore, Bulk simplifies bulk synchronous message passing and it enables sending data to different remote queues (instead of only one queue, as in BSPlib). Bulk is highly portable: backends exist both for shared memory (through C++ threads) and distributed memory (through MPI). As a demonstration of how to use Bulk, the authors have ported several programs from BSPedupack, which accompanies this book.

The Scientific Python package by Konrad Hinsen [156] combines BSP with the increasingly popular Python language. Its aim is to make parallel computing easier, avoiding deadlocks and other errors, simply by synchronizing implicitly, at the end of a superstep. The package provides a mechanism for communicating arbitrary objects, based on the `pickle` module from the Python standard library. The package runs in parallel on top of BSPlib or MPI, and sequentially on any system, in which case it can simulate an arbitrary number of processors. This provides an easy tool for testing and debugging. Parallelism is expressed in Scientific Python by manipulating global objects called a **parallel vector** with local values on each processor, for instance in a block distribution. A parallel program is thus formulated as a program for p processors, and not as a parameterized SPMD program for one processor out of p processors. This lockstep approach works well for regular algorithms, but it may lack the flexibility to accommodate highly irregular algorithms such as graph algorithms.

BSP has also been used in combination with functional programming languages, in addition to its use in imperative programming languages such as C, C++, Fortran, Java, and Python. BSML [200] is a library for parallel programming with the functional programming language Objective Caml; it is based on the λ-calculus [201]. BSML has been extended with BSPlib-style primitives by Loulergue [199], who also presents an inner-product program in BSML based on the program `bspip` from Section 1.4. Recently, Hains wrote a textbook (in French) on PRAM, BSP, and BSML [136]. Multi-ML [5] is an adaptation of BSML for the multi-BSP model [292] which allows exploitation of a hierarchical machine architecture, thereby increasing performance but also making programming harder. A BSP library also exists for Haskell [222].

NestStep [180] is a parallel programming language that extends the BSP model by allowing the nesting of supersteps, where processors split up into subgroups, each performing a sequence of supersteps, and then recombine after a global barrier synchronization of the subgroups. The splitting can be carried out dynamically at runtime. The language prototype was initially based on Java but was later replaced by a C version for reasons of performance.

Hamidouche, Falcou, and Etiemble [138] present an object-oriented library BSP++ for C++ which was inspired by BSML. It supports hybrid programming with shared-memory parallelism on top of OpenMP and distributed-memory parallelism on top of MPI, but with a unified BSP API. Hamidouche *et al.* [139] demonstrate the efficiency of their approach in a genomics application where they parallelize the Smith–Waterman dynamic programming algorithm for sequence alignment of DNA. They achieve a speedup of 116 on 128 cores for aligning two *Chlamydia* sequences of 1 million base pairs using a hybrid OpenMP/MPI approach, thereby outperforming a purely MPI approach that achieves a speedup of only 73. This shows that a hybrid approach may extend the parallel scalability of algorithms, due to the lower values of g and l for shared memory.

Several communication libraries and language extensions exist that enable programming in BSP style but do not fly the BSP flag. They fall within the category of Partitioned Global Address Space (PGAS) languages, which assume a common global memory that is addressable by all processors, but that has been partitioned so that each processor has a part. These languages may be used on both shared-memory and distributed-memory architectures. Two of the most popular PGAS languages are Universal Parallel C (UPC) and Coarray Fortran (CAF).

The UPC language [104] is a parallel extension of C that provides put and get primitives, remote assignments, and distributed arrays. Programs written in UPC are parameterized using parameters p = THREADS and s = MYTHREAD. Data distributions available for arrays are the cyclic and block distribution and, as an intermediate, also block-cyclic distributions. UPC provides global synchronization in the form of a barrier, which can be split into two parts: notify, the processor notifying the others that it has reached the barrier, and wait, the processor waiting until it can proceed. In between, some useful local computation can be carried out. Furthermore, the language provides a **for all**-loop which is a parallel loop with an **affinity expression** determining whether a processor $P(s)$ has to carry out a particular loop iteration. Recently, the UPC++ language [321] has been developed which provides an object-oriented version of UPC, with extensions such as multidimensional arrays and asynchronous remote function invocation.

Coarray Fortran [232], formerly called F^{--}, is a parallel extension of Fortran 95, included in current Fortran [219]. It represents a strict version of an SPMD approach: all program variables exist on all processors; remote variables can be accessed by appending the processor number in square brackets, for example, x(3)[2] is the variable x(3) on $P(2)$. A put is concisely formulated by using such brackets on the left-hand side of an assignment, for example, x(3)[2]=y(3), and a get by using them on the right-hand side. Processors can be synchronized in subsets or even in pairs. The programmer needs to be aware of the cost implications of the various types of assignments.

1.11.3 The non-BSP world: message passing and threads

For distributed-memory parallel computing, message passing is widely used. In contrast to the one-sided communication of BSP programming, traditional message passing uses two-sided communication, which involves both an active sender and an active receiver. The underlying model is that of communicating sequential processes (CSP) by Hoare [158].

Communication of a message synchronizes the sender and the receiver. The cost of communicating a message of length n is typically modelled as

$$T(n) = \alpha + n\beta, \tag{1.19}$$

with a fixed startup cost α and additional cost β per data word. Cost analysis in this model requires a detailed study of the order in which the messages are sent, their lengths, and the computations that are interleaved between the communications. In its most general form, this can be expressed by a directed acyclic graph with chunks of computation as vertices and messages as directed edges.

The first portable communication library, parallel virtual machine (PVM), was developed by Sunderam [282] and became a standard in 1994 [120]. PVM is a message-passing library that enables computing on **heterogeneous networks**, that is, networks of computers with different architectures. PVM also allows for dynamic creation and removal of processes.

The Message-Passing Interface (MPI), based on traditional message passing, was defined as a standard in 1994 by the MPI Forum, a committee of users of parallel computers, manufacturers, and tool developers. The initial definition is now known as MPI-1, and it provides an interface for parallel programming in C and Fortran 77. MPI-2 became a standard in 1997, adding functionality in the areas of one-sided communications, dynamic process management, and parallel input/output (I/O), and adding bindings for the languages Fortran 90 and C++. Because the C++ bindings were hardly used, they were subsequently removed from MPI-3, released in 2012. The current bindings of MPI are C and Fortran 90 (with some additional features from Fortran 2003/2008).

MPI is available on many different parallel computers. Important implementations are Open MPI [237] and MPICH [307]. Most likely MPI has already been installed on the parallel computer you use, perhaps even in a well-optimized version provided by the hardware vendor. (In contrast, often you have to install BSPlib yourself or request this from your systems administrator.) Much parallel software has already been written in MPI, a prime example being the numerical linear algebra library ScaLAPACK [35, 66]. The availability of such a library may sometimes be a compelling reason for using MPI in a parallel application. For the complete, most recent MPI-3.1 standard from 2015 with annotations, see [218]. For a tutorial introduction of the basics of MPI-3, see the book by Gropp, Lusk, and Skjellum [132]; for the advanced features, see [131]. The sheer size of MPI, and its backwards compatibility stretching over several decades have given rise to some criticism, and to an increase in the popularity of alternatives such as BSP-based approaches. Because MPI is so widely used, especially in high-performance computing, we will present a more extensive discussion of MPI, viewed from a BSP perspective. This may be a fresh view for those readers who are already familiar with MPI. We will also highlight the differences between BSPlib and MPI and also their common features.

MPI is a software interface, and not a parallel programming model. It enables programming in many different styles, including the bulk synchronous parallel style. A particular algorithm can typically be implemented in many different ways using MPI, which is the strength but also the difficulty of MPI.

In MPI, the archetypical primitives for the message-passing style, based on the message-passing model, are `MPI_Send` and `MPI_Recv`. An example of their use is

```
if (s==2)
    MPI_Send(x, 5, MPI_DOUBLE, 3, 0, MPI_COMM_WORLD);
if (s==3)
    MPI_Recv(y, 5, MPI_DOUBLE, 2, 0, MPI_COMM_WORLD,
             &status);
```

which sends five doubles from $P(2)$ to $P(3)$, reading them from an array x on $P(2)$ and writing them into an array y on $P(3)$. Here, the integer '0' is a tag that can be used to distinguish between different messages transferred from the same source processor to the same destination processor. Furthermore, `MPI_COMM_WORLD` is the communicator consisting of all the processors. A **communicator** is a subset of processors forming a communication environment with its own processor numbering.

Despite the fundamental importance of the `MPI_Send`/`MPI_Recv` pair in MPI, it is best to avoid its use if possible, as extensive use of such pairs may lead to unstructured programs that are hard to read, prove correct, or debug. Similar to the `goto`-statement, which was considered harmful in sequential programming by Dijkstra [86], the explicit send/receive pair can be considered harmful in parallel programming [125]. In the parallel case, the danger of **deadlock** always exists; deadlock may occur for instance if $P(0)$ wants to send a message to $P(1)$, and $P(1)$ to $P(0)$, and both processors want to send before they receive.

If you want to use MPI (no bias here!), I advocate using the collective and the one-sided communications of MPI-3 where possible, and to limit the use of the send/receive pair to exceptional situations. (Note that the `goto`-statement still exists in C, for good reasons, but it is hardly used anymore.) Collective communication requires the participation of all the processors of a communicator. An example of a collective communication is the broadcast `MPI_Bcast` from a **root processor** such as $P(0)$ to all other processors.

To model the cost of an MPI program written in BSP style, we need to obtain the BSP parameters r,p,g,l of the MPI system used. The main question then is which communication method from MPI to benchmark. In the BSPlib case, we opted for benchmarking a typical user program, where the user does not care about communication optimization such as combining messages to the same destination, but instead relies on the BSPlib system to do this for her. When writing a program in MPI, a typical user would look first if there is a collective-communication function that can perform the job for him. This would lead to shorter program texts, and is good practice from the BSP point of view as well. Therefore, we should choose a collective communication as the operation to be benchmarked for MPI.

The BSP superstep, where every processor can communicate in principle with all the others, is reflected best by the **all-to-all** primitives from MPI, also called **total-exchange** primitives. Using an all-to-all primitive gives the MPI system the best opportunities for optimization, similar to the opportunities that the superstep gives to the BSPlib system. The best choice is the most flexible variant, `MPI_Alltoallv`, which allows a varying number of data to be sent (or even no data).

Given the ubiquity of MPI, which road should we take when programming in bulk synchronous parallel style? In the past years, two main approaches have emerged: **MPI as a**

backend, and **BSP First, MPI Second**. MPI as a backend means building a BSP-like system that uses MPI at a lower level, thus guaranteeing portability but providing at the same time a high-level interface to the user. Examples of such BSP systems are BSPonMPI [281] and Bulk [52]. The small size of BSPlib makes the development of such systems relatively easy, and many started off as student projects and then matured (together with their designers!). The main advantage of this approach is ease of use, and automatic enforcement of the BSP style. Another important advantage is the impossibility of introducing deadlock in BSPlib programs. Optimization by a clever BSPlib system could even lead to faster communication compared with using the MPI backend directly. As a result, a BSPlib application program can be viewed as an MPI program when compiled for instance with the BSPonMPI library.

BSP First, MPI Second means first developing a program using BSPlib and, when the need arises, converting it to MPI. I did this for the programs from BSPedupack accompanying the first edition of this book. To give an idea, it took me only about a week (human processing time) to convert the whole of BSPedupack, version 1.0, to MPI, including all driver programs, and to compile and test the resulting programs. The conversion time is far less than the time it took me to develop BSPedupack. The extra human time incurred by having to convert the final result to MPI is more than compensated for by the quicker development of the original program. In my experience with the conversion of BSPedupack to MPIedupack, the differences are often limited: the main differences are in the I/O parts of the programs, and in communication parts that are well-isolated because of the structured approach inherent in the bulk synchronous parallel style. An additional advantage of this approach is that it encourages programming in this style also in the MPI part of programs, where the temptation of using matching send/receive pairs always lures.

The strength of MPI is its wide availability and broad functionality. You can do almost anything in MPI, except cook dinner. The weakness of MPI is its size: the present MPI-3.1 standard [218] is a huge book weighing 1066 gram (to save the Planet, it is best used as an online reference manual) and it has 868 pages, which is much more than the 34 pages of the BSPlib standard [153] plus four pages of the modernization presented in [318]. The size of MPI may lead to developers of system software implementing only a subset of the MPI primitives (often from MPI-1.2), which harms portability. It also forces users to learn only a subset of the primitives, which makes it more difficult to read programs written by others, since different programmers will most likely choose a different subset. Every implemented MPI primitive is likely to be optimized independently, with a varying rate of success. This makes it impossible to develop a uniform cost model that realistically reflects the performance of every primitive. In contrast, the small size of BSPlib and the underlying cost model provide a better focus to the implementer and make theoretical cost analysis and cost predictions feasible.

A fundamental difference between MPI and BSPlib is that MPI provides more opportunities for optimization by the user, by allowing many different ways to tackle a given programming task, whereas BSPlib provides more opportunities for optimization by the system. For an experienced user, MPI may achieve better results than BSPlib, but for an inexperienced user this may be the reverse. Using MPI as a backend is then the ideal combination: experts can optimize the use of the backend, whereas novices can quickly get started writing parallel programs that perform well.

MPI software can be used for programming in BSP style, even though it was not specifically designed for this purpose. Using collective communication wherever possible leads to supersteps and global synchronizations. Puts and gets are available since MPI-2 and can be used in the same way as BSPlib high-performance puts and gets. Still, in using MPI one would miss the imposed discipline provided by BSPlib. A small, paternalistic library such as BSPlib steers programming efforts in the right direction, unlike a large library such as MPI, which allows many different styles of programming and is more tolerant of deviations from the right path.

For shared-memory programming, communication with the shared memory is faster than communication through a network, and this is exploited by **threads** (lightweight processes) running computations in parallel. An efficient BSP library makes use of these threads. It is possible to program either directly using threads, such as POSIX threads (Pthreads) or threads from the newer versions of the C++ language, or instead make use of a system built on top of these threads, of which the most popular is OpenMP [238]. The basics of OpenMP are discussed in the book by Chapman, Jost, and van der Pas [62], and newer features in the book by van der Pas, Stotzer, and Terboven [296]. Graphics processing units (GPUs) also execute threads, in fact many of them, but these are very special and this type of parallelism is not easily captured within the BSP model. Therefore, we leave GPUs outside the scope of this book.

For hybrid shared/distributed-memory programming, users often employ MPI+X, where X stands for a shared-memory API such as OpenMP or Pthreads. In principle, this can achieve the ultimate in performance, but it requires familiarity with two APIs. The BSP approach is to unify these and, for instance, Bulk [52] tries to deliver the same performance with a single API.

An introduction to parallel programming that uses MPI-1 is the textbook by Pacheco [240]. An introduction that uses MPI for distributed-memory parallel programming and OpenMP for shared-memory programming is the textbook by Wilkinson and Allen [312]. The same choice is made in the textbook by Quinn [257] and the online textbook by Eijkhout [103]. An introduction that uses MPI for distributed memory and Pthreads, and OpenMP for shared memory, is the textbook by Grama *et al.* [129]. A recent book by Czarnul [75] presents a wide range of hardware devices and parallel programming APIs, including MPI, Pthreads, Open MPI for CPUs, and OpenCL and CUDA for GPUs.

1.11.4 Benchmarking

The BSPlib definition [153] presents results obtained by the optimized benchmarking program bspprobe, which is included in the Oxford BSP toolset [151]. Values of r and l measured by bspprobe will usually agree well with those of bspbench, but values of g will be lower for bspprobe due to more extensive optimization: data are sent as multiple-word packets instead of single words and high-performance puts are used instead of buffered puts. The goal of bspprobe is to measure communication performance for optimized programs and hence its bottom line takes as g-value the asymptotic value for large packets.

Benchmark results for machines ranging from personal computers to massively parallel supercomputers have been collected and regularly updated in the LINPACK report by Jack

Dongarra [92] since 1985. These results represent the total execution rates for solving a dense $n \times n$ linear system of equations with $n = 100$ and $n = 1000$ by the LINPACK software and with unlimited n by any suitable software. The High-Performance LINPACK (HPL) benchmark [90] became available in 2003; it can be used to measure linear system solving speed on parallel computers. HPL allows supercomputers to show off and demonstrate their top capabilities.

The LINPACK report gives the following parameters for each benchmarked computer: r_{max}, the maximum computing rate achieved; r_{peak}, the theoretical peak rate; n_{max}, the size of the system at which r_{max} is achieved; and $n_{1/2}$, the size at which half of r_{max} is obtained. The $n_{1/2}$ parameter is widely used as a measure of startup overhead. Low $n_{1/2}$ values promise top rates already for moderate problem sizes, see *The Science of Computer Benchmarking* by Hockney [159]. The value of r_{max} is the basis for the TOP500 list of supercomputers [279].

These days, to be called a supercomputer and enter the TOP500, a computer must achieve at least 1.142 Pflop/s. The fastest existing number cruncher (in November 2019) is Summit, an IBM Power system at Oak Ridge National Laboratory in the USA, a system with $p = 2\,414\,592$ processor cores. This computer solves a large linear system of size $n_{max} = 16\,473\,600$ at $r_{max} = 148.6$ Pflop/s. For comparison, its theoretical peak speed is $r_{peak} = 200.8$ Pflop/s.

For top speed in dense linear algebra, the BLAS (Basic Linear Algebra Subprograms) library [93, 94, 193] provides a complete and portable interface to a set of subroutines for the most common vector and matrix operations, such as DAXPY and DGEMM. A complete BLAS list is given in [95, Appendix C]. Efficient BLAS implementations exist for most machines. The ATLAS project [311] automatically tunes BLAS to the machine used by running initial tests to benchmark the machine and then choosing the best parameters and the best implementation for the BLAS.

Supercomputers consume vast amounts of energy, leading to large electricity bills and also plenty of CO_2 emission. To encourage efforts to become more energy-efficient, the Green500 list was introduced at the Supercomputing Conference in 2007 [105]. The greenest supercomputer in November 2019 [106] is the Fujitsu A64FX prototype installed at Fujitsu, Japan, which delivers 16.9 Gflop/watt. Its maximum speed is $r_{max} = 2.0$ Pflop/s and its total energy use is only 118 kwatt. To give an idea what this means: about 400 solar panels of 300 watt each would be needed to run this computer on a sunny day. (Full disclosure: I have seven such panels on the roof of my house, supplying power to the computers on which I write this book and all my other electrical equipment.)

1.11.5 Sorting

Many sequential algorithms exist for sorting, each with its own range of application, see Cormen *et al.* [72, Chapters 2, 6, 7, 8] for an introduction to mergesort, heapsort, quicksort, and counting/radix sort, respectively.

Early work on parallel sorting algorithms mainly concerned **sorting networks** consisting of **compare-and-swap** devices, which take as input a pair of numbers (x, y) and produce as output a pair $(\min(x, y), \max(x, y))$. The whole network takes as input n arbitrary numbers and produces as output the numbers sorted in increasing order. Since many devices can work at the same time, this can be viewed as a parallel computation. A simple (but not very efficient) example is the odd-even sorting transposition network [187] which implements a parallel variant of the $\mathcal{O}(n^2)$ bubblesort algorithm. In the even phases of the algorithm, compare-and-swap operations are carried out on pairs (x_{2i}, x_{2i+1}) for $i = 0, 1, \ldots, n/2 - 1$, and in the odd phases on pairs (x_{2i-1}, x_{2i}) for $i = 1, \ldots, n/2 - 1$. After n phases, the algorithm is finished. This parallel algorithm costs $\mathcal{O}(n)$ time, which is faster than the $\mathcal{O}(n \log n)$ of mergesort, quicksort, and heapsort, and it performs $p = n/2$ comparisons simultaneously. This achieves a speedup of $\mathcal{O}(\log n)$ on $n/2$ processors, but it also means a waste of processors. A faster algorithm is Batcher's odd-even mergesort [22], which takes $\mathcal{O}(\log^2 n)$ time for the same number of processors. Batcher also presents an algorithm with the same complexity based on **bitonic** sequences (which first increase, then decrease, possibly after a rotation of the sequence). Note that an increasing or decreasing sequence is **monotonic**.

Research on sorting networks has inspired the development of many PRAM algorithms for sorting, such as $\mathcal{O}(\log n)$ algorithms for n processors by Cole [69] for the CREW and EREW variants of the PRAM model. PRAM algorithms in turn have served as a source of inspiration for developing more practical parallel algorithms that take communication into account and run on fewer than n processors.

Shi and Schaeffer [266] introduced and analysed the parallel sort by regular sampling (PSRS) algorithm we presented here. They choose the global splitters in a slightly more sophisticated way than we do, taking special care of the first and last block of data. In a follow-up paper [198], the authors and their collaborators sharpen their bounds on the block size and they analyse the impact of duplicate array values.

Solomonik and Kalé [274] investigate the scalability of various parallel sorting algorithms. They show that for large p, storing and sorting the p^2 samples becomes a bottleneck in PSRS, and they provide an alternative, histogram sort. In this sorting method, a central processor $P(0)$ repeatedly makes informed guesses to find suitable splitters, until all p splitters are within a margin of 5% from their ideal position, which is at equal distances n/p. On an IBM Blue Gene/P computer using 32 768 cores, they achieve an impressive speedup of about 15 000 for histogram sort of an array of length $n = 8 \cdot 10^6$. (For this rather small length, the PSRS range of efficiency $p \leq n^{1/3}$ is equivalent to $p \leq 200$.) The paper extensively discusses user optimizations of the communication superstep that moves all the data; BSP systems do this automatically. The authors also exploit overlap between communication and computation.

Axtmann et al. [12] present a multilevel generalization for the case that p becomes very large, to reduce the total startup cost of sending up to $p(p - 1)$ messages in the main communication superstep of the PSRS algorithm. They analyse the cost of the algorithm within the BSP framework, but with an extra parameter to account for the maximum number of messages that a processor has to send or receive in a superstep. (Note that we simply lump all startup costs into l.) For two levels, the multilevel algorithm divides the processors into groups of size $\sqrt{p}$. After the local sort, each processor splits its data into $\sqrt{p}$ parts instead of p, based on $\sqrt{p}$ local samples. Then, the $p^{3/2}$ samples are used together to determine $\sqrt{p}$ global splitters, and the data is communicated to their responsible group. In a next superstep, the data is sent to their responsible processor. The group size can be chosen different from $\sqrt{p}$, for instance to reflect the architecture of the computer. The two-level algorithm would fit well in the hybrid-BSP framework that we present in Section 4.10. The authors present experimental results using C++ and MPI achieving a speedup of 6164 on 32 768 processors for $n = 10^6$, compared to a sequential sort from the C++ Standard Template Library.

In their article [122] from 1994 on **direct** BSP algorithms (with user control of the memory allocation), Gerbessiotis and Valiant present a multilevel sorting algorithm based on random samples, with oversampling to achieve a good load balance with high probability. Hill, Donaldson, and Skillicorn [152] present experimental results for a randomized BSP samplesort. Gerbessiotis developed several BSP sorting algorithms based on random or deterministic (regular) sampling. He uses a deterministic oversampling sort algorithm as an example when introducing his multicore BSP variant (MBSP) [121].

· ·

1.12 EXERCISES

Exercise 1.1 Algorithm 1.1 can be modified to combine the partial sums into one global sum by a different method. Let $p = 2^q$, with $q \geq 0$. Modify the algorithm to combine the partial sums by repeated pairing of processors. Take care that every processor obtains the final result. Formulate the modified algorithm exactly, using the same notation as in the original algorithm. Explain why your algorithm is correct. Compare the BSP cost of the two algorithms. For which ratio l/g is the pairwise algorithm faster? (If needed, approximate the BSP costs in this comparison.)

Exercise 1.2 Analyse the following operations and derive the BSP cost for a parallel algorithm. Let **x** be the input vector (of size n) of the operation and **y** the output vector. Assume that both these vectors are block distributed over p processors, with $p \leq n$. Furthermore, k is an integer with $1 \leq k \leq n$. The operations are:

(a) Minimum finding: determine the index j of the component with the minimum value and subtract this value from every component: $y_i = x_i - x_j$, for all i.
(b) Rotating to the right: assign $y_{(i+k) \bmod n} = x_i$.
(c) Smoothing: replace each component by a moving average $y_i = \frac{1}{k+1} \sum_{j=i-k/2}^{i+k/2} x_j$, where k is even. Assume here that $x_j = 0$ for $j < 0$ or $j \geq n$.
(d) Partial summing: compute $y_i = \sum_{j=0}^{i} x_j$, for all i. (This problem is an instance of the **parallel prefix** problem.)

Exercise 1.3 Get acquainted with your parallel computer before you use it.

(a) Run the program `bspbench` on your parallel computer. Measure the values of g and l for various numbers of processors. How does the performance of your machine scale with p?
(b) Modify `bspbench` to measure `bsp_gets` instead of `bsp_puts`. Think carefully about the required changes! Run the modified program for various p. Compare the results with those of the original program.

(c) Similarly, modify bspbench to measure bsp_sends, using messages with a long integer as the tag and a double as the payload.

(d) Modify bspbench to measure g in the case where the number of bytes in a single bsp_put operation is larger than the size of a double. How does the number of bytes influence g? We call the asymptotic value g_∞ for a very large number of bytes the **optimistic** g-value. The value g_1 for one double is then the **pessimistic** g-value. Draw conclusions on how to use measured g-values to predict the actual running time of a BSP algorithm.

Exercise 1.4 Since their invention, computers have been used as tools in cryptanalytic attacks on secret messages; parallel computers are no exception. Assume that a plain text has been encrypted by the classic method of monoalphabetic substitution, where each letter from the alphabet is replaced by another one and where blanks and punctuation characters are deleted. For such a simple encryption scheme, we can apply statistical methods such as frequency analysis to uncover the message. See Bauer [23] for more details and also for a fascinating history of cryptology.

(a) Let $\mathbf{t} = (t_0, \ldots, t_{n-1})^{\mathrm{T}}$ be a cryptotext of n letters and $\mathbf{t}'$ another cryptotext, of the same length, language, and encryption alphabet. With a bit of luck, we can determine the language of the texts by computing Friedman's Kappa value, also called the index of coincidence,

$$\kappa(\mathbf{t}, \mathbf{t}') = \frac{1}{n} \sum_{i=0}^{n-1} \delta(t_i, t_i').$$

Here, $\delta(x, y) = 1$ if $x = y$, and $\delta(x, y) = 0$ otherwise. The value of κ tells us how likely it is that two letters in the same position of the texts are identical. Write a parallel program that reads an encrypted text, splits it into two parts $\mathbf{t}$ and $\mathbf{t}'$ of equal size (dropping the last letter if necessary), and computes $\kappa(\mathbf{t}, \mathbf{t}')$. Motivate your choice of data distribution.

(b) Download the file crypto.txt from my personal book website (where you can also download BSPedupack). Use it as cryptotext input and compute its κ. Guess its language by comparing the result with the κ-values found by Kullback (reproduced in [23, Chapter 16]): Russian 5.29%, English 6.61%, German 7.62%, French 7.78%.

(c) Find out whether the Dutch language is closer to English or German by computing its κ-value.

(d) Extend your program to compute all letter frequencies in the input text. In English, the 'e' is the most frequent letter; its frequency is about 12.5%.

(e) Run your program on some large plain texts in the language guessed in (b) to obtain a frequency profile of that language. Run your program on the cryptotext and establish its letter frequencies. Now break the code by matching the letters.

Exercise 1.5 (*) We have analysed the parallel regular samplesort of Algorithm 1.4 and found an upper bound $b_s \leq 2n/p - p$ for the output block size, under the assumptions $n \bmod p^2 = 0$ and no duplicate values.

(a) Give a sharper upper bound for b_0.

(b) Give a lower bound for b_{p-1}.

(c) Assume that we **oversample** the data by a factor of two, generating $q = 2p$ samples (and subblocks) per processor. Adapt the algorithm accordingly. What is the new bound b_s? Analyse the BSP cost.

(d) What are the advantages and disadvantages of increasing the oversampling factor?

(e) Modify `bspsort` to incorporate oversampling by a factor of two.

(f) Test your modified program using a set of real-world data instead of the random data created by `bspsort_test`, and check how close the output block sizes are to the upper bound. Also, construct an artificial worst-case data set to obtain the upper bound on $\max_s b_s$ for regular sampling, and use it to investigate the benefits of oversampling.

(g) Optimize the `bspsort` program by filtering the set of p^2 samples (or $2p^2$ in case of twofold oversampling) before sorting them in superstep (2), keeping only the samples that are relevant for the range of local data values of a processor; the samples below the minimum local value or above the maximum just need to be counted. What cost savings can be obtained in the best case? Construct an artificial data set that would maximally benefit from the filtering. Note that this optimization would be impossible if we only made $P(0)$ responsible for sorting the samples.

Exercise 1.6 (∗) Data compression is widely used to reduce the size of data files, for instance texts or pictures to be transferred over the Internet. Compression can either be lossless (keeping all information) or lossy (allowing for some hardly noticeable degradation in quality, especially in pictures). The LZ77 algorithm by Ziv and Lempel [322] is a lossless compression algorithm that passes through a text and uses the most recently accessed portion as a reference dictionary to shorten the text, replacing repeated character strings by pointers to their first occurrence. The popular compression programs PKZIP, gzip, and 7-Zip are all based on LZ77; they incorporate various enhancements to achieve further compression or greater speed.

Consider the text

‘yabbadabbadoo’

(Fred Flintstone, Stone Age). Assume that we arrive at the second occurrence of the string ‘abbad’. By going back five characters, we find a matching string of length five. We can code this as the triple of decimal numbers $(5,5,111)$, where the first number in the triple is the number of characters we have to go back and the second number the length of the matching string. The number 111 is the ASCII code for the lowercase ‘o’, which is the next character after the second ‘abbad’. (The lowercase characters ‘a’–‘z’ are numbered 97–122 in the ASCII set.) Giving the next character ensures progress, even if no match was found. The output for this example is: $(0,0,121), (0,0,97), (0,0,98), (1,1,97), (0,0,100), (5,5,111), (1,1,-1)$. The ‘−1’ means end of input. If more matches are possible, the longest one is taken. For longer texts, the search for a match is limited to the last m characters before the current character (the search window); the string to be matched is limited to the first n characters starting at the current character (the look-ahead window).

(a) Write a sequential function that takes as input a character sequence and writes as output an LZ77 sequence of triples (o, l, c), where o is the offset, that is, the number of characters to be moved back, l the length of the matching substring, and c the code for the next character. Use suitable data types for o, l, and c to save space. Take $m = n = 512$. Also write a sequential function that decompresses the LZ77 sequence. Which is faster, compression or decompression? What is the computation complexity of compression and decompression?

(b) Design and implement a parallel LZ77 compression algorithm. You may adapt the original algorithm if needed for parallelization as long as the output can be read by the sequential LZ77 program. Derive the BSP cost, assuming that the file to be compressed has already been suitably distributed on input.

(c) Now design a parallel algorithm that produces exactly the same output sequence as the sequential algorithm. You may need several passes through the data.

(d) Compare the compression ratio of your compression programs with that of gzip. Use a suitable data set such as plain-text books from Project Gutenberg [141], or DNA sequences. How could you improve the performance?

(e) Is it worthwhile to parallelize the decompression?

Exercise 1.7 (∗) The sieve of Eratosthenes (276–194 BC) is a method for generating all prime numbers up to a certain bound n. It works as follows. Start with the integers from 2 to n. The number 2 is a prime; cross out all larger multiples of 2. The smallest remaining number, 3, is a prime; cross out all larger multiples of 3. The smallest remaining number, 5, is a prime, etc.

(a) When can we stop?

(b) Write a sequential sieve program. Represent the integers by a suitable array.

(c) Analyse the cost of the sequential algorithm. Hint: the probability of an arbitrary integer $x \geq 2$ to be prime is about $1/\log x$, where $\log = \log_e$ denotes the natural logarithm. Estimate the total number of cross-out operations and use some calculus to obtain a simple formula. Add operation counters to your program to check the accuracy of your formula.

(d) Design a parallel sieve algorithm. Would you distribute the array of integers over the processors by blocks, cyclically, or in some other fashion? The resulting set of primes need not be replicated across the processors; it is sufficient to obtain them in distributed form.

(e) Write a parallel sieve program bspsieve and measure its execution time for $n = 10^3, 10^4, 10^5, 10^6, 10^7$ and $p = 1, 2, 4, 8, 16, 32$, or use as many processors as you can lay your hands on.

(f) Estimate the BSP cost of the parallel algorithm and use this estimate to explain your time measurements.

(g) Can you reduce the cost further? Hints: for the prime q, do you need to start crossing out at $2q$? Does every processor cross out the same number of integers? Is all communication really necessary?

(h) Modify your program to generate twin primes, that is, pairs of primes that differ by two, such as 4 ± 1 or $2\,996\,863\,034\,895 \cdot 2^{1290000} \pm 1$, the largest known twin prime at the time of writing; this twin was discovered on September 14, 2016 by Tom Greer, participant in the Sophie Germain Prime search organized through the distributed computing project PrimeGrid [271]. It is still unknown whether there are infinitely many twin primes, but much progress has been made since the breakthrough paper by Yitang Zhang [320] in 2014, who showed that there are infinitely many pairs of subsequent primes (p_k, p_{k+1}) with a distance $p_{k+1} - p_k < 7 \cdot 10^7$. This distance has been reduced to at most 246 by the Polymath8b project, and the aim in proving the twin prime conjecture is eventually to reach 2. Give the BSP cost of your modified program and test it.

(i) Extend your program to check the Goldbach conjecture: every even $k > 2$ is the sum of two primes. Choose a suitable range of integers to check. Try to keep the number of operations low. (The conjecture has been an open question since 1742.) Give the BSP cost of the Goldbach program and test it.

2

$\cdot$ $\cdot$ $\bullet$ $\cdot$ $\cdot$

LU decomposition

2.1 The problem

Take a close look at your favourite scientific computing application. Whether it originates in ocean modelling, oil refinery optimization, electronic circuit simulation, or in another application area, most likely you will find on close inspection that at its heart lies the solution of large systems of linear equations. Indeed, solving linear systems is the most time-consuming part of many scientific computing applications. This motivates our choice of the LU decomposition problem for the present chapter.

In case you are more interested in Big Data computations such as those performed in machine learning and artificial intelligence, here too you will encounter much linear algebra and matrix decompositions such as QR and SVD, which can be parallelized using the same techniques as presented for LU decomposition.

Consider a system of linear equations

$$A\mathbf{x} = \mathbf{b}, \tag{2.1}$$

where A is a given $n \times n$ nonsingular matrix, $\mathbf{b}$ a given vector of length n, and $\mathbf{x}$ the unknown solution vector of length n. An $n \times n$ matrix A is called **nonsingular** (or **invertible**) if there exists a matrix A^{-1} such that $AA^{-1} = A^{-1}A = I_n$, where I_n denotes the $n \times n$ **identity matrix** which has ones on the diagonal and zeros everywhere else.

One method for solving the system (2.1) is by using **LU decomposition**, that is, decomposition of the matrix A into an $n \times n$ unit lower triangular matrix L and an $n \times n$ upper triangular matrix U such that

$$A = LU. \tag{2.2}$$

An $n \times n$ matrix L is called **unit lower triangular** if $l_{ii} = 1$ for all i, $0 \le i < n$, and $l_{ij} = 0$ for all i,j with $0 \le i < j < n$. An $n \times n$ matrix U is called **upper triangular** if $u_{ij} = 0$ for all i,j with $0 \le j < i < n$. Note that we always start counting at zero—my daughter Sarai was raised that way—and this will turn out to be an advantage later in life, when encountering parallel computations. (For instance, it becomes easier to define the cyclic distribution.)

Parallel Scientific Computation: A Structured Approach Using BSP. Second Edition. Rob H. Bisseling,
Oxford University Press (2020). © Rob H. Bisseling.
DOI: 10.1093/oso/9780198788348.001.0001

Example 2.1 For $A = \begin{bmatrix} 1 & 4 & 6 \\ 2 & 10 & 17 \\ 3 & 16 & 31 \end{bmatrix}$, we obtain $L = \begin{bmatrix} 1 & 0 & 0 \\ 2 & 1 & 0 \\ 3 & 2 & 1 \end{bmatrix}$,

$$U = \begin{bmatrix} 1 & 4 & 6 \\ 0 & 2 & 5 \\ 0 & 0 & 3 \end{bmatrix}.$$

The linear system $Ax = \mathbf{b}$ can be solved by first decomposing A into $A = LU$ and then solving the triangular systems $Ly = \mathbf{b}$ and $Ux = \mathbf{y}$. The advantage of LU decomposition over similar methods such as Gaussian elimination is that the factors L and U can be reused, to solve different systems $Ax = \mathbf{b}'$ with the same matrix but different right-hand sides. The main text of the present chapter only deals with LU decomposition. Exercise 2.10 treats the parallel solution of triangular systems.

2.2 Sequential LU decomposition

In this section, we derive the sequential algorithm that is the basis for developing our parallel algorithm. By expanding (2.2) and using the fact that $l_{ir} = 0$ for $i < r$ and $u_{rj} = 0$ for $r > j$, we get

$$a_{ij} = \sum_{r=0}^{n-1} l_{ir} u_{rj} = \sum_{r=0}^{\min(i,j)} l_{ir} u_{rj}, \quad \text{for } 0 \le i,j < n. \tag{2.3}$$

In the case $i \le j$, we split off the ith term and substitute $l_{ii} = 1$, to obtain

$$u_{ij} = a_{ij} - \sum_{r=0}^{i-1} l_{ir} u_{rj}, \quad \text{for } 0 \le i \le j < n. \tag{2.4}$$

Similarly,

$$l_{ij} = \frac{1}{u_{jj}} \left(a_{ij} - \sum_{r=0}^{j-1} l_{ir} u_{rj} \right), \quad \text{for } 0 \le j < i < n. \tag{2.5}$$

Equations (2.4) and (2.5) lead to a method for computing the elements of L and U. For convenience, we first define the intermediate $n \times n$ matrices $A^{(k)}$, $0 \le k \le n$, by

$$a_{ij}^{(k)} = a_{ij} - \sum_{r=0}^{k-1} l_{ir} u_{rj}, \quad \text{for } 0 \le i,j < n. \tag{2.6}$$

Note that $A^{(0)} = A$ and $A^{(n)} = 0$. In this notation, (2.4) and (2.5) become

$$u_{ij} = a_{ij}^{(i)}, \quad \text{for } 0 \le i \le j < n, \tag{2.7}$$

and

$$l_{ij} = \frac{a_{ij}^{(j)}}{u_{jj}}, \quad \text{for } 0 \leq j < i < n. \tag{2.8}$$

Algorithm 2.1 produces the elements of L and U in stages. Stage k first computes the elements u_{kj}, $j \geq k$, of row k of U and the elements l_{ik}, $i > k$, of column k of L. Then, it computes $A^{(k+1)}$ in preparation for the next stage. Since only values $a_{ij}^{(k)}$ with $i,j \geq k$ are needed in stage k, only the relevant values $a_{ij}^{(k+1)}$ with $i,j \geq k+1$ are prepared. It can easily be verified that this order of computation is indeed feasible: in each assignment of the algorithm, the values on the right-hand side have already been computed.

To assist in seeing the correctness of the algorithm, we inserted a loop invariant at the start and end of the main loop, which expresses the current relation between the relevant variables,

$$\text{Invariant}(k): \qquad a_{ij}^{(k)} = a_{ij} - \sum_{r=0}^{k-1} l_{ir}u_{rj}, \quad \text{for } k \leq i,j < n. \tag{2.9}$$

At the start of the loop, the invariant is trivially true, as it merely states that $a_{ij}^{(0)} = a_{ij}$ for all i,j. This is guaranteed by the **precondition** $A^{(0)} = A$, made true just before the loop. During the loop, the invariant is maintained when going from stage k to stage $k+1$ by subtracting one term $l_{ik}u_{kj}$ from every relevant matrix element. The use of a loop invariant in proving an algorithm correct thus resembles the use of induction in mathematical proofs. At the end, we obtain the **postcondition**, Invariant(n), which is trivially true as it states nothing. The validity of the invariant during the algorithm tells us that we indeed retrieve the correct values l_{ik} and u_{kj} in every stage k. This is one of the rare occasions where we will indulge in formal correctness proving, and the main goal is to illustrate the use of loop invariants as a tool.

Figure 2.1 illustrates how computer memory can be saved by storing all currently available elements of L, U, and $A^{(k)}$ in one working matrix, which we call A. Thus, we obtain

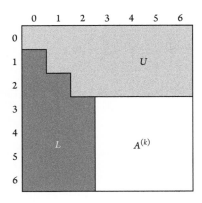

Figure 2.1 LU decomposition of a 7×7 matrix at the start of stage $k = 3$. The values of L and U computed so far and the computed part of $A^{(k)}$ fit exactly into one matrix.

Algorithm 2.1 Sequential LU decomposition.

---

input: $A : n \times n$ matrix.

output: $L : n \times n$ unit lower triangular matrix,
$\qquad U : n \times n$ upper triangular matrix,
$\qquad$ such that $LU = A$.

$A^{(0)} := A;$
for $k := 0$ **to** $n - 1$ **do**
$\qquad$ { Invariant(k) }

$\qquad$ **for** $j := k$ **to** $n - 1$ **do**
$\qquad\qquad u_{kj} := a_{kj}^{(k)};$
$\qquad$ **for** $i := k + 1$ **to** $n - 1$ **do**
$\qquad\qquad l_{ik} := a_{ik}^{(k)} / u_{kk};$
$\qquad$ **for** $i := k + 1$ **to** $n - 1$ **do**
$\qquad\qquad$ **for** $j := k + 1$ **to** $n - 1$ **do**
$\qquad\qquad\qquad a_{ij}^{(k+1)} := a_{ij}^{(k)} - l_{ik} u_{kj};$

$\qquad$ { Invariant($k + 1$) }

Algorithm 2.2. On input, A contains the original matrix $A^{(0)}$, whereas on output it contains the values of L below the diagonal and the values of U above and on the diagonal. Since L is unit lower triangular, its diagonal values are 1, so they need not be stored. In other words, the output matrix equals $L - I_n + U$. Note that stage $n - 1$ of the algorithm does nothing, so we can skip it if idling hurts.

This is a good moment for introducing our matrix/vector notation, which is similar to the MATLAB[1] notation commonly used in the field of numerical linear algebra. For an excellent introduction to MATLAB, see the book by Desmond and Nick Higham [150]. This notation makes it easy to describe submatrices and subvectors. The subvector $x(i_0 : i_1)$ is a vector of length $i_1 - i_0 + 1$, which contains all components of $\mathbf{x}$ from i_0 up to and including i_1. The (noncontiguous) subvector $x(i_0 : stride : i_1)$ contains the components $i_0, i_0 + stride, i_0 + 2 \cdot stride, \ldots$ not exceeding i_1. The subvector $x(*)$ contains all components and hence it equals $\mathbf{x}$. The subvector $x(i)$ contains one component, the ith. The submatrix $A(i_0 : i_1, j_0 : j_1)$ contains all elements a_{ij} with $i_0 \leq i \leq i_1$ and $j_0 \leq j \leq j_1$. The ranges for the matrix indices can be written in the same way as for the vector indices. For example, the submatrix $A(i, *)$ denotes row i of the matrix A. Using our matrix/vector notation, we can write the submatrix used to store elements of $A^{(k)}$ as $A(k : n - 1, k : n - 1)$. We can also write the part of U computed in stage k as $U(k, k : n - 1)$ and the part of L computed in stage k as $L(k + 1 : n - 1, k)$.

---

[1] MATLAB is a registered trademark of The MathWorks, Inc.

Algorithm 2.2 Memory-efficient sequential LU decomposition.

input: $A : n \times n$ matrix, $A = A^{(0)}$.
output: $A : n \times n$ matrix, $A = L - I_n + U$, with
$\qquad$ $L : n \times n$ unit lower triangular matrix,
$\qquad$ $U : n \times n$ upper triangular matrix,
$\qquad$ such that $LU = A^{(0)}$.

$\quad$ **for** $k := 0$ **to** $n - 1$ **do**
$\qquad$ **for** $i := k + 1$ **to** $n - 1$ **do**
$\qquad\quad$ $a_{ik} := a_{ik}/a_{kk}$;
$\qquad$ **for** $i := k + 1$ **to** $n - 1$ **do**
$\qquad\quad$ **for** $j := k + 1$ **to** $n - 1$ **do**
$\qquad\qquad$ $a_{ij} := a_{ij} - a_{ik}a_{kj}$;

Example 2.2 The matrix A of Example 2.1 is transformed into a matrix holding the L and U factors, as follows:

$$A = \begin{bmatrix} 1 & 4 & 6 \\ 2 & 10 & 17 \\ 3 & 16 & 31 \end{bmatrix} \xrightarrow{(0)} \begin{bmatrix} 1 & 4 & 6 \\ 2 & 2 & 5 \\ 3 & 4 & 13 \end{bmatrix} \xrightarrow{(1)} \begin{bmatrix} 1 & 4 & 6 \\ 2 & 2 & 5 \\ 3 & 2 & 3 \end{bmatrix} = L - I_n + U.$$

Example 2.3 No LU decomposition exists for

$$A = \begin{bmatrix} 0 & 1 \\ 1 & 0 \end{bmatrix}.$$

The last example shows that Algorithm 2.2 may break down, even in the case of a nonsingular matrix. This happens if $a_{kk} = 0$ for a certain k, so that division by zero is attempted. A remedy for this problem is to permute the rows of the matrix A in a suitable way, giving a matrix PA, before computing an LU decomposition. This yields

$$PA = LU, \tag{2.10}$$

where P is an $n \times n$ **permutation matrix**, that is, a matrix obtained by permuting the rows of I_n. A useful property of a permutation matrix is that its inverse equals its transpose, $P^{-1} = P^T$. The effect of multiplying A from the left by P is to permute the rows of A.

Every permutation matrix corresponds to a unique permutation, and vice versa. Let $\sigma : \{0, \ldots, n - 1\} \rightarrow \{0, \ldots, n - 1\}$ be a permutation. We define the permutation matrix P_σ corresponding to σ as the $n \times n$ matrix with elements

$$(P_\sigma)_{ij} = \begin{cases} 1 & \text{if } i = \sigma(j) \\ 0 & \text{otherwise,} \end{cases} \quad \text{for } 0 \leq i,j < n. \tag{2.11}$$

This means that column j of P_σ has an element 1 in row $\sigma(j)$, and zeros everywhere else.

Example 2.4 Let $n = 3$ and $\sigma(0) = 1, \sigma(1) = 2$, and $\sigma(2) = 0$. Then

$$
P_\sigma = \begin{bmatrix} \cdot & \cdot & 1 \\ 1 & \cdot & \cdot \\ \cdot & 1 & \cdot \end{bmatrix},
$$

where the dots in the matrix denote zeros.

The permutation matrix P_σ has the following useful properties:

Lemma 2.5 Let $\sigma : \{0, \dots, n-1\} \to \{0, \dots, n-1\}$ be a permutation. Let $\mathbf{x}$ be a vector of length n and A an $n \times n$ matrix. Then

$$
(P_\sigma \mathbf{x})_i = x_{\sigma^{-1}(i)}, \text{ for } 0 \le i < n,
$$
$$
(P_\sigma A)_{ij} = a_{\sigma^{-1}(i),j}, \text{ for } 0 \le i,j < n,
$$
$$
(P_\sigma A P_\sigma^{\mathrm{T}})_{ij} = a_{\sigma^{-1}(i),\sigma^{-1}(j)}, \text{ for } 0 \le i,j < n.
$$

Proof We will prove the first part of the lemma:

$$
(P_\sigma \mathbf{x})_i = \sum_{j=0}^{n-1} (P_\sigma)_{ij} x_j = x_{\sigma^{-1}(i)},
$$

because only the term with $\sigma(j) = i$ contributes, i.e., the term $j = \sigma^{-1}(i)$. The proof of the other parts of the lemma is similar. $\square$

Lemma 2.6 Let $\sigma, \tau : \{0, \dots, n-1\} \to \{0, \dots, n-1\}$ be permutations. Then

$$
P_\tau P_\sigma = P_{\tau\sigma},
$$
$$
(P_\sigma)^{-1} = P_{\sigma^{-1}}.
$$

Here, $\tau\sigma$ denotes σ followed by τ.

Proof The first part of the lemma follows from

$$
(P_\tau P_\sigma)_{ij} = \sum_{k=0}^{n-1} (P_\tau)_{ik} (P_\sigma)_{kj} = (P_\sigma)_{\tau^{-1}(i),j},
$$

because only one term $k = \tau^{-1}(i)$ contributes. By the definition of P_σ, the result is 1 if $\tau^{-1}(i) = \sigma(j)$, i.e., $i = \tau(\sigma(j)) = (\tau\sigma)(j)$, and 0 otherwise. This is the same as for $(P_{\tau\sigma})_{ij}$. The second part of the lemma follows from the first by taking $\tau = \sigma^{-1}$ and using the fact that $P_{\mathrm{id}} = I_n$, where id is the identity permutation. $\square$

Usually, it is impossible to determine a suitable complete row permutation before the LU decomposition has been carried out, because the choice may depend on the evolving computation of L and U. A common procedure, which works well in practice, is **partial**

row pivoting. The computation starts with the original matrix A. At the start of stage k, the element with the largest absolute value among the elements a_{ik} in column k with $i \geq k$ is chosen as the **pivot element** a_{rk}. We express this concisely in the program text by stating that $r = \text{argmax}(|a_{ik}| : k \leq i < n)$, that is, r is the **argument** (or index) of the element having the maximum absolute value. If A is nonsingular, it is guaranteed that $a_{rk} \neq 0$. Furthermore, taking the largest instead of an arbitrary nonzero element keeps us farthest from dividing by zero and hence improves the numerical stability. Swapping row k and the **pivot row** r now makes it possible to perform stage k.

A word of caution. Theoretically, partial row pivoting can go wrong, in rare cases such as the following matrix example given by Golub and Van Loan [124, Section 3.4.6]. If you ever encounter such a matrix in practice, Wilkinson's saying applies:

'Anyone that unlucky has already been run over by a bus.'

Example 2.7 Define an $n \times n$ matrix A with elements 1 on the diagonal and in the last column, -1 below the diagonal, and 0 otherwise. During LU decomposition, the maximum size of an element grows as 2^{n-1}. For $n = 4$, the LU decomposition is

$$
A = \begin{bmatrix} 1 & 0 & 0 & 1 \\ -1 & 1 & 0 & 1 \\ -1 & -1 & 1 & 1 \\ -1 & -1 & -1 & 1 \end{bmatrix} = \begin{bmatrix} 1 & 0 & 0 & 0 \\ -1 & 1 & 0 & 0 \\ -1 & -1 & 1 & 0 \\ -1 & -1 & -1 & 1 \end{bmatrix} \begin{bmatrix} 1 & 0 & 0 & 1 \\ 0 & 1 & 0 & 2 \\ 0 & 0 & 1 & 4 \\ 0 & 0 & 0 & 8 \end{bmatrix}.
$$

LU decomposition with partial row pivoting produces the L and U factors of a permuted matrix PA, for a given input matrix A. These factors can then be used to solve the linear system $PA\mathbf{x} = P\mathbf{b}$ by permuting the vector $\mathbf{b}$ and solving two triangular systems. To perform the permutation, we need to know P. We can find P by introducing a permutation vector π of length n. We denote the components of π by π_i or $\pi(i)$, whichever is more convenient in the context. We determine P by registering the swaps executed in the stages of the computation. For instance, we can start with the identity permutation stored as a vector $\mathbf{e} = (0, 1, \ldots, n - 1)^{\mathrm{T}}$ in π. We swap the components k and r of π whenever we swap a row k and a row r of the working matrix. On output, the working matrix holds the L and U factors of PA, and π holds the vector $P\mathbf{e}$. Assume $P = P_\sigma$ for a certain permutation σ. Applying Lemma 2.5 gives $\pi(i) = (P_\sigma \mathbf{e})_i = \mathbf{e}_{\sigma^{-1}(i)} = \sigma^{-1}(i)$, for all i. Therefore, $\sigma = \pi^{-1}$ and $P_{\pi^{-1}}A = LU$. Again applying the lemma, we see that this is equivalent with $a_{\pi(i),j} = (LU)_{ij}$, for all i, j.

The resulting LU decomposition with partial pivoting is given as Algorithm 2.3. Its cost is determined as follows. The floating-point operations in stage k are: $n - k - 1$ divisions, $(n - k - 1)^2$ multiplications, and $(n - k - 1)^2$ subtractions. We ignore all other operations, such as comparisons, assignments, and integer operations, because taking these into account would make our analysis laborious and unnecessarily complicated. The cost of Algorithm 2.3, measured in flops, is therefore:

$$
T_{\text{seq}} = \sum_{k=0}^{n-1} (2(n - k - 1)^2 + n - k - 1) = \sum_{k=0}^{n-1} (2k^2 + k) = \frac{2n^3}{3} - \frac{n^2}{2} - \frac{n}{6}. \tag{2.12}
$$

Algorithm 2.3 Sequential LU decomposition with partial row pivoting.

---

input: $\quad A : n \times n$ matrix, $A = A^{(0)}$.
output: $A : n \times n$ matrix, $A = L - I_n + U$, with
$\qquad\quad L : n \times n$ unit lower triangular matrix,
$\qquad\quad U : n \times n$ upper triangular matrix,
$\qquad\quad \pi :$ permutation vector of length n,
$\qquad\quad$ such that $a^{(0)}_{\pi(i),j} = (LU)_{ij}$, for $0 \leq i,j < n$.

$\quad$ **for** $i := 0$ **to** $n - 1$ **do**
$\qquad \pi_i := i;$
$\quad$ **for** $k := 0$ **to** $n - 1$ **do**
$\qquad r := \mathrm{argmax}(|a_{ik}| : k \leq i < n);$
$\qquad \mathrm{swap}(\pi_k, \pi_r);$
$\qquad$ **for** $j := 0$ **to** $n - 1$ **do**
$\qquad\quad \mathrm{swap}(a_{kj}, a_{rj});$
$\qquad$ **for** $i := k + 1$ **to** $n - 1$ **do**
$\qquad\quad a_{ik} := a_{ik}/a_{kk};$
$\qquad$ **for** $i := k + 1$ **to** $n - 1$ **do**
$\qquad\quad$ **for** $j := k + 1$ **to** $n - 1$ **do**
$\qquad\qquad a_{ij} := a_{ij} - a_{ik}a_{kj};$

In the summation, we used two formulae so important for analysing the complexity of matrix computations that you should know them by heart:

Lemma 2.8 *Let $n \geq 0$ be an integer. Then*

$$\sum_{k=0}^{n} k = \frac{n(n+1)}{2}, \qquad \sum_{k=0}^{n} k^2 = \frac{n(n+1)(2n+1)}{6}.$$

Proof By induction on n. $\qquad\qquad\qquad\qquad\qquad\qquad\qquad\qquad\qquad\qquad$ □

Sometimes, it may be useful to perform an LU decomposition on a rectangular matrix of size $m \times n$ with $m \geq n$, for instance as part of a larger sequential or parallel LU decomposition algorithm of a square matrix. The cost formula for rectangular LU decomposition is a generalization of eqn (2.12),

$$T_{\mathrm{seq}}(m,n) = \sum_{k=0}^{n-1}(2(m-k-1)(n-k-1)+m-k-1) = mn^2 - \frac{n^3}{3} - \frac{n^2}{2} - \frac{n}{6}.$$

$$(2.13)$$

2.3 Basic parallel algorithm

Design your parallel algorithms backwards! We follow this motto by first transforming a sequential step into a computation superstep and then inserting preceding communication supersteps to obtain nonlocal data where needed.

The design process of our parallel LU decomposition algorithm is as follows. First, we introduce a general data distribution scheme that reflects the problem and restricts the possible communication patterns, but also leaves sufficient freedom for optimization. Second, we derive a basic parallel algorithm, directly from the sequential algorithm and the data distribution scheme; we do this mostly in the backwards direction. Third, we analyse the cost of the basic parallel algorithm and use the results of this analysis to choose a data distribution with optimal load balance and low communication overhead. Fourth, we restructure the algorithm to reduce its cost further. This section presents the first three phases of the design process; the fourth phase is presented in the next section.

The data to be distributed for parallel LU decomposition are the matrix A and the vector π. Clearly, the most important decision is how to distribute A. The bulk of the computational work in stage k of the sequential algorithm is the modification of the matrix elements a_{ij} with $i, j \geq k + 1$. Therefore, our choice of distribution will be based on an analysis of this part of the algorithm. It is easy to distribute the computational work of this part evenly over the processors; this can simply be done by evenly distributing the corresponding data. Distribution of the matrix elements over different processors, however, will give rise to communication, because in general the matrix elements a_{ij}, a_{ik}, and a_{kj} involved in an update $a_{ij} := a_{ij} - a_{ik}a_{kj}$ will not reside on the same processor. There are $(n - k - 1)^2$ elements a_{ij} to be updated, using only $n - k - 1$ elements a_{ik} from column k of A and $n - k - 1$ elements a_{kj} from row k. Therefore, to prevent communication of large amounts of data, the update $a_{ij} := a_{ij} - a_{ik}a_{kj}$ must be performed by the processor that contains a_{ij}. This ensures that only elements of column k and row k of A need to be communicated in stage k. This approach is illustrated in Fig. 2.2.

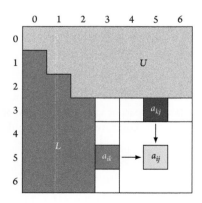

Figure 2.2 Matrix update by operations $a_{ij} := a_{ij} - a_{ik}a_{kj}$ at the end of stage $k = 3$. Arrows denote communication.

An important observation is that the modification of the elements in row $A(i, k+1 : n-1)$ uses only one value from column k of A, namely a_{ik}. If we distribute each matrix row over a limited set of N processors, then the communication of an element from column k can be restricted to a broadcast to N processors. Similarly, the modification of the elements in column $A(k+1 : n-1, j)$ uses only one value from row k of A, namely a_{kj}. If we distribute each matrix column over a limited set of M processors, then the communication of an element from row k can be restricted to a broadcast to M processors.

For matrix computations, it is natural to number the processors by two-dimensional (2D) identifiers $P(s, t)$, $0 \leq s < M$ and $0 \leq t < N$, where $MN = p$ is the number of processors. We define **processor row** $P(s, *)$ as the group of N processors $P(s, t)$ with $0 \leq t < N$, and **processor column** $P(*, t)$ as the group of M processors $P(s, t)$ with $0 \leq s < M$. This is just a 2D numbering of the processors and has no physical meaning in the BSP model. Any resemblance to actual parallel computers, such as a rectangular processor network, is purely coincidental and, for the sake of portability, such resemblance should not be exploited. To make it easier to resist the temptation, BSP veterans always tell newcomers to the BSP world that BSPlib software randomly renumbers the processors before it starts executing.

A **matrix distribution** is a mapping

$$\phi : \{(i,j) : 0 \leq i,j < n\} \rightarrow \{(s,t) : 0 \leq s < M \wedge 0 \leq t < N\}$$

from the set of matrix index pairs to the set of processor identifiers. The mapping function ϕ has two coordinates,

$$\phi(i,j) = (\phi_0(i,j), \phi_1(i,j)), \quad \text{for } 0 \leq i,j < n. \tag{2.14}$$

A matrix distribution is called **Cartesian** if $\phi_0(i,j)$ is independent of j and $\phi_1(i,j)$ is independent of i, so that we can write

$$\phi(i,j) = (\phi_0(i), \phi_1(j)), \quad \text{for } 0 \leq i,j < n. \tag{2.15}$$

Figure 2.3 shows a Cartesian distribution of a 7×7 matrix over 2×3 processors. Cartesian distributions allocate matrix rows to processor rows. This is good for LU decomposition, because in stage k an element a_{ik} of column k needs to be communicated only to the owners of matrix row i, that is, to processor row $P(\phi_0(i), *)$, which is a group of N processors. Similarly, Cartesian distributions allocate matrix columns to processor columns, which reduces the communication of an element from row k to a broadcast to M processors. In both cases, the destination is only a subset of all the processors. Therefore, we decide to use a Cartesian matrix distribution. For the moment, we do not specify the distribution further, to leave us the freedom of tailoring it to our future needs.

An initial parallel algorithm can be developed by parallelizing the sequential algorithm step by step, using data parallelism to derive computation supersteps and the **need-to-know principle** to obtain the necessary communication supersteps. According to this principle, exactly the nonlocal data that is needed in a computation superstep should be fetched in preceding communication supersteps.

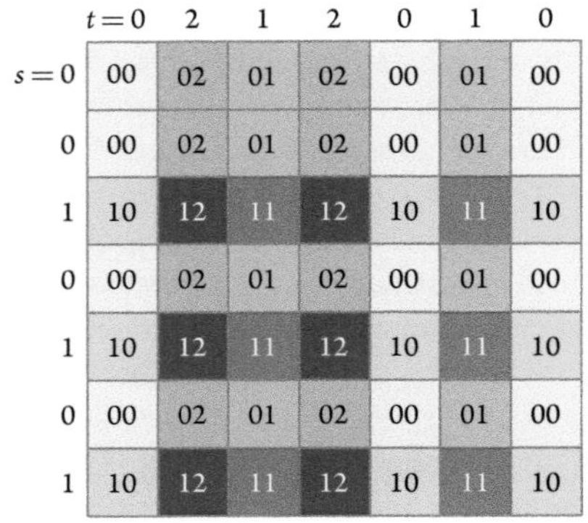

$t=0$	2	1	2	0	1	0
$s=0$ 00	02	01	02	00	01	00
0 00	02	01	02	00	01	00
1 10	12	11	12	10	11	10
0 00	02	01	02	00	01	00
1 10	12	11	12	10	11	10
0 00	02	01	02	00	01	00
1 10	12	11	12	10	11	10

Figure 2.3 A Cartesian distribution of a 7×7 matrix over 2×3 processors. The label 'st' in a cell denotes its owner, processor $P(s, t)$. The shade (light or dark) gives the processor row and the colour (yellow, blue, or red) gives the processor column.

One parallelization method based on this approach is to allocate a computation to the processor that possesses the variable on the left-hand side of an assignment and to communicate beforehand the nonlocal data appearing on the right-hand side. An example is the superstep pair (10)–(11) of Algorithm 2.4, which is a parallel version of the matrix update from stage k of the LU decomposition. (The superstep numbering corresponds to that of the complete basic parallel algorithm.) In superstep (11), the local elements a_{ij} with $i, j \geq k + 1$ are modified. In superstep (10), the elements a_{ik} and a_{kj} with $i, j \geq k + 1$ are communicated to the processors that need them. It is guaranteed that all values needed have been sent, but depending on the distribution and the stage k, certain processors actually may not need all of the communicated elements. (This mild violation of the strict need-to-know principle is common in **dense** matrix computations, where all matrix elements are treated as nonzero; for **sparse** matrices, however, where many matrix elements are zero, the communication operations should be precisely targeted, see Chapter 4.) Another example of this parallelization method is the superstep pair (8)–(9). In superstep (9), the local elements of column k are divided by a_{kk}. This division is performed only by processors in processor column $P(*, \phi_1(k))$, since these processors together possess matrix column k. In superstep (8), the element a_{kk} is obtained.

An alternative parallelization method based on the same need-to-know approach is to allocate a computation to the processor that contains part or all of the data on the right-hand side, and then to communicate partial results to the processors in charge of producing the final result. This may be more efficient if the number of result values is less than the number of input data values involved. An example is the sequence of supersteps (0)–(3) of Algorithm 2.5, which is a parallel version of the pivot search from stage k of the LU decomposition. First, a local element with maximum absolute value is determined, whose index and value are then sent to all processors in $P(*, \phi_1(k))$. (In our cost model, this takes the same time as sending them to only one master processor $P(0, \phi_1(k))$; a similar situation occurs for the inner product algorithm in Section 1.3.) All processors in the processor

---

Algorithm 2.4 Parallel matrix update in stage k for $P(s,t)$.

---

if $\phi_0(k) = s \land \phi_1(k) = t$ **then** $\triangleright$ Superstep (8)
    put a_{kk} in $P(*,t)$;

if $\phi_1(k) = t$ **then** $\triangleright$ Superstep (9)
    for all $i : k < i < n \land \phi_0(i) = s$ **do**
        $a_{ik} := a_{ik}/a_{kk}$;

if $\phi_1(k) = t$ **then** $\triangleright$ Superstep (10)
    for all $i : k < i < n \land \phi_0(i) = s$ **do**
        put a_{ik} in $P(s,*)$;
if $\phi_0(k) = s$ **then**
    for all $j : k < j < n \land \phi_1(j) = t$ **do**
        put a_{kj} in $P(*,t)$;

for all $i : k < i < n \land \phi_0(i) = s$ **do** $\triangleright$ Superstep (11)
    for all $j : k < j < n \land \phi_1(j) = t$ **do**
        $a_{ij} := a_{ij} - a_{ik}a_{kj}$;

Algorithm 2.5 Parallel pivot search in stage k for $P(s,t)$.

---

if $\phi_1(k) = t$ **then** $\triangleright$ Superstep (0)
    $r_s := \mathrm{argmax}(|a_{ik}| : k \leq i < n \land \phi_0(i) = s)$;

if $\phi_1(k) = t$ **then** $\triangleright$ Superstep (1)
    put r_s and $a_{r_s,k}$ in $P(*,t)$;

if $\phi_1(k) = t$ **then** $\triangleright$ Superstep (2)
    $s_{\max} := \mathrm{argmax}(|a_{r_q,k}| : 0 \leq q < M)$;
    $r := r_{s_{\max}}$;

if $\phi_1(k) = t$ **then** $\triangleright$ Superstep (3)
    put r in $P(s,*)$;

---

column redundantly determine the processor $P(s_{\max}, \phi_1(k))$ and the global row index r of the maximum value. The index r is then broadcast to all processors.

The part of stage k that remains to be parallelized consists of index and row swaps. To parallelize the index swaps, we must first choose the distribution of π. It is natural to store π_k together with row k, that is, somewhere in processor row $P(\phi_0(k), *)$; we could choose $P(\phi_0(k), 0)$ as the location. Alternatively, we can replicate π_k and store a copy in every processor of $P(\phi_0(k), *)$, which makes program texts more readable, as it saves some **if**-statements. (Strictly speaking, this is not a distribution anymore.) We choose the alternative in our algorithm and replicate/distribute π. The index swaps are performed by superstep pair (4)–(5) of Algorithm 2.6. The components π_k and π_r of the permutation vector are swapped by first putting each component into its destination processor and then assigning it to the appropriate component of the array π. Temporary variables (denoted by hats) are used to help distinguish between the old and new contents of a variable. The same is done for the row swaps in supersteps (6)–(7).

To make the algorithm efficient, we must choose a distribution ϕ that incurs low BSP cost. To do this, we first analyse stage k of the algorithm and identify the main contributions to its cost. Stage k consists of 12 supersteps, so that its synchronization cost equals $12l$. Sometimes, a superstep may be empty so that it can be deleted. For example, if $N = 1$, superstep (3) is empty. In the extreme case $p = 1$, all communication supersteps can be deleted and the remaining computation supersteps can be combined into one superstep. For $p > 1$, however, the number of supersteps in one stage remains a small constant, which should not influence the choice of distribution. Therefore, we consider $12nl$ to be an upper

---

Algorithm 2.6 Index and row swaps in stage k for $P(s,t)$.

---

if $\phi_0(k) = s$ **then**   ▷ Superstep (4)
    put π_k as $\hat{\pi}_k$ in $P(\phi_0(r),t)$;
if $\phi_0(r) = s$ **then**
    put π_r as $\hat{\pi}_r$ in $P(\phi_0(k),t)$;

if $\phi_0(k) = s$ **then** $\pi_k := \hat{\pi}_r$;   ▷ Superstep (5)
if $\phi_0(r) = s$ **then** $\pi_r := \hat{\pi}_k$;

if $\phi_0(k) = s$ **then**   ▷ Superstep (6)
    for all $j : 0 \leq j < n \wedge \phi_1(j) = t$ **do**
        put a_{kj} as $\hat{a}_{kj}$ in $P(\phi_0(r),t)$;
if $\phi_0(r) = s$ **then**
    for all $j : 0 \leq j < n \wedge \phi_1(j) = t$ **do**
        put a_{rj} as $\hat{a}_{rj}$ in $P(\phi_0(k),t)$;

if $\phi_0(k) = s$ **then**   ▷ Superstep (7)
    for all $j : 0 \leq j < n \wedge \phi_1(j) = t$ **do**
        $a_{kj} := \hat{a}_{rj}$;
if $\phi_0(r) = s$ **then**
    for all $j : 0 \leq j < n \wedge \phi_1(j) = t$ **do**
        $a_{rj} := \hat{a}_{kj}$;

---

bound on the total synchronization cost of the algorithm, and we exclude terms in l from the following analysis of the separate supersteps.

The computation and communication cost can concisely be expressed using

$$R_k = \max_{0 \leq s < M} |\{i : k \leq i < n \wedge \phi_0(i) = s\}|, \tag{2.16}$$

that is, the maximum number of local matrix rows with index $\geq k$, taken over all processor rows, and

$$C_k = \max_{0 \leq t < N} |\{j : k \leq j < n \wedge \phi_1(j) = t\}|, \tag{2.17}$$

that is, the maximum number of local matrix columns with index $\geq k$, taken over all processor columns.

Example 2.9 In Fig. 2.3, $R_0 = 4, C_0 = 3$ and $R_4 = 2, C_4 = 2$.

Lower bounds for R_k and C_k are given by

$$R_k \geq \left\lceil \frac{n-k}{M} \right\rceil, \qquad C_k \geq \left\lceil \frac{n-k}{N} \right\rceil. \tag{2.18}$$

Proof Assume $R_k < \lceil (n-k)/M \rceil$. Because R_k is an integer, we even have that $R_k < (n-k)/M$, so that each processor row has fewer than $(n-k)/M$ matrix rows. Therefore, the M processor rows together possess fewer than $n - k$ matrix rows, which contradicts the fact that they hold the whole range $k \leq i < n$. A similar proof holds for C_k. □

The computation supersteps of the algorithm are (0), (2), (5), (7), (9), and (11). Supersteps (0), (2), (5), and (7) are for free in our benign cost model, since they do not involve floating-point operations. (A more detailed analysis taking all types of operations into account would yield a few additional lower-order terms.) Computation superstep (9) costs R_{k+1} time units, since each processor performs at most R_{k+1} divisions. Computation superstep (11) costs $2R_{k+1}C_{k+1}$ time units, since each processor performs at most $R_{k+1}C_{k+1}$ multiplications and $R_{k+1}C_{k+1}$ subtractions. The cost of (11) clearly dominates the total computation cost.

Table 2.1 presents the cost of the communication supersteps of the basic parallel LU decomposition. It is easy to verify the cost values given by the table. For the special case $N = 1$, the h_r value given for (3) in the table should in fact be 0 instead of 1, but this does not affect the resulting value of h. A similar remark should be made for supersteps (4), (8), and (10). During most of the algorithm, the largest communication superstep is (10), while the next-largest is (6). Near the end of the computation, (6) becomes dominant.

To minimize the total BSP cost of the algorithm, we must take care to minimize the cost of both computation and communication. First, we consider the computation cost, and in particular the cost of the dominant computation superstep,

$$T_{(11)} = 2R_{k+1}C_{k+1} \geq 2 \left\lceil \frac{n-k-1}{M} \right\rceil \left\lceil \frac{n-k-1}{N} \right\rceil. \tag{2.19}$$

Table 2.1 Cost (in g) of communication supersteps in stage k of basic parallel LU decomposition.

Superstep	h_s	h_r	$h = \max\{h_s, h_r\}$
(1)	$2(M-1)$	$2(M-1)$	$2(M-1)$
(3)	$N-1$	1	$N-1$
(4)	1	1	1
(6)	C_0	C_0	C_0
(8)	$M-1$	1	$M-1$
(10)	$R_{k+1}(N-1)+$ $C_{k+1}(M-1)$	$R_{k+1}+C_{k+1}$	$R_{k+1}(N-1)+$ $C_{k+1}(M-1)$

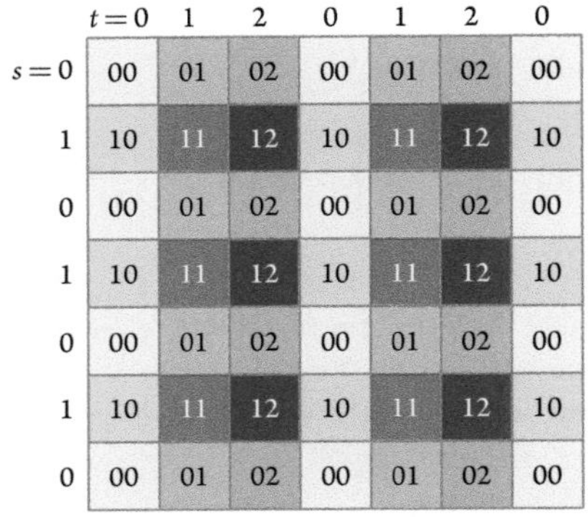

Figure 2.4 The 2×3 cyclic distribution of a 7×7 matrix.

This cost can be minimized by distributing the matrix rows cyclically over the M processor rows and the matrix columns cyclically over the N processor columns. In that case, matrix rows $k+1$ to $n-1$ are evenly or nearly evenly divided over the processor rows, with at most a difference of one matrix row between the processor rows, and similarly for the matrix columns. Thus,

$$T_{(11),\text{cyclic}} = 2 \left\lceil \frac{n-k-1}{M} \right\rceil \left\lceil \frac{n-k-1}{N} \right\rceil. \tag{2.20}$$

The resulting matrix distribution is the $M \times N$ **cyclic distribution**, defined by

$$\phi_0(i) = i \bmod M, \quad \phi_1(j) = j \bmod N, \text{ for } 0 \leq i,j < n. \tag{2.21}$$

Figure 2.4 shows the 2×3 cyclic distribution of a 7×7 matrix.

The cost of (11) for the $M \times N$ cyclic distribution is bounded between

$$
\frac{2(n-k-1)^2}{p} \leq T_{(11),\text{cyclic}} < 2 \left(\frac{n-k-1}{M} + 1 \right) \left(\frac{n-k-1}{N} + 1 \right)
$$

$$
= \frac{2(n-k-1)^2}{p} + \frac{2(n-k-1)}{p}(M+N) + 2, \tag{2.22}
$$

where we have used that $MN = p$. The upper bound is minimal if $M = N = \sqrt{p}$, that is, if the distribution is **square**. The resulting second-order term $4(n-k-1)/\sqrt{p}$ in the upper bound can be viewed as the additional computation cost caused by imbalance of the work load.

Next, we examine the cost of the dominant communication superstep,

$$
T_{(10)} = (R_{k+1}(N-1) + C_{k+1}(M-1))g
$$

$$
\geq \left(\left\lceil \frac{n-k-1}{M} \right\rceil (N-1) + \left\lceil \frac{n-k-1}{N} \right\rceil (M-1) \right) g
$$

$$
= T_{(10),\text{cyclic}}. \tag{2.23}
$$

Again, we can minimize the cost by using the $M \times N$ cyclic distribution. To find optimal values for M and N, we consider the upper bound

$$
T_{(10),\text{cyclic}} < \left(\left(\frac{n-k-1}{M} + 1 \right) N + \left(\frac{n-k-1}{N} + 1 \right) M \right) g
$$

$$
= \left((n-k-1) \left(\frac{N}{M} + \frac{M}{N} \right) + M + N \right) g. \tag{2.24}
$$

We now minimize this simple upper bound on the cost, instead of the more complicated true cost itself. (This approximation is valid because the bound is not too far from the true cost.) From $(M - N)^2 \geq 0$, it immediately follows that $N/M + M/N = (M^2 + N^2)/(MN) \geq 2$. For $M = N = \sqrt{p}$, the inequality becomes an equality. For this choice, the term $N/M + M/N$ is minimal. The same choice also minimizes the term $M + N$ under the constraint $MN = p$. This implies that the square cyclic distribution is a good choice for the basic LU decomposition algorithm, on the grounds of both computation cost and communication cost.

2.4 Two-phase broadcasting and other improvements

Can the basic parallel algorithm be improved? The computation cost cannot be reduced by much, because the computation part is already well-balanced and little is computed redundantly. Therefore, the question is whether the communication and synchronization costs can be reduced. To answer this, we take a closer look at the communication supersteps.

The **communication volume** V of an h-relation is defined as the total number of data words communicated. Using a one-dimensional (1D) processor numbering, we can express this as

$$V = \sum_{s=0}^{p-1} h_s(s) = \sum_{s=0}^{p-1} h_r(s), \tag{2.25}$$

where $h_s(s)$ is the number of data words sent by processor $P(s)$ and $h_r(s)$ is the number received. In this notation, $\max_s h_s(s) = h_s$ and $\max_s h_r(s) = h_r$. Note that $V \le \sum_{s=0}^{p-1} h = ph$. We call an h-relation **balanced** if $V = ph$, that is, $h = V/p$. Equality can only hold if $h_s(s) = h$ for all s. Therefore, a balanced h-relation has $h_s(s) = h$ for all s, and, similarly, $h_r(s) = h$ for all s. These necessary conditions for balance are also sufficient and hence an h-relation is balanced if and only if every processor sends and receives exactly h words. But this is precisely the definition of a full h-relation, see Section 1.2. It is just a matter of viewpoint whether we call an h-relation balanced or full. The communication volume provides us with a measure for imbalance: we call $h - V/p$ the **communication imbalance**. This is analogous to the **computation imbalance**, which commonly (but often tacitly) is defined as $w - w_{seq}/p$, where w denotes the maximum amount of work of a processor.

If an h-relation is balanced, then $h = h_s = h_r$. The reverse is not true: it is possible that $h = h_s = h_r$ but that the h-relation is still unbalanced: some processors may be overloaded sending and some receiving. In that case, $h > V/p$. To reduce communication cost, one can either reduce the volume, or improve the balance for a fixed volume.

Consider the basic parallel LU decomposition algorithm with the cyclic distribution. Assume for diagnostic purposes that the distribution is square. (Later, in developing our improved algorithm, we shall assume the more general $M \times N$ cyclic distribution.) Super-steps (3), (8), and (10) perform h-relations with $h_s \gg h_r$, see Table 2.1. Such a discrepancy between h_s and h_r is a clear symptom of imbalance. The three unbalanced supersteps are candidates for improvement. We concentrate our efforts on the dominant communication superstep, (10), which has $h_s = (\sqrt{p} - 1)h_r$ and $h \approx 2(n - k - 1)$, see (2.23). The contribution of superstep (10) to the total communication cost of the basic algorithm is about $\sum_{k=0}^{n-1} 2(n - k - 1)g = 2g \sum_{k=0}^{n-1} k = 2g(n-1)n/2 \approx n^2 g$, irrespective of the number of processors. With an increasing number of processors, the fixed contribution of $n^2 g$ to the total communication cost will soon dominate the total computation cost of roughly $T_{seq}/p \approx 2n^3/3p$, see (2.12). This back-of-the-envelope analysis suffices to reveal the undesirable scaling behaviour of the row and column broadcasts.

The imbalance in the broadcasts of superstep (10) is caused by the fact that only $2\sqrt{p} - 1$ out of p processors send data: the sending processors are $P(*, \phi_1(k)) = P(*, k \bmod \sqrt{p})$ and $P(\phi_0(k), *) = P(k \bmod \sqrt{p}, *)$. The receive operations are spread better: the majority of the processors receive $2R_{k+1}$ data elements, or one or two elements less. The communication volume equals $V = 2(n - k - 1)(\sqrt{p} - 1)$, because $n - k - 1$ elements of row k and column k must be broadcast to $\sqrt{p} - 1$ processors. It is impossible to reduce the communication volume significantly: all communication operations are really necessary, except in the last few stages of the algorithm. The communication balance, however, has potential for improvement.

To find ways to improve the balance, let us first examine the problem of broadcasting a vector $\mathbf{x}$ of length n from a processor $P(0)$ to all p processors of a parallel computer, where $n \geq p$. For this problem, we use a 1D processor numbering. The simplest approach is that processor $P(0)$ creates $p - 1$ copies of each vector component and sends these copies out. This method concentrates all sending work at the source processor. A better balance can be obtained by sending each component to a randomly chosen intermediate processor and making this processor responsible for copying and sending the copies to their final destinations. This method is similar to two-phase randomized routing [288], where packets are sent from source to destination through a randomly chosen intermediate location, to avoid congestion in the routing network. It is also similar to recent peer-to-peer file sharing methods, such as the BitTorrent protocol, which distribute a file by cutting it into pieces, sending these to clients, who receive the pieces and at the same time distribute them further. The new method for our vector broadcast splits the original h-relation into two phases: phase 0, an unbalanced h-relation with small volume that randomizes the location of the data elements; and phase 1, a well-balanced h-relation that performs the broadcast itself. We call the resulting pair of h-relations a **two-phase broadcast**.

An optimal balance during phase 1 can be guaranteed by choosing the intermediate processors deterministically instead of randomly. For instance, this can be achieved by spreading the vector in phase 0 according to the block distribution, defined by (1.7). (An equally suitable choice is the cyclic distribution.) The resulting two-phase broadcast is given as Algorithm 2.7; it is illustrated by Fig. 2.5. The notation $\text{repl}(\mathbf{x}) = P(*)$ means that $\mathbf{x}$ is replicated such that each processor has a copy. (This is in contrast to $\text{distr}(\mathbf{x}) = \phi$, which means that $\mathbf{x}$ is distributed according to the mapping ϕ.) Phase 0 is an h-relation with $h = n - b$, where $b = \lceil n/p \rceil$ is the block size, and phase 1 has $h = (p - 1)b$. The upper bound of h communicated data words is attained in both phases by $P(0)$, which has a complete block of b vector components and sends out $n - b$ data in phase 0 and $(p - 1)b$ data in phase 1. Note that both phases cost about ng. The total cost of the two-phase broadcast of a vector of length n to p processors is

$$T_{\text{broadcast}} = \left(n + (p-2)\left\lceil\frac{n}{p}\right\rceil\right)g + 2l \approx 2n\left(1 - \frac{1}{p}\right)g + 2l \approx 2ng + 2l. \qquad (2.26)$$

This is much less than the cost $(p - 1)ng + l$ of the straightforward **one-phase broadcast** (except when l is large and n is small).

The t-loops in both phases of Algorithm 2.7 display a small optimization: they start at $t = 1$ instead of $t = 0$. This has no influence on the BSP cost, but it reduces the communication volume (and removes clutter in Fig. 2.5), so that it may yield some gains in practice while it can never hurt.

The two-phase broadcast can be used to broadcast column k and row k of the matrix A in stage k of the parallel LU decomposition. The broadcasts are performed in supersteps (6) and (7) of the improved algorithm, Algorithm 2.8. The column part to be broadcast from processor $P(s, k \bmod N)$ is the subvector $(a_{ik} : k < i < n \wedge i \bmod M = s)$, which has length R_{k+1} or $R_{k+1} - 1$, and this subvector is broadcast to the whole processor row $P(s, *)$. Every processor row performs its own broadcast of a column part and every processor column its own broadcast of a row part. Phase 0 of the row broadcast is carried out together with phase

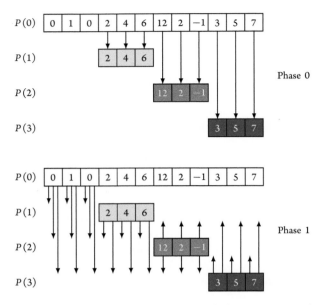

Figure 2.5 Two-phase broadcast of a vector of size twelve to four processors. The processors are shown by colours. The block size is $b = 3$. The arrows denote communication. In phase 0, the vector is spread over the four processors. In phase 1, each processor broadcasts its subvector to all processors except the source processor $P(0)$.

0 of the column broadcast and phase 1 with phase 1 of the column broadcast. This saves two synchronizations. (In an implementation, such optimizations are worthwhile, but they harm modularity: the complete broadcast cannot be invoked by one function call; instead, we need to make the phases available as separately callable functions.)

The improved algorithm has eight supersteps in the main loop, whereas the basic algorithm has twelve. The number of supersteps has been reduced as follows. First, we observe that the row swap of the basic algorithm turns element a_{rk} into the pivot element a_{kk}. The element a_{rk}, however, is already known by all processors in $P(*, k \bmod N)$, because it is one of the elements broadcast in superstep (1). Therefore, we divide column k immediately by a_{rk}, instead of dividing by a_{kk} after the row swap. This saves the pivot broadcast (8) of the basic algorithm and the synchronization of superstep (9). Second, the index and row swaps are now combined and performed in two supersteps, numbered (4) and (5). This saves two synchronizations. Third, the last superstep of stage k of the algorithm is combined with the first superstep of stage $k + 1$. We express this by numbering the last superstep as $(0')$, that is, superstep (0) of the next stage.

The BSP cost of the improved algorithm is computed in the same way as before. The cost of the separate supersteps is given by Table 2.2. Now, $R_{k+1} = \lceil (n - k - 1)/M \rceil$ and $C_{k+1} = \lceil (n - k - 1)/N \rceil$, because we use the $M \times N$ cyclic distribution. The cost expressions for supersteps (6) and (7) are obtained as in the derivation of (2.26).

The dominant computation superstep in the improved algorithm remains the matrix update; the choice $M = N = \sqrt{p}$ remains optimal for computation. The costs of the row

---

Algorithm 2.7 Two-phase broadcast for $P(s)$.

---

input: $\mathbf{x}$: vector of length n, $\mathrm{repl}(\mathbf{x}) = P(0)$.
output: $\mathbf{x}$: vector of length n, $\mathrm{repl}(\mathbf{x}) = P(*)$.

    function BROADCAST$(\mathbf{x}, P(0), P(*))$

        $b := \lceil n/p \rceil$;
        { Spread the vector }
        if $s = 0$ **then** $\triangleright$ Superstep (0)
           for $t := 1$ **to** $p - 1$ **do**
               for $i := tb$ **to** $\min\{(t+1)b, n\} - 1$ **do**
                   put x_i in $P(t)$;

        { Broadcast the subvectors }
        for $t := 1$ **to** $p - 1$ **do** $\triangleright$ Superstep (1)
           for $i := sb$ **to** $\min\{(s+1)b, n\} - 1$ **do**
               put x_i in $P(t)$;

Table 2.2 Cost of supersteps in stage k of the improved parallel LU decomposition algorithm, Algorithm 2.8.

Superstep	Cost
(0)	l
(1)	$2(M-1)g + l$
(2)	$R_k + l$
(3)	$(N-1)g + l$
(4)	$(C_0 + 1)g + l$
(5)	l
(6)	$(R_{k+1} - \lceil R_{k+1}/N \rceil + C_{k+1} - \lceil C_{k+1}/M \rceil)g + l$
(7)	$((N-1)\lceil R_{k+1}/N \rceil + (M-1)\lceil C_{k+1}/M \rceil)g + l$
(0')	$2R_{k+1}C_{k+1}$

and column broadcasts do not dominate the other communication costs anymore, since they have decreased to about $2(R_{k+1} + C_{k+1})g$ in total, which is of the same order as the cost $C_0 g$ of the row swap. To find optimal values of M and N for communication, we consider the upper bound

$$R_{k+1} + C_{k+1} < \left(\frac{n-k-1}{M} + 1 \right) + \left(\frac{n-k-1}{N} + 1 \right)$$
$$= (n-k-1)\frac{M+N}{p} + 2, \tag{2.27}$$

Algorithm 2.8 Improved parallel LU decomposition algorithm for $P(s,t)$.

---

input: $A: n \times n$ matrix, $A = A^{(0)}$, distr$(A) = M \times N$ cyclic.

output: $A: n \times n$ matrix, distr$(A) = M \times N$ cyclic, $A = L - I_n + U$, with

      $L: n \times n$ unit lower triangular matrix,

      $U: n \times n$ upper triangular matrix,

      $\pi:$ permutation vector of length n,

      distr$(\pi) =$ cyclic in $P(*, t)$, for $0 \leq t < N$,

      such that $a^{(0)}_{\pi(i),j} = (LU)_{ij}$, for $0 \leq i, j < n$.

    for all $i: 0 \leq i < n \wedge i \bmod M = s$ **do**

      $\pi_i := i;$

    for $k := 0$ **to** $n - 1$ **do**

      if $k \bmod N = t$ **then** $\triangleright$ Superstep (0)

        $r_s := \mathrm{argmax}(|a_{ik}| : k \leq i < n \wedge i \bmod M = s);$

      if $k \bmod N = t$ **then** $\triangleright$ Superstep (1)

        put r_s and $a_{r_s,k}$ in $P(*, t)$;

      if $k \bmod N = t$ **then** $\triangleright$ Superstep (2)

        $s_{\max} := \mathrm{argmax}(|a_{r_q,k}| : 0 \leq q < M);$

        $r := r_{s_{\max}};$

        for all $i: k \leq i < n \wedge i \bmod M = s \wedge i \neq r$ **do**

          $a_{ik} := a_{ik}/a_{rk};$

      if $k \bmod N = t$ **then** $\triangleright$ Superstep (3)

        put r in $P(s, *)$;

      if $k \bmod M = s$ **then** $\triangleright$ Superstep (4)

        put π_k as $\hat{\pi}_k$ in $P(r \bmod M, t)$;

        for all $j: 0 \leq j < n \wedge j \bmod N = t$ **do**

          put a_{kj} as $\hat{a}_{kj}$ in $P(r \bmod M, t)$;

      if $r \bmod M = s$ **then**

        put π_r as $\hat{\pi}_r$ in $P(k \bmod M, t)$;

        for all $j: 0 \leq j < n \wedge j \bmod N = t$ **do**

          put a_{rj} as $\hat{a}_{rj}$ in $P(k \bmod M, t)$;

      if $k \bmod M = s$ **then** $\triangleright$ Superstep (5)

        $\pi_k := \hat{\pi}_r;$

        for all $j: 0 \leq j < n \wedge j \bmod N = t$ **do**

          $a_{kj} := \hat{a}_{rj};$

      if $r \bmod M = s$ **then**

        $\pi_r := \hat{\pi}_k;$

        for all $j: 0 \leq j < n \wedge j \bmod N = t$ **do**

          $a_{rj} := \hat{a}_{kj};$

                                       $\triangleright$ Superstep (6)–(7)

      Broadcast$((a_{ik} : k < i < n \wedge i \bmod M = s), P(s, k \bmod N), P(s, *));$

      Broadcast$((a_{kj} : k < j < n \wedge j \bmod N = t), P(k \bmod M, t), P(*, t));$

      for all $i: k < i < n \wedge i \bmod M = s$ **do** $\triangleright$ Superstep $(0')$

        for all $j: k < j < n \wedge j \bmod N = t$ **do**

          $a_{ij} := a_{ij} - a_{ik}a_{kj};$

---

which is minimal for $M = N = \sqrt{p}$. The row swap in superstep (4) prefers large values of N, because $C_0 = \lceil n/N \rceil$. The degenerate choice $N = p$ even gives a free swap, but at the price of an expensive column broadcast. Overall, the choice $M = N = \sqrt{p}$ is close to optimal and we shall adopt it in the following analysis.

The total BSP cost of the improved algorithm with the square cyclic distribution is obtained by summing the contributions of all supersteps. This gives

$$T_{LU} = \sum_{k=0}^{n-1} (2R_{k+1}^2 + R_k) + 2 \sum_{k=0}^{n-1} \left(R_{k+1} + (\sqrt{p} - 2) \left\lceil \frac{R_{k+1}}{\sqrt{p}} \right\rceil \right) g$$
$$+ (R_0 + 3\sqrt{p} - 2)ng + 8nl. \tag{2.28}$$

To compute $\sum_{k=0}^{n-1} R_k = \sum_{k=0}^{n-1} \lceil (n-k)/\sqrt{p} \rceil = \sum_{k=1}^{n} \lceil k/\sqrt{p} \rceil$ and the sums of R_{k+1} and R_{k+1}^2, we need the following generalization of Lemma 2.8.

Lemma 2.10 *Let $n, q \geq 1$ be integers with $n \bmod q = 0$. Then*

$$\sum_{k=0}^{n} \left\lceil \frac{k}{q} \right\rceil = \frac{n(n+q)}{2q}, \qquad \sum_{k=0}^{n} \left\lceil \frac{k}{q} \right\rceil^2 = \frac{n(n+q)(2n+q)}{6q^2}.$$

Proof

$$\sum_{k=0}^{n} \left\lceil \frac{k}{q} \right\rceil = \left\lceil \frac{0}{q} \right\rceil + \left(\left\lceil \frac{1}{q} \right\rceil + \cdots + \left\lceil \frac{q}{q} \right\rceil \right) + \cdots + \left(\left\lceil \frac{n-q+1}{q} \right\rceil + \cdots + \left\lceil \frac{n}{q} \right\rceil \right)$$
$$= q \cdot 1 + q \cdot 2 + \cdots + q \cdot \frac{n}{q} = q \sum_{k=1}^{n/q} k = q \frac{n}{2q} \left(\frac{n}{q} + 1 \right), \tag{2.29}$$

where we have used Lemma 2.8. The proof of the second equation is similar. $\qquad \square$

Provided $n \bmod \sqrt{p} = 0$, the resulting sums are:

$$\sum_{k=0}^{n-1} R_k = \frac{n(n+\sqrt{p})}{2\sqrt{p}}, \tag{2.30}$$

$$\sum_{k=0}^{n-1} R_{k+1} = \frac{n(n+\sqrt{p})}{2\sqrt{p}} - \frac{n}{\sqrt{p}}, \tag{2.31}$$

$$\sum_{k=0}^{n-1} R_{k+1}^2 = \frac{n(n+\sqrt{p})(2n+\sqrt{p})}{6p} - \frac{n^2}{p}. \tag{2.32}$$

Using Lemma 1.2 with $q = r = \sqrt{p}$ and Lemma 2.10 with $q = p$, we also obtain

$$\sum_{k=0}^{n-1} \left\lceil \frac{R_{k+1}}{\sqrt{p}} \right\rceil = \sum_{k=0}^{n-1} \left\lceil \frac{\lceil (n-k-1)/\sqrt{p} \rceil}{\sqrt{p}} \right\rceil = \sum_{k=0}^{n-1} \left\lceil \frac{\lceil k/\sqrt{p} \rceil}{\sqrt{p}} \right\rceil = \sum_{k=0}^{n-1} \left\lceil \frac{k}{p} \right\rceil$$
$$= \frac{n(n+p)}{2p} - \frac{n}{p}. \tag{2.33}$$

Note that Lemma 2.10 can only be applied for $q = p$ if we assume that $n \bmod p = 0$ (which also guarantees that $n \bmod \sqrt{p} = 0$). This assumption is made solely for the purpose of simplifying our analysis; in an implementation, such a restriction would hinder practical application and hence it should be avoided there.

The total BSP cost expressed as a function of n and p is obtained by substituting the results of (2.30)–(2.33) and the value $R_0 = n/\sqrt{p}$ into (2.28). This gives

$$T_{\mathrm{LU}} = \frac{2n^3}{3p} + \left(\frac{3}{2\sqrt{p}} - \frac{2}{p} \right) n^2 + \frac{5n}{6}$$
$$+ \left(\left(\frac{3}{\sqrt{p}} - \frac{2}{p} \right) n^2 + \left(4\sqrt{p} - \frac{4}{\sqrt{p}} + \frac{4}{p} - 3 \right) n \right) g + 8nl. \tag{2.34}$$

For many purposes, it suffices to approximate the total cost of an algorithm by taking into account only the highest-order computation term and the highest-order **overhead** terms, that is, the terms representing load imbalance, communication, and synchronization. In this case, an approximate cost estimate, valid for $p \ll n$, is

$$T_{\mathrm{LU}} \approx \frac{2n^3}{3p} + \frac{3n^2}{2\sqrt{p}} + \frac{3n^2 g}{\sqrt{p}} + 8nl. \tag{2.35}$$

Note that the row swaps, row broadcasts, and column broadcasts each contribute $n^2 g/\sqrt{p}$ to the communication cost of the improved algorithm.

2.5 High-performance LU decomposition

Not all floating-point operations are created equal. Flops from matrix operations can often be performed at much higher computing rates than flops from vector or scalar operations. This motivates the restructuring of algorithms into blocking form which is common in modern numerical linear algebra packages, such as LAPACK [7], ScaLAPACK [35, 66], PLAPACK [293], and Elemental [251], and also in the High-Performance LINPACK benchmark (HPL) [90] which performs an LU decomposition and solves a triangular system in order to solve a large dense linear system. The HPL benchmark is most famous as the benchmark used to rank the worldwide TOP500 of supercomputers [279].

We can exploit blocking in a rudimentary form already by selective procrastination: we postpone all updates of the submatrix $A(k_1 : n-1, k_1 : n-1)$ from stages k with

$k_0 \leq k < k_1$ of the algorithm, but perform the other operations as before, and then we combine the $b = k_1 - k_0$ matrix updates into a single update

for $k := k_0$ **to** $k_1 - 1$ **do**
   for $i := k_1$ **to** $n - 1$ **do**
      for $j := k_1$ **to** $n - 1$ **do**
         $a_{ij} := a_{ij} - a_{ik}a_{kj};$

We call b the **algorithmic block size**.

The triple update loop can concisely be expressed as a matrix update

$$A_{22} := A_{22} - A_{21}A_{12},$$

where the submatrices A_{12}, A_{21}, A_{22} correspond to the submatrices of the current matrix A depicted in Fig. 2.6 and defined by $A_{12} = A(k_0 : k_1 - 1, k_1 : n - 1)$, $A_{21} = A(k_1 : n - 1, k_0 : k_1 - 1)$, and $A_{22} = A(k_1 : n - 1, k_1 : n - 1)$. Here, the main operation is multiplying a so-called **tall-and-skinny** matrix A_{21} of size $(n - k_1) \times b$ with a matrix A_{12} of size $b \times (n - k_1)$ (the transpose of a tall-and-skinny matrix). This costs $2(n - k_1)^2 b$ flops.

In the matrix multiplication, the $(n - k_1)^2$ matrix data can be reused b times, which reduces the number of cache misses on a cache-based computer by a factor of b. As a consequence, both in sequential and parallel LU decomposition, all the flops of these block operations can be carried out at an increased flop rate of $r_{MM} \gg r$, that is, at the speed of matrix multiplication, which approaches the peak speed of the computer for sufficiently large b. At some point, the gains of further increasing b diminish, since then the processor speed is the limiting factor, not the movement of data into and out of the cache.

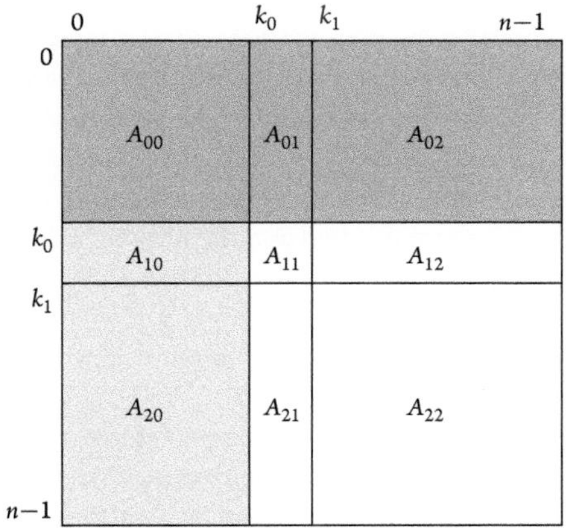

Figure 2.6 Submatrices created by combining the operations from stages $k_0 \leq k < k_1$ of the LU decomposition. The submatrices in darker grey have obtained their final values at the start of stage k_0; those in lighter grey can still change by row permutations.

The total number of flops carried out at peak speed can be obtained by adding the number of flops of the matrix multiplications for $k_0 = 0, b, \ldots, n - b$, where we assume that $n \bmod b = 0$. This gives

$$T_{\text{blocks}} = \frac{2n^3}{3} - bn^2 + \frac{b^2 n}{3}. \tag{2.36}$$

Comparing eqns (2.36) and (2.12), we see that for small b, most of the flops are performed at peak speed. Only a fraction of about $bn^2/(2n^3/3) = 1.5b/n$ is performed at lower speed. If we choose a too small b, the gains of blocking are limited as data are reused only b times during the matrix multiplications. If we choose a too large b, more flops remain that are carried out at lower speed. A good choice of b satisfies $1 \ll b \ll n$, and for instance in runs of the HPL benchmark, often a value in the range $b = 32$–256 is chosen. The value of b need not be constant during the algorithm and if desired it can be chosen smaller near the end.

Procrastination works both in the sequential and the parallel case. In the parallel case, it has even more benefits than just faster flops: all operations involving matrix elements a_{ij} with $j \geq k_1$ can be postponed until stage k_1, and then all delayed swaps of row parts can be done by all processors at the same time, at lower communication cost than in the original algorithm (where only two rows are swapped at a time, involving at most $2N$ processors out of p). The extra cost of the delay is at most $2nl/b$ for the whole LU decomposition algorithm, caused by performing the delayed operations in $2n/b$ extra supersteps.

To reduce the total run time of a parallel algorithm, we need to minimize, or **avoid**, all three contributing cost factors: computation, communication, and synchronization. In sequential computing, it is obvious that we need to avoid computation if we want our algorithms to be fast, although we do not speak about **computation-avoiding algorithms**. Many decades ago, just minimizing the total flop count would do the job of making an algorithm fast. This situation has completely changed and increasingly we must take the cost of data transfer into account.

In parallel computing based on the message-passing paradigm, every communication of a message entails an implicit synchronization between the sender and the receiver, and this gave rise to the notion of **communication-avoiding algorithms** [82]. The motto here is to avoid communication even if this is at the expense of an increase in flop count, because communication is much more expensive than computation. Often, lower bounds can be proven for the number of data words communicated and the number of messages exchanged for a given amount of memory available per processor and the goal of communication-avoiding algorithms is to attain both lower bounds. An example is a lower bound of $\mathcal{O}(n^2/\sqrt{p})$ data words communicated per processor [166] for an amount of n^2/p memory per processor, which corresponds to the third term in eqn (2.35).

Within the BSP paradigm, however, we try to avoid global synchronizations. If we got carried away, we would call our algorithms **synchronization-avoiding**. Such algorithms may be based on communication-avoiding techniques, but they are still different because they try to reduce the number of global synchronizations, not the number of pairwise synchronizations.

To avoid synchronization in LU decomposition, let us first consider the case where pivoting is not needed: a case without pivot search and row swaps. This means that we can skip supersteps (0)–(5) in Algorithm 2.8 but leave the divisions by a_{kk}. Still, we would need $\mathcal{O}(n)$ synchronizations for the remaining supersteps. A remedy would be to choose a different data distribution that increases the bulk of a superstep, but is still based on the cyclic distribution. The straightforward choice is to use the **block-cyclic distribution**, which assigns blocks of size β in a cyclic way to processors. For a vector of length n, and p processors, it is defined by

$$x_i \longmapsto P((i \operatorname{div} \beta) \operatorname{mod} p), \quad \text{for } 0 \leq i < n. \tag{2.37}$$

For an $n \times n$ matrix and $p = MN$ processors, we define

$$\phi_0(i) = (i \operatorname{div} \beta) \operatorname{mod} M, \quad \text{for } 0 \leq i < n,$$
$$\phi_1(j) = (j \operatorname{div} \beta) \operatorname{mod} N, \quad \text{for } 0 \leq j < n. \tag{2.38}$$

We modify Algorithm 2.8 accordingly, which is rather straightforward. The modification reduces the number of synchronizations of the algorithm by a factor of β, as there are n/β stages in the computation, each starting with the decomposition of a diagonal block of size $\beta \times \beta$. A disadvantage is that the load imbalance is magnified by a factor of β^2; this puts an upper limit on the block size β that can be used to our advantage. The communication cost does not change, because the same data has to be broadcast as before. The algorithm for the block-cyclic distribution is said to have a larger grain size, since it processes submatrices of size $\beta \times \beta$ instead of single matrix elements.

Unfortunately, if we insist on partial row pivoting for reasons of numerical stability, this spoils all the gains with regard to the number of supersteps. The reason is that we need to find the best pivot in a matrix column before we can start updating it and we need to update a matrix column completely before we can find the best pivot in the next matrix column. Each pivot search involves communication between all processors in a processor column and hence requires a synchronization of those processors before we can move on to the next matrix column. In our BSP approach, this incurs a global synchronization. The total number of synchronizations will thus be at least n.

The HPL benchmark requires partial row pivoting, because this type of pivoting has proven itself to be numerically stable in practice, and because the HPL benchmark was designed to be backwards compatible, to enable comparison of results over many decades. In parallel LU decomposition programs in general, we are not limited to partial row pivoting, and we can devise pivoting variants that are more friendly towards parallelism. We feel liberated to do so, since we use partial row pivoting in practice even though partial row pivoting can be unstable in rare cases, see Example 2.7.

Within the school of communication-avoiding algorithms, an alternative pivoting variant called **tournament pivoting** [130] has been proposed for the block-cyclic distribution, which works as follows in the BSP setting. Assume that the distribution block size is β. The tournament has as its goal to determine β good pivots so that we can perform β stages of the LU decomposition, stages $k_0 \leq k < k_0 + \beta$. In the pivoting part, we only perform operations on columns j with $k_0 \leq j < k_0 + \beta$. Assume that $k_0 \operatorname{mod} \beta = 0$, which will be true if we start with stage $k = 0$ and process blocks of β columns at a time. The pivot search is thus carried out in one processor column, $P(*, (k_0/\beta) \bmod N)$. Each processor $P(s,t)$ with $t = (k_0/\beta) \bmod N$ performs a local LU decomposition with partial row pivoting on the submatrix of elements a_{ij} with $k_0 \leq i < n$, $k_0 \leq j < k_0 + \beta$, $\phi_0(i) = s$, and $\phi_1(j) = t$. This yields β local pivot rows; their row indices are registered and the corresponding rows of the current matrix $A^{(k_0)}$ survive in the tournament. These rows are then broadcast to all processors in the processor column, and the $M\beta$ surviving rows enter a global tournament which is run redundantly on all processors in the processor column. This approach avoids global synchronization as much as possible. (In the original communication-avoiding LU approach, called CALU, a pairwise knock-out tournament is held, repeatedly pairing processors with β candidate pivot rows each.) The algorithm finishes with an update of the local rows by the winning pivot rows, in a procedure similar to the local tournament.

To determine the cost of a BSP tournament, we compute the main cost terms of the LU decomposition for a block of β columns. We use eqn (2.13) for the local tournament with $m = (n - k_0)/M$ and $n = \beta$, giving a main cost term of $(n - k_0)\beta^2/M$, and for the global tournament with $m = M\beta$, giving $(M - 1)\beta^3$. The cost of the final update is at most that of the local tournament. The row broadcast sends β local rows of length β to all processors in the processor column, at cost $(M - 1)\beta^2 g$. The synchronization cost is $3l$, because we have a computation superstep, followed by the row broadcast, and another computation superstep. Therefore, we achieve the desired number of $\mathcal{O}(n/\beta)$ supersteps. Note that a column broadcast is not needed here, as all β matrix columns in the range reside in the same processor column.

A good choice for β must be a compromise between synchronization considerations, which favour a larger β value, and load imbalance and numerical considerations, which both favour a smaller value. For the extreme choice $\beta = 1$, we obtain the cyclic distribution of the previous sections, which is simpler and requires fewer index computations. This is the choice we made for BSPedupack (in both versions 1.0 and 2.0). Van de Geijn and co-workers [251] also chose $\beta = 1$ for their package Elemental (a name referring to the cyclic distribution of matrix elements), and they attained higher speeds than ScaLAPACK in a number of linear algebra computations. Since computation scales with the problem size n as $\mathcal{O}(n^3)$, imbalance and communication scale as $\mathcal{O}(n^2)$, and synchronization only scales as $\mathcal{O}(n)$, reducing the lowest-order term to $\mathcal{O}(n/\beta)$ will hardly ever be worthwhile, so that it is better to use $\beta = 1$ with all its advantages: simplicity, good load balance, numerical stability, and no need to fight in tournaments.

2.6 Example function `bsplu`

This section presents the program text of the function `bsplu`, which is a BSPlib implementation of Algorithm 2.8, extended with algorithmic blocking as described in Section 2.5. The distribution used is the same square cyclic distribution as before, which corresponds to the choice $\beta = 1$ in the block-cyclic distribution (2.38). This section also presents the function `matmat_tall_skinny`, which multiplies a tall-and-skinny matrix with the transpose of another tall-and-skinny matrix, the function `bsp_permute_rows`, which permutes a set of rows of the matrix in a range of columns, and the collective-communication function `bsp_broadcast`.

The sequential function `matmat_tall_skinny` is a cache-friendly implementation of a matrix multiplication $C := C - AB^T$, where A and B are tall-and-skinny (I love that name), with sizes $m \times b$ and $n \times b$, respectively. The function picks a $b \times b$ block from A, a block of the same size from B^T, multiplies them, and subtracts the result from the corresponding block of C. The value of b is chosen small enough so that each block fits in cache, and large enough to benefit from cache reuse (each matrix element is used b times in a block multiplication). The innermost loop (over k) accesses both A and B by row, which is the way we store matrices. This increases the number of **cache hits** because matrix elements are stored in cache as **cache lines**, contiguous sets of data, here containing several matrix elements. In most cases, moving one matrix element into cache also brings in the next element from its row.

The function `bsp_permute_rows` permutes the rows of the matrix A. It puts `nperm` local rows with global row index `Src[i]` into their destination row `Dest[i]`. Because the matrix A is the target of put operations in this function, A must have been registered beforehand. The easiest and cheapest way of registering a 2D array representing A is by exploiting the fact that the utility function `matallocd` from `bspedupack.c` (see Appendix A) allocates a contiguous array of length mn to store an $m \times n$ matrix. We can address this matrix in a 1D fashion, if we wish to do so, and communication is one of the few occasions where this is worthwhile. We introduce a variable pa, which stands for 'pointer to A'; it is a pointer that stores the address of the first matrix row, a [0]. We can put data into every desired matrix row i by putting them into the space pointed to by pa and using a suitable offset i*nc, where nc is the number of columns, that is the row length, of the destination processor. (Watch out: the putting processor must know the row length of the remote processor. Fortunately, in the present case the local and remote row lengths are the same, because the rows are swapped.) This way of registering a matrix requires only one registration, instead of one registration per row. As a result, we save much communication time, because registration is expensive: each registration costs at least $(p-1)g$ because every processor broadcasts the address of its own variable to all other processors.

The function `bsp_broadcast` implements a slight generalization of Algorithm 2.7: it broadcasts the vector x from processor $P(\text{src})$ instead of $P(0)$, and the set of destination processors is $\{P(\text{s0} + t * \text{stride}): 0 \leq t < \text{p0}\}$ instead of the set of all p processors. (Sometimes, the term '**multicast**' is used to describe such an operation with a limited number of destination processors; the term 'broadcast' is then reserved for the case with p destination processors. We do not make this distinction.) Within the broadcast function, processors are numbered in 1D fashion. The broadcast as we formulate it is flexible and it can be applied in many situations: for instance, it can be used to broadcast a vector within one processor row of a parallel computer numbered in 2D fashion; for the standard identification $P(s,t) \equiv P(s+tM)$, the parameter s0 equals the processor row number of the single processor row involved, and furthermore $\text{stride} = M$, and p0 $= N$. The parameter src depends on the chosen source processor.

The broadcast function can also be used to perform several broadcasts simultaneously, for example, one broadcast within each processor row. In that case, $P(s,t)$ executes the function with the parameter $s0 = s$. This feature must be used with caution: the simultaneous broadcast works well as long as the set of processors can be partitioned into disjoint subsets, each including a source and a destination set. The processors within a subset should all be able to determine their source, destination set, and vector length uniquely from the function parameters. A processor can then decide to participate as source and/or destination in its subset or to remain idle. In the LU decomposition program, processors are partitioned into processor rows for the purpose of column broadcasts, and into processor columns for row broadcasts.

The broadcast function is designed such that it can perform the phases of the broadcast separately; a complete broadcast is done by calling the function twice, first with a value $phase = 0$, then with $phase = 1$. The synchronization terminating the phase is not done by the broadcast function itself, but is left to the calling program. The advantage of this approach is that unnecessary synchronizations can be avoided. For instance, phase 0 of the row and column broadcasts can be combined into one superstep, thus needing only one synchronization.

The program text of the broadcast function is a direct implementation of Algorithm 2.7 in the general context described above. The program texts of the two phases are similar and hence they are merged. The difference between the phases is twofold: in phase 0 only the source processor participates, whereas in phase 1 all destination processors participate; furthermore, in phase 0 the number of the block to be put is determined by the destination processor, whereas in phase 1 this is the local processor. Note that the size of the data vector to be put is the minimum of the broadcast block size $b = n/p$ and the number $n - tb$ of components that would remain if all preceding processors had put b components. The size thus computed may be negative or zero, so that we must make sure that the put is carried out only for positive size. All processors avoid sending data to the source processor, which would be superfluous. This optimization has no effect on the BSP cost, since the (cost-determining) source processor itself does not benefit, as can be seen by studying the role of $P(0)$ in Fig. 2.5. Still, the optimization reduces the overall communication volume, making it equal to that of the one-phase broadcast. This may make believers in other models than BSP happy, and give some BSP believers cold feet as well!

The basic structure of the LU decomposition algorithm and the function bsplu are the same, with two exceptions: First, operations are postponed for matrix elements a_{ij} with $j \geq k_1 = k_0 + b$, where b is the algorithmic block size, and also row swaps are postponed for matrix elements a_{ij} with $j < k_0$. The postponed operations are carried out at the end of stage $k_1 - 1$. In Fig. 2.6, these operations modify the submatrices A_{10}, A_{20}, A_{12}, and A_{22}. Second, computation supersteps and communication supersteps are combined into a single mixed superstep for the pairs $(0)/(1)$, $(2)/(3)$, and $(4)/(5)$. For the pairs $(0)/(1)$ and $(2)/(3)$, this could be done because BSPlib allows computation and communication to be mixed; for $(4)/(5)$, this could be done because bsp_puts are buffered automatically, so that we do not have to take care of that ourselves. Note that the superstep $(0')/(0)$ of the algorithm is delimited quite naturally in the program text by the common terminating bsp_sync of superstep $(0)/(1)$. As a result, each stage of the function bsplu has five bsp_syncs, not counting the synchronizations for the postponed operations.

The relation between the variables of Algorithm 2.8 and those of the function bsplu is as follows. The variables $M, N, s, t, n, k, s_{max}, r$ of the algorithm correspond to the variables M, N, s, t, n, k, smax, r of the function. The global row index used in the algorithm is $i =$ i*M+s, where i is the local row index used in the function. The global column index is $j =$ j*N+t, where j is the local column index. The matrix element a_{ij} corresponds to a[i][j] on the processor that owns a_{ij}, and the permutation component π_i corresponds to pi[i]. The global row index of the local element in column k with largest absolute value is $r_s =$ imax*M+s. The numerical value $a_{r_s,k}$ of this element corresponds to the variable max in the function. The arrays Max and Imax store the local maxima and their index for the M processors that contain part of column k. The maximum for processor $P(s, k \bmod N)$ is stored in Max[s]. The global row index of the overall winner is $r =$ Imax[smax]*M+smax and its value is $a_{rk} =$ pivot.

The arrays Lk and Uk store the local parts to be broadcast from column k of L and row k of U. The array L stores the local rows of b columns of L, created in stages $k_0, \ldots, k_1 - 1$. The array UT stores the local columns of b rows of U, in transposed format, and it is created only at the end of stage $k_1 - 1$.

The function nloc introduced in the program bspinprod of Section 1.4 is used here as well, for instance to compute the number of local rows nloc(M,s,n) of processor row $P(s, *)$ for an $n \times n$ matrix in the $M \times N$ cyclic distribution. The local rows have local indices i $= 0, 1, \ldots,$ nloc(M,s,n) $- 1$. It holds that i < nloc(M,s,k) if and only if $i < k$. Thus, i=nloc(M,s,k) is the first local row index for which the corresponding global row index satisfies $i \geq k$. We will denote this local row index by kr; similarly we define kc=nloc(N,t,k) for columns. Furthermore, we write k0r=nloc(M,s,k0) for the first local row index corresponding to a global row index $i \geq k_0$.

Variables must have been registered before they can be used as the destination of put operations. For example, the arrays Lk, Uk, Max, Imax are registered immediately upon allocation. Thus, registration takes place outside the main loop, which is much cheaper than registering an array each time it is used in communication. The exact length of the array is also registered so that we can be warned if we attempt to put data beyond the end of the array. (Some hardware uses this length to lock a given amount of memory space, so be careful in setting this length.) The permutation array pi must be allocated outside bsplu because it is an output array. Nevertheless, its registration takes place inside bsplu, because this is the only place where it is used in communication.

The supersteps of the function bsplu are a straightforward implementation of the supersteps in the LU decomposition algorithm. Two details might need additional explanation. First, the division by the pivot in superstep $(2)/(3)$ is also carried out for the pivot element itself, yielding $a_{rk}/a_{rk} = 1$, despite the fact that this element should keep its original value a_{rk}. Later, this value must be swapped into a_{kk}. This problem is solved by simply reassigning the original value stored in the temporary variable pivot to a_{rk}. Second, all processors need the index r, which is broadcast by using a get operation. Note that r is determined and communicated by a get operation in the same superstep; this does not cause any conflict because get operations are only executed after all computations of their superstep have been completed.

The postponed operations are performed at the end of stage $k_1 - 1 = k_0 + b - 1$. First, the function swaps2perm translates the b row swaps of stages $k_0, \ldots, k_1 - 1$ to a single permutation, given by arrays Src and Dest. (This function is included in the driver program bsplu_test and is not printed here.) After that, the permutation is carried out, but only for column indices $j < k_0$ or $j \geq k_1$, because for $k_0 \leq j < k_1$ the swaps were already done. Then, b rows of U are computed for $j \geq k_1$, similar to the case $k_0 \leq j < k_1$, and these rows are broadcast immediately after they have been computed, which requires $2b$ synchronizations overall. The total synchronization cost of the program is thus about $7nl$. A complication arises because some elements of L, which had been stored previously, are not valid anymore. They should have been permuted after their computation, but they were frozen in place instead. A simple remedy is to obtain them again by individual get operations. Since at most $2b$ rows are affected, with b elements in each row, the additional overhead of obtaining these data is small, and it is expected to be about $2b^2 g / M$.

The final bang is the call to the tall-and-skinny matrix multiplication, which performs a large number of floating-point operations at a high computing rate, which was indeed the purpose of our whole postponement approach.

The program contains only rudimentary error handling. For the sake of brevity, we have only included a crude test for numerical singularity. If no pivot can be found with an absolute value larger than EPS, the program is aborted and an error message is printed. The program text of bsplu is:

```
#include "bspedupack.h"

#define EPS 1.0e-15
#define BLOCK 16

void matmat_tall_skinny (double **A, double **B,
                         double **C, long m, long n, long b,
                         long i0 , long j0 ){

    /* This function multiplies the m by b matrix A and
       the transpose of the n by b matrix B and subtracts
       the result A(B^T) from the submatrix C(i0:i0+m-1,
       j0:j0+n-1).

       The function is written in a cache-friendly way
       for tall-and-skinny matrices A and B (b << m,n),
       using a block size b.
    */

    if (m < 1 || n < 1 || b < 1)
        return ;
```

```
for (long ia=0; ia<m; ia+=b){
    long imax= MIN(ia+b,m);
    for (long jb=0; jb<n; jb+=b){
        long jmax= MIN(jb+b,n);

        /* Multiply a block from A with a block from
           B */
        for (long i=ia; i<imax; i++){
            for (long j=jb; j<jmax; j++){
                double sum= 0.0;
                for (long k=0; k<b; k++)
                    sum += A[i][k]*B[j][k];
                C[i0+i][j0+j] -= sum;
            }
        }
    }
}

} /* end matmat_tall_skinny */


void bsp_permute_rows(long M, long *Src, long *Dest,
                      long nperm, double *pa, long nc,
                      long jc, long jc1){

    /* This function permutes the rows of matrix A such
       that local row Src[i] moves to row Dest[i],
       for 0 <= i < nperm. This is only done for local
       column indices jc <= j < jc1.
       M = number of processor rows,
       nc = length of local rows of matrix A,
       A is stored as a 1D array pa, which must have been
       registered previously.
    */

    if (jc1 <= jc)
        return;

    long pid= bsp_pid();
    long t= pid/M;

    for (long i=0; i<nperm; i++){
        /* Store row Src[i] of A in row r=Dest[i] on
           P(r%M, t) */
```

```
            long  r= Dest[i];
            bsp_put(r%M+t*M,&pa[(Src[i]/M)*nc+jc],pa,
                    ((r/M)*nc+jc)*sizeof(double),
                    (jc1-jc)*sizeof(double));
    }

}  /* end bsp_permute_rows */


void  bsp_broadcast(double *x, long n, long src, long s0,
                    long stride, long p0, long phase){

    /* Broadcast the vector x of length n from processor
       src to processors s0+t*stride, 0 <= t < p0. Here n,
       p0 >= 1. The vector x must have been registered
       previously. Processors are numbered in 1D fashion.

       phase = phase of two-phase broadcast (0 or 1)
       Only one phase is performed, without
       synchronization.
    */

    if (n < 1 || p0 < 1)
        return;

    long s= bsp_pid();  // processor number
    long b= (n%p0==0 ?  n/p0 : n/p0+1);  // broadcast
                                         // block size

    if ((phase==0 && s==src) ||
        (phase==1 && s0 <= s && s < s0+p0*stride &&
                        (s-s0)%stride==0)){
        /* Participate */

        for (long t=0; t<p0; t++){
            long dest= s0+t*stride;
            long t1 = (phase==0 ? t : (s-s0)/stride);
                // in phase 1: s= s0+t1*stride

            long nbytes= MIN(b,n-t1*b)*sizeof(double);
            if (nbytes>0 && dest!=src)
                bsp_put(dest,&x[t1*b],x,
                        t1*b*sizeof(double),nbytes);
        }
```

```
        }

} /* end bsp_broadcast */


void bsplu(long M, long N, long n, long *pi, double **a){

    /* Compute LU decomposition of n by n matrix A with
       partial row pivoting. The processors are numbered
       in 2D fashion. Program text for P(s,t) = processor
       s+t*M, with 0 <= s < M and 0 <= t < N.
       A is distributed by the M by N cyclic distribution.
       pi stores the output permutation, with a cyclically
       distributed copy in every processor column.
    */

    void swaps2perm(long M, long k0, long b, long *R,
                    long *Src, long *Dest, long *nperm);

    long pid= bsp_pid();
    long s= pid%M;
    long t= pid/M;

    long nr= nloc(M,s,n); // number of local rows
    long nc= nloc(N,t,n); // number of local columns

    long r; /* index of pivot row */
    bsp_push_reg(&r, sizeof(long));

    /* Set pointer for 1D access to A */
    double *pa= NULL;
    if (nr>0)
        pa= a[0];
    bsp_push_reg(pa, nr*nc*sizeof(double));

    /* Initialize permutation vector pi */
    for (long i=0; i<nr; i++)
        pi[i]= i*M+s; /* global row index */
    bsp_push_reg(pi, nr*sizeof(long));

    /* Allocate memory for BLOCK columns of L and U^T */
    double **UT= matallocd(nc,BLOCK);
    double **L= matallocd(nr,BLOCK);
```

```
long *R= vecalloci(BLOCK); // global indices of
                           // pivot rows
long *Src= vecalloci(2*BLOCK); // source indices
                               // of rows
                               // to be swapped
long *Dest= vecalloci(2*BLOCK); // destination indices

double *Uk= vecallocd(nc);
bsp_push_reg(Uk,nc*sizeof(double));
double *Lk= vecallocd(nr);
bsp_push_reg(Lk,nr*sizeof(double));
double *Max= vecallocd(M);
bsp_push_reg(Max,M*sizeof(double));
long *Imax= vecalloci(M);
bsp_push_reg(Imax,M*sizeof(long));

bsp_sync();

long k0= 0;
long b= MIN(BLOCK,n); // algorithmic block size

for (long k=0; k<n; k++){

    /****** Superstep (0)/(1) ******/
    long kr=   nloc(M,s,k); // first local row
                            // with global index >= k
    long kr1=  nloc(M,s,k+1);      // >= k+1
    long k0rb= nloc(M,s,k0+b);     // >= k0+b
    long kc=   nloc(N,t,k); // first local column
    long kc1=  nloc(N,t,k+1);
    long k0c=  nloc(N,t,k0);
    long k0cb= nloc(N,t,k0+b);

    if (k%N==t){    /* k=kc*N+t */
        /* Search for local absolute maximum
           in column k of A */
        double absmax= 0.0;
        long imax= DUMMY;
        for (long i=kr; i<nr; i++){
            if (fabs(a[i][kc])>absmax){
                absmax= fabs(a[i][kc]);
                imax= i;
            }
        }
```

```
    double max= 0.0;
    if (absmax>0.0)
        max= a[imax][kc];

    /* Broadcast value and local index
       of maximum to P(*,t) */
    for (long s1=0; s1<M; s1++){
        bsp_put(s1+t*M,&max,Max,
                s*sizeof(double),sizeof(double));
        bsp_put(s1+t*M,&imax,Imax,
                s*sizeof(long),sizeof(long));
    }
}
bsp_sync();

/****** Superstep (2)/(3) ******/
if (k%N==t){
    /* Determine global absolute maximum
       (redundantly) */
    double absmax= 0.0;
    long smax= DUMMY;
    for (long s1=0; s1<M; s1++){
        if (fabs(Max[s1])>absmax){
            absmax= fabs(Max[s1]);
            smax= s1;
        }
    }
    if (absmax > EPS){
        long imax= Imax[smax];
        r= imax*M+smax; // global index
        double pivot= Max[smax];
        for (long i=kr; i<nr; i++)
            a[i][kc] /= pivot;
        if (s==smax)
            a[imax][kc]= pivot; // Restore value
                                // of pivot
    } else {
        bsp_abort("bsplu at stage %d:"
                  " matrix is singular\n",k);
    }
}
/* Obtain index of pivot row */
bsp_get(s+(k%N)*M,&r,0,&r,sizeof(long));
bsp_sync();
```

```
/****** Superstep (4)/(5) ******/
R[k−k0]= r; /* store index of pivot row */

long nperm= 0;
long Src2[2], Dest2[2];
if (k%M==s && r!=k){
    /* Store pi(k) in pi(r) on P(r%M,t) */
    bsp_put(r%M+t*M,&pi[k/M],pi,(r/M)*sizeof(long),
            sizeof(long));
    Src2[nperm]= k; Dest2[nperm]= r; nperm++;
}
if (r%M==s && r!=k){
    bsp_put(k%M+t*M,&pi[r/M],pi,(k/M)*sizeof(long),
            sizeof(long));
    Src2[nperm]= r; Dest2[nperm]= k; nperm++;
}
/* Swap rows k and r for columns in range
   k0..k0+b−1 */
bsp_permute_rows(M,Src2,Dest2,nperm,
                    pa,nc,k0c,k0cb);
bsp_sync();

/****** Superstep (6) ******/
/* Phase 0 of two−phase broadcasts */
if (k%N==t){
    /* Store new column k in Lk */
    for (long i=kr1; i<nr; i++)
        Lk[i−kr1]= a[i][kc];
}
if (k%M==s){
    /* Store new row k in Uk for columns
       in range k+1..k0+b−1 */
    for (long j=kc1; j<k0cb; j++)
        Uk[j−kc1]= a[kr][j];
}
bsp_broadcast(Lk,nr−kr1,s+(k%N)*M,s,M,N,0);
bsp_broadcast(Uk,k0cb−kc1,(k%M)+t*M,t*M,1,M,0);
bsp_sync();

/****** Superstep (7) ******/
/* Phase 1 of two−phase broadcasts */
bsp_broadcast(Lk,nr−kr1,s+(k%N)*M,s,M,N,1);
bsp_broadcast(Uk,k0cb−kc1,(k%M)+t*M,t*M,1,M,1);
bsp_sync();
```

```
/****** Superstep (0') ******/
/* Update of A for columns in range
   k+1..k0+b−1 */
for (long i=kr1; i<nr; i++){
    for (long j=kc1; j<k0cb; j++)
        a[i][j] −= Lk[i−kr1]*Uk[j−kc1];
}

/* Store column k in L for rows in range
   k0+b..n−1 */
for (long i=k0rb; i<nr; i++)
    L[i−k0rb][k−k0]= Lk[i−kr1];

/* Perform postponed operations of stages
   k0,..., k0+b−1 */
if (k==k0+b−1){
    /****** Superstep (8) ******/
    nperm=0;
    swaps2perm(M,k0,b,R,Src,Dest,&nperm);
    bsp_permute_rows(M,Src,Dest,nperm,pa,nc,0,k0c);
    bsp_permute_rows(M,Src,Dest,nperm,pa,nc,k0cb,nc);

    for (long q=0; q<nperm; q++){
        if (Src[q] >= k0+b){
            /* Obtain row Src[q] of L for columns
               in range k0..k0+b−1 again */
            for (long j=k0; j<k0+b; j++){
                long tj= j%N;
                long ncj= nloc(N,tj,n);
                long i= Src[q]/M;
                bsp_get(s+tj*M,pa,
                        (i*ncj+j/N)*sizeof(double),
                        &(L[i−k0rb][j−k0]),
                        sizeof(double));
            }
        }
    }
    bsp_sync();

    if (k < n−1){
        for (long q=0; q<b; q++){
            /****** Superstep (9) ******/
            if ((k0+q)%M==s){
                /* Store row k0+q in Uk for
```

```
                    columns  in  range  k0+b..n−1 */
              for (long j=k0cb; j<nc; j++)
                  Uk[j−k0cb]= a[(k0+q)/M][j];
        }
        bsp_broadcast(Uk,nc−k0cb,
                       (k0+q)%M+t*M,t*M,1,M,0);
        bsp_sync();

        /****** Superstep (10) ******/
        bsp_broadcast(Uk,nc−k0cb,(k0+q)%M+t*M,
                       t*M,1,M,1);

        /* Obtain column k0+q of L
           in range k0+q+1..k0+b−1 */
        long k0rq1= nloc(M,s,k0+q+1);
        for (long i= k0rq1; i<k0rb; i++){
            long tj= (k0+q)%N;
            long ncj= nloc(N,tj,n);
            bsp_get(s+tj*M,pa,
                     (i*ncj+(k0+q)/N)*sizeof
                     (double),
                     &Lk[i−k0rq1],sizeof
                     (double));
        }
        bsp_sync();

        /****** Superstep (9') ******/
        /* Store row k0+q in UT for columns
           in range k0+b..n−1 */
        for (long j=0; j<nc−k0cb; j++)
            UT[j][q]= Uk[j]; // Store as
                             // a column of UT

        /* Update of A in rows
           k0+q+1..k0+b−1 */
        for (long i= k0rq1; i<k0rb; i++){
            for (long j=k0cb; j<nc; j++)
                a[i][j] −= Lk[i−k0rq1]*
                           Uk[j−k0cb];
        }
    }

    /* Rank−b update of the matrix A */
    matmat_tall_skinny(L,UT,a, nr−k0rb,
```

```
                    nc−k0cb ,  b ,  k0rb ,  k0cb );
            /* Prepare for next block */
            k0 += b;
            b= MIN(BLOCK, n−k0 );
        }
    }
}

bsp_pop_reg (Imax );   vecfreei (Imax );
bsp_pop_reg (Max );    vecfreed (Max );
bsp_pop_reg (Lk );     vecfreed (Lk );
bsp_pop_reg (Uk );     vecfreed (Uk );
bsp_pop_reg ( pi );  bsp_pop_reg (pa );  bsp_pop_reg(&r );
vecfreei ( Dest );  vecfreei ( Src );  vecfreei (R );
matfreed (L );  matfreed (UT );

} /* end bsplu */
```

2.7 Experimental results on the Cori supercomputer

Experiment does to computation models what the catwalk does to fashion models: it subjects the models to critical scrutiny, exposes their good and bad sides, and makes the better models stand out. In this section, we put the predictions of the BSP model for LU decomposition to the test. We perform numerical experiments to check whether the theoretical benefits of two-phase broadcasting promised in Section 2.4 can be observed in practice. To do this, we measure the performance of the function bsplu with the two-phase broadcasting function bsp_broadcast, and also with a one-phase broadcasting function. Furthermore, we try to achieve high performance for our LU decomposition program by varying the algorithmic block size b and the aspect ratio M/N between the number of processor rows M and the number of processor columns N, where we will be guided by our theoretical cost analysis. This is another test of our cost model.

We performed our experiments on the Cori supercomputer of the National Energy Research Scientific Computing Center (NERSC) located in Berkeley, CA. Cori is named after Nobel-prize-winning biochemist Gerty Cori. It is a Cray XC40 architecture consisting of 2388 Intel Dual Socket Xeon (Haswell) nodes, each with 32 cores running at 2.3 GHz, and 9688 Intel Xeon Phi (Knights Landing) nodes, each with 68 cores running at 1.4 GHz. The Haswell nodes were installed in 2015, and the Knights Landing nodes were added in 2016. We will use a small subset of the Haswell nodes in our experiments. Each Haswell node has a small L1 (level 1) data cache of 32 kB, which exactly fits a 64×64 matrix of doubles, and an L2 cache of 256 kB. The 16 cores of a single CPU socket share a 40 MB L3 cache. Each node has 128 GB memory. The nodes are connected by a Cray Aries network with a Dragonfly topology. We ignore the shared-memory access available within a node, and we use the Haswell nodes as a distributed-memory machine.

We transformed Cori into a BSP computer by using version 1.1β of BSPonMPI [281] released in 2019, which runs on top of the default Cray MPICH implementation of MPI, version 3.1, that is provided by the Cray programming environment, version 2.5.15C. We compiled our LU program using the Intel 18.0.1 C compiler.

A good habit is to run the benchmark program bspbench just before running an application program such as bsplu. This helps detecting system changes (improvements or degradations) and tells you what BSP machine you have today. The measured BSP parameters of our computer for two Haswell nodes are $p = 64, r = 9.32$ Gflop/s, $g = 1066$ (114 ns), $l = 1\,842\,436$ (198 μs).

In all our experiments, the test matrix A is distributed by the $M \times N$ cyclic distribution. The matrix is chosen such that the pivot row in stage k is row $k + 1$; for $M > 1$, this forces a row swap with communication in every stage of the algorithm, because rows k and $k + 1$ reside on different processor rows.

Table 2.3 presents the broadcast time and the total execution time of LU decomposition with one-phase and two-phase broadcasts on 64 cores of Cori. To isolate the broadcast, we choose $M = 1$ and $N = 64$, a column distribution of the matrix. This removes the communication of row broadcasts and row swaps and keeps the pivot search local, and it also makes the column broadcast more prominent: the column broadcast becomes a broadcast from one source processor to all other processors. The time given for the two-phase broadcast is the accumulated time of all column broadcasts during the whole LU decomposition, split into time spent in superstep (6), i.e. phase 0, and superstep (7), phase 1. For the one-phase broadcast, the accumulated time is given for the single phase 0. The supersteps have been timed by inserting a bsp_time statement after every bsp_sync, taking the time difference between subsequent synchronizations, and adding the times for the same program superstep during all stages of the algorithm.

Table 2.3 Broadcast time and total time T (in s) of LU decomposition with one-phase and two-phase broadcasts on 64 cores of Cori, with $M = 1, N = 64$, and $b = 16$.

n	One-phase		Two-phase		
	phase 0	T	phase 0	phase 1	T
1 000	0.36	1.64	0.23	0.23	1.75
2 000	0.75	3.30	0.49	0.51	3.57
3 000	1.33	5.19	0.77	0.80	5.53
4 000	2.09	7.33	1.07	1.12	7.53
5 000	2.99	9.78	1.40	1.46	9.72
6 000	4.02	12.53	1.75	1.82	12.16
7 000	5.20	15.60	2.11	2.20	14.75
8 000	6.53	18.81	2.53	2.64	17.55
9 000	8.00	22.38	2.98	3.34	20.85
10 000	9.64	26.47	3.44	4.42	24.80

The difference in performance between the two types of broadcast is clearly visible. For $n \leq 4000$, LU decomposition with the one-phase broadcast is faster because it requires less synchronization; this is important for small problems, where the vectors to be broadcast are too small to justify an extra synchronization. For $n > 4000$, however, LU decomposition with the two-phase broadcast is faster, which is due to better spreading of the communication. For $n = 10\,000$, the savings in broadcast time are 18.5%, and the resulting savings in total execution time are 6.3%. Note that the contribution of broadcast time to the total time is significant, more so than we have observed in the past, due to the relatively slower improvements in communication rate of recent architectures compared to the improvements in computation rate. Moving data around takes much more time these days, relatively speaking!

The theoretical asymptotic gain factor in broadcast time for column-distributed matrices is $p/2 = 32$, cf. eqn (2.26); the observed gain factor of about 1.23 at $n = 10\,000$ is still far from that asymptotic value. This can, to some extent, be explained by the small average vector length of $n/2 = 5000$ in a broadcast, so that the average communication cost of a column broadcast is about $2 \cdot 5000g \approx 10.7$ Mflop, whereas $l \approx 1.8$ Mflop. Thus, l cannot yet be ignored. Still, the gain factor is much less than we would expect, which may be caused by underlying hardware characteristics, such as the hierarchical nature of the Cori partition used (two nodes, possibly at some distance, each node with two sockets, each socket with 16 cores). It may also be caused by the underlying system software characteristics, such as the implementation of an h-relation in BSPonMPI or the implementation of the MPI primitives called from BSPonMPI to carry out an h-relation.

Another test of the BSP model is how it predicts the time of separate supersteps. The model predicts that phase 0 and phase 1 of a two-phase broadcast take equal time, see eqn (2.26), despite very different communication patterns; for instance, phase 1 has a $p - 1$ times larger communication volume than phase 0. Indeed, we observe that for $n \leq 8000$ the timings are almost equal and for larger n they differ by at most 28%, which reasonably confirms the prediction of the BSP model. We may also conclude that communication volume is definitely not a good predictor of communication time, and that the BSP cost is a much better predictor.

We introduced algorithmic blocking in Section 2.5 to execute most of the flops at a higher computing rate. To do so, we formulated the matrix update as a rank-b update by the product of two tall-and-skinny matrices with b columns or b rows. Figure 2.7 shows how the choice of b influences the total execution time for $n = 10\,000$ and $p = 64$, with $M = N = 8$. A rapid decrease of the runtime until the minimum of 23.3 s for $b = 64$ is followed by a slow increase. Moving from $b = 1$ to $b = 64$ enhances cache reuse, but this effect saturates around $b = 64$. Moving further to even larger values of b slowly decreases the computation rate, because a decreasing part of the flops is contained in the postponed rank-b updates, and an increasing part in the instant rank-1 updates. Note that for small b, the number of fast in-cache flops is about $2n^3/3$, see eqn (2.36); this number decreases only slowly with b due to the second-order term $-bn^2$. Figure 2.7 also displays the time of the rank-b update, which decreases in the same way as the total time: for $b = 1$, the update takes 54.4 s (out of a total time of 78.5 s), whereas for $b = 64$, it takes only 1.68 s (out of 23.3 s). Although the choice of

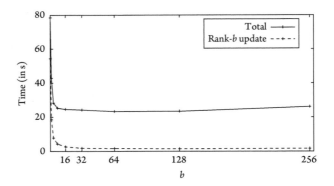

Figure 2.7 Time of a parallel LU decomposition of length $n = 10\,000$ on 64 cores of Cori as a function of the algorithmic block size b. Also given is the time spent in the rank-b update of the matrix. The matrix distribution is 8×8 cyclic.

Table 2.4 Broadcast time and total time T (in s) of LU decomposition with two-phase broadcasts on 64 cores of Cori for different aspect ratios M/N. The matrix size is $n = 10\,000$ and the algorithmic block size is $b = 64$.

M	N	Column broadcast		Row broadcast		T
		phase 0	phase 1	phase 0	phase 1	
1	64	3.52	4.51	1.29	5.23	27.37
2	32	2.66	4.41	1.68	3.46	23.55
4	16	2.23	3.62	1.64	2.72	21.27
8	8	2.06	3.02	1.63	2.29	20.17
16	4	2.04	2.50	1.79	2.14	19.51
32	2	2.08	2.21	2.28	2.69	20.71
64	1	1.96	2.00	3.25	4.37	24.10

$b = 64$ is optimal, we note that any value in the range 16–256 can safely be chosen without much loss.

Table 2.4 presents the measured time of the column and row broadcasts and the total time for all the $M \times N$ cyclic distributions with $MN = 64$. The broadcasts have two phases, for which the time is given separately. The column broadcast includes not only the time of broadcasting l_{ik} for $k + 1 \leq i < n$, but also the time of broadcasting a small part of row k, namely the values u_{kj} for $k + 1 \leq j < k + b$. The table to a large extent confirms the theoretical analysis of Section 2.4 which says that the square distribution with $M = N = \sqrt{p}$ is best: the 8×8 distribution reduces the broadcast time by 38.1% compared to the 1×64 distribution and it also causes a better load balance in other parts of the algorithm (leading to a further reduction in the total time). Still, the 16×4 distribution is slightly better, which is due to the behaviour of phase 1 of the row broadcast. This phase has a small column rebroadcast mixed in, for column values that became invalid; the rebroadcast is relatively costly as it involves b separate get operations. This also explains the relatively high cost of phase 1 of the row broadcast for $M = 1$. One might expect the column broadcast time to vanish for $M = 64$, but this does not happen because of the small row broadcast mixed in. Note that for the current problem size $n = 10\,000$ and the choice $M = 8$, the maximum broadcast length of a row or column is only $n/M = 1250$, so that using a one-phase broadcast would be a bit faster.

Our ultimate goal is to reach the highest possible performance for LU decomposition, tackling large problems and using a large number of processors. As a result of the numerical experiments carried out so far, we know that the best route towards our goal requires two-phase broadcasts, an algorithmic block size $b \approx 64$, and a (nearly) square distribution.

Table 2.5 presents the time of all the supersteps of the LU decomposition for a run with a large matrix of size $n = 100\,000$ on a large number of processor cores, $p = 256$. This problem is solved in about 19 minutes, which translates into a computing rate of 0.594 Tflop/s (1 Tflop = 1 teraflop = 10^{12} flop). We also ran the problem on 1024 cores, but this slowed the computation down, as it took 4206 s. To achieve even higher rates, the problem size must be enlarged and the number of cores increased. Also, the use of optimized BLAS functions instead of our plain C functions would further increase the speed. Exercise 2.11 shows how to do this.

For comparison, Cori ranks number 13 on the TOP500 list of supercomputers (November 2019, [279]), and this ranking has been obtained by running the High-Performance LINPACK benchmark (HPL) [90] with $n = 6\,984\,960$ and $p = 622\,336$, thereby reaching a supersonic speed of 14 015 Tflop/s.

Table 2.5 Breakdown of execution time (in s) of LU decomposition with two-phase broadcasts on 256 cores of Cori. The matrix size is $n = 100\,000$ and the algorithmic block size is $b = 64$. The matrix distribution is 16×16 cyclic.

Superstep	Operation	Time
(0)/(1)	local pivot search	69
(2)/(3)	global pivot search	71
(4)/(5)	row swap	51
(6)	phase 0 of column broadcast	72
(7)	phase 1 of column broadcast	189
(0′)	instant matrix update	73
(8)	postponed row permutation	2
(9)	phase 0 of postponed row broadcast	49
(10)	phase 1 of postponed row broadcast	73
(9′)	postponed rank-1 update	48
(Rb)	postponed rank-b update	424
Total	LU decomposition	1122

To understand the results of Table 2.5, we benchmarked the partition of eight Haswell nodes used, which gave the BSP parameters $p = 256$, $r = 9.363$ Gflop/s, $g = 1845$ (197 ns), and $l = 5\,077\,339$ (542 μs). All supersteps from the table are performed n times, except supersteps (8) and (Rb), which are performed n/b times. The predicted time for n synchronizations is $n \cdot 542$ μs $= 54.2$ s. Supersteps $(0')$, $(9')$, and (Rb) were measured separately by adding an extra synchronization. As in quantum mechanics, measuring a system disturbs it! Superstep (8) shows the benefits of procrastination: the superstep has become cheap, because many rows are permuted at the same time. Although the communication cost of a single row swap and a row broadcast is the same, $n^2 g/\sqrt{p}$, see the derivation of eqn (2.35), the time required for n/b times permuting $b = 64$ rows is a factor 51 times less than the time of n row broadcasts, mainly due to the removed synchronizations. Superstep (Rb) takes 424 s, which means that it performs its roughly $2n^3/3$ flops at a rate of 1.57 Tflop/s, or 6.14 Gflop/s per core, somewhat below the benchmarked rate of 9.363 Gflop/s.

We can predict the time of the row and column broadcasts in a more precise, quantitative way by using the theoretical cost $n^2 g/\sqrt{p} + 2nl$ together with benchmark results for r, g, and l. To do this, the BSP cost in flops is converted into a time in seconds by multiplying with $t_{\text{flop}} = 1/r$. The predicted communication time of the row broadcasts is 123 s, and the predicted synchronization time 108 s, summing up to 231 s, whereas the measured time is 122 s. The prediction for the column broadcasts is also 231 s, whereas the measured time is 261 s. Here, we observe that synchronization is expensive and that it still has an impact for a problem size as large as $n = 100\,000$.

The theoretical BSP model does not take **header overhead** into account, that is, the cost of sending address information together with the data itself. The BSP cost model is solely based on the amount of data sent, not on that of the associated headers. In most practical cases, this matches reality, because the header overhead is often insignificant. If we benchmark g also in such a situation, and use this (lower) value of g, the BSP model will predict communication time well. We may call this value the **optimistic g-value**. If, however, the data is communicated by put or get operations of very small size, say fewer than five reals, such overhead becomes significant. In the extreme case of single words as data, we have a high header overhead which is proportional to the amount of data sent. We can then just include this overhead in the cost of sending the data itself, which leads to a higher, **pessimistic g-value**. This is the value measured by bspbench. Exercise 1.3 asks you to modify bspbench to measure optimistic g-values. The header overhead actually includes more than just the cost of sending header information; for instance, it also includes the overhead of a call to the bsp_put function. Such costs are conveniently lumped together. In the transition range, for a data size in the range 1–5 reals, the BSP model does not accurately predict communication time, but we have an upper and a lower bound. It would be easy to extend the model to include an extra parameter (called the block size B in the BSP* model [24]), but this would be at the expense of simplicity. We shall stick to the simple BSP model, and rely on our common sense to choose between optimism and pessimism.

For LU decomposition, using the optimistic g-value would be more appropriate than using the pessimistic value as we did, since we send data in large blocks. This would lower the predicted time of the row and column broadcasts.

Returning to the fashion world, did the BSP model survive the catwalk? Guided by the BSP model, we obtained a theoretically superior algorithm with a better spread of the communication tasks over the processors. Our experiments show that this algorithm is also superior in practice for large enough problem sizes. The BSP model helped explain our experimental results, and it can tell us when to expect significant benefits. The superstep concept of the BSP model helped us to zoom in on certain parts of the computation and enabled us to understand what happens in those parts. Qualitatively speaking, we can say that the BSP model passed an important test. The BSP model also gave us a rough indication of the expected time for different parts of the algorithm. These quantitative predictions were reasonably close to our measurements.

2.8 Bibliographic notes

2.8.1 Matrix distributions

Almost all matrix distributions that have been proposed for use in parallel dense matrix computations are Cartesian. The term 'Cartesian' was first used in this context by Bisseling and van de Vorst [34] and Van de Velde [294] in articles on LU decomposition. Van de Velde even defines a matrix distribution as being Cartesian. (Still, non-Cartesian matrix distributions exist and they are useful for sparse matrices, see Chapter 4.) An early example of a Cartesian distribution is the cyclic row distribution, which is just the $p \times 1$ cyclic distribution. Chu and George [67] use this distribution to show that explicit row swaps lead to a good load balance during the whole LU decomposition and that the resulting savings in computation time outweigh the additional communication time.

In 1985, O'Leary and Stewart [234] introduced the square cyclic distribution in the field of parallel matrix computations; they called it **torus assignment**. In their scheme, the matrix elements and the corresponding computations are assigned to a torus of processors, which executes a data-flow algorithm. Over the years, this distribution has acquired names such as **cyclic storage** [169], **grid distribution** [295], **scattered square decomposition** [113], and **torus-wrap mapping** [148], and it has been used in a wide range of matrix computations. The name 'cyclic distribution' is in general use now, and therefore we use it as well.

Several algorithms based on the square cyclic distribution have been proposed for parallel LU decomposition. Van de Vorst [295] compares the square cyclic distribution with other distributions, such as the square block distribution, which allocates submatrices of size $n/\sqrt{p} \times n/\sqrt{p}$ to processors. The square block distribution leads to a bad load balance, because more and more processors become idle as the computation proceeds. As a result, the computation takes three times longer than with the square cyclic distribution. Fox et al. [113, Chapter 20] present an algorithm for LU decomposition of a banded matrix. They perform a theoretical analysis and give experimental results on a hypercube computer. (A matrix A is **banded** with **lower bandwidth** $b_L \geq 0$ and **upper bandwidth** $b_U \geq 0$ if $a_{ij} = 0$ for $i > j + b_L$ and for $i < j - b_U$.) Bisseling and van de Vorst [34] prove optimality with respect to load balance of the square cyclic distribution, within the class of Cartesian distributions. They also show that the communication time on a square mesh of processors is of the same order, $\mathcal{O}(n^2/\sqrt{p})$, as the load imbalance and that on a complete network the communication volume is $V = \mathcal{O}(n^2\sqrt{p})$. Extending these results, Hendrickson and

Womble [148] show that the square cyclic distribution is advantageous for a large class of matrix computations, including LU decomposition, QR decomposition, and Householder tridiagonalization. They present experimental results for various ratios M/N of the $M \times N$ cyclic distribution.

O'Leary and Stewart [235] proposed the block-cyclic distribution back in 1986, giving it the name **block-torus assignment**. It is widely used, for example in the Scalable Linear Algebra Package (ScaLAPACK) [35, 66] and in the High-Performance LINPACK benchmark (HPL) [90]. Both ScaLAPACK and HPL impose an equal algorithmic and distribution block size: $b = \beta$. Hendrickson, Jessup, and Smith [144] present a blocked parallel eigensystem solver based on the square cyclic distribution, and they argue in favour of blocking of algorithms but not of distributions, that is taking $b > 1$ and $\beta = 1$. PLAPACK [293] from 1997 allows an arbitrary choice $b \neq \beta$. The recent package Elemental [251] from 2013 with a simpler design based on the choice $\beta = 1$ outperforms ScaLAPACK on several dense matrix computations (including Cholesky factorization) on 8192 cores of an IBM Blue Gene/P.

2.8.2 Collective communication

The idea of spreading data of long vectors before broadcasting them was proposed by Barnett *et al.* [17, 18], who call the two phases of their broadcast 'scatter' and 'collect' (the latter is now known as 'allgather'). Their Interprocessor Collective Communication library is an implementation of broadcasting and related operations; it also implements hybrid methods for broadcasting vectors of medium length. Chan *et al.* [61] survey collective communication operations within the message-passing model for multidimensional processor meshes. They extensively analyse the broadcast, reduce, allreduce, scatter, gather, allgather, reduce-scatter, and allreduce operations. The reduce operation is an associative operation such as summing, with one input operand from each processor; the output ends up on one root processor. The allreduce is the same, except that the result ends up on all processors.

In the BSP model, the cost analysis of a two-phase broadcast becomes easy. Juurlink [170] presents and analyses a set of communication primitives including broadcasts for different vector lengths. Bisseling [29] implements a two-phase broadcast and shows that it reduces communication time significantly in LU decomposition. This implementation, however, has not been optimized by sending data in blocks, and hence the g-values involved are pessimistic.

The collective communications of the MPICH2 implementation of MPI have been optimized by Thakur, Rabenseifner, and Gropp [285]. Their broadcast for long vectors and large p has two phases, starting with a scatter phase using a **binomial tree** algorithm, followed by an allgather phase based on either **recursive doubling** ($P(s)$ communicating with $P(s + 2^k)$ or $P(s - 2^k)$ in step k) or a **ring algorithm** (which moves blocks of size n/p around a processor ring). This gains a factor of two compared to the old MPICH1 implementation and it also beats the vendor's implementation by a factor of 1.5 on an IBM SP machine. The MPICH2 implementation distinguishes between short and long vectors, with experimentally determined switching points. It also distinguishes between the case where p is a power of two, and the case where it is not; the latter case complicates collective communication algorithms.

Nishtala *et al.* [231] developed a set of one-sided collective communication algorithms for the Partitioned Global Address Space (PGAS) programming model and implemented them in the UPC language [104]. They applied the collectives in matrix multiplication, Cholesky factorization, and 3D fast Fourier transform; often the UPC collectives outperformed the MPI ones.

2.8.3 Parallel matrix computations

The handbook on matrix computations by Golub and Van Loan [124] is a standard reference for the field of numerical linear algebra. It treats sequential LU decomposition in full detail, discussing issues such as roundoff errors, partial and complete pivoting, matrix scaling, and iterative improvement. The book provides a wealth of references for further study. Section 1.6 of this handbook treats parallel matrix multiplication and Section 3.6 looks at parallel LU decomposition with tournament pivoting and the block-cyclic distribution with block size $b = \beta$. The cost analysis is based on the message-passing model, with the cost of a message given by eqn (1.19). The book on matrix algorithms by Stewart [276] also treats many different matrix computations, such as LU and QR decomposition and the singular value decomposition (SVD). The book by Dongarra, Duff, Sorensen, and van der Vorst [95] is a very readable introduction to numerical linear algebra on high-performance computers. It treats architectures, parallelization techniques, BLAS, and the direct and iterative solution of linear systems and eigensystems, with particular attention to sparse systems.

Software for sequential LU decomposition and other matrix computations is provided by LAPACK [7], which also has a limited capability for exploiting shared-memory parallelism through the use of parallel BLAS. A distributed-memory fully parallel version is ScaLAPACK [35, 66]. These two widely used packages contain solvers for linear systems, eigenvalue systems, linear least-squares problems, and singular-value problems, for dense symmetric and unsymmetric matrices. The packages also contain several solvers for banded, triangular, and tridiagonal matrices. The current version of ScaLAPACK is available on top of the portability layer MPI. Horvitz and Bisseling [163] discuss how ScaLAPACK can be ported to BSPlib and they show for LU decomposition that savings in communication time can be obtained by using BSPlib.

Several BSP algorithms have been designed for LU decomposition. Gerbessiotis and Valiant [122] present a BSP algorithm for Gauss–Jordan elimination, a matrix computation that is quite similar to LU decomposition; their algorithm uses the square cyclic distribution and a binary tree-based broadcast (which is less efficient than a two-phase broadcast). McColl [213] offers a BSP algorithm for LU decomposition without pivoting that is very different from other LU decomposition algorithms. He views the computation as a directed acyclic graph forming a regular 3D mesh of $n \times n \times n$ vertices, where vertex (i, j, k) represents matrix element a_{ij} in stage k. The absence of pivoting allows for more flexibility in scheduling the computation. Instead of processing the vertices layer by layer, that is, stage after stage, as is done in other algorithms, McColl's algorithm processes the vertices in cubic blocks, each representing a **task**, with at most p blocks handled in parallel. This algorithm has time complexity $\mathcal{O}(n^3/p + n^2g/\sqrt{p} + \sqrt{p}l)$, which may be attractive because of the low synchronization cost. The same method is also applicable to Cholesky factorization for symmetric positive definite matrices.

Ashcraft [10] was the first to show theoretically that LU decomposition can be carried out with a communication cost less than $\mathcal{O}(n^2g/\sqrt{p})$: by aggregating matrix updates he reduces the communication volume to $V = \mathcal{O}(n^2p^{1/3})$, which means that the communication cost becomes $V/p = \mathcal{O}(n^2/p^{2/3})$. He proposes the same basic idea as used in 3D matrix multiplication (see Exercise 2.6), namely replicating the target update matrix to introduce a third dimension, thereby reducing the total communication requirements in all dimensions together. This is at the expense of extra required memory. Solomonik and Demmel [273] incorporate this basic idea into a practical LU decomposition, by replicating the update matrix A_{22} from Fig. 2.6 to reduce communication compared to the common 2D algorithm. They provide a generalization called 2.5D which allows to tune the amount of replication, creating $c \le p^{1/3}$ copies of A_{22}, thereby reducing the communication cost by a factor of $\sqrt{c}$. The algorithm uses tournament pivoting and it employs a block-cyclic distribution with block size $b = \beta = n/\sqrt{pc}$.

Ballard *et al.* [16] provide lower bounds on communication for many different parallel dense matrix computations. A lower bound on the number of data words sent or received by a processor with local memory of size M is $\Omega(N_{\text{flops}}/\sqrt{M})$ and a lower bound on the number of messages is $\Omega(N_{\text{flops}}/M^{3/2})$, where N_{flops} is the number of flops to be performed by the processor. A common case is $M = n^2/p$ and $N_{\text{flops}} = 2n^3/p$ for 2D matrix multiplication, and $M = n^2/p^{2/3}$ for 3D matrix multiplication.

Parallel Linear Algebra Software for Multicore Architectures (PLASMA) [4, 51] is a software package for shared-memory parallel computers that relies on a task scheduler for efficient multithreading of algorithms, with tasks defined by operations on **tiles** (small square matrix blocks). PLASMA has recently been ported to use OpenMP and in particular its dynamic task scheduler [314]. Other parallel matrix computation packages are ELPA (Eigenvalue soLvers for Petascale Applications)[210] for the direct, massively parallel solution of symmetric or Hermitian dense eigenvalue problems, such as those that occur in electronic structure theory, and Elemental [251].

. . . .

2.9 EXERCISES

Exercise 2.1 Find a matrix distribution for parallel LU decomposition that is optimal with respect to computational load balance in all stages of the computation. The distribution need not be Cartesian. When would this distribution be applicable?

Exercise 2.2 Describe a BSP algorithm for the pivot search part of an LU decomposition with **complete pivoting**, that is searching the whole active submatrix for the largest pivot element. This gives additional stability to the LU decomposition, because it limits the growth of matrix elements in the algorithm. Analyse the BSP cost of the search. Assume that the matrix is distributed by a square cyclic distribution. How does complete pivoting affect the other parts of the LU decomposition algorithm?

Exercise 2.3 The ratio $M/N = 1$ is close to optimal for the $M \times N$ cyclic distribution used in Algorithm 2.8 and hence this ratio was assumed in our cost analysis. The optimal ratio, however, may be slightly different. This is mainly due to an asymmetry in the communication requirements of the algorithm. Explain this by using Table 2.2. Find the ratio M/N with the lowest communication cost, for a fixed number of processors $MN = p$. What is the reduction in communication cost for the optimal ratio, compared with the cost for the ratio $M/N = 1$?

Exercise 2.4 Take a critical look at the benefits of two-phase broadcasting by first running `bsplu` on your own parallel computer for a range of problem sizes and then replacing the two-phase broadcast by a simple one-phase broadcast. Measure the run time for both programs and explain the difference. Gain more insight by timing the broadcast parts separately.

Exercise 2.5 (∗) The **Cholesky factor** of a symmetric positive definite matrix A is defined as the lower triangular matrix L with positive diagonal entries that satisfies $A = LL^T$. (A matrix A is **symmetric** if it equals its transpose, $A = A^T$, and it is **positive definite** if $x^T A x > 0$ for all $x \neq 0$.)

(a) Derive a sequential Cholesky factorization algorithm that is similar to the sequential LU decomposition algorithm without pivoting, Algorithm 2.2. The Cholesky algorithm should save half the flops, because it does not have to compute the upper triangular matrix L^T. Furthermore, pivoting is not needed in the symmetric positive definite case, see [124].

(b) Design a parallel Cholesky factorization algorithm that uses the $M \times N$ cyclic distribution. Take care to communicate only where needed. Analyse the BSP cost of your algorithm.

(c) Implement and test your algorithm.

Exercise 2.6 (∗) Matrix–matrix multiplication is a basic building block in linear algebra computations. The highest computing rates can be achieved by constructing algorithms based on this operation. Consider the matrix product $C = AB$, where A, B, and C are $n \times n$ matrices. We can divide the matrices into submatrices of size $n/q \times n/q$, where we assume that $n \bmod q = 0$. Thus we can write $A = (A_{st})_{0 \le s,t < q}$, and similarly for B and C. We can express the matrix product in terms of submatrix products,

$$C_{st} = \sum_{u=0}^{q-1} A_{su} B_{ut}, \quad \text{for } 0 \le s,t < q. \tag{2.39}$$

On a sequential computer with a cache, this is even the best way of computing C, since we can choose the submatrix size such that two submatrices and their product fit into the cache. On a parallel computer, we can compute the product in 2D or 3D fashion; the latter approach was proposed by Aggarwal, Chandra, and Snir [3], as an example of the use of their LPRAM model. (See also [2] for experimental results, [213, 216] for a BSP analysis, and [166] for an analysis of the trade-off between available memory and necessary communication volume for 2D and 3D algorithms.)

(a) Let $p = q^2$ be the number of processors. Assume that the matrices are distributed by the square block distribution, so that processor $P(s, t)$ holds the submatrices A_{st} and B_{st} on input, and C_{st} on output. Design a BSP algorithm for the computation of $C = AB$ where $P(s, t)$ computes C_{st}. Analyse the cost and memory use of your algorithm.

(b) Let $p = q^3$ be the number of processors. Design a BSP algorithm for the computation of $C = AB$ where processor $P(s, t, u)$ with $0 \leq s, t, u < q$ computes the product $C_{stu} = A_{su}B_{ut}$. Choose a suitable distribution for the input and output matrices that spreads the data evenly. Analyse the cost and memory use of your algorithm. When is the 3D algorithm preferred? Hint: assume that on input the submatrix A_{su} is distributed over $P(s, *, u)$.

(c) Implement your 2D and 3D algorithms and compare their performance.

Exercise 2.7 (∗) A **boolean matrix** contains values 0 (**false**) and 1 (**true**). Assume that A and B are dense boolean matrices of size $n \times n$. The **boolean matrix product** $C = AB$ is the $n \times n$ boolean matrix defined by

$$c_{ij} = \bigvee_{k=0}^{n-1} (a_{ik} \wedge b_{kj}), \quad \text{for } 0 \leq i, j < n. \tag{2.40}$$

Boolean matrix multiplication has numerous applications, for instance in finding the transitive closure of a directed graph, and in recognizing context-free languages in a text.

(a) Design an efficient sequential algorithm for boolean matrix multiplication based on executing a triple loop over the indices i, j, k. Be sure to perform computations only if they are really needed. What is the best ordering of the indices, for the moment ignoring cache issues? What is the worst-case time complexity of your algorithm? And the best-case complexity?

(b) Design a parallel algorithm for boolean matrix multiplication. Assume that we have worst-case input, so that we cannot benefit from exploiting any specific bit pattern of the input matrices. Assume that A and B are distributed by the square block distribution for $p = q^2$ processors and that C also has to be distributed in this way. For simplicity, assume that n and q are powers of two. Denote the local submatrix of A on processor $P(s, t)$ by A_{st}, and similarly for B and C.

(c) Implement your algorithm using an unsigned integer to store a number of bits. Choose this number on the basis of the word size of your machine. Use the bit-wise operations & and | of the C language to implement the logical operations $\wedge$ and $\vee$. The C language stores 2D arrays by rows, so it is easy to access a matrix by rows. If you need to access a matrix by columns, however, it is best to store its transpose.

(d) Test your implementation by using dense input matrices that are randomly filled with binary values. Perform numerical experiments for various matrix sizes n.

(e) Assume that we only have $\mathcal{O}(n^2/p)$ memory available per processor. Split your algorithm into q computation supersteps and $q - 1$ communication supersteps. In superstep $(2r)$, $0 \leq r < q$, processor $P(s,t)$ uses submatrices $A_{s,(t+r) \bmod q}$ and $B_{(s+r) \bmod q,t}$ to update C_{st}. It obtains these submatrices beforehand in superstep $(2r - 1)$, $1 \leq r < q$. This yields a variant of Cannon's algorithm [55]. Superstep (0) does not need to obtain data by communication, because all the necessary data is already available locally. What is the BSP cost of this algorithm? Can you think of a (rare) situation where you do not need to obtain a complete submatrix $A_{s,(t+r) \bmod q}$ or $B_{(s+r) \bmod q,t}$?

(f) To optimize the parallel algorithm, we can use a technique introduced by Arlazarov and three colleagues [9] that became known as the Four-Russians method. (It is uncertain, however, whether all authors are actually Russian.) Split the matrix A into small $b \times b$ blocks, with b a power of two, and consider the data obtained by processor $P(s,t)$ from A as a collection of blocks. For each block X obtained from A, precompute and store $X\mathbf{v}$ for all 2^b possible vectors $\mathbf{v}$ in a lookup table. Use this table for multiplying X by column parts (of length b) of the matrix B, giving column parts (also of length b) to be $\vee$-ed into the matrix C. Furthermore, create a 2D lookup table of all 4^b possible operations $\mathbf{u} \vee \mathbf{v}$ for use in updates of the matrix C. To keep memory scalable, the block size must satisfy $b \leq \log_2(n/q)$.

Analyse the total cost of creating the lookup tables, and the cost of using them. In the analysis, you can assume that all operations, whether bit operations or integer operations, have the same unit cost. Try to find an optimal value of b, both theoretically and experimentally.

Exercise 2.8 (**) Once upon a time, there was a Mainframe computer that had great difficulty in multiplying floating-point numbers and preferred to add or subtract them instead. So the Queen decreed that computations should be carried out with a minimum of multiplications. A young Prince, Volker Strassen [278], set out to save multiplications in the Queen's favourite pastime, computing the product of 2×2 matrices on the Royal Mainframe,

$$\begin{bmatrix} c_{00} & c_{01} \\ c_{10} & c_{11} \end{bmatrix} = \begin{bmatrix} a_{00} & a_{01} \\ a_{10} & a_{11} \end{bmatrix} \begin{bmatrix} b_{00} & b_{01} \\ b_{10} & b_{11} \end{bmatrix}. \tag{2.41}$$

At the time, this took eight multiplications and four additions. The young Prince slew one multiplication, but at great cost: fourteen new additions sprang up. Nobody knew how he had obtained his method, but there were rumours and speculations, and indeed the Prince had drunk from the magic potion. Later, three additions were slain by the Princes Paterson and Winograd and the resulting Algorithm 2.9 was announced in the whole Kingdom. The Queen's subjects happily noted that the new method, with seven multiplications and fifteen additions, performed the same task as before. No more additions could be slain with simple means. The Queen herself lived happily ever after and multiplied many more 2×2 matrices.

(a) Join the inhabitants of the Mainframe Kingdom and check that the task is carried out correctly.

Algorithm 2.9 Strassen 2×2 matrix–matrix multiplication.

---

input: $A, B : 2 \times 2$ matrix.
output: $C : 2 \times 2$ matrix, $C = AB$.

$$
\begin{aligned}
&l_0 := a_{00}; && r_0 := b_{00}; \\
&l_1 := a_{01}; && r_1 := b_{10}; \\
&l_2 := a_{10} + a_{11}; && r_2 := b_{01} - b_{00}; \\
&l_3 := a_{00} - a_{10}; && r_3 := b_{11} - b_{01}; \\
&l_4 := l_2 - a_{00}; && r_4 := r_3 + b_{00}; \\
&l_5 := a_{01} - l_4; && r_5 := b_{11}; \\
&l_6 := a_{11}; && r_6 := b_{10} - r_4;
\end{aligned}
$$

for $i := 0$ **to** 6 **do**
 $m_i := l_i r_i;$

$$
\begin{aligned}
&t_0 := m_0 + m_4; \\
&t_1 := t_0 + m_3;
\end{aligned}
$$

$$
\begin{aligned}
&c_{00} := m_0 + m_1; \\
&c_{01} := t_0 + m_2 + m_5; \\
&c_{10} := t_1 + m_6; \\
&c_{11} := t_1 + m_2;
\end{aligned}
$$

(b) Now replace the matrix elements by submatrices of size $n/2 \times n/2$,

$$
\begin{bmatrix} C_{00} & C_{01} \\ C_{10} & C_{11} \end{bmatrix} = \begin{bmatrix} A_{00} & A_{01} \\ A_{10} & A_{11} \end{bmatrix} \begin{bmatrix} B_{00} & B_{01} \\ B_{10} & B_{11} \end{bmatrix}. \tag{2.42}
$$

The Strassen method can be applied here as well, because it does not rely on the commutativity of the real numbers. (Commutativity, $ab = ba$, holds for real numbers a and b, but in general not for matrices A and B.) This should be beneficial, because multiplication of submatrices is much more expensive than addition of submatrices (and not only on mainframes!). The method requires the multiplication of smaller submatrices. This can again be done using Strassen's method, and so on, until the remaining problem is small and traditional matrix–matrix multiplication is used. The resulting matrix–matrix multiplication algorithm is the Strassen algorithm. We say that the method is applied **recursively**, that is, calling itself on smaller problem sizes. The number of times the original matrix size must be halved to reach the current matrix size is called the **level** of the recursion.

Assume that n is a power of two. Derive a formula that expresses $T(n)$, the time needed to multiply two $n \times n$ matrices, in terms of $T(n/2)$. Use this formula to count the number of flops of the Strassen algorithm with a switch to the traditional method at size $r \times r$, $1 \le r \le n$. (The traditional method computes an $r \times r$ matrix product by performing $r - 1$ floating-point additions and r floating-point multiplications for each of the r^2 elements of the output matrix, thus requiring a total of $2r^3 - r^2$ flops.)

(c) Prove that the Strassen algorithm with $r = 1$ requires $\mathcal{O}(n^{\log_2 7}) \approx \mathcal{O}(n^{2.81})$ flops, which scales better than the $\mathcal{O}(n^3)$ flops of traditional matrix–matrix multiplication. What is the optimal value of the switching parameter r and the corresponding total number of flops? The lowest possible exponent for the cost of matrix–matrix multiplication is commonly called ω. The proof for the Strassen algorithm implies that $\omega < 2.81$, and of course $\omega \geq 2$ must also hold. The current record upper bound, obtained by Le Gall [194], is $\omega < 2.3728639$. Strassen's algorithm is widely used in practice, whereas most algorithms with a lower exponent are mainly of theoretical interest.

(d) Write a traditional matrix–matrix multiplication function and a recursive sequential function that implements the Strassen algorithm. Compare their accuracy for some test matrices.

(e) The addition of two $n/2 \times n/2$ submatrices of an $n \times n$ matrix A, such as the computation of $A_{10} + A_{11}$, is a fundamental operation in the Strassen algorithm. Assume that this is done in parallel by $p = q^2$ processors, where q, n are powers of two with $q \leq n/2$. Which distribution for A is better: the square block distribution or the square cyclic distribution? Why? (Loyens and Moonen [202] answered this question first.)

(f) Recursion is a gift to the programmer, because it takes the burden of data management from her shoulders. For parallelism, recursion is not always a blessing, because it zooms in on one task to be carried out while a parallel computation tries to perform many tasks at the same time. (This is explained in more detail in Section 3.3, where a recursive fast Fourier transform is cast into nonrecursive form to prepare the ground for parallelization.) We can create parallelism by stopping the recursion early, at matrix size $r' \times r'$, and outputting a pair of matrices (L_i, R_i) each time the recursion reaches that size. The output can be stored in two arrays of matrices, where each array will contain $7^{\log_2(n/r')}$ matrices of size $r' \times r'$. The multiplications $M_i := L_i R_i$ can then be carried out in parallel. The matrices M_i can be read as input by a recursive algorithm that combines them appropriately, similar to the recursive splitting algorithm. (This approach was proposed by McColl [214].)

Implement a parallel Strassen algorithm. Use the distribution found in (e) for all submatrices that occur in the splitting and combining parts of the algorithm. Redistribute the data before and after the multiplications $M_i := L_i R_i$ at matrix size $r' \times r'$. Perform each such multiplication on one processor, using the sequential recursive Strassen algorithm and switching to the traditional algorithm at size $r \times r$, where $r \leq r'$. In your implementation, generalize the function `matallocd` from BSPedupack to the 3D case and use the resulting function to allocate space for the two arrays of matrices.

(g) Analyse the BSP cost of the parallel algorithm. Find an upper bound for the load imbalance that occurs because p (a power of four) does not divide the number of multiplication tasks (a power of seven). Discuss the trade-off between computational load imbalance and communication cost and their scaling behaviour as a function of the number of splitting levels. Also analyse the memory requirements. In practice, how would you choose r'?

(h) Measure the run time of your program for different parameters n, p, r, r'. Explain your results.

Exercise 2.9 (∗∗) Householder tridiagonalization decomposes an $n \times n$ symmetric matrix A into $A = Q_1 T Q_1^T$, where Q_1 is an $n \times n$ orthogonal matrix and T an $n \times n$ symmetric tridiagonal matrix. To recall some linear algebra: a square matrix Q is **orthogonal** if $Q^T Q = I$, which is equivalent to $Q^{-1} = Q^T$; a matrix T is **tridiagonal** if $t_{ij} = 0$ for $|i - j| > 1$. (Do not confuse the T in italic font denoting the tridiagonal matrix with the superscript in roman font denoting transposition!)

Tridiagonalization is often a stepping stone to achieving a larger goal, namely solving a real symmetric eigensystem. This problem amounts to decomposing a real symmetric matrix A into $A = QDQ^T$, where Q is orthogonal and D is **diagonal**, that is, $d_{ij} = 0$ for $i \neq j$. The eigenvalues of A are the diagonal elements of D and the corresponding eigenvectors are the columns of Q. It is much easier to solve a symmetric tridiagonal eigensystem and decompose T into $T = Q_2 D Q_2^T$ than to solve the original system. As a result, we obtain $A = (Q_1 Q_2) D (Q_1 Q_2)^T$, which has the required form. Here, we concentrate on the tridiagonalization part of the eigensystem solution, which accounts for the majority of the flops. See [124] for more details.

(a) The central operation in Householder tridiagonalization is the application of a Householder reflection

$$P_{\mathbf{v}} = I_n - \frac{2}{\|\mathbf{v}\|^2} \mathbf{v}\mathbf{v}^T. \tag{2.43}$$

Here, $\mathbf{v} \neq 0$ is a vector of length n with **Euclidean norm** $\|\mathbf{v}\| = \|\mathbf{v}\|_2 = (\sum_{i=0}^{n-1} v_i^2)^{1/2}$. For brevity, we drop the subscript '2' from the norm. As with all our vectors, $\mathbf{v}$ is a column vector, and hence it can also be viewed as an $n \times 1$ matrix. Note that $\mathbf{v}\mathbf{v}^T$ represents an $n \times n$ matrix, in contrast to $\mathbf{v}^T\mathbf{v}$, which is the scalar $\|\mathbf{v}\|^2$. Show that $P_{\mathbf{v}}$ is symmetric and orthogonal. We can apply $P_{\mathbf{v}}$ to a vector $\mathbf{x}$ and obtain

$$P_{\mathbf{v}}\mathbf{x} = \mathbf{x} - \frac{2}{\|\mathbf{v}\|^2} \mathbf{v}\mathbf{v}^T\mathbf{x} = \mathbf{x} - \frac{2\mathbf{v}^T\mathbf{x}}{\mathbf{v}^T\mathbf{v}}\mathbf{v}. \tag{2.44}$$

(b) Let $\mathbf{e}_0 = (1, 0, 0, \ldots, 0)^T$. Show that the choice $\mathbf{v} = \mathbf{x} - \|\mathbf{x}\|\mathbf{e}_0$ implies $P_{\mathbf{v}}\mathbf{x} = \|\mathbf{x}\|\mathbf{e}_0$. This means that we have an orthogonal transformation that sets all components of $\mathbf{x}$ to zero, except the first.

(c) Algorithm 2.10 is a sequential algorithm that determines a vector $\mathbf{v}$ such that $P_{\mathbf{v}}\mathbf{x} = \|\mathbf{x}\|\mathbf{e}_0$. For convenience, the algorithm also outputs the corresponding scalar $\beta = 2/\|\mathbf{v}\|^2$ and the norm of the input vector $\mu = \|\mathbf{x}\|$. The vector has been normalized such that $v_0 = 1$. For the memory-conscious, this can save one memory cell when storing $\mathbf{v}$. The algorithm contains a clever trick proposed by Parlett [241] to avoid subtracting nearly equal quantities (which would result in so-called **subtractive cancellation** and severe loss of significant digits). Extend the algorithm to treat the special case $x(1 : n - 1) = 0$ in a sensible way. Now design and implement a parallel version of this algorithm. Assume that the input vector $\mathbf{x}$ is distributed by the cyclic

---

Algorithm 2.10 Sequential Householder reflection.

---

input: $\mathbf{x}$: vector of length n, $n \geq 2$, $x(1 : n-1) \neq 0$.

output: $\mathbf{v}$: vector of length n, such that $v_0 = 1$ and $(I - \beta \mathbf{v}\mathbf{v}^{\mathrm{T}})\mathbf{x} = \mu \mathbf{e}_0$, where $\beta = \frac{2}{\|\mathbf{v}\|^2}$
and $\mu = \|\mathbf{x}\|$.

    function HOUSEHOLDER$(\mathbf{x}, n)$

        {Compute $\alpha = \|x(1 : n-1)\|^2$ and $\mu = \|\mathbf{x}\|$}
        $\alpha := 0$;
        for $i := 1$ **to** $n - 1$ **do**
            $\alpha := \alpha + x_i^2$;
      $\mu := \sqrt{x_0^2 + \alpha}$;

        {Compute $\mathbf{v} = \mathbf{x} - \|\mathbf{x}\|\mathbf{e}_0$}
        if $x_0 \leq 0$ **then**
            $v_0 := x_0 - \mu$;
        else
            $v_0 := \frac{-\alpha}{x_0 + \mu}$;
        for $i := 1$ **to** $n - 1$ **do**
            $v_i := x_i$;

        {Compute β and normalize $\mathbf{v}$}
        $\beta := \frac{2v_0^2}{v_0^2 + \alpha}$;
        for $i := 1$ **to** $n - 1$ **do**
            $v_i := v_i / v_0$;
        $v_0 := 1$;

        return $(\mathbf{v}, \beta, \mu)$

---

distribution over M processors. The output vector $\mathbf{v}$ should become available in the same distribution. Try to keep communication to a minimum. What is the BSP cost?

(d) In stage k of the tridiagonalization, a Householder vector $\mathbf{v}$ is determined for column k of the current matrix A below the diagonal. The matrix is then transformed into $P_k A P_k$, where $P_k = \mathrm{diag}(I_{k+1}, P_{\mathbf{v}})$ is a symmetric matrix. (The notation $\mathrm{diag}(A_0, \ldots, A_r)$ stands for a block-diagonal matrix with blocks $A_0, \ldots, A_r$ on the diagonal.) This sets the elements a_{ik} with $i > k + 1$ to zero, and also the elements a_{kj} with $j > k + 1$; furthermore, it sets $a_{k+1,k}$ and $a_{k,k+1}$ to $\mu = \|A(k + 1 : n - 1, k)\|$. The vector $\mathbf{v}$ without its first component can be stored precisely in the space of the zeros in column k. Our memory-frugality paid off! As a result, we obtain the matrix $Q_1 = P_{n-3} \cdots P_0$, but only in factored form: we have a record of all the $P_{\mathbf{v}}$ matrices used in the process. In most cases, this suffices and Q_1 never needs to be computed explicitly. To see how the current matrix is transformed efficiently into $P_k A P_k$, we only have to look at the submatrix $B = A(k+1: n-1, k+1: n-1)$, which is transformed into $P_v B P_v$. Prove that $P_v B P_v = B - vw^T - wv^T$, where $w = p - (\beta p^T v / 2) v$ with $p = \beta B v$.

(e) Algorithm 2.11 is a sequential tridiagonalization algorithm based on Householder reflections. Verify that this algorithm executes the method just described. Note that in the algorithm we use indices starting from $k+1$ instead of 0. The algorithm does not make use of symmetry yet, but this is easy to achieve, by only performing operations on the lower triangular and diagonal part of A.

(f) Design, implement, and test a parallel version of this algorithm that exploits the symmetry. Assume that A is distributed by the square cyclic distribution, as in the case of LU decomposition. Why do these reasons apply here as well? Choose a suitable vector distribution, assuming that the vectors v, p, and w are distributed over all p processors, for their relevant part starting at index $k+1$, and that this is done in the same way for all three vectors. (We could have chosen to distribute the vectors in the way the vector $v(k+1: n-1)$ becomes available, i.e., in the distribution of column part $A(k+1: n-1, k)$. Why is this a bad idea?) Design the communication supersteps by following the need-to-know principle.

Exercise 2.10 (**) Usually, the decomposition $PA = LU$ is followed by the solution of two triangular systems, $Ly = Pb$ and $Ux = y$; this solves the linear system $Ax = b$. In the parallel case, the distribution in which the triangular matrices L and U are produced by the LU decomposition must be used when solving the triangular systems, because it would be too expensive to redistribute the n^2 matrix elements involved, compared with the $2n^2$ flops required by the triangular system solutions.

(a) Design a basic parallel algorithm for the solution of a lower triangular system $Lx = b$, where L is an $n \times n$ lower triangular matrix, b a given vector of length n, and x the unknown solution vector of length n. Assume that the number of processors is $p = M^2$ and that the matrix is distributed by the square cyclic distribution. Hint: the computation and communication can be organized in a wavefront pattern where, in stage k of the algorithm, computations are carried out for matrix elements l_{ij} with $i+j = k$. After these computations, communication is performed: the owner $P(s,t)$ of an element l_{ij} on the wavefront puts x_j into $P((s+1) \bmod M, t)$, which owns $l_{i+1,j}$, and it also puts $\sum_{r=0}^{j} l_{ir} x_r$ into $P(s, (t+1) \bmod M)$, which owns $l_{i,j+1}$.

(b) Reduce the amount of communication. Communicate only when this is really necessary.

(c) Which processors are working in stage k? Improve the load balance. Hint: consider blocks of size $M \times M$ in the matrix.

(d) Determine the BSP cost of the improved algorithm.

(e) Now assume that the matrix is distributed by the square block-cyclic distribution, defined by eqn (2.38) with $M = N = \sqrt{p}$. How would you generalize your algorithm for solving lower triangular systems to this case? Determine the BSP cost of the generalized algorithm and find the optimal distribution block size β for a computer with given BSP parameters p, g, and l.

Algorithm 2.11 Sequential Householder tridiagonalization.

---

input: $A : n \times n$ symmetric matrix, $A = A^{(0)}$.
output: $A : n \times n$ symmetric matrix, $A = V + T + V^{\mathrm{T}}$, with
$T : n \times n$ symmetric tridiagonal matrix,
$V : n \times n$ matrix with $v_{ij} = 0$ for $i \leq j + 1$,
such that $Q_1 T Q_1^{\mathrm{T}} = A^{(0)}$, where $Q_1 = P_{n-3} \cdots P_0$,
with $P_k = \mathrm{diag}(I_{k+1}, P_{\mathbf{v}^{(k)}})$ and $\mathbf{v}^{(k)} = \begin{bmatrix} 1 \\ V(k+2 : n-1, k) \end{bmatrix}$.

for $k := 0$ **to** $n - 3$ **do**
  $(v(k+1 : n-1), \beta, \mu) := \text{Householder}(A(k+1 : n-1, k), n-k-1)$;

  for $i := k + 1$ **to** $n - 1$ **do**
    $p_i := 0$;
    for $j := k + 1$ **to** $n - 1$ **do**
      $p_i := p_i + a_{ij} v_j$;
    $p_i := \beta p_i$;

  $\gamma := 0$;
  for $i := k + 1$ **to** $n - 1$ **do**
    $\gamma := \gamma + p_i v_i$;
  $\gamma := \beta \gamma / 2$;
  for $i := k + 1$ **to** $n - 1$ **do**
    $w_i := p_i - \gamma v_i$;

  $a_{k+1,k} := \mu; a_{k,k+1} := \mu$;
  for $i := k + 2$ **to** $n - 1$ **do**
    $a_{ik} := v_i; a_{ki} := v_i$;

  for $i := k + 1$ **to** $n - 1$ **do**
    for $j := k + 1$ **to** $n - 1$ **do**
      $a_{ij} := a_{ij} - v_i w_j - w_i v_j$;

(f) To avoid redistributing matrices, the same distribution should be used for the triangular system solution as for the LU decomposition, that is the distribution should be square cyclic. Implement your algorithm for this distribution in a function bspltriang. Write a similar function bsputriang that solves upper triangular systems. Combine bsplu, bspltriang, and bsputriang into one program bsplinsol that solves a linear system of equations $A\mathbf{x} = \mathbf{b}$. The program has to permute $\mathbf{b}$ into $P_{\pi^{-1}}\mathbf{b}$, where π is the partial pivoting permutation produced by the LU decomposition. Measure the execution time of the LU decomposition and the triangular system solutions for various p and n.

Exercise 2.11 ($**$) The LU decomposition function `bsplu` is educational and it can be optimized further. Your goal now is to turn `bsplu` into a fast program that is suitable for a production environment where every flop/s counts. Optimize the program gradually, taking care to observe the effect of each modification separately. Measure the gains (or losses) achieved and explain your results.

(a) Replace the matrix multiplication function of `bsplu` by a call to the DGEMM function from the BLAS library. The syntax of DGEMM is

$$\text{DGEMM}\quad(\text{transa}, \quad \text{transb}, \quad \text{m}, \quad \text{n}, \quad \text{k}, \quad \text{alpha}, \quad \text{pa}, \quad \text{lda},$$
$$\text{pb}, \quad \text{ldb}, \quad \text{beta}, \quad \text{pc}, \quad \text{ldc});$$

This corresponds to the operation $C := \alpha \hat{A}\hat{B} + \beta C$, where $\hat{A}$ is an $m \times k$ matrix, $\hat{B}$ a $k \times n$ matrix, C an $m \times n$ matrix, and α and β are scalars. Here, $\hat{A} = A$ if `transa='n'` and $\hat{A} = A^T$ if `transa='t'`, where the matrix A is the matrix that is actually stored in the memory, and similarly for $\hat{B}$. The parameter `pa` is a pointer to the 1D array that stores the matrix A. The integer `lda` is the leading dimension of A, that is, `lda` determines how the 2D matrix A is stored in the 1D array `pa`: element a_{ij} is located in position $i + j \cdot$`lda`. This means that matrix elements are stored column-wise. Similarly, `ldb` and `ldc` determine the storage format of B and C.

The data format assumed by DGEMM is that of the Fortran language, with matrices stored by columns, whereas in the C language matrices are stored by rows. To hand over a matrix A stored by rows from the calling C program to the Fortran-speaking DGEMM subroutine, we just tell the subroutine that it receives the matrix A^T stored by columns. Therefore, the subroutine should perform the update $C^T := \alpha \hat{B}^T \hat{A}^T + \beta C^T$, multiplying A and B in the reverse order. No explicit transposition is needed, and both `trans` parameters should therefore be set to `'n'`.

(b) Try to find a version of DGEMM that is tuned to your machine. Most machine vendors provide extremely efficient BLAS in assembler language; DGEMM is their showcase function which should approach theoretical peak performance. If such a tuned version is not available, use the autotuning ATLAS package [311] to create one. Find the optimal algorithmic block size when using DGEMM, for a suitable choice of n and p. Explain the relation between algorithmic block size and performance.

(c) Where possible, replace other computations by calls to BLAS functions. In the current version of the program, how much time is spent in computation? How much in communication?

(d) The **high-performance put** function `bsp_hpput` of BSPlib has exactly the same syntax as the `bsp_put` function:

$$\text{bsp\_hpput}(\text{pid}, \quad \text{source}, \quad \text{dest}, \quad \text{offset}, \quad \text{nbytes});$$

It does not provide the safety of buffering at the source and destination that `bsp_put` gives. The read and write operations can in principle occur at any time during the superstep. Therefore, the user must ensure safety by taking care that different communication operations do not interfere. The primary aim of using this primitive is to save the memory of the buffers. Sometimes, this makes the difference between being able to solve a problem or not. A beneficial side effect is that this saves time as well. There also exists a `bsp_hpget` operation, with syntax

`bsp_hpget(pid, source, offset, dest, nbytes);`

which should be used with the same care as `bsp_hpput`.

In the LU decomposition program, matrix data is often put into temporary arrays and not directly into the matrix itself, so that there is no need for additional buffering by the system. Change the `bsp_puts` into `bsp_hpputs` wherever this is useful and allowed, perhaps after a few minor modifications. What is the effect?

(e) Any ideas for further improvement?

3

The fast Fourier transform

3.1 The problem

Fourier analysis studies the decomposition of functions into their frequency components. The functions may represent a piano sonata by Mozart recorded 50 years ago, a blurred picture of a star taken by the Hubble Space Telescope before its mirrors were repaired, or a computed tomography (CT) scan of your chest. It is often easier to improve a function if we can work directly with its frequency components. Enhancing desired frequencies or removing undesired ones makes the music more pleasing to your ears. Fourier methods help in deblurring satellite pictures and they are crucial in the filtered backprojection method for reconstructing medical images from tomographic measurements.

Let $f : \mathbf{R} \to \mathbf{C}$ be a **T-periodic** function, that is, a function with $f(t + T) = f(t)$ for all $t \in \mathbf{R}$. The **Fourier series** associated with f is defined by

$$\tilde{f}(t) = \sum_{k=-\infty}^{\infty} c_k e^{2\pi i k t / T}, \tag{3.1}$$

where the **Fourier coefficients** c_k are given by

$$c_k = \frac{1}{T} \int_0^T f(t) e^{-2\pi i k t / T} \, dt \tag{3.2}$$

and i denotes the complex number with $i^2 = -1$. (To avoid confusion, we ban the index i from this chapter.) Coefficient c_k can be viewed as the amplitude of the function component with frequency k/T. Under relatively mild assumptions, such as piecewise smoothness, it can be proven that the Fourier series converges for every t. A function is called **smooth** if it is continuous and differentiable, and its derivative is also continuous. A property is said to hold **piecewise** if each finite interval of its domain can be cut up into a finite number of pieces where the property holds; it need not hold at the end points of the pieces. A piecewise smooth function satisfies $\tilde{f}(t) = f(t)$ in points of continuity; in the other points, $\tilde{f}$ is the average of the left and right limit of f. (For more details, see [46, Chapter 2].) If f is

Parallel Scientific Computation: A Structured Approach Using BSP. Second Edition. Rob H. Bisseling,
Oxford University Press (2020). © Rob H. Bisseling.
DOI: 10.1093/oso/9780198788348.001.0001

real-valued, we can use Euler's formula $e^{i\theta} = \cos\theta + i\sin\theta$, and eqns (3.1) and (3.2) to obtain a real-valued Fourier series expressed in sine and cosine functions.

On digital computers, signal or image functions are represented by their values at a finite number of sample points. A compact disc contains 44 100 sample points for each second of recorded music. A high-resolution digital image may contain 4096 by 4096 picture elements (**pixels**). On an unhappy day in the future, you might find your chest being cut by a CT scanner into slices, resulting in a discretized volume with 1024 by 1024 by 1024 volume elements (**voxels**). In all these cases, we obtain a discrete approximation to the continuous world.

Suppose we are interested in computing the Fourier coefficients of a T-periodic function f which is sampled at n points $t_j = jT/n$, with $j = 0, 1, \ldots, n-1$. Using the trapezoidal rule for numerical integration on the interval $[0, T]$ and using $f(0) = f(T)$, we obtain an approximation

$$c_k = \frac{1}{T} \int_0^T f(t)e^{-2\pi ikt/T} \, dt$$

$$\approx \frac{1}{T} \cdot \frac{T}{n} \left(\frac{f(0)}{2} + \sum_{j=1}^{n-1} f(t_j)e^{-2\pi ikt_j/T} + \frac{f(T)}{2} \right)$$

$$= \frac{1}{n} \sum_{j=0}^{n-1} f(t_j)e^{-2\pi ijk/n}. \tag{3.3}$$

The **discrete Fourier transform** (DFT) of a vector $\mathbf{x} = (x_0, \ldots, x_{n-1})^T \in \mathbf{C}^n$ can be defined as the vector $\mathbf{y} = (y_0, \ldots, y_{n-1})^T \in \mathbf{C}^n$ with

$$y_k = \sum_{j=0}^{n-1} x_j e^{-2\pi ijk/n}, \quad \text{for } 0 \le k < n. \tag{3.4}$$

(Different conventions exist regarding the sign of the exponent.) Thus, eqn (3.3) has the form of a DFT, with $x_j = f(t_j)/n$ for $0 \le j < n$. It is easy to see that the inverse DFT is given by

$$x_j = \frac{1}{n} \sum_{k=0}^{n-1} y_k e^{2\pi ijk/n}, \quad \text{for } 0 \le j < n. \tag{3.5}$$

A straightforward implementation of eqn (3.4) would require $n-1$ complex additions and n complex multiplications for each vector component y_k, assuming that factors of the form $e^{-2\pi ik/n}$ with k an integer have been precomputed and are available in a table. A complex addition has the form $(a + bi) + (c + di) = (a + c) + (b + d)i$, which requires two real additions. A complex multiplication has the form $(a + bi)(c + di) = (ac - bd) + (ad + bc)i$, which requires one real addition, one real subtraction, and four real multiplications, that is, a total of six flops. Therefore, the straightforward computation of the DFT costs $n(2(n-1) + 6n) = 8n^2 - 2n$ flops.

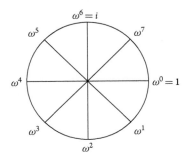

Figure 3.1 Roots of unity ω^k, with $\omega = \omega_8 = e^{-2\pi i/8}$, shown in the complex plane.

It is often convenient to use matrix notation to express DFT algorithms. Define the $n \times n$ **Fourier matrix** F_n by

$$(F_n)_{j,k} = \omega_n^{j \cdot k}, \quad \text{for } 0 \leq j, k < n, \tag{3.6}$$

where

$$\omega_n = e^{-2\pi i/n}. \tag{3.7}$$

We write the definition this way, to emphasize that the power of ω_n in row j and column k of the matrix is determined by the product $j \cdot k$. Figure 3.1 illustrates the powers of ω_n occurring in the Fourier matrix; these are sometimes called the **roots of unity**.

Example 3.1 Let $n = 4$. Because $\omega_4 = e^{-2\pi i/4} = e^{-\pi i/2} = -i$, it follows that

$$F_4 = \begin{bmatrix} \omega_4^0 & \omega_4^0 & \omega_4^0 & \omega_4^0 \\ \omega_4^0 & \omega_4^1 & \omega_4^2 & \omega_4^3 \\ \omega_4^0 & \omega_4^2 & \omega_4^4 & \omega_4^6 \\ \omega_4^0 & \omega_4^3 & \omega_4^6 & \omega_4^9 \end{bmatrix} = \begin{bmatrix} 1 & 1 & 1 & 1 \\ 1 & -i & -1 & i \\ 1 & -1 & 1 & -1 \\ 1 & i & -1 & -i \end{bmatrix}. \tag{3.8}$$

Useful properties of the Fourier matrix are $F_n^T = F_n$ and $F_n^{-1} = \overline{F_n}/n$, where the bar on F_n denotes the complex conjugate and the superscript 'T' denotes the transposed. The transform $\mathbf{y} := \mathrm{DFT}(\mathbf{x})$ can be written as $\mathbf{y} := F_n\mathbf{x}$, so that the DFT becomes a matrix–vector multiplication. The computation of the DFT is the problem studied in this chapter.

3.2 Sequential recursive fast Fourier transform

The **fast Fourier transform** (FFT) is a fast algorithm for the computation of the DFT. The basic idea of the algorithm is surprisingly simple, which does not mean that it is easy to discover if you have not seen it before. In this section, we apply the idea recursively, as was done by Danielson and Lanczos [76] in 1942. (We have seen a recursive algorithm before, namely quicksort, presented as Algorithm 1.2.)

Assume that n is even. We split the sum of eqn (3.4) into sums of even-indexed and odd-indexed terms, which gives

$$y_k = \sum_{j=0}^{n-1} x_j \omega_n^{jk} = \sum_{j=0}^{n/2-1} x_{2j} \omega_n^{2jk} + \sum_{j=0}^{n/2-1} x_{2j+1} \omega_n^{(2j+1)k}, \quad \text{for } 0 \le k < n. \tag{3.9}$$

By using the equality $\omega_n^2 = \omega_{n/2}$, we can rewrite (3.9) as

$$y_k = \sum_{j=0}^{n/2-1} x_{2j} \omega_{n/2}^{jk} + \omega_n^k \sum_{j=0}^{n/2-1} x_{2j+1} \omega_{n/2}^{jk}, \quad \text{for } 0 \le k < n. \tag{3.10}$$

In the first sum, we recognize a Fourier transform of length $n/2$ of the even components of $\mathbf{x}$. To cast the sum exactly into this form, we must restrict the output indices to the range $0 \le k < n/2$. In the second sum, we recognize a transform of the odd components. This leads to a method for computing the set of coefficients y_k, $0 \le k < n/2$, which uses two Fourier transforms of length $n/2$.

To obtain a method for computing the remaining coefficients y_k, $n/2 \le k < n$, we have to rewrite eqn (3.10). Let $k' = k - n/2$, so that $0 \le k' < n/2$. Substituting $k = k' + n/2$ into eqn (3.10) gives

$$y_{k'+n/2} = \sum_{j=0}^{n/2-1} x_{2j} \omega_{n/2}^{j(k'+n/2)} + \omega_n^{k'+n/2} \sum_{j=0}^{n/2-1} x_{2j+1} \omega_{n/2}^{j(k'+n/2)},$$

$$\text{for } 0 \le k' < n/2. \tag{3.11}$$

By using the equalities $\omega_{n/2}^{n/2} = 1$ and $\omega_n^{n/2} = -1$, and by dropping the primes we obtain

$$y_{k+n/2} = \sum_{j=0}^{n/2-1} x_{2j} \omega_{n/2}^{jk} - \omega_n^k \sum_{j=0}^{n/2-1} x_{2j+1} \omega_{n/2}^{jk}, \quad \text{for } 0 \le k < n/2. \tag{3.12}$$

Comparing eqns (3.10) and (3.12), we see that the sums appearing on the right-hand sides are the same; if we add the sum terms we obtain y_k and if we subtract them we obtain $y_{k+n/2}$. Here, the savings become apparent: we need to compute the sums only once.

Following the basic idea, we can compute a Fourier transform of length n by first computing two Fourier transforms of length $n/2$ and then combining the results, where we assume that the powers of ω needed are available as a table of weights, see Section 3.5. Combining the results requires $n/2$ complex multiplications, $n/2$ complex additions, and $n/2$ complex subtractions, that is, a total of $(6+2+2) \cdot n/2 = 5n$ flops. If we use the DFT for the half-length Fourier transforms, the total flop count is already reduced from $8n^2 - 2n$ to $2 \cdot [8(n/2)^2 - 2(n/2)] + 5n = 4n^2 + 3n$, thereby saving almost a factor of two in computing time. Of course, we can apply the idea recursively, computing the half-length transforms by the same splitting method. The recursion ends when the input length

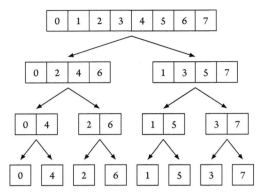

Figure 3.2 Recursive computation of the DFT for $n = 8$. The numbers shown are the indices in the original vector, that is, the number j denotes the index of the vector component x_j (and not the numerical value). The arrows represent the splitting operation. The combining operation is executed in the reverse direction of the arrows.

becomes odd; in that case, we switch to a straightforward DFT algorithm. If the original input length is a power of two, the recursion ends with a DFT of length one, which is just a trivial copy operation $y_0 := x_0$. Figure 3.2 shows how the problem is split up recursively for $n = 8$. Algorithm 3.1 presents the recursive FFT algorithm for an arbitrary input length.

For simplicity, we assume from now on that the original input length is a power of two. The flop count of the recursive FFT algorithm can be computed as follows. Let $T(n)$ be the number of flops of an FFT of length n. Then

$$T(n) = 2T\left(\frac{n}{2}\right) + 5n,$$

$$(3.13)$$

because an FFT of length n requires two FFTs of length $n/2$ and the combination of the results requires $5n$ flops. Since the half-length FFTs are split again, we substitute eqn (3.13) into itself, but with n replaced by $n/2$. This gives

$$T(n) = 2\left(2T\left(\frac{n}{4}\right) + 5\frac{n}{2}\right) + 5n = 4T\left(\frac{n}{4}\right) + 2 \cdot 5n.$$

$$(3.14)$$

Repeating this process until the input length becomes one, and using $T(1) = 0$, we obtain

$$T(n) = nT(1) + (\log_2 n) \cdot 5n = 5n\log_2 n.$$

$$(3.15)$$

The gain of the FFT compared with the straightforward DFT is huge: only $5n\log_2 n$ flops are needed instead of $8n^2 - 2n$. For example, on a single core of a personal computer running at a rate of 1 Gflop/s, we can transform an entire array of $n = 2^{27} = 134\,217\,728$ samples, representing about 50 minutes of music on a compact disc, in about 18 s by using an FFT, whereas we would have to wait 4.6 years if we were to use a DFT instead.

Algorithm 3.1 Sequential recursive FFT.

---

input: $\mathbf{x}$: vector of length n.
output: $\mathbf{y}$: vector of length n, $\mathbf{y} = F_n\mathbf{x}$.

 function $\text{FFT}(\mathbf{x}, n)$

  if $n \bmod 2 = 0$ **then**
   $\mathbf{x}^e := x(0 : 2 : n - 1)$; ▷ pick the even components
   $\mathbf{x}^o := x(1 : 2 : n - 1)$; ▷ pick the odd components
   $\mathbf{y}^e := \text{FFT}(\mathbf{x}^e, n/2)$;
   $\mathbf{y}^o := \text{FFT}(\mathbf{x}^o, n/2)$;
   for $k := 0$ **to** $n/2 - 1$ **do**
    $\tau := \omega_n^k y_k^o$;
    $y_k := y_k^e + \tau$;
    $y_{k+n/2} := y_k^e - \tau$;
  else
   $\mathbf{y} := \text{DFT}(\mathbf{x}, n)$;

3.3 Sequential nonrecursive algorithm

With each recursive computation, a computational tree is associated. The nodes of the tree are the calls to the recursive function that performs the computation. The root of the tree is the first call and the leaves are the calls that do not invoke the recursive function themselves. Figure 3.2 shows the tree for an FFT of length eight; the tree is binary, since each node has at most two children.

The tree-like nature of recursive computations may lead us into thinking that such algorithms are straightforward to parallelize. Indeed, it is clear that the computation can be split up easily. A difficulty arises, however, because a recursive algorithm traverses its computation tree sequentially, visiting different subtrees one after the other. This corresponds to a depth-first traversal of the tree. For a parallel algorithm, we ideally would like to access many subtrees simultaneously. One approach towards parallelization of a recursive algorithm is therefore to reformulate it first in nonrecursive form. In this section, we derive a nonrecursive FFT algorithm, which is known as the Cooley–Tukey algorithm [71]. An alternative approach would be to treat the top level of the tree in breadth-first fashion to create sufficient parallelism, and then to process the subtrees at the bottom in parallel; see for example Exercise 2.8 on Strassen matrix multiplication.

Van Loan [303] presents a unifying framework in which the Fourier matrix F_n is factorized as the product of permutation matrices and structured sparse matrices. This helps in concisely formulating FFT algorithms, classifying the huge amount of existing FFT variants, and identifying the fundamental variants. We adopt this framework in deriving our parallel algorithm.

The computation of $F_n\mathbf{x}$ by the recursive algorithm can be expressed in matrix language as

$$F_n\mathbf{x} = \begin{bmatrix} I_{n/2} & \Omega_{n/2} \\ I_{n/2} & -\Omega_{n/2} \end{bmatrix} \begin{bmatrix} F_{n/2} & 0 \\ 0 & F_{n/2} \end{bmatrix} \begin{bmatrix} x(0:2:n-1) \\ x(1:2:n-1) \end{bmatrix}. \tag{3.16}$$

Here, Ω_n denotes the $n \times n$ diagonal matrix with the first n powers of ω_{2n} on the diagonal,

$$\Omega_n = \mathrm{diag}(1, \omega_{2n}, \omega_{2n}^2, \ldots, \omega_{2n}^{n-1}). \tag{3.17}$$

Please verify that eqn (3.16) indeed corresponds to Algorithm 3.1.

We examine the three parts on the right-hand side of eqn (3.16) starting from the right. The rightmost part is just the vector $\mathbf{x}$ with its components sorted into even and odd components. We define the **even–odd sort matrix** S_n by

$$S_n = \begin{bmatrix} 1 & 0 & 0 & 0 & \cdots & 0 & 0 & 0 \\ 0 & 0 & 1 & 0 & \cdots & 0 & 0 & 0 \\ & & \vdots & & & & \vdots & \\ 0 & 0 & 0 & 0 & \cdots & 0 & 1 & 0 \\ 0 & 1 & 0 & 0 & \cdots & 0 & 0 & 0 \\ 0 & 0 & 0 & 1 & \cdots & 0 & 0 & 0 \\ & & \vdots & & & & \vdots & \\ 0 & 0 & 0 & 0 & \cdots & 0 & 0 & 1 \end{bmatrix}, \tag{3.18}$$

that is, S_n is the $n \times n$ permutation matrix that contains the even rows of I_n followed by the odd rows. (Note that the indices start at zero, so that the even rows are rows $0, 2, 4, \ldots,$ $n - 2$.) Using this notation, we can write

$$S_n\mathbf{x} = \begin{bmatrix} x(0:2:n-1) \\ x(1:2:n-1) \end{bmatrix}. \tag{3.19}$$

The middle part on the right-hand side of eqn (3.16) is a block-diagonal matrix with two identical blocks $F_{n/2}$ on the diagonal. The off-diagonal blocks, which are zero, can be interpreted as 0 times the submatrix $F_{n/2}$. The matrix therefore consists of four submatrices that are scaled copies of the submatrix $F_{n/2}$. In such a situation, it is convenient to use the Kronecker matrix product notation. If A is a $q \times r$ matrix and B an $m \times n$ matrix, then the **Kronecker product** (also called **tensor product**, or **direct product**) $A \otimes B$ is the $qm \times rn$ matrix defined by

$$A \otimes B = \begin{bmatrix} a_{00}B & \cdots & a_{0,r-1}B \\ \vdots & & \vdots \\ a_{q-1,0}B & \cdots & a_{q-1,r-1}B \end{bmatrix}. \tag{3.20}$$

Example 3.2 Let $A = \begin{bmatrix} 0 & 1 \\ 2 & 4 \end{bmatrix}$ and $B = \begin{bmatrix} 1 & 0 & 2 \\ 0 & 1 & 0 \end{bmatrix}$. Then

$$A \otimes B = \begin{bmatrix} 0 & B \\ 2B & 4B \end{bmatrix} = \begin{bmatrix} 0 & 0 & 0 & 1 & 0 & 2 \\ 0 & 0 & 0 & 0 & 1 & 0 \\ 2 & 0 & 4 & 4 & 0 & 8 \\ 0 & 2 & 0 & 0 & 4 & 0 \end{bmatrix}.$$

The Kronecker product has many useful properties (but, unfortunately, it does not possess commutativity). For an extensive list, see Van Loan [303]. Here, we only mention the three properties that we shall use.

Lemma 3.3 Let A, B, C be matrices. Then

$$(A \otimes B) \otimes C = A \otimes (B \otimes C).$$

Lemma 3.4 Let A, B, C, D be matrices such that AC and BD are defined. Then

$$(A \otimes B)(C \otimes D) = (AC) \otimes (BD).$$

Lemma 3.5 Let $m, n \in \mathbf{N}$. Then

$$I_m \otimes I_n = I_{mn}.$$

Proof Boring. □

Lemma 3.3 saves some ink because we can drop brackets and write $A \otimes B \otimes C$ instead of having to give an explicit evaluation order such as $(A \otimes B) \otimes C$. Using the Kronecker product notation, we can write the middle part on the right-hand side of eqn (3.16) as

$$I_2 \otimes F_{n/2} = \begin{bmatrix} F_{n/2} & 0 \\ 0 & F_{n/2} \end{bmatrix}. \tag{3.21}$$

The leftmost part on the right-hand side of eqn (3.16) is the $n \times n$ **butterfly matrix**

$$B_n = \begin{bmatrix} I_{n/2} & \Omega_{n/2} \\ I_{n/2} & -\Omega_{n/2} \end{bmatrix}. \tag{3.22}$$

The butterfly matrix obtains its name from the butterfly-like pattern in which it transforms input pairs $(x_j, x_{j+n/2}), 0 \le j < n/2$, into output pairs, see Fig. 3.3. The butterfly matrix is sparse because only $2n$ of its n^2 elements are nonzero. It is also structured, because its nonzeros form three diagonals.

Example 3.6

$$B_4 = \begin{bmatrix} 1 & 0 & 1 & 0 \\ 0 & 1 & 0 & -i \\ 1 & 0 & -1 & 0 \\ 0 & 1 & 0 & i \end{bmatrix}.$$

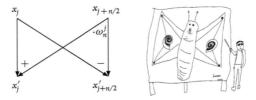

Figure 3.3 Butterfly operation transforming an input pair $(x_j, x_{j+n/2})$ into an output pair $(x'_j, x'_{j+n/2})$. Right butterfly: © 2002 Sarai Bisseling, reproduced with sweet permission.

Using our new notations, we can rewrite eqn (3.16) as

$$F_n\mathbf{x} = B_n(I_2 \otimes F_{n/2})S_n\mathbf{x}. \tag{3.23}$$

Since this holds for all vectors $\mathbf{x}$, we obtain the matrix factorization

$$F_n = B_n(I_2 \otimes F_{n/2})S_n, \tag{3.24}$$

which expresses the Fourier matrix in terms of a smaller Fourier matrix. We can reduce the size of the smaller Fourier matrix further by repeatedly factorizing the middle factor on the right-hand side. For a factor of the form $I_k \otimes F_{n/k}$, this is done by applying Lemmas 3.4 (twice), 3.3, and 3.5, giving

$$\begin{aligned}
I_k \otimes F_{n/k} &= [I_k I_k I_k] \otimes \big[B_{n/k}(I_2 \otimes F_{n/(2k)})S_{n/k}\big] \\
&= (I_k \otimes B_{n/k})\big([I_k I_k] \otimes \big[(I_2 \otimes F_{n/(2k)})S_{n/k}\big]\big) \\
&= (I_k \otimes B_{n/k})(I_k \otimes I_2 \otimes F_{n/(2k)})(I_k \otimes S_{n/k}) \\
&= (I_k \otimes B_{n/k})(I_{2k} \otimes F_{n/(2k)})(I_k \otimes S_{n/k}). \tag{3.25}
\end{aligned}$$

After repeatedly eating away at the middle factor, from both sides, we finally reach $I_n \otimes F_{n/n} = I_n \otimes I_1 = I_n$. Collecting the factors produced in this process, we obtain the following theorem, which is the so-called **decimation in time** (DIT) variant of the Cooley–Tukey factorization. (The name 'DIT' comes from splitting—decimating—the samples taken over time, cf. eqn (3.9).)

Theorem 3.7 (Cooley and Tukey [71]—DIT) *Let n be a power of two with $n \geq 2$. Then*

$$F_n = (I_1 \otimes B_n)(I_2 \otimes B_{n/2})(I_4 \otimes B_{n/4}) \cdots (I_{n/2} \otimes B_2)R_n,$$

where

$$R_n = (I_{n/2} \otimes S_2) \cdots (I_4 \otimes S_{n/4})(I_2 \otimes S_{n/2})(I_1 \otimes S_n).$$

Note that the factors $I_k \otimes S_{n/k}$ are permutation matrices, so that R_n is a permutation matrix.

Example 3.8

$$R_8 = (I_4 \otimes S_2)(I_2 \otimes S_4)(I_1 \otimes S_8) = (I_4 \otimes I_2)(I_2 \otimes S_4)S_8 = (I_2 \otimes S_4)S_8$$

$$
= \begin{bmatrix}
1 & \cdot & \cdot & \cdot & \cdot & \cdot & \cdot & \cdot \\
\cdot & \cdot & 1 & \cdot & \cdot & \cdot & \cdot & \cdot \\
\cdot & 1 & \cdot & \cdot & \cdot & \cdot & \cdot & \cdot \\
\cdot & \cdot & \cdot & 1 & \cdot & \cdot & \cdot & \cdot \\
\cdot & \cdot & \cdot & \cdot & 1 & \cdot & \cdot & \cdot \\
\cdot & \cdot & \cdot & \cdot & \cdot & \cdot & 1 & \cdot \\
\cdot & \cdot & \cdot & \cdot & \cdot & 1 & \cdot & \cdot \\
\cdot & \cdot & \cdot & \cdot & \cdot & \cdot & \cdot & 1
\end{bmatrix}
\begin{bmatrix}
1 & \cdot & \cdot & \cdot & \cdot & \cdot & \cdot & \cdot \\
\cdot & \cdot & 1 & \cdot & \cdot & \cdot & \cdot & \cdot \\
\cdot & \cdot & \cdot & \cdot & 1 & \cdot & \cdot & \cdot \\
\cdot & \cdot & \cdot & \cdot & \cdot & \cdot & 1 & \cdot \\
\cdot & 1 & \cdot & \cdot & \cdot & \cdot & \cdot & \cdot \\
\cdot & \cdot & \cdot & 1 & \cdot & \cdot & \cdot & \cdot \\
\cdot & \cdot & \cdot & \cdot & \cdot & 1 & \cdot & \cdot \\
\cdot & \cdot & \cdot & \cdot & \cdot & \cdot & \cdot & 1
\end{bmatrix}
$$

$$
= \begin{bmatrix}
1 & \cdot & \cdot & \cdot & \cdot & \cdot & \cdot & \cdot \\
\cdot & \cdot & \cdot & \cdot & 1 & \cdot & \cdot & \cdot \\
\cdot & \cdot & 1 & \cdot & \cdot & \cdot & \cdot & \cdot \\
\cdot & \cdot & \cdot & \cdot & \cdot & \cdot & 1 & \cdot \\
\cdot & 1 & \cdot & \cdot & \cdot & \cdot & \cdot & \cdot \\
\cdot & \cdot & \cdot & \cdot & \cdot & 1 & \cdot & \cdot \\
\cdot & \cdot & \cdot & 1 & \cdot & \cdot & \cdot & \cdot \\
\cdot & \cdot & \cdot & \cdot & \cdot & \cdot & \cdot & 1
\end{bmatrix}. \tag{3.26}
$$

Here, we write dots instead of zeros to facilitate pattern recognition by the reader.

The permutation matrix R_n is known as the **bit-reversal** matrix. Multiplying an input vector by this matrix first permutes the vector by splitting it into even and odd components, moving the even components to the front, then treats the two parts separately in the same way, splitting each half into its own even and odd components, and so on. The bit-reversal matrix has a useful property relating it to smaller bit-reversal matrices, given by the following lemma.

Lemma 3.9 *Let n be a power of two with $n \geq 4$. Then*

$$R_n = (I_2 \otimes R_{n/2})S_n.$$

Proof

$$
\begin{aligned}
R_n &= (I_{n/2} \otimes S_2) \cdots (I_4 \otimes S_{n/4})(I_2 \otimes S_{n/2})(I_1 \otimes S_n) \\
&= (I_2 \otimes I_{n/4} \otimes S_2) \cdots (I_2 \otimes I_2 \otimes S_{n/4})(I_2 \otimes I_1 \otimes S_{n/2})S_n \\
&= (I_2 \otimes [(I_{n/4} \otimes S_2) \cdots (I_1 \otimes S_{n/2})])S_n \\
&= (I_2 \otimes R_{n/2})S_n.
\end{aligned}
$$

$\square$

The name 'bit reversal' stems from viewing this permutation in terms of binary digits. We can write an index j, $0 \leq j < n$, as

$$j = \sum_{k=0}^{m-1} b_k 2^k, \tag{3.27}$$

where $b_k \in \{0, 1\}$ is the kth bit and $n = 2^m$. We call b_0 the **least significant bit** and b_{m-1} the **most significant bit**. We express the binary expansion by the notation

$$(b_{m-1} \cdots b_1 b_0)_2 = \sum_{k=0}^{m-1} b_k 2^k. \tag{3.28}$$

Example 3.10

$$(10100101)_2 = 2^7 + 2^5 + 2^2 + 2^0 = 165.$$

Let $n = 2^m$, with $m \geq 1$. The **bit-reversal permutation** $\rho_n : \{0, \ldots, n-1\} \rightarrow \{0, \ldots, n-1\}$ is then defined by

$$\rho_n((b_{m-1} \cdots b_0)_2) = (b_0 \cdots b_{m-1})_2. \tag{3.29}$$

The bit-reversal permutation for $n = 8$ is displayed in Table 3.1. It is convenient to define ρ_n also for the special case $n = 1$. The only possible choice is to let ρ_1 be the identity permutation of one element, $\rho_1(0) = 0$. This can be interpreted as the permutation that reverses zero bits.

The bit-reversal permutation is related to smaller bit-reversal permutations by the property

$$\rho_n(j) = \begin{cases} 2\rho_{n/2}(j) & \text{for } 0 \leq j < n/2, \\ 2\rho_{n/2}(j - n/2) + 1 & \text{for } n/2 \leq j < n. \end{cases} \tag{3.30}$$

This is easily proven by writing $j = (0 b_{m-2} \cdots b_0)_2$ for $j < n/2$, and $j = (1 b_{m-2} \cdots b_0)_2$ for $j \geq n/2$.

Table 3.1 Bit-reversal permutation for $n = 8$.

j	$(b_2 b_1 b_0)_2$	$(b_0 b_1 b_2)_2$	$\rho_8(j)$
0	000	000	0
1	001	100	4
2	010	010	2
3	011	110	6
4	100	001	1
5	101	101	5
6	110	011	3
7	111	111	7

Multiplying a vector by R_n starts by splitting the vector into a subvector of components $x_{(b_{m-1}\cdots b_0)_2}$ with $b_0 = 0$ and a subvector of components with $b_0 = 1$. This means that the most significant bit of the new position of a component becomes b_0. Each subvector is then split according to bit b_1, and so on. Thus, the final position of the vector component with index $(b_{m-1}\cdots b_0)_2$ becomes $(b_0 \cdots b_{m-1})_2$, that is, the bit reverse of the original position; hence the name. The splittings of the bit reversal are exactly the same as those of the recursive procedure, but now they are lumped together. For this reason, Fig. 3.2 can also be viewed as an illustration of the bit-reversal permutation, where the bottom row gives the bit reverses of the indices shown at the top.

The following theorem states formally that R_n corresponds to a bit-reversal permutation ρ_n, where the correspondence between a permutation σ and a permutation matrix P_σ is given by eqn (2.11).

Theorem 3.11 Let $n = 2^m$, with $m \geq 1$. Then

$$R_n = P_{\rho_n}.$$

Proof By induction on m. For $m = 1$, we note that $R_2 = S_2 = I_2$, which is the identity matrix, and also that ρ_2 is the identity permutation, since reversing one bit has no effect. Thus, the statement is true. Now assume that $m > 1$ and that the statement is true for $m - 1$. Because of Lemma 3.9 we have to prove that

$$(I_2 \otimes R_{n/2})S_n = P_{\rho_n}. \tag{3.31}$$

Because of the induction hypothesis, this is equivalent to proving

$$(I_2 \otimes P_{\rho_{n/2}})S_n = P_{\rho_n}. \tag{3.32}$$

First, consider element (j, k) of the left-hand side matrix, with k even. Its value can either be 0 or 1, and it is given by

$$[(I_2 \otimes P_{\rho_{n/2}})S_n]_{jk} = \sum_{r=0}^{n-1}(I_2 \otimes P_{\rho_{n/2}})_{jr}(S_n)_{rk}. \tag{3.33}$$

Inspecting the matrix S_n in eqn (3.18) shows that for even k the only possible nonzero term satisfies $r = k/2$, so that the value becomes

$$[(I_2 \otimes P_{\rho_{n/2}})S_n]_{jk} = (I_2 \otimes P_{\rho_{n/2}})_{j,k/2}. \tag{3.34}$$

This value can only be nonzero if $j < n/2$, in which case it simplifies to $(P_{\rho_{n/2}})_{j,k/2}$, which equals 1 if and only if $j = \rho_{n/2}(k/2)$ (by eqn (2.11)). This in turn is equivalent to $2\rho_{n/2}(j) = k$ and hence to $\rho_n(j) = k$ (by eqn (3.30)), and hence to $(P_{\rho_n})_{jk} = 1$. This proves equality for matrix elements (j, k) with even k. The proof for odd k is similar, and involves a single term $r = (k - 1 + n)/2$. $\qquad\square$

Algorithm 3.2 Sequential nonrecursive FFT.

input: $\mathbf{x}$: vector of length $n = 2^m$, $m \geq 1$, $\mathbf{x} = \mathbf{x}_0$.
output: $\mathbf{x}$: vector of length n, such that $\mathbf{x} = F_n\mathbf{x}_0$.

> **function** FFT$(\mathbf{x}, n)$
>
>> Bitrev$(\mathbf{x}, n)$;
>> UFFT$(\mathbf{x}, n)$;

Algorithm 3.2 is an FFT algorithm based on the Cooley–Tukey theorem. The algorithm overwrites the input vector $\mathbf{x}$ with the output vector $F_n\mathbf{x}$. The algorithm uses the function Bitrev$(\mathbf{x}, n)$, given as Algorithm 3.3, which performs a bit reversal of length n, and the function UFFT$(\mathbf{x}, n)$, given as Algorithm 3.4, which performs an **unordered FFT** of length n, that is, an FFT without bit reversal. Since the bit reversal is its own inverse, $R_n^{-1} = R_n$, we can express the unordered FTT in a fancy way as a matrix $F_nR_n = F_nR_n^{-1}$.

The bit reversal permutation can be determined efficiently by using eqn (3.30). The bit reversal algorithm, Algorithm 3.3, first computes ρ_2 for a vector of length 2, then ρ_4 for a vector of length 4, etc., until it finally computes ρ_n for a vector of length n. If we define $T(k)$ as the time (in integer operations) needed for computing $\rho_k(0: k - 1)$, we have

---

Algorithm 3.3 Bit reversal.

input: $\mathbf{x}$: vector of length $n = 2^m$, $m \geq 1$, $\mathbf{x} = \mathbf{x}_0$.
output: $\mathbf{x}$: vector of length n, such that $\mathbf{x} = R_n\mathbf{x}_0$.

> **function** BITREV$(\mathbf{x}, n)$
>
>> $\rho_1(0) := 0$;
>> $k := 2$;
>> **while** $k \leq n$ **do**
>>> $\{$ Compute $\rho_k(0: k - 1)$ $\}$
>>> **for** $j := 0$ **to** $k/2 - 1$ **do**
>>>> $\rho_k(j) := 2\rho_{k/2}(j)$;
>>>> $\rho_k(j + k/2) := 2\rho_{k/2}(j) + 1$;
>>> $k := 2k$;
>>
>> $\{$ Swap components of $\mathbf{x}$ based on $\rho_n\}$
>> **for** $j := 0$ **to** $n - 1$ **do**
>>> **if** $j < \rho_n(j)$ **then**
>>>> swap $(x_j, x_{\rho_n(j)})$;

$$T(k) = T\left(\frac{k}{2}\right) + 2\frac{k}{2} = T\left(\frac{k}{2}\right) + k = T\left(\frac{k}{4}\right) + \frac{k}{2} + k = \cdots$$
$$= T(1) + 2 + 4 + \cdots + k = 2k - 2, \tag{3.35}$$

where in the computation of ρ_k we charge a multiplication and an addition for each of the $k/2$ components of $\rho_{k/2}$: a multiplication by 2 to compute $2\rho_{k/2}(j)$, and an increment by 1 to obtain $\rho_k(j + k/2)$. We also charge $T(1) = 0$ for the initialization of ρ_1.

In Algorithm 3.4, the multiplication by the butterfly matrix B_k combines components at distance $k/2$, where k is a power of two. In the inner loop, the subtraction $x_{rk+j+k/2} := x_{rk+j} - \tau$ is performed before the addition $x_{rk+j} := x_{rk+j} + \tau$, because the old value of x_{rk+j} must be used in the computation of $x_{rk+j+k/2}$. (Performing these statements in the reverse order would require the use of an extra temporary variable.) A simple count of the floating-point operations shows that the cost of the unordered FFT algorithm is the same as that of the recursive algorithm. The bit-reversal cost is linear, so that the total cost of the nonrecursive FFT is almost the same as that of the recursive FFT.

The symmetry of the Fourier matrix F_n and the bit-reversal matrix R_n gives us an alternative form of the Cooley–Tukey FFT factorization, the so-called **decimation in frequency** (DIF) variant.

Corollary 3.12 (Cooley and Tukey [71]—DIF) *Let n be a power of two with $n \geq 2$. Then*

$$F_n = R_n(I_{n/2} \otimes B_2^{\mathsf{T}})(I_{n/4} \otimes B_4^{\mathsf{T}})(I_{n/8} \otimes B_8^{\mathsf{T}}) \cdots (I_1 \otimes B_n^{\mathsf{T}}).$$

Algorithm 3.4 Unordered FFT.

---

input: $\mathbf{x}$: vector of length $n = 2^m$, $m \geq 1$, $\mathbf{x} = \mathbf{x}_0$.
output: $\mathbf{x}$: vector of length n, such that $\mathbf{x} = F_n R_n \mathbf{x}_0$.

    function UFFT$(\mathbf{x}, n)$

        $k := 2$;
        while $k \leq n$ **do**
            { Compute $\mathbf{x} := (I_{n/k} \otimes B_k)\mathbf{x}$ }
            for $r := 0$ **to** $\frac{n}{k} - 1$ **do**
                { Compute $x(rk : rk + k - 1) := B_k x(rk : rk + k - 1)$ }
                for $j := 0$ **to** $\frac{k}{2} - 1$ **do**
                    { Compute $x_{rk+j} \pm \omega_k^j x_{rk+j+k/2}$ }
                    $\tau := \omega_k^j x_{rk+j+k/2}$;
                    $x_{rk+j+k/2} := x_{rk+j} - \tau$;
                    $x_{rk+j} := x_{rk+j} + \tau$;
        $k := 2k$;

Proof

$$
\begin{aligned}
F_n = F_n^{\mathrm{T}} &= \left[(I_1 \otimes B_n)(I_2 \otimes B_{n/2})(I_4 \otimes B_{n/4}) \cdots (I_{n/2} \otimes B_2) R_n \right]^{\mathrm{T}} \\
&= R_n^{\mathrm{T}} (I_{n/2} \otimes B_2)^{\mathrm{T}} \cdots (I_4 \otimes B_{n/4})^{\mathrm{T}} (I_2 \otimes B_{n/2})^{\mathrm{T}} (I_1 \otimes B_n)^{\mathrm{T}} \\
&= R_n (I_{n/2} \otimes B_2^{\mathrm{T}}) \cdots (I_4 \otimes B_{n/4}^{\mathrm{T}})(I_2 \otimes B_{n/2}^{\mathrm{T}})(I_1 \otimes B_n^{\mathrm{T}}).
\end{aligned}
$$
$\square$

3.4 Parallel algorithm

The first question to answer when parallelizing an existing sequential algorithm is: which data should be distributed? The vector **x** must certainly be distributed, but it may also be necessary to distribute the table containing the powers of ω_n that are used in the computation, the so-called **weights**. (A table must be used because it would be too expensive to compute the weights each time they are needed.) We defer the weights issue to Section 3.5, and for the moment we assume that the table of weights is replicated on every processor.

A suitable distribution should make the operations of the algorithm local. For the FFT, the basic operation is the butterfly, which modifies a pair $(x_j, x_{j+k/2})$, where k is the butterfly size. This is done in **stage** k of the algorithm, that is, the iteration corresponding to parameter k of the main loop of Algorithm 3.4. Let the length of the Fourier transform be $n = 2^m$, with $m \geq 1$, and let the number of processors be $p = 2^q$, with $0 \leq q < m$. We restrict the number of processors to a power of two because this matches the structure of our sequential FFT algorithm. Furthermore, we require that $q < m$, or equivalently $p < n$, because in the pathological case $p = n$ there is only one vector component per processor, and we need at least a pair of vector components to perform a sensible butterfly operation.

A block distribution of the vector **x**, with n/p components per processor, makes butterflies with $k \leq n/p$ local. This is because k and n/p are powers of two, so that $k \leq n/p$ ensures that k divides n/p, thus making each butterfly block $x(rk: rk + k - 1)$ fit completely into a processor block $x(sn/p: sn/p + n/p - 1)$; no butterfly blocks cross the processor boundaries.

Example 3.13 Let $n = 8$ and $p = 2$ and assume that **x** is block distributed. Stage $k = 2$ of the FFT algorithm is a multiplication of $\mathbf{x} = x(0: 7)$ with

$$
I_4 \otimes B_2 =
\begin{bmatrix}
1 & 1 & \cdot & \cdot & \cdot & \cdot & \cdot & \cdot \\
1 & -1 & \cdot & \cdot & \cdot & \cdot & \cdot & \cdot \\
\cdot & \cdot & 1 & 1 & \cdot & \cdot & \cdot & \cdot \\
\cdot & \cdot & 1 & -1 & \cdot & \cdot & \cdot & \cdot \\
\cdot & \cdot & \cdot & \cdot & 1 & 1 & \cdot & \cdot \\
\cdot & \cdot & \cdot & \cdot & 1 & -1 & \cdot & \cdot \\
\cdot & \cdot & \cdot & \cdot & \cdot & \cdot & 1 & 1 \\
\cdot & \cdot & \cdot & \cdot & \cdot & \cdot & 1 & -1
\end{bmatrix}.
$$

The butterfly blocks of **x** that are multiplied by a block of $I_4 \otimes B_2$ are $x(0: 1), x(2: 3)$, $x(4: 5)$, and $x(6: 7)$. The first two blocks are contained in processor block $x(0: 3)$, which belongs to $P(0)$. The last two blocks are contained in processor block $x(4{:}7)$, which belongs to $P(1)$.

In contrast to the block distribution, the cyclic distribution makes butterflies with $k \geq 2p$ local, because $k/2 \geq p$ ensures that $k/2$ is a multiple of p, so that the vector components x_j and $x_{j+k/2}$ reside on the same processor.

Example 3.14 Let $n = 8$ and $p = 2$ and assume that $\mathbf{x}$ is cyclically distributed. Stage $k = 8$ of the FFT algorithm is a multiplication of $\mathbf{x} = x(0{:}\,7)$ with

$$
B_8 = \begin{bmatrix}
1 & \cdot & \cdot & \cdot & 1 & \cdot & \cdot & \cdot \\
\cdot & 1 & \cdot & \cdot & \cdot & \omega & \cdot & \cdot \\
\cdot & \cdot & 1 & \cdot & \cdot & \cdot & \omega^2 & \cdot \\
\cdot & \cdot & \cdot & 1 & \cdot & \cdot & \cdot & \omega^3 \\
1 & \cdot & \cdot & \cdot & -1 & \cdot & \cdot & \cdot \\
\cdot & 1 & \cdot & \cdot & \cdot & -\omega & \cdot & \cdot \\
\cdot & \cdot & 1 & \cdot & \cdot & \cdot & -\omega^2 & \cdot \\
\cdot & \cdot & \cdot & 1 & \cdot & \cdot & \cdot & -\omega^3
\end{bmatrix},
$$

where $\omega = \omega_8 = e^{-\pi i/4} = (1 - i)/\sqrt{2}$. The component pairs (x_0, x_4) and (x_2, x_6) are combined on $P(0)$, whereas the pairs (x_1, x_5) and (x_3, x_7) are combined on $P(1)$.

Now, a parallelization strategy emerges: start with the block distribution and finish with the cyclic distribution. If $p \leq n/p$ (i.e., $p \leq \sqrt{n}$), then these two distributions suffice for the butterflies and we need to redistribute only once. In this case, we can start with the block distribution for $k = 2, 4, \ldots, n/p$ and use the cyclic distribution for $k = 2n/p, 4n/p, \ldots, n$. This requires $2n/p > p$, which is equivalent to $n/p \geq p$ because p and n are powers of two. We have some freedom here in choosing the moment of redistribution, which can be at any desired time after stage p but before stage $2n/p$. In the opposite case $p > n/p$, however, we are lucky to have so many processors to solve such a small problem, but we are unlucky in that we have to use more distributions. For the butterflies of size $n/p < k \leq p$, we need one or more intermediates between the block and cyclic distribution.

The **group-cyclic distribution** with cycle c first splits the vector $\mathbf{x}$ into blocks of size $\lceil cn/p \rceil$, and then assigns each block to a group of c processors using the cyclic distribution. The group-cyclic distribution is defined by the mapping

$$
x_j \longmapsto P\left(\left(j \operatorname{div} \left\lceil \frac{cn}{p} \right\rceil \right) c + \left(j \bmod \left\lceil \frac{cn}{p} \right\rceil \right) \bmod c \right), \quad \text{for } 0 \leq j < n. \tag{3.36}
$$

This distribution is defined for every c with $1 \leq c \leq p$ and $p \bmod c = 0$. Note that for $c = 1$ this reduces to the block distribution, see (1.7), and for $c = p$ to the cyclic distribution, see (1.6). In the special case $n \bmod p = 0$, the group-cyclic distribution reduces to

$$
x_j \longmapsto P\left(\left(j \operatorname{div} \frac{cn}{p} \right) c + j \bmod c \right), \quad \text{for } 0 \leq j < n. \tag{3.37}
$$

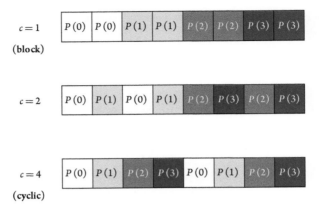

Figure 3.4 Group-cyclic distribution with cycle c of a vector of size eight over four processors. Each cell represents a vector component; the number in the cell and the colour denote the processor that owns the cell.

This case is relevant for the FFT, because n and p are both powers of two. Figure 3.4 illustrates the group-cyclic distribution for $n = 8$ and $p = 4$. The group-cyclic distribution is a new generalization of the block and cyclic distributions; note that it differs from the block-cyclic distribution introduced earlier,

$$x_j \longmapsto P((j \text{ div } b) \bmod p), \quad \text{for } 0 \leq j < n, \tag{3.38}$$

where b is the block size.

In the FFT case, n and p and hence c are powers of two and we can write each global index j uniquely as the sum of three terms,

$$j = j_2 \frac{cn}{p} + j_1 c + j_0, \tag{3.39}$$

where $0 \leq j_0 < c$ and $0 \leq j_1 < n/p$. The processor that owns the component x_j in the group-cyclic distribution with cycle c is $P(j_2 c + j_0)$; the processor allocation is not influenced by j_1. We can retrieve j_0 and j_2 from the processor number s by

$$j_0 = s \bmod c, \qquad j_2 = s \text{ div } c. \tag{3.40}$$

As always, the components are stored locally in order of increasing global index. Thus, x_j ends up in local position $\hat{\jmath} = j_1 = (j \bmod cn/p) \text{ div } c$ on processor $P(j_2 c + j_0)$. (The relation between global and local indices is explained in Fig. 1.9.)

To make a butterfly of size k local in the group-cyclic distribution with cycle c, two constraints must be satisfied. First, the butterfly block $x(rk : rk + k - 1)$ of size k should fit completely into one block of size cn/p, which is assigned to a group of c processors. This is guaranteed if $k \leq cn/p$. Second, $k/2$ must be a multiple of the cycle c, so that the components

x_j and $x_{j+k/2}$ reside on the same processor from the group. This is guaranteed if $k/2 \geq c$. As a result, we find that a butterfly of size k is local in the group-cyclic distribution with cycle c if

$$2c \leq k \leq \frac{n}{p}c. \tag{3.41}$$

This result includes as a special case our earlier results for the block and cyclic distributions. In Fig. 3.4, it can be seen that for $c = 1$ butterflies of size $k = 2$ are local, since they combine pairs (x_j, x_{j+1}); the same holds for $c = 2$ and $k = 4$ with pairs (x_j, x_{j+2}) and for $c = 4$ and $k = 8$ with pairs (x_j, x_{j+4}). In this particular example, the range of (3.41) consists of only one value of k, namely $k = 2c$.

A straightforward strategy for the parallel FFT is to start the butterflies with the group-cyclic distribution with cycle $c = 1$, and continue as long as possible with this distribution, that is, in stages $k = 2, 4, \ldots, n/p$. At the end of stage n/p, the vector $\mathbf{x}$ is redistributed into the group-cyclic distribution with cycle $c = n/p$, and then stages $k = 2n/p, 4n/p, \ldots, n^2/p^2$ are performed. Then c is again multiplied by n/p, $\mathbf{x}$ is redistributed, stages $k = 2n^2/p^2, 4n^2/p^2, \ldots, n^3/p^3$ are performed, and so on. Since $n/p \geq 2$ the value of c increases strictly monotonically. When multiplying c by n/p would lead to a value $c = (n/p)^t \geq p$, the value of c is set to $c = p$ instead and the remaining stages $2(n/p)^t, \ldots, n$ are performed in the cyclic distribution.

Until now, we have ignored the bit reversal preceding the butterflies. The bit reversal is a permutation, which in general requires communication. We have been liberal in allowing different distributions in different parts of our algorithm, so why not use different distributions before and after the bit reversal? This way, we might be able to avoid communication.

Let us try our luck and assume that we have the cyclic distribution before the bit reversal. This is the preferred starting distribution of the overall computation, because it is the distribution in which the FFT computation ends. It is advantageous to start and finish with the same distribution, because then it is easy to apply the FFT repeatedly. This would make it possible, for instance, to execute a parallel inverse FFT by using the parallel forward FFT with conjugated weights; this approach is based on the property $F_n^{-1} = \overline{F_n}/n$.

Consider a component x_j with index $j = (b_{m-1} \cdots b_0)_2$ of a cyclically distributed vector $\mathbf{x}$. This component is stored on processor $P((b_{q-1} \cdots b_0)_2)$ in location $\hat{j} = (b_{m-1} \cdots b_q)_2$. In other words, the least significant q bits of j determine the processor number and the most significant $m - q$ bits the local index, see the top line of Fig. 3.5. Since our aim is to achieve a global bit reversal, it seems natural to start with a local bit reversal; this already reverses part of the bits and it does not incur communication. The local bit reversal moves x_j into local position $(b_q \cdots b_{m-1})_2$, see the second line of Fig. 3.5. The local position consists of the least significant $m - q$ bits of the global destination index $\rho_n(j) = (b_0 \cdots b_{m-1})_2$. The least significant $m - q$ bits also happen to be those that determine the local position in the block distribution. Therefore, the local position would be correct if we declared the distribution to be by blocks. Unfortunately, the processor would still be wrong: in the block distribution after the global bit reversal, the original x_j should find itself in processor $P(b_0 \cdots b_{q-1})$, determined by the most significant q bits of the destination index $(b_0 \cdots b_{m-1})_2$, but of course x_j did not leave the original processor

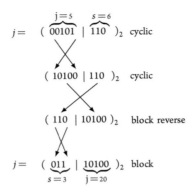

Figure 3.5 Parallel bit-reversal permutation starting with the cyclic distribution and finishing with the block distribution. Shown are the movements of component x_j with index $j = 46 = (00101110)_2$, which ends up in position $j = 116 = (01110100)_2$. The vector length is $n = 256$, corresponding to $m = 8$, and the number of processors is $p = 8$.

$P((b_{q-1} \cdots b_0)_2)$. Note that the correct processor number is the bit-reverse of the actual processor number. Therefore, we call the current distribution after the local bit reversal the **block distribution with bit-reversed processor numbering**, see the third line of Fig. 3.5. Swapping the data between each processor and its bit-reverse partner finally results in the block distribution, see the bottom line of Fig. 3.5.

Can we use the current distribution instead of the block distribution for the first set of butterflies, with size $k = 2, 4, \ldots, n/p$? We have to check whether these butterflies remain local when using the block distribution with bit-reversed processor numbering. Fortunately, for these k, every processor carries out exactly the same operations, but on its own data. This is because $k \le n/p$, so that every butterfly block fits completely into a processor block. As a consequence, the bit-reversed processor numbering does not affect the local computations. Every processor $P(s)$ thus performs the operations of its bit-reverse partner $P(\rho_p(s))$, following the motto 'You scratch my back, and I'll scratch yours'. At the first redistribution, the vector is moved into the standard group-cyclic distribution without bit-reversed processor numbering, and then the algorithm returns to the original strategy outlined above.

By a stroke of luck, we now have a complete parallel FFT algorithm that starts and ends with the same distribution, the cyclic distribution, and that performs only a limited number of redistributions. The result is given as Algorithm 3.5. In stage k of the algorithm, there are n/k butterfly blocks, each of size k, which are numbered from $r = 0$ to $n/k - 1$. Each of the p/c processor groups handles $b = (n/k)/(p/c) = nc/(kp)$ butterfly blocks.

The processors in the processor group of $P(s) = P(j_2c + j_0)$ have the same value j_2 but different values j_0. We can view j_2 as the group number. The group handles the butterfly blocks numbered from $r = j_2b$ to $(j_2 + 1)b - 1$.

Processor $P(s)$ participates in the computations of every butterfly block of its group, with the loop index j running from j_0, through $j_0 + c, j_0 + 2c, \ldots$, to $j_0 + k/2 - c$. Note that the loop index j differs from the j in eqn (3.39) by a constant term rk, but this should not cause any confusion. We could have called this dummy index $\hat{j}$ instead, but omitted the hat for brevity. (For dummies, what's in a name anyway?)

The redistribution function used in Algorithm 3.5 is given as Algorithm 3.6. It takes a boolean variable *rev* as parameter which causes a reversal of the processor number during the first call of the function. The function puts every component x_j in the destination processor determined by the new distribution with cycle c, where the source is determined by the old distribution with cycle c_0. We do not specify where exactly in the destination processor the component x_j is placed. Strictly speaking this has nothing to do with the distribution; rather, it is related to the data structure used to store the local values. Still, our convention

---

Algorithm 3.5 Parallel FFT algorithm for processor $P(s)$.

---

input: $\mathbf{x}$: vector of length $n = 2^m$, $m \geq 1$, $\mathbf{x} = \mathbf{x}_0$,
     $\text{distr}(\mathbf{x}) = $ cyclic over $p = 2^q$ processors with $0 \leq q < m$.
output: $\mathbf{x}$: vector of length n, $\text{distr}(\mathbf{x}) = $ cyclic, such that $\mathbf{x} = F_n \mathbf{x}_0$.

$\quad$ Bitrev$(x(s : p : n - 1), n/p)$;
$\quad$ { $\text{distr}(\mathbf{x}) = $ block with bit-reversed processor numbering }

$\quad$ $k := 2$;
$\quad$ $c := 1$;
$\quad$ $rev := true$;
$\quad$ **while** $k \leq n$ **do**
$\quad\quad$ $j_0 := s \bmod c$; $\hfill \triangleright$ Superstep (0)
$\quad\quad$ $j_2 := s \operatorname{div} c$;
$\quad\quad$ **while** $k \leq \frac{n}{p}c$ **do**
$\quad\quad\quad$ $b := \frac{nc}{kp}$;
$\quad\quad\quad$ **for** $r := j_2 b$ **to** $(j_2 + 1)b - 1$ **do**
$\quad\quad\quad\quad$ { Compute local part of $B_k x(rk : (r + 1)k - 1)$ }
$\quad\quad\quad\quad$ **for** $j := j_0$ **to** $\frac{k}{2} - 1$ **step** c **do**
$\quad\quad\quad\quad\quad$ $\tau := \omega_k^j x_{rk+j+k/2}$;
$\quad\quad\quad\quad\quad$ $x_{rk+j+k/2} := x_{rk+j} - \tau$;
$\quad\quad\quad\quad\quad$ $x_{rk+j} := x_{rk+j} + \tau$;
$\quad\quad\quad$ $k := 2k$;

$\quad\quad$ { Redistribute $\mathbf{x}$ } $\hfill \triangleright$ Superstep (1)
$\quad\quad$ **if** $c < p$ **then**
$\quad\quad\quad$ $c_0 := c$;
$\quad\quad\quad$ $c := \min(\frac{n}{p}c, p)$;
$\quad\quad\quad$ Redistr$(\mathbf{x}, n, p, c_0, c, rev)$;
$\quad\quad\quad$ $rev := false$;
$\quad\quad$ { $\text{distr}(\mathbf{x}) = $ group-cyclic with cycle c }

Algorithm 3.6 Redistribution from group-cyclic distribution with cycle c_0 to cycle c for processor $P(s)$.

---

input: **x** : vector of length $n = 2^m$, $m \geq 0$,

   distr(**x**) = group-cyclic with cycle c_0 over $p = 2^q$ processors with $0 \leq q \leq m$.

   If *rev* is true, the processor numbering is assumed bit-reversed, otherwise it is standard.

output: **x** : vector of length n, distr(**x**) = group-cyclic with cycle c with standard processor numbering.

   function REDISTR($\mathbf{x}, n, p, c_0, c, rev$)

   　　if *rev* **then**

   　　　　$j_0 := \rho_p(s) \bmod c_0$;

   　　　　$j_2 := \rho_p(s) \operatorname{div} c_0$;

   　　else

   　　　　$j_0 := s \bmod c_0$;

   　　　　$j_2 := s \operatorname{div} c_0$;

   　　for $j := j_2 \frac{c_0 n}{p} + j_0$ **to** $(j_2 + 1)\frac{c_0 n}{p} - 1$ **step** c_0 **do**

   　　　　$dest := (j \operatorname{div} \frac{cn}{p})c + j \bmod c$;

   　　　　put x_j in $P(dest)$;

---

that components are ordered locally by increasing global index determines the local index, $(j \bmod cn/p) \operatorname{div} c$, as we saw above, and this will be used later on in the implementation. Note that the redistribution also works in the trivial case $p = 1$, because we suitably defined ρ_1 as an identity permutation.

Finally, we determine the cost of Algorithm 3.5. First, we consider the synchronization cost. Each iteration of the main loop has two supersteps: a computation superstep that computes the butterflies and a communication superstep that redistributes the vector **x**. The computation superstep of the first iteration also includes the local bit reversal. The last iteration, with $c = p$, does not perform a redistribution anymore. The total number of iterations equals $t + 1$, where t is the smallest integer such that $(n/p)^t \geq p$. By taking the $\log_2$ of both sides and using $m = 2^n$ and $p = 2^q$, we see that this inequality is equivalent to $t \geq q/(m - q)$, so that $t = \lceil q/(m - q) \rceil$. Therefore, the total synchronization cost is

$$T_{\text{sync}} = \left(2 \left\lceil \frac{q}{m - q} \right\rceil + 1\right) l. \tag{3.42}$$

Second, we examine the communication cost. Communication occurs only within the redistribution, where in the worst case all n/p old local vector components are sent away, and n/p new components are received from another processor. Each vector component is a complex number, which consists of two real numbers. The redistribution is therefore a $2n/p$-relation. (The cost is actually somewhat lower than $2ng/p$, because certain data remain local. For example, component x_0 remains on $P(0)$ in all group-cyclic distributions, even when the processor numbering is bit-reversed. This is a small effect, which we can neglect.) Thus, the communication cost is

$$T_{\text{comm}} = \left\lceil \frac{q}{m-q} \right\rceil \cdot \frac{2n}{p} g. \tag{3.43}$$

Third, we focus on the computation cost. In stage k, each processor group handles $b = nc/(kp)$ butterfly blocks, each of size k. Each processor handles a fraction $1/c$ of the $k/2$ component pairs in a butterfly block. Each pair requires a complex multiplication, addition, and subtraction, that is, a total of 10 real flops. We do not count indexing arithmetic or the computation of the weights. As a consequence, the total number of flops per processor in stage k equals $(nc/(kp)) \cdot (k/(2c)) \cdot 10 = 5n/p$. Since there are m stages, the computation cost is

$$T_{\text{comp}} = 5mn/p. \tag{3.44}$$

The total BSP cost of the algorithm as a function of n and p is obtained by summing the three costs and substituting $m = \log_2 n$ and $q = \log_2 p$, giving

$$T_{\text{FFT}} = \frac{5n \log_2 n}{p} + 2 \cdot \left\lceil \frac{\log_2 p}{\log_2 (n/p)} \right\rceil \cdot \frac{n}{p} g + \left(2 \left\lceil \frac{\log_2 p}{\log_2 (n/p)} \right\rceil + 1 \right) l. \tag{3.45}$$

Budgets for the acquisition of parallel computers are growing these days, but often they are still tight. You, the user of a parallel computer, may however be insatiable in your computing demands. In that case, p remains small, n becomes large, and you may find yourself performing FFTs with $1 < p \leq \sqrt{n}$. The good news is that then you only need one communication superstep and two computation supersteps. The BSP cost of the FFT reduces to

$$T_{\text{FFT}, 1<p\leq\sqrt{n}} = \frac{5n \log_2 n}{p} + 2\frac{n}{p} g + 3l. \tag{3.46}$$

This happens because $p \leq \sqrt{n}$ implies $p \leq n/p$ and hence $\log_2 p \leq \log_2 (n/p)$, so that the ceiling expression in (3.45) becomes 1.

3.5 Weight reduction

The **weights** of the FFT are the powers of ω_n that are needed in the FFT computation. These powers $1, \omega_n, \omega_n^2, \ldots, \omega_n^{n/2-1}$ are usually precomputed and stored in a table, thus saving trigonometric evaluations when repeatedly using the same power of ω_n. This table can be reused in subsequent FFTs. In a sequential computation, the table requires a storage space of $n/2$ complex numbers, which is half the space needed for the vector $\mathbf{x}$; such an overhead is usually acceptable. For small n, the $\mathcal{O}(n)$ time of the weight initializations may not be negligible compared with the $5n \log_2 n$ flops of the FFT itself. The reason is that each weight computation requires the evaluation of two trigonometric functions,

$$\omega_n^j = \cos \frac{2\pi j}{n} - i \sin \frac{2\pi j}{n}, \tag{3.47}$$

which might cost anywhere in the range of 10–50 flops per evaluation. The required number of flops depends very much on the hardware and the implementation of the trigonometric functions in the mathematical library used. Let us be optimistic here and charge 10 flops per evaluation.

The precomputation of the weights can be accelerated by using symmetries. For example, the property

$$\omega_n^{n/2-j} = -\overline{(\omega_n^j)} \tag{3.48}$$

ensures that only the weights ω_n^j with $0 \leq j \leq n/4$ have to be computed. The remaining weights can then be obtained by negation and complex conjugation, which are cheap operations. Symmetry can be exploited further by using the property

$$\omega_n^{n/4-j} = -i\overline{(\omega_n^j)}, \tag{3.49}$$

which is also cheap to compute. The set of weights can thus be computed by eqn (3.47) with $0 \leq j \leq n/8$, eqn (3.49) with $0 \leq j < n/8$, and eqn (3.48) with $0 < j < n/4$. This way, the initialization of the $n/2$ weights in double precision costs about $2 \cdot 10 \cdot n/8 = 2.5n$ flops.

An alternative method for precomputation of the weights would be to compute the powers of ω_n by successive multiplication, computing $\omega_n^2 = \omega_n \cdot \omega_n$, $\omega_n^3 = \omega_n \cdot \omega_n^2$, and so on. Unfortunately, this propagates roundoff errors and hence produces less accurate weights and a less accurate FFT. This method is not recommended [303].

In the parallel case, the situation is more complicated. For example, in the first iteration of the main loop of Algorithm 3.5, $c = 1$ and hence $j_0 = 0$ and $j_2 = s$, so that all processors perform the same set of butterfly operations, but on different data. Each processor performs an unordered sequential FFT of length n/p on its local part of $\mathbf{x}$. This implies that the processors need the same weights, so that the weight table for these butterflies must be replicated, instead of being distributed. The local table should at least contain the weights $\omega_{n/p}^j = \omega_n^{jp}, 0 \leq j < n/(2p)$, so that the total memory used by all processors for this iteration alone is already $n/2$ complex numbers. Clearly, in the parallel case care must be taken to avoid excessive memory use and initialization time.

A brute-force approach would be to store on every processor the complete table of all $n/2$ weights that could possibly be used during the computation. This has the disadvantage that every processor has to store almost the same amount of data as needed for the whole sequential problem. Therefore, this approach is not scalable in terms of memory usage. Besides, it is also unnecessary to store all weights on every processor, since not all of them are used. Another disadvantage is that for small n the $2.5n$ flops of the weight initializations can easily dominate the $(5n\log_2 n)/p$ flops of the FFT itself.

At the other extreme is the simple approach of recomputing the weights whenever they are needed, thus discarding the table. This attaches a weight computation of about 20 flops to the 10 flops of each pairwise butterfly operation, thereby approximately tripling the total computing time. This approach wastes a constant factor in computing time, but it is scalable in terms of memory usage. Still, this may have advantages for certain cache-based architectures with a small cache, where it may be cheaper to recompute data than retrieve them from a table stored in faraway main memory.

Our main aim in this section is to find a scalable approach in terms of memory usage. We call the memory requirements of a BSP algorithm **scalable** if the maximum memory space $M(n,p)$ required per processor satisfies

$$M(n,p) = \mathcal{O}\left(\frac{M_{\text{seq}}(n)}{p} + p\right),\tag{3.50}$$

where $M_{\text{seq}}(n)$ is the memory space required by the sequential algorithm for an input size n, and p is the number of processors. This definition allows for $\mathcal{O}(p)$ overhead, reflecting the philosophy that BSP algorithms are based on all-to-all communication supersteps, where each processor deals with $p-1$ others, and also reflecting the practice of current BSP implementations where each processor stores several arrays of length p. For example, each registration of a variable by the BSPlib primitive `bsp_push_reg` gives rise to an array of length p on every processor, which contains the p addresses of the variable on all processors. Another example is the common implementation of a communication superstep where the number of data to be sent is announced to each destination processor before the data themselves are sent. This information needs to be stored in an array of length p on the destination processor.

Note that in defining scalability, we assume that all processors are equal in memory size (as well as in computing rate), so that it is not really worthwhile to save memory for some processors when this is not possible for the others. After all, this would not increase the size of the largest problem that can be solved. The moral: stick to the SPMD style of programming and do not try to be clever by saving memory space (or computing time) for specific processors.

We can achieve memory scalability by performing a dry run of the algorithm just for computing and storing the weights needed in the order of their use, without actually using them to transform a data vector $\mathbf{x}$. In stage k of the algorithm in the group-cyclic distribution with cycle c, this means we need to compute the $k/(2c)$ complex weights of the local part of the butterfly matrix B_k.

In the computation supersteps with $c < p$, we perform stages $k = 2c, \ldots, (n/p)c$, with $1, 2, 4, \ldots, n/(2p)$ weights, respectively, adding up to a total of $n/p - 1$ complex weights for the whole superstep. We can therefore bound the memory usage for the weights of such a superstep by $2n/p$ reals. The last superstep, which has $c = p$, performs the remaining stages in the cyclic distribution. It starts at stage $k = 2(n/p)c_0 \geq 2p$, where c_0 is the cycle of the previous superstep, and this stage needs $(c_0/c)(n/p)$ weights. The last superstep ends at stage $k = n$, which needs $k/(2c) = n/(2p)$ complex weights. The memory usage for the weights of the last superstep is therefore also at most $2n/p$ reals.

By invoking some basic algebra, we can find a simple upper bound on the memory requirements of the weights. If $t = \lceil \log_2 p/\log_2(n/p) \rceil$, that is the smallest integer for which $(n/p)^t \geq p$ (see the derivation of eqn (3.42)), we have $t+1$ computation supersteps. Then it holds that

$$(t-1)\frac{n}{p} \leq \left(\frac{n}{p}\right)^{t-1} < p,\tag{3.51}$$

where we have used the inequality $rx \leq x^r$ for $x \geq 2$ and integer $r \geq 1$, with substitution of $r = t - 1$ and $x = n/p$. This leads to a total memory for the weights of at most

$$2(t+1)\frac{n}{p} = \frac{4n}{p} + 2(t-1)\frac{n}{p} < \frac{4n}{p} + 2p. \tag{3.52}$$

Adding the $2n/p$ memory needed for the vector $\mathbf{x}$, we decree the total memory use of Algorithm 3.5 to be

$$M_{\text{FFT}} = \frac{6n}{p} + 2p, \tag{3.53}$$

which is scalable. Therefore, we have achieved our initial aim.

An additional benefit of this approach is that the weights used for the butterflies of stage k are packed closely together in the table and that their repeated use enhances the number of cache hits on cache-based architectures. This is in contrast to an approach where the weights are retrieved while jumping through a larger table, which may cause more cache misses.

3.6 Example function `bspfft`

This section presents the program text of the function `bspfft`, which is a straightforward implementation of Algorithm 3.5. This function was written to explain the implementation of the algorithm, and hence its formulation emphasizes clarity and brevity rather than efficiency, leaving room for further optimization (mainly in the computation part). Throughout, the data structure used to store a complex vector of length n is an array of size n containing values of type `double complex`, which is a double-precision type provided by the C99 standard. To use it, we included the header file `complex.h` in `bspedupack.h`, see Appendix A.

The function `bspfft` can also compute an inverse FFT, and it does this by performing all operations of the forward FFT with conjugated weights and scaling the output vector by $1/n$. Before we can use `bspfft`, the function `bspfft_init` must have been called to initialize the weight table and two bit-reversal tables.

The function `butterfly_stage` is a faithful implementation of the kth iteration of the UFFT function in Algorithm 3.4. Depending on the contents of the weights table w, a sequential butterfly stage can be performed or a local part of a parallel butterfly. The table is initialized by the function `bspfft_init`. The function `ufft` shows the use of `butterfly_stage` in a sequential unordered FFT.

The function `permute` permutes a vector by a given permutation σ that swaps component pairs independently; an example of such a permutation is the bit-reversal permutation ρ_n. This type of permutation has the advantage that it can be done in place, requiring only one complex number as extra storage but no additional temporary array. The condition $j < \text{sigma}[j]$ ensures that the swap is executed only if the indices involved are different and that this is done only once per pair. Without the condition the overall effect of the function would be nil!

The bit-reversal initialization function `bitrev_init` fills an array `rho` with bit reverses of indices used in the FFT. The function implements the first part of Algorithm 3.3, which computes ρ_n. Note that in this computation, ρ_k overwrites $\rho_{k/2}$ in the array `rho`, as $\rho_{k/2}$ is not needed anymore. Of course, the bit reverse of an index can also be computed when needed, saving the memory of `rho`, but this would be more costly in computer time. Therefore, we use a table so that the bit reversal is computed only once and its cost can be amortized over several FFTs.

The function `bspredistr` redistributes the vector **x** from the group-cyclic distribution with cycle c_0 to the group-cyclic distribution with cycle c, for a ratio $c/c_0 \geq 1$, as illustrated in Fig. 3.6. (We can derive a similar redistribution function for $c/c_0 < 1$, but we do not need it.) The function is an implementation of Algorithm 3.6, but with one important optimization (I could not resist the temptation!): vector components to be redistributed are sent in blocks, rather than individually. The aim is, of course, to reach a communication rate that corresponds to optimistic values of g, see Section 2.7.

The parallel FFT, like the parallel LU decomposition, is a **regular parallel algorithm**, for which the communication pattern can be predicted exactly, and each processor can determine exactly where every communicated data element goes. In such a case, it is always possible for the user to combine data for the same destination in a block, or **packet**, and communicate them using one put operation. In general, this requires **packing** at the source processor and **unpacking** at the destination processor. No identifying information needs to be sent together with the data since the receiver knows their meaning. (In contrast, for certain irregular algorithms, sending such information cannot be avoided, in which case there is no advantage in packaging by the user and this is better left up to the BSP system. If, furthermore, the size of the data items is small compared with the identifying information, we must sadly communicate at a rate corresponding to pessimistic values of g.)

To perform the packing, we have to answer the question: which vector components move to the same processor? Consider two components, x_j and $x_{j'}$, that reside on the same processor in the old distribution with cycle c_0. Obviously, these components are in the same block of size nc_0/p handled by a group of c_0 processors. Because $c_0 \leq c$, the block size increases on moving to the new distribution, or it stays the same, and because n, p, c_0, c

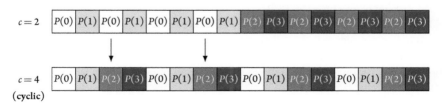

Figure 3.6 Redistribution from group-cyclic distribution with cycle $c_0 = 2$ to cycle $c = 4$ for a vector of size $n = 16$. The number of processors is $p = 4$. Each cell represents a vector component; the number in the cell and the colour denote the processor that owns the cell. The initial distribution has two blocks of size eight; the final distribution has one block of size 16. The arrows show a packet sent by $P(0)$ to $P(2)$.

are powers of two, each block of the old distribution fits entirely into a block of the new distribution. Thus, x_j and $x_{j'}$ will automatically be in the same new block of size nc/p handled by a group of c processors. Furthermore, they will be on the same processor in the new distribution if and only if j and j' differ by a multiple of c. Using eqn (3.39) with c_0 instead of c for j and j', and noting that $j_0 = j_0'$ and $j_2 = j_2'$ because these indices depend only on the processor number, we see that this is equivalent to $j_1 c_0$ and $j_1' c_0$ differing a multiple of c, that is, j_1 and j_1' differing a multiple of $\mathtt{ratio} = c/c_0$. Thus, we can pack components with local indices $\mathtt{j}, \mathtt{j} + \mathtt{ratio}, \mathtt{j} + 2 * \mathtt{ratio}, \ldots$, into a temporary array and then put all of these together, as a packet, into the destination processor, which is determined by component $\mathtt{j}$. The size of a packet is $(n/p)/\mathtt{ratio} = nc_0/(pc)$. If $nc_0 < pc$, components are sent individually. The destination index must be chosen such that two different processors do no write into the same memory location. In general, this can be done by assigning on each receiving processor a piece of memory for each of the other processors. Because of the regularity, the starting point and size of such a location can be computed by the source processor. Since this computation is closely related to the unpacking, we shall treat it together with that operation.

To perform the unpacking, we have to move data from the location they were put into, to their final location on the same processor. Let x_j and $x_{j'}$ be two adjacent components in a packet, with $\mathtt{j'} = \mathtt{j} + \mathtt{ratio}$, and hence $j' = j + (c/c_0)c_0 = j + c$. Since these components are in the same new block, and their global indices differ by c, their new local indices differ by one, $\mathtt{j'} = \mathtt{j} + 1$. We are lucky: if we put x_j into its final location, and the next component of the packet into the next location, and so on, then all components of the packet immediately reach their final destination. In fact, this means that we do not have to unpack!

The function $\mathtt{bspfft}$ performs the FFT computation itself. It follows Algorithm 3.5 and contains no surprises. The local bit reversal and the unordered FFT of length n/p at the start can be combined, yielding a sequential ordered FFT of length n/p. This has the benefit that in this part of the program we can exploit the tremendous amount of available sequential FFT software such as FFTW [115, 116] and various highly tuned programs provided by computer vendors for their hardware. In case $p \ll n/p$, this FFT of $\log_2(n/p)$ stages will account for the vast majority of the flops, and the remainder, a superstep with the last $\log_2 n - \log_2(n/p) = \log_2 p$ stages, will be less important. The variable $\mathtt{start}$ tells where the weights of the current stage k start; after the stage has completed, it is incremented by the number of weights used, $k/(2c)$.

The function $\mathtt{bspfft\_init}$ initializes all tables used. It also follows Algorithm 3.5. The function assumes that the calling program has allocated a suitable amount of storage for the tables. For the weights, the allocated amount is $(t + 1)n/p$ complex numbers, cf. eqn (3.52). In the program, the complex number i is represented by $\mathtt{I}$. The program text of $\mathtt{bspfft}$ is:

```
#include "bspedupack.h"

void butterfly_stage(double complex *x, long n, long k,
                     bool forward, double complex *w){

    /* This sequential function computes one butterfly
```

*stage k of a complex vector x of length n, where k
is even and n mod k = 0. The output overwrites x.*

*The function uses a table w of k/2 complex weights
which must have been initialized beforehand.*

*Each pair (x[j], x[j+k/2]) with 0 <= j < n and
j mod k < k/2 is transformed into a pair
    (x[j] + weight*x[j+k/2], x[j] − weigth*x[j+k/2]),
where weight = w[j mod k] in the forward case
and its complex conjugate otherwise.*

```
*/

for (long r=0; r<n/k; r++){
    for (long j=0; j<k/2; j++){
        double complex weight;
        if (forward) {
            weight= w[j];
        } else {
            weight= conj(w[j]);
        }

        double complex tau= weight * x[r*k+j+k/2];
        x[r*k+j+k/2]= x[r*k+j] − tau;
        x[r*k+j] += tau;
    }
}

} /* end butterfly_stage */


void ufft(double complex *x, long n, bool forward,
          double complex *w){
```

  / This sequential function computes the unordered
    discrete Fourier transform of a complex vector x
    of length n, where n=2^m, m >= 0.
    The output overwrites x.*

    *If forward, then the forward unordered DFT is
    computed, and otherwise the backward unordered DFT.*

    w is a table of complex weights of length n−1,

which must have been suitably initialized before calling this function.
```
*/

long start= 0;
for (long k=2; k<=n; k *=2){
    butterfly_stage(x,n,k,forward,&w[start]);
    start += k/2;
}

} /* end ufft */


void permute(double complex *x, long n, long *sigma){
```

/* *This in-place sequential function permutes a complex vector x of length n >= 1 by the permutation sigma,*
      y[j] = x[sigma[j]], 0 <= j < n.
   The output overwrites the vector x.

   sigma is a permutation of length n that must be decomposable into disjoint swaps; an example is the bit-reversal permutation.
*/

```
for (long j=0; j<n; j++){
    long sigmaj = sigma[j];
    if (j<sigmaj){
        /* swap components j and sigma[j] */
        double complex tmp= x[j];
        x[j]= x[sigmaj];
        x[sigmaj]= tmp;
    }
}

} /* end permute */


void bitrev_init(long n, long *rho){
```

/* *This function initializes the bit-reversal permutation rho of length n, where n=2^m, m >= 0.* */

```
rho[0]= 0;
for (long k=2; k<=n; k *=2){
    for (long j=0; j<k/2; j++){
        rho[j] *= 2;
        rho[j+k/2]= rho[j] + 1;
    }
}

} /* end bitrev_init */


void bspredistr(double complex *x, long n, long c0,
                long c, bool rev, long *rho_p){

    /* This function redistributes the complex vector x
       of length n, from group−cyclic distribution over
       p processors with cycle c0 to cycle c, where
       c0, c, p, n are powers of two with
           1 <= c0 <= c <= p <= n.
       If rev, the function assumes the processor
       numbering is bit−reversed on input.
       rho_p is the bit−reversal permutation of length p.
    */

    long p= bsp_nprocs();
    long s= bsp_pid();
    long np= n/p;

    long j0, j2;
    if (rev) {
        j0= rho_p[s]%c0;
        j2= rho_p[s]/c0;
    } else {
        j0= s%c0;
        j2= s/c0;
    }

    long ratio= c/c0;
    long size= (np >= ratio ? np/ratio : 1 );
    long npackets= np/size;
    double complex *tmp= vecallocc(size);

    for (long j=0; j<npackets; j++){
        long jglob= j2*c0*np + j*c0 + j0;
```

```
        long destproc= (jglob/(c*np))*c + jglob%c;
        long destindex= (jglob%(c*np))/c;
        for (long r=0; r<size; r++)
            tmp[r]=    x[j+r*ratio];

        bsp_put(destproc,tmp,x,destindex*sizeof
            (double complex), size*sizeof(double complex));
    }
    bsp_sync();
    vecfreec(tmp);

} /* end bspredistr */



void bspfft(double complex *x, long n, bool forward,
            double complex *w, long *rho_np, long *rho_p){

    /* This parallel function computes the discrete
       Fourier transform of a complex vector x of length
       n=2^m, m >= 1.
       x must have been registered before calling this
       function. The number of processors p must be a
       power of two.

       The function uses a weight table w which stores
       in sequence all the weights used locally in the
       butterfly stages of the FFT.

       The function uses two bit-reversal permutations:
           rho_np of length n/p,
           rho_p of length p.
       The weight table and bit-reversal permutations
       must have been initialized before calling this
       function.

       If forward, then the DFT is computed,
           y[k] = sum j=0 to n-1 exp(-2*pi*i*k*j/n)*x[j],
       for 0 <= k < n.
       Otherwise, the inverse DFT is computed,
           y[k] = (1/n) sum j=0 to n-1
                            exp(+2*pi*i*k*j/n)*x[j],
       for 0 <= k < n.
       Here, i=sqrt(-1). The output vector y overwrites x.
    */
```

```
long p= bsp_nprocs ();
long np= n/p;
long c= 1;
bool rev= true;

/* Perform a local ordered FFT of length n/p.
   This part can be replaced easily by your favourite
   sequential FFT */
permute(x,np,rho_np);
ufft (x,np,forward ,w);

long k= 2*np;
long start= np−1; // start of current weights in w
while (c < p){
    long c0= c;
    c= ( np*c <= p ? np*c : p);
    bspredistr (x,n,c0 ,c ,rev ,rho_p );
    rev= false ;

    while (k <= np*c){
        butterfly_stage (x,np,k/c ,forward,&w[start ]);
        start += k/(2*c);
        k *= 2;
    }
}

/* Normalize the inverse FFT */
if (!forward){
    double ninv= 1 / (double)n;
    for (long j=0; j<np; j++)
        x[j] *= ninv;
}

} /* end bspfft */


void bspfft_init (long n, double complex *w, long *rho_np ,
                  long *rho_p ){

/* This parallel function initializes all the tables
   used in the FFT. */

long p= bsp_nprocs ();
```

```
long s= bsp_pid ();
long np= n/p;

/* Initialize bit-reversal tables */
bitrev_init (np, rho_np);
bitrev_init (p, rho_p);

/* Initialize weight tables */
long c= 1;
long k= 2;
long start= 0;

while (c <= p){
    /* Initialize weights for superstep with cycle
       c */
    long j0= s%c;
    while (k <= np*c){
        /* Initialize k/(2c) weights for stage k */
        double theta= -2.0 * M_PI / (double)k;

        for (long j=0; j<k/(2*c); j++, start++){
            double jtheta= (j0 + j*c) * theta;
            w[start]= cexp(jtheta*I);
        }

        k *= 2;
    }
    if (c < p)
        c= ( np*c <= p ? np*c : p);
    else
        c= 2*p; //done
}

} /* end bspfft_init */
```

3.7 Experimental results on the Cartesius supercomputer

In this section, we take a critical look at parallel computing. We introduce several new ways of presenting experimental results, and furthermore we will try to explain the results we obtain for our FFT program, which is not always an easy task. Surprises lurk everywhere.

The experiments of this section were performed on up to 512 processors of Cartesius, the national supercomputer in the Netherlands, which was introduced in Section 1.7. This Atos Bullx machine was extended in 2016 by adding a BullSequana X1000 cell with 177 thin nodes, each with two 16-core 2.6 GHz Intel Xeon E5-2697A v4 (Broadwell) CPUs and a memory of 64 GB. The clock speed of a core can be increased from 2.6 to 3.6 GHz when the Turbo Booster is switched on. It is unknown when exactly the booster is working; this makes understanding performance measurements more difficult and harms the reproducibility of results. We used up to eight Broadwell nodes for testing the program bspfft of this chapter. Each CPU core has a theoretical peak performance of 41.7 Gflop/s, so that a 32-core Broadwell node has a peak computing rate of 1.3 Tflop/s. The 16 cores of a single CPU share a 40 MB L3 (level 3) cache. Each core also has a smaller (and faster) L1 cache of 32 kB, and an L2 cache of 256 kB. For inter-node communication, each node has a Mellanox ConnectX-4 InfiniBand adapter providing 100 Gbit/s inter-node bandwidth. Individual Broadwell nodes are allocated entirely to a single user, but this does not hold for the whole BullSequana cell, so that inter-node communication may share resources such as communication links, which may affect results for $p \geq 64$.

In our experiments, we ignore the shared-memory access available within a node, and we use the Broadwell nodes as a distributed-memory machine. We transformed the architecture into a BSP computer by using version 1.1 of BSPonMPI [281]. We compiled our programs using the Intel C compiler, version 15.0.0, with optimization flag -O3. BSPonMPI is run on top of the Intel MPI library for Linux, version 5.0.3. BSPonMPI tries to make best use of the different types of communication offered by the invoked MPI implementation, collective as well as one-sided communications, and it tries to switch between them at an optimal point. The user can provide information to the BSPonMPI runtime system to help in determining good switching points. For this purpose, BSPonMPI provides the bompiprobe tool. More in general, BSPlib implementations such as BSPonMPI and MulticoreBSP for C can often be fine-tuned for a particular architecture.

The BSP parameters of the BullSequana submachine obtained by bspbench for various values of p are given by Table 3.2. Note that g is fairly constant for $p \leq 64$ but that it jumps up for $p = 128$. The value of l grows about linearly with p, but with a big jump when moving from $p = 32$ to $p = 64$, that is when using more than one node. For $p = 32$, the synchronization time of 469 605 flop units is equivalent to about 79 μs.

The measurement of g for $p = 128$ is clearly an outlier, which I investigated further. I repeated the measurement a week after the first measurement, on a quiet, sunny holiday in June 2019. I did not have to wait for long in the queue to run my job, and I got access to consecutively numbered nodes (tcn1708-1711) of the machine, which I did not get the first time. The results, however, were the same. The cause may still be interference by other users, but more likely it may be due to underlying system software, either BSPonMPI or MPI. Plotting the benchmark results showed that in the range of h-values measured, the time of an h-relation follows two straight lines with a jump between them; thus, the higher g-value is a compromise. Measuring in a larger range would give a more accurate (and lower) g-value. I looked further into this problem and noted that an MPI benchmark based on the MPI_Alltoallv primitive displayed even wilder jumps, both upwards and downwards, for $p = 256, 512$. Therefore, the outlier for BSPonMPI is most likely due to the underlying MPI switching from one communication algorithm to a different one with a suboptimal choice of switching parameters. Because of the problem being elsewhere, we will consider the BSP parameters just as given. They might be improved by running bompiprobe for

Table 3.2 Benchmarked BSP parameters p, g, l and the time of a 0-relation for a BullSequana cell consisting of 32-core 2.6 GHz Intel Xeon E5-2697A (Broadwell) nodes. All times are in flop units and they are normalized to the same computing rate ($r = 5.912$ Gflop/s).

p	g	l	$T_{\text{comm}}(0)$
1	315	25 999	16 270
2	352	63 146	47 270
4	333	122 716	96 964
8	328	216 380	146 945
16	350	330 632	221 014
32	450	469 605	312 097
64	500	2 437 872	1 733 434
128	1 800	2 646 273	2 647 049
256	756	5 045 305	4 310 730
512	1 114	4 098 700	3 078 612

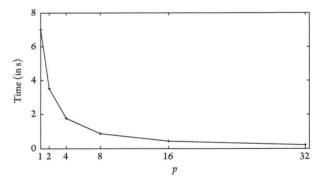

Figure 3.7 Time of a parallel FFT of length $n = 2^{26}$.

a certain period of time to obtain more knowledge of the actual MPI behaviour, and use this knowledge to optimize the installation. Thus we can also view BSPonMPI as a system to tame MPI, providing the best possible h-relations to the user of a particular machine and MPI implementation by employing several possible MPI communication primitives, without the user having to worry too much about any wild MPI behaviour.

Figure 3.7 shows a set of timing results $T_p(n)$ for an FFT of length $n = 2^{26} = 67\,108\,864$. What is your first impression? Does the performance scale well? It seems that for larger numbers of processors the improvement levels off. Well, let me reveal that this figure represents the time of a theoretical, perfectly parallelized FFT, based on a time of 7.035 s for $p = 1$. Thus, we conclude that presenting results in this way may deceive the human eye.

Table 3.3 presents the raw data of our time measurements for the program bspfft of Section 3.6. The results for the sequential program and the parallel program for $p = 1$ are very close, and the parallel overhead must be less than the measurement error, because sometimes the parallel program run on just one processor is even faster than the sequential program. The data for $p \leq 32$ is fairly consistent and displays the expected reduction in execution time. The data for $p > 32$ has to be taken with a grain of salt, because of the problems exposed by the benchmark results from Table 3.2. Still, using more than 32 processors can be beneficial, provided the problem size is large enough; for $n = 2^{26}$, it is even best to use all 512 processors.

Cache effects play a major role in our results, and we need to investigate these to understand some of the observed behaviours. The L1, L2, and L3 caches each fit a complex vector of size $n = 2^{11}, 2^{14}, 1.25 \cdot 2^{21}$, respectively. Note, however, that we also need to store the weights of the FFT, which consume twice the amount of memory as used for x, see eqn (3.53). For $p = 32$, that is one complete node, we have 32 L1 caches, 32 L2 caches, and two L3 caches, so that we can fit problems of size $n \leq 1.33 \cdot 2^{14}$ into the L1 caches, $n \leq 1.33 \cdot 2^{17}$ into the L2 caches, and $n \leq 1.67 \cdot 2^{20}$ into the L3 caches. For larger p, the local data vector of a processor is smaller, and this benefits use of the smaller L1 and L2 caches, leading to higher computing rates. For the largest problem size $n = 2^{26}$, the computation is totally out of cache.

Figure 3.8 compares the actual measured execution time for $n = 2^{26}$ on a Broadwell node with the ideal time. Note that for this large n, the measured time is reasonably close to the ideal time, except perhaps for $p = 32$.

Table 3.3 Time $T_p(n)$ (in ms) of a sequential and parallel FFT on p processors of a BullSequana cell consisting of 32-core 2.6 GHz Intel Xeon E5-2697A (Broadwell) nodes. Problem instances that locally fit into the L1 cache are shown in bold, others that fit into the L2 cache are shown in italic.

p		Length n					
		2^{16}	2^{18}	2^{20}	2^{22}	2^{24}	2^{26}
1	(seq)	2.6	13.9	67.6	356	1 603	7 035
1	(par)	2.6	13.5	65.9	372	1 603	7 017
2		1.6	6.9	37.3	177	927	3 972
4		0.9	3.5	18.9	90	510	2 160
8		0.4	1.9	9.2	48	278	1 238
16		0.2	1.0	4.4	25	195	842
32		0.2	0.6	2.5	16	172	743
64		4.3	4.5	5.5	12	85	382
128		**0.8**	12.8	13.0	17	36	214
256		**1.1**	*1.3*	32.1	33	45	147
512		**1.4**	**0.8**	*1.3*	72	76	107

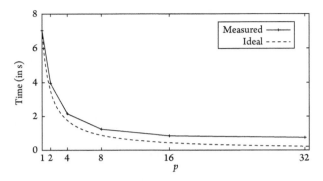

Figure 3.8 Time T_p of an actual parallel FFT of length 2^{26}.

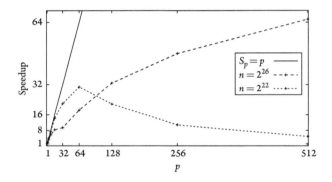

Figure 3.9 Measured speedup $S_p(n)$ of parallel FFT. The ideal value is p.

The **speedup** $S_p(n)$ of a parallel program has been defined in eqn (1.16) as the increase in speed of the program running on p processors compared with the speed of a sequential program. Figure 3.9 gives the speedup for $n = 2^{22}, 2^{26}$ and $p \leq 512$ and compares it to the ideal speedup $S_p = p$. The largest speedup obtained is about 65.6 for $n = 2^{26}$.

The **efficiency** $E_p(n) = S_p(n)/p$, defined in eqn (1.17), gives the fraction of the total computing power that is usefully employed. Figure 3.10 gives the efficiency for $n = 2^{22}, 2^{26}$ and $p \leq 512$.

Another related performance metric is the **normalized cost** $C_p(n)$, which is just the time of the parallel program divided by the time that would be taken by a perfectly parallelized version of the sequential program. This cost is defined as

$$C_p(n) = \frac{T_p(n)}{T_{\text{seq}}(n)/p}. \tag{3.54}$$

Note that $C_p(n) = 1/E_p(n)$, which explains why this cost is sometimes called the **inefficiency**. Figure 3.11 gives the cost of the FFT program for $n = 2^{22}, 2^{26}$ and $p \leq 512$. The

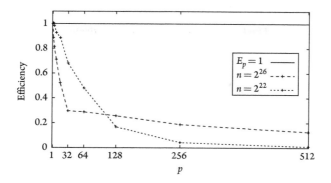

Figure 3.10 Measured efficiency $E_p(n)$ of parallel FFT. The ideal value is 1.

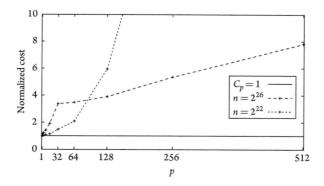

Figure 3.11 Normalized cost $C_p(n)$ of parallel FFT. The ideal value is 1.

difference between the normalized cost and the ideal value of 1 is the parallel **overhead**, which usually consists of load imbalance, communication time, and synchronization time.

A breakdown of the parallel overhead into its main parts can be obtained in practice by performing additional measurements, or theoretically by predictions based on the BSP model. Table 3.4 predicts the computation, communication, and synchronization time of the FFT for $n = 2^{26}$ and $p \leq 32$, based on the costs $5n\log_2 n + 0g + l$ for $p = 1$ and $(5n\log_2 n)/p + 2ng/p + 3l$ for $p > 1$, cf. eqn (3.46). The table also presents the measured times, where we have not inserted any extra synchronizations to measure the separate supersteps. We have taken the computation and communication time of $P(0)$ as our measured timing value, which is a good approximation of the corresponding superstep time; the times of the other processors do not differ much from this value. For the total time T, we did synchronize and hence the given time is exact (and the value is usually a bit higher than the sum of the computation and communication times).

The first observation we can make from Table 3.4 is that it is difficult to predict the computation time accurately just based on the BSP parameters. Our program `bspfft` takes about 4.8 times the computation time predicted for $p = 1$. This is because our benchmark

Table 3.4 Breakdown of predicted and measured execution time (in ms) of the parallel FFT program for $n = 2^{26}$ into computation, communication, and synchronization time, and the total time T.

p	Predicted				Measured		
	T_{comp}	T_{comm}	T_{sync}	T	T_{comp}	T_{comm} $+T_{sync}$	T
1	1 476	0	0.004	1 476	7 048	0	7 048
2	738	4 004	0.032	4 742	3 548	593	4 141
4	369	1 882	0.062	2 251	1 788	428	2 223
8	184	925	0.109	1 109	942	315	1 268
16	92	492	0.167	584	640	209	852
32	46	319	0.238	365	601	154	757

program measured a computing rate of 5.91 Gflop/s for a small DAXPY of length 2^{10}, which fits into the L1 cache, but for an FFT of length 2^{26}, the computations are done out of cache and the rate reduces to 1.26 Gflop/s. Thus, the prediction considerably underestimates the actual computing time T_{comp}.

From Table 3.4, we also learn that the FFT is such a data-intensive computation that one permutation of the data vector already has a serious impact on the total execution time of a parallel FFT program. The prediction overestimates the communication time T_{comm}, because it is based on a pessimistic g-value, whereas the actual parallel FFT was optimized to send data in large packets. The prediction also overestimates the synchronization time T_{sync}, because for $p = 1$ we counted l (for a computation superstep) but in reality there is no synchronization, and for $p > 1$ we counted $3l$ (for two computation supersteps and one communication superstep) where there is only one synchronization. This does not matter much, because the synchronization time is insignificant, even with the high value of l measured in flop time units.

The prediction of the total time T for $p > 1$ reasonably agrees with the measured total time, because the errors made in estimating computation time and communication time partly cancel each other. Of course, it is possible to predict better, for example by measuring the computing rate for this particular application and using that rate instead of r, and perhaps even using a rate that depends on the local vector length. The communication prediction can be improved by measuring optimistic g-values.

Table 3.5 shows the computing rate $R_p(n)$ of all processors together for this application, defined by

$$R_p(n) = \frac{5n \log_2 n}{T_p(n)}, \qquad (3.55)$$

where we take the standard flop count $5n \log_2 n$ as basis (as is customary for all FFT counts, even for highly optimized FFTs that perform fewer flops). The flop rate is useful in com-

Table 3.5 Computing rate $R_p(n)$ (in Gflop/s) of a sequential and parallel FFT on p processors of a BullSequana cell consisting of 32-core 2.6 GHz Intel Xeon E5-2697A (Broadwell) nodes.

p		Length n					
		2^{16}	2^{18}	2^{20}	2^{22}	2^{24}	2^{26}
1	(seq)	2.04	1.74	1.58	1.32	1.28	1.26
1	(par)	2.10	1.79	1.62	1.26	1.28	1.26
2		3.32	3.47	2.87	2.66	2.21	2.23
4		6.28	6.83	5.65	5.19	4.01	4.10
8		12.64	12.70	11.59	9.79	7.37	7.16
16		21.65	24.90	24.37	18.70	10.47	10.52
32		27.48	41.63	42.23	28.76	11.90	11.92
64		1.24	5.42	19.44	40.52	24.15	23.16
128		6.96	1.89	8.22	28.45	56.76	41.36
256		5.02	18.94	3.33	14.33	45.74	60.40
512		3.78	28.44	83.85	6.49	27.05	82.54

paring results for different problem sizes and also for different applications. Furthermore, it tells us how far we are from the advertised peak performance. It is a sobering thought that we need at least four processors to exceed the top computing rate of 5.91 Gflop/s measured for an in-cache DAXPY operation on a single processor. Thus, instead of parallelizing, it may be preferable first to make our sequential program more cache-friendly. If we still need more speed, we turn to parallelism and make our parallel program more cache-friendly. This will decrease the running time and hence increase the computing rate, but paradoxically it will also decrease the speedup and the efficiency, because the communication part remains the same while the computing part is made faster in both the parallel program and the sequential reference program.

To conclude, use of a parallel computer for the 1D FFT can only be justified for very large problems, where the $(5n \log_2 n)/p$ cost of the computation outweighs the $2ng/p$ cost of the communication. But were not parallel computers made exactly for that purpose?

3.8 Bibliographic notes

3.8.1 Sequential FFT algorithms

The basic idea of the FFT was discovered back in 1805 by (who else?) Gauss [119]. It has been rediscovered several times: by Danielson and Lanczos [76] in 1942 and by Cooley and Tukey [71] in 1965. Because Cooley and Tukey's rediscovery took place in the age of digital computers, their FFT algorithm found immediate widespread use in computer programs. As a result, the FFT became connected to their name. Cooley [70] tells the whole story of the discovery in a paper *How the FFT gained acceptance*. He states that one reason for the widespread use of the FFT is the decision made at IBM, the employer of Cooley at that time, to put the FFT algorithm in the public domain and not to try to obtain a patent on this algorithm. In concluding his paper, Cooley recommends not to publish papers in neoclassic Latin (as Gauss did). Heideman, Johnson, and Burrus [142] dug up the prehistory of the FFT and wrote a historical account on the FFT from Gauss to modern times. Some entrance points into the vast FFT literature can be found below.

A large body of work such as the work done on FFTs inevitably contains much duplication. Identical FFT algorithms have appeared in completely different formulations. Van Loan in his book *Computational Frameworks for the Fast Fourier Transform* [303] has rendered us the great service of providing a unified treatment of many different FFT algorithms. This treatment is based on factorizing the Fourier matrix and using powerful matrix notations such as the Kronecker product. The book contains a wealth of material and it is the first place to look for suitable variants of the FFT. We have adopted this framework where possible, and in particular we have used it in describing sequential FFTs and their parallelization using the block distribution.

Karp [171] compares many different ways of performing a sequential bit reversal, and he shows how to compute the bit reversal permutation in linear time, as we do in eqn (3.30).

For those who want to learn more about using the DFT, but care less about how it is actually computed, the book by Briggs and Henson [46] is a good source. It discusses the various forms of the DFT and their relation with continuous Fourier transforms, 2D DFTs, applications such as the reconstruction of images from projections, and related transforms. Bracewell [42] gives a detailed discussion of the continuous Fourier transform; a good understanding of the continuous case is necessary for explaining the results of a discrete transform. The book by Bracewell includes a series of pictures of functions and their continuous Fourier transforms and also a biography of Fourier.

Sequential implementations of various FFTs can be found in *Numerical Recipes: The Art of Scientific Computing* by Press, Teukolsky, Vetterling, and Flannery [253]. This book devotes two chapters to FFTs and their application. Programs included are, among others, complex-valued FFT, real-valued FFT, fast sine transform, fast cosine transform, multidimensional FFT, out-of-core FFT, and convolution.

The fastest Fourier transform in the West (FFTW) package by Frigo and Johnson [115] is an extremely fast sequential program. The latest version is FFTW3, described in [116]. The speed of FFTW comes from the use of hardware-independent **codelets**, straight inline code without loops, in core parts of the software and from the program's ability to adapt itself to the hardware used. Instead of using flop counts or user-provided knowledge about the hardware (such as cache sizes) to optimize performance, the program carries out a set of FFT timings on the hardware, resulting in a **computation plan** for each FFT length. Using actual timings is better than counting flops, since most of the execution time of an FFT is spent in moving data around between registers, caches, and main memory, and not in floating-point operations. A plan is used in all subsequent FFT runs of the corresponding length. An optimal plan is chosen by considering several possible plans: an FFT of length $n = 128$ can be split into two FFTs of length 64 by a so-called radix-2 approach (used in this chapter) but it can also be split into four FFTs of length 32 by a radix-4 approach, and so on. Optimal plans for smaller FFTs are used in determining plans for larger FFTs. Thus, the plans are computed bottom-up, starting with the smallest lengths. The large number of possibilities to be considered is reduced by **dynamic programming**, that is, the use of optimal solutions to subproblems when searching for an optimal solution to a larger problem. (If a solution to a problem is optimal, its solutions of subproblems must also be optimal; otherwise, the overall solution could have been improved.) FFTW is recursive, with the advantage that sufficiently small subproblems fit completely into the cache. The program can handle all FFT lengths n in $\mathcal{O}(n \log n)$ time, not only powers of two. Parallel versions of FFTW exist for shared memory (based on Pthreads or OpenMP) and distributed memory (based on MPI). The latter uses the block distribution on input and has two or three communication supersteps, depending on whether the output must be redistributed into blocks or can remain scrambled.

Xiong, Johnson, Johnson, and Padua [313] describe the Signal Processing Language (SPL), a domain-specific programming language that can be used to implement factorization formulae directly for transform matrices (such as Fourier and Walsh–Hadamard matrices) arising in digital signal processing applications. SPL uses a Lisp-like prefix notation, with an operator preceding its operands, for example (tensor (I 2) (F 2)) to denote $I_2 \otimes F_2$. Many different factorization formulae for the same matrix F_n can be generated automatically using mathematical transformation rules such as the properties of Kronecker products and the radix-m splitting formula,

$$F_{mn} = (F_m \otimes I_n) T_{m,mn} (I_m \otimes F_n) S_{m,mn},$$ (3.56)

which is the basis for the Cooley–Tukey approach [71]. Here, the **twiddle matrix** $T_{m,N}$ is an $N \times N$ diagonal matrix defined by

$$(T_{m,N})_{jj} = \omega_N^{(j \bmod \frac{N}{m})(j \operatorname{div} \frac{N}{m})}, \text{ for } 0 \leq j < N.$$ (3.57)

Furthermore, $S_{m,N}$ is the **mod-m sort matrix**, that is the $N \times N$ permutation matrix defined by

$$S_{m,N}\mathbf{x} = \begin{bmatrix} x(0: m: N-1) \\ x(1: m: N-1) \\ \vdots \\ x(m-1: m: N-1) \end{bmatrix},$$ (3.58)

which has as inverse $S_{m,N}^{-1} = S_{N/m,N}$. Note that $T_{2,N} = \operatorname{diag}(I_{N/2}, \Omega_{N/2})$ and $S_{2,N} = S_N$.

Spiral [255, 256] is a software package based on SPL that translates factorization formulae into a C or Fortran program. In the same spirit as FFTW, an extensive search is carried out over the space of possible factorization formulae and compiler techniques (such as loop unrolling). Here, the search space is restricted in an intelligent way by using dynamic programming or reinforcement learning. Each formula is tested on the specific hardware of the user, and the best formula is taken as the basis for the implementation. A Kronecker-product property used by Spiral which is important for a parallel context is: for every $m \times m$

matrix A and $n \times n$ matrix B,

$$A \otimes B = S_{m,mn}(I_n \otimes A)S_{n,mn}(I_m \otimes B). \tag{3.59}$$

As a special case, we have

$$F_m \otimes I_n = S_{m,mn}(I_n \otimes F_m)S_{n,mn}. \tag{3.60}$$

Equation (3.56) is an example of a **breakdown rule** in Spiral, which decomposes a transform into smaller transforms, whereas eqn (3.59) is a **manipulation rule**, which can be used to find equivalent formulae. As we have seen throughout this chapter, an expression of the form $I_n \otimes F_m$ indicates that we have n-fold parallelism available. In contrast, an expression $F_m \otimes I_n$ points towards opportunities for vectorization, since we can perform the same Fourier transform on m vectors of length n instead of m scalars.

3.8.2 Parallel FFT algorithms

Cooley and Tukey [71] have already observed that all butterflies of one stage can be computed in parallel. The first parallel FFT algorithm was published by Pease [243] in 1968, a few years after the Cooley–Tukey paper. Pease presents a matrix decomposition of the Fourier matrix in which he uses the Kronecker-product notation. Each of the $\log_2 n$ stages of his algorithm requires a so-called **perfect shuffle** permutation S_n^{-1}; this would make an actual implementation on a general-purpose computer expensive. The algorithm, however, was aimed at implementation in special-purpose hardware, with specialized circuitry for butterflies, shuffles, and twiddles.

The parallel FFT algorithms proposed in the earlier literature typically perform $\log_2 (n/p)$ stages locally without communication and $\log_2 p$ stages nonlocally involving both communication and computation, thus requiring a total of $\mathcal{O}(\log_2 p)$ communication supersteps. These algorithms were mostly designed targeting the hypercube architecture, where each processor $s = (b_{q-1} \cdots b_0)_2$ is connected to the $q = \log_2 p$ processors that differ exactly one bit with s in their processor number. Examples of algorithms from this category are discussed by Van Loan [303, Algorithm 3.5.3], by Dubey, Zubair, and Grosch [98], who present a variant that can use every input and output distribution from the block-cyclic family, and by Gupta and Kumar [133] (see also [129, Chapter 13]), who describe the so-called **binary exchange** algorithm. Gupta and Kumar analyse the scalability of this algorithm by using the **isoefficiency** function $f_E(p)$, which expresses how fast the amount of work of a problem must grow with p to maintain a constant efficiency E.

We can make parallel FFT algorithms more efficient if we manage to combine many butterfly stages into one superstep (or pair of supersteps); this way, they require less communication and synchronization. Under mild assumptions, such as $p \leq \sqrt{n}$, this leads to algorithms with only $\mathcal{O}(1)$ supersteps. The BSP algorithm presented in this chapter falls into this category.

The original BSP paper by Valiant [290] discusses briefly the BSP cost of an FFT algorithm that is within a constant factor of optimal, provided $g = \mathcal{O}(\log(n/p))$ and

$l = \mathcal{O}((n/p)\log(n/p))$; for such a ratio n/p, our algorithm also achieves optimality, cf. eqn (3.45). For the common special case $p \leq \sqrt{n}$, this method has been implemented in an unordered DIF FFT by Culler *et al.* [73], demonstrating the application of the LogP model. The computation starts with a cyclic distribution and then switches to a block distribution. The authors avoid contention during the redistribution by scheduling the communications carefully and by inserting additional global synchronizations to enforce strict adherence to the communication schedule. (A good BSPlib system would do this automatically.)

McColl [215] presents a detailed BSP algorithm for an ordered FFT, which uses the block distribution on input and output. The algorithm starts with an explicit bit-reversal permutation and it finishes with a redistribution from cyclic to block distribution. Thus, for $p > 1$ the algorithm needs at least three communication supersteps. Except for the extra communication at the start and finish, the algorithm of McColl is quite similar to our algorithm. His algorithm stores and communicates the original index of each vector component together with its numerical value. This facilitates the description of the algorithm, but the resulting communication should be removed in an implementation because the original indices can in principle be computed by every processor. Furthermore, the exposition is simplified by the assumption that $m - q$ is a divisor of m. This implies that $p = 1$ or $p \geq \sqrt{n}$; it is easy to generalize the algorithm so that it can handle the most common case $1 < p < \sqrt{n}$ as well.

The algorithm presented in this chapter is largely based on work by Inda and Bisseling [164]. This work introduces the group-cyclic distribution and formulates redistributions as permutations of the data vector. For example, changing the distribution from block to cyclic has the same effect as keeping the distribution by blocks but performing an explicit permutation $S_{p,n}$. To be more precise, in both cases the original data element x_j ends up in the same processor $P(j \bmod p)$ at the same local index j div p. The algorithm can handle any number of processors $p \leq n/2$.

Yzelman *et al.* [318] try to obtain state-of-the-art performance for the parallel FFT algorithm of this chapter (in the first edition), by replacing the sequential unordered FFT at the start of the program `bspfft` by a call to FFTW3 and by formulating the butterflies of the later stages using a twiddle approach, which also enables calling FFTW3. Since FFTW3 does not support unordered FFTs, this requires inserting an extra (small) bit reversal before each call to FFTW3. The implementation can handle any number of processors $p \leq n/2$, although results are given only for the common case $p \leq \sqrt{n}$. The package Spiral can also be called if desired, instead of FFTW3. Experimental results for $n = 2^{26}$ show a speedup of 24.4 (compared to sequential FFTW3) for $p = 64$ using BSPonMPI on a distributed-memory machine and a speedup of 13.7 using MulticoreBSP for C on a shared-memory machine. The program reaches a computing rate of 31 Gflop/s on $p = 64$ cores of the shared-memory machine, outperforming the shared-memory parallel version of FFTW3, which reaches 22 Gflop/s. Buurlage and coworkers [52] take a similar approach, using FFTW3 as a sequential kernel within `bspfft`, but they port the program from BSPlib/C to Bulk/C++. Experimental results for $n = 2^{26}$ show a speedup of 5.5 (compared to sequential FFTW3) on a dual-socket shared-memory machine with 16 cores, reaching 24.8 Gflop/s.

A related algorithm is the **transpose** algorithm, which calculates a 1D FFT of size mn by storing the vector **x** as a 2D matrix of size $m \times n$. Component x_j is stored as matrix element

$X(j_0, j_1)$, where $j = j_0 n + j_1$ with $0 \leq j_0 < m$ and $0 \leq j_1 < n$. This algorithm is based on the observation that in the first part of an unordered FFT components within the same matrix row are combined, whereas in the second part components within the same column are combined. The matrix can be transposed between the two parts of the algorithm, so that all butterflies can be done within rows. In the parallel case, each processor can then handle one or more rows. The only communication needed is in the matrix transposition and the bit reversal. For a description and experimental results, see for example Gupta and Kumar [133]. This algorithm works for $p \leq \min(m, n)$. Otherwise, the transpose algorithm must be generalized to a higher dimension. A detailed description of such a generalization can be found in the book by Grama and coworkers [129, Chapter 13]. Note that their algorithm is similar to the BSP algorithm presented here, except that their bit-reversal permutation requires communication.

The 2D view of a 1D FFT can be carried one step further by formulating the algorithm such that it uses explicit shorter-length FFTs on the rows or columns of the matrix storing the data vector. Van Loan [303, Section 3.3.1] calls the corresponding approach the **four-step framework** and the **six-step framework**. The six-step framework is equivalent to a factorization into six factors,

$$F_{mn} = S_{m,mn}(I_n \otimes F_m)S_{n,mn}T_{m,mn}(I_m \otimes F_n)S_{m,mn}. \tag{3.61}$$

This factorization follows immediately from eqns (3.56) and (3.60). In a parallel algorithm based on eqn (3.61), with the block distribution used throughout, the only communication occurs in the permutations $S_{m,mn}$ and $S_{n,mn}$ and hence there are three communication supersteps. These permutations are called **transpositions**, as they correspond to a matrix transposition in the 2D storage view of the vector. The four-step framework is equivalent to the factorization

$$F_{mn} = (F_m \otimes I_n)S_{m,mn}T_{n,mn}(F_n \otimes I_m), \tag{3.62}$$

which also follows from eqns (3.56) and (3.60) and from the symmetry of the Fourier matrix. Note that now the shorter-length Fourier transforms need strided access to the data vector, with stride n for $F_m \otimes I_n$. In a parallel implementation, such access is local if a cyclic distribution is used, provided $p \leq \min(m, n)$.

The four-step and six-step frameworks are cache-friendly: whereas a full-length FFT of size n may not fit into the cache of a computer, shorter-length FFTs of size $\sqrt{n}$ are much more likely to fit, which will result in higher computing rates. The use of genuine FFTs in this approach makes it possible to call fast system-specific FFTs in an implementation. A disadvantage is that the multiplication by the twiddle factors takes an additional $6n$ flops above the $5n \log_2 n$ flops of the original FFT. In a parallel implementation of the four-step and six-step frameworks, the communication is nicely isolated in the permutations.

Once there exists a fastest Fourier transform in the West, we may expect to see a fastest Fourier transform in the East, and indeed Daisuke Takahashi developed FFTE. Takahashi, Uno, and Yokokawa [284] present a parallel 1D FFT from FFTE based on recursive application of the six-step framework, where the Fourier transform of length n is decomposed into smaller transforms of lengths $n^{1/2}, n^{1/4}, \ldots$, until the vector to be transformed fits in cache. The decomposition is mixed-radix, each time choosing between radix 2, 3, 4, 5, and 8. In the parallel algorithm, each global transposition consists of an all-to-all communication superstep followed by a local transposition. Numerical experiments were carried out on the K computer at the RIKEN institute in Japan, ranked first on the TOP500 list in 2011 [279]. Results for $n = 2^{41}$ on 8192 nodes, each with 8 cores, achieve a speed of 18 Tflop/s with the recursive six-step FFT, using MPI for inter-node communication and OpenMP within a node. The running time for $n = 2^{41}$ is 25 s, of which 12.7 s represents communication time.

FFTS, the fastest Fourier transform in the South, has been developed by Blake, Witten, and Cree [36] in New Zealand. It is based on a depth-first recursive conjugate-pair FFT algorithm, which splits an FFT of length n in a single split into one FFT of length $n/2$ and two FFTs of length $n/4$. In contrast to an iterative approach, a recursive approach always exploits the cache hierarchy of the computer used, without being aware of the exact cache sizes; we call such an approach **cache-oblivious**. Another advantage of a recursive approach is that it removes explicit bit reversals, which may take extra time and which may also be difficult to implement for more complicated algorithms such as mixed-radix or conjugate-pair algorithms. In almost all cases, FFTS outperforms the autotuned libraries FFTW, Spiral, UHFFT, and the tested vendor-tuned libraries.

3.8.3 Applications

Applications of the FFT are ubiquitous. Here, we mention only two, very demanding application areas. The spectral transform method for solving partial differential equations on a sphere is widely used in numerical weather prediction and future climate simulation. The spectral transform for a 2D latitude/longitude grid consists of a DFT along each latitude (i.e., in the east–west direction) and a discrete Legendre transform (DLT) along each longitude (i.e., in the north–south direction). In early work, Barros et al. [20] and Foster and Worley [112] parallelized the spectral transform. For over 30 years now, this transform has been a core computation of the Integrated Forecasting System (IFS) [309] of the European Centre for Medium-Range Weather Forecasts (ECMRWF) in Reading, UK. The $\mathcal{O}(n^2)$ computation time of a standard DLT grows faster than the $\mathcal{O}(n \log n)$ time of the FFT, and hence the DLT may become a computational bottleneck especially for high-resolution models. To mitigate this, Wedi and coworkers [310] present a fast spherical harmonics transform. Another potential bottleneck for weather prediction based on parallel spectral transforms is the large amount of communication required, which may reach up to 75% of the total run time for a 2.5 km resolution model [309]. Reducing this amount would speed up the whole computation and would also make it more energy-efficient. The spectral transform has been used by Shingu et al. [267] in a climate simulation on the Earth Simulator, a top-ranking supercomputer in Japan.

The FFT is the computational workhorse in grid methods for quantum molecular dynamics, where the time-dependent Schrödinger equation is solved numerically on a multidimensional grid, see a review by Kosloff [189] and a comparison of different time propagation schemes by Leforestier et al. [195]. In each time step, a potential-energy operator is multiplied by a wave function, which is a local (i.e. point-wise) operation in the spatial domain. This means that every possible distribution including the cyclic one can be used in a parallel implementation. The kinetic-energy operator is local in the transformed domain, that is, in momentum space. The transformation between the two domains is done efficiently using the FFT. A recent example applying this method is the parallel program wavepacket by Dion, Hashemloo, and Rahali [87], which simulates the dynamics of a (1D, 2D, or 3D) wave packet interacting with a time-dependent potential. This program uses FFTW for the FFTs and MPI for parallelism.

Another quantum molecular dynamics example is the parallel computation of a Hamiltonian operator (the sum of the potential-energy and kinetic-energy operators) for a wave function on a 6D grid by Borowski and Klüner [41]. The data are distributed in all dimensions and they are communicated by one-sided communications before and after performing an FFT in each separate dimension. The method is applied in a large-scale 4D quantum dynamical simulation of CO molecules desorbing from a $Cr_2O_3(0001)$ surface after laser irradiation. For actual quantum dynamical applications, today's dimensional frontier is 4D or 5D. For example, Petersen, Mischker, and Klüner [247] simulate the photodissociation of water on a titanium dioxide catalyst with a 4D simulation, motivated by possible future use of hydrogen as a green fuel. They use a 5D potential-energy surface, but fix one coordinate to make the whole calculation feasible.

....

3.9 EXERCISES

Exercise 3.1 The recursive FFT, Algorithm 3.1, splits vectors repeatedly into two vectors of half the original length. For this reason, we call it a **radix-2 FFT**. We can generalize the splitting method by allowing the vectors to be split into r parts of equal length. This leads to a radix-r algorithm.

(a) How many flops are actually needed for the computation of $F_4\mathbf{x}$, where $\mathbf{x}$ is a vector of length four? Where does the gain in this specific case come from compared to the $5n\log_2 n$ flops of an FFT of arbitrary length n?

(b) Let n be a power of four. Derive a sequential recursive radix-4 FFT algorithm. Analyse the computation time and compare the number of flops with that of a radix-2 algorithm. Is the new algorithm faster?

(c) Let n be a power of four. Formulate a sequential nonrecursive radix-4 algorithm. Invent an appropriate name for the new starting permutation. Can you modify the algorithm to handle all powers of two, for example by ending with a radix-2 stage if needed?

(d) Let n be a power of two. Implement your nonrecursive radix-4 algorithm in a sequential function fft4. Compare its performance with a sequential radix-2 function based on functions used in bspfft. Explain your results. Is the difference in performance only due to a difference in flop count?

(e) Modify bspfft to create a parallel radix-4 FFT program bspfft4. Compare the performance of bspfft and bspfft4.

Exercise 3.2 Algorithm 3.5 starts with a sequential FFT of length n/p on every processor. Its implementation in the program bspfft uses a home-brewed FFT, which has not been optimized yet. Assume that $p \leq \sqrt{n}$; this will often hold in practice.

(a) Optimize `bspfft` by replacing the starting part by a call to FFTW [115, 116] or another fast sequential FFT.
(b) Check the gains for various values of n and p.
(c) Any ideas for optimizing the remaining part?

Exercise 3.3 (∗) Let f be a T-periodic smooth function. The Fourier coefficients c_k of f are given by eqn (3.2).

(a) Let d_k be the kth Fourier coefficient of the derivative f'. Prove that $d_k = 2\pi i k c_k / T$. How can you use this relation to differentiate f?
(b) The Fourier coefficients c_k, $k \in \mathbf{Z}$, can be obtained in approximation by eqn (3.3). The quality of the approximation depends on how well the trapezoidal rule estimates the integral of the function $f(t) e^{-2\pi i k t / T}$ on the subintervals $[t_j, t_{j+1}]$. The average of the two function values in the endpoints t_j and t_{j+1} is a good approximation of the integral on $[t_j, t_{j+1}]$ if the function $f(t) e^{-2\pi i k t / T}$ changes slowly on the subinterval. On the other hand, if the function changes quickly, the approximation is poor. Why is the approximation meaningless for $|k| > n/2$? For which value of k is the approximation best? In answering these questions, you may assume that f itself behaves well and is more or less constant on each subinterval $[t_j, t_{j+1}]$. The frequency k/T corresponding to the value $k = n/2$ is known as the **Nyquist frequency** [46].
(c) Let n be even. How can you compute (in approximation) the set of coefficients $c_{-n/2+1}, \ldots, c_{n/2}$ by using a DFT? Hint: relate the y_k's of eqn (3.4) to the approximated c_k's.
(d) Write a parallel program for differentiation of a function f sampled in $n = 2^m$ points. The program should use a forward FFT to compute the Fourier coefficients c_k, $-n/2+1 \leq k \leq n/2$, then compute the corresponding d_k's, and finally perform an inverse FFT to obtain the derivative f' in the original sample points. Use the cyclic distribution. Test the accuracy of your program by comparing your results with analytical results, using a suitable test function. Take for instance the Gaussian function $f(t) = e^{-\alpha(t-\beta)^2}$, and place it in the middle of your sampling interval $[0, T]$ by choosing $\beta = T/2$.

Exercise 3.4 (∗) The **two-dimensional discrete Fourier transform** (2D DFT) of an $n_0 \times n_1$ matrix X is defined as the $n_0 \times n_1$ matrix Y given by

$$Y(k_0, k_1) = \sum_{j_0=0}^{n_0-1} \sum_{j_1=0}^{n_1-1} X(j_0, j_1) \omega_{n_0}^{j_0 k_0} \omega_{n_1}^{j_1 k_1}, \tag{3.63}$$

for $0 \leq k_0 < n_0$ and $0 \leq k_1 < n_1$. We can rewrite this as

$$Y(k_0, k_1) = \sum_{j_0=0}^{n_0-1} \left(\sum_{j_1=0}^{n_1-1} X(j_0, j_1) \omega_{n_1}^{j_1 k_1} \right) \omega_{n_0}^{j_0 k_0}, \tag{3.64}$$

showing that the 2D DFT is equivalent to a set of n_0 1D DFTs of length n_1, each in the row direction of the matrix, followed by a set of n_1 1D DFTs of length n_0, each in the column direction.

(a) Write a function `bspfft2d` that performs a 2D FFT, assuming that X is distributed by the $M \times N$ cyclic distribution with $1 \leq M < n_0$ and $1 \leq N < n_1$. Assume that n_0, n_1, M, N are powers of two. The result Y must be in the same distribution as X. Use the function `bspfft` to perform parallel 1D FFTs, but modify it to perform several FFTs together in an efficient manner. In particular, avoid unnecessary synchronizations.

(b) As an alternative, write a function `bspfft2d_transpose` that first performs sequential 1D FFTs on the rows of X, assuming that X is distributed by the cyclic row distribution, then transposes the matrix, performs sequential 1D FFTs on its rows, and finally transposes back to return to the original distribution.

(c) Let $n_0 \geq n_1$. For each function, how many processors can you use? Compare the theoretical cost of the two implemented algorithms. In particular, which algorithm is better in the important case $p \leq \sqrt{n_0}$? Hint: you can choose M, N freely within the constraint $p = MN$; use this freedom well.

(d) Compare the performance of the two functions experimentally.

(e) Optimize the best of the two functions.

Exercise 3.5 (∗) The **three-dimensional discrete Fourier transform** (3D DFT) of an $n_0 \times n_1 \times n_2$ array X is defined as the $n_0 \times n_1 \times n_2$ array Y given by

$$Y(k_0, k_1, k_2) = \sum_{j_0=0}^{n_0-1} \sum_{j_1=0}^{n_1-1} \sum_{j_2=0}^{n_2-1} X(j_0, j_1, j_2) \omega_{n_0}^{j_0 k_0} \omega_{n_1}^{j_1 k_1} \omega_{n_2}^{j_2 k_2}, \qquad (3.65)$$

for $0 \leq k_d < n_d$, for dimensions $d = 0, 1, 2$.

(a) Write a function `bspfft3d`, similar to `bspfft2d` from Exercise 3.4, that performs a 3D FFT, assuming that X is distributed by the $M_0 \times M_1 \times M_2$ cyclic distribution with $1 \leq M_d < n_d$, for $d = 0, 1, 2$. Assume that n_d and M_d are powers of two, for all d. The result Y must be in the same distribution as X.

(b) Explain why each communication superstep of the parallel 3D FFT algorithm has the same cost.

(c) In the case $n_0 = n_1 = n_2 = n$ and p a power of eight, how do you choose the M_d? Hint: for $p \leq \sqrt{n}$ you need only one communication superstep; for $p \leq n$ only two.

(d) For arbitrary n_0, n_1, n_2, what is the maximum number of processors you can use? Write a function that determines, for a given p, the triple (M_0, M_1, M_2) with $M_0 M_1 M_2 = p$ that causes the least number of communication supersteps.

(e) Test your parallel 3D FFT and check its performance. Is the theoretically optimal triple indeed optimal?

Exercise 3.6 (∗∗) Let **x** be a real vector of length n. We could compute the Fourier transform **y** = F_n**x**, which is complex, by using a straightforward complex FFT. Still, we may hope to do better and accelerate the computation by exploiting the fact that **x** is real.

(a) Show that $y_{n-k} = \overline{y_k}$, for $k = 1, \ldots, n-1$. This implies that the output of the FFT is completely determined by $y_0, \ldots, y_{n/2}$. The remaining $n/2 - 1$ components of **y** can be obtained cheaply by complex conjugation, so that they need not be stored. Also show that y_0 and $y_{n/2}$ are real.

(b) We can preprocess the input data by packing the real vector **x** of length n as a complex vector $\mathbf{x}'$ of length $n/2$ defined by $x'_j = x_{2j} + ix_{2j+1}$, for $0 \le j < n/2$. It turns out that if we perform a complex FFT of length $n/2$ on the conjugate of $\mathbf{x}'$, yielding $\mathbf{y}' = F_{n/2}\overline{\mathbf{x}'}$, we can retrieve the desired vector **y** by

$$ y_k = y'_k - \tfrac{1}{2}(1 - i\omega_n^k)(y'_k - \overline{y'_{n/2-k}}), \tag{3.66} $$

for $0 \le k \le n/2$. Prove by substitution that the postprocessing by (3.66) is correct. The variable $y'_{n/2}$ appearing on the right-hand side for $k = 0$ and $k = n/2$ is defined in a periodic fashion by $y'_{n/2} = y'_0$.

(c) Formulate a sequential algorithm for a real FFT based on the procedure above and count its number of flops. Take care to perform the postprocessing efficiently by computing pairs $(y_k, y_{n/2-k})$ together, using only one complex multiplication. Store constants such as $\tfrac{1}{2}(1 - i\omega_n^k)$ in a table.

(d) Design and implement a parallel algorithm. Assume that n and p are powers of two. You may also assume that p is so small that only one communication superstep is needed in the complex FFT. Start the complex FFT with the cyclic distribution of $\mathbf{x}'$ (which is equivalent to the cyclic distribution of component pairs in **x**). Finish the complex FFT with the zig-zag cyclic distribution shown in Fig. 3.12(b). The **zig-zag cyclic distribution** of a vector **x** of length n over p processors is defined by the mapping

$$ x_j \longmapsto \begin{cases} P(j \bmod p) & \text{if } j \bmod 2p < p \\ P((-j) \bmod p) & \text{otherwise,} \end{cases} \quad \text{for } 0 \le j < n. \tag{3.67} $$

The local index of x_j on the processor that owns it is $\tilde{\jmath} = j \operatorname{div} p$, just as in the cyclic case. This distribution was proposed for use in FFT-based transforms in [165]. What is the main advantage of the zig-zag cyclic distribution? Which operations are local

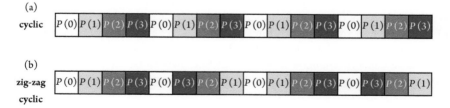

(a)

cyclic

(b)

zig-zag cyclic

Figure 3.12 Distribution of a vector of size 16 over four processors. Each cell represents a vector component; the number in the cell and the colour denote the processor that owns the cell. (a) Cyclic distribution; (b) zig-zag cyclic distribution.

in this distribution? Take care in designing your algorithm: a subtle point is to decide when exactly to redistribute the data.

(e) For which p is your algorithm valid? What is the BSP cost of your algorithm?

(f) Design and implement an inverse real FFT algorithm by inverting each of the main phases of your real FFT and performing them in reverse order.

Exercise 3.7 (∗∗) The **discrete cosine transform** (DCT) can be defined in several ways. One version, which is often used in image processing and data compression, is as follows. Let $\mathbf{x}$ be a real vector of length n. The DCT of $\mathbf{x}$ is the real vector $\mathbf{y}$ of length n given by

$$y_k = \sum_{j=0}^{n-1} x_j \cos \frac{\pi k(j+1/2)}{n}, \quad \text{for } 0 \le k < n. \tag{3.68}$$

(a) In our pursuit of a **fast cosine transform** (FCT), we try to pack the vector $\mathbf{x}$ in a suitable form into another vector $\mathbf{x}'$ of length n, then compute the Fourier transform $\mathbf{y}' = F_n \mathbf{x}'$, and hope to be able to massage $\mathbf{y}'$ into $\mathbf{y}$. By way of miracle, we can indeed succeed if we define

$$x_j' = x_{2j},$$
$$x_{n-1-j}' = x_{2j+1}, \quad \text{for } 0 \le j < n/2. \tag{3.69}$$

We can retrieve $\mathbf{y}$ by

$$y_k = \text{Re}(\omega_{4n}^k y_k'), \quad \text{for } 0 \le k < n/2,$$
$$y_{n-k} = -\text{Im}(\omega_{4n}^k y_k'), \quad \text{for } 1 \le k \le n/2. \tag{3.70}$$

Prove by substitution that this method, due to Narasimha and Peterson [227], is correct.

(b) Formulate a sequential FCT algorithm based on the procedure above and count its number of flops. Since $\mathbf{x}'$ is real, it is best to perform the Fourier transform by using the real FFT of Exercise 3.6.

(c) Describe how you would perform a parallel FCT. Which distributions do you use for input and output? They need not be the same. Motivate your choices and give your distributions a meaningful name. Hint: try to avoid redistribution as much as possible. You may assume that p is so small that only one communication superstep is needed in the complex FFT used by the real FFT.

(d) Analyse the cost of your parallel algorithm, implement it, and test the resulting program. How does the computing time scale with n and p?

(e) Refresh your trigonometry and formula manipulation skills by proving that the inverse DCT is given by

$$x_j = \frac{y_0}{n} + \frac{2}{n}\sum_{k=1}^{n-1} y_k \cos\frac{\pi k(j+1/2)}{n}, \quad \text{for } 0 \le j < n. \qquad (3.71)$$

Hint: Use the formula $\cos\alpha\cos\beta = [\cos(\alpha+\beta)+\cos(\alpha-\beta)]/2$ to remove products of cosines. Derive and use a simple expression for $\sum_{k=1}^{n-1}\cos(\pi kr/n)$, for integer r.

(f) How would you compute the inverse FCT in parallel?

Exercise 3.8 ($**$) The discrete Fourier transform can be generalized from the special case of the field **C** of complex numbers to a **ring**, which is a set R with two binary operations, addition and multiplication, that satisfy certain axioms such as additive commutativity, see any textbook on abstract algebra.

For our generalization of the DFT, we make an even stronger assumption on the ring: we assume that it is a **field F** (with more nice properties, like the existence of a multiplicative inverse) and that it contains a **primitive nth root of unity**, which is an element $\omega \in \mathbf{F}$ that satisfies

$$\omega^n = 1,$$
$$\omega^k \ne 1, \quad \text{for } 1 \le k < n. \qquad (3.72)$$

For $\mathbf{F} = \mathbf{C}$, $\omega = \omega_n$ is a primitive nth root of unity, see Fig. 3.1. (Which other such roots are there in the figure?) The generalized DFT is then defined by

$$y_k = \sum_{j=0}^{n-1} x_j \omega^{jk}, \quad \text{for } 0 \le k < n. \qquad (3.73)$$

(a) Let n be a power of two. Convince yourself that the derivation of the recursive and nonrecursive sequential FFT algorithms from Sections 3.2 and 3.3 still holds for the generalized case, with proper adaptation to computation in a field with a primitive root of unity.

(b) Choose $\mathbf{F} = \mathbf{F}_q = \mathbf{Z}/q\mathbf{Z}$, where q is a prime. Thus, $\mathbf{F}$ is the finite field of integers modulo q. Assume additionally that $q \bmod n = 1$. This guarantees that there exists a primitive nth root of unity ω; for a proof, see e.g. [188, Chapter 2]. Show that $\omega^{n/2} = q - 1 \pmod{q}$. Give a primitive root for the case $q = 17$ and $n = 8$.

(c) Assuming that your machine has a word size of 64 bits, let $\beta = 2^{64}$, so that we can store unsigned integers between 0 and $\beta - 1$. Assume that $q < \beta/2$, so that we can add two numbers from $\mathbf{F}_q$ without overflow and store the result in a 64-bit integer. We can then reduce the result to an integer in the range $[0, q-1]$ by subtracting q if needed. For multiplication, we need a 128-bit integer to store the result; this integer type is provided for instance by the gcc compiler. Write C functions for adding or multiplying two numbers in $\mathbf{F}_q$.

(d)   Modify the program bspfft to perform a fast parallel **number-theoretic transform** (NTT), which is the generalized DFT for a finite field $\mathbf{F}_q$. Also provide an inverse NTT. Test your program for various values of n. Use a suitable value of q, preferably close to $\beta/2$.

(e)   Applications of the fast NTT in computational number theory and cryptography are numerous. For instance, the widely used number theory library NTL written by Victor Shoup[268] is based on a fast NTT. Find an interesting application for your own parallel NTT.

Exercise 3.9 ($**$) Today, wavelet transforms are a popular alternative to Fourier transforms: wavelets are commonly used in areas such as image compression and video compression. An interesting application is the storage and recognition of fingerprints. Wavelets are suitable for dealing with short-lived or transient signals, and for analysing images with highly localized features. Probably the best-known wavelet is the wavelet of order four (DAUB4) proposed by Ingrid Daubechies [77]. A nice introduction to DAUB4 is given in *Numerical Recipes: The Art of Scientific Computing* [253, Section 13.10]. The DAUB4 wavelet transform is defined as follows. For $k \geq 4$, k even, let W_k denote the $k \times k$ matrix given by

$$
W_k = \begin{bmatrix}
c_0 & c_1 & c_2 & c_3 & & & & & \\
c_3 & -c_2 & c_1 & -c_0 & & & & & \\
 & & c_0 & c_1 & c_2 & c_3 & & & \\
 & & c_3 & -c_2 & c_1 & -c_0 & & & \\
 & & & & \ddots & & & & \\
 & & & & & & c_0 & c_1 & c_2 & c_3 \\
 & & & & & & c_3 & -c_2 & c_1 & -c_0 \\
c_2 & c_3 & & & & & & & c_0 & c_1 \\
c_1 & -c_0 & & & & & & & c_3 & -c_2
\end{bmatrix},
$$

where the coefficients are given by $c_0 = (1 + \sqrt{3})/(4\sqrt{2})$, $c_1 = (3 + \sqrt{3})/(4\sqrt{2})$, $c_2 = (3 - \sqrt{3})/(4\sqrt{2})$, and $c_3 = (1 - \sqrt{3})/(4\sqrt{2})$. For this choice of wavelet, the discrete wavelet transform (DWT) of a real input vector $\mathbf{x}$ of length $n = 2^m$ can be obtained by: first multiplying $\mathbf{x}$ with W_n and then moving the even components of the result to the front, that is, multiplying the result with S_n; repeating this procedure on the first half of the current vector, using $W_{n/2}$ and $S_{n/2}$; and so on. The algorithm terminates after multiplication by W_4 and S_4. We denote the result, obtained after $m - 1$ stages, by $W\mathbf{x}$.

(a)   Factorize W in terms of matrices W_k, S_k, and I_k of suitable size, similar to the sequential factorization of the Fourier matrix F_n. You can use the notation $\mathrm{diag}(A_0, \ldots, A_r)$, which stands for a block-diagonal matrix with blocks $A_0, \ldots, A_r$ on the diagonal.

(b)   How many flops are needed to compute $W\mathbf{x}$? How does this scale compared with the FFT? What does this mean for communication in a parallel algorithm?

(c)   Formulate a sequential algorithm that computes $W\mathbf{x}$ in place, without performing permutations. The output data will become available in scrambled order. Usually, there is no need to unscramble. Still, to unscramble the data in one final permutation, where would we have to move the output value at location $28 = (0011100)_2$ for length $n = 128$? And at $j = (b_{m-1} \cdots b_0)_2$ for arbitrary length n?

(d) Choose a data distribution that enables the development of an efficient parallel in-place DWT algorithm. This distribution must be used on input and as long as possible during the algorithm.

(e) Formulate a parallel DWT algorithm. Hint: avoid communicating data at every stage of your algorithm. Instead, be greedy and compute what you can from several stages without communicating in between. Then communicate and finish the stages you started. Furthermore, find a sensible way of finishing the whole algorithm.

(f) Analyse the BSP cost of the parallel DWT algorithm.

(g) Compare the characteristics of your DWT algorithm to those of the parallel FFT, Algorithm 3.5. What are the essential similarities and differences?

(h) Implement and test your algorithm.

(i) Prove that the matrix W_k is orthogonal (i.e., $W_k^T W_k = I_k$, or equivalently $W_k W_k^T = I_k$) by showing that its rows are mutually orthogonal and have unit norm. Thus W is orthogonal and $W^{-1} = W^T$. Extend your program so that it can also compute the inverse DWT.

(j) Take a picture of a beloved person or animal, translate it into a matrix A, where each element represents a pixel, and perform a 2D DWT by carrying out 1D DWTs over the rows, followed by 1D DWTs over the columns. Choose a threshold value $\tau > 0$ and set all matrix elements a_{jk} with $|a_{jk}| \leq \tau$ to zero. What would the compression factor be if we stored A as a sparse matrix by keeping only the nonzero values a_{jk} together with their index pairs (j, k)? What does your beloved one look like after an inverse 2D DWT? You may vary τ.

Exercise 3.10 (∗∗) The **discrete convolution** of two vectors $\mathbf{u}$ and $\mathbf{v}$ of length n is defined as the vector $\mathbf{u} * \mathbf{v}$ of length n with

$$(\mathbf{u} * \mathbf{v})_k = \sum_{j=0}^{n-1} u_j v_{k-j}, \quad \text{for } 0 \leq k < n, \tag{3.74}$$

where v_j for $j < 0$ is defined by periodic extension with period n, $v_j = v_{j+n}$.

(a) Prove the convolution theorem:

$$(F_n(\mathbf{u} * \mathbf{v}))_k = (F_n \mathbf{u})_k (F_n \mathbf{v})_k, \quad \text{for } 0 \leq k < n. \tag{3.75}$$

How can we use this to perform a fast convolution? An important application of convolutions is high-precision arithmetic, used for instance in the record computation of π in zillions of decimals. This will become clear in the following.

(b) A large nonnegative integer can be stored as a sequence of coefficients, which represents its expansion in a radix-r digit system,

$$x = (x_{m-1} \cdots x_1 x_0)_r = \sum_{k=0}^{m-1} x_k r^k, \tag{3.76}$$

where $0 \leq x_k < r$, for all k. We can view the integer x as a vector $\mathbf{x}$ of length m with integer components. Show that we can use a convolution to compute the product xy of two integers x and y. Hint: pad the vectors of length m with at least $m - 1$ zeros, giving the vector $\mathbf{x} = (x_0, \ldots, x_{m-1}, 0, \ldots, 0)^T$ of length $n \geq 2m - 1$, and a similar vector $\mathbf{y}$ of length n. The vector $\mathbf{x} * \mathbf{y}$ then contains the coefficients of xy in the form (3.76), although they may be larger than or equal to r. The coefficients can be reduced to values between 0 and $r - 1$ by performing carry-add operations, similar to those used in ordinary decimal arithmetic.

(c) Use a parallel FFT to multiply two large integers in parallel. Choose $r = 256$, so that an expansion coefficient can be stored in a byte, that is, a `char`. Take n as a power of two. Choose a suitable distribution for the FFTs and the carry-adds, not necessarily the same distribution. On input, each coefficient x_k is stored as a complex number, and on output the result must be rounded to the nearest integer. Check the maximum rounding error incurred during the convolution, to see whether the components of the result vector are sufficiently close to the nearest integer, with a solid safety margin.

(d) Check the correctness of the result by comparing with an ordinary (sequential) large-integer multiplication program, based on the $\mathcal{O}(m^2)$ algorithm you learned at primary school. Sequentially, which m is the break-even point between the two multiplication methods?

(e) Multiply

334780716989568987860441698482126908177047949837137685
689124313889828837938780022876147116525317430877378144
67999489

and

367460436667995904282446337996279526322791581643430876
426760322838157396665112792333734171433968102700927987
36308917

using your parallel large integer multiplication function. The answer should equal

123018668453011775513049495838496272077285356959533479
219732245215172640050726365751874520219978646938995647
494277406384592519255732630345373154826850791702612214
291346167042921431160222124047927473779408066535141959
7459856902143413,

a number known as RSA-768 (with 768 bits and 232 decimal digits). The reverse computation, finding the two prime factors of RSA-768 was posed as a cryptanalytic challenge by RSA Security. Its solution was announced in December 2009 by Kleinjung et al. [184]. The solution of RSA-768 took two years of coordinated computation on many different computers, comprising the equivalent of about 2000 CPU years on a single-core 2.2 GHz AMD Opteron processor. This is the largest RSA challenge solved so far. Solving RSA-1024 with 1024 bits would achieve a real breakthrough. (In the past, it would also have given you a prize of $100 000, but alas, the prizes have been withdrawn by RSA Security, which considers the challenges now obsolete.)

(f) Develop parallel functions for addition and subtraction operations on large integers using the block distribution. Allow for negative integers by storing the sign of an integer separately.

(g) The **Newton–Raphson** method for finding a zero of a function f, that is, an x with $f(x) = 0$, computes successively better approximations

$$x^{(k+1)} = x^{(k)} - \frac{f(x^{(k)})}{f'(x^{(k)})}. \tag{3.77}$$

Apply this method with $f(x) = 1/x - a$ and $f(x) = 1/x^2 - a$ to compute $1/a$ and $1/\sqrt{a}$, respectively, with high precision for a given fixed real a using your parallel functions. Choose a suitable representation of a as a finite sequence of bytes. Pay special attention to termination of the Newton–Raphson iterations.

(h) At the time of writing, the world record in π computation is held by Emma Haruka Iwao from Google, who used the program y-cruncher written by Alexander Yee to compute 31 415 926 535 897 decimal digits of π on π-day (March 14) 2019. Her computation took 121 days on 25 Google Cloud virtual machines running on Intel Skylake processors with AVX-512 support. It required a total memory of 170 TB (1 TB = 1 terabyte = 10^{12} byte). The algorithm used is based on the Chudnovsky formula [68]. A previous record, by Kanada and Takahashi who got 206 158 430 000 digits right in 1999 used the Gauss–Legendre method proposed by Brent [45] and Salamin [264], which works as follows. Define sequences $a_0, a_1, a_2, \ldots$ and $b_0, b_1, b_2, \ldots$ by $a_0 = \sqrt{2}$, $b_0 = 1$, $a_{k+1} = (a_k + b_k)/2$ is the **arithmetic mean** of the pair (a_k, b_k), and $b_{k+1} = \sqrt{a_k b_k}$ is its **geometric mean**, for $k \geq 0$. Let $c_k = 2^k(a_k^2 - b_k^2)$. Define the sequence $d_0, d_1, d_2, \ldots$ by $d_0 = 1$ and $d_{k+1} = d_k - c_{k+1}$. Then $\lim_{k\to\infty} 2a_k^2/d_k = \pi$, with fast convergence: the number of digits of π produced doubles at every iteration. Use your own parallel functions to compute as many decimal digits of π as you can. You need an efficient conversion from binary to decimal digits to produce human-readable output, or you have to waste some memory and reduce the radix to $r = 100$.

4

. . • . .

Sparse matrix–vector multiplication

4.1 The problem

Sparse matrices are matrices that are, well, sparsely populated by nonzero elements. The vast majority of their elements are zero. This is in contrast to **dense matrices**, which have mostly nonzero elements. The borderline between sparse and dense may be hard to draw, but it is usually clear whether a given matrix is sparse or dense.

For a sparse $n \times n$ matrix A, we denote the number of nonzeros by

$$nz(A) = |\{a_{ij} : 0 \leq i, j < n \wedge a_{ij} \neq 0\}|, \tag{4.1}$$

the average number of nonzeros per row or column by

$$c(A) = \frac{nz(A)}{n}, \tag{4.2}$$

and the **density** by

$$d(A) = \frac{nz(A)}{n^2}. \tag{4.3}$$

In this terminology, a matrix is sparse if $nz(A) \ll n^2$, or equivalently $c(A) \ll n$, or $d(A) \ll 1$. We drop the A and write $nz, c,$ and d in cases where this does not cause confusion. For simplicity, we stick to square $n \times n$ matrices, but it is easy to extend our treatment to rectangular matrices of size $m \times n$ with $m \neq n$. An example of a small sparse matrix is given by Fig. 4.1.

Sparse matrix algorithms are much more difficult to analyse than their dense matrix counterparts. Still, we can get a bit of a grip on their time and memory requirements by analysing them in terms of n and c, while making simplifying assumptions. For instance, we may assume that c remains constant during a computation, or even that each matrix row has a fixed number of nonzeros c.

In practical applications, sparse matrices are the rule rather than the exception. A sparse matrix arises in every situation where each variable from a large set of variables is connected to only a few others. For example, in a computation scheme for the heat equation discretized on a two-dimensional (2D) grid, the temperature at a grid point may be related to the

Parallel Scientific Computation: A Structured Approach Using BSP. Second Edition. Rob H. Bisseling, Oxford University Press (2020). © Rob H. Bisseling.
DOI: 10.1093/oso/9780198788348.001.0001

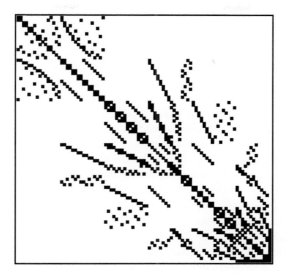

Figure 4.1 Sparse matrix cage6 with $n = 93$, $nz = 785$, $c = 8.4$, and $d = 9.1\%$, generated in a DNA electrophoresis study by van Heukelum, Barkema, and Bisseling [302]. The matrix can be downloaded from the SuiteSparse Matrix Collection [79], formerly known as the University of Florida sparse matrix collection. Black squares denote nonzero elements; white squares denote zeros. This transition probability matrix represents the movement of a DNA polymer in a gel under the influence of an electric field. Matrix element a_{ij} represents the probability that a polymer in state j moves to a state i. The matrix is **stochastic**, i.e., $0 \leq a_{ij} \leq 1$ for all i,j, and $\sum_{i=0}^{n-1} a_{ij} = 1$ for all j. The matrix has the name cage6 because the model used is the cage model and the polymer modelled contains six monomers. The sparsity pattern of this matrix is symmetric (i.e., $a_{ij} \neq 0$ if and only if $a_{ji} \neq 0$), but the matrix itself is unsymmetric (since in general $a_{ij} \neq a_{ji}$). In this application, the eigensystem $Ax = x$ is solved by the power method, which computes $Ax, A^2x, A^3x, \ldots$, until convergence. Solution component x_i represents the frequency of state i in the steady-state situation.

temperatures at the neighbouring grid points to the north, east, south, and west. This can be expressed by a sparse linear system involving a sparse matrix with $c = 5$.

The problem studied in this chapter is the multiplication of a sparse square matrix A and a dense vector $\mathbf{v}$, yielding a dense vector $\mathbf{u}$,

$$\mathbf{u} := A\mathbf{v}. \tag{4.4}$$

The size of A is $n \times n$ and the length of the vectors is n. The components of $\mathbf{u}$ are defined by

$$u_i = \sum_{j=0}^{n-1} a_{ij} v_j, \quad \text{for } 0 \leq i < n. \tag{4.5}$$

Of course, we can exploit the sparsity of A by summing only those terms for which $a_{ij} \neq 0$.

Sparse matrix–vector multiplication (SpMV) is almost trivial as a sequential problem, but it is surprisingly rich as a parallel problem. Different sparsity patterns of A lead to a wide variety of communication patterns during a parallel computation. The main task then is to keep this communication within bounds.

The SpMV operation is important in a range of computations, most notably in the iterative solution of linear systems and eigensystems. **Iterative solution methods** start with an initial guess $\mathbf{x}^0$ of the solution and then successively improve it by finding better approximations $\mathbf{x}^k$, $k = 1, 2, \ldots$, until convergence within a prescribed error tolerance; however, convergence is not always guaranteed. Examples of such methods are the conjugate gradient method for solving symmetric positive definite sparse linear systems $A\mathbf{x} = \mathbf{b}$ and the Lanczos method for solving symmetric sparse eigensystems $A\mathbf{x} = \lambda\mathbf{x}$; for an introduction, see [124]. The attractive property of SpMV as the main kernel of these solvers is that the matrix does not change, and in particular that it remains sparse throughout the computation. This is in contrast to **direct solution methods** such as sparse LU decomposition that create **fill-in**, that is, new nonzeros.

An application of SpMV that has a daily impact on our lives is web search. The importance of web pages can be determined by the **PageRank** algorithm proposed by Google founders Sergey Brin and Larry Page in 1998 [47]. PageRank exploits the hyperlink structure of the World Wide Web to quantify the importance of all web pages; the resulting ranking value is used to decide the order in which search results are presented for a certain query, the top-10 being the most important. Has anyone ever looked at results beyond the top-30?

We can capture the structure of the World Wide Web in an $n \times n$ matrix A, defined by

$$a_{ij} = \begin{cases} 1 & \text{if there is a hyperlink from page } j \text{ to page } i \\ 0 & \text{otherwise,} \end{cases} \quad \text{for } 0 \leq i, j < n. \quad (4.6)$$

This matrix is sparse because pages usually link to a limited number of other pages. The matrix is also huge: at the time of writing, there exist about 10^9 websites, containing many more individual web pages, so we easily reach $n = 10^{10}$. The hyperlinks (**links**, for short) starting at a page are called the page's **outlinks**, and those pointing towards it are called its **inlinks**. The average number of outlinks per page is somewhere in the range of $c = 10$ (Google once recommended keeping the number below a 100). There may be large deviations from the average because relatively few pages have many outlinks, and many pages have few outlinks. Figure 4.2 gives an example of a link matrix obtained by crawling the web starting at a particular URL.

The matrix A can tell us a lot about the importance of web pages. For instance, if we compute $A\mathbf{e}$, where $\mathbf{e} = (1, 1, \ldots, 1)^{\mathrm{T}}$, we obtain

$$(A\mathbf{e})_i = \sum_{j=0}^{n-1} a_{ij}, \quad (4.7)$$

that is, the total number of inlinks of page i, which can serve as a first, crude measure of its importance. A more realistic measure is obtained by taking into account that a link from a page with many outlinks is less meaningful than a link from a page with only a few outlinks.

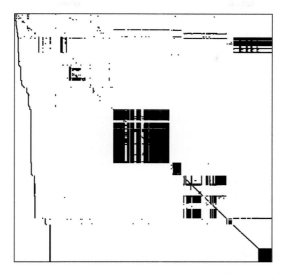

Figure 4.2 Link matrix `bspww500` of size 500×500 with $13\,400$ nonzeros. The matrix represents 500 web pages and the links connecting them. It was obtained by a breadth-first search of the World Wide Web starting at `http://www.bsp-worldwide.org`. The search was performed on May 22, 2017 using the web crawler `surfer.m` written in MATLAB by Cleve Moler [226, Chapter 7].

If $c_j = \sum_{i=0}^{n-1} a_{ij}$ is the number of outlinks of page j, i.e., the number of nonzeros in matrix column j, we can define an $n \times n$ diagonal matrix D by $d_{jj} = \max(1, c_j)$, and then scale A, giving the matrix AD^{-1}. This divides the contribution of each outlink by the total number of outlinks on its web page. Note that we put a 1 on the diagonal for pages without outlinks (so-called **dangling nodes**, often a PDF file or an image file) to prevent division by zero.

The importance of web pages as obtained by multiplying AD^{-1} with a uniform input vector can be interpreted within a **random surfer** model, where a web surfer moves from page to page following one of the outlinks of the current page at random. If we start with a vector $\mathbf{x}^0 = \mathbf{e}/n$, where x_i represents the fraction of surfers currently at page i, then $AD^{-1}\mathbf{x}$ is the vector with fractions after an iteration where every surfer moves once. Of course, we can repeat the process, and after a sufficient number of iterations we obtain the fraction of surfers expected to be at each web page in the steady state.

A small complication arises because a surfer cannot escape from dangling nodes. Page and Brin remedied this problem (and some other problems as well) by letting the surfer follow a random outlink with a probability α (magically set to a value $\alpha = 0.85$) and jump ('teleport') to a random page with a probability $1 - \alpha$. The jump is supposed to model a **bored surfer**. The resulting Google matrix is thus

$$G = \alpha AD^{-1} + (1 - \alpha)\frac{1}{n}\mathbf{e}\mathbf{e}^{\mathrm{T}}. \qquad (4.8)$$

Note that the $n \times n$ matrix $\mathbf{ee}^{\mathrm{T}}$ consists of all ones; it has rank 1 and is dense, but it need not be stored explicitly. Instead, multiplying a vector $\mathbf{x}$ by this matrix is carried out as

$$\mathbf{ee}^{\mathrm{T}}\mathbf{x} = \mathbf{e}(\mathbf{e}^{\mathrm{T}}\mathbf{x}) = \left(\sum_{i=0}^{n-1} x_i\right)\mathbf{e}. \tag{4.9}$$

For more details, see the book by Langville and Meyer [192].

The Hyperlink-Induced Topic Search (HITS) algorithm [183] is an important algorithm from the area of web search that is an alternative to PageRank and that requires multiplication of a vector by the matrix $A^{\mathrm{T}}A$, where A is the link matrix defined by eqn (4.6). This algorithm assigns two importance values to each web page i: an **authority** value u_i which expresses how authoritative the page is as a source of information, and a **hub** value v_i which expresses how far its hyperlinks point to authorities. An authority vector $\mathbf{u}$ can be computed from a hub vector $\mathbf{v}$ by $\mathbf{u} := A\mathbf{v}$, and a hub vector from an authority vector by $\mathbf{v} := A^{\mathrm{T}}\mathbf{u}$. Repeated application of $A^{\mathrm{T}}A$ (with suitable normalization) to an initial hub vector $\mathbf{v}^0 = \mathbf{e}/n$ will, after a sufficient number of iterations, lead to the desired hub vector $\mathbf{v}$. The corresponding authority vector is then $A\mathbf{v}$.

A very different reason for studying SpMV is that it yields more insight into other areas of scientific computation. In a molecular dynamics simulation, or an n-body simulation in general, the interaction between particles i and j can be described by a force f_{ij}. For short-range interactions, this force is zero if the particles are far apart. This implies that the force matrix F is sparse. The computation of the new positions and velocities of particles moving under two-particle forces is similar to the multiplication of a vector by $F + I$, where a unit diagonal is included to represent the contribution of a particle to its own new position and velocity. A 2D particle domain and the corresponding matrix are shown in Fig. 4.3.

Algorithm 4.1 is a sequential SpMV algorithm. The 'for all'-statement of the algorithm must be interpreted such that all index pairs involved are handled in some arbitrary sequential order. Tests such as '$a_{ij} \neq 0$' need never be performed in an actual implementation, since only the nonzeros of A are stored in the data structure used. The formulation '$a_{ij} \neq 0$' is a simple notational device for expressing sparsity without having to specify the details of a data structure. This allows us to formulate sparse matrix algorithms that are data-structure independent. The algorithm costs $2cn$ flops.

Algorithm 4.1 Sequential sparse matrix–vector multiplication.

---

input: A : sparse $n \times n$ matrix,
          $\mathbf{v}$: dense vector of length n.
output: $\mathbf{u}$: dense vector of length n, $\mathbf{u} = A\mathbf{v}$.

```
for i := 0 to n − 1 do
    u_i := 0;
    for all (i, j) : 0 ≤ i, j < n ∧ a_ij ≠ 0 do
        u_i := u_i + a_ij v_j;
```

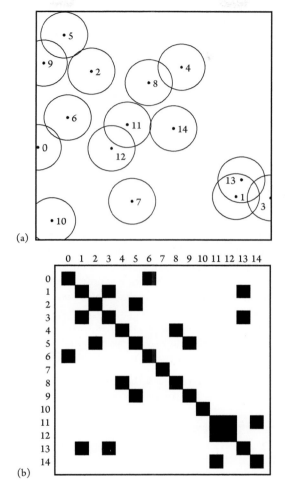

(a)

(b)

Figure 4.3 (a) Two-dimensional molecular dynamics domain of size 1.0×1.0 with 15 particles. Two particles interact if they are within a distance $r_c = 0.2$ from each other, where r_c is the cut-off radius of a short-range potential function. Each circle depicts a region of radius $r_c/2$ around a particle; thus, two particles interact if their circles intersect. (b) The matrix $F + I$, where F is the sparse 15×15 force matrix corresponding to interactions in (a). If a particle i interacts with another particle j, nonzeros f_{ij} and f_{ji} appear in F.

4.2 Sparse matrices and their data structures

The main advantage of exploiting sparsity is a reduction in memory usage (zeros are not stored) and computation time (operations with zeros are skipped or simplified). There is, however, a price to be paid, because sparse matrix algorithms are more complicated than their dense equivalents. Developing and implementing sparse algorithms costs more human time and effort. Furthermore, sparse matrix computations have a larger integer overhead associated with each floating-point operation. This implies that sparse matrix algorithms are less efficient than dense algorithms on sparse matrices that are relatively dense, with a density approaching one.

In this section, we discuss a few basic concepts from sparse matrix computations. For an extensive coverage of this field, see for instance the books by Duff, Erisman, and Reid [99] on direct methods and by Saad [262] and van der Vorst [298] on iterative methods. To illustrate a fundamental sparse technique, we first study the addition of two sparse vectors.

Assume that we have to add an input vector $\mathbf{y}$ of length n to an input vector $\mathbf{x}$ of length n, overwriting $\mathbf{x}$, that is, we have to perform $\mathbf{x} := \mathbf{x} + \mathbf{y}$. The vectors are sparse, which means that $x_i = 0$ for most i and $y_i = 0$ for most i. We denote the number of nonzeros of $\mathbf{x}$ by c_x and that of $\mathbf{y}$ by c_y.

To store $\mathbf{x}$ as a sparse vector, we only need $2c_x$ memory cells: for each nonzero, we store its index i and numerical value x_i as a pair (i, x_i). Since storing $\mathbf{x}$ as a dense vector requires n cells, we save memory if $c_x < n/2$. There is no need to order the pairs. In fact, ordering is sometimes disadvantageous in sparse matrix computations, for instance when the benefit from ordering the input is small but the obligation to order the output is costly. In the sparse data structure for the vector $\mathbf{x}$, it is stored as an array x of c_x nonzeros. For a nonzero x_i stored in position j, $0 \le j < c_x$, it holds that $x[j].i = i$ and $x[j].a = x_i$.

The computation of the new component x_i requires a floating-point addition only if both $x_i \ne 0$ and $y_i \ne 0$. The case $x_i = 0$ and $y_i \ne 0$ does not require a flop because the addition reduces to an assignment $x_i := y_i$. For $y_i = 0$, nothing needs to be done.

Example 4.1 Vectors $\mathbf{x}, \mathbf{y}$ have length $n = 8$; their number of nonzeros is $c_x = 3$ and $c_y = 4$, respectively. Let $\mathbf{z} = \mathbf{x} + \mathbf{y}$. The sparse data structure for $\mathbf{x}, \mathbf{y}$, and $\mathbf{z}$ is:

$x[j].a =$	2	5	1		
$x[j].i =$	5	3	7		

$y[j].a =$	1	4	1	4	
$y[j].i =$	6	3	5	2	

$z[j].a =$	3	9	1	1	4
$z[j].i =$	5	3	7	6	2

Now, I suggest you pause for a moment to think about how you would add two vectors $\mathbf{x}$ and $\mathbf{y}$ that are stored in the data structure described above. When you are done contemplating this, you may realize that the main problem is to find the matching pairs (i, x_i) and (i, y_i) without incurring excessive costs; this precludes for instance sorting. The magic trick is to use an auxiliary array of length n that has been initialized already. We can use this array to register the location of the components of the vector $\mathbf{y}$ in its sparse data structure, so that for a given i, we can directly find the location $j = yloc[i]$ where y_i is stored. A value $yloc[i] = -1$ denotes that y_i is not stored in the data structure, implying that $y_i = 0$. After the computation, $yloc$ must be left behind in the same state as before the computation, that

---

Algorithm 4.2 Addition of two sparse vectors.

---

input: $\mathbf{x}$: sparse vector with $c_x \geq 0$ nonzeros, $\mathbf{x} = \mathbf{x}_0$,
        $\mathbf{y}$: sparse vector with $c_y \geq 0$ nonzeros,
        $yloc$: dense vector of length n, $yloc[i] = -1$, for $0 \leq i < n$.
output: $\mathbf{x} = \mathbf{x}_0 + \mathbf{y}$, $yloc[i] = -1$, for $0 \leq i < n$.

     { Register location of nonzeros of $\mathbf{y}$}
     for $j := 0$ **to** $c_y - 1$ **do**
        $yloc[y[j].i] := j;$

     { Add matching nonzeros of $\mathbf{x}$ and $\mathbf{y}$ }
     for $j := 0$ **to** $c_x - 1$ **do**
        $i := x[j].i;$
        if $yloc[i] \neq -1$ **then**
           $x[j].a := x[j].a + y[yloc[i]].a;$
           $yloc[i] := -1;$

     { Append remaining nonzeros of $\mathbf{y}$ to $\mathbf{x}$ }
     for $j := 0$ **to** $c_y - 1$ **do**
        $i := y[j].i;$
        if $yloc[i] \neq -1$ **then**
           $x[c_x].i := i;$
           $x[c_x].a := y[j].a;$
           $c_x := c_x + 1;$
           $yloc[i] := -1;$

---

is, with every array element set to -1. For each nonzero y_i, the addition method modifies the component x_i if it is already nonzero and otherwise creates a new nonzero in the data structure of $\mathbf{x}$. Algorithm 4.2 gives the details of the method.

This sparse vector addition algorithm is more complicated than the straightforward dense algorithm, but it has the advantage that the computation time is only proportional to the sum of the input lengths. The total number of operations is $\mathcal{O}(c_x + c_y)$, since there are $c_x + 2c_y$ loop iterations, each with a small constant number of operations. The number of flops equals the number of nonzeros in the intersection of the sparsity patterns of $\mathbf{x}$ and $\mathbf{y}$. The initialization of array $yloc$ costs n operations, and this cost will dominate that of the algorithm itself if only one vector addition has to be performed. Fortunately, $yloc$ can be reused in subsequent vector additions, because each modified array element is reset to -1. For example, if we add two $n \times n$ matrices row by row, we can amortize the initialization cost over n vector additions. The relative cost of initialization then becomes insignificant.

The addition algorithm does not check its output for **accidental zeros**, that is, elements that are numerically zero but still present as a nonzero pair $(i, 0)$ in the data structure. Such accidental zeros are created, for instance, when a nonzero $y_i = -x_i$ is added to a nonzero x_i and the resulting zero is retained in the data structure. Furthermore, accidental zeros can propagate: if y_i is an accidental zero included in the data structure of $\mathbf{y}$, and $x_i = 0$ is not in the data structure of $\mathbf{x}$, then Algorithm 4.2 will insert the accidental zero into the data structure of $\mathbf{x}$. Still, testing all operations in a sparse matrix algorithm for zero results is more expensive than computing with a few additional nonzeros, so accidental zeros are usually kept. Another reason for keeping accidental zeros is that removing them would make the output data structure dependent on the numerical values of the input and not on their sparsity pattern alone. This may cause problems for certain computations, for example if the same program is executed repeatedly for a matrix with different numerical values but the same sparsity pattern and if knowledge obtained from the first program run is used to speed up subsequent runs. (Often, the first run of a sparse matrix program uses a dynamic data structure, but subsequent runs use a simplified static data structure based on the sparsity patterns encountered in the first run.) In our terminology, we ignore accidental zeros and we just assume that they do not exist.

Sparse matrices can be stored using many different data structures; the best choice depends on the particular computation at hand. Some of the most common data structures are:

The **coordinate scheme,** or **triple scheme.** Every nonzero element a_{ij} is represented by a triple (i, j, a_{ij}), where i is the row index, j the column index, and a_{ij} the numerical value. The triples are stored in an array in arbitrary order. This data structure is easiest to understand and is therefore often used for input/output, for instance in Matrix Market [37], a web-based repository of sparse test matrix collections. The Matrix Market format is one of the three formats used in the SuiteSparse Matrix Collection [79]. It is also suitable for input to a parallel computer, since all information about a nonzero is contained in its triple. The triples can be sent directly and independently to the responsible processors. It is difficult, however, to perform row-wise or column-wise operations on this data structure.

Compressed row storage (CRS), sometimes called compressed sparse row (CSR), which can be confusing; we will use the initialism CRS throughout this book. Each row i of the matrix is stored as a sparse vector consisting of pairs (j, a_{ij}) representing nonzeros. In the data structure, $a[k]$ denotes the numerical value of the nonzero numbered k, and $j[k]$ its column index. Rows are stored consecutively, in order of increasing row index. The address of the first nonzero of row i is given by $start[i]$; the number of nonzeros of row i equals $start[i+1] - start[i]$, where by convention $start[n] = nz(A)$.

Example 4.2

$$
A = \begin{bmatrix} 0 & 3 & 0 & 0 & 1 \\ 4 & 1 & 0 & 0 & 0 \\ 0 & 5 & 9 & 2 & 0 \\ 6 & 0 & 0 & 5 & 3 \\ 0 & 0 & 5 & 8 & 9 \end{bmatrix}, \quad n = 5, \quad nz(A) = 13.
$$

The CRS data structure for A is:

$a[k] =$	3	1	4	1	5	9	2	6	5	3	5	8	9
$j[k] =$	1	4	0	1	1	2	3	0	3	4	2	3	4
$k =$	0	1	2	3	4	5	6	7	8	9	10	11	12

$start[i] =$	0	2	4	7	10	13
$i =$	0	1	2	3	4	5

The CRS data structure has the advantage that the elements of a row are stored consecutively, so that row-wise operations are easy. If we compute $\mathbf{u} := A\mathbf{v}$ by components of $\mathbf{u}$, then the nonzero elements a_{ij} needed to compute u_i are conveniently grouped together, so that the value of u_i can be kept in cache on a cache-based computer, thus speeding up the computation. Algorithm 4.3 shows a sequential SpMV that uses CRS.

Algorithm 4.3 Sequential sparse matrix–vector multiplication for the CRS data structure.

input: A : sparse $n \times n$ matrix,
　　　　$\mathbf{v}$: dense vector of length n.
output: $\mathbf{u}$: dense vector of length n, $\mathbf{u} = A\mathbf{v}$.

for $i := 0$ **to** $n - 1$ **do**
　　$u_i := 0$;
　　for $k := start[i]$ **to** $start[i + 1] - 1$ **do**
　　　　$u[i] := u[i] + a[k] \cdot v[j[k]]$;

Compressed column storage (CCS). Similar to CRS, but with columns instead of rows. This is the data structure employed by the Harwell–Boeing collection [100], later called the Rutherford–Boeing collection [101], the first sparse matrix test collection that found widespread use. The motivation for building such a collection is that researchers testing different algorithms on different machines should at least be able to use a common set of test problems, in particular in the sparse matrix field where rigid analysis is rare and where heuristics reign.

Incremental compressed row storage (ICRS) [190]. A variant of CRS, where the index pair (i,j) of a nonzero a_{ij} is encoded as a one-dimensional (1D) index $i \cdot n + j$, and the difference with the 1D index of the previous nonzero is stored (except for the first nonzero, where the 1D index itself is stored). The nonzeros within a row are ordered by increasing column index, so that the 1D indices form a monotonically increasing sequence. Thus, their differences are positive integers, which are called the **increments** and are stored in an array *inc*. This technique is sometimes called **delta-indexing** and has been proposed before in the context of sparse matrices [248] to save memory. A dummy nonzero is added at the end, representing a dummy index pair $(n,0)$; this is useful in addressing the *inc* array. The ordering imposed by ICRS may also be beneficial for cache-based computers, as consecutively accessed vector components v_j will be closer together in memory. Note that the increment is less than n if the next nonzero is in the same row as the previous one, which usually will be the case. If the matrix does not have empty rows, all increments will be less than $2n$. If there are many empty rows, increments can become large (but still at most n^2), so then we must make sure that each increment fits into a data word.

Example 4.3 The matrix A is the same as in Example 4.2. The ICRS data structure for A is given by the arrays a and inc from:

$a[k] =$	3	1	4	1	5	9	2	6	5	3	5	8	9	0
$j[k] =$	1	4	0	1	1	2	3	0	3	4	2	3	4	0
$i[k] \cdot n + j[k] =$	1	4	5	6	11	12	13	15	18	19	22	23	24	25
$inc[k] =$	1	3	1	1	5	1	1	2	3	1	3	1	1	1
$k =$	0	1	2	3	4	5	6	7	8	9	10	11	12	13

The ICRS data structure has been used in Parallel Templates [190], a parallel version of the Templates package for iterative solution of sparse linear systems [19]. ICRS does not need the *start* array and its implementation in C was found to be somewhat faster than that of CRS because the increments translate well into the pointer arithmetic of the C language. Algorithm 4.4 shows a sequential SpMV that uses ICRS. Note that the algorithm avoids the indirect addressing of the vector $\mathbf{v}$ in the CRS data structure, replacing access to $v[j[k]]$ by access to $v[j]$.

Jagged diagonal storage (JDS) [261]. The matrix A is permuted into a matrix PA by ordering the rows by decreasing number of nonzeros, where P is the corresponding permutation matrix. The first jagged diagonal is formed by taking the first nonzero element of every row in PA. If the matrix does not have empty rows, the length of the first jagged diagonal is n. The second jagged diagonal is formed by taking the second nonzero of every row. The length may now be less than n. This process continues until all c_0 jagged diagonals have been formed, where c_0 is the number of nonzeros of row 0 in PA. As in CRS, for each element the numerical value and column index are stored. The main advantage of JDS is the large average length of the jagged diagonals (of order n) that occurs if the number of

---

Algorithm 4.4 Sequential sparse matrix–vector multiplication for the ICRS data structure.

input: A : sparse $n \times n$ matrix,
        $\mathbf{v}$: dense vector of length n.
output: $\mathbf{u}$: dense vector of length n, $\mathbf{u} = A\mathbf{v}$.

$j := inc[0];$
$k := 0;$
for $i := 0$ **to** $n - 1$ **do**
     $u_i := 0;$
     while $j < n$ **do**
         $u[i] := u[i] + a[k] \cdot v[j];$
         $k := k + 1;$
         $j := j + inc[k];$
     $j := j - n;$

nonzeros per row does not vary too much. In that case, the SpMV can be done using efficient operations on long vectors.

Gustavson's data structure [135]. This data structure combines CRS and CCS, except that it stores the numerical values only for the rows. It provides row-wise and column-wise access to the matrix, which is useful for sparse LU decomposition.

The **2D doubly linked list**. Each nonzero is represented by a tuple, which includes i, j, a_{ij}, and links to a next and a previous nonzero in the same row and column. The elements within a row or column need not be ordered. This data structure gives maximum flexibility: row-wise and column-wise access are easy and elements can be inserted and deleted in $\mathcal{O}(1)$ operations. Therefore, it is applicable in dynamic computations where the matrix changes. The 2D doubly linked list was proposed as the best data structure for parallel sparse LU decomposition with pivoting [297], where rows or columns have to move frequently from one set of processors to another. (A 2D singly linked list for sparse linear system solving was presented by Knuth back in 1968 in the first edition of [186].) A disadvantage of linked list data structures is the amount of storage needed, for instance seven memory cells per nonzero for the doubly linked case, which is much more than the two cells per nonzero for CRS. A severe disadvantage is that following the links causes arbitrary jumps in the computer memory, thus often incurring cache misses.

Matrix-free storage. In certain applications such as in computed tomography, it may be too costly or unnecessary to store the matrix explicitly. Instead, each matrix element is recomputed every time it is needed. This may enable the solution of huge problems that otherwise could not have been solved. For instance, in computed tomography the projection matrix W is computed row by row, where each row represents an X-ray and each column a **voxel** of the 3D region of interest. The weight w_{ij} represents the length of the segment of ray i in voxel j. Typically, the number of nonzeros per row of W is $c = \mathcal{O}(n^{1/3})$. In an image reconstruction, the matrices W and W^{T} are repeatedly multiplied by a vector, but they are never stored.

Sampled storage. The matrix may be very large, coming from a Big Data application, so that only a sample can be taken when performing an operation such as SpMV. An example is computing the PageRank of a large collection of pages on the World Wide Web, where the random surfer process is mimicked using a set of surfers each performing one move in an iteration. This samples the nonzeros of the matrix.

4.3 Parallel algorithm

How can we distribute a sparse matrix over the processors of a parallel computer? Should we first build a data structure and then distribute it, or should we start with the distribution? The first approach constructs a global data structure and then distributes its components; a parallelizing compiler would take this road. Unfortunately, this requires global collaboration between the processors, even for basic operations such as insertion of a new nonzero. For example, if the nonzeros of a matrix row are linked in a list with each nonzero pointing to the next, then the predecessor and the successor in the list, and the nonzero to be inserted may reside on three different processors. This means that three processors have to communicate to adjust their link information.

The alternative approach starts with the distribution of the sparse matrix by assigning a subset of nonzeros to each processor. The subsets are disjoint, and together they contain all nonzeros. (This means that the subsets form a **partitioning** of the nonzero set.) Each subset can be viewed as a smaller sparse submatrix containing exactly those rows and columns that have nonzeros in the subset and exactly those nonzeros that are part of the subset. Submatrices can then be stored using a familiar sequential sparse matrix data structure. This approach has the virtue of simplicity: it keeps basic operations such as insertion and deletion local. When a new nonzero is inserted, the distribution scheme first determines which processor is responsible, and then this processor inserts the nonzero in its local data structure without communicating. Because of this, our motto is: distribute first, represent later.

We have already encountered Cartesian matrix distributions (see Section 2.3), which are suitable for dense LU decomposition and many other matrix computations, sparse as well as dense. Here, however, we would like to remain as general as possible and remove the restriction of Cartesianity. This will give us, in principle, more possibilities of finding a good distribution. We do not fear the added complexity of non-Cartesian distributions because the SpMV is a relatively simple problem, and because the matrix does not change in this computation (unlike, for instance, in LU decomposition). Our general scheme maps nonzeros to processors by

$$a_{ij} \longmapsto P(\phi(i,j)), \quad \text{for } 0 \le i,j < n \quad \text{and} \quad a_{ij} \ne 0, \tag{4.10}$$

where $0 \le \phi(i,j) < p$. Zero elements of the matrix are not assigned to processors. For notational convenience, we define ϕ also for zeros: $\phi(i,j) = -1$ if $a_{ij} = 0$. Note that we use a 1D processor numbering for our general matrix distribution. For the moment, we do not specify ϕ further. Obviously, it is desirable that the nonzeros of the matrix are evenly spread over the processors. Figure 4.4 shows a non-Cartesian matrix distribution. (Note that the distribution in the figure is indeed not Cartesian, since a Cartesian distribution over two processors must be either a 2×1 row distribution or a 1×2 column distribution, and clearly neither is the case.)

Each nonzero a_{ij} is used only once in the SpMV. Furthermore, usually $nz(A) \gg n$ holds, so that there are many more nonzeros than vector components. For these reasons, we perform the computation of $a_{ij} v_j$ on the processor that possesses the nonzero element. Thus, we bring the vector component to the matrix element, and not the other way round. We add products $a_{ij} v_j$ belonging to the same row i; the resulting sum is the **local contribution** to u_i, which is sent to the owner of u_i. This means that we do not have to communicate elements of A, but only components of **v** and contributions to components of **u**.

How do we distribute the input and output vectors of an SpMV? In most iterative linear system solvers and eigensystem solvers, the same vector is repeatedly multiplied by a matrix A, with a few vector operations interspersed. These vector operations are mainly DAXPYs (additions of a scalar times a vector to a vector) and inner product computations. In such

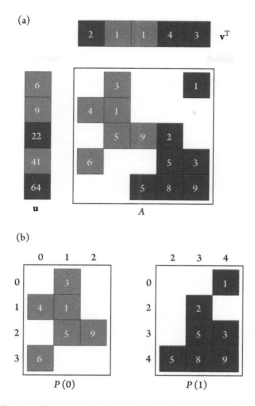

Figure 4.4 (a) Distribution of a sparse 5×5 matrix A and vectors $\mathbf{u}$ and $\mathbf{v}$ of length five over two processors. The matrix nonzeros and vector components of processor $P(0)$ are shown as red cells; those of $P(1)$ as blue cells. The numbers in the cells denote the numerical values a_{ij}. The matrix is the same as in Example 4.2. Vector component u_i is shown to the left of the matrix row that produces it; vector component v_j is shown above the matrix column that needs it. (b) The local matrix part of the processors. Processor $P(0)$ has six nonzeros; its row index set is $I_0 = \{0, 1, 2, 3\}$ and its column index set $J_0 = \{0, 1, 2\}$. Processor $P(1)$ has seven nonzeros; $I_1 = \{0, 2, 3, 4\}$ and $J_1 = \{2, 3, 4\}$.

a situation, it is most natural to distribute all vectors in the same way, and in particular the input and output vectors of the SpMV, thus requiring distr($\mathbf{u}$) = distr($\mathbf{v}$).

Another common situation is that the multiplication by A is followed by a multiplication by A^T (or vice versa). This happens for instance when a vector has to be multiplied by a matrix $B = A^T A$, where B itself is not explicitly stored but only its factor A. An example is the HITS algorithm [183], discussed in Section 4.1. The output vector of the multiplication by A is thus the input vector of the multiplication by A^T, so that we do not need to revert immediately to the same distribution. In this situation, we can use two different distributions, so that distr($\mathbf{u}$) $\neq$ distr($\mathbf{v}$) is allowed.

For a vector **u** of length n, we map components to processors by

$$u_i \longmapsto P(\phi_{\mathbf{u}}(i)), \quad \text{for } 0 \leq i < n, \tag{4.11}$$

where $0 \leq \phi_{\mathbf{u}}(i) < p$. To remain as general as possible, we assume that we have two mappings, $\phi_{\mathbf{u}}$ and $\phi_{\mathbf{v}}$, describing the vector distributions; these can be different, as happens in Fig. 4.4. Often, it is desirable that vector components are evenly spread over the processors, to balance the work load of vector operations in other parts of an application.

It becomes straightforward to derive a parallel algorithm, once we have chosen the distribution of the matrix and the vectors and once we have decided to compute the product $a_{ij}v_j$ on the processor that contains a_{ij}. Let us first focus on the main computation, which is a local SpMV. Processor $P(s)$ multiplies each local nonzero element a_{ij} by v_j and adds the result into a local partial sum,

$$u_{is} = \sum_{\substack{j=0 \\ \phi(i,j)=s}}^{n-1} a_{ij}v_j, \tag{4.12}$$

for all i with $0 \leq i < n$. As in the sequential case, only terms for which $a_{ij} \neq 0$ are summed. Furthermore, only the local partial sums u_{is} for which the set $\{j : 0 \leq j < n \wedge \phi(i,j) = s\}$ is nonempty are computed. (The other partial sums are zero.) If there are fewer than p nonzeros in row i, then certainly one or more processors will have an empty row part. For $c \ll p$, this will happen in many rows. To exploit this, we introduce the index set I_s of the rows that are locally nonempty in processor $P(s)$. We compute u_{is} if and only if $i \in I_s$. An example of row index sets is depicted in Fig. 4.4(b). Superstep (1) of Algorithm 4.5 is the resulting local SpMV.

A suitable sparse data structure must be chosen to implement superstep (1). Since we formulate our algorithm by rows, row-based sparse data structures such as CRS and ICRS are a good choice, see Section 4.2. The data structure should, however, only include nonempty local rows, to avoid unacceptable overhead for very sparse matrices. To achieve this, we can number the nonempty local rows from 0 to $|I_s| - 1$. The corresponding indices i are the **local indices**. The original **global indices** from the set I_s are stored in increasing order in an array *rowindex* of length $|I_s|$. For $0 \leq i < |I_s|$, the global row index is $i = rowindex[\mathtt{i}]$. If for instance CRS is used, the address of the first local nonzero of row i is $start[\mathtt{i}]$ and the number of local nonzeros of row i is $start[\mathtt{i} + 1] - start[\mathtt{i}]$.

The vector component v_j needed for the computation of $a_{ij}v_j$ must be obtained before the start of superstep (1). This is done in communication superstep (0), see the vertical arrows in Fig. 4.5. The processor that has to receive v_j knows from its local sparsity pattern that it needs this component. In contrast to this, the processor that has to send the value is not aware of the needs of the receiver. This implies that the receiver should be the initiator of the communication, that is, we should use a 'get' primitive. Here, we encounter an important difference between dense and sparse algorithms. In dense algorithms, the communication patterns are predictable and thus known to every processor, so that we can formulate communication supersteps exclusively in terms of 'put' primitives. In sparse algorithms, this is often not the case, and we have to use 'get' primitives as well.

Component v_j has to be obtained only once by every processor that needs it, even if it is used repeatedly for different local nonzeros a_{ij} in the same matrix column j. If column j contains at least one local nonzero, then v_j must be obtained; otherwise, v_j is not needed. Therefore, it is convenient to define the index set J_s of the locally nonempty columns, similar to the row index set I_s. We get v_j if and only if $j \in J_s$. This gives superstep (0) of Algorithm 4.5. We call superstep (0) the **fanout**, because vector components fan out from their initial location. The set J_s can be represented by an array *colindex* of length $|J_s|$, similar to *rowindex*. An example of column index sets is also depicted in Fig. 4.4(b). We consider the arrays *rowindex* and *colindex* to be part of the data structure for the local sparse matrix.

The partial sum u_{is} must be contributed to u_i if the local row i is nonempty, that is, if $i \in I_s$. In that case, we call u_{is} nonzero, even if accidental cancellation of terms $a_{ij}v_j$ has occurred. Each nonzero partial sum u_{is} should be sent to the processor that possesses u_i. In this case, the sender has the knowledge about the existence of a nonzero partial sum, so that we have to use a 'put' primitive. The resulting communication superstep is superstep (2), which we call the **fanin**, see the horizontal arrows in Fig. 4.5.

Algorithm 4.5 Parallel sparse matrix–vector multiplication for $P(s)$.

input: A : sparse $n \times n$ matrix, $\mathrm{distr}(A) = \phi$,
           $\mathbf{v}$: dense vector of length n, $\mathrm{distr}(\mathbf{v}) = \phi_{\mathbf{v}}$.
output: $\mathbf{u}$: dense vector of length n, $\mathbf{u} = A\mathbf{v}$, $\mathrm{distr}(\mathbf{u}) = \phi_{\mathbf{u}}$.

$I_s = \{i : 0 \le i < n \wedge (\exists j : 0 \le j < n \wedge \phi(i,j) = s)\}$
$J_s = \{j : 0 \le j < n \wedge (\exists i : 0 \le i < n \wedge \phi(i,j) = s)\}$

{ Fanout }   ▷ Superstep (0)
for all $j \in J_s$ **do**
     get v_j from $P(\phi_{\mathbf{v}}(j))$;

{ Local sparse matrix–vector multiplication }   ▷ Superstep (1)
for all $i \in I_s$ **do**
     $u_{is} := 0$;
     for all $j : 0 \le j < n \wedge \phi(i,j) = s$ **do**
         $u_{is} := u_{is} + a_{ij}v_j$;

{ Fanin }   ▷ Superstep (2)
for all $i \in I_s$ **do**
     put u_{is} in $P(\phi_{\mathbf{u}}(i))$;

{ Summation of nonzero partial sums }   ▷ Superstep (3)
for all $i : 0 \le i < n \wedge \phi_{\mathbf{u}}(i) = s$ **do**
     $u_i := 0$;
     for all $t : 0 \le t < p \wedge u_{it} \ne 0$ **do**
         $u_i := u_i + u_{it}$;

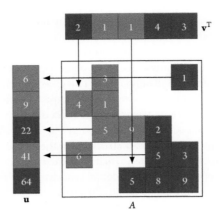

Figure 4.5 Communication during sparse matrix–vector multiplication. The matrix is the same as in Fig. 4.4. Vertical arrows denote communication of components v_j: v_0 must be sent from its owner $P(1)$ to $P(0)$, which owns the nonzeros $a_{10} = 4$ and $a_{30} = 6$; v_2 must be sent from $P(0)$ to $P(1)$; v_1, v_3, v_4 need not be sent. Horizontal arrows denote communication of partial sums u_{is}: $P(1)$ sends its contribution $u_{01} = 3$ to $P(0)$; $P(0)$ sends $u_{20} = 14$ to $P(1)$; and $P(1)$ sends $u_{31} = 29$ to $P(0)$; u_1 and u_4 are computed locally, without contribution from the other processor. The total communication volume is $V = 5$ data words.

Finally, the processor responsible for u_i computes its value by adding the previously received nonzero contributions u_{it}, $0 \le t < p$ with $t \ne s$, and the local contribution u_{is}. This is superstep (3). Similar to the test '$a_{ij} \ne 0$' in Algorithm 4.1, the test '$u_{it} \ne 0$' need never be performed in an actual implementation. The formulation '$u_{it} \ne 0$' is merely a simple notational device for expressing that the received (nonzero) contributions must be added.

'*Wat kost het?*' is an often-used Dutch phrase meaning 'How much does it cost?' Unfortunately, the answer here is, 'It depends', because the cost of Algorithm 4.5 depends on the matrix A and the chosen distributions ϕ, ϕ_v, ϕ_u. Assume that the matrix nonzeros are evenly spread over the processors, each processor having $nz(A)/p = cn/p$ nonzeros. Assume that the vector components are also evenly spread over the processors, each processor having n/p components. Under these two load balancing assumptions, we can obtain an upper bound on the cost. This bound may be far too pessimistic, since distributions may exist that reduce the communication cost by a large factor.

The cost of superstep (0) is as follows. In the worst case, $P(s)$ must receive all n components v_j except the n/p locally available components. Therefore, in the worst case $h_r = n - n/p$; also, $h_s = n - n/p$, because the n/p local vector components must be sent to the other $p - 1$ processors. The resulting cost is $T_{(0)} = (1 - 1/p)ng + l$. The cost of superstep (1) is $T_{(1)} = 2cn/p + l$, since two flops are needed for each local nonzero. The cost of superstep (2) is $T_{(2)} = (1 - 1/p)ng + l$, similar to $T_{(0)}$. The cost of superstep (3) is $T_{(3)} = n + l$, because each of the n/p local vector components is computed by adding at most p partial sums. The total cost of the algorithm is thus bounded by

$$T_{MV} \le \frac{2cn}{p} + n + 2\left(1 - \frac{1}{p}\right)ng + 4l. \qquad (4.13)$$

Examining the upper bound (4.13), we see that the computation cost dominates if $2cn/p >$ $2ng$, that is, if $c > pg$. In that (rare) case, a distribution is already efficient if it only satisfies the two load balancing assumptions. Note that it is the number c of nonzeros per row and not the density d that directly determines the efficiency. Here, and in many other cases, we see that the parameter c is the most useful one to characterize the sparsity of a matrix. The synchronization cost of $4l$ is usually insignificant and it does not grow with the problem size.

To achieve efficiency for smaller c, we can use a Cartesian distribution and exploit its 2D nature, see Section 4.4, or we can refine the general distribution scheme using an automatic procedure to detect the underlying structure of the matrix, see Section 4.5. We can also exploit known properties of specific classes of sparse matrices, such as random sparse matrices, see Section 4.8, and Laplacian matrices, see Section 4.9.

In our model, the cost of a computation is the BSP cost. A closely related metric is the communication volume V, which is the total number of data words sent. The volume depends on ϕ, $\phi_{\mathbf{u}}$, and $\phi_{\mathbf{v}}$. For a given matrix distribution ϕ, a lower bound V_ϕ on V can be obtained by counting for each i the number of processors λ_i with a nonzero a_{ij} in matrix row i, and similarly for each j the number of processors μ_j with a nonzero a_{ij} in matrix column j. The lower bound equals

$$V_\phi = \sum_{\substack{i=0 \\ \lambda_i \geq 1}}^{n-1} (\lambda_i - 1) + \sum_{\substack{j=0 \\ \mu_j \geq 1}}^{n-1} (\mu_j - 1), \tag{4.14}$$

because every processor that has a nonzero in a matrix row i must send a value u_{is} in superstep (2), except perhaps one processor (the owner of u_i), and similarly every processor that has a nonzero in a matrix column j must receive v_j in superstep (0), except perhaps one processor (the owner of v_j). An upper bound is $V_\phi + 2n$, because in the worst case all n components u_i are owned by processors that do not have a nonzero in row i, and similarly for the components v_j. Therefore,

$$V_\phi \leq V \leq V_\phi + 2n. \tag{4.15}$$

We can achieve $V = V_\phi$ by choosing the vector distribution after the matrix distribution, taking care that u_i is assigned to one of the processors that owns a nonzero a_{ij} in row i, and similarly for v_i and column i. We can always do this if u_i and v_i can be assigned independently; if, however, they have to be assigned to the same processor, and $a_{ii} = 0$, then achieving the lower bound may be impossible. If $\text{distr}(\mathbf{u}) = \text{distr}(\mathbf{v})$ must be satisfied, we can achieve

$$V = V_\phi + |\{i : 0 \leq i < n \wedge a_{ii} = 0\}| \tag{4.16}$$

(how?) and hence certainly $V \leq V_\phi + n$. In the example of Fig. 4.5, the communication volume could be reduced from $V = 5$ to $V_\phi = 4$ if we were to assign v_0 to $P(0)$ instead of $P(1)$.

4.4 Cartesian matrix distribution

For sparse matrices, a Cartesian distribution is defined in the same way as for dense matrices, by mapping an element a_{ij} (whether it is zero or not) to a processor $P(\phi_0(i), \phi_1(j))$ with $0 \leq \phi_0(i) < M$, $0 \leq \phi_1(j) < N$, and $MN = p$. We can fit this assignment into our general scheme by identifying 1D and 2D processor numbers. An example is the natural column-wise identification

$$P(s, t) \equiv P(s + tM), \quad \text{for } 0 \leq s < M \quad \text{and} \quad 0 \leq t < N, \tag{4.17}$$

which can also be written as

$$P(s) \equiv P(s \bmod M, s \operatorname{div} M), \quad \text{for } 0 \leq s < p. \tag{4.18}$$

Thus, we map nonzeros a_{ij} to processors $P(\phi(i,j))$ with

$$\phi(i,j) = \phi_0(i) + \phi_1(j)M, \quad \text{for } 0 \leq i, j < n \quad \text{and} \quad a_{ij} \neq 0. \tag{4.19}$$

Again we define $\phi(i,j) = -1$ if $a_{ij} = 0$. In this section, we examine only Cartesian distributions, and use both 1D and 2D processor numberings, choosing the numbering that is most convenient in the given situation.

Cartesian distributions have the same advantage for sparse matrices as for dense matrices: row-wise operations require communication only within processor rows, and column-wise operations only within processor columns, and this restricts the amount of communication. For the SpMV, this means that a vector component v_j has to be sent to at most M processors, and a vector component u_i is computed using contributions received from at most N processors. Another advantage is simplicity: Cartesian distributions partition the matrix orthogonally into rectangular submatrices (with rows and columns that are not necessarily consecutive in the original matrix). In general, non-Cartesian distributions create arbitrarily shaped matrix parts, see Fig. 4.4. We can view the local part of a processor $P(s)$ as a submatrix $\{a_{ij} : i \in I_s \wedge j \in J_s\}$, but in the non-Cartesian case the local submatrices may overlap. For instance, in Fig. 4.4(b), we note that column 2 has three overlapping elements (a_{02}, a_{22}, and a_{32}). In the Cartesian case, however, the local submatrix of a processor $P(s)$ equals its Cartesian submatrix $\{a_{ij} : \phi_0(i) = s \bmod M \wedge \phi_1(j) = s \operatorname{div} M\}$ with the empty rows and columns removed. Since the Cartesian submatrices are disjoint, the local submatrices are also disjoint. Figure 4.6 shows a Cartesian distribution of the matrix cage6.

An advantage of Cartesian distributions which lies outside the BSP cost model is that they have a nontrivial bound on the **total number of messages** exchanged between processors. If a processor has to communicate data to another processor in a superstep, this generates one message, irrespective of how many data words have to be sent. The trivial upper bound for a superstep is $p(p - 1)$ messages, and the BSP cost model includes the corresponding cost of generating messages for all-to-all communication in the synchronization parameter l. For square Cartesian distributions, the total number of messages of the fanout is at most $p(\sqrt{p} - 1)$, and the same holds for the fanin. This reduction in number of messages may be

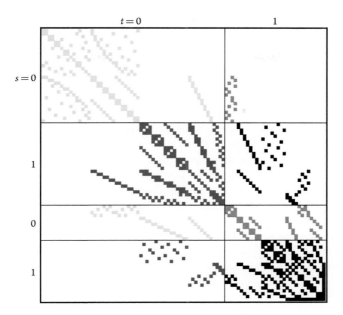

Figure 4.6 Sparse matrix cage6 with $n = 93$ and $nz = 785$, distributed in a Cartesian manner over four processors with $M = N = 2$; the matrix is the same as that shown in Fig. 4.1. Coloured or black squares denote nonzero elements; white squares denote zeros. Lines denote processor boundaries. The processor row of a matrix element a_{ij} is denoted by $s = \phi_0(i)$, and the processor column by $t = \phi_1(j)$. The distribution has been determined visually, by trying to create blocks of rows and columns that fit the sparsity pattern of the matrix. Note that the matrix diagonal is assigned in blocks to the four processors, in the order $P(0) \equiv P(0,0)$ (yellow), $P(1) \equiv P(1,0)$ (blue), $P(2) \equiv P(0,1)$ (red), and $P(3) \equiv P(1,1)$ (black). The number of nonzeros of the processors is 216, 236, 76, 257, respectively. The number of diagonal elements is 32, 28, 12, 21, respectively; these are all nonzero. Assume that the vectors $\mathbf{u}$ and $\mathbf{v}$ are distributed in the same way as the matrix diagonal. In that case, 64 (out of 93) components of $\mathbf{v}$ must be communicated in superstep (0) of the SpMV, and 72 contributions to $\mathbf{u}$ in superstep (2). For example, components $v_0, \ldots, v_{15}$ are only needed locally. The total communication volume is $V = 136$ and the BSP cost is $24g + 2 \cdot 257 + 28g + 28 \cdot 2 + 4l = 570 + 52g + 4l$. Try to verify these numbers by clever counting!

important for certain architectures, especially if p is large. We will further ignore the message count metric and concentrate on the metrics of communication volume and BSP cost.

To reduce communication, the matrix distribution and the vector distribution should match. The vector component v_j is needed only by processors that possess an $a_{ij} \neq 0$ with $0 \leq i < n$, and these processors are contained in processor column $P(*, \phi_1(j))$. Assigning component v_j to one of the processors in that processor column reduces the upper bound on the communication, because then v_j has to be sent to at most $M - 1$ processors, instead of M. This decrease in upper bound may hardly seem worthwhile, especially for large M, but the lower bound also decreases, from one to zero, and this is crucial. If v_j were assigned to a different processor column, it would always have to be communicated (assuming that matrix column j is nonempty). If component v_j is assigned to processor column $P(*, \phi_1(j))$, then there is a chance that it is needed only by its own processor, so that no communication is required. A judicious choice of distribution may enhance this effect. This is the main reason why, for Cartesian matrix distributions, we impose the constraint that v_j resides in $P(*, \phi_1(j))$. If we are free to choose the distribution of $\mathbf{v}$, we assign v_j to one of the owners of nonzeros in matrix column j, thereby satisfying the constraint.

We impose a similar constraint on the output vector $\mathbf{u}$. To compute u_i, we need contributions from the processors that compute the products $a_{ij}v_j$, for $0 \leq j < n$ and $a_{ij} \neq 0$. These processors are all contained in processor row $P(\phi_0(i), *)$. Therefore, we assign u_i to a processor in that processor row. The number of contributions sent for u_i is thus at most $N - 1$. If we are free to choose the distribution of $\mathbf{u}$, we assign u_i to one of the owners of nonzeros in matrix row i.

If the requirement distr($\mathbf{u}$) = distr($\mathbf{v}$) has to be satisfied, our constraints on $\mathbf{u}$ and $\mathbf{v}$ imply that u_i and v_i must be assigned to $P(\phi_0(i), \phi_1(i))$, which is the processor that owns the diagonal element a_{ii} in the Cartesian distribution of A. In that case,

$$\phi_{\mathbf{u}}(i) = \phi_{\mathbf{v}}(i) = \phi_0(i) + \phi_1(i)M, \quad \text{for } 0 \leq i < n. \tag{4.20}$$

As a result, for a fixed M and N, the choice of a Cartesian matrix distribution determines the vector distribution. The reverse is also true: an arbitrary matrix element a_{ij} is assigned to the processor row that possesses the vector component u_i and to the processor column that possesses u_j.

A nonzero a_{ij} does not cause communication in the parallel SpMV if a_{ij}, u_i, and v_j are all assigned to the same processor. The following trivial but powerful theorem states that the amount of communication can be restricted based on a suitable distribution of the vectors.

Theorem 4.4 *Let A be a sparse $n \times n$ matrix and $\mathbf{u}, \mathbf{v}$ vectors of length n. Assume that:*

(i) *the distribution of A is Cartesian, $\text{distr}(A) = (\phi_0, \phi_1)$;*

(ii) *the distribution of $\mathbf{u}$ is such that u_i resides in $P(\phi_0(i), *)$, for all i;*

(iii) *the distribution of $\mathbf{v}$ is such that v_j resides in $P(*, \phi_1(j))$, for all j.*

Then: if u_i and v_j are assigned to the same processor, the matrix element a_{ij} is also assigned to that processor.

Proof Component u_i is assigned to a processor $P(\phi_0(i), t)$ and component v_j to a processor $P(s, \phi_1(j))$. Since this is the same processor, it follows that $(s, t) = (\phi_0(i), \phi_1(j))$, so that this processor also owns matrix element a_{ij}. $\qquad\qquad\square$

Example 4.5 Let A be the $n \times n$ tridiagonal matrix defined by

$$A = \begin{bmatrix} -2 & 1 & & & & & & \\ 1 & -2 & 1 & & & & & \\ & 1 & -2 & 1 & & & & \\ & & & \ddots & & & & \\ & & & 1 & -2 & 1 & & \\ & & & & 1 & -2 & 1 \\ & & & & & 1 & -2 \end{bmatrix}.$$

This matrix represents a Laplacian operator on a 1D grid of n points. (Section 4.9 treats Laplacian operators on multidimensional grids.) The nonzeros are the elements on the main diagonal and on the diagonals immediately above and below it, so that $a_{ij} \neq 0$ if and only if $i - j = 0, \pm 1$. Assume that we have to find a suitable Cartesian matrix distribution (ϕ_0, ϕ_1) and a single distribution for the input and output vectors. Theorem 4.4 says that here it is best to assign u_i and u_j to the same processor if $i = j \pm 1$. Therefore, a suitable vector distribution over p processors is the block distribution,

$$u_i \longmapsto P\left(i \operatorname{div} \left\lceil \frac{n}{p} \right\rceil \right), \quad \text{for } 0 \leq i < n. \tag{4.21}$$

Communication takes place only on the boundary of a block. Each processor has to send and receive at most two components v_j, and to send and receive at most two contributions to a component u_i. If we choose M and N, the vector distribution then completely determines the matrix distribution.

For $n = 12$ and $M = N = 2$, the matrix distribution corresponding to the block distribution of the vectors is

$$\operatorname{distr}(A) = \left[\begin{array}{ccc|ccccccccc} 0 & 0 & & & & & & & & & & \\ 0 & 0 & 0 & & & & & & & & & \\ & 0 & 0 & 0 & & & & & & & & \\ \hline & & 1 & 1 & 1 & & & & & & & \\ & & & 1 & 1 & 1 & & & & & & \\ & & & & 1 & 1 & 3 & & & & & \\ \hline & & & & & 0 & 2 & 2 & & & & \\ & & & & & & 2 & 2 & 2 & & & \\ & & & & & & & 2 & 2 & 2 & & \\ \hline & & & & & & & & 3 & 3 & 3 & \\ & & & & & & & & & 3 & 3 & 3 \\ & & & & & & & & & & 3 & 3 \end{array} \right].$$

Position (i,j) of $\operatorname{distr}(A)$ gives the 1D identity of the processor that possesses matrix element a_{ij}. The matrix distribution is obtained by first distributing the matrix diagonal in the same way as the vectors, and then translating the corresponding 1D processor numbers into 2D numbers by $P(0) \equiv P(0,0)$, $P(1) \equiv P(1,0)$, $P(2) \equiv P(0,1)$, and $P(3) \equiv P(1,1)$. After that, the off-diagonal nonzeros are assigned to processors: for instance a_{56} is in the same processor row as a_{55}, which is owned by $P(1) = P(1,0)$, and it is in the same processor column as a_{66}, which is owned by $P(2) = P(0,1)$. Thus, a_{56} is owned by $P(1,1) = P(3)$. Note that this distribution differs only slightly from the row distribution defined by $M = 4, N = 1$; the only elements distributed differently are a_{56} and a_{65} (marked in boldface), which in the row distribution are assigned to $P(1)$ and $P(2)$, respectively.

The cost of Algorithm 4.5 for a Cartesian distribution depends on the matrix A and the chosen distribution. Because of our additional assumptions, we can improve the upper bound (4.13). As before, we assume a good spread of the matrix elements and vector components over the processors, but now we also assume a good spread of the matrix rows over the processor rows and the matrix columns over the processor columns. In superstep (0), $P(s,t)$ must receive at most all components v_j with $\phi_1(j) = t$, except the n/p locally available components. Therefore, in the worst case $h_r = n/N - n/p = (M-1)n/p = h_s$. The cost is at most $T_{(0)} = (M-1)ng/p + l$. As before, $T_{(1)} = 2cn/p + l$. The cost of superstep (2) is at most $T_{(2)} = (N-1)ng/p + l$, similar to $T_{(0)}$. The cost of superstep (3) is at most $T_{(3)} = Nn/p + l = n/M + l$, because each of the n/p local vector components is computed by adding at most N partial sums. The total cost of the algorithm is thus bounded by

$$T_{MV, M \times N} \leq \frac{2cn}{p} + \frac{n}{M} + \frac{M+N-2}{p}ng + 4l. \tag{4.22}$$

The communication term of the upper bound (4.22) is minimal for $M = N = \sqrt{p}$. For that choice, the bound reduces to

$$T_{MV, \sqrt{p} \times \sqrt{p}} \leq \frac{2cn}{p} + \frac{n}{\sqrt{p}} + 2\left(\frac{1}{\sqrt{p}} - \frac{1}{p}\right)ng + 4l. \tag{4.23}$$

Examining the upper bound (4.23), we see that the computation cost dominates if $2cn/p > 2ng/\sqrt{p}$, that is, if $c > \sqrt{p}g$. This is an improvement of the critical c-value by a factor $\sqrt{p}$ compared with the value for the general upper bound (4.13).

Dense matrices can be considered as the extreme limit of sparse matrices, with $c = n$. Analysing the dense case is easier and it can give us insight into the sparse case as well. Let us therefore examine a dense $n \times n$ matrix A. Assume that we have to use the same distribution for the input and output vectors, which therefore must be the distribution of the matrix diagonal. Assume for simplicity that n is a multiple of p and p is a square.

In our study of dense LU decomposition, see Chapter 2, we extolled the virtues of the square cyclic distribution for parallel linear algebra. One may ask whether this is also a good distribution for dense matrix–vector multiplication by Algorithm 4.5. Unfortunately, the answer is negative. The reason is that element a_{ii} from the matrix diagonal is assigned to processor $P(i \bmod \sqrt{p}, i \bmod \sqrt{p})$, so that the matrix diagonal is assigned to the **diagonal processors**, that is, the processors $P(s,s)$, $0 \leq s < \sqrt{p}$. This implies that only $\sqrt{p}$ out of p processors own part of the matrix diagonal, and hence of the vectors, so that the load balancing assumption for vector components is not satisfied. Diagonal processors have to send out $\sqrt{p} - 1$ copies of $n/\sqrt{p}$ vector components, so that $h_s = n - n/\sqrt{p}$ in superstep (0) and h is $\sqrt{p}$ times larger than the h of a well-balanced distribution. The total cost for a dense matrix with the square cyclic distribution becomes

$$T_{\text{MV, dense, } \sqrt{p} \times \sqrt{p} \text{ cyclic}} = \frac{2n^2}{p} + n + 2\left(1 - \frac{1}{\sqrt{p}}\right)ng + 4l. \tag{4.24}$$

The communication cost for this unbalanced distribution is a factor $\sqrt{p}$ higher than the upper bound (4.23) for balanced distributions, with $c = n$. The total communication volume is $V_\phi = 2(\sqrt{p} - 1)n$. For dense matrices with the square cyclic distribution, the communication imbalance can be reduced by changing the algorithm and using two-phase broadcasting for the fanout and a similar technique, two-phase combining, for the fanin. This, however, does not solve the problem of vector imbalance in other parts of the application, and of course it would be better to use a good distribution in the first place, instead of redistributing the data during the fanout or fanin.

The communication balance can be improved by choosing a distribution that spreads the vectors and hence the matrix diagonal evenly, for example choosing the 1D distribution $\phi_{\mathbf{u}}(i) = \phi_{\mathbf{v}}(i) = i \bmod p$ and using the 1D–2D identification (4.18). We still have the freedom to choose M and N, where $MN = p$. For the choice $M = p$ and $N = 1$, this gives $\phi_0(i) = i \bmod p$ and $\phi_1(j) = 0$, which is the same as the cyclic row distribution. It is easy to see that now the cost is

$$T_{\text{MV, dense, } p \times 1 \text{ cyclic}} = \frac{2n^2}{p} + \left(1 - \frac{1}{p}\right)ng + 2l. \tag{4.25}$$

This distribution disposes of the fanin and the summation of partial sums, since each matrix row is completely contained in one processor. Therefore, the last two supersteps are empty and can be deleted. Still, this is a bad distribution, since the gain from fewer synchronizations is lost due to the much more expensive fanout: each processor has to send n/p vector components to all other processors. The communication volume is large: $V_\phi = (p - 1)n$.

For the choice $M = N = \sqrt{p}$, we obtain $\phi_0(i) = (i \bmod p) \bmod \sqrt{p} = i \bmod \sqrt{p}$ and $\phi_1(j) = (j \bmod p) \operatorname{div} \sqrt{p}$ by applying eqn (4.18). The costs of the fanout and fanin for this distribution are given by $h_s = h_r = (\sqrt{p} - 1)n/p$, so that we get

$$T_{\text{MV, dense}} = \frac{2n^2}{p} + \frac{n}{\sqrt{p}} + 2\left(\frac{1}{\sqrt{p}} - \frac{1}{p}\right)ng + 4l, \tag{4.26}$$

which equals the upper bound (4.23) for $c = n$. We see that this distribution is much better than the square cyclic distribution and the cyclic row distribution. The communication volume is $V_\phi = 2(\sqrt{p} - 1)n$. Figure 4.7 illustrates this data distribution. Note that we could also have distributed the matrix diagonal by blocks and carry out the same procedure, to obtain an alternative data distribution that performs equally well.

Figure 4.8 shows an important application of dense matrix–vector multiplication in **machine learning**, namely the computation of signal values in the next layer of an artificial

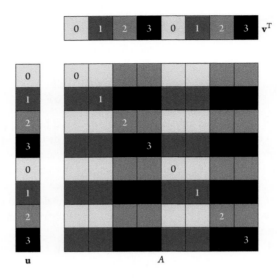

Figure 4.7 Dense 8×8 matrix distributed over four processors using a square Cartesian distribution based on a cyclic distribution of the matrix diagonal. The vectors are distributed in the same way as the matrix diagonal. The processors are shown by colours; the 1D processor numbering is shown as numbers in the cells of the matrix diagonal and the vectors. The corresponding 2D numbering is given by $\phi_0(i) = i \bmod 2$ and $\phi_1(j) = (j \bmod 4) \operatorname{div} 2$. Thus, the 1D–2D correspondence is $P(0) \equiv P(0,0)$, $P(1) \equiv P(1,0)$, $P(2) \equiv P(0,1)$, and $P(3) \equiv P(1,1)$.

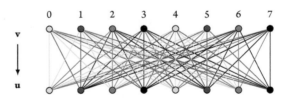

Figure 4.8 Two layers of an artificial neural network, both with eight neurons. Each neuron in the top layer is connected to all neurons of the bottom layer. The vector **v** of length 8 represents signal strengths for neurons in the top layer, and the vector **u** of length 8 represents strengths for the bottom layer. The strength v_j of a signal fired by neuron j in the top layer is an input to the strength u_i of neuron i in the bottom layer. The connection between top neuron j and bottom neuron i carries a weight a_{ij} which has been determined during a training phase of the network. The value u_i is typically given by a formula of the form $u_i = f(\sum_{j=0}^{n-1} a_{ij}v_j + b_i)$, where f is an activation function such as the Rectified Linear Unit (ReLU) function $f(x) = \max(0, x)$ and b_i is a component of a bias vector **b**. The neurons and their connections have been distributed over four processors of a parallel computer in correspondence with the vectors and the matrix from Fig. 4.7.

neural network from the values of the previous layer. The quality of the network is determined by its weights, which are attached to the connections between the neurons and which have between determined previously in a training phase. Commonly, a neural network has one input layer, several so-called hidden layers, and one output layer. In **deep learning**, many layers are used.

We may conclude that the case of dense matrices is a good example where Cartesian matrix partitioning is useful in deriving an optimal distribution, a square Cartesian distribution based on a cyclic distribution of the matrix diagonal. (Strictly speaking, we did not give an optimality proof; it seems, however, that this distribution is hard to beat.)

4.5 Mondriaan distribution for general sparse matrices

Sparse matrices usually have a special structure in their sparsity pattern. Sometimes this structure is known, but more often it has to be detected by use of an automatic procedure. The aim of this section is to present an algorithm that finds the underlying structure of an arbitrary sparse matrix and exploits this structure to generate a good distribution for the SpMV. We name the resulting distribution **Mondriaan distribution**, honouring the Dutch painter Piet Mondriaan (1872–1944) who is most famous for his compositions of brightly coloured rectangles.

Suppose we have to find matrix and vector distributions for a sparse matrix A where we have the freedom to distribute the input and output vectors independently. Thus, we can first concentrate on the matrix distribution problem and try to find a matrix distribution ϕ that minimizes the communication volume V_ϕ, defined by eqn (4.14), while balancing the computational work. We define $A_s = \{(i,j) : 0 \leq i,j < n \wedge \phi(i,j) = s\}$ as the set of index pairs corresponding to the nonzeros of $P(s)$, $0 \leq s < p$. Thus, $A_0, \ldots, A_{p-1}$ forms a **p-way partitioning** of $A = \{(i,j) : 0 \leq i,j < n \wedge a_{ij} \neq 0\}$. (For the purpose of partitioning, we identify a nonzero with its index pair and a sparse matrix with its set of index pairs.) We use the notation $V(A_0, \ldots, A_{p-1}) = V_\phi$ to express the explicit dependence of the communication volume on the partitioning.

For mutually disjoint subsets of nonzeros $A_0, \ldots, A_{k-1}$, where $k \geq 1$, not necessarily with $A_0 \cup \cdots \cup A_{k-1} = A$, we define the communication volume $V(A_0, \ldots, A_{k-1})$ as the volume of the SpMV for the matrix $A_0 \cup \cdots \cup A_{k-1}$ where subset A_s is assigned to $P(s)$, $0 \leq s < k$. For $k = p$, this reduces to the original definition. When we split a subset of a k-way partitioning of A, we obtain a $(k+1)$-way partitioning. The following theorem says that the new communication volume equals the old volume plus the volume incurred by splitting the subset as a separate problem, ignoring all other subsets.

Theorem 4.6 (*Vastenhouw and Bisseling [304]*) Let A be a sparse $n \times n$ matrix and let $A_0, \ldots, A_k \subseteq A$ be mutually disjoint subsets of nonzeros, where $k \geq 1$. Then

$$V(A_0, \ldots, A_k) = V(A_0, \ldots, A_{k-2}, A_{k-1} \cup A_k) + V(A_{k-1}, A_k). \qquad (4.27)$$

Proof The number of processors that contribute to a vector component u_i depends on the partitioning assumed, $\lambda_i = \lambda_i(A_0, \ldots, A_{k-1})$ for the k-way partitioning $A_0, \ldots, A_{k-1}$, and similarly $\mu_j = \mu_j(A_0, \ldots, A_{k-1})$ is the number of processors that need a vector component v_j. Let $\lambda_i' = \max(\lambda_i - 1, 0)$ and $\mu_j' = \max(\mu_j - 1, 0)$. We are done if we prove

$$\lambda_i'(A_0, \ldots, A_k) = \lambda_i'(A_0, \ldots, A_{k-2}, A_{k-1} \cup A_k) + \lambda_i'(A_{k-1}, A_k), \tag{4.28}$$

for $0 \leq i < n$, and a similar equality for μ_j', because the result then follows from summing over $i = 0, \ldots, n-1$ for λ_i' and $j = 0, \ldots, n-1$ for μ_j'. We only prove the equality for the λ_i', and do this by distinguishing two cases. If row i has a nonzero in A_{k-1} or A_k, then $\lambda_i' = \lambda_i - 1$ in all three terms of eqn (4.28). Thus,

$$
\begin{aligned}
\lambda_i'(A_0, &\ldots, A_{k-2}, A_{k-1} \cup A_k) + \lambda_i'(A_{k-1}, A_k) \\
&= \lambda_i(A_0, \ldots, A_{k-2}, A_{k-1} \cup A_k) - 1 + \lambda_i(A_{k-1}, A_k) - 1 \\
&= \lambda_i(A_0, \ldots, A_{k-2}) + 1 - 1 + \lambda_i(A_{k-1}, A_k) - 1 \\
&= \lambda_i(A_0, \ldots, A_{k-2}) + \lambda_i(A_{k-1}, A_k) - 1 \\
&= \lambda_i(A_0, \ldots, A_k) - 1 \\
&= \lambda_i'(A_0, \ldots, A_k). \tag{4.29}
\end{aligned}
$$

If row i has no nonzero in A_{k-1} or A_k, then

$$
\begin{aligned}
\lambda_i'(A_0, &\ldots, A_{k-2}, A_{k-1} \cup A_k) + \lambda_i'(A_{k-1}, A_k) \\
&= \lambda_i'(A_0, \ldots, A_{k-2}) + 0 \\
&= \lambda_i'(A_0, \ldots, A_k). \tag{4.30}
\end{aligned}
$$

$\square$

The proof of Theorem 4.6 shows that the theorem also holds for the communication volume of the fanout and fanin separately. The theorem ensures that we only have to look at the subset we want to split when trying to optimize the split, and not at the effect such a split has on communication for other subsets.

The theorem helps us to achieve our goal of minimizing the communication volume. Of course, we must at the same time also consider the load balance of the computation; otherwise, the problem is easily solved: assign all nonzeros to the same processor *et voilà*, no communication whatsoever! We specify the allowed load imbalance by a parameter $\epsilon \geq 0$, requiring that the p-way partitioning of the nonzeros satisfies the computational balance constraint

$$\max_{0 \leq s < p} nz(A_s) \leq (1 + \epsilon) \frac{nz(A)}{p}. \tag{4.31}$$

We usually choose $\epsilon > 0$, because obtaining a perfect load balance is often impossible, and even when it is possible, the demand for perfect balance does not leave much room for minimizing communication. In the words of a great poet (Leonard Cohen, *Anthem*, 1992):

There is a crack in everything.
That's how the light gets in.

The load imbalance achieved for the matrix cage6 for $p = 4$ and $\epsilon = 0.03$ using the Mondriaan partitioner [304] is $\epsilon' \approx 0.0293$: the matrix has 785 nonzero, the maximum number of nonzeros per processor is 202, and the average is 785/4=196.25. We denote the achieved imbalance by ϵ', to distinguish it from the allowed imbalance ϵ. The partitioning obtained is displayed in Fig. 4.9, in **global view**, that is with the matrix in its original ordering and showing the nonzeros in their original position with colours denoting the processors.

The best choice of the imbalance parameter ϵ is machine-dependent and can be found by using the BSP model. Suppose we have obtained a matrix distribution with volume V that satisfies the constraint (4.31). Assuming that the subsequent vector partitioning does a good job, balancing the communication well and thus achieving a communication cost of Vg/p, we have a BSP cost of

$$T_{\text{MV, Mondriaan}} = 2(1 + \epsilon')\frac{nz(A)}{p} + \frac{V}{p}g + 4l. \tag{4.32}$$

To get a good trade-off between computation imbalance and communication, the corresponding overhead terms should be about equal, that is,

$$\epsilon' \approx \frac{Vg}{2nz(A)}. \tag{4.33}$$

If this is not the case, we can increase or decrease ϵ and obtain a lower BSP cost. We cannot determine ϵ beforehand, because we cannot predict exactly how its choice affects V.

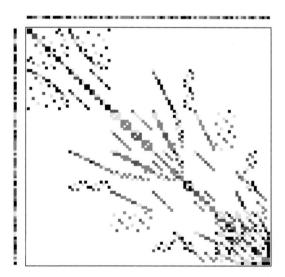

Figure 4.9 Matrix and vector distributions in global view for the sparse matrix cage6 for $p = 4$ and $\epsilon = 0.03$. The processors are $P(0)$ (yellow), $P(1)$ (blue), $P(2)$ (red), and $P(3)$ (black). The number of nonzeros per processor is 196, 202, 199, 188, respectively.

How to split a given subset? Without loss of generality, we may assume that the subset is A itself. In principle, we can assign every individual nonzero to one of the two available processors. The number of possible two-way partitionings, however, is huge, namely $2^{nz(A)-1}$. (We saved a factor of two by using symmetry: we can always assign the first nonzero to $P(0)$, without loss of generality.) Trying all partitionings and choosing the best is usually impossible, even for modest problem sizes. In the small example of Fig. 4.4, we already have $2^{12} = 4096$ possibilities (one of which is shown). Thus, our only hope is to develop a **heuristic method**, that is, a method that gives an approximate solution, hopefully close to the optimum and computed within reasonable time. A good start is to try to limit the search space by imposing a sensible restriction on the possible solutions, for example, by assigning complete columns to processors; the number of possibilities then decreases to 2^{n-1}. A major advantage of assigning complete columns is that it prevents communication in the fanout. In the example, we now have $2^4 = 16$ possibilities. In general, the number of possibilities is still large, and heuristics are still needed, but the problem is more manageable now. One reason is that bookkeeping is simpler for n columns than for $nz(A)$ nonzeros. Thus, we decide to perform each split by complete columns, or, alternatively, by complete rows. We can express the splitting by the assignment

$$(A_0, A_1) := Bipartition(A, dir, \epsilon), \qquad (4.34)$$

where $dir \in \{row, col\}$ is the splitting direction and ϵ the allowed load imbalance. Since we do not know beforehand which of the two splitting directions is better, we try both, and choose the direction with the lower communication volume.

Example 4.7 Let

$$A = \begin{bmatrix} 0 & 3 & 0 & 0 & 1 \\ 4 & 1 & 0 & 0 & 0 \\ 0 & 5 & 9 & 2 & 0 \\ 6 & 0 & 0 & 5 & 3 \\ 0 & 0 & 5 & 8 & 9 \end{bmatrix}.$$

For $\epsilon = 0.1$, the maximum number of nonzeros per processor must be seven and the minimum six. For a column split, this implies that one processor must have two columns with three nonzeros and the other processor the remaining columns. A solution that minimizes the communication volume V is to assign columns 0, 1, 2 to $P(0)$ and columns 3, 4 to $P(1)$. This gives $V = 4$. For a row split, assigning rows 0, 1, 3 to $P(0)$ and rows 2, 4 to $P(1)$ is optimal, giving $V = 3$. Puzzle: if you are allowed to assign nonzeros individually to processors, can you find a better solution?

The function *Bipartition* can be applied repeatedly, giving a method for partitioning a matrix into several parts. The method can be formulated concisely as a recursive computation. For convenience, we assume that $p = 2^q$, but the method can be adapted to handle other values of p as well. (This would also require generalizing the bipartitioning function, so that for instance in the first split for $p = 3$, it can produce two subsets with a nonzero ratio of about $2 : 1$.) The recursive method should work for a rectangular input matrix, since the submatrices involved may be rectangular (even though the initial matrix is square). Because of the splitting into sets of complete columns or rows, we can view the resulting p-way partitioning as a splitting into p mutually disjoint submatrices (not necessarily with consecutive rows and columns): we start with a complete matrix, split it into two submatrices, split each submatrix, giving four submatrices, and so on. The number of times the original submatrix must be split to reach a given submatrix is called the **recursion level** of the submatrix. The level of the original matrix is 0. The final result for processor $P(s)$ is a submatrix defined by an index set $\bar{I}_s \times \bar{J}_s$. This index set is different from the index set $I_s \times J_s$ of pairs (i,j) with $i \in I_s$ and $j \in J_s$ defined in Algorithm 4.5, because the submatrices $\bar{I}_s \times \bar{J}_s$ may contain empty rows and columns; removing these gives $I_s \times J_s$. Thus, we have

$$A_s \subseteq I_s \times J_s \subseteq \bar{I}_s \times \bar{J}_s, \quad \text{for } 0 \le s < p. \tag{4.35}$$

Furthermore, all the resulting submatrices are mutually disjoint, that is,

$$(\bar{I}_s \times \bar{J}_s) \cap (\bar{I}_t \times \bar{J}_t) = \varnothing, \quad \text{for } 0 \le s < t < p, \tag{4.36}$$

and together they comprise the original matrix,

$$\bigcup_{s=0}^{p-1} (\bar{I}_s \times \bar{J}_s) = \{0, \ldots, n-1\} \times \{0, \ldots, n-1\}. \tag{4.37}$$

The resulting Mondriaan distribution can be viewed as the outcome of an **orthogonal recursive bisection** of a sparse matrix.

To achieve a final load imbalance of at most ϵ, we must take care that the maximum number of nonzeros per matrix part grows slowly enough with the recursion level. If the growth factor at each level is $1 + \delta$, then the overall growth factor is $(1 + \delta)^q \approx 1 + q\delta$ in a first-order approximation; for $p = 2$ (i.e., $q = 1$), the approximation is exact. This motivates our choice of starting with $\delta = \epsilon/q$. After the first split, a new situation arises. One part has at least half the nonzeros, and the other part at most half. Assume that the matrix parts, or subsets, are B_0 and B_1. Subset B_s, $s = 0, 1$, has $nz(B_s)$ nonzeros and will be partitioned over $p/2$ processors with a load imbalance parameter ϵ_s. Equating the maximum number of nonzeros per processor specified for the remainder of the partitioning process to the maximum specified at the beginning,

$$(1 + \epsilon_s) \frac{nz(B_s)}{p/2} = (1 + \epsilon) \frac{nz(A)}{p}, \tag{4.38}$$

gives the value ϵ_s to be used in the remainder. In this way, the allowed load imbalance is dynamically adjusted during the partitioning. A matrix part that has fewer nonzeros than the average will have a larger ϵ in the remainder, giving more freedom to minimize communication for that part. The deepest splits of the recursion have $\delta = \epsilon$, and hence they impose the exact desired upper bound on the number of nonzeros of the resulting submatrices. The recursive algorithm is given as Algorithm 4.6.

Algorithm 4.6 Recursive matrix partitioning.

---

input: A: sparse $m \times n$ matrix,
   p: number of processors, $p = 2^q$ with $q \geq 0$,
   ϵ = allowed load imbalance, $\epsilon > 0$.
output: $(A_0, \ldots, A_{p-1})$: p-way partitioning of A,
   satisfying $\max_{0 \leq s < p} nz(A_s) \leq (1 + \epsilon) \frac{nz(A)}{p}$.

   function MATRIXPARTITION(A, p, ϵ)

   if $p > 1$ **then**
     $maxnz := (1 + \epsilon) \frac{nz(A)}{p}$;
     $(B_0^{\text{row}}, B_1^{\text{row}}) := Bipartition(A, \text{row}, \frac{\epsilon}{q})$;
     $(B_0^{\text{col}}, B_1^{\text{col}}) := Bipartition(A, \text{col}, \frac{\epsilon}{q})$;
     if $V(B_0^{\text{row}}, B_1^{\text{row}}) \leq V(B_0^{\text{col}}, B_1^{\text{col}})$ **then**
       $(B_0, B_1) := (B_0^{\text{row}}, B_1^{\text{row}})$;
     else
       $(B_0, B_1) := (B_0^{\text{col}}, B_1^{\text{col}})$;
     $\epsilon_0 := \frac{maxnz}{nz(B_0)} \cdot \frac{p}{2} - 1$;
     $\epsilon_1 := \frac{maxnz}{nz(B_1)} \cdot \frac{p}{2} - 1$;
     $(A_0, \ldots, A_{p/2-1}) := \text{MatrixPartition}(B_0, \frac{p}{2}, \epsilon_0)$;
     $(A_{p/2}, \ldots, A_{p-1}) := \text{MatrixPartition}(B_1, \frac{p}{2}, \epsilon_1)$;
   else
     $A_0 := A$;

The matrix and vector partitioning of Fig. 4.9 were computed by the Mondriaan partitioner [304], version 4.1, with the *localbest* strategy, which is an implementation of Algorithm 4.6. The communication volume of the fanout is 58 and that of the fanin is 55, so that $V = 113$. The BSP cost is $404 + 34g + 4l$. The matrix cage6 is structurally symmetric, the nonzero pattern being symmetric, and although the Mondriaan partitioner has an option to produce symmetric partitionings, we did not use it for our example. We also did not impose an equal distribution for the input and output vectors.

Figure 4.10 presents a **local view**, or **processor view**, of cage6. For processor $P(s)$, $s = 0, 1, 2, 3$, the local submatrix $\bar{I}_s \times \bar{J}_s$ is shown. Together, these submatrices fit into the space of the original matrix. The global indices of a submatrix are not consecutive in the original matrix, but scattered. For instance, $\bar{I}_2 = \{36, 37, 38, 39, 44, 45, \ldots, 87, 90, 91\}$, cf. Fig. 4.9. The partitioning directions chosen for cage6 corresponded to first splitting in the column direction, and then twice, independently, in the row direction. A column split creates empty rows in the submatrix to the left and to the right. Empty rows and columns in a submatrix are the aim of a good partitioner, because they do not incur communication. An empty row is created by a column split in which all nonzeros of a row are assigned to the same processor, leaving the other processor empty-handed. These empty rows are not assigned

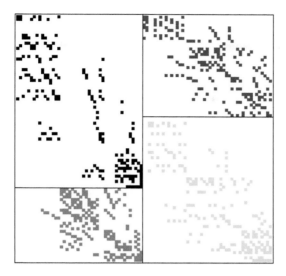

Figure 4.10 Same matrix and distribution as in Fig. 4.9, but in local view. The size of the local submatrix shown is 55 × 48 for $P(0)$ (yellow), 38 × 48 for $P(1)$ (blue), 28 × 45 for $P(2)$ (red), and 65 × 45 for $P(3)$ (black).

to a processor by Mondriaan, but we have assigned them arbitrarily to $P(3)$ (black) and $P(0)$ (yellow), mainly for artistic reasons. By construction, processors $P(1)$ and $P(2)$ then contain no empty rows, so that $\bar{I}_1 = I_1$ and $\bar{I}_2 = I_2$. The sizes of the submatrices without empty rows and columns are: 38 × 42 for $I_0 \times J_0$, 38 × 41 for $I_1 \times J_1$, 28 × 34 for $I_2 \times J_2$, and 44 × 34 for $I_3 \times J_3$.

The high-level recursive matrix partitioning algorithm does not specify the inner workings of the *Bipartition* function that splits a matrix into two parts. To find a good split, we need a bipartitioning method based on the exact communication volume. It is convenient to express our problem in terms of hypergraphs, as was first done for matrix partitioning problems by Çatalyürek and Aykanat [56, 57]. A **hypergraph** $\mathcal{H} = (\mathcal{V}, \mathcal{N})$ consists of a set of **vertices** $\mathcal{V}$ and a set of **hyperedges**, or **nets**, $\mathcal{N}$, which are subsets of $\mathcal{V}$. Figure 4.11 illustrates the definition of a hypergraph. A hypergraph is a generalization of an **undirected graph** $\mathcal{G} = (\mathcal{V}, \mathcal{E})$, where $\mathcal{E}$ is a set of **undirected edges**, which are unordered pairs (i,j) with $i,j \in \mathcal{V}$. Thus, an undirected edge $(i,j) = (j,i)$ can be identified with a subset $\{i,j\}$ of two elements, which is a net with two vertices.

Our splitting problem is to assign each of the n columns of a sparse $m \times n$ matrix to either processor $P(0)$ or $P(1)$. We can identify a matrix column j with a vertex j of a hypergraph with vertex set $\mathcal{V} = \{0, \ldots, n-1\}$, so that our problem translates into assigning each vertex to a processor. We have to minimize the communication volume of the fanin: assigning the nonzeros of a row to different processors gives rise to one communication, whereas assigning them to the same processor avoids communication. We can identify a matrix row i with a net n_i, defining

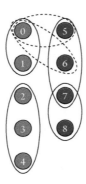

Figure 4.11 Hypergraph with nine vertices and six nets. Each circle represents a vertex. Each ellipse enclosing a set of vertices represents a net. The vertex set is $V = \{0,\dots,8\}$ and the nets are $n_0 = \{0,1\}$, $n_1 = \{0,5\}$, $n_2 = \{0,6\}$, $n_3 = \{2,3,4\}$, $n_4 = \{5,6,7\}$, and $n_5 = \{7,8\}$. The vertices have been coloured to show a possible assignment to processors, where $P(0)$ has the red vertices and $P(1)$ the blue vertices. Cut nets, with vertices in different colours, are shown as dashed ellipses; uncut nets as solid ellipses. Can you improve the assignment?

$$n_i = \{j : 0 \le j < n \wedge a_{ij} \ne 0\}, \quad \text{for } 0 \le i < m. \tag{4.39}$$

Here, we have used the so-called **row-net model** [57] to convert a sparse matrix into a hypergraph. A communication arises if a net is **cut**, that is, not all its vertices are assigned to the same processor. The total communication volume incurred by the split thus equals the number of cut nets of the hypergraph. In the assignment of Fig. 4.11, two nets are cut: n_1 and n_2.

Example 4.8 The hypergraph that corresponds to the column partitioning problem of Example 4.7 is $\mathcal{H} = (\mathcal{V}, \mathcal{N})$, where $\mathcal{V} = \{0,1,2,3,4\}$ and $\mathcal{N} = \{n_0, n_1, n_2, n_3, n_4\}$, with $n_0 = \{1,4\}$, $n_1 = \{0,1\}$, $n_2 = \{1,2,3\}$, $n_3 = \{0,3,4\}$, and $n_4 = \{2,3,4\}$. The optimal column solution has four cut nets: n_0, n_2, n_3, n_4.

We have to assign the vertices of the hypergraph in a balanced way, so that both processors receive about the same number of nonzeros. This is best modelled by making the vertices weighted, defining the weight c_j of vertex j to be the number of nonzeros in column j,

$$c_j = |\{i : 0 \le i < m \wedge a_{ij} \ne 0\}|, \quad \text{for } 0 \le j < n. \tag{4.40}$$

The splitting has to satisfy

$$\sum_{\substack{j=0 \\ \phi(j)=s}}^{n-1} c_j \le (1+\epsilon)\frac{nz(A)}{2}, \quad \text{for } s = 0,1. \tag{4.41}$$

Having converted our problem to a hypergraph bipartitioning problem, we can apply algorithms developed for such problems. An excellent approach is to use the **multilevel** method [48], which consists of three phases: coarsening, initial partitioning, and uncoarsening. During the **coarsening phase**, the problem is reduced in size by merging similar vertices, that is, vertices representing columns with similar sparsity patterns. A natural heuristic is to do this pairwise, halving the number of vertices at each coarsening level. The best match for column j is an unmatched column j' with maximal overlap in the sparsity pattern, that is, maximal $|\{i : 0 \leq i < m \land a_{ij} \neq 0 \land a_{ij'} \neq 0\}|$. This value can be computed as the inner product of columns j and j', taking all nonzeros to be ones. The result of the merger is a column which has a nonzero in row i if $a_{ij} \neq 0$ or $a_{ij'} \neq 0$. In Example 4.7, the best match for column 2 is column 3, since their sparsity patterns have two nonzeros in common. For the purpose of load balancing, the new column gets a weight equal to the sum of the weights of the merged columns.

The **initial partitioning** phase starts when the problem is sufficiently reduced in size, typically when a few hundred columns are left. Each column is then assigned to a processor. The simplest initial partitioning method is by random assignment, but more sophisticated methods give better results. Care must be taken to obey the load balance criterion for the weights.

The initial partitioning for the smallest problem is transferred to the larger problems during the **uncoarsening phase**, which is similar to the coarsening phase but is carried out in the reverse direction. At each level, both columns of a matched pair are assigned to the same processor as their merged column. The resulting partitioning of the larger problem is refined, for instance by trying to move columns or vertices, to the other processor. A simple approach would be to try a move of all vertices that are part of a cut net. Note that a vertex can be part of several cut nets. Moving a vertex to the other processor may increase or decrease the number of cut nets. The **gain** of a vertex is the reduction in cut nets obtained by moving it to the other processor. The best move has the largest gain, for example, moving vertex 0 to $P(1)$ in Fig. 4.11 has a gain of 1. (Yes, the assignment of the figure could be improved!) The gain may be zero, such as in the case of moving vertex 5 or 6 to $P(0)$. The gain may also be negative, for example, moving vertex 1, 2, 3, 4, or 8 to the other processor has a gain of -1. The worst move is that of vertex 7, since its gain is -2.

Figure 4.12 shows an example of a column bipartitioning by the multilevel method. The matrix is first coarsened. After that, an initial partitioning is performed, leading to an initial communication volume of $V = 3$, which is caused by rows 1, 2, and 7. Then the matrix is uncoarsened and refined. The first refinement does not change the partitioning, because the only move of a single column that reduces the communication is moving the last merged column to $P(0)$ and this would cause an unacceptable load imbalance (17 vs. 5 nonzeros). The second refinement moves column 0 to $P(1)$, giving a partitioning with $V = 2$ and $\epsilon' \approx 0.18$ as the final result.

The Kernighan–Lin algorithm [179], originally developed for graph bipartitioning, can be applied to hypergraph bipartitioning. It can be viewed as a method for improving a given bipartitioning. The algorithm consists of several passes. Fiduccia and Mattheyses [108] give an efficient implementation of the Kernighan–Lin algorithm based on a priority-queue data structure for which one pass costs $\mathcal{O}(nz(A) + n)$. In a pass, all vertices are first marked as movable and their gain is computed. The vertex with the largest gain among the movable vertices is moved, provided this does not violate the load balance constraint. The vertex

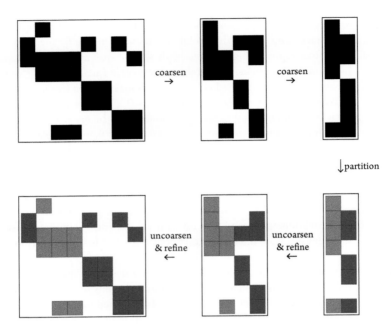

Figure 4.12 A column bipartitioning of an 8×8 matrix by the multilevel method. The allowed imbalance is $\epsilon = 0.2$, so that no processor can have more than 13 out of 22 nonzeros. During the coarsening, columns are matched in even–odd pairs, column 0 with 1, 2 with 3, and so on. The initial partitioning assigns columns to processors. Columns owned by $P(0)$ are shown in red; those owned by $P(1)$ in blue.

is then marked as nonmovable for the remainder of the current pass; this is to guarantee termination of the pass. The gains of the other vertices are then updated and a new move is determined. This process continues until no more moves can be carried out. The best partitioning encountered during the pass (not necessarily the final partitioning) is saved and used as the starting point for the next pass. Note that moves with negative gain are allowed and that they occur when no moves with positive or zero gain are available. A move with negative gain may still be advantageous, for instance if it is followed by a move of **adjacent** vertices (i.e., vertices that share a net with the moved vertex).

The Kernighan–Lin algorithm can be used in the initial partitioning and uncoarsening phases of the multilevel method. In the initial partitioning, the algorithm can be applied several times, each time to improve a different random assignment of the vertices to the processors. The best result is chosen. In the uncoarsening phase, the algorithm is commonly applied only once, and often with the movable vertices restricted to those that are part of a cut net. This cheaper variant is called the boundary Kernighan–Lin algorithm. Its use is motivated by the larger problem sizes involved and by the limited purpose of the uncoarsening phase, which is to refine a partitioning, and not to compute a completely new one.

4.6 Fine-grain and medium-grain matrix distribution

We have seen that keeping rows (or columns) of a sparse matrix together is a good idea. Ideally, we would like to keep both rows and columns together, but we would also like to have our cake and eat it too. If we keep everything together, all nonzeros will end up on the same processor. In this section, we will present two methods that try to get the best in both directions: the fine-grain approach which equally penalizes cut rows and columns, and the medium-grain approach which tries to keep parts of rows together as well as parts of columns. In particular for $p = 2$, we hope to do better by such an approach than just taking the best of both directions.

The **fine-grain model** [58] is a model for converting a sparse matrix into a hypergraph based on identifying individual nonzeros of the matrix with vertices of the hypergraph. Thus, the number of vertices is $|\mathcal{V}| = nz(A)$. Each nonempty row i becomes a row net, which contains the vertices corresponding to the nonzeros of row i, and each nonempty column becomes a column net. The vertices of the hypergraph can then be partitioned by any existing hypergraph partitioner, and the result converted back to a partitioning of the matrix nonzeros. The communication volume incurred by a nonempty row i is then $\lambda_i - 1$, where λ_i is the number of processors having a nonzero in row i; λ_i equals the **connectivity** of row net i, that is its number of parts. A similar statement holds for columns and column nets. The total communication volume V of the matrix partitioning then equals the total of the *connectivity* $- 1$ terms of the hypergraph; this metric is also called the $\lambda - 1$ **metric**. As a result, the fine-grain model allows any possible partitioning, including those produced by the row-net and column-net models, and it represents the communication volume objective exactly. In theory, the fine-grain model is the appropriate model. Note that the hypergraph created by the fine-grain model is special: every vertex is contained in exactly two nets. A general hypergraph partitioner will most likely not exploit this property; a specialized one should.

To perform a fine-grain partitioning in practice, we will restrict ourselves to bipartitioning, and use it as the function *Bipartition* in Algorithm 4.6. An alternative would be to use a **direct p-way** hypergraph partitioner, but this is much less common in practice, for instance because it is more difficult to carry out an efficient Kernighan–Lin refinement procedure for more than two parts.

The **medium-grain method** [245] tries to keep a subset of nonzeros from each row together and a subset from each column, taking care to assign each nonzero a_{ij}, by some criterion, to either row subset i or column subset j. This means that the criterion partitions the matrix A into $A = A^r \cup A^c$, viewed as sets of index pairs of nonzeros. We can also write this as a matrix sum, $A = A^r + A^c$, where all three matrices have the same size. To keep our explanation simple, we assume that A is square, but the method can easily be extended to rectangular matrices. An example split of a matrix A is given by Fig. 4.13(a). After the split, the method forms a new matrix B of size $2n \times 2n$,

$$B = \left[\begin{array}{cc} I_n & (A^r)^T \\ A^c & I_n \end{array} \right]. \tag{4.42}$$

Every nonzero of A thus ends up as a nonzero in B. The matrix B is converted to a hypergraph by the row-net model, so that every column becomes a vertex. Thus, the number of vertices is $|\mathcal{V}| = 2n$. This hypergraph is then bipartitioned. Nonzeros from the same column j of A^c all end up in column j of B, and hence will stay together during the partitioning. Nonzeros from the same row i of A^r will end up in the same column $n + i$ of B, and hence will also stay together.

To ensure a proper load balance for the bipartitioning of the original matrix A, cf. eqn (4.31), the balance constraint for bipartitioning the matrix B should only count the nonzeros originating in A and not those of the added identity matrices I_n. This requires just a slight modification of the vertex weights given as input to the hypergraph partitioner. The corresponding column nonzero counts c_j are shown in Fig. 4.13(b).

As a result of the hypergraph bipartitioning, the matrix B is bipartitioned column-wise into submatrices B_0 and B_1, and an owner is assigned to every nonzero of B, and hence to the corresponding nonzero of A. This leads to a bipartitioning of A into A_0 and A_1. Figure 4.14 shows the result of a bipartitioning, in panel (a) as a bipartitioning of the matrix B and in panel (b) converted back to the original matrix A.

The purpose of introducing the identity matrix I_n into the left upper block of B is to connect, for each column j of A, the nonzeros in A^c with the other nonzeros of that column, that is those included in A^r. Assume for a moment that column j of A has at least one nonzero in A^c and one in A^r. Thinking alert! Now note that the number $\mu_j(A_0, A_1)$ of processors having part of column j in the bipartitioning of A is the same as the number $\lambda_j(B_0, B_1)$ having part of row j in the bipartitioning of B:

$$\mu_j(A_0, A_1) = \lambda_j(B_0, B_1), \text{ for } 0 \leq j < n. \tag{4.43}$$

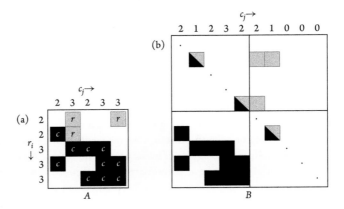

Figure 4.13 (a) Simple split of a 5×5 sparse matrix A based on the number r_i of nonzeros of row i and c_j of column j. Nonzero a_{ij} is assigned to A^r (light grey) if $r_i < c_j$, and to A^c (black) otherwise. (b) The resulting 10×10 matrix B with unnecessary diagonal entries (denoted by a dot) removed. The column nonzero counts c_j of B exclude the diagonal nonzeros. The block structure corresponds to eqn (4.42).

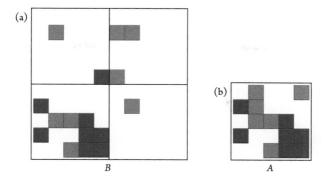

Figure 4.14 (a) Column-wise bipartitioning of the matrix B from Fig. 4.13, produced by a run of Mondriaan, version 4.2, with allowed imbalance $\epsilon = 0.1$. (b) The corresponding bipartitioning of the matrix A. Both bipartitionings have volume $V = 4$.

This is because the nonzeros in column j of B have all been assigned to the same processor, the owner of nonzero b_{jj}, and this processor is one of the processors owning row j of B. The nonzeros in row j of B in turn are the nonzeros of column j of A^r, extended with b_{jj}. If our assumption above does not hold, so that all nonzeros of column j of A are in A^c or all are in A^r, the connecting nonzero b_{jj} must be removed, because it may cause an extra, unnecessary communication.

The identity matrix I_n in the right lower block of B connects, for each row i of A, the nonzeros in A^r with the other nonzeros of that row, that is those included in A^c. As a result, we have

$$\lambda_i(A_0, A_1) = \lambda_{n+i}(B_0, B_1), \text{ for } 0 \leq i < n. \tag{4.44}$$

Here, the diagonal nonzero $b_{n+i,n+i}$ must be removed if all nonzeros of row i are in A^r or all are in A^c.

Because of eqns (4.43) and (4.44), the communication volume of the bipartitioning of A satisfies

$$V(A_0, A_1) = V(B_0, B_1). \tag{4.45}$$

(This result also holds more generally, for rectangular matrices and for $p \geq 2$, see [245].)

How can we split the matrix A in a suitable fashion into A^c and A^r? If we choose $A^c = A$ and $A^r = 0$, we compute a 1D column partitioning of A. If we choose $A^r = A$ and $A^c = 0$ instead, we compute a 1D row partitioning. The Mondriaan method tries both, but here we would like to get even better than the best of both dimensions, creating a true 2D distribution even for $p = 2$. It turns out that a very good heuristic is to assign nonzero a_{ij} to A^r if row i has fewer nonzeros than column j, and to A^c otherwise. This is because the nonzeros of a sparser row have a higher likelihood to be together in a good partitioning. Such an initial split is easy to compute and in general leads to a lower communication volume than a 1D initial split with all nonzeros in either A^c or A^r.

Comparing the fine-grain and medium-grain approaches, we see that using the fine-grain model can in theory yield any possible partitioning as outcome, and hence it is more general and may achieve a lower communication volume. It is also slower, however, since the corresponding hypergraph has many more vertices. In practice, implementations of the medium-grain method outperform implementations based on the fine-grain model [245] considering both quality (communication volume) and speed (partitioning time). Note that implementations of both methods are inevitably heuristic in nature as they cannot explore the whole solution space of possible partitionings, except for very small problems, and the initial split of the medium-grain method just works very well as a starting heuristic.

The medium-grain method can be applied repeatedly to improve a given bipartitioning, because it takes as input a bipartitioning of A into A^c and A^r, and it yields as output also a bipartitioning of A, into A_0 and A_1. We can then feed the output of one bipartitioning as input into the next. Here, we must ensure that the subsequent applications are indeed improvements; we can achieve this by only performing the Kernighan–Lin refinement from the uncoarsening phase of the multilevel method (see Section 4.5), and then only for the finest level, that is with the original uncoarsened hypergraph. An additional benefit is that such a refinement iteration is much faster than a full medium-grain bipartitioning. The resulting **iterative refinement** procedure starts with $A^c = A_0$ and $A^r = A_1$, then performs a Kernighan–Lin refinement iteration, and after that uses the new A_0 and A_1 again as initial split. This is repeated until no more improvement can be obtained. Then the roles of A^c and A^r are reversed, and so on, alternating roles until no more improvement can be obtained in any way. Note that iterative refinement can also be applied if the first bipartitioning is done by a different method, for instance by fine-grain bipartitioning. Also in that case, the solution quality is considerably improved, at little extra cost, as shown in [245].

To check the performance of the different partitioning algorithms, we carried out some numerical experiments on a small test set of sparse matrices from the SuiteSparse Matrix Collection [79]. We used one core of an Apple iMac computer with a 3.4 GHz Intel Core i5 quadcore processor with 32 GB RAM running MacOs 10.12.5. We selected five square matrices with 10–30 million nonzeros originating in different application areas and we show their size and number of nonzeros in Table 4.1. The matrices have been ordered by increasing number of nonzeros. We used version 4.2 of the Mondriaan sparse matrix partitioner, with its own hypergraph bipartitioner, and performed experiments for three methods. The localbest (LB) method described in Section 4.5 tries both row and column directions and chooses the best, thus yielding a Mondriaan distribution. Note that for $p = 2$, this gives either a 1D row distribution or a 1D column distribution, whichever is better. The other two methods in our experiments are fine-grain (FG) and medium-grain (MG).

Table 4.2 compares the three partitioning methods and it shows that the 2D methods FG and MG yield a lower communication volume than the 1D method LB, with one exception (asia_osm), and that LB and MG are significantly faster than FG. We may conclude that MG is the method of choice, being fast and giving the lowest volume; it has become the default in Mondriaan, starting from version 4.0. This comparison does not do complete justice to the FG method, however, because a highly optimized implementation with specialized hypergraph bipartitioning such as provided by PaToH [57, 58] will improve the volume results for FG, see [245].

Table 4.1 Test set of sparse square matrices selected from the SuiteSparse Matrix Collection [79]. The parameters given are: the number of rows/columns n, the number of nonzeros nz, the average number c of nonzeros per row/column.

Name	n	nz	c	Origin
mip1	66 463	10 352 819	155.8	mixed integer programming
in-2004	1 382 908	16 917 053	12.2	web links India 2004
asia_osm	11 950 757	25 423 206	2.1	road network Asia
cage14	1 505 785	27 130 349	18.0	DNA electrophoresis
rgg_n_2_21_s0	2 097 152	28 975 990	13.8	random geometric graph

The partitioning times in our experiments depend very much on the structure of the input matrix. For example, road networks such as the Open Street Map of Asia are easy to partition, whereas web link matrices such as the India subdomain crawled in 2004 are hard and take more time. The matrix cage14 is the second-largest matrix from the DNA electrophoresis series, see Fig. 4.1. This matrix represents transition probabilities between the configurations (states) of a polymer with 14 monomers. It has an underlying 13-dimensional state space which makes partitioning hard and time-consuming, and also causes the outcome to have a high communication volume. The partitioning time should roughly grow with the number of parts p in proportion to $\log_2 p$, meaning a factor of 5 when going from $p = 2$ to $p = 64$. This is because there are $\log_2 p$ levels of bipartitioning in a recursive partitioning algorithm. At each level, a set of bipartitionings is performed, together doubling the number of parts. These bipartitionings access the whole matrix once, albeit split up into smaller submatrices. The time of a deeper level of the recursion is thus about the same as that of the highest level. For a more detailed theoretical complexity analysis, see [30]. Experimentally, in Table 4.2, we indeed observe a growth factor that is reasonably close to 5. We also see that all matrices could be partitioned within 1–10 minutes.

To summarize the results of the five matrices for $p = 2$ and $p = 64$ given in Table 4.2, we compute the geometric mean of the ten values in each column, and normalize it so that the geometric mean for the localbest method is 1. The **geometric mean** of k values $x_0, \ldots, x_{k-1} > 0$ is defined as

$$GM(x_0, \ldots, x_{k-1}) = (x_0 \cdot x_1 \cdots x_{k-1})^{\frac{1}{k}}. \tag{4.46}$$

This type of average is able to handle widely differing scales, such as the communication volumes generated for the different matrices and different p. It gives each matrix/p pair equal influence. Furthermore, it has the useful property that

$$GM\left(\frac{x_0}{y_0}, \ldots, \frac{x_{k-1}}{y_{k-1}}\right) = \frac{GM(x_0, \ldots, x_{k-1})}{GM(y_0, \ldots, y_{k-1})}, \tag{4.47}$$

for all sequences x_i and y_i, so that it is irrelevant whether we normalize the values first or only after computing the mean. This ensures that it does not matter to which method we

Table 4.2 Communication volume V and partitioning time using Mondriaan, version 4.2, for the test set of Table 4.1, comparing the localbest (LB), fine-grain (FG), and medium-grain with iterative refinement (MG) methods. The results are averaged over 10 runs; the allowed load imbalance is $\epsilon = 0.03$. The bottom line summarizes the results of each column as a normalized geometric mean.

Name	p	Volume			Time (in s)		
		LB	FG	MG	LB	FG	MG
mip1	2	9 099	3 929	2 109	94	291	98
	64	120 636	90 133	56 864	350	1 059	230
in-2004	2	1 158	637	558	81	376	89
	64	18 247	16 345	14 425	401	1 774	397
asia_osm	2	91	120	130	61	48	48
	64	2 291	2 667	2 538	271	206	258
cage14	2	195 912	172 091	154 962	153	232	109
	64	1 436 410	1 161 269	980 957	664	1 035	516
rgg_n_2_21_s0	2	3 364	3 322	2 976	47	111	64
	64	46 192	44 049	41 249	234	613	345
Norm. geom. mean		1.00	0.83	0.70	1.00	2.10	0.95

normalize the results: the relative performance ratios are the same. For a further motivation with compelling examples why the geometric mean (and not the arithmetic mean) is the right tool to summarize normalized results, see [109]. The bottom line summarizing our results clearly indicates that the medium-grain method is superior to the other two methods, with respect to both communication volume and partitioning time.

Figure 4.15 presents a visual comparison of the obtained communication volumes in the form of a **performance profile**, first proposed as a tool by Dolan and Moré [88]. A performance profile allows for the comparison of several methods for many different problem instances (e.g., all the matrices in the SuiteSparse collection, for all $p = 1–1024$). A data point (x, y) for a given method means that a fraction y of the problem instances has a value within a factor x of the best value obtained by the compared methods. Here, the LB method solves 70% of the ten problem instances within 1.5 times the lowest volume achieved by any of the three methods. The MG method is better, since it solves *all* instances within that factor 1.5. Furthermore, note that MG solves 80% of the instances as the best method. Visually, the higher the curve of a method, the better. If a method fails on a particular problem instance, this instance can still be included in the performance profile, in contrast to the geometric mean where it must be excluded. A profile can be created by first dividing the result (here, the volume) for each instance by the result of the best method for that instance, then sorting the normalized results in increasing order, for each method separately, and finally plotting the normalized results along the x-axis and their rank expressed as a fraction along the y-axis.

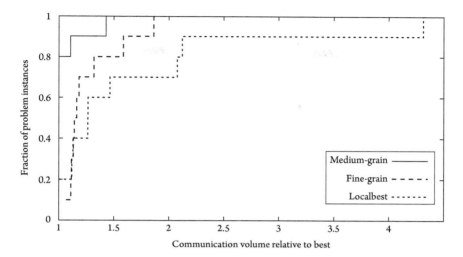

Figure 4.15 Performance profile of the communication volume V from Table 4.2 comparing the localbest, fine-grain, and medium-grain with iterative refinement methods.

4.7 Vector distribution

The matrix distribution algorithms of Sections 4.5 and 4.6 should lead to an SpMV with low communication volume and a good computational load balance. What remains to be done is to partition the input and output vectors such that the communication is balanced as well. In other words, given a matrix distribution ϕ, we have to determine a vector distribution $\phi_{\mathbf{v}}$ that minimizes the value h of the fanout and that satisfies

$$j \in J_{\phi_{\mathbf{v}}(j)}, \quad \text{for } 0 \leq j < n. \tag{4.48}$$

This **consistency constraint** says that the processor $P(s) = P(\phi_{\mathbf{v}}(j))$ that obtains v_j must own a nonzero in matrix column j, that is, $j \in J_s$. We also have to find a vector distribution $\phi_{\mathbf{u}}$ that minimizes the value h of the fanin and that satisfies the consistency constraint

$$i \in I_{\phi_{\mathbf{u}}(i)}, \quad \text{for } 0 \leq i < n. \tag{4.49}$$

These are two independent vector distribution problems, except if the requirement $\text{distr}(\mathbf{u}) = \text{distr}(\mathbf{v})$ must be satisfied; we assume that this is not the case.

Figure 4.9 gives a possible vector distribution in the global view. The vectors in this figure are depicted in the familiar way, cf. Fig. 4.5. It is easy to verify that the two consistency constraints mentioned above are satisfied: one of the nonzeros in each matrix column has the colour of the corresponding component v_j, and one of the nonzeros in each row has the colour of the corresponding component u_i.

Table 4.3 Components of vectors **u** and **v** owned and communicated by the different processors for the matrix cage6 in the distribution of Fig. 4.9. The number of components owned by processor $P(s)$ is $N(s)$; the number sent is $h_s(s)$; the number received is $h_r(s)$.

	u			**v**		
s	$N(s)$	$h_s(s)$	$h_r(s)$	$N(s)$	$h_s(s)$	$h_r(s)$
0	23	15	15	24	18	18
1	26	12	13	23	18	18
2	16	12	11	23	11	11
3	28	16	16	23	11	11

With some stamina, or by writing a helpful small computer program, we can count the number of components, sends, and receives of every processor for the vector distribution of Fig. 4.9. Table 4.3 summarizes those statistics. The table shows that the communication cost of the fanout is $18g$ and the cost of the fanin $16g$. The total communication cost of $34g$ is thus only slightly above the average $Vg/p = 113g/4 = 28.25g$, which means that the communication is well-balanced.

Table 4.3 also shows that the number of vector components of the vector **v** is well-balanced, with one processor having 24 components and the others 23. If we introduce a load imbalance parameter ϵ' for the vector distribution, in the same way as we did for the matrix distribution, we can say that we achieved a value $\epsilon' \approx 0.03$. The vector **u** is less well-balanced, with $\epsilon' \approx 0.20$, but this does not influence the cost of the SpMV. It influences the cost of other operations, however, such as the vector operations accompanying the SpMV in an iterative solver. For an iterative solver such as GMRES [263], where DAXPY vector operations consume a significant portion of the computation time, we may have to take this balance into account as well; the necessary modification of our vector distribution methods is sketched at the end of the present section.

The vector distribution problems for **u** and **v** are similar; it is easy to see that we can solve the problem of finding a good distribution $\phi_{\mathbf{u}}$ given $\phi = \phi_A$ by finding a good distribution $\phi_{\mathbf{v}}$ given $\phi = \phi_{A^T}$. This is because the nonzero pattern of row i of A is the same as the nonzero pattern of column i of A^T, so that a partial sum u_{is} is sent from $P(s)$ to $P(t)$ in the multiplication by A if and only if a vector component v_i is sent from $P(t)$ to $P(s)$ in the multiplication by A^T. Therefore, we only treat the problem for $\phi_{\mathbf{v}}$ and hence only consider the communication in the fanout.

Let us assume without loss of generality that we have a vector distribution problem with $\mu_j \geq 2$, for all j. Columns with $\mu_j = 0$ or $\mu_j = 1$ do not cause communication and hence may be omitted from the problem formulation. (A good matrix distribution method will give rise to many columns with $\mu_j = 1$.) Without loss of generality we may also assume that the columns are ordered by increasing μ_j; this can be achieved by renumbering. Then the h-values for the fanout are

$$h_s(s) = \sum_{\substack{j=0 \\ \phi_v(j)=s}}^{n-1} (\mu_j - 1), \quad \text{for } 0 \le s < p, \tag{4.50}$$

and

$$h_r(s) = |\{j : j \in J_s \wedge \phi_v(j) \ne s\}|, \quad \text{for } 0 \le s < p. \tag{4.51}$$

Me first! Consider what would happen if a processor $P(s)$ becomes utterly egoistic and tries to minimize its own $h(s) = \max(h_s(s), h_r(s))$ without consideration for the other processors. To minimize $h_r(s)$, it just has to maximize the number of components v_j with $j \in J_s$ that it owns, irrespective of which they are. To minimize $h_s(s)$, it has to minimize the total weight of these components, where we define the weight of v_j as $\mu_j - 1$. An optimal strategy would thus be to start with $h_s(s) = 0$ and $h_r(s) = |J_s|$ and grab the components in increasing order (and hence increasing weight), while increasing $h_s(s)$ and decreasing $h_r(s)$ to account for each newly owned component. The processor grabs components as long as $h_s(s) \le h_r(s)$, the new component included. We denote the resulting optimal value of $h_s(s)$ by $\hat{h}_s(s)$, that of $h_r(s)$ by $\hat{h}_r(s)$, and that of $h(s)$ by $\hat{h}(s)$. Thus,

$$\hat{h}_s(s) \le \hat{h}_r(s) = \hat{h}(s), \quad \text{for } 0 \le s < p. \tag{4.52}$$

The value $\hat{h}(s)$ is indeed optimal for an egoistic $P(s)$, because stopping earlier would result in a higher $h_r(s)$ and hence a higher $h(s)$, and because stopping later would not improve matters either: if for instance $P(s)$ were to grab one component more, then $h_s(s) > h_r(s)$ so that $h(s) = h_s(s) \ge h_r(s) + 1 = \hat{h}_r(s)$, so that $h(s) \ge \hat{h}(s)$. The value $\hat{h}(s)$ is a local lower bound on the actual value that can be achieved in the fanout,

$$\hat{h}(s) \le h(s), \quad \text{for } 0 \le s < p. \tag{4.53}$$

Example 4.9 The following table gives the input of a vector distribution problem. If a processor $P(s)$ owns a nonzero in matrix column j, this is denoted by a 1 in the corresponding location; if it does not own such a nonzero, this is denoted by a dot. This problem could for instance be the result of a matrix partitioning for $p = 4$ with all splits in the row direction. (We can view the input itself as a sparse $p \times n$ matrix.)

$s = 0$	1	.	1	.	1	1	1	1
1	1	1	.	1	1	1	1	.
2	.	1	.	.	.	1	1	1
3	.	.	1	1	1	.	.	1
$\mu_j =$	2	2	2	2	3	3	3	3
$j =$	0	1	2	3	4	5	6	7

Processor $P(0)$ egoistically wants v_0 and v_2, so that $\hat{h}_s(0) = 2, \hat{h}_r(0) = 4$, and $\hat{h}(0) = 4$; $P(1)$ wants v_0, v_1, and v_3, so that $\hat{h}(1) = 3$; $P(2)$ wants v_1, giving $\hat{h}(2) = 3$; and $P(3)$ wants v_2 and v_3, giving $\hat{h}(3) = 2$. The fanout will cost at least $4g$.

More in general, we can compute a lower bound $\hat{h}(J, ns_0, nr_0)$ for a given index set $J \subseteq J_s$ and a given initial number of sends, ns_0, and receives, nr_0. We denote the corresponding send and receive values by $\hat{h}_s(J, ns_0, nr_0)$ and $\hat{h}_r(J, ns_0, nr_0)$. The initial communications may be due to columns outside J. This bound is computed by the same method, but starting with the values $h_s(s) = ns_0$ and $h_r(s) = nr_0 + |J|$. Note that $\hat{h}(s) = \hat{h}(J_s, 0, 0)$. The generalization of eqn (4.52) is

$$\hat{h}_s(J, ns_0, nr_0) \le \hat{h}_r(J, ns_0, nr_0) = \hat{h}(J, ns_0, nr_0). \tag{4.54}$$

Think about the others! Every processor would be happy to own the lighter components and would rather leave the heavier components to the others. Since every component v_j will have to be owned by exactly one processor, we must devise a mechanism to resolve conflicting desires. A reasonable heuristic seems to be to give preference to the processor that faces the toughest future, that is, the processor with the highest value $\hat{h}(s)$. Our aim in the vector distribution algorithm is to minimize the highest $h(s)$, because $(\max_{0 \le s < p} h(s)) \cdot g$ is the communication cost of the fanout.

Algorithm 4.7 is a vector distribution algorithm based on the local-bound heuristic; we have proposed it in joint work with Wouter Meesen [33]. The algorithm successively assigns components v_j; the set L_s is the index set of components that may still be assigned to $P(s)$. The number of send operations caused by the assignments is registered as $h_s(s)$ and the number of receive operations as $h_r(s)$. The processor with the highest local lower bound $\hat{h}_r(L_s, h_s(s), h_r(s))$ becomes the happy owner of the lightest component available. The values $\hat{h}_r(L_s, h_s(s), h_r(s))$ and $\hat{h}_s(L_s, h_s(s), h_r(s))$ may change after every assignment. A processor will not accept components anymore from the moment it knows that it has achieved its optimum, which happens when $h_s(s) = \hat{h}_s(L_s, h_s(s), h_r(s))$. (Note that $ns_0 \le \hat{h}_s(J, ns_0, nr_0)$ by construction, so that for $ns_0 = h_s(s)$ we obtain $h_s(s) \le \hat{h}_s(L_s, h_s(s), h_r(s))$.) Accepting additional components would raise its final $h(s)$. This egoistic approach is taken by every processor, and not only the one with the highest current bound. (Accepting more components for altruistic reasons may be well-intended, but is still a bad idea because the components thus accepted may be more useful to other processors.) The algorithm terminates when no processor is willing to accept components any more.

After termination, a small fraction of the vector components may remain unassigned. These will be the heavier components. We can assign the remaining components in a greedy fashion, each time assigning a component v_j to the processor $P(s)$ for which this would result in the lowest new value $h(s)$.

A special case occurs if the matrix partitioning has the property $\mu_j \le 2$, for all j. This case can be solved to optimality by an algorithm Opt2 [33] that has as input the undirected communication graph $\mathcal{G} = (\mathcal{V}, \mathcal{E})$ defined by a vertex set $\mathcal{V} = \{0, \ldots, p-1\}$ representing the processors and an edge set $\mathcal{E}$ representing matrix columns shared by a pair of processors. Here, an edge (s, t) represents one communication, either from $P(s)$ to $P(t)$, or vice versa.

Algorithm 4.7 Local-bound based vector partitioning [33].

---

input: $\phi = \text{distr}(A)$, matrix distribution over p processors, $p \geq 1$, where A is a sparse $n \times n$ matrix.

output: $\phi_\mathbf{v} = \text{distr}(\mathbf{v})$: vector distribution over p processors, satisfying $j \in J_{\phi_\mathbf{v}(j)}$, for $0 \leq j < n$, where $J_s = \{j : 0 \leq j < n \wedge (\exists i : 0 \leq i < n \wedge \phi(i,j) = s)\}$, for $0 \leq s < p$.

{ Initialize }
for $s := 0$ **to** $p - 1$ **do**
    $L_s := J_s$;
    $h_s(s) := 0$;
    $h_r(s) := 0$;
    if $h_s(s) < \hat{h}_s(L_s, h_s(s), h_r(s))$ **then**
        active$(s) := true$;
    else
        active$(s) := false$;

while $\exists s : 0 \leq s < p \wedge$ active(s) **do**
    { Choose processor with highest local bound }
    $s_{\max} := \text{argmax}(\hat{h}_r(L_s, h_s(s), h_r(s)) : 0 \leq s < p \wedge$ active$(s))$;
    $j := \min(L_{s_{\max}})$;
    $\phi_\mathbf{v}(j) := s_{\max}$;

    { Update sends and receives }
    $h_s(s_{\max}) := h_s(s_{\max}) + \mu_j - 1$;
    for all $s : 0 \leq s < p \wedge s \neq s_{\max} \wedge j \in J_s$ **do**
        $h_r(s) := h_r(s) + 1$;

    { Remove index }
    for all $s : 0 \leq s < p \wedge j \in J_s$ **do**
        $L_s := L_s \setminus \{j\}$;
        if $h_s(s) = \hat{h}_s(L_s, h_s(s), h_r(s))$ **then**
            active$(s) := false$;

Multiple edges between the same pair of vertices are possible, see Fig. 4.16(a); such edges are commonly called **parallel edges**. The algorithm first removes all parallel edges in pairs: if matrix column j and j' are both shared by $P(s)$ and $P(t)$, then v_j is assigned to $P(s)$ and $v_{j'}$ to $P(t)$. This gives rise to one send and one receive operation for both processors, balancing their communication obligations. The undirected graph that remains has at most one edge between each pair of vertices, see Fig. 4.16(b), and hence it is a **simple graph**, that is it does not have parallel edges or self-edges.

The algorithm now picks an arbitrary vertex with odd degree as the starting point for a path. The **degree** of a vertex is the number of edges connected to it, for example, the degree

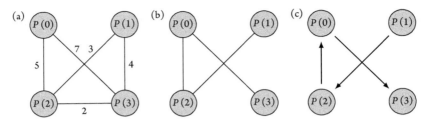

Figure 4.16 Transforming the undirected communication graph of a matrix distribution into a directed graph. (a) The original undirected communication graph with parallel edges shown as edge weights; (b) the undirected graph after removal of all pairs of edges; (c) the final directed graph. As a result, $P(0)$ has to send two values to $P(2)$ and receive three values from $P(2)$; it has to send four values to $P(3)$ and receive three.

of vertex 0 in Fig. 4.16(b) is two. A **path** is a sequence of vertices that are connected by edges. Edges along the path are transformed into directed edges in a new, directed graph, see Fig. 4.16(c). (In a **directed graph**, each edge has a direction. Thus an edge is an ordered pair (s, t), which differs from (t, s).) The direction of the created edge is the same as that of the path. The path ends when a vertex is reached that has no more undirected edges connected to it. This procedure is repeated until no more odd-degree vertices are present. It is easy to see that our procedure cannot change the degree of a vertex from even to odd. Finally, the same procedure is carried out starting at even-degree vertices.

Once all undirected edges have been transformed into directed edges, we have obtained a directed graph, which determines the owner of every remaining vector component: component v_j corresponding to a directed edge (s, t) is assigned to $P(s)$, causing a communication from $P(s)$ to $P(t)$. The resulting vector distribution has minimal communication cost; for a proof of optimality of Opt2, see [33]. The vector distribution shown in Fig. 4.9 has been determined by using Opt2. The matrix cage6 indeed has the property $\lambda_i \leq 2$ for all i and $\mu_j \leq 2$ for all j, as a consequence of the different splitting directions of the matrix, first vertically, then twice horizontally.

The appendix of [33] contains a proof provided by Ali Pinar for the NP-completeness of the general vector distribution problem. This NP-completeness property implies that we will have to resort to a heuristic algorithm for the vector distribution, as we had to do for the matrix distribution.

If the vector components have to be balanced to accommodate vector operations, besides balancing the communication, we should modify the vector distribution algorithms by imposing a balance constraint on the number of vector components, similar to the constraint on the number of matrix nonzeros, eqn (4.31). For example, we can run the same heuristic algorithm for the fanout as before, but we stop assigning vector components to a processor once it reaches its allowed maximum. It may then happen that a vector component cannot be assigned anymore to one of the processors in its column, so that we have to violate the consistency constraint eqn (4.48) and incur an extra communication of one data word. We then have the freedom to assign the vector component to any one of the remaining processors.

Our algorithms are not applicable for the case distr($\mathbf{u}$) = distr($\mathbf{v}$), since we have less freedom there to assign vector components to processors. A vector component v_i must then be assigned to a processor that has a nonzero both in row i and in column i of the matrix. If $a_{ii} \neq 0$, $P(\phi(i,i))$ is such a processor, but otherwise it may not exist and we will have to violate a consistency constraint.

A humbling final note on the communication balance achieved: even though we may solve the vector distribution problem to optimality, this does not mean that the balance will always be perfect. After all, the matrix distribution does not take communication balance into account, only total communication volume, and it may prevent achieving a good communication load balance in the ensuing vector distribution.

4.8 Random sparse matrices

A **random sparse matrix** A can be obtained by determining randomly and independently for each matrix element a_{ij} whether it is zero or nonzero. If the probability of creating a nonzero is d and hence that of creating a zero is $1 - d$, the matrix has an expected density $d(A) = d$ and an expected number of nonzeros $nz(A) = dn^2$. This definition of randomness only concerns the sparsity pattern, and not the numerical values of the nonzeros.

Historically, the first sparse matrix algorithms were tested using random sparse matrices. Later, one realized that these matrices constitute a very particular class and that many sparse matrices from practical applications fall outside this class. This led to the development of the Harwell–Boeing collection [100, 101] of sparse matrices, now called the Rutherford–Boeing collection.

If nothing is known about a given sparse matrix A, except its size $n \times n$ and its sparsity pattern, and if no structure is discernible, then a first approximation would be to consider A as a random sparse matrix with density $d = nz(A)/n^2$. Still, it is best to call such a sparse matrix **unstructured**, and not random sparse, because random sparse matrices have a very special structural property: every subset of the matrix elements, chosen independently from the sparsity pattern, has an expected fraction d of nonzeros. This property provides us with a powerful tool for analysing algorithms aimed at handling random sparse matrices and for finding good distributions for these matrices.

The question whether a given sparse matrix such as the one shown in Fig. 4.17 is random is tricky and just as hard to answer as the question whether a given random number generator generates a true sequence of random numbers. A **random number generator** (RNG) produces a sequence of real numbers, in most cases uniformly distributed over the interval $[0,1]$, that are uncorrelated and at least appear to be random. A truly random sequence can be produced by a **quantum** random number generator (QRNG) such as the online QRNG at Australian National University [283]. In most cases, the sequence is generated by a computer in a completely deterministic manner, and then the generator is called a **pseudorandom** number generator (PRNG). High-quality PRNGs are essential for obtaining reliable results in Monte Carlo simulations.

If a random number generator passes a battery of tests and has a long enough period so that it will not repeat itself during the simulations to be carried out, then for all practical

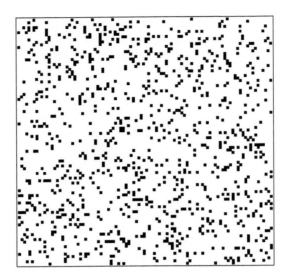

Figure 4.17 Sparse matrix random100 with $n = 100$, $nz = 982$, $c = 9.82$, generated by creating a nonzero a_{ij} in position (i, j) of the matrix if a random number r_{ij} drawn satisfies $r_{ij} < d = 0.1$. The random number generator used is Ran from Numerical Recipes [253].

purposes we consider the pseudorandom number generator to be a true random number generator. The same pragmatic approach can be taken for checking the randomness of sparse matrices. One test could be to split the matrix into four submatrices of equal size, and check whether each has about $dn^2/4$ nonzeros, within a certain tolerance given by probability theory. In this section, we do not have to check randomness, since we assume that the sparse matrix is random by construction. We have faith in the random number generator we use, Ran from [253], which we converted from C++ to C for use in our programs. Ran was constructed by combining four different random number generators. One of its characteristics is a period of about 3.138×10^{57}, meaning that it will not repeat itself for a very long time.

Now, let us study the parallel SpMV for random sparse matrices. Suppose we have constructed a random sparse matrix A by drawing for each index pair (i, j) a random number $r_{ij} \in [0, 1]$, doing this independently and **uniformly** (i.e., with each outcome equally likely), and then creating a nonzero a_{ij} if $r_{ij} < d$. Furthermore, suppose that we have distributed A over the p processors of a parallel computer in a manner that is independent of the sparsity pattern, by assigning an equal number of matrix elements (whether zero or nonzero) to each processor. For simplicity, assume that $n \bmod p = 0$. Therefore, each processor has n^2/p elements. Examples of such a distribution are the square block distribution and the cyclic row distribution.

First, we investigate the effect of such a fixed, pattern-independent distribution scheme on the spread of the nonzeros, and hence on the load balance in the main computation part of Algorithm 4.5, the local SpMV of superstep (1). The load balance can be estimated by using probability theory. The problem here is to determine the expected maximum, taken over all the processors, of the local number of nonzeros. We cannot solve this problem exactly, but we can still obtain a useful bound on the probability of the maximum exceeding a certain value, by applying a theorem of Chernoff, which is often used in the analysis of randomized algorithms. A proof, related bounds, and applications can be found in [225].

Theorem 4.10 (*Chernoff* [63]). *Let* $0 < d < 1$. *Let* $X_0, X_1, \ldots, X_{m-1}$ *be independent Bernoulli trials with outcome 0 or 1, such that* $\Pr[X_k = 1] = d$, *for* $0 \le k < m$. *Let* $X = \sum_{k=0}^{m-1} X_k$ *and* $\mu = md$. *Then for every* $\epsilon > 0$,

$$\Pr[X > (1+\epsilon)\mu] < \left(\frac{e^\epsilon}{(1+\epsilon)^{1+\epsilon}}\right)^\mu.$$

If we flip a biased coin which produces heads with probability d, then the Chernoff bound tells us how small the probability is of getting $\epsilon\mu$ more heads than the expected number μ. The bound for $\epsilon = 1$ tells us that the probability of getting more than twice the expected number of heads is less than $(e/4)^\mu \approx (0.68)^{md}$. Often, we apply the bound for smaller values of ϵ.

In the case of a random sparse matrix distributed over p processors, every processor has $m = n^2/p$ elements, each being nonzero with a probability d. The expected number of nonzeros per processor is $\mu = dn^2/p$. Let E_s be the event that processor $P(s)$ has more than $(1+\epsilon)\mu$ nonzeros and E the event that at least one processor has more than $(1+\epsilon)\mu$ nonzeros, that is, $E = \cup_{s=0}^{p-1} E_s$. The probability that at least one event from a set of events happens is less than or equal to the sum of the separate probabilities of the events, so that $\Pr[E] \le \sum_{s=0}^{p-1} \Pr[E_s]$. All separate events E_s have the same probability, which we denote by q, so that $\Pr[E] \le pq$. In fact, we can compute an even sharper upper bound by using the exact probability $\Pr[E] = 1 - (1-q)^p$, obtained by looking at the probability that no event E_s occurs in any processor. Since each nonzero causes two flops in superstep (1), we get as a result

$$\Pr\left[T_{(1)} > \frac{2(1+\epsilon)dn^2}{p}\right] < 1 - \left(1 - \left(\frac{e^\epsilon}{(1+\epsilon)^{1+\epsilon}}\right)^{\frac{dn^2}{p}}\right)^p = F(\epsilon). \qquad (4.55)$$

Here, we defined a function F that represents the upper bound for p processors as a function of the imbalance parameter ϵ. The bound for $\epsilon = 1$ tells us that the extra time caused by load imbalance exceeds the ideal time of the computation itself with probability less than $1 - (1 - (0.68)^{dn^2/p})^p$.

Figure 4.18 plots the function $F(\epsilon)$ against the normalized computation cost $1 + \epsilon$, for $n = 1000$, $p = 100$, and three different choices of d. The normalized computation cost of superstep (1) is the computation cost in flops divided by the cost of a perfectly parallelized computation. The figure shows for instance that for $d = 0.01$ the expected normalized cost is at most 1.5; this is because the probability of exceeding 1.5 is almost zero.

The expected normalized computation cost for given n, p, and d can be estimated more accurately by performing a simulation experiment. In this experiment, a set of random

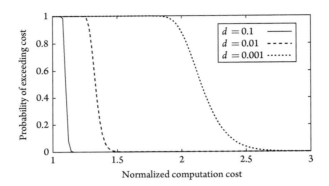

Figure 4.18 Chernoff bound $F(\epsilon)$ on the probability that a given normalized computation cost $1 + \epsilon$ is exceeded, for a random sparse matrix of size $n = 1000$ and density d distributed over $p = 100$ processors.

sparse matrices is created by using the random number generator Ran from Numerical Recipes [253]. Each matrix is distributed by a fixed scheme that is independent of the sparsity pattern (e.g. by a square block distribution), and its maximum local number of nonzeros is determined in this scheme. The average over the whole set of matrices is an estimate of the expected maximum number of nonzeros; dividing the average by dn^2/p gives an estimate of the expected normalized cost. For the matrices of Fig. 4.18, the average normalized computation costs are: 1.076 for $d = 0.1$; 1.258 for $d = 0.01$; and 1.875 for $d = 0.001$. These values were obtained by creating 10 000 matrices.

Figure 4.19 shows the measured probability that a given normalized computation cost $1 + \epsilon$ is exceeded for $d = 0.01$, obtained by creating 100 000 matrices in a simulation experiment. The most frequent result in our simulation is a maximum local nonzero count of 124; this occurred 9305 times. Translated into normalized costs and probabilities, this means that a normalized cost of 1.24 has the highest probability, namely 9.3%. The probability of having more than 124 nonzeros is about 57.1%, which can be read off directly from the figure (provided you have discerning eyes). For comparison, the figure also shows the Chernoff bound $F(\epsilon)$. Since the curve of the measured values is shifted by a distance of about 0.1 (corresponding to ten nonzeros) to the left, we may conclude that our Chernoff bound is somewhat pessimistic, as bounds tend to be.

Based on the above, we may expect that distributing a random sparse matrix independently of its sparsity pattern spreads the computation well; we can quantify this expectation using the Chernoff bound. The same quality of load balance is expected for every distribution scheme with an equal number of matrix elements assigned to the processors. For the communication, however, the choice of distribution scheme makes a difference. The communication volume for a dense matrix is an upper bound on the volume for a sparse matrix distributed by the same fixed, pattern-independent distribution scheme. For a random sparse matrix with a high density, the communication obligations will be the same as for a dense matrix. Therefore, the best we can do to find a good fixed distribution

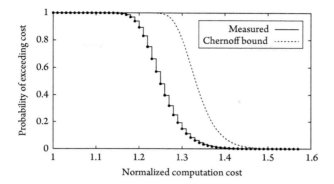

Figure 4.19 Measured probability that a given normalized computation cost $1 + \epsilon$ is exceeded, for a random sparse matrix of size $n = 1000$ and density $d = 0.01$ distributed over $p = 100$ processors. Also given is the corresponding Chernoff bound $F(\epsilon)$. The measured values are shown as black circles. They create a step function with intervals of length $\Delta \epsilon = 0.01$ (corresponding to one nonzero).

scheme for random sparse matrices is to apply methods for reducing communication in the dense case. A good choice is a square Cartesian distribution based on a cyclic distribution of the matrix diagonal, cf. Fig. 4.7, where each processor has an $n / \sqrt{p} \times n / \sqrt{p}$ submatrix. A suitable corresponding choice of vector distribution is to distribute the vectors $\mathbf{u}$ and $\mathbf{v}$ in the same cyclic way as the matrix diagonal. Unfortunately, this choice does have a slight disadvantage: since diagonal elements may be zero, the owner of a vector component v_j may not own a matrix nonzero in column j, thus necessitating an extra communication for v_j.

To obtain the communication cost of Algorithm 4.5 for this distribution, we first examine superstep (0). Vector component v_j is needed only by processors in $P(*, \phi_1(j))$. A processor $P(s, \phi_1(j))$ does not need the component v_j if all $n / \sqrt{p}$ elements in the local part of matrix column j are zero; this event has probability $(1 - d)^{n/\sqrt{p}}$. The probability that $P(s, \phi_1(j))$ needs v_j is $1 - (1 - d)^{n/\sqrt{p}}$. Since $\sqrt{p} - 1$ processors each have to receive v_j with this probability, the expected number of receives for component v_j is $(\sqrt{p} - 1)(1 - (1 - d)^{n/\sqrt{p}})$. The owner of v_j does not have to receive it. The expected communication volume of the fanout is therefore $n(\sqrt{p} - 1)(1 - (1 - d)^{n/\sqrt{p}})$. Since no processor is preferred, the h-relation is expected to be balanced, so that the expected communication cost of superstep (0) is

$$T_{(0)} = n \left(\frac{1}{\sqrt{p}} - \frac{1}{p} \right) (1 - (1 - d)^{n/\sqrt{p}}) g. \qquad (4.56)$$

Communication superstep (2) is similar to (0), with the operation of sending vector components replaced by the operation of receiving partial sums. The communication cost of superstep (2) is

$$T_{(2)} = T_{(0)}. \qquad (4.57)$$

Superstep (3) adds the nonzero partial sums, both those just received and those present locally. This costs

$$T_{(3)} = \frac{n}{\sqrt{p}}(1 - (1 - d)^{n/\sqrt{p}}). \tag{4.58}$$

If $g \gg 1$, which is often the case, then $T_{(3)} \ll T_{(2)}$, so that the cost of superstep (3) can be neglected. Finally, the synchronization cost of the whole algorithm is $4l$.

For our example of $n = 1000$ and $p = 100$, the matrix with highest density, $d = 0.1$, is expected to cause a communication cost of $179.995g$, which is close to the cost of $180g$ for a completely dense matrix. The corresponding expected normalized communication cost is $(T_{(0)} + T_{(2)})/(2dn^2/p) \approx 0.09g$. This means that we need a parallel computer with $g \leq 11$ to run our algorithm with more than 50% efficiency.

For matrices with very low density, the local part of a matrix column is unlikely to have more than one nonzero. Every nonzero will thus incur a communication. In that case, a row distribution is better than a square matrix distribution, because this saves the communications of the fanin. For our example of $n = 1000$ and $p = 100$, the matrix with lowest density, $d = 0.001$, is expected to cause a normalized communication cost of $0.86g$ for a square matrix distribution and $0.49g$ for the cyclic row distribution.

One way of improving the performance is by tailoring the distribution used to the sparsity pattern of the random sparse matrix. Figure 4.20 shows a tailored distribution produced by the Mondriaan partitioner for the matrix random100. The figure gives a global permuted view of the matrix, showing the **Separated Block Diagonal** (SBD) structure [316] obtained by moving cut (mixed) rows and columns to the middle. The row separator is relatively wide, since it contains 48 cut rows, giving rise to 48 communications in the fanin, with each processor sending and receiving 24 partial sums. The column separator is also wide, causing 41 communications, with each processor sending and receiving at most 21 vector components. This shows that just splitting the matrix into two parts already causes much communication for a random sparse matrix.

As we can see, an SBD matrix ordering is useful for visualizing the communication requirements of a parallel SpMV. It can also be used to speed up a sequential SpMV, as this ordering is more cache-friendly than the original one. Imagine that we have a cache that can fit roughly 2/3 of the components of $\mathbf{v}$. At the start of the computation, the red rows of the permuted matrix can then be processed while the relevant, leftmost part of $\mathbf{v}$ is kept in cache. At the end, the blue rows can be processed while the rightmost part of $\mathbf{v}$ is kept in cache. In between, there is a gradual transition. Of course, this works best if the separator is relatively narrow. Splitting and permuting recursively in this manner, we obtain a **cache-oblivious** ordering which will exploit the cache of the computer irrespective of its size, also if there are multiple caches that form a hierarchical-memory architecture.

Table 4.4 compares the theoretical communication volume for the best pattern-independent distribution scheme, the square Cartesian distribution based on a cyclic distribution of the matrix diagonal, with the volume for the distribution produced by the Mondriaan partitioner (run with default parameters), averaged over a set of 1000 random sparse matrices. The volume for the Cartesian distribution is based on the cost formula eqn (4.56), generalized to handle nearly square distributions as well, such as the

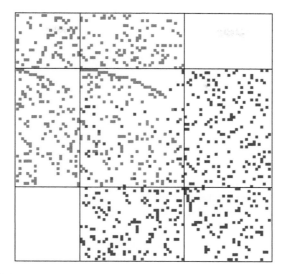

Figure 4.20 Global permuted view of the sparse matrix `random100` from Fig. 4.17 with $n = 100$, $nz = 982$, and $d = 0.1$, distributed over $p = 2$ processors by the Mondriaan partitioner (version 4.2, with the default medium-grain method). The allowed imbalance is $\epsilon = 0.03$; the achieved imbalance is $\epsilon' = 0$. Both processors have 491 nonzeros. The matrix A has been permuted by moving cut rows to the middle, rows owned completely by $P(0)$ (red rows) to the top, and those owned completely by $P(1)$ (blue rows) to the bottom, and similarly for the columns. This yields a Separated Block Diagonal (SBD) structure [316] for the matrix. The communication volume of the fanout is 41 and that of the fanin is 48, so that $V = 89$. The BSP cost is $982 + 45g + 4l$.

Table 4.4 Communication volume for a random sparse matrix of size $n = 1000$ and density $d = 0.01$ distributed over p processors, for a pattern-independent Cartesian distribution and a pattern-dependent distribution produced by the Mondriaan partitioner, version 4.2.

p	ϵ (in %)	ϵ' (in %)	V (Cartesian)	V (Mondriaan)
2	0.8	0.005	993	862
4	2.1	0.015	1 987	1 765
8	4.0	0.048	3 750	2 696
16	7.1	4.318	5 514	3 611
32	11.8	10.874	7 764	4 461

8×4 distribution for $p = 32$. For ease of comparison, the value of ϵ specified as input to Mondriaan equals the expected load imbalance for the Cartesian distribution, as obtained by a simulation. The imbalance ϵ' achieved by Mondriaan is below that value.

For small p, the load balance achieved is close to perfect, which is due to a feature introduced in version 4.2 of the Mondriaan package: after a bipartitioning, **free nonzeros** may occur, that is nonzeros that are assigned to one processor, say $P(0)$, but have both in their row and column another nonzero that is assigned to $P(1)$. This sets the nonzero free to move to the other processor without harming the communication volume. Such a move can be used to reduce the load imbalance. For small p (and small allowed imbalance ϵ), this feature has much effect; for large p, we observe only a limited effect.

It is clear from the table that the distribution obtained by Mondriaan causes less communication, demonstrating that on average the package succeeds in tailoring a better distribution to the sparsity pattern. For $p = 32$, we gain about 43%. Still, we may conclude from these results that the parallel multiplication of a random sparse matrix and a vector is a difficult problem, most likely leading to much communication. Only low values of g or high nonzero densities can make this operation efficient. Using the fixed, pattern-independent Cartesian distribution scheme based on a cyclic distribution of the matrix diagonal already brings us close to the best distribution we can achieve. The load balance of this distribution is expected to be good in most cases, as the numerical simulation and the Chernoff bound showed. The distribution can be improved by tailoring it to the sparsity pattern, for example, by using the Mondriaan partitioner, but the improvement is only modest.

4.9 Laplacian matrices

In many applications, a physical domain exists that can be distributed naturally by assigning a contiguous subdomain to every processor. Communication is then only needed for exchanging information across the subdomain boundaries. Often, the domain is structured as a multidimensional rectangular grid, where grid points interact only with a set of immediate neighbours. In the 2D case, this set could for instance contain the neighbours to the north, east, south, and west. One example of a grid application is the Ising model used to study ferromagnetism, in particular phase transitions and critical temperatures. Each grid point in this model represents a particle with positive or negative spin; neighbours tend to prefer identical spins. (For more on the Ising model, see [230].) Another example is the heat equation, where the value at a grid point represents the temperature at the corresponding location. The heat equation can be solved iteratively by a relaxation procedure that computes the new temperature at a point using the old temperatures of that point and its neighbours.

An important operation in the solution of the 2D heat equation is the application of the 2D **Laplacian operator** to the grid, computing

$$\Delta_{i,j} = x_{i-1,j} + x_{i+1,j} + x_{i,j+1} + x_{i,j-1} - 4x_{i,j}, \quad \text{for } 0 \le i, j < k, \tag{4.59}$$

where $x_{i,j}$ denotes the temperature at grid point (i,j). The difference $x_{i+1,j} - x_{i,j}$ approximates the derivative of the temperature in the i-direction, and the difference $(x_{i+1,j} -$

$x_{i,j}) - (x_{i,j} - x_{i-1,j}) = x_{i-1,j} + x_{i+1,j} - 2x_{i,j}$ approximates the second derivative. This kind of approximation is the essence of **finite difference methods** for the solution of partial differential equations. By convention, we assume that $x_{i,j} = 0$ outside the $k \times k$ grid; in practice, we just ignore zero terms on the right-hand side of eqn (4.59).

We can view the $k \times k$ array of values $x_{i,j}$ as a vector $\mathbf{v}$ of length $n = k^2$ by the identification

$$v_{i+jk} \equiv x_{i,j}, \quad \text{for } 0 \le i, j < k, \tag{4.60}$$

and, similarly, we can identify the $\Delta_{i,j}$ with a vector $\mathbf{u}$.

Example 4.11 Consider the 3×3 grid shown in Fig. 4.21. Equation (4.59) now becomes $\mathbf{u} = A\mathbf{v}$, where

$$A = \begin{bmatrix} -4 & 1 & \cdot & 1 & \cdot & \cdot & \cdot & \cdot & \cdot \\ 1 & -4 & 1 & \cdot & 1 & \cdot & \cdot & \cdot & \cdot \\ \cdot & 1 & -4 & \cdot & \cdot & 1 & \cdot & \cdot & \cdot \\ 1 & \cdot & \cdot & -4 & 1 & \cdot & 1 & \cdot & \cdot \\ \cdot & 1 & \cdot & 1 & -4 & 1 & \cdot & 1 & \cdot \\ \cdot & \cdot & 1 & \cdot & 1 & -4 & \cdot & \cdot & 1 \\ \cdot & \cdot & \cdot & 1 & \cdot & \cdot & -4 & 1 & \cdot \\ \cdot & \cdot & \cdot & \cdot & 1 & \cdot & 1 & -4 & 1 \\ \cdot & \cdot & \cdot & \cdot & \cdot & 1 & \cdot & 1 & -4 \end{bmatrix} = \begin{bmatrix} B & I_3 & 0 \\ I_3 & B & I_3 \\ 0 & I_3 & B \end{bmatrix}.$$

The matrix A is pentadiagonal because vector components (representing grid points) are only connected to components at distance ± 1 or ± 3. The holes in the subdiagonal and superdiagonal occur because points (i,j) with $i = 0, 2$ do not have a neighbour at distance -1 and $+1$, respectively. As a result, the matrix has a block-tridiagonal structure with 3×3 blocks B on the main diagonal and 3×3 identity matrices just below and above it.

The matrix A in Example 4.11 is a particular instance of the more general class of **Laplacian matrices**, which originate in a graph. The **graph Laplacian** L is commonly defined as a matrix with the vertex degrees of a graph as diagonal elements, and the edges as off-diagonal elements with value -1. The matrix representing our Laplacian operator is then given by $A = -L$. (For more on the general class of Laplacian matrices, see for example [229, Chapter 6].) In this section, we will be concerned only with Laplacian matrices that originate in regular, rectangular grids of dimension two or three, and we will choose the sign following the Laplacian operator, not the graph Laplacian, so that we have negative diagonal values and positive off-diagonal values.

In general, it is best to view the application of the Laplacian operator as an operation on the physical domain. This domain view has the advantage that it naturally leads to the use of a regular data structure for storing the data. Occasionally, however, it may also be beneficial to view the Laplacian operation as a matrix operation, so that we can apply our knowledge about the SpMV operation and gain from insights obtained in that context.

Let us try to find a good distribution for the $k \times k$ grid. We adopt the domain view, and not the matrix view, and therefore we must assign each grid point to a processor. The

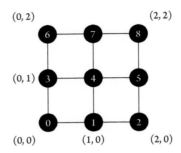

Figure 4.21 A 3×3 grid. For each grid point (i,j), the index $i + 3j$ of the corresponding vector component is shown.

resulting distribution of the grid should uniquely determine the distribution of the matrix and the vectors in the corresponding SpMV. We assign the values $x_{i,j}$ and $\Delta_{i,j}$ to the owner of grid point (i,j), and this leads to distr($\mathbf{u}$) = distr($\mathbf{v}$). It is easiest to use a row distribution for the matrix and assign row $i + jk$ to the same processor as vector component u_{i+jk} and hence grid point (i,j). (For low dimensions and large k, using a square matrix distribution does not give much advantage over a row distribution.) The resulting parallel SpMV algorithm has two supersteps, the fanout and the local SpMV. If a neighbouring point is on a different processor, its value must be obtained during the fanout. The computation time assuming an equal spread of grid points is $5k^2/p$, since eqn (4.59) gives rise to five flops per grid point. Note that in this specific application, we use the flop count corresponding to the domain view, and not the more general count of two flops per matrix nonzero used in other sections of this chapter; the latter count yields ten flops per grid point. Furthermore, we do not have to store the matrix elements explicitly, that is, we may use matrix-free storage, cf. Section 4.2.

The simplest distribution of the grid can be obtained by dividing it into p strips, each of size $k \times k/p$, assuming that $k \bmod p = 0$, see Fig. 4.22(a). The advantages are, indeed, simplicity and the fact that communication is only needed in the east–west direction, between a grid point (i,j) on the eastern border of a strip and its neighbour $(i + 1, j)$, or between a point on the western border and its neighbour $(i - 1, j)$. The northern and southern neighbours of a grid point are on the same processor as the point itself and hence do not cause communication. The main disadvantage will immediately be recognized by every Norwegian or Chilean: relatively long borders. Each processor, except the first and the last, has to send and receive $2k$ boundary values. Therefore,

$$T_{\text{comm, strips}} = 2kg. \tag{4.61}$$

A related disadvantage is that $p \leq k$ should hold, because otherwise processors would be idle, giving a bad load balance. Even if $p \leq k$ holds, load balance may be a serious problem: if $k \bmod p \neq 0$, some processors will contain one extra column of k points. This problem can be solved by border corrections, jumping one point to the east or west somewhere along the border, as shown in Fig. 4.22(b).

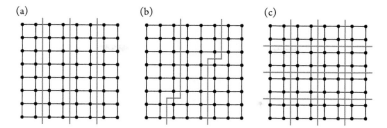

Figure 4.22 Distribution of an 8×8 grid (a) by strips for $p = 4$ processors; (b) by strips with border corrections for $p = 3$; (c) by square blocks for $p = 16$.

A better distribution can be obtained by dividing the grid into p square blocks, each of size $k/\sqrt{p} \times k/\sqrt{p}$, where we assume that p is a square number and that $k \bmod \sqrt{p} = 0$, see Fig. 4.22(c). The borders are shorter now. Consider the general case $p > 4$. Processors not on the boundary are the busiest communicating, having to send and receive $4k/\sqrt{p}$ values, so that

$$T_{\text{comm, squares}} = \frac{4k}{\sqrt{p}} g. \tag{4.62}$$

This is a factor $\sqrt{p}/2$ less than for division into strips. The resulting communication-to-computation ratio is

$$\frac{T_{\text{comm, squares}}}{T_{\text{comp, squares}}} = \frac{4k/\sqrt{p}}{5k^2/p} g = \frac{4\sqrt{p}}{5k} g. \tag{4.63}$$

The communication-to-computation ratio of a subdomain is often called its **surface-to-volume** ratio. This term originates in the 3D case, where the volume of a subdomain represents the amount of computation of a processor and the surface represents its communication with other processors.

Not only are square blocks better with respect to communication, but they are also better with respect to computation: in case of load imbalance, the surplus of the busiest processor is only $2\lceil k/\sqrt{p}\rceil - 1$ grid points, instead of k. This is because the busiest processor has a square block of $\lceil k/\sqrt{p}\rceil \times \lceil k/\sqrt{p}\rceil$ grid points, while the least busy processor has $\lfloor k/\sqrt{p}\rfloor \times \lfloor k/\sqrt{p}\rfloor$.

It may seem that the best we can do is to distribute the grid by square blocks. This intuitive belief may be even stronger if you happen to use a square grid of processors or processor cores and are tempted to exploit hardware connectivity to optimize communication. In the BSP model, however, there is no particular advantage in using such regular schemes. Therefore, we can freely try other shapes for the area allocated to one processor. Consider what the computer scientist would call the **digital diamond**, and the mathematician the **closed l_1-sphere**, defined by

$$B_r(c_0, c_1) = \{(i,j) \in \mathbf{Z}^2 : |i - c_0| + |j - c_1| \leq r\}, \tag{4.64}$$

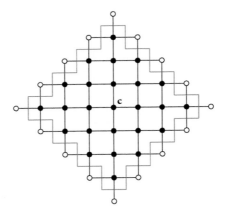

Figure 4.23 Digital diamond $B_r(\mathbf{c})$ of radius $r = 3$ centred at $\mathbf{c}$. Points inside the diamond are shown in black; neighbouring points are shown in white.

for integer radius $r \geq 0$ and centre $\mathbf{c} = (c_0, c_1) \in \mathbf{Z}^2$. This is the set of points with Manhattan distance at most r to the central point $\mathbf{c}$, see Fig. 4.23. The number of points of $B_r(\mathbf{c})$ is $1 + 3 + 5 + \cdots + (2r - 1) + (2r + 1) + (2r - 1) + \cdots + 1 = 2r^2 + 2r + 1$. The number of neighbouring points is $4r + 4$. If $B_r(\mathbf{c})$ represents a set of grid points allocated to one processor, then the fanout involves receiving $4r + 4$ values. Just on the basis of receive operations, we may conclude that this processor has a communication-to-computation ratio

$$\frac{T_{\text{comm, diamonds}}}{T_{\text{comp, diamonds}}} = \frac{4r + 4}{5(2r^2 + 2r + 1)}g \approx \frac{2}{5r}g \approx \frac{2\sqrt{2p}}{5k}g, \tag{4.65}$$

for large enough r, where we use the approximation $r \approx k/\sqrt{2p}$, obtained by assuming that the processor has its fair share $2r^2 + 2r + 1 = k^2/p$ of the grid points. The resulting asymptotic ratio is a factor $\sqrt{2}$ lower than for square blocks, cf. eqn (4.63). This reduction is caused by using each received value twice. Diamonds are a parallel computing scientist's best friend.

The gain of using diamonds can only be realized if the outgoing traffic is balanced with the incoming traffic, that is, if the number $h_s(s)$ of send operations of processor $P(s)$ is the same as the number $h_r(s) = 4r + 4$ of receive operations. The number of send operations of a processor depends on which processors own the neighbouring points. Each of the $4r$ border points of a diamond has to be sent to at least one processor and at most two processors, except corner points, which may have to be sent to three processors. Therefore, $4r \leq h_s(s) \leq 8r + 4$.

To find a distribution that balances the sends and the receives, we try to fit the diamonds into a regular pattern. Consider first the infinite lattice $\mathbf{Z}^2$; to make mathematicians cringe, we view it as a $k \times k$ grid with $k = \infty$; to make matters worse, we let the grid start at $(-\infty, -\infty)$. We try to partition this $\infty \times \infty$ grid over an infinite number of processors using diamonds. It turns out that we can do this by placing the diamonds in a periodic

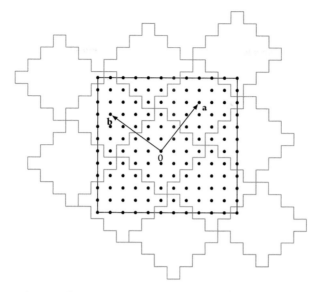

Figure 4.24 Distribution of a 12×12 grid by digital diamonds of radius $r = 3$. Grid points are connected to their neighbours to the north, east, south, and west, but only the connections along the grid boundary are shown. The central diamond is complete and has 25 grid points; the other diamonds are only partially contained in the grid. Pieces of incomplete diamonds can be combined, assigning them to the same processor.

fashion at centres $\mathbf{c} = \lambda \mathbf{a} + \mu \mathbf{b}$, $\lambda, \mu \in \mathbf{Z}$, where $\mathbf{a} = (r, r + 1)$ and $\mathbf{b} = (-r - 1, r)$. Part of this infinite partitioning is shown (in red) in Fig. 4.24. The centres of the diamonds form a lattice defined by the orthogonal basis vectors $\mathbf{a}, \mathbf{b}$. We leave it to the mathematically inclined reader to verify that the diamonds $B_r(\lambda \mathbf{a} + \mu \mathbf{b})$ are indeed mutually disjoint and that they fill the whole domain. It is easy to see that each processor sends $h_s(s) = 4r + 4$ values. This distribution of an infinite grid over an infinite number of processors achieves the favourable ratio of eqn (4.65).

Practical computational grids and processor sets are, alas, finite and therefore the region of interest must be covered using a finite number of diamonds. Sometimes, the shape of the region allows us to use diamonds directly without too much waste. In other situations, many points from the covering diamonds fall outside the region of interest. These points are then discarded and the remaining pieces of diamonds are combined, assigning several pieces to one processor, such that each processor obtains about the same number of grid points.

Figure 4.24 also shows a 12×12 grid partitioned by using the infinite diamond tiling of the plane. The partitioning has one complete diamond with 25 grid points and 11 pieces of diamonds. The partitioning can be transformed into a partitioning for $p = 6$ by assigning several pieces to the same processor. To minimize communication, adjacent pieces such as the four-point piece at the left boundary and the 21-point piece above it should preferably be assigned to the same processor. If we do this, and combine the four-point piece at the bottom with its left neighbour, the single point in the bottom-right corner with its 23-point neighbour, and collect the four remaining small pieces into a 22-point non-connected processor part, then we obtain a partitioning for $p = 6$ with 25, 25, 24, 24, 24, 22 grid points per processor. Note that points on the boundary have fewer flops associated with them, so that the resulting work load may not be exactly proportional to the counts of the grid points. The processor with the original complete diamond has to compute most, because it has the largest number of grid points and none of them is a boundary point or corner point. This processor has to send and receive 16 data words, so that it attains the minimum achievable number of $4r + 4 = 16$ data words communicated for a complete diamond of radius $r = 3$. The processor that collects the four remaining parts, however, has to receive 17 data words, which is the maximum for this particular six-way partitioning. Therefore, the total BSP cost is $125 + 17g + 2l$. It is possible to improve this partitioning, for instance by border corrections.

To find an optimal assignment of pieces to processors while allowing border corrections is a hard optimization problem, and perhaps the best approach would be to use a suitable heuristic. In a few exceptional cases, we are lucky and we can fit all the pieces exactly together creating complete diamonds. An example is the 25×25 grid, which can be covered exactly with 25 diamonds of radius $r = 3$. (For the curious, a picture can be found in [32].) For the general case, we take a slightly different approach based on modifying the basic cell of the partitioning.

The main disadvantage of using diamonds is that it is much more complicated than using blocks. To make the partitioning method based on diamonds practical, it must be simplified. Fortunately, this can be done by a small modification, discarding one layer of points from the north-eastern and south-eastern border of the diamond, as shown in Fig. 4.25. For $r = 3$, the number of points decreases from 25 (see Fig. 4.23) to 18. The resulting set of points can be seen as the set of points closer to the centre than to a corner of the enclosing large square, and such a set is called a **Voronoi cell**. Ties are broken by assigning border points to the interior for the western borders, and to the exterior for the eastern borders. Only one corner of the enclosed (rotated) square is assigned to the interior, namely the western corner. This way, we obtain a basic cell that can be repeated and used to tile the whole space. We can place the diamonds in a periodic fashion at centres $\mathbf{c} = \lambda\mathbf{a} + \mu\mathbf{b}$, $\lambda, \mu \in \mathbf{Z}$, where $\mathbf{a} = (r,r)$ and $\mathbf{b} = (-r,r)$. Figure 4.26 shows how the basic cell is used to distribute a 12×12 grid over eight processors. The periodic assignment of boundary pieces guarantees that processors never have more computation or communication work than processors possessing a complete basic cell.

A different way of partitioning a $k \times k$ grid is to translate it into the corresponding $k^2 \times k^2$ matrix and vectors of length k^2, then let the Mondriaan partitioner find a good data distribution for the corresponding SpMV, and translate this back into a distribution for the grid. As before, we impose $\mathrm{distr}(\mathbf{u}) = \mathrm{distr}(\mathbf{v})$ for the vectors and use a row distribution for the matrix. Figure 4.27 shows the result for an allowed load imbalance $\epsilon = 6\%$. Note that Mondriaan (the partitioner!) prefers stepwise borders, similar to the borders of a digital diamond. The communication volume $V = 83$ is significantly lower than the volume $V = 104$ for the regular distribution of Fig. 4.26. The reason is that Mondriaan manages to make good use of the grid boundaries.

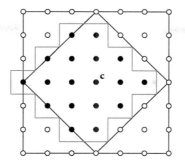

Figure 4.25 Basic cell of radius $r = 3$ assigned to a processor. The cell has 18 grid points, shown in black. Grid points outside the cell are shown in white. Grid points on the left diagonal lines are included; those on the right diagonal lines are excluded. The cell contains 13 grid points that are closer to the centre **c** than to a corner of the enclosing square and it contains five points at equal distance to the centre and a nearest corner. The cell has 14 neighbouring grid points.

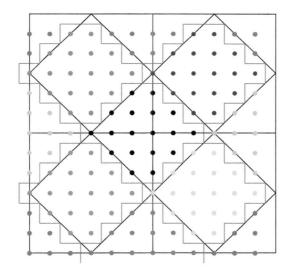

Figure 4.26 Distribution of a 12×12 grid over eight processors, obtained by using the basic cell from Fig. 4.25. Five cells are complete (green, blue, black, cyan, yellow); the pink processor has points near the left and right border of the grid; the grey processor near the top and bottom; and the red processor near the four corners. Incomplete cells have been combined by treating the grid boundaries as periodic. Each processor has 18 grid points. The communication volume is 104 and $h_s = h_r = 14$; the BSP cost of the computation is $90 + 14g + 2l$.

To use Mondriaan for finding a good distribution, we had to allow a relatively large load imbalance, because otherwise Mondriaan could not have succeeded in keeping the communication low. (For $\epsilon = 3\%$, the result is a high volume of $V = 331$ and a cost of $86 + 51g + 2l$.) We came to the choice of $\epsilon = 6\%$ by trial and error, where we tried to find a low communication volume and an acceptable load imbalance. Exercise 4.2 poses the

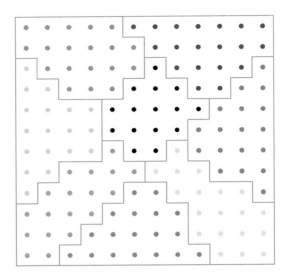

Figure 4.27 Distribution of a 12 × 12 grid over eight processors, produced by the Mondriaan partitioner, version 4.2. The allowed load imbalance is $\epsilon = 6\%$ and the achieved imbalance is $\epsilon' = 5.95\%$. The number of flops per processor ranges from 75 (black) to 89 (yellow); the average is 84 flops. The maximum number of grid points per processor is 19 (for the green, blue, and yellow processors); the average is 18. The communication volume is 83, $h_s = 14$ and $h_r = 13$; the BSP cost of the computation is $89 + 14g + 2l$.

challenge to improve on this and find an optimal solution for the 12 × 12 grid in the specific case of $g = 10$ and $l = 50$.

Running Mondriaan takes much more time than performing one Laplacian operation on the grid, but the effort of finding a good distribution has to be spent only once, and the cost can be amortized over many parallel computations on the same grid.

The crucial property of our parallel SpMV algorithm applied to grid computation is that a value needed by another processor is sent only once, even if it is used several times. Our cost model reflects this, thus encouraging reuse of communicated data. If a partitioning method based on this cost model is applied to a regular grid, then the result will be diamond-like shapes of the subdomain, especially for large grids. The small example of Fig. 4.27 already shows this type of shape in a rough approximation. For larger grids and a larger number of processors, boundary effects become less important and more diamond-like shapes appear, as we can see in Fig. 4.28.

The prime application of diamond-shaped partitioning will most likely lie in three dimensions, where the number of grid points at the boundary of a subdomain is relatively large compared to the number of interior points. If a processor has a cubic block of $N = k^3/p$ points, about $6k^2/p^{2/3} = 6N^{2/3}$ are boundary points; in the 2D case, this is only $4N^{1/2}$. For example, if a processor has a 10 × 10 × 10 block, 488 points lie on the processor boundary. In 3D, communication is even more important than in 2D and it may easily dominate computation. Based on the surface-to-volume ratio of a 3D digital diamond, we can expect a reduction by a factor $6^{1/3} \approx 1.82$ in communication cost, which is certainly worthwhile.

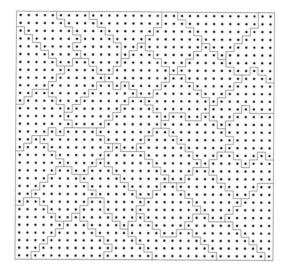

Figure 4.28 Distribution of a 32×32 grid over 32 processors, produced by the Mondriaan partitioner, version 4.2. The allowed load imbalance is $\epsilon = 6\%$ and the achieved imbalance is $\epsilon' = 5.77\%$. The number of flops per processor ranges from 135 to 165; the average is 156 flops. The communication volume is 532, $h_s = 23$ and $h_r = 20$; the BSP cost of the computation is $165 + 23g + 2l$.

This factor can be computed from an approximate volume of $4r^3/3$ points, each with 7 flops, and a surface of $4r^2$ points and hence a surface-to-volume ratio of $4r^2/(28r^3/3) = 3/(7r) \approx 6^{2/3}p^{1/3}/(7k)$ for digital diamonds, vs. $6p^{1/3}/(7k)$ for cubic blocks. The reduction achieved in reality depends on whether we manage to fill 3D space with shapes that closely resemble digital diamonds.

The basic cell that suits our purpose is a **truncated octahedron**, shown in Fig. 4.29. The surface parts have been carefully assigned to the interior or exterior, so that the whole space can be filled with nonoverlapping copies of the cell, that is, with each point in space belonging to exactly one cell. This has been achieved by a fair assignment of the faces, edges, and vertices of the cell. For instance, the front square is included in the cell, but the back square is not. A cell of radius r is enclosed by a cube with edge length $2r$, where we assume that r is an even integer; the case of odd r is similar. We can fill space with such cubes, and place copies of the basic cell at the corners and centres of these cubes. As a result, cells are centred at points $(\lambda r, \mu r, \nu r)$, with λ, μ, ν three even integers, or three odd integers. This set of centre points is called the **body-centred cubic** (BCC) lattice. Each centre point represents a processor. As in the 2D case, the basic cell is a Voronoi cell, since grid points of the cell are closer to its centre than to the centres of other cells (with fair tie breaking).

The number of grid points of the basic cell is $4r^3$, half the number of points of the enclosing cube. A careful count shows that the number of points on the surface is $9r^2 - 6r + 2$ and

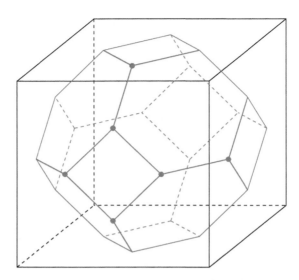

Figure 4.29 Basic 3D cell assigned to a processor. The cell (in red) is defined as the set of grid points that fall within a truncated octahedron. The boundaries of this truncated octahedron are included/excluded as follows, in case the cube has edge length $2r$ with r even. Included are the four hexagons and three squares visible from the front (which are enclosed by solid lines), the twelve edges shown as thick solid lines, and the six vertices marked by red circles. The other faces, edges, and vertices are excluded. The enclosing cube (in black) is shown for reference only. Neighbouring cells are centred at the eight corners of the cube and the six centres of neighbouring cubes. Solid lines of an object are visible from the front; dashed lines are invisible.

that the number of send operations and receive operations is $9r^2 + 6r + 2$. The resulting communication-to-computation ratio is

$$\frac{T_{\text{comm, truncated octahedra}}}{T_{\text{comp, truncated octahedra}}} = \frac{9r^2 + 6r + 2}{7 \cdot 4r^3} g \approx \frac{9}{28r} g \approx \frac{9(4p)^{1/3}}{28k} g, \tag{4.66}$$

which is better by a factor of 1.68 than the ratio $6p^{1/3}/(7k)$ for cubic blocks. In an actual implementation, it may be most convenient to use a cubic array as local data structure, with an extra layer of points along each border, and to fill this array only partially. This enables the use of a regular array structure while still reducing the communication.

Table 4.5 shows the communication cost for various distributions of a 2D grid with $k = 4096$ and a 3D grid with $k = 256$. For both grids, the total number of points equals $N = 16\,777\,216$. For the 2D Laplacian, the ideal case for the rectangular block distribution occurs for $p = q^2$, that is, for $p = 16, 64$, since the local subdomains then become square blocks. For $p = 2q^2$, that is, for $p = 8, 32, 128$, the blocks become rectangles with an aspect ratio 2 : 1. In contrast, the ideal case for the diamond distribution is $p = 2q^2$. To handle the nonideal case $p = q^2$ as well, the diamond distribution is generalized by stretching the basic cell in one direction, giving a communication cost of $(4k/\sqrt{p})g$. The table shows that the diamond

Table 4.5 Communication cost (in g) for a Laplacian operation on a grid, using distributions based on rectangular blocks and diamond cells, and a distribution produced by the Mondriaan partitioner, version 4.2, with $\epsilon = 6\%$. For comparison, the cost V/p is also given for the achieved communication volume V.

Grid	p	Rect.	Diam.	Mondriaan	
		h	h	h	V/p
4096×4096	8	5 120	4 098	5 587	4 106
	16	4 096	4 096	4 306	3 100
	32	3 072	2 050	3 303	2 468
	64	2 048	2 048	2 383	1 797
	128	1 536	1 026	1 728	1 313
$256 \times 256 \times 256$	16	49 152	37 250	50 676	38 474
	128	16 384	9 410	16 568	12 312

distribution is better than the rectangular block distribution for $p = 2q^2$ (with a reduction by a factor 1.50 for $p = 32, 128$) and that both distributions perform the same for $p = q^2$.

For the 3D Laplacian, only the ideal case for the diamond distribution, $p = 2q^3$, is shown. (The other cases $p = q^3$ and $p = 4q^3$ are more difficult to treat, requiring a generalization of the diamond distribution based on stretching the basic cell.) We observe a reduction by a factor of 1.74 for $p = 128$ compared with the block distribution. For $p = 16$, the reduction is less because of boundary effects. Asymptotically, for large radius r, the reduction factor is $16/9 \approx 1.78$ in the case $p = 2q^3$. Note that the total amount of communication is much larger for 3D than for 2D, for the same number of grid points, so that a communication reduction is certainly worth the effort of using a nonstandard distribution.

For comparison, Table 4.5 also presents results obtained by using the Mondriaan partitioner to produce a row distribution of the Laplacian matrix and a corresponding distribution of the grid. The communication cost given is the average over 10 runs of the Mondriaan partitioner, each time with a different seed of the random number generator used. The distribution generated by Mondriaan performs about the same as blocks for the communication cost metric (h), but it is closer to diamonds for the communication volume metric (V). This shows that there is potential for improvement, which may be achieved by better balancing of the communication load even if this is at the expense of a slight increase in communication volume.

4.10 Parallel algorithm for hybrid-BSP

Modern supercomputers often have thousands of nodes, each with many cores, and thus they have a clear hierarchical architecture, which we cannot ignore if we want to model our parallel computations on such a computer in a realistic fashion. Communication within a supercomputer node is fast, because the cores have access to a shared memory on the node, and communication between nodes is slower, because data has to travel through a network and it also has to travel farther. The aggregated memory of the nodes can be viewed as a distributed memory, so that we may view the architecture as a hybrid shared/distributed-memory parallel computer. To complicate matters even more, often accelerators are attached in the form of a large set of graphics processing units (GPUs), but we will ignore these, as they have quite different characteristics than CPUs. (Treating GPUs adequately would justify a separate book, and is outside our scope.)

To write efficient programs for a hybrid architecture, we need to take the hybrid nature into account. In this section, we will present hybrid-BSP, which is our generalization of the flat BSP model of Section 1.2. Several generalizing variants of BSP already exist, including decomposable BSP and Y-BSP [81], NestStep [180], multi-BSP [292], and MBSP [121], and we apply their basic idea of a hierarchical BSP architecture with several levels, aiming at the common hybrid architecture and trying to keep the design as simple as possible, as this is the main strength of the original BSP model. Thus, we restrict the number of levels of the hierarchy by allowing just one extra level beyond flat BSP, and we allow one level of nesting of supersteps. To define the hybrid-BSP model, we will describe the hybrid-BSP computer architecture, the structure of hybrid-BSP algorithms, and the cost of running such an algorithm on a hybrid-BSP computer.

The architecture of a hybrid-BSP computer comprises a set of p_2 nodes, where each node is itself a $BSP(p_1, r, g_1, l_1)$ computer with p_1 processors (which in fact are usually processor cores). The total number of processors is $p = p_1 p_2$. Each processor has its own memory. Communication between the nodes costs g_2 flop time units per data word and synchronization of all the nodes costs l_2 flops. Figure 4.30 illustrates this architecture. In this model, we view the memory as a distributed memory, which simplifies matters tremendously. The underlying shared-memory architecture of a node is still exploited, namely by faster communication through this memory, expressed by the parameter $g_1 \ll g_2$. For a user, it is beneficial to keep communication within a node as much as possible, because this is cheaper. We number the processors in 2D fashion, with processor $P(s, t)$ representing processor t in node s, where $0 \le s < p_2$ and $0 \le t < p_1$. Note that this 2D numbering is different from the 2D numbering used with Cartesian matrix distributions: it is based on a decomposition of the machine used, not of a matrix.

An algorithm in the hybrid-BSP model consists of a sequence of **global supersteps**. A global superstep is either a **global communication superstep**, where processors communicate with processors in another node, or a **global computation superstep**, where each of the p_2 nodes simultaneously executes a BSP algorithm consisting of **local supersteps**. At the end of a global superstep, all processors synchronize. Within a global computation superstep, processors only synchronize with processors in the same node, at the end of every local superstep. Figure 4.31 shows the structure of an algorithm in the hybrid-BSP model. Note that in the global superstep of the figure, we let processors only communicate with processors in another node, because local communication (within a node) can be done in a local communication superstep at a much lower cost of g_1 flops per data word. This is similar to our assumption that a processor does not communicate with itself in the flat BSP model, because this requires only a memory copy.

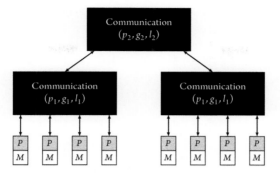

Figure 4.30 Architecture of a hybrid-BSP computer. The computer consists of p_2 nodes, each of which comprises a BSP computer with p_1 processors denoted by 'P'. Each processor has a memory, denoted by 'M'. The processors within a node communicate with each other according to the BSP parameters p_1, g_1, and l_1; the nodes communicate with each other according to p_2, g_2, and l_2. Here, $p_1 = 4$ and $p_2 = 2$.

The cost function corresponding to the hybrid-BSP model is based on the cost function for the original, flat BSP model, but now with additional parameters. A global communication superstep that is an h-relation between the p_2 nodes costs

$$T_{\text{comm, global}}(h) = hg_2 + l_2, \tag{4.67}$$

where l_2 is the global synchronization cost. We assume that $l_2 \gg l_1$. The cost of a global computation superstep, in which node $P(s, *)$, $0 \le s < p_2$, executes a BSP algorithm with cost $a_s + b_s g_1 + c_s l_1$ is

$$T_{\text{comp, global}} = \max_{0 \le s < p_2} (a_s + b_s g_1 + c_s l_1) + l_2. \tag{4.68}$$

For simplicity, we disallow mixed global supersteps. Since the cost expression of eqn (4.68) is far more complicated than expression eqn (1.3) for the flat BSP model, analysing the cost of a hybrid-BSP algorithm will be more difficult. It may facilitate the analysis if all nodes perform the same BSP algorithm with the same number of local supersteps.

Algorithm 4.8 presents an SpMV in the hybrid-BSP framework. It is a generalization of Algorithm 4.5 that targets both levels of the hybrid-BSP architecture. The algorithm has seven supersteps, which are marked as either local or global. A **local superstep** is ended by a synchronization of the p_1 processors in node $P(s, *)$. A **global superstep** is ended by a synchronization of all p_2 nodes, which is in fact a synchronization of all p processors. The algorithm uses a sparse matrix distribution ϕ, where we define $\phi(i, j) = (\phi_0(i, j), \phi_1(i, j))$ for $a_{ij} \neq 0$, and a dummy value $\phi(i, j) = (-1, -1)$ for $a_{ij} = 0$.

Algorithm 4.8 starts with a fanout, where each processor obtains the vector components v_j that it needs. This happens in two phases: first, a global communication superstep where every node $P(s, *)$ obtains the components v_j that it needs, directly from the source processor $P(\phi_v(j))$. Component v_j is stored at one designated processor in the node, $P(s, \phi_v^s(j))$,

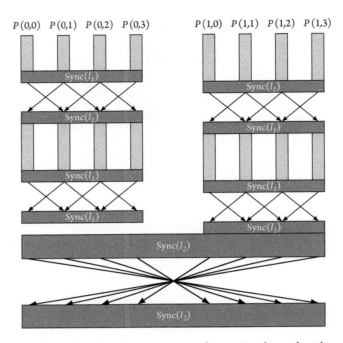

$P(0,0)$ $P(0,1)$ $P(0,2)$ $P(0,3)$ $P(1,0)$ $P(1,1)$ $P(1,2)$ $P(1,3)$

Figure 4.31 Hybrid-BSP algorithm for a computer with $p_2 = 2$ nodes, each with $p_1 = 4$ processors. The processors first perform a sequence of four local supersteps (two communication and two computation supersteps), and they do this independently in two nodes, $P(0, *)$ and $P(1, *)$. At the end of each local superstep, the processors of a node synchronize, at cost l_1. Node $P(0, *)$ finishes a bit earlier than $P(1, *)$, and has to wait until $P(1, *)$ finishes its local supersteps. All processors then synchronize, at cost $l_2 \gg l_1$. The processors within a node communicate with each other at a cost of g_1 per data word; the nodes communicate with each other at a much higher cost g_2, denoted by thicker arrows.

which becomes the local owner of a copy of v_j. After that, every processor that needs v_j obtains it from the local owner in a local communication superstep. If a node $P(s, *)$ does not need v_j, we set $\phi_\mathbf{v}^s(j) = -1$. The fanin is done in a similar way, with a local designated processor $P(s, \phi_\mathbf{u}^s(i))$ responsible for computing the contribution u_{is} of node $P(s, *)$ to the output component u_i. It does this by adding contributions u_{ist} from all the processors in node $P(s, *)$. If a node $P(s, *)$ does not contribute to u_i, we set $\phi_\mathbf{u}^s(i) = -1$.

Algorithm 4.8 contains the original BSP algorithm, Algorithm 4.5, as a series of four local supersteps, namely (1)–(4). Algorithm 4.8 is adapted from an MPI-oriented algorithm by Bienz, Gropp, and Olson [26] called **node-aware** SpMV, which uses a 1D row distribution (with only a fanout and no fanin).

A question that remains to be answered is: how do we partition the data for the hybrid parallel SpMV given as Algorithm 4.8? We can use the Mondriaan sparse matrix partitioner for this purpose, but we have to take into account that global communication is much more expensive than local communication. This requires a different trade-off between

---

Algorithm 4.8 Hybrid parallel sparse matrix–vector multiplication for $P(s,t)$.

---

input: A : sparse $n \times n$ matrix, $\text{distr}(A) = \phi = (\phi_0, \phi_1)$,
$\qquad$ $\mathbf{v}$: dense vector of length n, $\text{distr}(\mathbf{v}) = \phi_\mathbf{v}$.
output: $\mathbf{u}$: dense vector of length n, $\mathbf{u} = A\mathbf{v}$, $\text{distr}(\mathbf{u}) = \phi_\mathbf{u}$.

$\quad I_{st} = \{i : 0 \le i < n \land (\exists j : 0 \le j < n \land \phi(i,j) = (s,t))\}$
$\quad I_s = \{i : 0 \le i < n \land (\exists j : 0 \le j < n \land \phi_0(i,j) = s)\}$
$\quad 0 \le \phi_\mathbf{u}^s(i) < p_1$, for all $i \in I_s$, otherwise $\phi_\mathbf{u}^s(i) = -1$

$\quad J_{st} = \{j : 0 \le j < n \land (\exists i : 0 \le i < n \land \phi(i,j) = (s,t))\}$
$\quad J_s = \{j : 0 \le j < n \land (\exists i : 0 \le i < n \land \phi_0(i,j) = s)\}$
$\quad 0 \le \phi_\mathbf{v}^s(j) < p_1$, for all $j \in J_s$, otherwise $\phi_\mathbf{v}^s(j) = -1$

$\quad$ { Global fanout } $\qquad\qquad\qquad\qquad\qquad\qquad\qquad$ ▷ Superstep (0)
$\quad$ **for all** $j : 0 \le j < n \land \phi_\mathbf{v}^s(j) = t$ **do**
$\qquad$ get v_j from $P(\phi_\mathbf{v}(j))$;

$\quad$ { Local fanout } $\qquad\qquad\qquad\qquad\qquad\qquad\qquad\quad$ ▷ Superstep (1)
$\quad$ **for all** $j \in J_{st}$ **do**
$\qquad$ get v_j from $P(s, \phi_\mathbf{v}^s(j))$;

$\quad$ { Local sparse matrix–vector multiplication } $\qquad\qquad$ ▷ Superstep (2)
$\quad$ **for all** $i \in I_{st}$ **do**
$\qquad$ $u_{ist} := 0$;
$\qquad$ **for all** $j : 0 \le j < n \land \phi(i,j) = (s,t)$ **do**
$\qquad\qquad$ $u_{ist} := u_{ist} + a_{ij}v_j$;

$\quad$ { Local fanin } $\qquad\qquad\qquad\qquad\qquad\qquad\qquad\qquad$ ▷ Superstep (3)
$\quad$ **for all** $i \in I_{st}$ **do**
$\qquad$ put u_{ist} in $P(s, \phi_\mathbf{u}^s(i))$;

$\quad$ { Local summation of nonzero partial sums } $\qquad\quad$ ▷ Superstep (4)
$\quad$ **for all** $i : 0 \le i < n \land \phi_\mathbf{u}^s(i) = t$ **do**
$\qquad$ $u_{is} := 0$;
$\qquad$ **for all** $t' : 0 \le t' < p_1 \land u_{ist'} \ne 0$ **do**
$\qquad\qquad$ $u_{is} := u_{is} + u_{ist'}$;

$\quad$ { Global fanin } $\qquad\qquad\qquad\qquad\qquad\qquad\qquad\quad$ ▷ Superstep (5)
$\quad$ **for all** $i : 0 \le i < n \land \phi_\mathbf{u}^s(i) = t$ **do**
$\qquad$ put u_{is} in $P(\phi_\mathbf{u}(i))$;

$\quad$ { Global summation of nonzero partial sums } $\qquad\;$ ▷ Superstep (6)
$\quad$ **for all** $i : 0 \le i < n \land \phi_\mathbf{u}(i) = (s,t)$ **do**
$\qquad$ $u_i := 0$;
$\qquad$ **for all** $s' : 0 \le s' < p_2 \land u_{is'} \ne 0$ **do**
$\qquad\qquad$ $u_i := u_i + u_{is'}$;

---

communication cost and load imbalance in the earlier stages of Mondriaan's recursive bipartitioning than in the later stages.

In the hybrid case, we use Mondriaan several times: first, we partition the matrix A into p_2 parts with an allowed imbalance $\epsilon_2 < \epsilon$, where ϵ_2 has a suitable value (to be discussed below), and then we partition each resulting part s using Mondriaan with an allowed imbalance $\epsilon_1(s)$ that corresponds to allowing at most $(1 + \epsilon)nz(A)/p$ nonzeros per processor, where $nz(A)$ is the number of nonzeros of the original matrix. The value of $\epsilon_1(s)$ may vary across the p_2 different parts.

A suitable value for ϵ_2 can be found as follows. The communication cost of global superstep (0) is $V_2 g_2/p_2$, where V_2 is the communication volume of that superstep and we assume perfect communication balance. The communication cost of local superstep (1) is $V_1 g_1/p$, where V_1 is the total communication volume of that superstep, for all the processors in all the nodes, and again we assume perfect communication balance. Note that here the communication volume within each node is V_1/p_2, and hence $h = (V_1/p_2)/p_1 = V_1/p$. Therefore, communication per data word is more expensive in the distributed-memory global superstep (0) than in the shared-memory local superstep (1) by a factor

$$\beta = \frac{g_2/p_2}{g_1/p} = \frac{g_2 p_1}{g_1}. \tag{4.69}$$

We call β the **distributed/shared-memory communication cost ratio**. Note that this ratio also depends on the number of processors, p_1; this is caused by our decision to model p_1 processors as a single node. A larger value of β means that communication becomes more important in the top levels of the partitioning, relative to the load imbalance, so that ϵ_2 should become a larger fraction of ϵ.

The relative importance of β in the hybrid parallel SpMV depends on the growth of the communication volume with the number of parts in the partitioning, which is unfortunate, since this growth depends on the matrix. Still, we can give some guidelines. For Laplacian matrices originating in 2D grids, quadrupling the number of processors leads to a doubling in total communication volume, as can be seen by studying Fig. 4.22(c). This means that the volume grows with p as $V = \mathcal{O}(p^{1/2})$. In 3D, this is $V = \mathcal{O}(p^{1/3})$. Such behaviour can also be seen, in rough approximation, in Table 4.5. For other types of problems, we can empirically determine a growth exponent α, such that $V = \mathcal{O}(p^\alpha)$. The effect of having a volume $V_2 = \beta p_2^\alpha = (\beta^{1/\alpha} p_2)^\alpha$ in the global fanout instead of p_2^α is the same as having $\hat{q} = \log_2 \beta^{1/\alpha}$ additional levels of recursive bipartitioning, interspersed with the top $q_2 = \log_2 p_2$ levels. The total number of levels now increases from $q = \log_2 p$ to $q + \hat{q}$, and treating all these levels equally leads to

$$\epsilon_2 = \frac{q_2 + \hat{q}}{q + \hat{q}} \epsilon. \tag{4.70}$$

The final allowed imbalance ϵ can be determined by comparing the total communication cost and the computation imbalance of a given partitioning by the procedure above, and adjusting the target value by trial and error to equalize these overhead costs.

For the vector distribution, we only discuss the fanout of the input vector, since the fanin is similar. Here, our goal is to determine the unique owner $P(\phi_v(j))$ of the component v_j

and for each node $P(s, *)$ with $j \in J_s$ the owner $P(s, \phi_v^s(j))$ of the local copy. Our matrix partitioning minimizes the communication volume, and the corresponding vector partitioning tries to balance the communication load. We can use the vector partitioning that follows the initial matrix partitioning (across the nodes) to determine for each vector component v_j the node $P(s, *)$ that owns it, and then we write $\phi_v(j) = (s, \phi_v^s(j))$, where $\phi_v^s(j)$ still has to be determined. In turn, we can use the vector partitioning that follows the matrix partitioning within a node $P(s, *)$ to balance the communication in the local fanout. This determines the local processor number $\phi_v^s(j)$ and in case the node is the owner of v_j, it fixes the second coordinate of $\phi_v(j)$.

As a final remark, note that our cost definition eqn (4.67) for communication between nodes enables an unmodified initial partitioning by Mondriaan, where we only need to consider inter-node communication, and not what happens within a node. In eqn (4.67), h is based on how much each node sends and receives, and not on how much each individual processor sends and receives. Thus, our cost definition nicely separates the communication concerns of the two levels of the hybrid model and in particular, it enables separate partitionings at the node and processor levels.

4.11 Example function bspmv

The function bspmv is an implementation of Algorithm 4.5 for the SpMV. It can handle every possible data distribution for the matrix and vectors. Before executing the algorithm, each processor builds its own local data structure for representing the local part of the sparse matrix. The local nonempty rows are numbered $i = 0, \ldots, \text{nrows} - 1$, where $\text{nrows} = |I_s|$. The global index of the row with local index i is given by $i = \text{rowindex}[i]$. Similarly, the global index of the column with local index j is given by $j = \text{colindex}[j]$, for $0 \le j < \text{ncols} = |J_s|$. (The local indices i and j of the matrix data structure are distinct from those of the vectors.) The nonzeros are stored in order of increasing local row index i. The nonzeros of each local row are stored consecutively in increasing order of local column index j, using the ICRS data structure presented in Section 4.2. The kth nonzero is stored as a pair (a[k], inc[k]), where a[k] is the numerical value of the nonzero and inc[k] the increment in the local column index.

This data structure is convenient for use in repeated SpMV operations. Building the structure, however, requires quite a bit of preprocessing on input. An outline of the input preprocessing is as follows. Each triple (i, j, a_{ij}) is read from an input file and sent to the responsible processor, as determined by the matrix distribution of the file. The local triples are then sorted by increasing global column index, which enables conversion to local column indices. During the conversion, the global indices are registered in colindex. The triples are sorted again, this time by global row index, taking care that the original mutual precedences are maintained between triples from the same matrix row. (Such a sort is called **stable**.) The global row indices are then converted to local ones and the array rowindex is initialized.

The nonzeros must be sorted with care. Sequentially, the $nz(A)$ nonzeros of a sparse matrix A can be sorted by row in time $\mathcal{O}(nz(A) + n)$, simply by counting the number of nonzeros in each row during one pass through the nonzeros, allocating exactly the right amount of memory space for each row, and filling the space in a second pass. In parallel, it is more difficult to sort efficiently, because the range of possible global indices remains $0, \ldots, n-1$, while the number of local nonzeros decreases to $nz(A)/p$. Clearly, such $\mathcal{O}(nz(A)/p + n)$ behaviour for a straightforward sort by row index is nonscalable and hence unacceptable. Fortunately, a radix sort (see [72, Chapter 8]) with radix $r = \sqrt{n}$ will do the job. This method first sorts the triples by using $i \bmod r$ as a key, and then in a second pass, sorts the indices by using $i \operatorname{div} r$ as a key, maintaining the original mutual precedences between triples that have the same key for the second pass. The total time and memory needed is about $\mathcal{O}(nz(A)/p + n/r + r)$, which is minimal for the choice $r = \sqrt{n}$. We choose the radix to be a power of two close to $\sqrt{n}$, because of the cheaper modular arithmetic for powers of two. This sorting procedure is scalable in time and memory by our definition (3.50), because $\sqrt{n} \leq (n/p + p)/2$. The driver program bspmv_test (not printed here because of its length, but included in BSPedupack) implements the complete input phase, for matrix as well as vectors. For vectors, the input and output distributions are read from file, but the input values are not; they are assigned by bspmv_test.

The relation between the vector variables of Algorithm 4.5 and the functions bspmv and bspmv_init is as follows. Vector component v_j corresponds to a local component v[k] in $P(\phi_\mathbf{v}(j))$, where $j = \mathtt{vindex[k]}$. All the needed vector components v_j, whether obtained from other processors or already present locally, are written into a local array vloc, which has the same local indices as the matrix columns; vloc[j] stores a copy of v_j, where $j = \mathtt{colindex[j]}$. This copy is obtained using a bsp_get, which is the most convenient option because the receiver knows it needs the value. The processor from which to get the value v_j has processor number $\phi_\mathbf{v}(j) = \mathtt{srcprocv[j]}$ and this number is stored beforehand by the initialization function bspmv_init. This way, the source processor needs to be determined only once and its processor number can be used without additional cost in repeated application of the SpMV. We also need to determine the location in the source processor where v_j resides. This location is stored as the local index srcindv[j]. We could also have used a bsp_put instead of a bsp_get, but this would require a bit more preprocessing and data storage. We could also have sent larger packets of data instead of single words, provided we carried out even more preprocessing. We did not implement these optimizations here. A small optimization that we did implement, however, is the direct assignment in the fanout of the value v_j to vloc[j] in case v_j is local. This avoids the overhead of a call to bsp_get, which may be substantial, and it may also save buffer memory in the underlying communication system.

The partial sum $u_{it} = \mathtt{sum}$ is computed by pointer magic, to be explained later on, and this sum is immediately sent to the processor $P(\phi_\mathbf{u}(i))$ that computes u_i. A convenient way of sending this value is by using bsp_send, which is the core primitive of bulk synchronous message passing, a style of communication introduced for the bspsort program in Section 1.9. The reason for the existence of bsp_send is illustrated here once more, namely in superstep $(1)/(2)$ of bspmv. The information whether a nonzero partial sum for a certain row exists is only available at the sender. As a consequence, a sending processor does not know what the other processors send. Furthermore, processors do not know what they will receive. If we were to use bsp_put statements, we would have to specify a destination address, which is not directly available. (It could be obtained, however, by additional preprocessing.)

The bsp_send primitive sends a message which consists of a tag and a payload. The tag is used to identify the message; the payload contains the actual data. In our case, the tag is an index corresponding to i and the payload is the partial sum u_{it}. The number of the destination processor is available as $\phi_{\mathbf{u}}(i) = $ destprocu[i], which has been initialized beforehand by the function bspmv_init. It is important to choose a tag that enables the receiver to handle the payload easily. Here, the receiver needs to know to which vector component the partial sum belongs. We could have used the global index i as a tag, but then this index would have to be translated on receipt into the local index i used to access u. Instead, we use the local index directly. Note that here the tag need not identify the source processor, since its number is irrelevant. In our case, the payload of a message is one double, which is written in its entirety into sum, so that the number of bytes is sizeof(double). Also here, we implemented the small optimization of avoiding a function call (to bsp_send) for the local case.

The status information obtained by the primitive bsp_get_tag(status, tag) can be used to decide whether there is an unread message, and if so, how much space to allocate for it. We could have used the status in the termination criterion of the loop in superstep (3) to determine whether we have handled all partial sums. Instead, we choose to use the enquiry primitive bsp_qsize to determine the number of iterations of the loop, that is, the number of partial sums received.

The local SpMV in superstep $(1)/(2)$ is an implementation of Algorithm 4.4 for the local data structure, modified to handle a rectangular nrows × ncols matrix. The inner loop of the multiplication has been optimized by using pointer arithmetic. For once, deviating from our declared BSPedupack principles, we sacrifice readability here because this loop is expected to account for a large proportion of the computing time spent, and because pointer arithmetic is the raison d'être of the ICRS data structure. The statement

sum += (*pa) * (*pvloc);

is a translation of

sum += a[k] * vloc[j];

We move through the array a by incrementing pa (i.e., the pointer to a) and do the same for the inc array. Instead of using an index j to access vloc, we use a pointer pvloc; after a nonzero has been processed, this pointer is moved *pinc = inc[k] places forwards.

The initialization function bspmv_init first reveals the owner of each global index i, storing its number in a temporary array tmpproc that can be queried by all processors. As a result, every processor can find answers to questions such as: who is the owner of u_i and where is this component parked? For scalability, the temporary array is itself distributed, and this is done by the cyclic distribution. In addition, the local index on the owning processor is stored in an array tmpind. The temporary arrays are then queried to initialize the local lists used for steering the communications. For example, vector component v_j with $j = $ jglob $= $ colindex[j], which is needed for local matrix column j, can be obtained from the processor whose number is stored in array tmpprocv on processor $P(j \bmod p)$, in location *j* div *p*. A suitable mental picture is that of a collection of noticeboards: every processor first announces the availability of its vector components on the appropriate noticeboards and then reads the announcements that concern the components it needs. We finish bspmv_init by deregistering and freeing memory.

It is possible to optimize the program bspmv further by performing a more extensive initialization, to enable packing as we did for the program bspfft in Section 3.6. As a result, all data for the same destination can be sent together in one packet. We did not include this optimization in our program. The program text of bspmv is:

```
#include "bspedupack.h"

void bspmv(long n, long nz, long nrows, long ncols,
           double *a, long *inc,
           long *srcprocv, long *srcindv,
           long *destprocu, long *destindu,
           long nv, long nu, double *v, double *u){

/* This function multiplies a sparse matrix A with a
   dense vector v, giving a dense vector u=Av.
   A is n by n, and u,v are vectors of length n.
   A, u, and v are distributed arbitrarily on input.
   They are all accessed using local indices, but the
   local matrix indices may differ from the local vector
   indices. The local matrix nonzeros are stored in an
   incremental compressed row storage (ICRS) data
   structure defined by nz, nrows, ncols, a, inc.

   All rows and columns in the local data structure
   are nonempty.

   n is the global size of the matrix A.
   nz is the number of local nonzeros.
   nrows is the number of local rows.
   ncols is the number of local columns.

   a[k] is the numerical value of the k'th local nonzero
       of the sparse matrix A, 0 <= k < nz.
   inc[k] is the increment in the local column index
       of the k'th local nonzero, compared to the column
       index of the (k-1)th nonzero if this nonzero is
       in the same row; otherwise, ncols is added
       to the difference.
       Here, the column index of the -1'th nonzero is 0.
```

```
srcprocv[j] is the source processor of the
    component in v corresponding to local
    column j, 0 <= j < ncols.
srcindv[j] is the local index on the source
    processor of the component in v corresponding
    to local column j.
destprocu[i] is the destination processor of
    the partial sum corresponding to local
    row i, 0 <= i < nrows.
destindu[i] is the local index in the vector
    u on the destination processor corresponding
    to local row i.

nv is the number of local components of the input
vector v. nu is the number of local components of
the output vector u.
v[k] is the k'th local component of v, 0 <= k < nv.
u[k] is the k'th local component of u, 0 <= k < nu.
*/

/* Allocate, register, and set tag size */
double *vloc= vecallocd(ncols);
bsp_push_reg(v,nv*sizeof(double));
bsp_size_t tagsize= sizeof(long);
bsp_set_tagsize(&tagsize);
bsp_sync();

/****** Superstep (0). Fanout ******/
long s= bsp_pid();
for (long j=0; j<ncols; j++){
    if (srcprocv[j] == s)
        vloc[j]= v[srcindv[j]];
    else
      bsp_get(srcprocv[j],v,srcindv[j]*sizeof(double),
              &vloc[j],sizeof(double));
}
bsp_sync();

/****** Superstep (1)/(2) ******/
/* Local matrix-vector multiplication and fanin */
double *pa= a;
long *pinc= inc;
double *pvloc= vloc;
```

```
    double *pvloc_end= pvloc + ncols;

    for (long i=0; i<nu; i++)
        u[i]= 0.0;

    pvloc += *pinc;
    for (long i=0; i<nrows; i++){
        double sum= 0.0;
        while (pvloc<pvloc_end){
            sum += (*pa) * (*pvloc);
            pa++;
            pinc++;
            pvloc += *pinc;
        }
        if (destprocu[i] == s)
            u[destindu[i]]= sum;
        else
            bsp_send(destprocu[i],&destindu[i],
                     &sum, sizeof(double));
        pvloc -= ncols;
    }
    bsp_sync();

    /****** Superstep (3) ******/
    /* Summation of nonzero partial sums */

    bsp_nprocs_t nsums;
    bsp_size_t nbytes, status;
    long i;
    bsp_qsize(&nsums,&nbytes);
    bsp_get_tag(&status,&i);
    for (long k=0; k<nsums; k++){
        /* status != -1, but its value is not used */
        double sum;
        bsp_move(&sum, sizeof(double));
        u[i] += sum;
        bsp_get_tag(&status,&i);
    }

    bsp_pop_reg(v);
    vecfreed(vloc);

} /* end bspmv */
```

```
void bspmv_init(long n, long nrows, long ncols,
                long nv, long nu,
                long *rowindex,
                long *colindex,
                long *vindex, long *uindex,
                long *srcprocv, long *srcindv,
                long *destprocu, long *destindu){
```

/* *This function initializes the communication data
   structure needed for multiplying a sparse matrix
   A with a dense vector v, giving a dense vector
   u=Av.*

   *Input: the arrays rowindex, colindex, vindex,
   uindex, containing the global indices
   corresponding to the local indices of the
   matrix and the vectors.*

   *Output: initialized arrays srcprocv, srcindv,
   destprocu, destindu containing the processor
   number and the local index on the remote
   processor of vector components corresponding
   to local matrix columns and rows.*

   n, nrows, ncols, nv, nu are the same as in bspmv.

*rowindex[i] is the global index of local row i,
            0 <= i < nrows.*
*colindex[j] is the global index of local column j,
            0 <= j < ncols.*
*vindex[j] is the global index of local component v[j],
            0 <= j < nv.*
*uindex[i] is the global index of local component u[i],
            0 <= i < nu.*

   *srcprocv, srcindv, destprocu, destindu
            are the same as in bspmv.*
*/

```
long p= bsp_nprocs();  // p = number of processors
                       //     obtained
long s= bsp_pid();     // s = processor number
```

```
/* Allocate and register temporary arrays */
long np= nloc(p,s,n);
long *tmpprocv=vecalloci(np);
long *tmpindv=vecalloci(np);
long *tmpprocu=vecalloci(np);
long *tmpindu=vecalloci(np);

bsp_push_reg(tmpprocv,np*sizeof(long));
bsp_push_reg(tmpindv,np*sizeof(long));
bsp_push_reg(tmpprocu,np*sizeof(long));
bsp_push_reg(tmpindu,np*sizeof(long));
bsp_sync();

/* Write my announcement into temporary arrays */
for (long j=0; j<nv; j++){
    long jglob= vindex[j];
    /* Use the cyclic distribution */
    bsp_put(jglob%p,&s,tmpprocv,
            (jglob/p)*sizeof(long),sizeof(long));
    bsp_put(jglob%p,&j,tmpindv,
            (jglob/p)*sizeof(long),sizeof(long));
}
for (long i=0; i<nu; i++){
    long iglob= uindex[i];
    bsp_put(iglob%p,&s,tmpprocu,
            (iglob/p)*sizeof(long),sizeof(long));
    bsp_put(iglob%p,&i,tmpindu,
            (iglob/p)*sizeof(long),sizeof(long));
}
bsp_sync();

/* Read announcements from temporary arrays */
for (long j=0; j<ncols; j++){
    long jglob= colindex[j];
    bsp_get(jglob%p,tmpprocv,(jglob/p)*sizeof(long),
            &srcprocv[j],sizeof(long));
    bsp_get(jglob%p,tmpindv, (jglob/p)*sizeof(long),
            &srcindv[j], sizeof(long));
}
for (long i=0; i<nrows; i++){
    long iglob= rowindex[i];
    bsp_get(iglob%p,tmpprocu,(iglob/p)*sizeof(long),
            &destprocu[i],sizeof(long));
    bsp_get(iglob%p,tmpindu, (iglob/p)*sizeof(long),
```

```
                &destindu[i], sizeof(long));
    }
    bsp_sync();

    /* Deregister temporary arrays */
    bsp_pop_reg(tmpindu); bsp_pop_reg(tmpprocu);
    bsp_pop_reg(tmpindv); bsp_pop_reg(tmpprocv);
    /* Free temporary arrays */
    vecfreei(tmpindu); vecfreei(tmpprocu);
    vecfreei(tmpindv); vecfreei(tmpprocv);

    bsp_sync();
} /* end bspmv_init */
```

4.12 Experimental results on the Cartesius supercomputer

In this section, we perform numerical experiments for the parallel SpMV on the supercomputer Cartesius, both for shared and distributed memory. We use the Broadwell nodes, which have been benchmarked in Section 1.7 for a single node with shared memory ($p \leq 32$), cf. Table 1.4, and in Section 3.7 for multiple nodes with distributed memory ($p \leq 512$), cf. Table 3.2.

Table 4.6 shows the set of sparse matrices used in our SpMV experiments. The set consists of the five SuiteSparse matrices from Table 4.1, supplemented with three larger matrices of our own concoction, namely the matrix random100k with density $d = 0.01$, which represents the random sparse matrices discussed in Section 4.8, and the matrices laplace2D_4096, corresponding to a 4096 × 4096 grid, and laplace3D_256, corresponding to a 256 × 256 × 256 grid, which represent the class of Laplacian matrices discussed in Section 4.9.

Table 4.6 Test set of sparse square matrices. The parameters given are: the number of rows/-columns n, the number of nonzeros nz, the average number c of nonzeros per row/column.

Name	n	nz	c	Origin
mip1	66 463	10 352 819	155.8	mixed integer programming
in-2004	1 382 908	16 917 053	12.2	web links India 2004
asia_osm	11 950 757	25 423 206	2.1	road network Asia
cage14	1 505 785	27 130 349	18.0	DNA electrophoresis
rgg_n_2_21_s0	2 097 152	28 975 990	13.8	random geometric graph
laplace2D_4096	16 777 216	83 869 696	5.0	2D Laplacian
random100k	100 000	100 004 125	1 000.0	random sparse matrix
laplace3D_256	16 777 216	117 047 296	7.0	3D Laplacian

Table 4.7 Computation and communication cost for sparse matrix–vector multiplication. The synchronization cost for $p > 1$ is $4l$.

p	mip1	in-2004	asia_osm
1	20 705 638	33 834 106	50 846 412
2	10 635 008 + 1 087g	17 402 680 + 319g	25 582 806 + 62g
4	5 321 972 + 2 152g	8 619 792 + 611g	12 847 854 + 62g
8	2 665 180 + 3 539g	4 354 756 + 832g	6 526 308 + 82g
16	1 332 106 + 2 603g	2 178 062 + 867g	3 272 994 + 97g
32	666 428 + 2 740g	1 089 034 + 832g	1 636 606 + 143g
64	333 156 + 2 000g	544 514 + 756g	818 266 + 96g
128	166 614 + 1 640g	272 258 + 777g	409 110 + 99g
256	83 304 + 1 380g	136 128 + 588g	204 564 + 132g

p	cage14	rgg_n_2_21_s0	laplace2D_4096
1	54 260 698	57 951 980	167 739 392
2	27 166 388 + 74 019g	29 832 972 + 1 578g	84 777 274 + 4 096g
4	13 565 176 + 99 763g	14 569 690 + 1 602g	43 065 966 + 4 634g
8	6 890 846 + 74 273g	7 440 620 + 1 784g	21 577 598 + 7 741g
16	3 391 294 + 49 716g	3 728 966 + 1 587g	10 797 944 + 5 956g
32	1 718 302 + 34 948g	1 864 464 + 1 409g	5 397 110 + 4 600g
64	859 872 + 19 192g	932 328 + 917g	2 699 434 + 3 339g
128	434 492 + 11 846g	465 786 + 830g	1 349 762 + 2 785g
256	215 784 + 9 402g	233 020 + 553g	674 844 + 1 869g

p	random100k	laplace3D_256
1	200 008 250	234 094 592
2	100 004 126 + 50 001g	117 124 986 + 65 942g
4	51 502 050 + 77 951g	59 819 416 + 72 363g
8	25 342 198 + 70 647g	30 138 652 + 78 441g
16	12 875 064 + 60 560g	15 065 066 + 59 840g
32	6 437 730 + 42 376g	7 532 394 + 44 229g
64	3 218 834 + 39 937g	3 766 718 + 30 805g
128	1 609 420 + 30 428g	1 883 288 + 18 681g
256	804 708 + 24 039g	941 610 + 12 726g

The matrices of the test set and the corresponding input and output vectors were partitioned in one run of the Mondriaan partitioner, version 4.2.1, for the purpose of a parallel SpMV with $p = 1, 2, 4, \ldots, 256$. The resulting BSP costs are given in Table 4.7. Note that every nonzero is counted as two flops, so that the cost for $p = 1$ equals $2nz(A)$. Mondriaan was run with $\epsilon = 3\%$ load imbalance allowed, with input and output vectors distributed independently, and with all parameters set to their default values. In particular, this means that the medium-grain method with iterative refinement was used. The load imbalance ϵ' achieved satisfied $\epsilon' \leq \epsilon$ for all problem instances. In most cases, ϵ' was close to this upper bound. Here, synchronization cost can be important: to make parallelization worthwhile, $T_2 \leq T_{\text{seq}}$ needs to hold, that is $2nz/2 + 4l \leq 2nz$, which is equivalent to $nz \geq 4l$. For shared memory, this means that the matrix must have at least 73 000 nonzeros, see Table 1.4, and for distributed memory at least 252 000 nonzeros, see Table 3.2.

The computation costs presented in Table 4.7 behave as expected because of the imposed load balance. The communication costs show remarkable differences, which depend on the sparsity structure of the matrices tested. The matrix asia_osm clearly has the lowest communication cost, which tells us that near-planar road networks are easy to partition. Comparing cage14 and rgg_n_2_21_s0, we see that although their size n and number of nonzeros nz are close to each other, they differ much in their communication cost. The matrix cage14 with its underlying high-dimensional structure has a 47 times higher communication cost for $p = 2$ and a 17 times higher cost for $p = 256$ than the random geometric matrix rgg_n_2_21_s0. The latter matrix represents 2^{21} points randomly placed on a 2D unit square, which are interacting within a short cut-off distance, similar to the molecular dynamics system shown in Fig. 4.3. Comparing the 2D and 3D Laplacian matrices, which represent exactly the same number of grid points and hence have the same size, we see that the computation cost is an expected factor 1.4 larger for 3D, but the communication cost is a factor 6.8 larger. The well-known **curse of dimensionality** also manifests itself in parallel computing!

The communication cost presented in Table 4.7 for this particular run of the Mondriaan partitioner can be compared to the average value V/p for perfectly balanced communication obtained for the medium-grain (MG) method shown in Table 4.2. For $p = 2$, communication is always perfectly balanced (why?) and any discrepancy is due to deviation from the average in a single Mondriaan run. The largest discrepancy observed for $p = 2$ is 14.3%, comparing the cost $319g$ of the matrix in-2004 to the average value $Vg/p = 279g$. For $p = 64$, however, discrepancies are mainly due to communication imbalance caused by an imperfect vector distribution. The largest discrepancy observed for $p = 64$ is a factor of 3.4 between the cost $756g$ of the matrix in-2004 and the average value $Vg/p = 225g$. For the Laplacian matrices, the communication cost presented in Table 4.7 can be compared to the average measured value h and the average value V/p shown in Table 4.5 for a row distribution. We observe that the communication cost in Table 4.5 is a bit lower: for the 3D case with $p = 128$ the cost in Table 4.5 is $16\,568g$ compared to $18\,681g$ in Table 4.7. This justifies our choice in Section 4.9 of a row distribution for Laplacian matrices instead of a more general matrix distribution.

Table 4.8 presents the timings for $p \leq 32$ on one Broadwell node of Cartesius, running the program bspmv from Section 4.11 on top of the shared-memory library MulticoreBSP for C [318], version 2.0.4. We used the gcc compiler, version 4.8.5, with the compiler optimization flag -O3. We created a sequential version of bspmv with the same level of program optimization by removing all BSP primitives and simplifying the program text wherever possible. The overhead of the parallel program for $p = 1$ relative to the sequential program can be significant: it ranges from 2.8% for the matrix random100k, which has the highest value of c, to 20.6% for asia_osm, which has the lowest value of c. This indicates that the overhead is related to the handling of the rows, which is relatively more important for a smaller number of nonzeros per row. The overhead mainly consists of checking

Table 4.8 Measured execution time (in ms) for sparse matrix–vector multiplication using the MulticoreBSP for C library.

p	mipl	in-2004	asia_osm	cage14	rgg_n_2_21_s0	laplace 2D_4096	random 100k	laplace 3D_256
1 (seq)	13.9	32.1	150.2	46.9	59.0	213.6	379.5	255.5
1 (par)	14.9	35.4	181.2	50.9	63.6	241.2	390.3	285.7
2	7.5	18.6	91.4	31.6	32.9	122.7	188.8	150.2
4	4.1	10.0	46.6	21.4	16.5	63.7	115.9	104.4
8	2.3	5.7	24.9	13.8	11.0	52.2	71.6	72.0
16	2.3	4.8	30.1	10.4	11.2	53.1	38.9	72.6
32	1.6	5.4	29.7	12.4	5.3	43.6	20.8	41.0

whether communication is really necessary, and if not replacing it by a local memory copy, as can be seen in the program text. As an alternative, we could remove this check and the program would still work, but it would carry out a superfluous function call to a BSP primitive, and we found that this entails a large overhead; such overhead is also visible in the relatively high value of g for $p = 1$ in Table 1.4.

The timings for $p > 1$ in Table 4.8 show modest speedups ranging from 4.5 for cage14 and $p = 16$ to 18.2 for random100k and $p = 32$. To obtain higher speedups, we would have to optimize the program by sending data in larger packets instead of single words, as we did for the FFT in the program bspfft of Chapter 3. This would also reduce the cost of the function calls to the BSP primitives bsp_get and bsp_send. The matrices with the largest communication cost are cage14, random100k, and laplace3D_256 and their speedups for $p = 32$ are 3.8, 18.2, and 6.2. The surprisingly high speedup of random100k is due to its high number of 1000 nonzeros per row, which reduces the relative influence of function-call overheads. The highest computing rate attained on one processor core is 1.489 Gflop/s for the smallest matrix mip1, which fits better in cache, and the lowest rate is 0.527 Gflop/s for the large matrix random100k, which suffers from a random cache-access pattern.

Table 4.9 presents the timings for $p \leq 256$ on up to eight Broadwell nodes of Cartesius, running the program bspmv from Section 4.11 on top of the distributed-memory library BSPonMPI [281], version 1.1, which, in turn, ran on top of OpenMPI, version 3.1.1. We used the gcc compiler, version 7.3.0, with the compiler optimization flag -O3.

The speedups displayed in Table 4.9 reach up to $S_{256} = 50$ for the matrix asia_osm, which has a very low communication cost. According to Table 4.7, the communication cost for asia_osm on 256 processors becomes dominant for machines with $g \geq 204564/132 \approx 1550$. Our computer has a lower value $g = 756$ and hence computation dominates. In contrast, the lowest maximum speedup achieved is $S_{64} = 6.3$ for the matrix mip1, which has a relatively high communication cost. For mip1 and $p = 64$, communication already dominates for $g \geq 167$. For the matrix cage14 and $p = 256$, the break-even point is even lower, at $g = 23$.

Table 4.9 exhibits several superlinear speedups, for instance a speedup of 4.0 for the matrix laplace2D_4096 and a speedup of 2.7 for cage14, both on doubling the number of processors from $p = 32$ to $p = 64$. Such superlinear speedups must be due to cache effects, which we can explain as follows. The matrix laplace2D_4096 needs about 2 GB storage space, assuming we use one double and two long integers (i.e., 24 bytes) to store a nonzero. For $p = 32$, the local matrix part thus needs about 64 MB storage space, which is well above the L3 cache size per core of 2.5 MB. Therefore, the matrix cannot benefit from any cache reuse. The situation is different, however, for the corresponding input and output vectors. Each such vector needs about 134 MB storage space. For $p = 32$, this means that a local vector needs about 4.2 MB storage space, just above the 2.5 MB L3 cache memory available per processor core. For $p = 64$, a local vector can fit into the L3 cache and this is clearly beneficial.

Comparing the results from Tables 4.8 and 4.9 for one Broadwell node ($p \leq 32$), we observe that their sequential results are almost the same. This is as expected, because no communication is carried out in that case. The shared-memory parallel computations

Table 4.9 Measured execution time (in ms) for sparse matrix–vector multiplication using the BSPonMPI library.

p	mip1	in-2004	asia _osm	cage14	rgg_n_2 _21_s0	laplace 2D_4096	random 100k	laplace 3D_256
1 (seq)	13.8	31.6	150.0	46.5	56.5	213.6	380.0	256.3
1 (par)	14.7	34.6	178.6	50.0	61.5	239.0	386.7	283.8
2	7.9	19.0	95.8	40.8	32.8	125.9	190.4	176.3
4	4.5	9.7	44.9	33.2	16.4	66.2	126.8	93.2
8	3.0	6.0	26.0	22.3	12.8	52.5	84.8	80.9
16	3.9	7.7	35.0	23.0	12.7	61.8	58.3	85.8
32	2.4	8.3	34.2	22.5	5.7	52.7	23.9	38.8
64	2.2	2.8	7.9	8.4	3.3	13.2	15.9	21.0
128	2.9	2.1	5.3	7.5	2.3	8.2	13.5	13.1
256	3.9	3.0	3.0	6.1	2.3	5.1	15.4	8.7

of Table 4.8 are in general faster than the distributed-memory parallel computations of Table 4.9, but not by much. There are even a few cases where the distributed-memory computation is faster. Note that the shared-memory values for g from Table 1.4 are somewhat lower than the distributed-memory values from Table 3.2, although for $p = 32$ they are nearly equal. The values of l are significantly lower for shared memory: for $p = 32$, this is by a factor of 3.5. The largest difference observed in our SpMV measurements is for the communication-intensive matrix `cage14`, which takes 12.4 ms per SpMV on 32 processor cores for shared memory, and 22.5 ms for distributed memory. This indicates that we can gain significantly by combining shared-memory and distributed-memory approaches into a unified hybrid-BSP approach, as outlined in Section 4.10.

It is quite common to finish research papers about parallel computing with a remark 'it has been shown that for large problem sizes the algorithm scales well.' If only all problems were large! More important than showing good speedups by enlarging problem sizes until the experimenter is happy, is gaining an understanding of what happens for various problem sizes, small as well as large.

Qualitatively, the BSP cost can be used to explain the timing results, or predict them. Quantitatively, the agreement is less than perfect. The reader can easily check this by substituting the measured values of g and l into the cost expressions of Table 4.7. The advantage of presenting BSP costs for sparse matrices as shown in Table 4.7 over presenting raw timings as is done in Table 4.8 and 4.9 is the longevity of the results: in 20 years from now, when all present supercomputers will rest in peace, when I shall be older and hopefully wiser, the results expressed as BSP costs can still be used to predict execution time on a state-of-the-art, completely solar-powered parallel computer.

4.13 Bibliographic notes

4.13.1 Sparse matrix computations

The book *Direct methods for sparse matrices* by Duff, Erisman, and Reid [99], is a good starting point for a study of sparse matrix computations of the direct type. Direct methods such as sparse LU decomposition for unsymmetric matrices and sparse Cholesky factorization for symmetric matrices are based on the Gaussian elimination method for solving linear systems. The unsymmetric case is characterized by the interplay between numerical stability and sparsity; in the symmetric case, it is often possible to separate these concerns by performing symbolic, sparsity-related computations before the actual numerical factorization. The book has a practical flavour, discussing in detail important issues such as sparse data structures, reuse of information obtained during previous runs of a solver, heuristics for finding good pivot elements that preserve both the numerical stability and the sparsity, and nested dissection techniques for matrix ordering and partitioning. The book also introduces graph-theoretic concepts commonly used in the sparse matrix field. The exploitation of parallelism is discussed throughout the book. In particular, the topic of parallel numerical factorization of an unsymmetric sparse matrix illustrates different sources of parallelism, such as node parallelism (originating in dense blocks) and tree parallelism (coming from sparsity).

Davis, Rajamanickam, and Sid-Lakhdar [80] present an extensive survey of direct methods for solving sparse linear systems, both sequential and parallel. They treat the topics of sparse triangular system solving, LU and QR decomposition, Cholesky factorization, frontal and multifrontal methods, and fill-reducing matrix orderings. The survey has over 600 references and it includes a useful list of software packages, categorized by problems that can be solved and by shared/distributed-memory type in case of a parallel solver.

The Templates project aims at providing precise descriptions in **template** form of the most important iterative solvers for linear systems and eigensystems, by giving a general algorithm with sufficient detail to enable customized implementation for specific problems. The book on templates for linear systems [19] contains a host of iterative linear system solvers, including the conjugate gradient (CG) [149], generalized minimal residual (GMRES) [263], and bi-conjugate gradient stabilized (Bi-CGSTAB) [299] methods. More recently, the induced dimension reduction method IDR(s) [275] has been added to the family of iterative linear system solvers. It is important to have a choice of solvers, since no single iterative method can solve all problems efficiently. Implementations of the complete templates for linear systems are available in C++, Fortran 77, and MATLAB. Most modern iterative methods build a **Krylov subspace**

$$K_m = \mathrm{span}\{\mathbf{r}, A\mathbf{r}, A^2\mathbf{r}, \dots, A^{m-1}\mathbf{r}\}, \tag{4.71}$$

where $\mathbf{r} = \mathbf{b} - A\mathbf{x}^0$ is the **residual** of the initial solution $\mathbf{x}^0$. The SpMV is the main building block of Krylov subspace methods. Preconditioning is often used to accelerate convergence of an iterative method, thus solving a system $K^{-1}A\mathbf{x} = K^{-1}\mathbf{b}$ instead of $A\mathbf{x} = \mathbf{b}$, where the $n \times n$ matrix K is the **preconditioner**, which must be a good approximation to A for which $K\mathbf{x} = \mathbf{b}$ is easy to solve. Many more details on iterative linear system solving methods can be found in the books by van der Vorst [298] and Saad [262]; Saad devotes a chapter to parallel implementations and another chapter to parallel preconditioners. The book on templates for algebraic eigensystems [15] treats the problem of solving eigensystems $A\mathbf{x} = \lambda\mathbf{x}$ and generalized eigensystems $A\mathbf{x} = \lambda B\mathbf{x}$, where A, B are square matrices, and it also treats the singular value decomposition (SVD) $A = U\Sigma V^{\mathrm{T}}$, where U and V are orthogonal matrices and Σ is a diagonal matrix.

Combinatorial scientific computing (CSC) is an area of research that contributes combinatorial models, algorithms, and implementations to applications from scientific computing, thus enabling the solution of much larger problems. A prime example is reordering of a sparse matrix to keep it sparse during the solution of a linear system. Another example is the partitioning of a sparse matrix for the sake of parallelism, based on graph or hypergraph partitioning. The book *Combinatorial Scientific Computing* [228] presents a broad overview of recent contributions by the CSC community covering, among others, sparse linear system solving, algorithmic differentiation, mesh generation, sparse matrix partitioning, graph partitioning, graph visualization, and large-scale data analysis.

The performance of sparse matrix algorithms achieved in practice depends to a large extent on the problem solved and hence it is important to use realistic test problems. The Harwell–Boeing collection was the first widely available set of sparse test matrices originating in real applications. Release 1, the version from 1989 described in [100], contained almost 300 matrices with the largest matrix bcsstk32 of size $n = 44\,609$ possessing $1\,029\,655$ stored nonzeros. (For this symmetric matrix, only the nonzeros below or on the main diagonal were stored.) The Harwell–Boeing input format is based on the CCS data structure, see Section 4.2. The original distribution medium of the 110-MB collection was a set of three nine-track tapes of 2400 feet length and 1600 bits-per-inch (bpi) density. Using the CCS format and not the triple scheme saved at least one tape! The original Harwell–Boeing collection has evolved into the Rutherford–Boeing collection [101], which in turn has been included in the Matrix Market repository [37]. Today, the largest and most-used repository is the SuiteSparse Matrix Collection [79], formerly called the University of Florida sparse matrix collection, which is maintained and continually expanded by Tim Davis. In May 2019, this online collection contained 2833 matrices with the largest matrix MOLIERE_2016 having $n = 30\,239\,687$ rows and columns and $nz = 6\,669\,254\,694$ true nonzeros. Matrices from the SuiteSparse collection are available in three formats: Rutherford–Boeing (based on CCS), Matrix Market (based on the triple scheme, a readable ASCII file with extension .mtx), and MATLAB (a binary file with extension .mat, obtainable by using the ss_get command from within MATLAB). The SuiteSparse collection can be searched by size (number of rows, columns, or nonzeros), shape (square or rectangular), symmetry, and keyword in the description. Useful statistics and pictures are provided for each matrix. Furthermore, the SuiteSparse website also provides beautiful images created by Yifan Hu of the graphs that correspond to the sparse matrices.

Langr and Tvrdík [191] survey many different data structures for storing sparse matrices. They present evaluation criteria for assessing the quality of these formats and any new *Yet Another Storage* (YAS) format. They recommend measuring the time needed to convert a sparse matrix from CRS to YAS, and express this time as the number of SpMVs using CRS that could have been performed during the conversion. This may help a potential user decide whether to use YAS. The authors also recommend comparing the computing rate in flop/s using YAS with the upper bound $r_{max} = 2B/d$ determined by the memory bandwidth B in bytes and the number of bytes d (usually 8) needed to store a numerical value. The bound is due to the fact that every nonzero has to be brought in from (cache) memory and is then used in one floating-point addition and one multiplication.

4.13.2 Parallel sparse matrix–vector multiplication algorithms

Back in 1988, Fox and collaborators [113, Section 21–3.4] presented a parallel algorithm for dense matrix–vector multiplication that distributes the matrix in both dimensions. They assume that a block-distributed copy of the complete input vector **v** is available in every processor row. Their algorithm starts with a local SpMV, then performs a so-called **fold operation** which gathers and adds partial sums $u_{it}, 0 \le t < N$, into a sum u_i, spreading the responsibility for computing the sums u_i of a processor row over all its processors, and finally performs an **expand operation** to broadcast the sums within their processor row. Thus, a block-distributed copy of the output vector **u** becomes available in every processor column. If **v** and **u** are needed in exactly the same distribution, the broadcast must be preceded by a vector transposition.

The parallel SpMV algorithm described in this chapter, Algorithm 4.5, is based on previous work by Bisseling and McColl [28, 31, 32]. The Cartesian version of the algorithm was first presented in [28] as part of a parallel implementation of GMRES, an iterative solver for square unsymmetric linear systems. Bisseling [28] outlines the advantages of using a 2D Cartesian distribution and distributing the vectors in the same way as the matrix diagonal and suggests to use as a fixed matrix-independent distribution the **square block/cyclic distribution**, defined by assigning matrix element a_{ij} to processor $P(i \text{ div } (n/\sqrt{p}), j \text{ mod } \sqrt{p})$. The cost analysis of the algorithm in [28] and the implementation, however, are closely tied to a square mesh communication network with store-and-forward routing. Bisseling and McColl [31, 32] transfer the parallel SpMV algorithm from [28] to the BSP context. The matrix distribution is Cartesian and the vectors are distributed in the same way as the matrix diagonal. Now, the algorithm benefits from the complete communication network provided by the BSP architecture. Architecture-independent time analysis becomes possible because of the BSP cost function. This leads to a theoretical and experimental study of scientific computing applications such as molecular dynamics, partial differential equation solving on multidimensional grids, and linear programming, all interpreted as an instance of an SpMV. This work shows that the block/cyclic distribution is an optimal fixed Cartesian distribution for unstructured sparse matrices; also optimal is a Cartesian matrix distribution based on a balanced random distribution of the matrix diagonal. Bisseling and McColl propose using digital diamonds for the Laplacian operator on a square grid, cf. Section 4.9.

Ogielski and Aiello [233] present a four-superstep parallel algorithm for multiplication of a sparse rectangular matrix and a vector. The algorithm exploits sparsity in the computation, but not in the communication. The matrix is distributed in a Cartesian manner by first randomly permuting the rows and columns (independently from each other) and then using an $M \times N$ cyclic distribution. A probabilistic analysis shows that the randomization leads to good expected load balance in the computation, for every matrix with a limited number of nonzeros per row and column. The vectors are first permuted in correspondence with the matrix and then component v_i is assigned to $P(s \text{ div } N, s \text{ mod } N)$, where $s = i \text{ mod } p$, and u_i to $P(s \text{ mod } M, s \text{ div } M)$. Experimental results on a 16384-processor MasPar machine show better load balance than theoretically expected.

Lewis and van de Geijn [197] present several algorithms for SpMV on a parallel computer with a mesh or hypercube communication network. Their final algorithm distributes the matrix and the vectors by assigning a_{ij} to processor $P((i \text{ div } (n/p)) \text{ mod } M, j \text{ div } (n/N))$ and u_i and v_i to $P((i \text{ div } (n/p)) \text{ mod } M, i \text{ div } (n/N))$. This data distribution fits into the scheme of Section 4.4: the matrix distribution is Cartesian and the vectors are distributed in the same way as the matrix diagonal. The vector distribution uses blocks of size n/p. The resulting data distribution is similar to that of Fig. 4.6. The sparsity of the matrix is exploited in the computation, but not in the communication. Experimental results are given for the random sparse matrix with $n = 14\,000$ and $nz = 1\,853\,104$ from the conjugate gradient solver of the NAS benchmark. Such experiments were also carried out by Hendrickson, Leland, and Plimpton [146], using a sparse algorithm similar to the dense algorithm of Fox *et al.* [113]. Hendrickson and Plimpton [147] apply ideas from this matrix–vector multiplication algorithm to compute the operation of a dense $n \times n$ force matrix on n particles in a molecular dynamics simulation.

Dongarra, Heroux, and Luszczek [89] developed the High-Performance Conjugate-Gradients (HPCG) benchmark which measures the computation time of a fixed number of iterations of a distributed-memory parallel sparse linear system solver. The solver is iterative, and it is based on the conjugate-gradient algorithm (see Algorithm 4.9), where each iteration involves an SpMV and several inner-product computations. The sparse linear system is part of a partial differential equation solver on a 3D rectangular grid, where grid points are connected to 26 neighbours (instead of the six neighbours we studied in Section 4.9 for 3D Laplacian matrices). The sparse matrix computation should better model the current mix of applications run on supercomputers than the High-Performance Linpack (HPL) benchmark [90], which is based on dense matrix computations. Hopefully, HPCG will drive hardware development in a direction beneficial to sparse matrix computations. The fastest supercomputer on both the TOP500 HPCG list and the TOP500 HPL list [279] from November 2019 is Summit, an IBM Power system. Summit reaches 2926 Tflop/s for HPCG and 148 600 Tflop/s for HPL, meaning that the sparse computing rate is only 2% of the dense rate.

Yzelman and Roose [319] present several strategies for parallel SpMV in pursuit of both large parallel speedups and good single-processor performance. They compare eight different methods and find that the most successful method is based on a combination of strategies: first divide the matrix into $\beta \times \beta$ blocks, then assign block rows to processors, order the local blocks of each processor in a cache-oblivious fashion based on the Hilbert space-filling curve, and finally store the nonzeros using a two-level data structure. The blocks are stored according to bidirectional ICRS (BICRS), a variant of ICRS where the increments may be negative and where row jumps need not be to the next row, but can be to any row. The nonzeros within a block are stored in row-major order using a compressed form of ICRS. In shared-memory parallel programming, concurrent reading of an input variable v_j poses no problem, but concurrent writing into an output variable u_i must be avoided, and this can be done by first writing into a local variable u_{is}. Yzelman et al. [318] present an implementation of a parallel SpMV in BSPlib, and achieve state-of-the-art performance using MulticoreBSP for C, with 2D methods performing better than 1D methods. Using the new primitives `bsp_hpsend` and `bsp_direct_get`, a highest speedup of 46.6 is obtained for the matrix `road_usa` on a 64-core HP DL980 machine.

4.13.3 Partitioning methods

The multilevel partitioning method was proposed by Bui and Jones [48] and improved by Hendrickson and Leland [145]. Hendrickson and Leland present a multilevel scheme for partitioning a sparse undirected graph $\mathcal{G} = (\mathcal{V}, \mathcal{E})$ among the processors of a parallel computer, where the aim is to obtain subsets of vertices of roughly equal size and with a minimum number of **cut edges**, that is edges that connect pairs of vertices in different subsets (and hence on different processors). In the case of a square symmetric matrix, the data distribution problem for SpMV can be converted into a graph partitioning problem by identifying matrix row i with vertex i and matrix nonzero a_{ij}, $i < j$, with an edge $(i, j) \in \mathcal{E}$. (Self-edges (i, i) are not created.) The graph is partitioned and the processor that obtains a vertex i in the graph partitioning becomes the owner of matrix row i and vector components

u_i, v_i. For more detail on the relation between the number of cut edges and the communication volume, see Sections 5.7 and 5.8. Hendrickson and Leland [145] use a spectral method for the initial partitioning, based on solving an eigensystem for the Laplacian matrix connected to the graph. They implemented their partitioning algorithms in a package called Chaco.

Karypis and Kumar [172] investigate the three phases of multilevel graph partitioning, proposing new heuristics for each phase, based on extensive experiments. For the coarsening phase, they propose matching each vertex with the neighbouring vertex connected by the heaviest edge. For the initial partitioning, they propose growing a partition greedily by highest gain, starting from an arbitrary vertex, until half the total vertex weight is included in the partition. For the uncoarsening, they propose a boundary Kernighan–Lin algorithm. The authors implemented the graph partitioner in a package called Metis. Karypis and Kumar [174] also developed a parallel multilevel algorithm that performs the partitioning itself on a parallel computer, with p processors computing a p-way partitioning. The algorithm uses a **graph colouring**, that is, a colouring of the vertices such that neighbouring vertices have different colours. To avoid conflicts between processors when matching vertices in the coarsening phase, each coarsening step is organized by colour, trying to find a match for vertices of one colour first, then for those of another colour, and so on. This parallel algorithm has been implemented in the ParMetis package. The authors show that the quality of the partitioning obtained by ParMetis is close to that of its sequential counterpart, at least for $p \leq 128$. (For larger p, the quality may deteriorate.) An alternative, widely used parallel graph partitioner is PT-Scotch [64], which is based on the sequential partitioner Scotch [244]. Buluç et al. [49] survey recent methods for graph partitioning, both sequential and parallel.

Hendrickson [143] argues in a paper from 1998 that the standard approach to sparse matrix partitioning by using graph partitioners is flawed because it optimizes the wrong cost function and because it is unnecessarily limited to square symmetric matrices. In his view, the emperor wears little more than his underwear. The standard approach minimizes the number of nonzeros (edges) that induce communication, but not necessarily the number of communication operations themselves. Thus the cost function does not take into account that if there are two nonzeros a_{ij} and $a_{i'j}$ on the same processor, the value v_j need not be sent twice to that processor. (Note that our Algorithm 4.5 obeys the old rule *ne bis in idem*, because it sends v_j only once to the same processor, as a consequence of using the index set J_s.) Furthermore, Hendrickson states that the cost function of the standard approach only considers communication volume and not the imbalance of the communication load or the startup costs of sending a message. (Note that the BSP cost function is based on the maximum communication load of a processor, which naturally encourages communication balancing. The BSP model does not ignore startup costs, but lumps them together into one parameter l; BSP implementations such as BSPlib reduce startup costs by combining messages to the same destination in the same superstep. The user minimizes startup costs by minimizing the number of synchronizations.)

Çatalyürek and Aykanat [56, 57] model the total communication volume of the SpMV operation correctly by using hypergraphs. They present a multilevel hypergraph partitioning algorithm that minimizes the true communication volume. The algorithm has been implemented in a package called PaToH (Partitioning Tool for Hypergraphs). Experimental results show that PaToH reduces the communication volume by 30–40% compared with graph-based partitioners. PaToH is about four times faster than the hypergraph version of Metis, called hMetis [173], while it produces partitionings of about the same quality. The partitioning algorithm in [56, 57] is one-dimensional since all splits are carried out in the same direction, yielding a row or column distribution for the matrix with a corresponding vector distribution. Çatalyürek and Aykanat [58] also present a fine-grained approach to SpMV, where nonzeros are assigned individually to processors, which has been discussed in Section 4.6. Çatalyürek, Aykanat, and Uçar [60] compare the 1D row and 1D column methods with three 2D methods: fine-grain, jagged-like (first partition A into row blocks, then partition each row block independently into column blocks), and checkerboard (a Cartesian distribution obtained by multiconstraint partitioning). They also provide a recipe that helps in choosing the best method just based on a number of basic matrix characteristics. Hypergraph partitioning is commonly used in the design of electronic circuits and much improvement is due to work in that field. A hypergraph partitioner developed for circuit design is MLpart [54].

Parkway [287] is a parallel multilevel hypergraph partitioner developed by Trifunović and Knottenbelt. It has been applied to compute the PageRank of web link matrices [43], showing a large savings of a factor of 20.2 in communication volume for a 2D fine-grain matrix distribution compared to a 1D row distribution for the problem stanford_berkeley with $p = 16$. This led to savings in measured communication time of a factor 3.5. The authors attribute the smaller gain in measured time to high message-startup costs in the PC cluster used. For the matrix in-2004 with $p = 16$ (cf. Table 4.1), the communication volume showed a reduction from 14 433 for 1D to 11 684 for 2D.

The Zoltan load balancing toolkit [38, 84] provides various types of data partitioning, sparse matrix ordering, and graph colouring. It contains a parallel hypergraph partitioner (PHG) [85], which internally uses a 2D Cartesian distribution of the corresponding matrix (viewed in the row-net model). Bipartitioning experiments with Zoltan PHG using 64 processors for a few large matrices (including cage14) showed in most cases faster partitioning with a square 2D internal distribution than with 1D. Surprisingly, among the 1D distributions the 1D row distribution was faster than the 1D column distribution; thus, keeping hyperedge (net) information together works better than keeping vertex information together. Zoltan can be used for repartitioning of dynamically changing data [59], taking migration costs into account. This is achieved by introducing a special fixed vertex for each processor and a migration net for each original vertex. The trade-off between communication and migration cost can be controlled by the user. Rajamanickam and Boman [258] compare Zoltan PHG as a graph and hypergraph partitioner with the graph partitioner ParMetis, and they perform numerical experiments on a set of 22 matrices from the 10th DIMACS implementation challenge, using up to 1024 processors. They observe that for unsymmetric matrices hypergraph partitioning is superior to graph partitioning, as it reduces the communication volume by orders of magnitude, but that for symmetric matrices there is no benefit, possibly because hypergraph partitioning ignores the symmetry.

KaHyPar [265] is a sequential hypergraph partitioner, developed in Karlsruhe, which is based on the multilevel approach, but takes this approach to the extreme by creating

$\mathcal{O}(n)$ levels instead of $\mathcal{O}(\log n)$, where each level has one vertex less than the previous level. Through crafty engineering, KaHyPar attains low communication volumes at a reasonable cost in running time. Experiments on a set of hypergraphs from VLSI benchmarks, satisfiability (SAT) solving, and the SuiteSparse Matrix Collection show that KaHyPar beats hMetis, both in quality of the output and in running time. KaHyPar also beats PaToH on quality, but still lags behind in speed.

The 2D Mondriaan matrix distribution method described in Section 4.5 is due to Vastenhouw and Bisseling [304] and has been implemented as the `localbest` strategy in the Mondriaan package. The method used to split a matrix into two submatrices is based on the multilevel method for hypergraph bipartitioning by Çatalyürek and Aykanat [56, 57]. The Mondriaan package also implements a method based on the fine-grain model by Çatalyürek and Aykanat [58] and a hybrid method [30] that tries 1D row, 1D column, and fine-grain splitting at each bipartitioning step. The current default splitting strategy of Mondriaan, version 4.2.1, is the medium-grain method by Pelt and Bisseling [245], described in Section 4.6. The Mondriaan package can handle rectangular matrices as well as square matrices, and it allows the user to impose the condition distr(**u**) = distr(**v**). The package also has an option to exploit symmetry by assigning a_{ij} and a_{ji} to the same processor. Furthermore, it has an option to permute the matrix rows and columns after the partitioning into separated block diagonal (SBD) form [316] with cut rows in the middle, which enhances cache use, or bordered block diagonal (BBD) form with cut rows ordered last, which leads to a nested dissection ordering. Fortmeier *et al.* [110] introduce the $\lambda(\lambda - 1)$-metric, also available in Mondriaan, which punishes communication harder than the $(\lambda - 1)$-metric. It was developed to reflect all-to-all neighbour communications in a finite-element application, and it also turned out to reduce the total number of messages transferred. The vector distribution methods described in Section 4.7 are due to Bisseling and Meesen [33]; they improve on the method described in the original Mondriaan paper [304].

To assess the quality of the 2D bipartitioning function used in 2D sparse matrix partitioners, a subpackage MondriaanOpt [246] has been developed by Pelt and Bisseling, which produces an optimal partitioning (with provably lowest volume) for $p = 2$. Further improvement has been obtained by the Matrix Partitioner (MP) package by Knigge and Bisseling [185], which could solve (to optimality) 839 matrices out of 2833 from the SuiteSparse Matrix Collection [79].

An application of 2D sparse matrix partitioning to matrices originating in large scalefree graphs is presented by Boman, Devine, and Rajamanickam [39], who partition the symmetrized web link matrix uk-2005 with 1.6×10^9 nonzeros for 16 384 processor cores. They construct a 2D Cartesian distribution similar to Fig. 4.7 by first partitioning the vertices of the graph (i.e., the rows and columns of the matrix), and then assigning the nonzeros by looking at the matrix diagonal, as discussed in Section 4.4. This has the advantage that the total number of messages sent during fanout and fanin is at most $p(M + N - 2)$, instead of the general upper bound of $2p(p - 1)$ for an arbitrary distribution. The communication volume is reduced by using either a graph or hypergraph partitioning in the vertex partitioning phase.

Our approach to achieving an efficient parallel SpMV tries first to minimize the total communication volume in the matrix partitioning phase, and then to minimize the maximum send/receive volume per processor in the vector partitioning phase. The number of messages sent is ignored, assuming that their startup costs are accounted for by the global synchronization cost parameter l. For large p, however, the actual number of messages may be much lower than the assumed maximum number of messages $p(p-1)$ of an all-to-all superstep, which determines l. In the BSP context, this problem can be alleviated by using the hybrid-BSP model, see Section 4.10.

A different approach to achieving an efficient parallel SpMV, in the message-passing context, would be to minimize both the total communication volume and the total number of messages. This can be done in a single phase by using UMPa, a sequential hypergraph partitioner recently developed by Deveci *et al.* [83]. UMPa allows to choose a primary objective, for example communication volume or number of messages, and a secondary objective for breaking ties. It also allows to apply the chosen metric either as the total or the maximum over all the processors. To achieve this, it was necessary to add a direction to the hypergraphs: each net has a source vertex, representing a sender. UMPa is a direct p-way partitioner, which does not use recursive bipartitioning. Experimental results for UMPa show modest gains in the other metrics (10–20%), at the expense of a slight deterioration in the volume metric.

Acer, Selvitopi, and Aykanat [1] extend the fine-grain and medium-grain approaches, discussed in Section 4.6, to minimize both the total communication volume and the total number of messages. When bipartitioning, they add **message nets** to the regular nets, which are called **volume nets** by the authors. The aim of introducing the message nets is to penalize the creation of new messages. The communication cost of a message net is set at 50 times the cost of a volume net, reflecting the ratio α/β in eqn (1.19) between the startup cost of a message and the cost per data word. Furthermore, they add vertices representing the input and output vector components, so that the matrix and vector partitioning are carried out together in a single phase. The authors also treat the case distr($\mathbf{u}$) = distr($\mathbf{v}$), which they call **conformal partitioning**. In their partitioning taxonomy, the authors call the fine-grain and medium-grain approaches both **nonzero-based**. Numerical experiments using the hypergraph partitioner PaToH show a significant decrease in the number of messages, both for fine-grain and medium-grain, at the expense of an increase in total communication volume, eventually resulting in an average gain of 15% in actual runtime of a parallel SpMV from the PETSc package running on 512 processors. The medium-grain approach was found to perform slightly better than the fine-grain approach in both communication volume and number of messages and hence was used in the actual SpMV experiments.

....

4.14 EXERCISES

Exercise 4.1 Let A be a dense $m \times n$ matrix distributed by an $M \times N$ block distribution. Find a suitable distribution for the input and output vector of the dense matrix–vector multiplication $\mathbf{u} := A\mathbf{v}$; the input and output distributions can be chosen independently. Determine the BSP cost of the corresponding matrix–vector multiplication. What is the optimal ratio M/N and the BSP cost for this ratio?

Exercise 4.2 Find a distribution of a 12×12 grid for a BSP computer with $p = 8, g = 10$, and $l = 50$, such that the BSP cost of executing a 2D Laplacian operator is as low as possible. For the computation, we count five flops for an interior point, four flops for a boundary point that is not a corner point, and three flops for a corner point. Your distribution should be better than that of Fig. 4.27, which has a BSP cost of $89 + 14g + 2l = 329$ flops on this computer.

Exercise 4.3 ($*$) An $n \times n$ matrix A is **banded** with **lower bandwidth** $b_L \geq 0$ and **upper bandwidth** $b_U \geq 0$ if $a_{ij} = 0$ for $i > j + b_L$ and for $i < j - b_U$. Let $b_L = b_U = b$. The matrix A has a band of $2b + 1$ nonzero diagonals and hence it is sparse if b is small. Consider the multiplication of a banded matrix A and a vector $\mathbf{v}$ by Algorithm 4.5 using the 1D distribution $\phi(i) = i \operatorname{div}(n/p)$ for the matrix diagonal and the vectors, and a corresponding $M \times N$ Cartesian matrix distribution (ϕ_0, ϕ_1). For simplicity, assume that n is a multiple of p. Choosing M then completely determines the matrix distribution. (See also Example 4.5, where $n = 12, b = 1$, and $p = 4$.)

(a) Let $b = 1$, which means that A is tridiagonal. Show that the communication cost for the choice $M = p$ (i.e., a row distribution of the matrix) is lower than for the choice $M = \sqrt{p}$ (i.e., a square distribution).
(b) Let $b = n - 1$, which means that A is dense. Section 4.4 shows that now the communication cost for the choice $M = \sqrt{p}$ is lower than for $M = p$. We may conclude that for small bandwidth the choice $M = p$ is better, whereas for large bandwidth the choice $M = \sqrt{p}$ is better. Which value of b is the break-even point between the two methods?
(c) Implement Algorithm 4.5 for the specific case of band matrices. Drop the constraint on n and p. Choose a suitable data structure for the matrix: use an array instead of a sparse data structure.
(d) Run your program and obtain experimental values for the break-even point of b. Compare your results with the theoretical predictions.

Exercise 4.4 ($*$) Let A be a sparse $m \times m$ matrix and B a dense tall-and-skinny matrix of size $m \times n$, that is with $m \gg n$. Consider the matrix–matrix multiplication $C = AB$.

(a) What is the time complexity of a straightforward sequential algorithm?
(b) Choose distributions for A, B, and C, and formulate a corresponding parallel algorithm. Motivate your choice and discuss alternatives. Hint: draw a picture displaying the matrices A, B^T, and C in suitable positions.
(c) Analyse the time complexity of the parallel algorithm. How does the communication balance depend on the value of n? For what value of n would you consider switching to a different algorithm?
(d) Implement the algorithm. Measure the execution time for various values of m, n, and p. Explain the results.

Exercise 4.5 ($*$) The conjugate gradient (CG) algorithm by Hestenes and Stiefel [149] is an iterative algorithm for solving a symmetric positive definite linear system of equations $A\mathbf{x} = \mathbf{b}$. It is one of the Top-10 algorithms of the twentieth century, as proclaimed by *IEEE Computing in Science and Engineering* in January 2000 [91]. The

---

Algorithm 4.9 Sequential conjugate gradient algorithm.

---

input: A: sparse symmetric positive definite $n \times n$ matrix,
  $\mathbf{b}$: dense vector of length n.
output: $\mathbf{x}$: dense vector of length n, such that $A\mathbf{x} \approx \mathbf{b}$.

$\mathbf{x} := \mathbf{x}^0$;
$k := 0$;
$\mathbf{r} := \mathbf{b} - A\mathbf{x}$;
$\rho := \|\mathbf{r}\|^2$;
while $\sqrt{\rho} > \epsilon_{\mathrm{conv}} \|\mathbf{b}\| \wedge k < k_{\max}$ **do**
  if $k = 0$ **then**
    $\mathbf{p} := \mathbf{r}$;
  else
    $\beta := \rho / \rho_{\mathrm{old}}$;
    $\mathbf{p} := \mathbf{r} + \beta\mathbf{p}$;
  $\mathbf{w} := A\mathbf{p}$;
  $\gamma := \mathbf{p}^{\mathrm{T}}\mathbf{w}$;
  $\alpha := \rho / \gamma$;
  $\mathbf{x} := \mathbf{x} + \alpha\mathbf{p}$;
  $\mathbf{r} := \mathbf{r} - \alpha\mathbf{w}$;
  $\rho_{\mathrm{old}} := \rho$;
  $\rho := \|\mathbf{r}\|^2$;
  $k := k + 1$;

---

algorithm computes a sequence of approximations $\mathbf{x}^k, k = 0, 1, 2 \ldots$, that converges towards the solution $\mathbf{x}$. The algorithm is usually considered converged when $\|\mathbf{r}^k\| \leq \epsilon_{\mathrm{conv}} \|\mathbf{b}\|$, where $\mathbf{r}^k = \mathbf{b} - A\mathbf{x}^k$ is the residual. One can take, for example, $\epsilon_{\mathrm{conv}} = 10^{-12}$. A sequential (nonpreconditioned) CG algorithm is given as Algorithm 4.9. This algorithm is the basis for the High-Performance Conjugate-Gradient (HPCG) benchmark [89]. For more details and a proof of convergence, see Golub and Van Loan [124].

(a) Design a parallel CG algorithm based on the parallel SpMV of this chapter. How do you distribute the vectors $\mathbf{x}, \mathbf{r}, \mathbf{p}, \mathbf{w}$? Motivate your design choices. Analyse the time complexity.

(b) Implement your algorithm in a function bspcg, which uses bspmv for the SpMV and bspip from Chapter 1 for inner product computations.

(c) Write a test program that first generates a sparse $n \times n$ matrix B with a random sparsity pattern and random nonzero values in the interval $[-1, 1]$ and then turns B into a symmetric matrix $A = B + B^{\mathrm{T}} + \mu I_n$. Choose the scalar $\mu > 0$ sufficiently large to make A **strictly diagonally dominant**, that is, $|a_{ii}| > \sum_{j=0, j \neq i}^{n-1} |a_{ij}|$ for all i, and to make the diagonal elements a_{ii} positive. It can be shown that such a matrix is positive definite, which means that $\mathbf{x}^{\mathrm{T}} A\mathbf{x} > 0$, for all $\mathbf{x} \neq 0$. Use the Mondriaan partitioner with suitable options to distribute the matrix and the vectors.

(d) Experiment with your program and explain the results. Try different n and p and different nonzero densities. How does the run time of bspcg scale with p? What is the bottleneck? Does the number of iterations needed depend on the number of processors and the distribution?

Exercise 4.6 ($*$) Today, increasingly large volume images are created by high-resolution techniques such as 3D computed tomography and 3D fluorescence microscopy. A volume image typically contains $k \times k \times k$ voxels, where k can reach up to 4096. One form of processing a volume image is to label objects in the image by running a **connected components** algorithm. Consider a binary image, where each voxel is either white (has value 0) or black (value 1). Each maximal set of connected black voxels represents an object. (A set is **maximal** if it cannot be extended.) Two voxels **a** and **b** are **connected** if there exists a path of neighbouring black voxels from **a** to **b**. Here, we consider voxels as neighbours if they share a full face. Thus a voxel has at most six neighbours. (Voxels that only share an edge or a corner point merely touch one another, and are not considered neighbours.) The output of the algorithm is an assignment to each voxel of a label representing its component number.

(a) Design and implement a sequential algorithm that labels the objects in a $k \times k \times k$ image. One possible approach is first to build an auxiliary forest of segments. A **forest** is a set of trees. A **segment** is a set of consecutive black voxels in the same direction (e.g. the x-direction of the image). A child node in a tree points to a parent node if it is connected to that parent but has been numbered after that parent. The forest can then be used to construct the final labelling.

(b) Design and implement a parallel labelling algorithm. Use different distributions of the 3D array representing the image: slabs, piles, and cubes, obtained by cutting the image in one, two, and three directions, respectively. For the daring, try truncated octahedra as well.

(c) Compare the performance of the data distributions on a set of test images, which can either be obtained from publicly available repositories or created yourself by placing a large number of objects such as spheres in a 3D array, or by randomly assigning, with a certain probability, a binary value to each voxel.

Exercise 4.7 ($*$) In a typical molecular dynamics simulation, the movement of a large number of particles is followed for a long period of time. The aim is to gain insight into a physical process such as the folding of a protein in an aqueous solution. For an efficient parallel simulation, it is crucial to use a good data distribution, especially in three dimensions. We can base the data distribution on a suitable geometric partitioning of space, following [277].

Consider a simulation with a 3D simulation box of size $1.0 \times 1.0 \times 1.0$ containing n particles, spread homogeneously, which interact if their distance is less than a cut-off radius r_c, with $r_c \ll 1$, see Fig. 4.3. Assume that the box has periodic boundaries, meaning that a particle near a boundary interacts with particles near the opposite boundary; a particle that leaves the box at one boundary enters the box on the opposite boundary.

(a) Design a geometric distribution of the particles for $p = 2q^3$ processors based on the truncated octahedron, see Fig. 4.29. What is the difference with the case of the Laplacian operator on a 3D grid? For a given small value of r_c, how many nonlocal particles are expected to interact with the n/p local particles of a processor, in a first-order approximation? These neighbouring nonlocal particles form the **halo** of the local domain; their positions must be obtained by communication. Give the ratio between the number of halo particles and the number of local particles, which is proportional to the communication-to-computation ratio of a parallel simulation.

(b) Implement your distribution by writing a function that computes the processor responsible for a particle at location (x, y, z).

(c) Test your distribution function for a large ensemble of particles located at random positions in the box. Compare the corresponding ratio with the predicted ratio.

(d) Design a scaling procedure that transforms the cubic box to a suitable rectangular box to enable use of the distribution method for arbitrary even p. Hint: write $p = 2q_0 q_1 q_2$ where q_0, q_1, q_2 are integers with $q_0 \geq q_1 \geq q_2 \geq 1$. Give the corresponding particle ratio.

(e) How would you distribute the particles for $p = 8$? Surprise!

(f) Compare the output quality of the geometric distribution program to that of the distribution produced by running the Mondriaan partitioner in 1D mode for the matrix A defined by taking $a_{ij} \neq 0$ if and only if particles i and j interact. Use the option $\text{distr}(\mathbf{u}) = \text{distr}(\mathbf{v})$ in Mondriaan, and convert the output to a particle distribution by assigning particle i to the processor that owns u_i and v_i.

Exercise 4.8 ($**$) The sparse matrix partitioning methods of this chapter are heuristic in nature and they provide a good partitioning for large problems in a reasonable time. To assess the quality of a partitioning, however, we need to compare it to an optimal partitioning, which can be obtained by an **exact algorithm**. The optimal partitionings can be used as a quality benchmark, because they yield the minimum achievable communication volume for a specified maximum load imbalance. An exact algorithm can only handle relatively small problems. An example is the exact 2D sparse matrix bipartitioner MondriaanOpt [246], which is accompanied by an online data base of optimal 2-way partitionings for matrices from the SuiteSparse collection [79].

Here, we aim to develop a parallel k-way 1D sparse matrix partitioner, which we generalize by adding integer weights ω_j to the columns and integer costs γ_i to the rows. The partitioning is chosen to be by columns. The load balance criterion is

$$\max_{0 \leq t < k} \omega(A_t) \leq (1 + \epsilon) \frac{\omega(A)}{p}. \tag{4.72}$$

Here, $\omega(A_t)$ is the total weight of the matrix columns assigned to part t, and $\omega(A)$ is the total weight of all the matrix columns. The communication volume p_i caused by row i is multiplied by γ_i, to enable nonuniform row costs. We will run our partitioning on p processors, and do not require that $p = k$. With these definitions, we have a **parallel k-way hypergraph partitioner**, where the rows correspond to the nets of the hypergraph and the columns to the vertices. If we take $\omega_j = c_j$ (i.e., the number of nonzeros of column j) for all j, and $\gamma_i = 1$ for all i, the partitioning reduces to the sparse matrix partitioning we know. Note that if we choose ϵ too small, there may not be a feasible solution.

(a) Design and implement a sequential algorithm that partitions a sparse $m \times n$ matrix into k sets of columns satisfying the load imbalance constraint (4.72) and with guaranteed minimum communication volume in the corresponding SpMV with nonuniform row costs. Because of the strict demand for optimality, the algorithm should be based on some form of brute-force enumeration of all possible partitionings with selection of the best partitioning. Formulate the algorithm recursively, with the recursive task defined as assigning columns $j, \ldots, n-1$ to a part t, $0 \le t < k$.

(b) The assignment of columns $j = 0, 1, \ldots, n-1$ to k parts can be viewed as a k-ary computation tree. A node of the tree at depth j corresponds to an assignment of all columns up to and including column j to parts. The root of the tree, at depth 0, corresponds to an assignment of column 0 to part 0, which can be done without loss of generality. Each node at depth j with $j < n-1$ has k branches to children nodes, representing assignment of column $j+1$ to parts $0, 1, \ldots, k-1$, respectively. Nodes at depth $n-1$ are leaves, without children.

Accelerate the search for the best solution, that is, the best path to a leaf of the tree, by pruning part of the tree. For instance, when the imbalance exceeds ϵ after assigning a number of columns, further assignments can only make matters worse. Thus, there is no need to search the subtree corresponding to all possible assignments of the remaining columns. We may even take into account the total weight ω of the currently unassigned columns and exploit the fact that at least one part must be assigned a weight of at least $\lceil \omega/k \rceil$. A subtree can also be pruned when the number of communications incurred exceeds the minimum number found so far for a complete assignment of all columns. This pruning approach makes the search algorithm a so-called **branch-and-bound** method.

(c) Try to accelerate the search further by adding heuristics to the search method, such as choosing the branch to search first by some greedy criterion, or reordering the columns at the start of the algorithm by decreasing weight.

(d) Try to accelerate the search even further by sharpening the lower bound on the amount of communication that must be carried out. For instance, if all the assigned nonzeros of row i have been assigned to the same part t, then assigning the remaining nonzeros in row i without incurring additional communication would require assigning these nonzeros and their columns to part t. The weight of part t might then exceed the maximum allowed part weight. In that case, we would need an extra communication for row i.

(e) Compare the quality and computing time of your optimal partitioner to that of the 1D column partitioner of the Mondriaan package. What size of problems can you solve on your computer?

(f) From the $m \times n$ matrix A, create a fine-grain hypergraph, see Section 4.6, and in turn translate this hypergraph to a fine-grain matrix $F = F(A)$ of size $(m+n) \times nz(A)$, with one column per nonzero of A. The rth nonzero a_{ij} of A gives rise to two nonzeros $f_{ir} = 1$ and $f_{jr} = 1$ in F. ($F(A)$ can be viewed as an **incidence matrix**.) Partition this hypergraph optimally using your partitioner. Note that this approach provides a way of obtaining an optimal 2D sparse matrix partitioning for arbitrary (but small) k. Compare the quality and computing time of your optimal partitioner to that of MondriaanOpt, fixing the number of parts to $k = 2$.

(g) Parallelize your algorithm by assigning p disjoint subtrees of the computational tree to the p available processors. Organize your computation in supersteps, as we always do, synchronizing once in a while to exchange the best solution found so far to enable better pruning. If you are lucky, this might even lead to superlinear speedup compared to the sequential algorithm! (Why?) Methods for balancing the work load in such a situation will be discussed in detail in Section 5.7.

Exercise 4.9 ($\ast\ast$) Finding the best matrix distribution for a parallel SpMV $\mathbf{u} := A\mathbf{v}$ is a combinatorial optimization problem. It can be solved by recursive matrix partitioning using multilevel splitting (see Section 4.5) or optimal splitting by enumeration (see Exercise 4.8). We can also use the general-purpose combinatorial optimization method known as **simulated annealing** [182], which is based on the Metropolis algorithm [221]. This method simulates slow cooling of a liquid: the temperature is gradually lowered until the liquid freezes; at that point the molecules of the liquid lose their freedom to move and they line up to form crystals. If the liquid cools down slowly enough, the molecules have time to adapt to the changing temperature so that the final configuration will have the lowest possible energy.

(a) Implement the simulated annealing algorithm for parallel SpMV. Start with a random distribution ϕ of the matrix A. Write a sequential function that computes the corresponding communication volume V_ϕ, defined in eqn (4.14). For the purpose of optimization, take $V_\phi g/p$ as the communication cost and ignore the synchronization cost because it is either $2l$ or $4l$. Assume that the value of g is known. Try to improve the distribution by a sequence of moves, that is, assignments of a randomly chosen nonzero a_{ij} to a randomly chosen processor. A move is accepted if the BSP cost of the new distribution is lower than that of the old one. If, however, only cost decreases were allowed, the process could easily get stuck in a local minimum, and this will not always be a global minimum. Such a process would not be able to peek over the upcoming mountain ridge to see that there lies a deeper valley ahead. To escape from local minima, the method occasionally accepts an increase in cost. This is more likely at the beginning than at the end. Suppose we use as cost function the normalized cost C, that is, the BSP cost divided by $2nz(A)/p$. A move with cost increase ΔC is accepted with probability $e^{-\Delta C/T}$, where T is the current temperature of the annealing process. Write a sequential function that decides whether to accept a move with a given (positive or negative) cost increment ΔC.

(b) Write an efficient function that computes the cost increment for a given move. Note that simply computing the cost from scratch before and after the move and taking the difference is inefficient; this approach would be too slow for use inside a simulated annealing program, where many moves must be evaluated. Take care that updating the cost for a sequence of moves yields the same result as computing the cost from scratch. Hint: keep track of the contribution of each processor to the cost of the four supersteps of the SpMV.

(c) Put everything together and write a complete simulated annealing program. The main loop of your program should implement a **cooling schedule**, that is, a method for changing the temperature T during the course of the computation. Start with a temperature T_0 that is much larger than every possible increment ΔC to be encountered. Try a large number of moves at the initial temperature, for instance $p \cdot nz(A)$ moves, and then reduce the temperature, for example, to $T_1 = 0.99T_0$, thus making cost increases less likely to be accepted. Perform another round of moves, reduce the temperature further, and so on. Finding a good cooling schedule requires some trial and error.

(d) Compare the output quality and computing time of the simulated annealing program to that of the Mondriaan partitioner. Discuss the difference between the output distributions produced by the two programs.

Exercise 4.10 ($\ast\ast$) For C++ aficionados: port the program bspmv to C++ and Bulk [52], incorporating the hybrid-BSP SpMV algorithm given as Algorithm 4.8. Test your program on a hybrid shared/distributed-memory parallel computer, using C++17 threads as a Bulk backend for shared memory and MPI as a Bulk backend for distributed memory. (No need, however, to program directly using threads or MPI!) Partition your sparse test matrices by repeatedly applying Mondriaan with a suitable choice of ϵ, as described in Section 4.10.

5

Graph matching

5.1 The problem

People match with people all the time. Matchmakers endeavour to match people for the purpose of marriage, bringing suitable candidates together who look like a good match. The essence of matching is forming an exclusive pair, two persons that are matched to each other but not to anyone else. We are interested in the general weighted matching problem, where anyone can match with anyone, without restrictions, and where a positive weight expresses the mutual attraction of every candidate pair. Such weights have been considered for centuries in some form or another by matchmakers, a tradition that continues into modern times with online dating services. A good matchmaker considers not only the immediate preferences of every candidate, but also the interests of a community at large, perhaps leading to more and happier marriages. This can be expressed as maximizing the total weight of the matching.

Matching occurs not only in the romantic realm, but also elsewhere: human donor organs are matched with patients for transplants and students are matched with available places at universities for admissions. In 2012, a Nobel memorial prize in economics was awarded to Alvin Roth and Lloyd Shapley for their contributions to designing and implementing optimal matching processes, in particular for finding suitable kidney donors and for assigning medical-school graduates to residentships. This work was based on a seminal paper by Gale and Shapley [118] on the stable marriage problem and on research into applications by Roth [260].

The advent of social networks over the past decade and the associated flood of data becoming available to the curious network owners has led to an expansion of the field of **data analytics**, which tries to obtain knowledge from large amounts of raw unstructured data. Matching the people in a social network based on their friendships can help reveal communities of common interest, also called **clusters**. For the World Wide Web, with websites as nodes in the network, and hyperlinks connecting the websites, clustering based on repeatedly matching nodes with similar neighbour structure may help detect spam farms, groups of highly interconnected sites that merely exist to enhance the ranking of certain sites in web searches.

Parallel Scientific Computation: A Structured Approach Using BSP. Second Edition. Rob H. Bisseling,
Oxford University Press (2020). © Rob H. Bisseling.
DOI: 10.1093/oso/9780198788348.001.0001

We can formulate the matching problem more precisely. Assume that we have an **undirected graph** $\mathcal{G} = (\mathcal{V}, \mathcal{E})$, consisting of a set $\mathcal{V}$ of **vertices** (nodes) and a set $\mathcal{E}$ of **edges** (connections). An edge is a pair $e = (u, v)$ with $u, v \in \mathcal{V}$. Because the graph is undirected, we identify $(u, v) \equiv (v, u)$. Throughout this chapter, we assume that the graph is **simple**, meaning that it has no self-edges (hence $u \neq v$ for all $(u, v) \in \mathcal{E}$), and that at most one edge exists between the same pair of vertices. We also assume that the graph is **edge-weighted**, that is every edge $e = (u, v)$ has a weight $\omega(e) > 0$, which we also write as $\omega(u, v)$. As is common for graph algorithms, we will denote the number of vertices of the graph by $n = |\mathcal{V}|$, and the number of edges by $m = |\mathcal{E}|$.

A **matching** is a subset $\mathcal{M} \subseteq \mathcal{E}$ such that $(u, v) \in \mathcal{M}$ and $(u', v) \in \mathcal{M}$ implies $u = u'$. Thus, no two edges in the matching are incident to the same vertex v. The weight of a matching $\mathcal{M}$ is defined as

$$\omega(\mathcal{M}) = \sum_{e \in \mathcal{M}} \omega(e). \tag{5.1}$$

The problem we want to solve is finding a matching $\mathcal{M}$ with maximum possible weight $\omega(\mathcal{M})$; this is called the **edge-weighted maximum matching problem**. Figure 5.1 illustrates a maximum matching solution for a weighted cube graph. A matching with maximum possible edge weight is called a **maximum matching**. To confuse matters, there also exists the notion of **maximal matching**, which is a matching that cannot be extended by adding another edge. Every maximum matching is a maximal matching, but not vice versa. If all weights are equal, the problem reduces to the **maximum-cardinality problem**, finding as many matches as possible for the given graph.

We call a graph **bipartite** if the vertices can be split into two disjoint nonempty subsets $\mathcal{V}_0, \mathcal{V}_1$ such that all edges connect a vertex in $\mathcal{V}_0$ with a vertex in $\mathcal{V}_1$, i.e., $\mathcal{V}_0 \cup \mathcal{V}_1 = \mathcal{V}$, $\mathcal{V}_0 \cap \mathcal{V}_1 = \emptyset$, $\mathcal{V}_0 \neq \emptyset$, $\mathcal{V}_1 \neq \emptyset$, and $\mathcal{E} \subseteq \mathcal{V}_0 \times \mathcal{V}_1 = \{(v_0, v_1) : v_0 \in \mathcal{V}_0 \wedge v_1 \in \mathcal{V}_1\}$. An example is the situation where $\mathcal{V}_0$ represents organ donors and $\mathcal{V}_1$ patients. Bipartite graph matching is sometimes called the **assignment problem**; it is easier to solve than general

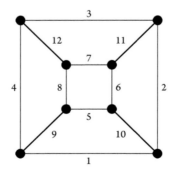

Figure 5.1 A maximum matching in the cube graph with eight vertices and twelve edges, with edge weights $1, 2, \ldots, 12$ as shown. The cube graph is depicted in planar form. Thick lines denote edges in the matching; thin lines denote edges outside the matching. All vertices are matched. The total weight of the matching is 42, which is optimal.

graph matching and it has numerous applications. Since we are interested in the general matching problem, where anyone can match with anyone, our graphs may be non-bipartite.

Matching also has applications in scientific computing. In sparse LU decomposition, every matrix row i is matched with exactly one matrix column j, such that a_{ij} is a good pivot (see also Section 2.2), i.e., a nonzero matrix element that has a sufficiently large absolute value and that preserves sparsity when used as a pivot. Here, the graph contains row vertices and column vertices, and the edges correspond to the nonzeros of the matrix. The graph is bipartite, with $\mathcal{V}_0$ containing the row vertices and $\mathcal{V}_1$ the column vertices. A **perfect matching** for an $n \times n$ matrix thus yields n matched pairs (i,j) and hence n mutually independent pivots a_{ij} (two pivots are **independent** if they do not occur in the same row or column). An example of this approach is the well-known MC64 subroutine by Duff and Koster from the HSL Mathematical Software Library [102].

Another example from scientific computing is the coarsening of a matrix in the multilevel method for sparse matrix partitioning, where pairs of similar columns are merged to reduce the size of the matrix (see Section 4.5). Columns j and j' can be merged if there exists at least one row i where both columns have a nonzero element (i.e., $a_{ij} \neq 0$ and $a_{ij'} \neq 0$), and we define the weight $\omega(j,j')$ of the column pair as the total number of such rows. A good matching will lead to highly similar columns being merged, ultimately resulting in a reduced communication volume for a parallel sparse matrix–vector multiplication (SpMV).

5.2 Sequential algorithm

From now on, we assume that the graph for which we are trying to find a matching is general, non-bipartite. The first choice we have to make is which sequential algorithm we are going to parallelize. We aim for Big Data sets, perhaps in the order of the number of people on Earth ($n = 10^{10}$). The number of friends, colleagues, or acquaintances each person has may vary, but a reasonable estimate is an average of about a thousand per person. If we matched everybody, this would mean matching in a graph with $n = 10^{10}$ vertices and $m = 10^{13}$ edges. Let us call this the **One-World matching problem**.

Surprisingly, despite all the different possibilities for matching, an optimal algorithm exists for general edge-weighted graph matching that runs in polynomial time. Gabow [117] designed an algorithm with time complexity $\mathcal{O}(mn + n^2 \log n)$ that provides a maximum-weight solution. Running this algorithm for the One-World problem, however, would require of the order of 10^{23} operations. Summit, ranked first on the TOP500 list (November 2019) [279] of supercomputers, runs at a speed of 2926 Tflop/s on the HPCG benchmark [89] solving a sparse linear system. This computer would need about a year to solve the One-World matching problem, assuming that graph computations and sparse matrix computations are equally fast. In principle, we can solve the One-World matching problem, but it is not very practical if we have to solve similar problems repeatedly. Furthermore, since the power consumption of Summit is 10.1 MWatt, it is doubtful whether one would want to spend the required large amount of energy on solving such a matching problem optimally.

Approximation algorithms provide problem solutions that differ at most by a guaranteed factor from the optimal solution. The hope here is to obtain solutions of good guaranteed quality within reasonable time. Note that heuristic algorithms have the same goal of providing good quality, but without the guarantee. An α-**approximation algorithm** for weighted matching gives a matching $\mathcal{M}$ with

$$\omega(\mathcal{M}) \geq \alpha \cdot \omega(\mathcal{M}^*), \tag{5.2}$$

where $\mathcal{M}^*$ denotes a maximum matching.

A family of algorithms that provide $1/2$-approximations for edge-weighted maximum matching is based on exploiting dominant edges. An edge (u, v) is **dominant** if $\omega(u, v) \geq \omega(e)$ for all edges e incident to u or v, as illustrated in Fig. 5.2(a). The basic dominant-edge algorithm is given as Algorithm 5.1.

Lemma 5.1 *Algorithm 5.1 yields a maximal matching.*

Proof Let $\mathcal{M}$ be the matching produced by Algorithm 5.1 and $\mathcal{E}$ the original edge set. Consider an edge $e \in \mathcal{E}$ to be added to $\mathcal{M}$. Since $e \notin \mathcal{M}$, it must have been removed by an edge (u, v) at some point during the algorithm. Then e must be incident to u or v and hence cannot be in the same matching as (u, v). Thus, the matching $\mathcal{M}$ cannot be extended. □

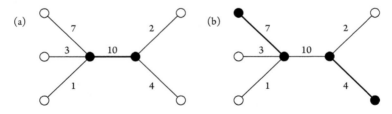

Figure 5.2 Two matchings in a graph with seven vertices and six edges. Black circles denote matched vertices; white circles denote unmatched vertices. (a) A maximal matching $\mathcal{M}$ consisting of one dominant edge with weight 10. (b) The unique maximum matching $\mathcal{M}^*$ of this graph with weight 11.

Algorithm 5.1 Basic dominant-edge algorithm [252].

input: $\mathcal{G}$: graph with vertex set V and edge set $\mathcal{E}$, $\mathcal{G} = (V, \mathcal{E})$.
output: $\mathcal{M}$: matching, $\mathcal{M} \subseteq \mathcal{E}$.

$\mathcal{M} := \emptyset$;
while $\mathcal{E} \neq \emptyset$ **do**
    pick a dominant edge $(u, v) \in \mathcal{E}$;
    $\mathcal{M} := \mathcal{M} \cup \{(u, v)\}$;
    $\mathcal{E} := \mathcal{E} \setminus \{(x, y) \in \mathcal{E} : x = u \vee x = v\}$;
    $V := V \setminus \{u, v\}$;
return $\mathcal{M}$;

Lemma 5.2 *Algorithm 5.1 is a $\frac{1}{2}$-approximation algorithm.*

Proof Let $\mathcal{M}$ be the matching produced by Algorithm 5.1, and let $\mathcal{M}^* = \{e_0^*,\ldots,e_{k-1}^*\}$ be a maximum matching with k edges. (An example is given by the matchings $\mathcal{M}$ and $\mathcal{M}^*$ in Fig. 5.2.) For each edge $e_i^* \in \mathcal{M}^*$, we define an edge e_i, as follows. If $e_i^* \in \mathcal{M}$, then $e_i = e_i^*$. Otherwise, let $e_i \in \mathcal{M}$ be the edge that removed e_i^* from $\mathcal{E}$ in Algorithm 5.1. This creates a list $e_0,\ldots,e_{k-1}$ of edges from $\mathcal{M}$. It may happen that $e_i = e_j$ for $i \neq j$, since several edges may be removed by the same edge in $\mathcal{M}$. However, at most two edges from $\mathcal{M}^*$ may be removed by the same edge in $\mathcal{M}$: e_i^* and e_j^* must be at opposite ends of the removing edge $e_i = e_j$, see Fig. 5.3, because otherwise they would share a vertex, and this is impossible because both are in the matching $\mathcal{M}^*$. As a consequence, an edge from $\mathcal{M}$ occurs at most twice in the list of the e_i, so that the total weight of the removing edges has an upper bound

$$\sum_{i=0}^{k-1} \omega(e_i) \leq 2\omega(\mathcal{M}). \tag{5.3}$$

It also holds that

$$\omega(e_i) \geq \omega(e_i^*), \text{ for } 0 \leq i < k, \tag{5.4}$$

because either $e_i = e_i^*$ or e_i is the dominant edge in the algorithm that removed e_i^*. Thus, we also obtain a lower bound on the weight of the removing edges,

$$\sum_{i=0}^{k-1} \omega(e_i) \geq \sum_{i=0}^{k-1} \omega(e_i^*) = \omega(\mathcal{M}^*). \tag{5.5}$$

Combining eqns (5.3) and (5.5) yields

$$\omega(\mathcal{M}) \geq \frac{1}{2}\omega(\mathcal{M}^*). \tag{5.6}$$

$\square$

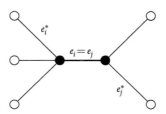

Figure 5.3 A dominant edge $e_i \in \mathcal{M}$ removes two edges, e_i^* and e_j^*, from the maximum matching $\mathcal{M}^*$, and three more edges as well.

Different matching algorithms with different time complexities can be designed starting from the basic dominant-edge algorithm, Algorithm 5.1. For example, if we first sort the edges by decreasing weight in $\mathcal{O}(m \log m)$ time, we can pick the current heaviest edge as the dominant edge, and then we can run the basic algorithm in linear time, $\mathcal{O}(m + n)$, giving a total time of $\mathcal{O}(m \log m + n) = \mathcal{O}(m \log n + n)$ (because $m = \mathcal{O}(n^2)$). This gives the **greedy matching algorithm**.

The first linear-time dominant-edge algorithm, called LAM, was presented by Preis in 1999 [252]. It does not require sorting, and hence the linear time complexity holds for the complete algorithm. It is based on a depth-first search, following paths in the graph of increasing weight. These paths may become very long, giving the algorithm a very nonlocal nature and thus making parallelization difficult.

The **local domination algorithm** by Manne and Bisseling [207], given as Algorithm 5.2, is a variant of Algorithm 5.1 where every vertex v has a current preference $pref(v)$, that is a neighbouring vertex u for which the weight $\omega(u, v)$ is highest, see Fig. 5.4. Domination is expressed by a mutual preference, $pref(pref(v)) = v$. To simplify our presentation, we want to avoid equal preferences (ties), which may complicate matters. To remove any chance of a tie, we will assume from now on that all edge weights are unique. Later we will relax this restriction, see Section 5.6 on tie-breaking.

Algorithm 5.2 computes a matching and stores it in a set $\mathcal{M}$, which initially is empty. The algorithm enters the vertices u, v of every encountered dominant edge (u, v) into a set D and removes them when they have been fully processed. Every vertex v has an adjacency set Adj_v which consists of all **adjacent vertices**, that is vertices connected to v by an edge. All the initial adjacency sets together correspond to the initial edge set $\mathcal{E}$ by

$$\mathcal{E} = \{(u, v) : v \in V \wedge u \in Adj_v\}. \tag{5.7}$$

The algorithm starts by setting the initial preferences and filling the set D. Matches are registered in $\mathcal{M}$ as they occur. The initial set D will have at least two vertices, as the overall heaviest edge will immediately be detected and its vertices included in D.

The main loop of the algorithm processes the matched vertices by removing each matched vertex v from the adjacency sets of its unmatched neighbours x. This may change the preference of x. The loop ends when D becomes empty, implying that for every unmatched vertex v, the adjacency set Adj_v must be empty.

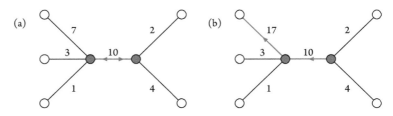

Figure 5.4 Preferences in two weighted graphs. A preference has been set for the red vertices; it is indicated by an arrow pointing to the preferred neighbour. The preferences in (a) are mutual; those in (b) are not.

Algorithm 5.2 Local domination algorithm [207].

input:	$\mathcal{G}$: graph with vertex set $\mathcal{V}$ and edge set $\mathcal{E}$, $\mathcal{G} = (\mathcal{V}, \mathcal{E})$.
output:	$\mathcal{M}$: matching, $\mathcal{M} \subseteq \mathcal{E}$.

$D := \emptyset;$
$\mathcal{M} := \emptyset;$
for all $v \in \mathcal{V}$ **do**
    $pref(v) := $ **nil**;

{ Find initial dominant edges }
for all $v \in \mathcal{V}$ **do**
    $Adj_v := \{u \in \mathcal{V} : (u,v) \in \mathcal{E}\};$
    if $Adj_v \neq \emptyset$ **then**
        $pref(v) := \text{argmax}\{\omega(u,v) : u \in Adj_v\};$
        if $pref(pref(v)) = v$ **then**
            $D := D \cup \{v, pref(v)\};$
            $\mathcal{M} := \mathcal{M} \cup \{(v, pref(v))\};$

{ Process matched vertices }
while $D \neq \emptyset$ **do**
    pick a vertex $v \in D;$
    $D := D \setminus \{v\};$
    for all $x \in Adj_v : (x, pref(x)) \notin \mathcal{M}$ **do**
        $Adj_x := Adj_x \setminus \{v\};$
        if $Adj_x \neq \emptyset$ **then**
            $pref(x) := \text{argmax}\{\omega(x,y) : y \in Adj_x\};$
            if $pref(pref(x)) = x$ **then**
                $D := D \cup \{x, pref(x)\};$
                $\mathcal{M} := \mathcal{M} \cup \{(x, pref(x))\};$
        else
            $pref(x) := $ **nil**;

Setting a new preference can be viewed as **proposing**, where the expressed preference is a proposal that remains valid until rejection. A proposal from a vertex x to a vertex $y = pref(x)$ becomes accepted at the moment y also proposes to x. A proposal from x to y becomes rejected at the moment vertex y is picked from D and processed and it turns out that $pref(y) \neq x$. This happens after y has matched to $pref(y)$, but not necessarily immediately.

Since setting a preference and examining whether a preference is mutual are local operations involving only a vertex and its neighbours, Algorithm 5.2 is a good basis for parallelization, provided that in most cases neighbouring vertices reside on the same processor. A good data partitioning will ensure this.

5.3 Suitors and sorting

To implement the local domination algorithm efficiently, we will have to choose a suitable data structure for storing all the data of the graph. In this section, we will design such a data structure and also refine the algorithm, improving the efficiency along the way. The input of the matching problem to be solved is given as a set of n vertices $v_0, \ldots, v_{n-1}$ and m undirected edges $e_0, \ldots, e_{m-1}$.

The information stored on input for an edge $e = (v_i, v_j)$ is:

- $\omega(e)$, the weight of the edge.

The information stored for a vertex v is tailored to facilitate the matching process, and it contains:

- $pref(v)$, the preferred partner, which is the neighbouring vertex still available with the highest connecting edge weight;
- $suitor(v)$, the **suitor**, i.e., the neighbouring vertex with the highest edge weight that prefers v.

These values may be **nil**, meaning there is no preference set by v, or no suitor has expressed an interest yet in v, in the respective cases. A vertex can have only one preference, and only one suitor. Note that

$$\omega(v, pref(v)) \geq \omega(v, suitor(v)) \tag{5.8}$$

if both the preference and the suitor of v have been set, because otherwise the suitor of v would be a better candidate than the preferred choice of v. Initially, all the preference and suitor values are **nil**. By convention, we define $\omega(u, v) = 0$ if $u = $ **nil** or $v = $ **nil**. This saves some checks for special cases in our program texts. Manne and Halappanavar [208] first proposed the use of a suitor in a shared-memory parallel matching algorithm based on local domination.

To exploit the suitor value, a vertex v that sets its preference to $u = pref(v)$ should make sure that the preference will not immediately be rejected, that is u must satisfy $\omega(u, v) > \omega(u, suitor(u))$ (by assumption, ties cannot occur). Otherwise, u will prefer $suitor(u)$ or an even better future suitor, so that it will never match with v. Figure 5.5 illustrates the case where u also prefers v and is already the suitor of v, which results in a match. Figure 5.6 illustrates the case where u had a suitor x with a lower weight $\omega(u, x)$, so that the edge (u, x) will be removed and x will have to set a new preference.

The case that vertex v wants to set its preference to u but u already has a better suitor causes an immediate rejection, which means that the edge (u, v) can be removed from the problem, or in other words, it will be declared dead. Once an edge becomes dead, it remains dead! Vertex v will try again, until it has set its preference or runs out of eligible neighbours.

An advantage of looking for a new preference that cannot be immediately rejected is that we need not store $pref(v)$ explicitly. Since only one vertex v can have a preference set for a vertex u, we have that $pref(v) = u$ if and only if $suitor(u) = v$. This advantage only holds

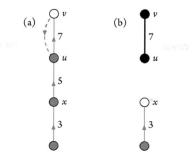

Figure 5.5 Setting a new preference u for a vertex v where the preference is mutual and v matches with u. The dashed arrow gives the new preference. Red circles denote vertices with a set preference. Black circles denote matched vertices. Each solid arrow points from a red vertex to its current preferred neighbour, for example u already prefers v. Vertex x loses its preference by the match. (a) Before the match; (b) afterwards.

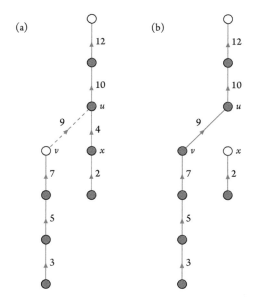

Figure 5.6 Setting a new preference u for a vertex v where the preference is not mutual. Vertex v becomes the new suitor of u, replacing the previous suitor x. The dashed arrow gives the new preference. Red circles denote vertices with a set preference. Each solid arrow points from a red vertex to its current preferred neighbour. (a) Before setting; (b) afterwards.

for a sequential algorithm, where information about possible immediate rejection is readily available. In the parallel case, this information may reside elsewhere.

Algorithm 5.3 gives a local domination algorithm which repeatedly picks a vertex and sets its preference. For each vertex v picked, the algorithm first removes its **dead edges**, that is edges connected to v that cannot be matched anymore or that were already matched to other vertices. After that, the algorithm finds the preference of v. The details of the function FindAlive are given in Algorithm 5.4, those of FindSplitter in Algorithm 5.5, and those of FindPref in Algorithm 5.6; all functions will be discussed later on.

In Algorithm 5.3, the set Q denotes the current set of unmatched but still matchable vertices without a preference. The set D of dominant vertices from Algorithm 5.2 is not needed anymore as all actions required upon finding a match are performed immediately and the required preference resets are entered into Q. In an implementation, Q can be represented by a list of vertex numbers. The list changes, as vertices are added and deleted, and it can be implemented as a **queue** (hence its name) following the First In, First Out (FIFO) principle, or as a **stack**, following Last In, First Out (LIFO). The size of Q either decreases from one iteration to the next, or it stays the same. There is freedom in the order of picking vertices from Q. One can start with a round of setting preferences for all vertices from the initial set V, as in Algorithm 5.2, but other orderings are possible.

In Algorithm 5.3, the adjacency set Adj_v of vertex v is implemented as an array of length d_v representing the edges of v, where d_v is the **degree** of v, that is its number of neighbours. This array is commonly called the **adjacency list** of v. The list simply contains the indices k of the edges e_k connected to v. One way of looking at this is that the adjacency list corresponds to a matrix row in the compressed row storage (CRS) scheme for sparse matrices, see Section 4.2: each edge (v_i, v_j) is represented twice, once corresponding to a nonzero a_{ij} in row i (the list of vertex v_i) and once corresponding to a_{ji} in row j (the list of vertex v_j).

The required adjacency lists can be constructed by sorting the nonzeros corresponding to the edges by row, in the same way as CRS is created. Because this sort is by index, with a limited range from 0 to $n - 1$, a **counting sort** can be used here: in a first pass through the nonzeros, we count the number of nonzeros in each row, and then we determine the start and end of the space needed for each row; in a second pass, we place the nonzeros in the space corresponding to their row. This takes $\mathcal{O}(m + n)$ time for all vertices of the graph, which is cheap since the input size is also $\mathcal{O}(m + n)$. The n adjacency lists for all the vertices can be stored together in one large array of length $2m$, as each edge is represented twice.

Adjacency lists can only shrink, since Algorithm 5.3 only deletes edges from a list, and never adds an edge. The easiest way to delete an edge is to use a boolean array $alive$ of length m, initially all **true**, to keep track of whether an edge is still alive. The value is changed to **false** when an edge is deleted. For an index k of an edge $e_k = (u, v)$ contained somewhere in the adjacency list of a vertex v, we can find out whether it represents a living edge by inspecting $alive(e_k)$, also written as $alive(u, v)$, and furthermore by checking whether $d_u > 0$. If $d_u = 0$ and $u \neq suitor(v)$, then the edge (u, v) is dead because u will never set a preference again, and its preference is not v. If $d_u = 0$ and $u = suitor(v)$, then the edge is still alive, because v can still set its preference to u so that we would have a match. The checks can be carried out irrespective of the ordering of the indices in the adjacency list.

Internally, the adjacency list of a vertex could remain unordered, but for the matching application we can benefit from partially sorting the list by increasing weight to help find a preference quickly. Note that we cannot use a counting sort here, because the weights can have in principle an unlimited range. The partial sort is expressed by using splitters that split

Algorithm 5.3 Local domination algorithm with suitor improvement and partial sorting.

input: $\mathcal{G}$: graph with vertex set $\mathcal{V}$ and edge set $\mathcal{E}$, $\mathcal{G} = (\mathcal{V}, \mathcal{E})$,
d: array of length n storing the vertex degrees,
Adj_v: adjacency list of length d_v containing neighbouring edges of v,
for all v.
output: $\mathcal{M}$: matching, $\mathcal{M} \subseteq \mathcal{E}$.

```
{ Initialize arrays }
for all v ∈ V do
    suitor(v) := nil;
    splitter_v(*) := false;
for all e ∈ E do
    alive(e) := true;

{ Set preferences and match }
M := ∅;
Q := V;
while Q ≠ ∅ do
    pick a vertex v ∈ Q;
    Q := Q \ {v};
    FindAlive(v, Adj_v, ω, alive, suitor, d);
    r := FindSplitter(v, Adj_v, ω, alive, splitter_v, suitor, d);

    { Set preference for v }
    if d_v > 0 then
        (u, v) := FindPref(Adj_v, ω, r, d_v − 1);
        d_v := d_v − 1;
        x := suitor(u);
        suitor(u) := v;
        if x ≠ nil then
            Q := Q ∪ {x};
            alive(u, x) := false;
        if u = suitor(v) then
            M := M ∪ {(u, v)};
            d_v := 0;
            d_u := 0;

    { Split adjacency list of v in range [r, d_v − 1] for future use }
    if r < d_v then
        SplitAdj(Adj_v, ω, splitter_v, r, d_v − 1);
```

the array into smaller pieces, similar to the splitters of the quicksort algorithm, see eqn (1.11) and Example 1.1. In this chapter, however, we call an index r a **splitter** of the array x if

$$x_i < x_j \text{ for } i < r \leq j. \tag{5.9}$$

The value x_r itself does not matter here, as our aim is not necessarily to sort the values, but to identify a range starting at index r where the maximum value of x can be found. Furthermore, because we assume there are no ties, we have strict inequality between the values.

Associated with the array Adj_v, we use a boolean array $splitter_v$ of length d_v to indicate whether an index is a splitter or not. If we define an array x by

$$x[i] = \omega(e_{Adj_v[i]}), \text{ for } 0 \leq i < d_v, \tag{5.10}$$

then x gives the weights of the neighbouring edges of v in the same order as that of the edges. The boolean $splitter_v[r]$ is **true** if and only if r is a splitter of array x. To find the edge with the highest weight, we only need to consider edges $e_{Adj[i]}$ with $i \geq r$, where r is the largest splitter, except if all these edges are dead.

Algorithm 5.4 finds the living edge with the highest index adjacent to a vertex v. Along the way, it removes dead edges from the adjacency list Adj_v, thus shortening the list to a new length d_v, to speed up future use. The main loop of the algorithm starts at the last position $d_v - 1$ in the adjacency list, and runs downwards until it finds a living edge. If an edge (u, v) is encountered with $d_u = 0$ and $suitor(v) \neq u$, or with u having a better suitor, then (u, v) is declared dead, as v will never match with u, and d_v is decremented.

Algorithm 5.5 is similar to Algorithm 5.4. It returns the starting point r of a range $[r, d_v - 1]$ to search for the heaviest edge connected to v. This starting point is the highest splitter i below or equal to the index of the highest living edge, if such a splitter exists, and the start of the list otherwise.

Algorithm 5.6 straightforwardly finds the preference of a vertex, that is the heaviest neighbouring edge, by searching a range $[lo, hi]$, where $lo = r$ and $hi = d_v - 1$; this is faster than searching the whole range $[0, d_v - 1]$. This algorithm also swaps the preference into the last position of the range, so it can easily be removed from the list by decrementing d_v.

To accelerate future searches for a preference of the same vertex, a nonempty range $[r, d_v - 1]$ without a splitter can be split into two parts by Algorithm 1.3 (from the quicksort example in Chapter 1), the lower part representing the edges with weight below that of a randomly chosen new splitter, and the upper part representing the edges with an equal or higher weight. The correspondence of the values in Algorithm 1.3 to the edge weights of the adjacency list is given by eqn (5.10), where the notations x_i and $x[i]$ denote the same. The index i returned by the split function is used to set $splitter_v[i] :=$ **true**. In our algorithms, we will call this variant of the Split function 'SplitAdj'.

The computation cost of the complete sequential matching algorithm can be determined as follows. The initializations of Algorithm 5.3 cost $\mathcal{O}(m + n)$ and the other operations, excluding the function calls, also cost $\mathcal{O}(m + n)$ since in each iteration of the main loop, either a vertex v is removed from Q and no vertex is put back, or a vertex x is put back but then also a living edge (u, x) is killed. Therefore, the total number of iterations is at most $m + n$.

Algorithm 5.4 Finding the highest living edge in an adjacency list.

---

input: v: a vertex,

        Adj: its adjacency list of length d_v containing neighbouring edges,

        ω: array storing edge weights,

        alive: boolean array stating whether edges are alive,

        suitor: array giving the suitor of each vertex,

        d: array storing the vertex degrees.

output: The living edge $e_{Adj[i]}$ with highest index i.

    function FINDALIVE$(v, Adj, \omega, alive, suitor, d)$

        for $i := d_v - 1$ **to** 0 **step** -1 **do**

           $(u, v) := e_{Adj[i]}$;

           if $(d_u = 0 \wedge suitor(v) \neq u) \vee \omega(u, suitor(u)) > \omega(u, v)$ **then**

               $alive(u, v) := $ **false**;

        if $alive(u, v)$ **then**

           return;

        else

           $d_v := d_v - 1$;

The range splitting of the function SplitAdj based on Algorithm 1.3 is the workhorse of the quicksort algorithm, Algorithm 1.2, which chooses a random splitter, splits the data into a lower and upper part and recursively splits these parts again. Here, we may have to split the upper part again, since we are interested in finding the highest weight, but we only split the lower part if this becomes necessary later on in the algorithm; hopefully, this will never happen. Thus, the sorting is only **partial**. In the worst case, we perform a full quicksort for every vertex v, with an expected cost of $d_v \log_2 d_v$ operations. The expected total time for the fully sorted case is of order

$$\sum_v d_v \log_2 d_v \leq \sum_v d_v \log_2 \Delta = 2m \log_2 \Delta, \tag{5.11}$$

where $\Delta = \max_v d_v$, the maximum vertex degree. This equation follows because every edge is counted twice when adding all the vertex degrees. Nevertheless, since we only need the highest weight, we may be lucky and never need to access any lower parts. In that favourable case, the expected time for vertex v will be about $d_v + d_v/2 + d_v/4 + \cdots + 1 \approx 2d_v$, so that the expected total time is about

$$\sum_v 2d_v = 4m. \tag{5.12}$$

Here, we make the implicit assumption that the splitters are perfect, so that each split halves the range. The time of the other parts of the preference-finding algorithm, namely finding the highest living edge, the highest splitter, and the heaviest edge in Algorithms 5.4–5.6, is

---

Algorithm 5.5 Finding the highest splitter in an adjacency list.

---

input: Same parameters as for Algorithm 5.4,
with additional boolean array *splitter* used for marking splitters.
$d_v > 0$, $alive[Adj[d_v - 1]]$.

output: The function returns the starting point $r \geq 0$ of a range $[r, d_v - 1]$.
All edges $e_{Adj[i]}$ with i in the range are alive.
One of these is the heaviest edge connected to v.

function FINDSPLITTER($v, Adj, \omega, alive, splitter, suitor, d$)

    for $i := d_v - 1$ **to** 0 **step** -1 **do**
      $(u, v) := e_{Adj[i]}$;
      if $(d_u = 0 \land suitor(v) \neq u) \lor \omega(u, suitor(u)) > \omega(u, v)$ **then**
        $alive(u, v) := \textbf{false}$;

      if not $alive(u, v)$ **then**
        $Adj[i] := Adj[d_v - 1]$;
        $d_v := d_v - 1$;
      if $splitter[i]$ **then**
        return i;

    return 0;

Algorithm 5.6 Finding the preference of a vertex in its adjacency list.

---

input: array Adj of length d, interval $[lo, hi]$ with $0 \leq lo \leq hi < d$.
output: The preferred edge is returned and moved to the end of Adj.

function FINDPREF(Adj, ω, lo, hi)

    $\omega_{max} := -\infty$;
    for $i := lo$ **to** hi **do**
      if $\omega(e_{Adj[i]}) > \omega_{max}$ **then**
        $i_{max} := i$;
        $\omega_{max} := \omega(e_{Adj[i]})$;
    $swap(Adj[i_{max}], Adj[hi])$;
    return $e_{Adj[hi]}$;

---

of the same order as that of the partial sorting. For the total time, we hope to attain the best case time complexity of $\mathcal{O}(m+n)$ operations, and we have a worst case of $\mathcal{O}(m\log\Delta + n)$. Practice will show whether our hopes will come true, see the operation counts for the experiments of Section 5.10.

5.4 Parallel algorithm

In the previous section, we have obtained a fast sequential algorithm that can in principle be parallelized because it is based on local domination, a property that can be checked for an edge by just checking its neighbouring edges. If we partition our data such that neighbouring vertices and edges often reside on the same processor, the check will in most cases be local to the processor and will hence avoid communication.

Let us assume that we have a given p-**way vertex partitioning**, where the vertex set $\mathcal{V}$ has been split into p disjoint nonempty subsets $\mathcal{V}_0, \ldots, \mathcal{V}_{p-1}$ such that

$$\mathcal{V} = \bigcup_{s=0}^{p-1} \mathcal{V}_s. \tag{5.13}$$

We denote the processor number of vertex v by $\phi(v)$. We also assume that the adjacency list Adj_v of a vertex v is stored on the same processor as v, i.e., on $P(\phi(v))$. Since every edge occurs in two adjacency lists, this means that every edge (and its weight) is stored twice, and in a good partitioning the two occurrences will often (but not always) be on the same processor. Note that we could also have chosen a more general edge partitioning where edges can be assigned to any processor, potentially reducing the communication volume, but also leading to more complicated parallel algorithms. In terms of the adjacency matrix A of the graph, with edge (i,j) represented by nonzeros a_{ij} and a_{ji}, a vertex partitioning leads to a one-dimensional (1D) row distribution of the matrix A, whereas an edge partitioning would lead to a two-dimensional (2D) distribution. Edge partitioning has many advantages, as shown in Chapter 4 for the corresponding case of sparse matrices. We will start with a vertex partitioning for the sake of simplicity; Section 5.8 presents an approach based on edge partitioning.

The **halo** of a processor is the set of data surrounding the processor that interacts directly with the processor, hence necessitating communication. The name comes from the halo that surrounds sacred persons in certain religious paintings. For our graph partitioning, the halo $\mathcal{H}_s$ of processor $P(s)$ is defined as the set of vertices

$$\mathcal{H}_s = \left(\bigcup_{v \in \mathcal{V}_s} Adj_v \right) \setminus \mathcal{V}_s. \tag{5.14}$$

The size of the set $\mathcal{H}_s$ depends on the partitioning: for a good partitioning, the size is relatively small, but for a random partitioning, it may be large and this will cause a parallel matching algorithm to perform mainly communication.

We define the set of edges of processor $P(s)$ by

$$\mathcal{E}_s = \{(u,v) \in \mathcal{E} : v \in \mathcal{V}_s\}, \tag{5.15}$$

so that we include **internal edges** (with both ends in $\mathcal{V}_s$) as well as **external edges** (with one end in $\mathcal{V}_s$ and one in $\mathcal{H}_s$, also called **cut edges** or **halo edges**). The set $\mathcal{E}_s$ corresponds to all the edges stored in the adjacency lists of processor $P(s)$. Figure 5.7 shows the halo vertices and cut edges of a partitioned graph.

Algorithm 5.7 presents the parallel local domination algorithm for a graph with vertices distributed over p processors. On input, each processor has the local vertex set $\mathcal{V}_s$ and the local edge set $\mathcal{E}_s$. (This implies that each cut edge is stored twice, that is on both processors that hold an endpoint.) On output, each processor locally contains a set of registered matches $\mathcal{M}_s \subseteq \mathcal{E}_s$. A match (u,v) will be registered twice if $u \in \mathcal{V}_s$ and $v \in \mathcal{V}_t$ where $s \neq t$.

The algorithm proceeds in a sequence of rounds, each consisting of computation followed by communication. The computation starts by processing the contents of messages received in the previous round, which are stored in a local receive buffer R_s, and then setting preferences for all vertices in the local work queue Q_s until it is depleted, similar to what happens in the sequential algorithm, Algorithm 5.3. The main difference is that a preferred vertex u may not reside on the same processor, and this leads to an explicit proposal to be sent to $P(\phi(u))$ at the end of the round, in the communication phase. Another difference is that a suitor x who is replaced by a better suitor may also reside on another processor, and hence needs to be told about this, necessitating a rejection message to $P(\phi(x))$. Whether such a vertex x resides on the same processor is easily checked by a test '$x \in \mathcal{V}_s$'. Otherwise, we know that $x \in \mathcal{H}_s$.

Since communication may be incurred from anywhere within a round, it becomes difficult to separate computation from communication in the program text of the algorithm,

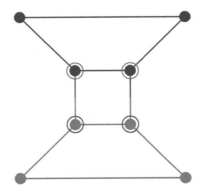

Figure 5.7 A graph with eight vertices and ten edges, partitioned into $p = 2$ parts. The vertices of $P(0)$ are shown in red and those of $P(1)$ in blue. The halo vertices of $P(0)$ are shown in blue with a red enclosing circle. The internal edges of $P(0)$ are shown in red; those of $P(1)$ in blue. External edges are displayed as a pair of red/blue half-edges.

and to distinguish between computation supersteps and communication supersteps. The natural separation of computation from communication that we encountered for instance in LU decomposition, fast Fourier transform, or even sparse matrix–vector multiplication does not occur here. Therefore, we will consider the complete round as one mixed superstep, where computation and communication can be mixed freely, and where the communication is actually carried out at the **Sync**-statement ending the round.

The possibility to mix computation and communication is one of the strongest points of BSP algorithms for graph computations, because we have the convenience of initiating communication from anywhere in the algorithm, and still achieve a superstep structure by assuming delayed communication executed at the next synchronization. This structure helps us in thinking about algorithms, and it facilitates analysing their time complexity and proving their correctness. One-sided communication as provided by BSP is the basis for the ability to send data from anywhere in a program text. Think of the difficulties we would face if we wanted to use two-sided communication and we had to match send-statements hidden somewhere with receive-statements hidden somewhere else!

The algorithm terminates when all processors have an empty receive buffer R_s and an empty work queue Q_s. Received messages can give rise to new work, hence we have to make sure both R_s and Q_s are empty when declaring the local work done. Termination is expressed in a boolean variable **done**, which is true if all local booleans **done**$_s$ are true. This can be checked without requiring extra synchronization by broadcasting the local booleans once every superstep. Note that it is important to terminate all the processors at the same time, so that they carry out the same number of supersteps.

In the parallel algorithm, as in life, it may be useful to remember to whom you proposed, just in case you get an answer back. That is why we reintroduce the variable *pref*, to express the preference of a vertex. (In the sequential algorithm, we have full information available and the variable *suitor* is all we need; in the parallel case, we possess only local information).

Algorithm 5.8 displays the processing of received messages. The messages have been sent in the previous superstep, and are now stored in the message buffer R_s. A message can give rise to a variety of actions, including sending a new message. Such a message will, however, only be sent at the next synchronization, that is at the end of the current superstep.

There are three types of messages: proposals, acceptances, and rejections. In case the message *msg* entails a proposal from u to v, it is determined whether u dislodges another suitor x. If so, x is placed back in the queue (for a local x), or a rejection message is sent (for a nonlocal x).

If a proposal comes from a nonlocal vertex u that is the preferred vertex of the local vertex v, this means that v must have set the preference and proposed to u in the previous superstep. This cannot have happened in the present superstep, because new preferences to vertices are only set in the main algorithm, Algorithm 5.7, not in Algorithm 5.8. It also cannot have happened earlier than in the previous superstep, because then u would simply have sent an acceptance message. This implies that both proposals have been sent in the same superstep. Therefore, v can accept u and we have a match. Since u is in the same situation, no acceptance message needs to be sent to u. The previous suitor is then rejected, using the function RejectSuitor, presented in Algorithm 5.9.

Algorithm 5.7 Parallel local domination algorithm for $P(s)$.

---

input: $\mathcal{G}$: graph with vertex set $\mathcal{V}$ and edge set $\mathcal{E}$, $\mathcal{G} = (\mathcal{V}, \mathcal{E})$, distr$(\mathcal{V}) = \phi$,
       d: array of length $|\mathcal{V}_s|$ storing the vertex degrees,
       Adj_v: adjacency list of length d_v containing neighbouring edges of v,
       for all $v \in \mathcal{V}_s$.
output: $\mathcal{M}$: matching, $\mathcal{M} \subseteq \mathcal{E}$, $\mathcal{M} = \cup_{t=0}^{p-1} \mathcal{M}_t$.

  for all $v \in \mathcal{V}_s$ **do**
    $suitor(v) := $ **nil**; $pref(v) := $ **nil**; $splitter_v(*) := $ **false**;
  for all $e \in \mathcal{E}_s$ **do**
    $alive(e) := $ **true**;
  $\mathcal{M}_s := \emptyset$; $R_s := \emptyset$; $Q_s := \mathcal{V}_s$;

  done := false;
  while not done do
    done$_s := (R_s = \emptyset \wedge Q_s = \emptyset)$;
    put **done**$_s$ in $P(*)$;
    ProcessReceivedMessages$(R_s, Q_s, \mathcal{M}_s, \mathcal{V}_s, \omega, alive, suitor, pref, d)$;
    while $Q_s \neq \emptyset$ **do**
      pick a vertex $v \in Q_s$;
      $Q_s := Q_s \setminus \{v\}$;
      FindAlive$(v, Adj_v, \omega, alive, suitor, d)$;
      $r := $ FindSplitter$(v, Adj_v, \omega, alive, splitter_v, suitor, d)$;

      if $d_v > 0$ **then**
        $(u, v) := $ FindPref$(Adj_v, \omega, r, d_v - 1)$;   ▷ Set preference for v
        $d_v := d_v - 1$;
        $pref(v) := u$;

        if $u = suitor(v)$ **then**   ▷ Register a match or propose
          $\mathcal{M}_s := \mathcal{M}_s \cup \{(u, v)\}$;
          $d_v := 0$;
          if $u \in \mathcal{V}_s$ **then**
            $d_u := 0$;
          else
            put accept(v, u) in $P(\phi(u))$;
        else if $u \notin \mathcal{V}_s$ **then**
          put propose(v, u) in $P(\phi(u))$;

        if $u \in \mathcal{V}_s$ **then**   ▷ Replace the previous suitor
          $x := suitor(u)$;
          $suitor(u) := v$;
          RejectSuitor$(u, x, Q_s, \mathcal{V}_s, alive, pref)$;

        if $r < d_v$ **then**   ▷ Split the adjacency list
          SplitAdj$(Adj_v, \omega, splitter_v, r, d_v - 1)$;
    Sync;
    done := $\bigwedge_{t=0}^{p-1}$ **done**$_t$;

Algorithm 5.8 Processing received messages.

input: R_s: buffer containing messages received by $P(s)$,
          Q_s: queue of vertices without a preference of $P(s)$,
          $\mathcal{M}_s$: set of registered matches of $P(s)$,
          $\mathcal{V}_s$: set of local vertices of $P(s)$.
output: All messages have been processed, $R_s = \emptyset$.

function PROCESSRECEIVEDMESSAGES$(R_s, Q_s, \mathcal{M}_s, \mathcal{V}_s, \omega, alive, suitor, pref, d)$

  while $R_s \neq \emptyset$ **do**
    pick a message $msg \in R_s$;
    $R_s := R_s \setminus \{msg\}$;

    if $msg = \text{propose}(u, v)$ **then** $\{ u$ proposes to $v \}$
      $\{$ Register a match $\}$
      if $u = pref(v)$ **then**
        $\mathcal{M}_s := \mathcal{M}_s \cup \{(u, v)\}$;
        $d_v := 0$;

      $\{$ Assign new suitor $\}$
      $x := suitor(v)$;
      if $\omega(u, v) > \omega(x, v)$ **then**
        $suitor(v) := u$;
        RejectSuitor$(v, x, Q_s, \mathcal{V}_s, alive, pref)$
      else
        put reject(v, u) in $P(\phi(u))$;
        $alive(u, v) := \textbf{false}$;

    else if $msg = \text{accept}(u, v)$ **then** $\{ u$ accepts $v \}$
      $\mathcal{M}_s := \mathcal{M}_s \cup \{(u, v)\}$;
      $d_v := 0$;
      $x := suitor(v)$;
      $suitor(v) := u$;
      RejectSuitor$(v, x, Q_s, \mathcal{V}_s, alive, pref)$;

    else if $msg = \text{reject}(u, v)$ **then** $\{ u$ rejects $v \}$
      $Q_s := Q_s \cup \{v\}$;
      $pref(v) := \textbf{nil}$;
      $alive(u, v) := \textbf{false}$;

Algorithm 5.9 Vertex v rejects suitor x.

---

function REJECTSUITOR$(v, x, Q_s, V_s, alive, pref)$

    if $x \neq$ **nil then**
        if $x \in V_s$ **then**
            $Q_s := Q_s \cup \{x\}$;
            $pref(x) :=$ **nil**;
        else
            put reject(v, x) in $P(\phi(x))$;
        $alive(v, x) :=$ **false**;

5.5 Correctness

An algorithm is **correct** if it does what it is supposed to do, for every legitimate input. This is one reason to require a specification for every algorithm designed; otherwise, we can only assume that the algorithm merely does what it does rather than what it should do. Once we have a specification, we can try to prove the algorithm correct. This can be done in a very formal way, perhaps even using automated program verifiers, or more informally, which is our approach. A correctness proof is best obtained during the process of designing an algorithm, and not after the process has completed. This is because higher-level, less optimized versions of an algorithm are usually easier to reason about, and easier to prove correct.

For our problem, we will give informal arguments that should convince the reader that our parallel matching algorithm is correct. First of all, we should prove that the algorithm terminates in a finite number of steps. For the sequential high-level algorithm, Algorithm 5.1, we start with a finite set $\mathcal{E}$ of m edges, and we remove at least one edge in every iteration of the main loop. Note that in a nonempty set $\mathcal{E}$, there must always exist a dominant edge, namely the edge (or edges) in $\mathcal{E}$ with largest weight. Therefore, the algorithm terminates after at most m iterations. In fact, since also two vertices are removed in every iteration, the total number of iterations is at most $\min(m, \lfloor n/2 \rfloor)$.

For the improved sequential algorithm, Algorithm 5.3, we start with n vertices in the queue Q. In every iteration of the main loop, we either remove a vertex v from Q, so the size of Q decreases, or we remove a vertex from Q and put a former suitor x back into Q, so the size stays the same, but in that case an edge (u, x) is removed, that is a living edge is declared dead. Thus, the number of iterations is at most $|\mathcal{V}| + |\mathcal{E}| = m + n$. In practice, the number of iterations required will often be much lower, because the functions FindAlive and FindSplitter also remove edges and because a match (u, v) removes all edges incident to u and v by setting d_u and d_v to 0.

For the parallel algorithm, Algorithm 5.7, we start with a total queue size $\sum_s |Q_s| = \sum_s |V_s| = n$. The local queues Q_s are disjoint, because they are subsets of the disjoint local vertex sets V_s. At the start of a superstep, a finite number $|R_s|$ of received messages is processed by processor $P(s)$, each in $\mathcal{O}(1)$ time, possibly filling the local queue Q_s.

This queue is then emptied in at most $|\mathcal{V}_s| + |\mathcal{E}_s|$ iterations, similar to the sequential case. Therefore, we may conclude that every computation superstep terminates in finite time.

All the communications initiated during a computation superstep are delayed and carried out in a subsequent communication superstep, just before the synchronization denoted by a **Sync**-statement in the program text. The algorithm terminates when no communications have been initiated during a computation superstep. In that case, R_s will be empty for all s at the start of the next computation superstep. (The queue Q_s will be empty at the start of every superstep, except the first.) An upper bound on the number of communicated words during the algorithm can be obtained by considering the three types of messages: proposals, accepts, and rejects. The total number of proposals sent during the algorithm is at most $2m$, since a vertex v proposes at most once to a neighbouring vertex u. Note that a mutual proposal can be made along the same edge (u, v), as discussed in Section 5.4. Accept or reject messages are only sent in response to a proposal, but not in case of a mutual proposal. Therefore, the total number of communicated words remains at most $2m$. We may conclude that the number of supersteps is finite and that the parallel algorithm terminates. Note that we do not have to worry about deadlock, as communications are always carried out and never have to wait for other communications to finish in the same superstep.

To check that the BSP algorithm does what it is supposed to do, we transform it into an equivalent sequential algorithm, a process we call **serialization**. (It can be considered as the reverse of parallelization.) The resulting sequential program is then checked for correctness, which can be done by any of the already available sequential verification methods, whether formal or informal. The serialization process is illustrated by Fig. 5.8.

Algorithm 5.10 displays the result of our serialization. The initialization superstep has been transformed into a sequential loop over all p processors, where the loop iterations are ordered by increasing processor number s. The order does not matter, as the superstep works

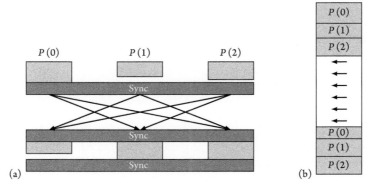

Figure 5.8 Serialization of a BSP algorithm for $p = 3$ processors. (a) The original BSP algorithm with two computation supersteps and one communication superstep. The colours are light grey for computation and dark grey for synchronization. Black arrows denote communication. (b) The resulting serialized algorithm, obtained by performing the computations of each superstep in sequence, instead of in parallel. The communications are replaced by a sequence of memory copies, the order of which should not matter.

on disjoint variables (a consequence of assuming a distributed memory and a corresponding partitioning of the data). Therefore, we can choose the simplest possible loop ordering. For the sake of brevity, we omit some lines that are identical to the corresponding lines in Algorithm 5.7. Next, each superstep of the main **while**-loop is transformed in a similar fashion into a loop over all processors.

The initiation of sending a proposal (v, u) to the owner of u, $P(\phi(u))$, is transformed into adding the proposal message to the set R_t, where $t = \phi(u)$. This set acts as a buffer, storing values to be communicated until the next synchronization point. When serializing, we must distinguish between messages received at the start of the current superstep, which we will denote by the set R_s, and those that will be sent at the end of the superstep, and hence will have been received at the start of the next superstep; we will denote the messages destined for processor $P(t)$ by R'_t and the union of all sets R'_t by R'. Without this distinction, it could happen that a message from $P(0)$ to $P(1)$ initiated in the current superstep is already processed in the same superstep, thereby breaking the equivalence between the parallel and the serialized algorithm. At the end of the superstep, the messages from R'_s are copied into R_s; at the start of the next superstep, R'_s is emptied. Note that this reflects the actual buffering happening in a BSPlib implementation of buffered one-sided communication.

The serialized algorithm retains the original superstep structure, with synchronizations replaced by copying of message buffers. The algorithm termination mechanism has been simplified, as there is no need to communicate to find out whether all processors are done.

The function ProcessReceivedMessages processes the messages from R_s and possibly generates new messages for the next superstep. The function can be serialized by changing the statement 'put reject(v, u) in $P(\phi(u))$' of Algorithm 5.8 into adding reject(v, u) to $R'_{\phi(u)}$, in the same way as we did for the main algorithm.

As a final step in our correctness proof, we verify the serialized algorithm, Algorithm 5.10, and show that it is a more detailed version of the basic dominant-edge algorithm, Algorithm 5.1, and thus produces a matching with at least half the maximum obtainable weight. Algorithm 5.10 only adds edges to the matching that are dominant, either when a vertex finds a mutual preference in the current superstep, or when it proposes and wins the heart of a mate in a future superstep. Edges incident to the matched vertices are either explicitly removed, when they are dislodged as a suitor or when dead edges are removed, or they are retained but implicitly assumed dead because they can never become a match. In any case, they will not be considered as candidates for dominant edges later on. Furthermore, if there exists a dominant edge, it will be discovered as a mutual preference, sooner or later, and processed. The algorithm finishes when there are no more dominant edges. As a consequence of Lemma 5.2, the serialized algorithm and hence the equivalent BSP algorithm is a $1/2$-approximation algorithm.

In algorithm design, we should in principle always strive for having a wider choice of possibilities; we should not be too picky. For instance, in the basic sequential algorithm we have the statement 'pick a dominant edge'. This means that every possible dominant edge is acceptable. Picking is arbitrary, and could even happen at random, so there may be no unique outcome and the algorithm may be nondeterministic. If there are ties, this will even be likely to happen. In the absence of ties, as we assumed so far, it can be proven that all dominant-edge algorithms produce the same matching, see Exercise 5.1.

Algorithm 5.10 Serialized BSP algorithm.

for $s := 0$ to $p - 1$ do
    for all $v \in \mathcal{V}_s$ do
        $suitor(v) := \textbf{nil}$; $pref(v) := \textbf{nil}$; $splitter_v(*) := \textbf{false}$;
    for all $e \in \mathcal{E}_s$ do
        $alive(e) := \textbf{true}$;
    $\mathcal{M}_s := \emptyset$; $R_s := \emptyset$; $Q_s := \mathcal{V}_s$;

while $\exists s : 0 \le s < p \wedge (R_s \ne \emptyset \vee Q_s \ne \emptyset)$ do
    $R' := \emptyset$;
    for $s := 0$ to $p - 1$ do
        ProcessReceivedMessages($R_s, R', Q_s, \mathcal{M}_s, \mathcal{V}_s, \omega, alive, suitor, pref, d$);

        while $Q_s \ne \emptyset$ do
            pick a vertex $v \in Q_s$;
            $Q_s := Q_s \setminus \{v\}$;
            FindAlive($v, Adj_v, \omega, alive, suitor, d$);
            $r :=$ FindSplitter($v, Adj_v, \omega, alive, splitter_v, suitor, d$);

            if $d_v > 0$ then
                $(u, v) :=$ FindPref($Adj_v, \omega, r, d_v - 1$);
                $d_v := d_v - 1$;
                $pref(v) := u$;

                { Register a match or propose }
                if $u = suitor(v)$ then
                    $\mathcal{M}_s := \mathcal{M}_s \cup \{(u, v)\}$;
                    $d_v := 0$;
                    if $u \in \mathcal{V}_s$ then
                        $d_u := 0$;
                    else
                      $R'_{\phi(u)} := R'_{\phi(u)} \cup \{accept(v, u)\}$;
                else if $u \notin \mathcal{V}_s$ then
                  $R'_{\phi(u)} := R'_{\phi(u)} \cup \{propose(v, u)\}$;

                { Replace the previous suitor }
                $\cdots$

            if $r < d_v$ then
                 SplitAdj($Adj_v, \omega, splitter_v, r, d_v - 1$);

    for $s := 0$ to $p - 1$ do
        $R_s := R'_s$;

The nondeterministic pick-statement creates a wider family of algorithms, which may make it easier to prove equivalence of algorithms. We use this to our advantage in our parallel matching algorithm where we pick a vertex v from the work queue Q_s, or pick a message msg from the receive queue R_s. For the serialized algorithm, we can view R_s as just another work queue, and because of this, the serialized algorithm fits into the overall family of dominant-edge algorithms.

When serializing BSP algorithms, we are forced to accept nondeterminism because the order in which messages arrive at their destination during the communication superstep is not fixed; this is exactly the feature that enables communication optimization by the BSP system. Transforming BSP algorithms to a sequential version thus means allowing permutation of the communications between the same source and destination processor.

5.6 Tie-breaking

So far, we have assumed that all edge weights are unique, so that no equal weights occur when comparing adjacent edges. Thus, we always have a unique preference, and **ties** (edges with equal weight) do not occur. Note that we can actually relax this assumption, by imposing uniqueness only for edges that share a vertex. Under this relaxed assumption, a vertex can still always set a unique preference or decide on the unique suitor. In practice, however, equal weights do occur, and this may happen also at neighbouring edges. In the extreme case of cardinality matching, all weights are equal. We would like our algorithm to work for such cases as well.

Arbitrarily picking one of the ties when setting a preference may cause the algorithm to fail, as this could create a cycle of preferences of length three (or larger). Figure 5.9 presents an example where three preferences have been set, but no matches can be made, despite the fact that we have three dominant edges. Note that a cycle of length two would pose no problem, as this would enable an immediate match.

Software writers sometimes debate whether certain unexpected program behaviour represents a bug or a feature, that is whether it is undesired behaviour or perhaps an opportunity.

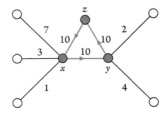

Figure 5.9 A preference cycle of length three, created by arbitrary tie-breaking when setting preferences as shown by the arrows. Red circles denote vertices with a set preference. The three edges marked by preference arrows all have weight 10 and they are all dominant edges.

The same holds for ties in matching. We can view ties as a disturbance that we must get rid of, or as an opportunity that broadens the scope for matches.

A simple strategy to break ties consistently is to use a secondary weight criterion when comparing edges. Besides the weight $\omega(u,v)$ of an edge, we can also consider the sum of vertex numbers,

$$\omega_2(u,v) = u + v, \text{ for } 0 \leq u,v < n, \tag{5.16}$$

where we assume that vertices have been identified with their index, and thus are numbers between 0 and $n-1$. In our algorithm, we only need to compare edges that share a vertex v, which makes the comparison even simpler:

$$\omega_2(u,v) > \omega_2(u',v) \iff u+v > u'+v \iff u > u'. \tag{5.17}$$

Using ω as a primary and ω_2 as a secondary weight criterion makes all weights of edges adjacent to a certain vertex unique again. Thus, preferring the highest-indexed partner breaks all ties and prevents cycles. This solution holds for both the sequential and the parallel algorithm.

In the sequential case, we can do a bit better than the simple tie-breaking strategy, by exploiting the opportunities that ties offer. When setting a preference for vertex v, we can first check whether $u = suitor(v)$ is among the ties with the highest weight, and if so, match v to u. Since (u,v) is then a dominant edge, this fits with the local domination scheme. If u is not among the ties, or there is no suitor yet, we can break ties arbitrarily. This feature will speed up the algorithm, as we match earlier than otherwise. Here, there is no danger of creating a cycle because a chain of tied edges can only grow at its tail; setting a preference at the head to a tied edge would result in an immediate match. As a consequence, the chain can never be closed to become a cycle.

In the parallel case, the simple strategy with ω_2 as secondary criterion will work just fine, as it removes all ties. The alternative strategy of checking your suitor first when setting a preference can, however, lead to a cycle: three vertices x,y, and z all on different processors could create a cycle as in Fig. 5.9. For instance, this can happen if x proposes to y, y proposes to z, and z proposes to x, all in the same superstep, where none has a suitor yet. In the next superstep, all three will have a suitor: $suitor(y) = x$, $suitor(z) = y$, and $suitor(x) = z$.

A better strategy for the parallel case is to use a secondary criterion that enhances locality, giving preference to internal edges (with both ends in V_s) over external edges. This can be achieved by defining the weight function

$$\omega_1(u,v) = \begin{cases} 1 & \text{if } \phi(u) = \phi(v) \\ 0 & \text{otherwise,} \end{cases} \quad \text{for } (u,v) \in \mathcal{E}. \tag{5.18}$$

Using ω_1 as secondary criterion leads to setting more local preferences, thereby avoiding the communication of proposals and rejections caused by nonlocal preferences. Besides saving communication time, this also prevents delays as local preferences can be checked immediately, for instance to see whether they are mutual.

Here, enhancing locality does not come at the cost of quality, as all ties have equal weight and are therefore, in principle, equally good. This would be different if we used ω_1 as a primary criterion; in that case the boy or girl next door would be preferred even if there were a better match in another village. In parallel computing in general, one should be careful not to trade off quality for locality; one should also avoid biased outcomes. Here, however, we benefit in terms of speed, and perhaps it is also desired to have more local matches (for instance if the resulting matching is subsequently used to improve the partitioning). Using locality introduces a new form of nondeterminism: the matching produced will have different characteristics for different p. Still, the matching guarantees at least half the optimal weight.

In an implementation, it is easiest to use $\omega, \omega_1, \omega_2$ as primary, secondary, and tertiary criterion, respectively. When setting a preference, we move all the ties to the top of the adjacency list, with the local ties nearest to the top. We set splitters to mark the start of the nonlocal ties and also for the local ones. As an optimization, we can still check a local suitor first when setting a preference, and match if the preference is mutual, thereby overruling the tertiary criterion.

5.7 Load balancing

The amounts of work that the processors have to carry out in a superstep of our parallel matching algorithm need not be the same, and hence some processors may spend time idling at the end of their superstep, waiting for others to finish. Even worse, if one processor has a lot more work in its work queue than the others, all others will be idling most of the time, as illustrated in Fig. 5.10(a). The only way we can try to prevent idling when running the present parallel algorithm is to give it a good partitioning, with an equal number of edges on each processor, and then hope for the best. Fortunately, we can build a load balancing mechanism into our algorithm based on the fact that a processor does not have to finish all the work in its work queue before synchronizing. This section will present such a mechanism.

Every processor $P(s)$ can keep track of the amount of work W_s it has carried out so far in the current superstep, for instance by adding operation counters to the algorithm, or by using the range sizes in the arrays processed when setting the next preference. If this is done accurately, the work counter can tell us when we should call for synchronization, namely when

$$W_s \geq W_{\max} \vee Q_s = \emptyset. \tag{5.19}$$

Here, $W_{\max}$ is the maximum amount of work to be done until the next synchronization; its value should be chosen carefully.

A slightly more elaborate and more robust load balancing mechanism can be obtained by using the work counter $W_{\max}$ to determine when to look at the system clock of $P(s)$ to obtain the time t_s elapsed since the start of the superstep. We can then call for synchronization if

$$t_s \geq t_{\max} \vee Q_s = \emptyset. \tag{5.20}$$

Here, $t_{\max}$ is a carefully chosen maximum superstep time. Using the work counter prevents us from looking at the clock all the time, which itself consumes precious computation

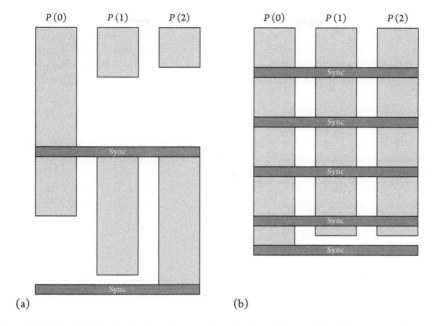

Figure 5.10 Load balancing by inserting synchronizations. The number of processors is $p = 3$. The colours are light grey for computation and dark grey for synchronization. Communication is omitted for the sake of clarity. (a) Computation with two larger supersteps, of cost $12l$ and $13l$, respectively, each followed by a synchronization of cost l. The total cost is $27l$. (b) Computation with five smaller supersteps, of cost $4l$, $4l$, $4l$, $4l$, and $2l$, respectively, each followed by a synchronization of cost l. The total computation and synchronization cost is $23l$.

time. This procedure also provides robustness against variation in the cost of the different operations of the algorithm, and even against variations in hardware performance, although this is beyond the scope of the BSP cost model, which assumes that all processors compute at exactly the same speed. (In particular, computing speeds may vary if dynamic frequency scaling is used to save energy.)

How can we determine the optimal value of $W_{\max}$? Certainly, we should not synchronize too often, otherwise we would spend most of our time synchronizing. To make this statement more precise, we can invoke the BSP model: if we choose $W_{\max} \geq 4l$, we will never spend more than 20% of the total time synchronizing, which should be acceptable to a typical user. Of course, we can change the constant factor in case we deem a different percentage acceptable. Furthermore, if we just want to minimize synchronization overhead, we can communicate additional information between the processors such as the queue sizes at the end of a superstep, and take $W_{\max} \geq \min_s |Q_s|$ for the next superstep, with $W_{\max}$ expressed as a maximum number of preferences to be set.

Executing many smaller supersteps has one main advantage over executing a few larger supersteps, namely the synchronization of the superstep effectuates communication, which in turn leads to new useful work in the work queues of the processors, in particular putting the processors without work back to work again. This effect, illustrated in Fig. 5.10(b), increases the chances of all processors performing useful work during the superstep. The hope is that all processors will be busy during most supersteps, and that only near the end of the whole computation processors start idling. For this reason, we will synchronize as often as possible and choose $W_{\max} = 4l$, the minimum acceptable value.

In our load balancing analysis above, we ignored communication cost. Nevertheless, communication also takes time, but its cost is hard to analyse exactly. The communication cost depends not only on the (static) partitioning, like in the case of an SpMV, see Chapter 4, but also on the (dynamic) flow of the algorithm, that is the sequence of operations carried out at each processor. The partitioning determines which edges are cut and hence can give rise to a proposal message sent and an answer received, but the flow of the algorithm decides which messages are actually sent. Minimizing the **edge cut** in the vertex partitioning of the graph,

$$ EC_\phi = |\{(u,v) \in \mathcal{E} : \phi(u) \neq \phi(v)\}|, \tag{5.21} $$

will minimize an upper bound $2EC_\phi$ on the communication volume of the algorithm, but not necessarily the volume itself. The factor of two occurs because every proposal sent along an edge may cause an answer to be sent back along the same edge.

For a good partitioning, the edge cut EC_ϕ will be small so that most preferences will be local and the number of proposals to be sent to nonlocal vertices will be limited. As a consequence, communication time will most likely be negligible. For a bad partitioning, however, all preferences may turn out to be nonlocal, and communication will most likely be dominant. This may happen, for instance, if computing a good partitioning beforehand would be too expensive, more expensive than the matching itself, and in practice this may often be the case. It may also happen if the number of processors is large compared to the number of vertices, for example if $p = n$. Systems like Pregel [205] and Giraph [211], with the motto 'think like a vertex', indeed impose $p = n$, identifying every vertex with a virtual processor, and hence accepting the fact that all edges between vertices cause communication. If it thinks like a vertex, it talks like a vertex! In that case, the work mainly consists of sending out proposals and receiving answers.

5.8 Further improvements

In the previous two sections, we have already improved our basic parallel matching algorithm by better tie-breaking and better load balancing. More can be done, however, to achieve further improvements, in particular by reducing the amount of communication. In this section, we present ways of reducing the number of proposals sent to other processors.

Receiving a negative answer to a matching proposal may never be a pleasure, but if the answer contains a motivation, we might be able to do something useful with it (except if it is 'I don't like your face'). For example, if vertex v proposes to u, but u rejects because it has a better suitor x, processor $P(\phi(u))$ can send back the weight $\omega(u,x)$ to $P(\phi(v))$, so that no vertex with a lower weight residing on $P(\phi(v))$ will ever propose again to vertex u.

This potentially saves many proposals, especially later on in the execution of the algorithm, when the suitor weights have increased. The additional communication cost incurred by sending the suitor weight back is one data word per reject message, which will at most double the cost of a rejection. Proposing to an already matched vertex on a remote processor also causes a rejection, and the motivation could then be given as an infinite weight, $\omega(u,x) = \infty$.

In an implementation of this motivated rejection method, we can store for each halo vertex $u \in \mathcal{H}_s$ the latest known value of its suitor in a variable $\omega_{\text{suitor}}(u)$. In case of a match, we can store the value ∞ (or the largest possible value that can be represented on our finite-precision computer). The stored value can be inspected before sending a proposal, and it can also be used for removing dead edges.

Another possible improvement, to express it in romantic terms, is to exchange wedding rings as a symbol of love and to tell all the world about the marriage, or, in algorithmic terms, to broadcast a match to all processors involved. Proposing marriage to someone already wearing a wedding ring does not make much sense, and, similarly, proposing to an already matched vertex is useless. Thus, we broadcast that vertex v has infinite suitor weight to all processors in the set $\{P(\phi(u)) : (u,v) \in \mathcal{E}_s\}$ at the moment $v \in \mathcal{V}_s$ becomes registered as matched. The gain of this broadcast is that it prevents futile proposals.

The broadcast requires additional communication, the cost of which can be found as follows. Assume that all vertices are matched during the algorithm, and that all matches are broadcast. Furthermore, assume as a worst case that this broadcast is based on the original edge set $\mathcal{E}_s$, before any edges have been removed. The additional communication volume then depends completely on the partitioning ϕ of the vertices. We can relate this volume conveniently to the communication volume of parallel SpMV, treated in Chapter 4, by the natural correspondence between a graph and its adjacency matrix. The **adjacency matrix** $A = A(\mathcal{G})$ of an undirected simple graph $\mathcal{G} = (\mathcal{V}, \mathcal{E})$ is defined by

$$a_{ij} = \begin{cases} 1 & \text{if } (i,j) \in \mathcal{E} \\ 0 & \text{otherwise,} \end{cases} \quad \text{for } 0 \le i,j < n. \tag{5.22}$$

The adjacency matrix is **binary** (having only values 0 and 1), sparse, symmetric, and it has a zero diagonal. We provide it with a unit diagonal, however, by adding the identity matrix $I = I_n$. We can now define a row distribution ϕ_{A+I} of the matrix $A + I$ induced by the vertex partitioning ϕ of the graph $\mathcal{G}$ by setting $\phi_{A+I}(i,j) = \phi(i)$ for each nonzero of the matrix $A + I$; we can also define a corresponding vector distribution by setting $\phi_v = \phi_u = \phi$. Here, v is the input vector and u the output vector of the SpMV $u := Av$. A social-network graph is shown in Fig. 5.11 and its adjacency matrix A is shown in Fig. 5.12. A row distribution of the matrix $A + I$ is shown in Fig. 5.13 and the corresponding vertex partitioning of the original graph is shown in Fig. 5.14.

From the correspondence between a graph and its adjacency matrix, it follows that the number of remote processors owning a vertex adjacent to a given vertex j on processor $P(\phi(j))$ equals the number of processors having nonzeros in column j of the matrix $A + I$, minus 1. The inclusion of the unit diagonal ensures that the processor owning vertex j is always represented in matrix column j, so that we always have to subtract 1 to account for

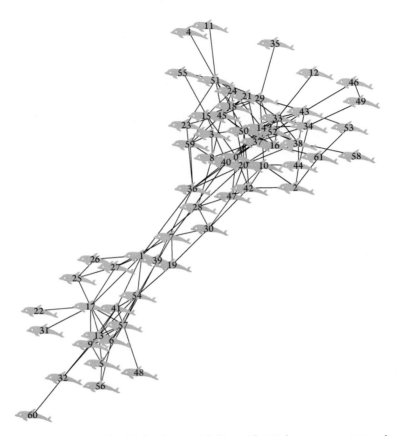

Figure 5.11 A social network of 62 bottlenose dolphins with 159 frequent associations between them in a community living off the Doubtful Sound fjord, New Zealand [204], represented by an undirected graph with 62 vertices and 159 edges. Vertex 0 is a dolphin named Beak, vertex 1 is called Beescratch, . . ., and vertex 61 is called Zipfel. The edges represent frequent associations and they have unit weight. The vertex coordinates in this drawing were obtained by using the Gephi software [21] with Yifan Hu's multilevel force-directed proportional layout algorithm.

local nonzeros. Thus, the number of remote processors is exactly the contribution to the fanout of column j in the SpMV, Algorithm 4.5. Since this algorithm has no fanin because of the 1D row distribution, the total communication volume of the fanout equals $V_{\phi_{A+I}}$; this is also the volume of the broadcast in the graph.

Partitioning the sparse matrix $A + I$ in one dimension, for instance by using the Mondriaan package, see Section 4.5, also yields a partitioning of the graph, with minimized communication volume. We impose that the distribution of the input and output vector of the matrix–vector multiplication must be the same; including a unit matrix diagonal makes sure that we can do this without incurring additional communication volume, cf. eqn (4.16).

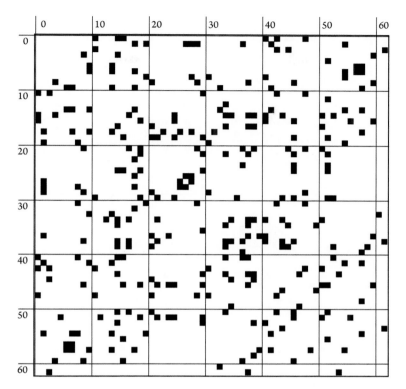

Figure 5.12 Adjacency matrix A corresponding to the dolphins network of Fig. 5.11. The matrix is symmetric and has size 62×62. It has 318 nonzeros. The horizontal and vertical lines are drawn to help identify the row and column indices of the nonzeros.

When partitioning the vertices of the graph, we have to decide on the most suitable load balancing constraint, the graph equivalent of the sparse matrix partitioning constraint eqn (4.31). We can either balance the number of vertices, or the number of edges (the nonzeros of the matrix A). Both numbers are only approximate indications of the amount of work of the matching algorithm, which is more dynamic in nature than sparse matrix–vector multiplication, for which the nonzero balance represents the true work balance. Indeed, for matching, the work balance in a series of separate supersteps determines the overall efficiency, and not the balance in the total amount of work. Because it is likely that processors with more edges will have more work searching and splitting adjacency lists, balancing the edges better reflects the balance of the work load of the matching algorithm. This choice has the additional advantage that it also balances the memory requirements, which allows us to solve larger problems in case all processors have the same amount of memory available.

How much can we gain by the broadcast of the matches, and how much can we lose? The following straightforward observation helps us in answering this question.

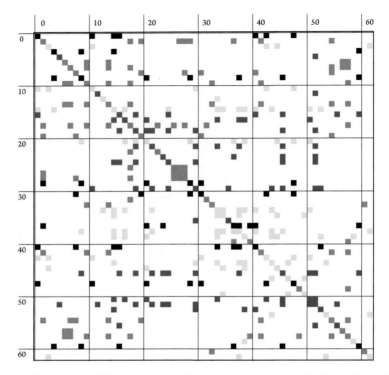

Figure 5.13 Partitioning of the adjacency matrix from Fig. 5.12 with an added unit diagonal, $A + I$, into four parts with a roughly equal number of nonzeros. We imposed a relatively high value $\epsilon = 0.2$, which is needed for this small matrix to give the partitioner more freedom to move vertices between the parts. The processors $P(0), \dots, P(3)$ are denoted by the colours red, black, yellow, and blue, respectively. The partitioning has been obtained by using the Mondriaan software package, version 4.2.1, in 1D mode, partitioning by rows. The communication volume is $V = 47$ and the edge cut is $EC = 47$ (it is a pure coincidence that these values are the same).

Theorem 5.3 *Let V_ϕ be the communication volume of a broadcast induced by vertex partitioning ϕ of an undirected graph $\mathcal{G} = (\mathcal{V}, \mathcal{E})$, defined by*

$$V_\phi = \sum_{v \in \mathcal{V}} |\{\phi(u) \; : \; (u, v) \in \mathcal{E} \wedge \phi(u) \neq \phi(v)\}|. \tag{5.23}$$

Let EC_ϕ be the edge cut of the vertex partitioning, defined by

$$EC_\phi = |\{(u, v) \in \mathcal{E} \; : \; \phi(u) \neq \phi(v)\}|. \tag{5.24}$$

Then

$$V_\phi \leq 2 \cdot EC_\phi. \tag{5.25}$$

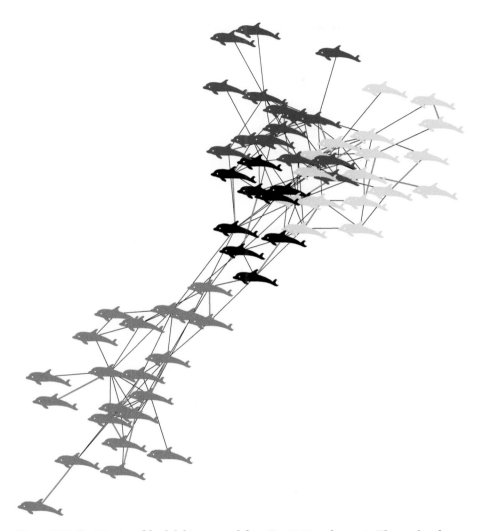

Figure 5.14 Partitioning of the dolphins network from Fig. 5.11 into four parts. The graph is shown in the original layout. Although this layout is not based on the given partitioning, the dolphins assigned to the same part can still be seen close together in the drawing. The dolphins have been matched by the program bspmatch (presented in the next section) and the resulting matching has a weight of 24. This means that 24 pairs of dolphins have been formed, and these pairs are shown by a green edge. Because all edge weights are the same, tie-breaking was invoked for all weight comparisons. Ties were broken in the first instance by using eqn (5.18), which gives preference to local matches. As a result, only one edge is external, between dolphins 16 (called Jet) and 20 (called MN105).

Proof Because every edge is connected to two vertices, we have that

$$2 \cdot EC_\phi = \sum_{v \in \mathcal{V}} \sum_{\substack{(u,v) \in \mathcal{E} \\ \phi(u) \neq \phi(v)}} 1$$

$$= \sum_{v \in \mathcal{V}} \sum_{\substack{s=0 \\ s \neq \phi(v)}}^{p-1} \sum_{\substack{(u,v) \in \mathcal{E} \\ \phi(u)=s}} 1$$

$$\geq \sum_{v \in \mathcal{V}} \sum_{\substack{s=0 \\ s \neq \phi(v)}}^{p-1} \mathbf{1}_{\exists u:(u,v) \in \mathcal{E} \wedge \phi(u)=s}$$

$$= \sum_{v \in \mathcal{V}} |\{\phi(u) \, : \, (u,v) \in \mathcal{E} \wedge \phi(u) \neq \phi(v)\}| = V_\phi. \qquad (5.26)$$

Here, we used the **indicator function** $\mathbf{1}_X$, defined as 1 if the statement X holds, and 0 otherwise. □

As a consequence of Theorem 5.3, the potential gain factor is much larger than the potential loss factor: in the worst case, the communication cost will be doubled, when a broadcast volume of $V_\phi = 2 \cdot EC_\phi$ is added to the volume of EC_ϕ proposals and EC_ϕ answers. But this is highly unlikely, because equality in eqn (5.25) would imply that all edges of each vertex must be connected to different processors. In the best case, most proposals are prevented and the communication volume is close to the much smaller volume V_ϕ of the broadcast of the matches. In that case, we have the additional advantage that the hypergraph-based partitioning obtained for parallel sparse matrix–vector multiplication is also the right partitioning for the graph matching algorithm.

A final possible improvement is the use of a 2D matrix distribution instead of a 1D row distribution, that is we partition the matrix nonzeros instead of the rows. In graph terms, this means that we partition the edges instead of the vertices. The 2D approach has more flexibility, and because it is more general, it will in principle give better partitionings with lower communication volume. This has been shown to be advantageous, for example in unweighted maximum-cardinality matching [242] (where the aim is to find as many matches as possible). The 2D approach may also be beneficial for very irregular graphs with widely varying vertex degrees, because in a 1D approach a high-degree vertex would require lots of memory on the processor that contains it, and it would also require a lot of computation because of its long adjacency list, which may harm load balance. An example is a so-called power-law network, which is a graph where the fraction of vertices of degree d scales as $\mathcal{O}(d^{-\alpha})$; in many networks occurring in practice, we have $2 \leq \alpha \leq 3$ [229, Chapter 10].

A 2D matching algorithm, based on edge partitioning, would be more complicated than a 1D matching algorithm. The main difference is that we need to find the preferences in a distributed manner, because the edges connected to a vertex v will not all be stored on processor $P(\phi(v))$. Thus, this processor will first have to request candidates for its new preference and only then can it decide on the best. For our matching program, presented in the next section, we choose the simpler, more educational 1D approach and we leave the 2D approach as Exercise 5.3 to the astute reader.

5.9 Example function bspmatch

The function bspmatch is an implementation of Algorithm 5.7 for parallel weighted graph matching. On input, it assumes a vertex distribution ϕ, which corresponds to a 1D row distribution of the adjacency matrix of the graph. The driver program bspmatch_test (not printed here, but included in BSPedupack) reads a sparse matrix in Matrix Market format, distributed by a 1D row distribution, without diagonal entries and with symmetric partner a_{ji} included for each nonzero a_{ij}. The distribution is represented by a list of nonzeros assigned to $P(0)$, followed by those assigned to $P(1)$, and so on. A warning: the input procedure does not check whether the distribution is truly a 1D row distribution: if two nonzeros from the same row are assigned to different processors, they may cause havoc. The nonzeros are then sent to the processors as prescribed by ϕ, where they become the edges in the edge lists of the vertices.

The input procedure of bspmatch has much in common with that of the sparse matrix–vector multiplication function bspmv; the common functions are included in the file bspsparse_input.c, see the description at the start of Section 4.11. A difference is that here we use the standard compressed row storage (CRS), instead of incremental CRS.

The driver program bspmatch_test builds the data structures needed by bspmatch, which are a list of internal edges, numbered $e = 0,\ldots,$ nedges $- 1$, followed by external (halo) edges, numbered $e =$ nedges$,\ldots,$nedges $+$ nhalo $- 1$. For each edge e, we can look up its weight weight[e] $= \omega(e)$, which is a double, and its secondary weight weight1[e] $= \omega_1(e) \cdot 2n + \omega_2(e)$, where ω_1 is defined by eqn (5.18) and ω_2 by eqn (5.16). The secondary weight is an integer and it is used for breaking all ties. If the edge is local, we can look up the local vertex numbers v0[e] and v1[e] of its two endpoints, where v0[e] $<$ v1[e]. If the edge is an external edge, we can look up its local vertex number v0[e], but the variable v1[e] then has a different meaning, namely the corresponding edge number e' on the remote processor $P(t)$ that shares the edge with the local processor $P(s)$. If we send a message such as a proposal to a remote processor involving an edge e, we communicate in the language of the receiver, who can look up all information concerning the corresponding edge e', such as its weight and its local vertex. For each halo edge e, we also store the processor number of the remote owner $P(t)$ as destproc[e $-$ nedges] $= t$. The numbering with local edges first makes it easy to see whether an edge is local or a halo edge, namely by the simple comparison $e <$ nedges.

Pleasing the receiver of a message by adopting her language is not always an easy task, and it requires setting up a translation beforehand. Here, this is done in the program bspmatch_test, which first finds out who the owners are of the halo vertices, in a procedure similar to the noticeboard procedure in the function bspmv_init, see Section 4.11. After that, the local edge numbers e of the halo edges are sent to the remote processors, where they are sorted lexicographically by their global indices. Since the local edge numbers e′ on the remote processor were already arranged in the same way, the edge numbers e and e′ can be coupled by setting $v1[e'] = e$ on the remote processor.

The driver program bspmatch_test also determines the number nvertices of local vertices with a nonempty edge list. The edges adjacent to a vertex with local vertex number v are stored by placing their local edge numbers in positions Start[v] to Start[v + 1] − 1 of the array Adj.

The function find_alive is a direct implementation of Algorithm 5.4, the function find_splitter implements Algorithm 5.5, find_pref implements Algorithm 5.6, and split_adj implements Algorithm 1.3. Furthermore, the function reject_suitor is a direct implementation of Algorithm 5.9.

In the main function bspmatch, the queue Q is implemented as a circular list, which wraps around at vertex number nvertices, by starting again at 0. The queue contains nq local vertices, starting at q_lo. A new vertex is pushed onto the queue at the tail, and a vertex is popped off at the head, that is at q_lo. A variable is set to **nil** by giving it a value DUMMY $= -1$, which is not a legitimate index. This happens when a vertex v is pushed onto the queue, and its preference is reset to **nil**. Note that in our functions we store the preference and the suitor of a vertex v as an edge number e. This facilitates looking up all relevant information, such as weights. This is in contrast to our algorithms, where we store preferences and suitors as vertex numbers.

Communication of proposals, acceptances, and rejections is carried out in bspmatch by bulk synchronous message passing, which is the most convenient choice because messages can be sent from anywhere within the program and the resulting communication pattern is totally irregular. It would for instance be hard to determine where exactly to put a proposal if we wanted to use a bsp_put primitive instead.

Function bspmatch needs no further explanation, as it closely resembles Algorithm 5.7. The same holds for the processing of received messages by the function bsp_process_recvd_msgs, which closely resembles Algorithm 5.8. The program has been optimized by including load balancing as outlined in Section 5.7. This is achieved through the parameter maxops, which sets a bound on the amount of work that can be carried out in a superstep. This amount is measured by counting the elemental $\mathcal{O}(1)$-operations executed by the loops of the superstep. The program could be further optimized by sending a motivation with each rejection or broadcasting matches to all concerned (remember the wedding ring from Section 5.8?), but we did not do this here for the sake of simplicity. The program text of bspmatch is:

```
#include "bspedupack.h"

#define PROPOSE 0 // possible  tags
#define ACCEPT 1
#define REJECT 2

#define SPLITMIN 5 // minimum  array  size
                   // for  splitting  to  be  worthwhile
```

```
bool  heavier(long e0, long e1, double *weight,
              long *weight1){

    /* This function checks whether edge e0 is heavier
       than edge e1 using weight as a primary criterion
       and weight1 for breaking ties. */

    if (e0 == DUMMY)
        return false;

    if (e1 == DUMMY || weight[e0] > weight[e1] ||
       (weight[e0] == weight[e1] && weight1[e0] >
        weight1[e1])) return true;

    return false;

} /* end heavier */


void find_alive (long v, long *Adj, long nedges,
                 double *weight, long *weight1,
                 long *v0, long *v1, bool *Alive,
                 long *Suitor, long lo, long *d){

    /* This function finds the highest index i of a
       living edge e=Adj[i] in the adjacency list
       of vertex v, with range [lo, lo+dv-1], where
       dv is the degree of v. It removes dead
       edges along the way and reduces the degree
       accordingly.

       Input:
           v is the local vertex number,
           Adj = adjacency list of vertex v, of length
           d[v], nedges is the number of internal (nonhalo)
           edges, weight[e] is the weight of edge e,
           where for internal edges, e = (v0[e],v1[e]),
           weight1[e] is a secondary weight used for
           breaking ties, Alive[e] is a boolean stating
           whether edge e is alive, Suitor[u] = edge
           number of suitor of local vertex u.

       Output:
           d[v] is the new vertex degree, d[v]>=0,
```

```
                    Alive[Adj[lo+d[v]−1]] holds if d[v]>0.
        */

        for (long i= lo+d[v]−1; i>=lo; i−−){
            long e = Adj[i];

                /* Kill internal edge if it cannot be matched
                   any more */
                if (e < nedges){
                    /* Determine other end point of edge e */
                    long u = (v0[e]==v ? v1[e] : v0[e]);
                    if ((d[u]==0 && Suitor[v]!=e) ||
                        heavier(Suitor[u], e, weight, weight1))
                        Alive[e] = false;
                }

                if (Alive[e]){
                    return;
                } else {
                    d[v]−−;
                }
        }

} /* end find_alive */


long find_splitter (long v, long *Adj, long nedges,
                    double *weight, long *weight1,
                    long *v0, long *v1, bool *Alive,
                    bool *Splitter, long *Suitor,
                    long lo, long *d){

    /* This function finds the highest splitter r of the
       adjacency list of vertex v, with range
       [lo, lo+d[v]−1], where d[v] is the degree of v.
       If no splitter exists, the function returns r=lo.

       The function removes dead edges along the way and
       reduces the degree accordingly. On output, it
           holds that lo <= r < lo+d[v].

       Input and output parameters are the same as for
       find_alive, except for an extra boolean array
       Splitter (of the same length as Adj) which denotes
```

```
        whether an index is a splitter.
    */

    for (long r= lo+d[v]−1; r>=lo; r−−){
        long e = Adj[r];

        /* Kill internal edge if it cannot be matched
           any more */
        if (e < nedges){
            /* Determine other end point of edge e */
            long u = (v0[e]==v ? v1[e] : v0[e]);
            if ((d[u]==0 && Suitor[v]!=e) ||
                heavier(Suitor[u], e, weight, weight1))
                Alive[e] = false;
        }

        if (!Alive[e]){
            Adj[r] = Adj[lo+d[v]−1]; // copy highest alive
            d[v]−−;
        }

        if (Splitter[r])
            return r;
    }

    return lo; // in case no splitter was found

} /* end find_splitter */


void swap (long *x, long i, long j){

    /* This function swaps x[i] and x[j] */

    long tmp = x[i];
    x[i] = x[j];
    x[j] = tmp;

} /* end swap */


void find_pref(long *Adj, double *weight, long *weight1,
               long lo, long hi){
```

```
/* This function finds the maximum weight[Adj[i]]
   with lo <= i <= hi and swaps Adj[i] and Adj[hi].
   Here, weight1 is a secondary weight criterion
   used for breaking ties. */

if (hi <= lo )
    return;

long imax= hi;
long emax= Adj[hi];
for (long i=lo; i<hi; i++){
    if (heavier(Adj[i], emax, weight, weight1)){
        imax= i;
        emax= Adj[i];
    }
}
swap(Adj, imax, hi);

return;

} /* end find_pref */


long split_adj(long *Adj, double *weight, long *weight1,
               long lo, long hi){

/* This function splits the range [lo,hi] with
   lo <= hi of the adjacency list Adj and returns
   a splitter r, such that
       weight[Adj[i]] < weight[Adj[j]],
   for all i < r <= j.
*/

if (hi-lo >= 2){
    long piv = (lo+hi)/2; // a simple random-like
                          // pivot

    /* Swap Adj[piv] and Adj[hi] */
    swap(Adj, piv, hi);
    long epiv= Adj[hi];
    long i = lo; // first free position
                 // for values < pivot weight
    for (long j=lo; j<hi; j++){
```

```
              /* Loop invariant: lo <= i <= j < hi,
                        weight[Adj[lo:i−1]] < wpiv,
                        weight[Adj[i:j−1]] >= wpiv */

        if (heavier(epiv, Adj[j], weight, weight1)){
            swap(Adj, i, j);
            i++;
        }
    }
    swap(Adj, i, hi);
    return i;

} else if (hi−lo == 1){
    if (heavier(Adj[lo], Adj[hi], weight, weight1))
        swap(Adj, lo, hi);
    return hi;
} else if (hi==lo){
    return hi;
}

return DUMMY; // in case hi < lo

} /* end split_adj */



void push(long v, long nvertices, long q_lo,
          long *nq, long *Q, long *Pref){

    /* This function pushes vertex v onto the queue
       and sets its preference to DUMMY.

       nvertices= number of vertices,
       q_lo= start of the queue,
       nq= number of queue entries,
       Q= array of size nvertices storing the queue,
       Pref= array of size nvertices storing preferences.
    */

    long q_hi= q_lo + (*nq); // first free position
    if (q_hi >= nvertices)
        q_hi −= nvertices;
    Q[q_hi]= v;
    (*nq)++;
    Pref[v]= DUMMY;
```

```
} /* end push */


long pop(long nvertices, long *q_lo, long *nq, long *Q){

    /* This function pops a vertex v from the queue */

    long i= *q_lo;
    (*q_lo)++;
    if (*q_lo >= nvertices)
        *q_lo -= nvertices;
    (*nq)--;

    return Q[i];

} /* end pop */

void reject_suitor(long v, long e, long q_lo, long *nq,
                   long *Q, long nvertices, long nedges,
                   long *v0, long *v1, long *destproc,
                   bool *Alive, long *Pref){

    /* This function rejects suitor e of vertex v.

       q_lo, nq, Q, nvertices, Pref are the same as
       in the push function.

       nedges= number of internal edges,
       For local edge e < nedges:
           v0[e], v1[e] are the vertices of edge e.
       For halo edge e >= nedges:
           v0[e]= the local vertex of edge e,
           v1[e]= the local edge number on the remote
               processor for edge e.
       destproc[e-nedges]= the remote processor that
           owns halo edge e. The shift by nedges is to
           save memory and store destproc only for halo
           edges.
       Alive[e]= boolean that says whether edge e is
           still alive.
    */

    if (e == DUMMY)
```

```
        return;

    if (e < nedges){
        /* Determine other end point of edge e */
        long x = (v0[e]==v ? v1[e] : v0[e]);
        push(x, nvertices, q_lo, nq, Q, Pref);
    } else {
        long tag= REJECT;
        bsp_send(destproc[e−nedges], &tag, &(v1[e]),
                sizeof(long));
    }
    Alive[e]= false;

} /* end reject_suitor */


void bsp_process_recvd_msgs(long q_lo, long *nq, long *Q,
                            long *nmatch, long *match,
                            long nvertices, long nedges,
                            long *v0, long *v1,
                            long *destproc, double *weight,
                            long *weight1, bool *Alive,
                            long *Suitor, long *Pref,
                            long *degree){
```

/* This function processes the messages received
   at the start of a superstep. The messages can
   be of three types: a proposal for a match
   (with a tag 0), acceptance (tag 1),
   or rejection (tag 2).

   In case of a proposal, the proposer either becomes
   the new suitor, a match, or the proposal is rejected.
   An acceptance message leads to the registration
   of a match. A rejection leads to the proposer being
   pushed back onto the queue.

   q_lo, nq, Q, nvertices, Pref are the same
       as in the push function.
   v0, v1, destproc, Alive are the same as in the
       reject_suitor function.
   nmatch= number of matches registered so far,
   match[i]= edge number of match i,
   weight[e]= weight of edge e,

```
    weight1 [e]= secondary weight of edge e,
                 used for breaking ties,
    Suitor [v]= edge corresponding to the suitor of
                 vertex v,
    degree [v]= the degree of vertex v.
*/

bsp_nprocs_t nmessages;   // total number of messages
                          // received
bsp_size_t nbytes;        // total size in bytes
                          // received
bsp_qsize(&nmessages,&nbytes);

for (long i=0; i<nmessages; i++){
    bsp_size_t status; // not used
    long tag;          // tag of received message
    bsp_get_tag(&status, &tag);

    long e; // local number of halo edge e received
    bsp_move(&e, sizeof(long));
    long v= v0[e]; // local vertex of halo edge e

    if (tag==PROPOSE){

        /* Register a match if the preference is
           mutual */
        if (e==Pref[v]){
            /* v has proposed to e in the previous
               superstep.
               No need to send an accept. */
            match[*nmatch]= e;
            (*nmatch)++;
            degree[v]= 0;
        }

        /* Assign new suitor */
        long e0= Suitor[v]; // previous suitor
        if (heavier(e, e0, weight, weight1)){
            Suitor[v]= e;
            reject_suitor(v,e0,q_lo,nq,Q,nvertices,
                    nedges, v0,v1,destproc,Alive,Pref);
        } else { // reject the proposal
            long tag_new= REJECT;
            bsp_send(destproc[e-nedges], &tag_new,
```

```
                              &(v1[e]) ,  sizeof(long));
                   Alive[e]= false;
              }

       } else if (tag==ACCEPT){
              match[*nmatch]= e;
              (*nmatch)++;
              degree[v]= 0;

              /* Reject previous suitor */
              long e0= Suitor[v];
              Suitor[v]= e;  // so future proposers know
              reject_suitor(v,e0,q_lo,nq,Q,nvertices,nedges,
                             v0,v1,destproc,Alive,Pref);

       } else if (tag==REJECT){
              push(v, nvertices, q_lo, nq, Q, Pref);
              Alive[e]= false;
       }
   }
}

} /* end bsp_process_recvd_msgs */


void bspmatch(long nvertices, long nedges, long nhalo,
              long *v0, long *v1, long *destproc,
              double *weight, long *weight1, long *Adj,
              long *Start, long *degree, long maxops,
              long *nmatch, long *match, long *nsteps,
              long *nops){

   /* This function matches the vertices of a graph
      by a local domination algorithm. This guarantees
      obtaining at least half the maximum possible weight.

      Input:
            nvertices is the number of local vertices,
            nedges is the number of internal (nonhalo) edges,
            nhalo is the number of external (halo) edges,
            degree[v] = degree of local vertex v,
                  0 <= v < nvertices,
            weight[e] = weight of edge e,
            weight1[e] = secondary weight of edge e,
                  used for breaking ties.
```

For internal edges, 0 <= e < nedges:
v0[e] = local vertex number of minimum
    end point of edge e,
v1[e] = local vertex number of maximum
    end point of edge e.

For external edges, nedges <= e < nedges+nhalo:
v0[e] = vertex number of the local end point
    of edge e,
v1[e] = local edge number on remote processor
    of edge e,
destproc[e−nedges] = destination processor
    that owns the nonlocal vertex of edge e.

*Adj is an array of length 2*nedges+nhalo,*
which contains the adjacency lists of all the
local vertices. The list of local vertex v
contains the local indices of the edges
incident to v. This list is initially stored
in positions Start[v]..Start[v+1]−1.
Adj may change during the matching.

maxops is the maximum number of elemental
operations carried out in a superstep, which
is a measure of the amount of work.
Once maxops is reached, a synchronization is
called. maxops=0 means no maximum number
is imposed.

Output:
    nmatch is the number of matches found locally,
    match[i] = local edge number of match i,
        0 <= i < nmatch,
    nsteps is the number of mixed supersteps taken,
        each consisting of processing the
        received messages and then setting
        preferences,
    nops is the total number of elemental operations
        carried out locally.
*/

```
long p= bsp_nprocs(); // p = number of processors
                      // obtained
```

```
long  s= bsp_pid ();      // s = processor number

/* Allocate, register, and set tag size */
long *Done= vecalloci(p);
bsp_push_reg(Done,p*sizeof(long));

bsp_size_t tagsize= sizeof(long);
bsp_set_tagsize(&tagsize);
bsp_sync();

/* Initialize vertices */
long *Suitor= vecalloci(nvertices);
long *Pref= vecalloci(nvertices);
long *Q= vecalloci(nvertices);
for (long v=0; v<nvertices; v++){
    Suitor[v]= DUMMY;
    Pref[v]= DUMMY;
    Q[v]= v;
}

/* Initialize edges */
bool *Alive= vecallocb(nedges+nhalo);
bool *Splitter= vecallocb(2*nedges+nhalo);
                             // same size as Adj
for (long e=0; e<nedges+nhalo; e++)
    Alive[e]= true;
for (long i=0; i<2*nedges+nhalo; i++)
    Splitter[i]= false;

long q_lo=0;         // start of the queue
long nq= nvertices;  // number of vertices in the queue
*nmatch= 0;          // number of matches registered
*nsteps= 0;          // number of supersteps taken
*nops= 0;            // number of operations

bool alldone= false;

while (!alldone){
    long nops_step= 0; // number of operations
                       // of this superstep

    /* Initialize all processors to not done yet */
    for (long t=0; t<p; t++)
        Done[t]= false;
```

```
/* Determine if the local processor is done
   for this superstep */
bsp_nprocs_t nmessages;  // total number of
                         // messages
bsp_size_t nbytes;       // total size in bytes
bsp_qsize(&nmessages,&nbytes);

if (nmessages==0 && nq==0){
    long done= true;
    for (long t=0; t<p; t++)
        bsp_put(t,&done,Done,s*sizeof(long),
                sizeof(long));
} else {
    bsp_process_recvd_msgs(q_lo,&nq,Q,nmatch,
        match,nvertices,nedges,v0,v1,destproc,
        weight,weight1,Alive,Suitor,Pref,degree);

    while (nq > 0 && (maxops==0 ||
            nops_step < maxops)){
        long v= pop(nvertices, &q_lo, &nq, Q);

        /* Find highest living edge */
        if (degree[v] > 0){
            long degree_old= degree[v];
                        // it may decrease
            find_alive (v,Adj,nedges,
                        weight,weight1,v0,v1,
                        Alive,Suitor,Start[v],
                        degree);
            nops_step += degree_old-degree[v]+1;
        }
        /* Find highest splitter r */
        long r= Start[v];
        if (degree[v] > 0){
            long hi= Start[v]+degree[v]-1;
            r= find_splitter (v,Adj,nedges,weight,
                              weight1, v0,v1,Alive,
                              Splitter,Suitor,
                              Start[v],degree);
            nops_step += hi-r+1;
        }

        /* Find preference */
        if (degree[v] > 0){
```

```
// Start[v] <= r <= hi
long hi= Start[v]+degree[v]−1;
find_pref(Adj, weight, weight1, r, hi);
nops_step += hi−r+1;
long e= Adj[hi];
Pref[v]= e;

/* Remove the top entry from
   the adjacency list of v */
degree[v]−−;

/* Register a match or propose */
if (e==Suitor[v]){
    match[*nmatch]= e;
    (*nmatch)++;
    if (e < nedges){ // internal edge
        degree[v0[e]]= 0;
        degree[v1[e]]= 0;
    } else {
        degree[v]= 0;
        long tag= ACCEPT;
        bsp_send(destproc[e−nedges],
        &tag,&(v1[e]), sizeof(long));
    }
} else if (e >= nedges){
    long tag= PROPOSE;
    bsp_send(destproc[e−nedges], &tag,
            &(v1[e]), sizeof(long));
}

/* Replace the previous suitor
   of the preference */
if (e < nedges){
    /* Determine other end point of
       edge e */
    long u = (v0[e]==v ? v1[e] :
                         v0[e]);
    long e0= Suitor[u];
    Suitor[u]= e;

    reject_suitor(u,e0,q_lo,&nq,
            Q,nvertices,nedges,
            v0,v1,destproc,Alive,Pref);
}
```

```
                        /* Split the top part of the
                        adjacency list of v if the part
                        is large enough */
                        hi= Start[v]+degree[v]−1; // new hi
                        if (hi−r >= SPLITMIN){
                            long r_new= split_adj(Adj, weight,
                                                weight1, r, hi);
                            nops_step += hi−r+1;
                            Splitter[r_new]= true;
                        }
                    }
                }
            }
        }
        *nops += nops_step;
        (*nsteps)++;
        bsp_sync();

        /* Determine if the algorithm has terminated */
        alldone= true;
        for (long t=0; t<p; t++){
            if(Done[t] == false){
                alldone= false;
                break;
            }
        }
    }
    bsp_pop_reg(Done);

    vecfreeb(Splitter);   vecfreeb(Alive);
    vecfreei(Q);          vecfreei(Pref);
    vecfreei(Suitor);     vecfreei(Done);

} /* end bspmatch */
```

5.10 Experimental results on the Cartesius supercomputer

In this section, we perform numerical experiments for parallel graph matching on the supercomputer Cartesius, which we use as a distributed-memory parallel computer. We run our experiments on the Broadwell nodes, which have been benchmarked in Section 3.7 for multiple nodes with distributed memory, cf. Table 3.2. We use up to 1024 processor cores.

Table 5.1 Test set of weighted graphs. The parameters given are: the number of vertices n, the number of edges m, the average degree d, and the maximum degree Δ.

Name	n	m	d	Δ	Origin
tx2010	914 231	2 228 136	4.9	121	redistricting Texas
mouse_gene	45 101	14 461 095	641.3	8 031	gene regulatory network
cage15	5 154 859	47 022 346	18.2	46	DNA electrophoresis
kmer_P1a	139 353 211	148 914 992	2.1	40	protein k-mer

Table 5.1 presents our test graphs, which originate in various data sets and which can be obtained through the SuiteSparse Matrix Collection [79]. The meaning of the vertices, edges, and weights of these graphs is as follows.

- tx2010: the vertices represent Texas land areas from the 2010 US Census, the edges represent connections to neighbouring areas, and the edge weights the length of the shared borders. The weights are integers in the range $[1, 10\ 149\ 954]$.

- mouse_gene: the vertices represent probes from a DNA microarray corresponding to mouse genes, the edges represent regulatory interactions between the genes, and the edge weights their mutual information values. Self-edges (corresponding to diagonal matrix elements) were removed. The weights are real numbers in the range $(0, 1]$.

- cage15: the vertices represent states of a polymer of length 15, the edges represent possible state transitions, and the edge weights their probabilities, see also Fig. 4.1. The edges and their weights were taken from the strictly lower triangular part of the corresponding matrix. The weights are real numbers in the range $(0, 1)$.

- kmer_P1a: the vertices represent segments of length k (so-called k-mers) of amino acids and the edges represent overlapping segment pairs. The weights are unit, since the corresponding matrix is a pattern (binary) matrix.

The graphs of the test set were partitioned by one run of the Mondriaan partitioner, version 4.2.1, in 1D row mode for the purpose of a parallel SpMV with $p = 1, 2, 4, \ldots, 1024$. On input, the graph was translated to a matrix by creating the corresponding sparse symmetric adjacency matrix A. Mondriaan was then set to add a dummy diagonal (with diagonal entries that count for communication but not for load balancing purposes) and to generate the same distribution for input and output vectors. This produced a proper vertex partitioning with each vertex stored together with its complete adjacency list on one of the processors.

Running Mondriaan to partition a test graph takes much longer than running a matching algorithm on the partitioned graph. Still, this resembles a likely use case, where the graph is available in a sensible distributed form, as part of a larger application. If we would not partition the graph beforehand, but instead would use a random distribution of the vertices, most edges would be cut and the algorithm would be communication-bound. The

Table 5.2 Measured execution time (in ms) for weighted graph matching using the BSPonMPI library.

p	tx2010	mouse_gene	cage15	kmer_P1a
1	208.5	671	2 358	59 057
2	107.0	356	1 237	32 473
4	52.4	322	646	17 618
8	28.1	305	424	9 054
16	15.1	251	194	4 454
32	9.1	317	178	2 756
64	7.5	538	88	911
128	7.9	836	76	561
256	8.3	2 005	77	299
512	15.1	2 526	129	204
1 024	29.3	6 295	218	302

advantage of parallel matching would then be that larger problems can be solved, because the graph would be distributed across the processor memories.

Table 5.2 presents the timings obtained for $p \leq 1024$ on up to 32 Broadwell nodes of Cartesius, running the program bspmatch from Section 5.9 on top of the distributed-memory BSPonMPI library [281], version 1.1, which, in turn, runs on top of OpenMPI, version 3.1.1. We used the gcc compiler, version 7.3.0, with the compiler optimization flag -O3. This is the same experimental setup as in Section 4.12. Note that the time of the preprocessing needed to partition and distribute the graph is not included, that is the time is only the time of the matching. We did not develop a separate sequential version of the bspmatch program because we expect the overhead of the parallel program to be small. The reason is that the program processes internal edges separately and that it does not invoke bsp_send primitives for them, and this is especially important for the case $p = 1$, where all edges are internal. As a result, the program for $p = 1$ almost runs like a sequential program.

The timings of Table 5.2 decrease monotonically for smaller values of p, until a minimum time is reached. For the largest problem kmer_P1a this is for $p = 512$, with a good speedup of a factor 289. For the smaller problem mouse_gene, however, the minimum is already reached for $p = 16$, with a speedup of only a factor 2.7. After reaching the minimum, using more processors becomes counterproductive, which is partly due to the increasing cost of communication and synchronization for larger p. Both g and l increase and also the communication volume increases with further splits of the input graph.

Table 5.3 presents the number of matches and the total matching weight for the four test graphs, as computed by bspmatch for $p = 1$. Because of the preference for a local match in tie-breaking, there is a slight variation (of at most 0.1%) in these numbers for varying p. Switching this preference off makes the matching outcome unique and renders the algorithm deterministic; we checked this for our runs by checking the matching weights in that case and indeed these are always the same.

Table 5.3 Total number of matches $|\mathcal{M}|$, total matching weight $\omega(\mathcal{M})$, and an upper bound on the achievable total weight, for the parallel program run with $p = 1$.

	tx2010	mouse_gene	cage15	kmer_P1a
Matches	375 342	18 273	2 575 446	59 735 594
Weight	28 933 021 703	1 287.998	76 890.186	59 735 594
Weight upper bound	39 547 303 682	1 553.424	77 709.076	69 676 605

Table 5.4 Total number of operations performed to compute the matching and a linear-time lower bound of $4m$ on the number of operations. The results are for the parallel program run on p processors.

	p	tx2010	mouse_gene	cage15	kmer_P1a
Operations lower bound ($\times 10^6$)		8.9	58	188	596
Operations ($\times 10^6$)	1	9.5	59	193	873
	32	9.5	148	206	872
	1 024	9.8	168	225	872

Table 5.3 also gives an upper bound on the matching weight,

$$\omega(\mathcal{M}) \leq \frac{1}{2} \sum_{v \in \mathcal{V}} \max \{\omega(u,v) \; : \; (u,v) \in \mathcal{E}\}. \tag{5.27}$$

This bound holds because every vertex $v \in \mathcal{V}$ contributes at most the weight of one half-edge to the total matching weight, and this contribution is at most half the weight of its heaviest edge. Here, we view an edge as a pair of half-edges, one half-edge connected to each endpoint. We observe that the matching weight is in the range from 73.2% of the upper bound (for tx2010) to 98.9% (for cage15). Note that this value is a percentage of an upper bound on the maximum weight, so that the percentage achieved for the maximum weight itself will even be higher. To find that percentage, however, we would have to solve these problems optimally, which is infeasible for such problem sizes.

Table 5.4 displays the number of operations performed during the whole algorithm, obtained by summing the sizes of the ranges encountered in finding living edges and splitters, setting preferences, and splitting adjacency lists. The operation counts for $p = 1$ fit remarkably well with the theoretical lower bound of $4m$ given by eqn (5.12). This means that in practice the partial sort leads to a linear-time sequential algorithm. The number of operations grows with p, because operations are performed on the basis of incomplete information, and some operations could have been avoided if new information such as a new suitor were already available locally. The growth, however, is limited and only for one problem, mouse_gene, is it significant, reaching a factor of 2.8. For mouse_gene and $p = 1\,024$, the total number of operations is still well below the upper bound $2m \log_2 \Delta$ of eqn (5.11), which amounts to about 375×10^6 operations.

Table 5.5 Number of supersteps needed to compute a parallel graph matching for p processors, and for comparison an estimate of $(\log_2 m)\log_2 \Delta$ representing the expected parallel depth for edge weights chosen uniformly at random.

	p	tx2010	mouse_gene	cage15	kmer_P1a
Supersteps	2	8	957	55	26
	32	10	1 613	69	67
	1 024	13	2 099	82	72
Parallel depth		146	309	141	145

Comparing Tables 5.2 and 5.4 for $p = 1$ gives the actual computing rate of the matching program. This rate is highest for mouse_gene, reaching 88 Mops/s (million operations per second), far below the benchmark rate of 5 912 Mflop/s given by Table 3.2. The reason for the much lower computing rate (by a factor of 67.2) is that here the operations are irregular, accessing arrays such as Alive in a rather random fashion, and also that each basic $\mathcal{O}(1)$-operation involves a function call, namely to heavier; as a further optimization, this call could be replaced by inline code, if desired.

Table 5.5 shows the number of supersteps needed to perform the parallel computation as a function of p. Clearly, this number grows with p, and the reason is the same as for the growth in number of operations, namely incomplete information. For comparison, we provide an estimate of the **parallel depth**, that is the length of the critical path in an algorithm, which is $\mathcal{O}((\log m)\log \Delta)$, provided the edge weights are chosen uniformly at random [107, Theorem 6.1]. This will be a lower bound on the number of supersteps for a graph with random edge weights. Although the weights are not random here, the estimate is quite reasonable for mouse_gene, cage15, and kmer_P1a, but it is far off for tx2010.

Table 5.6 presents results for load balancing by imposing a maximum number of operations carried out by a processor in a superstep, see Section 5.7; once this maximum has been exceeded, the processor calls for a synchronization. The bottom line of the table gives the time without any maximum imposed, which represents the same experiment as displayed for $p = 8$ in Table 5.2. Unfortunately, the results differ somewhat: 341 ms in the present table vs. 424 ms in the other table, indicating that it is hard to reproduce results exactly in different sets of experiments.

The total number of operations for cage15 and $p = 8$ is about 2×10^8, so that the average number of operations per processor and per superstep is about 413 000, which is close to the benchmarked cost of a synchronization, $l = 216 380$ (36.6 μs). Because the operations of our algorithm cost much more than the flops of our benchmark, this means that the cost of the synchronizations themselves is insignificant. Indeed, the total synchronization time for 60 supersteps based on the benchmark value of l is only 2.2 ms.

Despite the insignificant synchronization cost for the experiments of Table 5.6, we do not observe any gain from the load balancing procedure. The computing time and the number of supersteps simply decrease with a higher imposed limit and the best result is obtained if no limit is imposed. We found the same in all our other experiments. This indicates that our work counters are not accurate enough. Reasons may be that not all $\mathcal{O}(1)$-operations are created equal, some involving more comparisons than others, and also that operations

Table 5.6 Computing time and number of supersteps as a function of the maximum amount of work W_{max} for the graph cage15 and $p = 8$; W_{max} is expressed as a maximum allowed number of local operations per superstep.

Max operations ($\times 10^3$)	Time (in ms)	Supersteps
4	845	6 618
8	657	3 340
16	555	1 694
32	500	875
64	465	465
128	445	261
256	429	159
512	417	108
1 024	400	83
2 048	377	71
4 096	352	65
8 192	346	62
16 384	341	60
∞	341	60

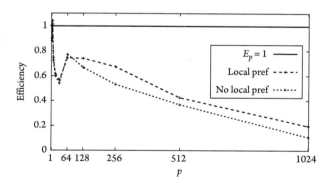

Figure 5.15 Efficiency for weighted matching for the graph kmer_P1a, with and without tie-breaking by preferring local matches. The efficiency is relative to the parallel program run with $p = 1$.

associated with message processing were not counted. To improve the procedure, we should refine our counting or use a timer, as outlined in Section 5.7. We did not pursue this further.

Figure 5.15 shows the efficiency of parallel matching for the graph kmer_P1a, which has unit weights so that all weight comparisons are ties. For this reason, we choose kmer_P1a to investigate the influence of tie-breaking with a local preference. For small p, we observe hardly any difference in efficiency. For $p \geq 128$, however, we clearly see the benefits of preferring local matches; for $p = 1\,024$, this yields an efficiency of 19.6% instead of the 10.7% in the case without a local preference. We also noted a tiny advantage of 0.04% in the number of matches found, with the number of matches growing steadily from 59 735 594 for $p = 1$ to 59 764 727 for $p = 1\,024$. Without the local preference, the number of matches always equals 59 735 594.

5.11 Bibliographic notes

5.11.1 Sequential graph matching

Berge [25] proved in 1957 that a matching in an unweighted graph has maximum cardinality if and only if no augmenting path exists. An $\mathcal{M}$-**augmenting path** for a given matching $\mathcal{M} \subseteq \mathcal{E}$ is a path of vertices $v_0, v_1, \ldots, v_r$ of odd length r, where $(v_k, v_{k+1}) \in \mathcal{M}$ for odd k and $(v_k, v_{k+1}) \in \mathcal{E} \backslash \mathcal{M}$ for even, and which starts and ends in an unmatched vertex. It alternates between edges inside and outside the matching. An augmenting path can be used to improve the matching, since flipping the edges of the path increases the cardinality of the matching by one.

Avis [11] showed that the greedy matching algorithm in an edge-weighted graph is a 1/2-approximation algorithm. Drake and Hougardy [96] showed that a 2/3-approximation can be achieved by applying seven local improvement operations, organized in rounds, until no such operation is possible anymore. In each round, all matched edges are considered, at a cost of $\mathcal{O}(m)$. The improvement operations flip the edges in a short alternating path or cycle with at most two edges outside the matching, such that the total weight increases. A restriction applies to the alternating paths: an alternating path ending with an unmatched edge cannot have its endpoint matched (by another matched edge). This procedure with short alternating paths or cycles could also be used to improve the matchings computed by our Algorithm 5.7, since short paths do not hinder parallelism too much. Longer paths, however, could wind through many processors parts and hence cause a lot of trouble.

Preis [252] proposed the first linear-time 1/2-approximation algorithm, LAM, based on local domination, and a few years later Drake and Hougardy [97] designed a much simpler linear-time 1/2-approximation algorithm, the path-growing algorithm (PGA). In PGA, edges are inserted alternatingly in matchings $\mathcal{M}$ and $\mathcal{M}'$, and at the end the heaviest matching $\mathcal{M}$ or $\mathcal{M}'$ is chosen. The algorithm starts at a vertex v_0, the heaviest edge (v_0, v_1) is chosen and included in $\mathcal{M}$, and then v_0 and all its incident edges are removed from the graph; this process is then repeated for v_1, where its heaviest edge (v_1, v_2) is included in $\mathcal{M}'$. After that, the heaviest edge (v_2, v_3) is included in $\mathcal{M}$, and so on. This grows a path until a dead end is reached, and then a new starting vertex with at least one incident edge is chosen. An enhanced version PGA' of PGA uses dynamic programming to find a maximum matching for each path in linear time, based on the formula

$$\omega(r) = \max\{\omega(r-1), \omega(r-2) + \omega(v_{r-1}, v_r)\} \tag{5.28}$$

for the maximum weight on a path $v_0, v_1, \ldots, v_r$ of length $r \geq 2$. The linear-time algorithms LAM, PGA, and PGA' all create long paths and hence are not easily amenable to parallelization.

Gale and Shapley [118] introduced in 1962 the procedure of proposals and deferred acceptance, as part of their elegant solution algorithm for the **stable marriage problem**. They formulate the problem and its solution as follows: n boys have to match with n girls, and each person has a sorted list of preferences for a marriage partner. (This traditional setting causes the corresponding graph to be bipartite. The general, non bipartite problem is known as the **stable roommate problem**.) A matching is called **unstable** if there exist two boy–girl pairs, (b_0, g_0) and (b_1, g_1), such that b_0 prefers g_1 over g_0, and g_1 prefers b_0 over b_1. If no such pairs exist, the matching is called **stable**. A stable, perfect matching can be obtained in a sequence of rounds. In each round, each boy who has not proposed yet, or whose proposals have all been rejected, proposes to his preferred girl, excluding girls that have already rejected him. (Of course, the roles of boys and girls can be reversed here.) The girls keep the best proposer (suitor) so far and reject a proposer once a better proposer arrives. This procedure terminates when no more proposals can be made and then each girl accepts her current proposer. The time complexity of this algorithm is $\mathcal{O}(n^2)$. The book by Manlove [206] covers the state-of-the-art in algorithms for matching with preferences, one-sided as well as two-sided, for both the bipartite and the general case.

Manne *et al.* [209] reveal the relation between recent algorithms for greedy matching (GM) and solutions of the classical stable marriage (SM) problem. They prove that the weighted matching problem can be formulated as a special case of the stable marriage problem with incomplete preference lists (i.e., the sparse version of SM), where each preference list corresponds to an adjacency list in the graph and where the preferences are based on the edge weights. If there are no ties for the weights, the solution $\mathcal{M}$ of the matching problem is unique, and it contains exactly those edges that correspond to the unique solution of the corresponding SM problem. The authors compare two approaches for handling rejected proposals: queue-based (Gale–Shapley [118]), that is waiting until the next round before proposing again, or stack-based (McVitie–Wilson [217]), that is immediately proposing again. In Algorithms 5.3 and 5.7, this means using either a queue or a stack as a data structure for the sets Q and Q_s. Given the similarities between the SM and GM problems, and the existence of linear-time algorithms for GM, the authors pose the (still open) question whether it is possible to design a linear-time SM algorithm with two sets of unsorted input weights, $\omega(b_i, g_j)$ and $\omega(g_i, b_j)$, instead of preference lists.

Pothen, Ferdous, and Manne [250] survey approximation algorithms for various graph matching problems, including maximum-cardinality matching, maximum edge-weighted matching (the problem treated in the present chapter), maximum vertex-weighted matching, and a generalization called b-matching, where every vertex v is allowed to have at most $b(v)$ incident edges. Choosing $b(v) = 1$ for all v reduces the b-matching to the standard matching as we know it. The authors present several sequential algorithms and they also explain the better amenability of certain approximation algorithms to parallelization. They extensively discuss the suitor algorithm (which we parallelized for distributed memory in Algorithm 5.7) and its b-suitor generalization. Experimental results show that the suitor algorithm achieves on average 94% of the optimal weight, which is much better than the guarantee of 50%. The suitor algorithm is by far the fastest, compared to several competitors, and an OpenMP implementation achieves a speedup of about 13 on 40 cores of a shared-memory parallel computer. The authors also provide a proof that a matching $\mathcal{M}$ attains at least $k/(k+1)$ times the optimal weight if there does not exist a weight-increasing k-**augmentation**, which is an alternating path or cycle with at most k edges outside $\mathcal{M}$, obeying the same endpoint restriction on alternating paths as in the $k = 2$ case of Drake and Hougardy [96] mentioned above.

An interesting application of b-matching treated in the survey by Pothen, Ferdous, and Manne [250] is in privacy protection: given a set of data, represented by an integer input matrix X, where x_{ij} represents feature j of individual i, create a masked output matrix Y with a minimum number of masked elements (denoted by '*'), such that each individual i is indistinguishable from at least $b(i) - 1$ other individuals. This problem is solved by creating a complete graph with vertices representing the individuals and weighted edges representing the dissimilarity (number of different features) between pairs of individuals, and then computing a minimum-weight b-edge cover for this graph, which can be done by solving a b-matching problem. In a b-**edge cover** problem, every vertex v must have at least $b(v)$ incident edges in the cover.

5.11.2 Parallel graph matching

The parallel edge-weighted matching algorithm described in this chapter, Algorithm 5.7, is based on a distributed-memory parallel algorithm by Manne and Bisseling [207], extended by the suitor idea from Manne and Halappanavar [208] for a shared-memory parallel algorithm. Hoepman [161] presented a precursor to these parallel algorithms in a distributed computing context, where every vertex is associated with a processor and where neighbouring vertices can communicate with each other. Note that this assumption of $p = n$ makes the algorithm impractical for parallel computation, and that proper partitioning is needed to handle the more realistic case of $p < n$.

Manne and Halappanavar [208] introduce a method to improve the quality of a given matching. After having obtained a matching $\mathcal{M} \subseteq \mathcal{E}$, they run their algorithm again, but now starting from the edge set $\mathcal{E} \backslash \mathcal{M}$. This way, they obtain a second matching $\mathcal{M}'$, which satisfies $\mathcal{M} \cap \mathcal{M}' = \emptyset$. The vertices of the graph $(\mathcal{V}, \mathcal{M} \cup \mathcal{M}')$ have degree at most two, since they possess at most one incident edge from $\mathcal{M}$ and at most one from $\mathcal{M}'$. This implies that $\mathcal{M} \cup \mathcal{M}'$ consists of vertex-disjoint paths and even-length cycles. They then apply dynamic programming to these paths and cycles; for a path as in the PGA' algorithm described above and for a cycle $v_0, v_1, \ldots, v_r, v_0$ by taking the heaviest of the two paths $v_0, v_1, \ldots, v_r$ and $v_1, \ldots, v_r, v_0$. Experimental results show that this improvement attains state-of-the-art quality, as measured by the relative **gap-to-optimality** metric $(\omega(\mathcal{M}^*) - \omega(\mathcal{M}))/\omega(\mathcal{M}^*)$. The extra cost incurred by the improvement method is at most twice the cost of the original matching algorithm.

Halappanavar et al. [137] present lessons learned from implementing weighted general graph matching and bipartite maximum-cardinality matching on multithreaded (shared-memory) architectures as a prototypical study into irregular applications. One lesson is that approximation algorithms localize the computation, making it more suitable for parallelization than exact, optimal algorithms, which are more global and lead to slower convergence at the end of the computation. Another lesson is that algorithms that follow the data flow, such as parallel matching using suitors (see Section 5.3), are superior to algorithms that maintain a work queue (such as the set D in Algorithm 5.2), especially if several processors share this queue. A final lesson is that switching to a sequential algorithm at the end of the computation may be beneficial, which is easier in the shared-memory setting where a single processor has direct access to all the data.

Khan *et al.* [181] implemented a local domination/suitor-based algorithm for weighted b-matching on a distributed-memory parallel computer. Their algorithm resembles the algorithm presented in this chapter; it uses a local queue Q_s for storing vertices that need to propose, and it partially sorts the neighbours of a vertex by increasing weight. Their implementation is based on MPI and OpenMP, and it tries to avoid synchronization by using nonblocking ('asynchronous') MPI send primitives, where the sender does not wait for the completion of the message transferral before proceeding with its tasks. The algorithm creates superstep-like rounds by handling a batch of vertices from the queue at the same time. Still, there is no global synchronization barrier, and this has its advantages (no unnecessary waiting at the barrier) and its disadvantages (no load balancing or communication optimization at the barrier). A b-matching problem on a large graph from the Graph500 benchmark with 268 million vertices and 2147 million edges was solved in less than four seconds on 16 384 cores of Cori (the supercomputer described in Section 2.7). Ghosh *et al.* [123] achieve a sixfold speedup for this algorithm on Cori by replacing the two-sided send/receive primitives of MPI by new one-sided primitives from MPI-3 and by new neighbourhood collectives (involving only a subset of the processors). As a bonus, the one-sided primitives reduced the energy consumption by a factor of 3.6: the Friendster social network graph of 1.8×10^9 edges was matched on 1024 cores consuming only 793 kJ of energy, compared to the 2868 kJ needed for the two-sided primitives.

5.11.3 GraphBLAS

Azad and Buluç [13] investigate maximal-cardinality matching for bipartite graphs by exploiting the duality between graphs and sparse matrices. They formulate their basic operations in terms of matrix and vector operations. A bipartite graph with vertex sets $\mathcal{V}_0$ and $\mathcal{V}_1$ is represented by a sparse $|\mathcal{V}_0| \times |\mathcal{V}_1|$ matrix A with $a_{ij} = 1$ if $(i,j) \in \mathcal{E}$, for $i \in \mathcal{V}_0$ and $j \in \mathcal{V}_1$, and $a_{ij} = 0$ otherwise. The vertices in $\mathcal{V}_0$ are called **row vertices** and those in $\mathcal{V}_1$ **column vertices**. In contrast to the standard sparse matrix–vector multiplication (SpMV) studied in Chapter 4 where the vector is assumed to be dense, the vectors can now be sparse, giving rise to an **SpMSpV** operation. To find the row vertices adjacent to the currently unmatched column vertices, they perform a generalized matrix–vector multiplication $\mathbf{u} = A\mathbf{v}$, where the input vector is defined by $v_j = j$ if j is unmatched, and v_j has a dummy (neutral) value otherwise. The multiply and add operations for computing and summing the products $a_{ij} \cdot v_j$ are redefined as **semiring** operations: the multiply becomes a **select2nd** operation, returning the second operand v_j if $a_{ij} \neq 0$, and the neutral element of the addition if $a_{ij} = 0$; the addition becomes a **min** operation, taking the minimum, or a **rand** operation, taking a random operand. As a result, u_i is the minimum index of an unmatched column adjacent to row vertex i, or the index of a random such column. This enables row vertex i to propose a match to a single unmatched column vertex u_i.

In their hybrid parallel implementation, Azad and Buluç [13] exploit both shared and distributed memory by using OpenMP as well as MPI. They formulate their algorithms in a bulk synchronous style, performing each basic graph operation simultaneously on a large set of vertices. The matrix A is distributed in a 2D Cartesian manner, by first randomly permuting the rows and columns to balance the work load, and then using a block distribution. This reduces communication to some extent by making use of both dimensions, and it has the advantage that it is easy to determine which processor a nonzero (an edge) belongs to. Since the maximal matching is often done only once, as a preprocessing step for another computation (e.g. linear-system solving), finding a full optimal partitioning specifically for the matching is in many cases not worthwhile, because its high costs cannot be recovered. The chosen distribution is then a good compromise. The speedup achieved by the authors in numerical experiments for matching on a Cray XC30 is on average 121 for $p = 2048$.

The matrix/semiring framework for graph algorithms has several advantages: a range of different algorithms can be formulated with only small differences in their program texts, and parallelism can be derived automatically from basic parallel sparse matrix computations. By design, the resulting parallel algorithms are BSP algorithms. A treatise on the matrix/semiring approach is the book *Graph Algorithms in the Language of Linear Algebra* [177], which states three advantages: (i) syntactic simplicity, making graph algorithms understandable to a wider audience with a basic linear algebra knowledge; (ii) ease of implementation, enabling reuse of existing sparse matrix software; (iii) higher performance, due to more opportunities for optimization. The basic connection between a graph $\mathcal{G}$ and its adjacency matrix $A(\mathcal{G})$ is given by eqn (5.22), where for a directed graph the direction of an edge (i,j) is from i to j. (Note that this is in contrast to the web link example of eqn (4.6), where we defined a sparse matrix based on links in the opposite direction.) As a basic example, one step of a breadth-first search from a vertex i is expressed by the operation $A^T \mathbf{e}_i$, where $\mathbf{e}_i$ is a vector with value 1 in position i, and 0 elsewhere. The introductory chapters of the book present the axioms of a semiring such as the addition being commutative, and give examples of a semiring such as $(\mathbf{R}, +, \times, 0, 1)$, the reals with the standard addition and multiplication and 0 and 1 as their respective neutral elements, and $(\mathbf{R} \cup \{\infty\}, \min, +, \infty, 0)$. Algorithms are formulated in this language for finding strongly connected components, shortest paths, specific subgraphs such as small trees, and also for determining betweenness centrality. The linear algebra approach facilitates parallelization and it naturally creates a 2D (edge-based) perspective for data distribution. A chapter on multilinear algebra treats **tensors**, a generalization of matrices to higher dimensions, which are popular in the field of Big Data. A tensor can capture a set of weights or attributes of different type associated with an edge in a graph. The book also treats **hypersparse** matrices, which are defined by $nz(A) < n$, and which may occur as submatrices assigned to a processor in a parallel computation.

The **GraphBLAS** [176] is a standard developed to capture the most fundamental graph operations and express them as matrix operations on semirings, so that a wide range of graph operations can be carried out by composing a small number of matrix operations. These matrix operations involve adjacency matrices and incidence matrices. An **incidence matrix** (or **edge matrix**) of a graph $\mathcal{G}$ is an $|\mathcal{E}| \times |\mathcal{V}|$ matrix where each row represents an edge and each column a vertex. Here, a graph $\mathcal{G}$ is associated with a pair of incidence matrices, $E_{\text{out}}(\mathcal{G})$ and $E_{\text{in}}(\mathcal{G})$. Edge $e_k = (i,j)$ defines $(E_{\text{out}})_{ki} = 1$ and $(E_{\text{in}})_{kj} = 1$; otherwise, the values in row k of these matrices are 0. The adjacency matrix A can be obtained from these incidence matrices by

$$A = (E_{\text{out}})^T E_{\text{in}}. \tag{5.29}$$

An early implementation of the GraphBLAS is the Combinatorial BLAS by Buluç and Gilbert [50]. A reference implementation of the GraphBLAS API is available for MATLAB, as part of the SuiteSparse library by Davis [78].

A possible field of application of the GraphBLAS is artificial neural networks. Kepner *et al.* [178] formulate an SpMV for a deep neural network using the standard semiring of the reals and they express the subsequent ReLU activation operation (see Fig. 4.8) using the semiring $(\mathbf{R} \cup \{-\infty\}, \max, +, -\infty, 0)$.

....

5.12 EXERCISES

Exercise 5.1 Prove that all runs of the basic dominant-edge algorithm, Algorithm 5.1, produce the same matching, irrespective of the picking order of the dominant edges, under the assumption that the weights of edges sharing the same vertex are all different. Hint: consider two runs of the algorithm and the set of edges that occur in one output matching but not in the other. What does the uniqueness result for the dominant-edge algorithm imply for the greedy matching algorithm?

Exercise 5.2 Consider an undirected graph $\mathcal{G} = (\mathcal{V}, \mathcal{E})$ that represents a square $k \times k$ grid. The graph has $n = k^2$ vertices, with vertex v_{i+jk} representing grid point (i,j). Therefore, the vertex set is

$$\mathcal{V} = \{(v_{i+jk} : 0 \leq i,j < k\}, \tag{5.30}$$

and the edge set is

$$\mathcal{E} = \{(v_{i+jk}, v_{i+(j+1)k}) : 0 \leq i < k \wedge 0 \leq j < k-1\} \cup$$
$$\{(v_{i+jk}, v_{i+1+jk}) : 0 \leq i < k-1 \wedge 0 \leq j < k\}. \tag{5.31}$$

Assume that the edge weights are given by $\omega(v_r, v_{r+k}) = r$ and $\omega(v_r, v_{r+1}) = r + 1/2$, provided that the corresponding edges exist. (Note that this problem is totally rigged!) Furthermore, assume that the graph has been partitioned over $p = 2$ processors and that the edge weights have already been sorted, so that no partial sorting or range splitting is needed.

(a) Draw the graph for $k = 8$ with vertex v_0 at the bottom left and v_{n-1} at the top right, and determine the matching obtained by Algorithm 5.3 for this graph.
(b) For an arbitrary k with $k \bmod 4 = 0$, let the graph be partitioned so that the vertex sets are $\mathcal{V}_0 = \{v_0, \ldots, v_{n/2-1}\}$ and $\mathcal{V}_1 = \{v_{n/2}, \ldots, v_{n-1}\}$. We call this a **horizontal**

partitioning. Analyse the behaviour of Algorithm 5.7 on this graph, assuming that setting a preference is one basic operation, which we simply call an 'op'. Use a true queue Q_s (with FIFO policy) for storing the local vertices that need to set a preference. Initialize the queue with the local vertices in increasing order. What is the situation after the first superstep, that is just before the first synchronization in the main loop of the algorithm? How many supersteps are needed? What is the total BSP cost? What is the speedup compared to a sequential algorithm?

(c) The same questions, but now for a vertical partitioning.

(d) Improve the load balance for the vertical partitioning by limiting the amount of work in a superstep. What is the resulting total cost?

(e) Give ideas for improving the queueing policy and motivate them.

Exercise 5.3 (∗) The program `bspmatch` is based on a vertex partitioning of the input graph with a conforming edge partitioning. Allowing an arbitrary edge partitioning may reduce computation time and memory use, as outlined at the end of Section 5.8. This means moving from a 1D to a 2D partitioning of the adjacency matrix A of the graph.

(a) Modify `bspmatch` to allow an arbitrary edge partitioning of the input graph in addition to the arbitrary vertex partitioning that was already allowed. Hint: the main program part affected is the function for finding a new preference, which now may become nonlocal, involving sending a request for best-preference candidates and responding in the next superstep. In other parts of the program, the adjacency lists may become shorter, but the operations carried out are still the same as before. You should introduce a new type of message for sending and answering candidate requests.

(b) Choose a suitable set of test graphs and use the Mondriaan package to partition each corresponding matrix $A + I$ by a symmetric 2D matrix partitioning. The off-diagonal nonzeros then determine the edge partitioning of the graph and the diagonal ones (those of I) the vertex partitioning.

(c) Test your modified program and compare its performance to the original program. Was it worth your efforts?

Exercise 5.4 (∗) An **independent set** in an undirected graph $\mathcal{G} = (\mathcal{V}, \mathcal{E})$ is a subset $\mathcal{I} \subseteq \mathcal{V}$ of vertices such that $u, v \in \mathcal{I}$ with $u \neq v$ implies $(u, v) \notin \mathcal{E}$. An independent set is **maximal** if it cannot be extended to a larger independent set. The maximal independent set (MIS) problem is to find a maximal independent set for a given graph.

(a) Design and implement a BSP algorithm for finding a MIS in a vertex-partitioned undirected unweighted graph based on Algorithm 5.11, which was adapted from [220, Algorithm $\mathcal{A}$]. This algorithm is a variant of Luby's algorithm [203].

(b) Test your program on a few large graphs from the Stanford Large Network Dataset Collection [196]. How many supersteps do you need to perform for each graph? Does this confirm the $\mathcal{O}(\log n)$ behaviour that is theoretically expected [220] for the number of rounds (supersteps)?

(c) Try to optimize your program, by improving either its speed or its output quality $|\mathcal{I}|$. One possibility is by **kernelization**, that is preprocessing to handle easy parts

---

Algorithm 5.11 Basic randomized maximal independent set algorithm [220].

---

input: $\mathcal{G}$: graph with vertex set $\mathcal{V}$ and edge set $\mathcal{E}$, $\mathcal{G} = (\mathcal{V}, \mathcal{E})$.
output: $\mathcal{I}$: maximal independent set, $\mathcal{I} \subseteq \mathcal{V}$.

$\mathcal{I} := \emptyset$;
while $\mathcal{V} \neq \emptyset$ **do**
    for all $v \in \mathcal{V}$ **do**
        pick a random real value $r(v) \in [0, 1]$;

    $\mathcal{V}_{\text{del}} := \emptyset$;
    for all $v \in \mathcal{V}$ **do**
        $Adj_v := \{u \in \mathcal{V} : (u, v) \in \mathcal{E}\}$;
        if $r(v) > \max\{r(u) : u \in Adj_v\}$ **then**
            $\mathcal{I} := \mathcal{I} \cup \{v\}$;
            $\mathcal{V}_{\text{del}} := \mathcal{V}_{\text{del}} \cup \{v\} \cup Adj_v$;

    $\mathcal{V} := \mathcal{V} \setminus \mathcal{V}_{\text{del}}$;
    $\mathcal{E} := \mathcal{E} \setminus \{(u, v) \in \mathcal{E} : v \in \mathcal{V}_{\text{del}}\}$;

---

of the graph first, thus reducing the size of the input given to the algorithm. For instance, we can include all vertices of degree 1 in the independent set at the start of the computation, while keeping the maximum achievable number of vertices in $\mathcal{I}$ the same. (Why?) Removing the edges connected to the degree-1 vertices may give rise to new degree-1 vertices (or even degree-0 vertices); these may be included in $\mathcal{I}$ as well, and so on. The preprocessing can also be inserted into the main loop of the algorithm. Note that computing a **maximum independent set** (with maximum cardinality) is extremely hard, so that we are satisfied with just a maximal set, hopefully with a large cardinality. How does the optimized program perform for your test graphs?

(d) Modify the MIS program to solve the weighted matching problem of this chapter indirectly, as follows. From the input graph $\mathcal{G} = (\mathcal{V}, \mathcal{E})$ construct a **line graph** $L(\mathcal{G})$, where edges from $\mathcal{G}$ become vertices in $L(\mathcal{G})$ and where edges in $L(\mathcal{G})$ represent pairs of edges from $\mathcal{G}$ that share a vertex in $\mathcal{G}$. The edge weights from $\mathcal{G}$ become vertex weights $r(v)$ in $L(\mathcal{G})$ that replace the random values. The resulting weighted MIS in $L(\mathcal{G})$ then corresponds to a weighted matching in $\mathcal{G}$. (This relation between Luby's algorithm and dominant-edge matching has already been observed in [207].) Compare the performance of your modified program with that of `bspmatch`, with respect to speed, output quality, and memory use. Explain the difference in performance.

Exercise 5.5 (∗) The 8-queens puzzle is the problem of putting eight queens on an 8×8 chessboard without any queens attacking any other, meaning that they are not allowed to be in the same row, column, or diagonal. This puzzle is commonly attributed to Max Bezzel who published it in 1848. The puzzle has 92 solutions, including the ones that can be created

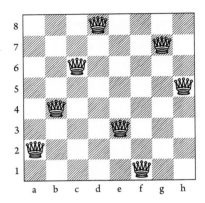

Figure 5.16 Eight nonattacking queens on a chessboard.

from another solution by rotating or reflecting the board. One of the 92 solutions is shown in Fig. 5.16.

(a) Design a recursive sequential algorithm for finding a solution to the n-queens problem on an $n \times n$ chessboard. Let $q(i)$ be the column number of the queen placed in row i, for $0 \le i < n$. A solution is then represented by a vector q of length n. Note that q must be a permutation of $0, 1, \ldots, n - 1$. A partial solution may have a dummy value $q(i) = -1$ for a row i without a queen. Hint: write an efficient function for checking whether a new queen attacks an existing queen along a diagonal. Backtrack the recursion if you get stuck and cannot add another queen. Declare victory when you reach n queens.

(b) Parallelize your algorithm by distributing the work over a set of processors. The recursive search can be seen as a **depth-first search** (DFS) in a tree. Assign the n children of the tree root cyclically over the p processors; these children represent the n possible choices for $q(0)$. If $p > n$, assign the nearly n^2 grandchildren cyclically. Measure the running time for various p and n.

(c) Build a mechanism into your program that detects if a processor has found a solution, so that others can then stop searching. This may be done by synchronizing at regular intervals as discussed in Section 5.7, or by some other clever mechanism. You might even try to abuse the `bsp_abort`.

(d) Insert some randomness into your algorithm by assigning the children randomly instead of cyclically, and by choosing the next row randomly. Does this improve the running time? Do you observe any **superlinear speedup**, that is a speedup $S_p > p$? Explain your results.

(e) Modify your algorithm so that it computes and counts all solutions. Verify your results using the On-Line Encyclopedia of Integer Sequences [272]. Does this modification make the load balancing easier or harder? What is the largest n you can reach now?

Exercise 5.6 (∗∗) A **self-avoiding walk** (SAW) on a regular lattice such as the square lattice is a walk along the edges of the lattice which never revisits a lattice point. Counting

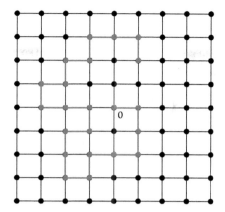

Figure 5.17 A self-avoiding walk of length $N = 21$ on the square lattice starting in the origin, one of $c_{21} = 2\,408\,806\,028$ possibilities. Only part of the lattice is shown.

the number of self-avoiding walks of a particular length has a long history which started in 1947 [239] and which has applications in polymer physics, see for example [168] for a recent monograph. Counting SAWs remains a challenging problem today, because there is no known formula for the total number of walks c_N of length N and this number grows exponentially as $\mathcal{O}(\mu^N)$, where μ is the so-called **connective constant** of the lattice. Figure 5.17 shows a SAW on the square lattice.

(a) Design a recursive sequential algorithm for counting the number of self-avoiding walks on an undirected simple graph $\mathcal{G} = (\mathcal{V}, \mathcal{E})$ starting in vertex $v \in \mathcal{V}$ and traversing N edges. Hint: use a boolean array *visited* of length $n = |\mathcal{V}|$ to mark the vertices visited so far. In graph terminology, a self-avoiding walk is called a **simple path**.

(b) Implement your algorithm in a sequential recursive program and test it for the square lattice with all walks starting in the origin. Include only reachable lattice points in the graph. Can you exploit symmetry, for example by only starting walks eastwards? Check your counts c_N against the numbers presented in the On-Line Encyclopedia of Integer Sequences (OEIS) [272]. Use your results to estimate

$$\mu = \lim_{N \to \infty} c_N^{1/N}. \tag{5.32}$$

(c) Test your program for another lattice of your choice (in any dimension) and check whether the OEIS has values c_N for this lattice. Compare the results. How does the run time of your program grow as a function of N?

(d) Parallelize your algorithm by distributing the work over a set of processors. Hint: you can store a copy of the graph (or the part that can be reached in N steps) at every processor, because its size will be small due to the exponential growth of the number of walks as a function of N, which limits N.

(e) Measure the load balance of your algorithm, both for a regular lattice and for an irregular input graph. How efficient is your program in terms of parallel performance?

(f) Build work counters into your parallel program, as discussed in Section 5.7, to detect idling processors as early as possible and redistribute work if needed. What do you need to communicate to offload work to another processor?

(g) Measure the load balance again and check whether it has improved.

Exercise 5.7 (**) A typical characteristic of social networks is that any two friends of a given person are more likely to be mutual friends as well: friendships do not occur randomly! This observation has led to the definition of the **local clustering coefficient** by Watts and Strogatz [308],

$$c_v = \frac{2t_v}{d_v(d_v - 1)}, \text{ for } v \in \mathcal{V}, \tag{5.33}$$

where t_v is the number of triangles containing v and d_v is the degree of v, with $d_v \geq 2$. If $d_v = 0$ or $d_v = 1$, no triangles are possible and $c_v = 0$. This coefficient compares the number of triangles to the maximum number $d_v(d_v - 1)/2$ possible and thus represents a fraction between 0 and 1. The average local clustering coefficient over all the vertices of a graph,

$$c = \frac{1}{|\mathcal{V}|} \sum_{v \in \mathcal{V}} c_v, \tag{5.34}$$

is a very useful metric. Newman [229, Table 10.1] gives values ranging from 0.001 for a student dating network up to 0.78 for a film actor network and even 0.88 for a company director network.

(a) Design an efficient sequential algorithm based on adjacency lists that takes as input an undirected graph and computes as output the average value c.

(b) To facilitate analysis, assume that the graph is **regular**, so that all vertices have the same degree d. What is the time complexity of your algorithm?

(c) Design and implement an algorithm that takes as input a vertex-partitioned undirected graph and computes in parallel the average value c and the total number of triangles.

(d) Now assume the graph has positive edge weights, normalized such that the largest occurring edge weight is $\omega_{max} = 1$. These edge weights might represent the strengths of the friendships in a social network. A good measure for the strength of a triangle (u, v, w) is the geometric mean of the three edge weights:

$$\omega(u, v, w) = (\omega(u, v) \cdot \omega(v, w) \cdot \omega(w, u))^{1/3}. \tag{5.35}$$

(The geometric mean has many nice properties, see eqns (4.46) and (4.47), and this may be the moment to review them.) Modify your parallel program to generalize the computation of c_v to the weighted case, replacing the counting of triangles by the summing of triangle weights. This computes the metric proposed by Onnela *et al.* [236].

(e) Test your program on the dolphins network of Fig. 5.11 and on the largest social-network graph you can lay your hands on.

Exercise 5.8 (∗∗) Let $\mathcal{G} = (\mathcal{V}, \mathcal{E})$ be an undirected unweighted graph. Assume that the graph is **connected**, so that there is a path from every source vertex s to every target vertex t. (In this exercise, s denotes the source vertex, and not a processor number.) Let σ_{st} be the number of shortest paths from s to t, and $\sigma_{st}(v)$ the number of such paths passing through vertex v. The fraction $\sigma_{st}(v)/\sigma_{st}$ tells us how important vertex v is for travelling from s to t. For instance, if $\sigma_{st}(v)/\sigma_{st} = 1$ and we remove vertex v and its adjacent edges, this means that the distance (in edges travelled) between s and t will increase at least by 1. On the other hand, if the fraction is zero, removing v has no effect. Note that for $v = s$ or $v = t$, the fraction trivially equals 1.

The **betweenness centrality** [8, 114] of vertex v is defined as

$$C_B(v) = \sum_{s \in \mathcal{V} \setminus \{v\}} \sum_{t \in \mathcal{V} \setminus \{v\}} \frac{\sigma_{st}(v)}{\sigma_{st}}. \tag{5.36}$$

In this definition, we exclude paths that start or end in v. The metric C_B expresses how important vertex v is to the connectivity of the whole graph along shortest paths. Knocking out vertices v with high $C_B(v)$ will increase the average shortest path length the most.

(a) Brandes [44] presents an algorithm for efficient computation of betweenness centrality based on the computation of the intermediate variable $\delta_s(v)$, which represents the **dependency** on vertex v for a single source s and the set of all possible targets t,

$$\delta_s(v) = \sum_{t \in \mathcal{V} \setminus \{v\}} \frac{\sigma_{st}(v)}{\sigma_{st}}. \tag{5.37}$$

How can you compute $C_B(v)$ from the $\delta_s(v)$ values?

(b) Now we can fix the source vertex s and drop it as a subscript if desired. We write $\delta(v)$ instead of $\delta_s(v)$, and σ_t instead of σ_{st}. Let $dist(x)$ denote the distance along a shortest path from the source vertex s to vertex x. Define the set of successors of vertex v,

$$Succ(v) = \{w \in \mathcal{V} : (v, w) \in \mathcal{E} \wedge dist(w) = dist(v) + 1\}. \tag{5.38}$$

If v has no successors, what is $\delta(v)$?

(c) Prove that

$$\delta(v) = \sum_{w \in Succ(v)} \frac{\sigma_v}{\sigma_w} (\delta(w) + 1), \tag{5.39}$$

for the case that v has at least one successor. Hint: note that $\sigma_t(v) = \sum_{w \in Succ(v)} \sigma_t(v, w)$, where $\sigma_t(v, w)$ is the number of shortest paths from s to t that pass both through v and w. Find a useful expression for $\sigma_t(v, w)$ in terms of σ_v, σ_w, and $\sigma_t(w)$.

(d) Assume that the graph $\mathcal{G}$ is vertex-partitioned. Design and implement a parallel algorithm for computing the distances from a given source vertex s to all other vertices. Hint: use a **breadth-first search** (BFS) with synchronization after computing a **level**, a set of vertices with the same distance to s.

(e) Extend your algorithm to compute all values $\delta(v)$ based on eqn (5.39), starting with the vertices v farthest from the source.

(f) Now compute the betweenness centrality of all vertices by using your algorithm for batches of k sources s at a time. Try to balance the work load. The batch size k may be limited by the available memory. How does the choice of k influence the speedup of your program?

Exercise 5.9 ($**$) Consider a bipartite undirected unweighted graph $\mathcal{G} = (\mathcal{V}_0 \cup \mathcal{V}_1, \mathcal{E})$. We would like to compute a maximum-cardinality matching for such a graph. Note that this means an optimal solution, not just an approximation. Such a matching can be computed in $\mathcal{O}(m\sqrt{n})$ operations by the Hopcroft–Karp algorithm [162], which is based on finding augmenting paths in the graph. However, other augmenting-path based algorithms with a higher complexity of $\mathcal{O}(mn)$ may still be competitive in practice.

(a) Let $v_0 \in \mathcal{V}_0$ be an unmatched source vertex. Design and implement a sequential algorithm that builds a special breadth-first search (BFS) tree with root v_0, where each path in the tree alternates between edges inside the matching and outside. When the search encounters an unmatched vertex other than the source, an augmenting path has been found and the matching is improved.

(b) Design and implement a BSP algorithm that starts from multiple sources, all in $\mathcal{V}_0$. (Without loss of generality we may assume that all augmenting paths start in $\mathcal{V}_0$ and end in $\mathcal{V}_1$.) The sequential algorithm can be used within a processor, but paths that cross processor boundaries will give rise to communication and hence require adaptation of the algorithm. Organize the computation in such a way that first only short paths are computed (initially, paths of length 1), and later the possible lengths are increased. Two paths that are created simultaneously must be vertex-disjoint, otherwise their edge flips will interfere with each other.

(c) Azad, Buluç, and Pothen [14] proved that if an unrestricted search (i.e., no restrictions on length or eligible vertices) terminates without finding an augmenting path, then all vertices in the search tree can be removed from the problem, as they will never be included anymore in an augmenting path. Use this fact to speed up the computation.

(d) Monitor the average augmenting-path length during the execution of your algorithm and explain its behaviour.

APPENDIX A
AUXILIARY BSPEDUPACK FUNCTIONS

A.1 Header file bspedupack.h

This header file is included in every program file of BSPedupack. It contains necessary file inclusions, useful definitions and macros, and prototypes for the memory allocation and deallocation functions.

```
/*
   ###########################################################
   ## BSPedupack Version 2.0                              ##
   ## Copyright (C) 2019 Rob H. Bisseling                 ##
   ##                                                     ##
   ## BSPedupack is released under the                    ##
   ## GNU GENERAL PUBLIC LICENSE                          ##
   ## Version 3, 29 June 2007 (given in the file          ##
   ##                                      LICENSE)       ##
   ###########################################################
*/

#include <stdio.h>
#include <stdlib.h>
#include <string.h>
#include <stdbool.h>
#include <stddef.h>
#include <complex.h>
#include <math.h>
#include <tgmath.h>

#include <bsp.h> // header file of the BSPlib
                 // implementation

#ifndef M_PI
#define M_PI 3.14159265358979323846
#endif
```

```
#define MAX(a,b)  ((a)>(b) ? (a) : (b))
#define MIN(a,b)  ((a)<(b) ? (a) : (b))
#define DUMMY -1 // dummy vertex

typedef struct item {
    double weight;
    long index;
} Item;

long nloc(long p, long s, long n);

long *vecalloci(size_t n);
bool *vecallocb(size_t n);
double *vecallocd(size_t n);
double complex *vecallocc(size_t n);
Item *vecallocitem(size_t n);
double **matallocd(size_t m, size_t n);

void vecfreei(long *pi);
void vecfreeb(bool *pb);
void vecfreed(double *pd);
void vecfreec(double complex *pc);
void vecfreeitem(Item *pitem);
void matfreed(double **ppd);
```

A.2 Utility file bspedupack.c

This file contains the functions used by BSPedupack to allocate and deallocate memory dynamically for storing vectors and matrices. The functions are suited for use in a parallel program, because they can abort a parallel computation on all processors if they detect a potential memory overflow on one of the processors. If zero memory space is requested, which could happen if the local part of a distributed vector or matrix is empty, a vector of length 1 or a matrix of size at least 1 in each dimension is still allocated. This creates a unique pointer and prevents problems with registering an array of length 0 for communication by puts or gets.

Allocating an $m \times n$ matrix reserves a contiguous chunk of mn memory cells and prepares it for row-wise matrix access. As a result, matrix element a_{ij} can conveniently be addressed as a[i][j] and row i as a[i].

For the sake of brevity, only the allocation and deallocation functions for vectors and matrices of doubles are shown. The file bspedupack.c also contains similar functions for allocating and deallocating vectors of booleans, long integers, complex numbers, and items containing a double and a long integer.

```c
#include "bspedupack.h"

long nloc(long p, long s, long n){
    /* Compute number of local components of processor s
       for vector of length n distributed cyclically
       over p processors. Also useful for block
       distribution with ceil(n/p) components if
       s < (n mod p), floor(n/p) components otherwise.
    */

    return (n+p-s-1)/p;

} /* end nloc */


/* The following functions can be used to allocate and
   deallocate vectors and matrices. If not enough
   memory is available, one processor halts them all. */

double *vecallocd(size_t n){
    /* This function allocates a vector of doubles of
       length n */
    double *pd;

    pd= malloc(MAX(n,1)*sizeof(double));
    if (pd==NULL)
        bsp_abort("vecallocd: not enough memory");
    return pd;

} /* end vecallocd */

double **matallocd(size_t m, size_t n){
    /* This function allocates an m x n matrix of
       doubles */
    size_t i, m1, n1;
    double *pd, **ppd;

    m1= MAX(m,1);
    n1= MAX(n,1);
    ppd= malloc(m1*sizeof(double *));
    if (ppd==NULL)
        bsp_abort("matallocd: not enough memory");
    pd= malloc(m1*n1*sizeof(double));
    if (pd==NULL)
```

```
        bsp_abort("matallocd: not enough memory");
    ppd[0]= pd;
    for (i=1; i<m1; i++)
        ppd[i]= ppd[i-1]+n1;

    return ppd;

} /* end matallocd */

void vecfreed(double *pd){
    /* This function frees a vector of doubles */

    if (pd!=NULL)
        free(pd);

} /* end vecfreed */

void matfreed(double **ppd){
    /* This function frees a matrix of doubles */

    if (ppd!=NULL){
        if (ppd[0]!=NULL)
            free(ppd[0]);
        free(ppd);
    }

} /* end matfreed */
```

APPENDIX B
A QUICK REFERENCE GUIDE TO BSPLIB

Table B.1 groups the primitives of BSPlib into three classes: Single Program Multiple Data (SPMD) for creating the overall parallel structure; Direct Remote Memory Access (DRMA) for communication with puts or gets; and Bulk Synchronous Message Passing (BSMP) for communication with sends. The table is meant as a memory aid to the syntax; for a full specification, see the given page.

Functions bsp_nprocs and bsp_pid return an unsigned int; bsp_time returns a double; bsp_hpmove returns a size_t; and all others return void. A parameter with an asterisk is a pointer; a parameter with two asterisks is a pointer to a pointer. The pointers occurring as parameters in the primitives are of type void *, so they can handle any type of variable, with a few exceptions: the functions bsp_set_tagsize, bsp_qsize, and bsp_get_tag expect a size_t * for their respective parameters tagsz, nbytes, and status; furthermore, bsp_qsize expects an unsigned int * for its parameter nmessages. The parameter spmd is a parameterless function returning void. The parameter error_message is a format string. The parameter pid is of type unsigned int. The parameters offset, nbytes, and maxnbytes are of type size_t.

The primitive bsp_direct_get, introduced in [318], is a get primitive with the same syntax as bsp_get, but it has a different meaning. It is executed immediately, without waiting for the next global synchronization. The local computation continues only after the remote read by bsp_direct_get has been completed, so that the direct get is **blocking**. The direct get was introduced as a lightweight primitive to enable reading on a shared-memory architecture, and it should be used with care. The direct get does not fit well within the BSP cost model, and its cost should merely be considered as that of a (slightly more expensive) local read operation. We have not used the direct get in this book, even though it might have been useful in certain cases.

The primitive bsp_hpsend, introduced in [318], is a high-performance version of bsp_send that does not use a send buffer and may send the message at any time between its function call and the end of the current superstep. It must be used with care: for example, the source cannot be reused until the end of the superstep.

The primitive bsp_hpmove was available in the original BSPlib, but it has not been explained before in this book. It receives the messages sent in the previous superstep without copying them. The primitive returns the payload size in bytes, except if the message queue is empty, in which case it returns SIZE_MAX, the maximum possible size_t value. It sets the tagptr to the address of the tag in the receive buffer and the payloadptr to the address of the payload.

Table B.1 The 22 primitives of modernized BSPlib [153, 318].

Class	Primitive	Meaning	Page
SPMD	`bsp_begin(reqprocs);`	Start of parallel part	14
	`bsp_end();`	End of parallel part	14
	`bsp_init(spmd, argc, **argv);`	Initialize parallel part	14
	`bsp_nprocs();`	Number of processors	15
	`bsp_pid();`	My processor number	15
	`bsp_time();`	My elapsed time (in s)	15
	`bsp_sync();`	Synchronize globally	15
	`bsp_abort(error_message, ...);`	One processor stops all	19
DRMA	`bsp_push_reg(*variable, nbytes);`	Register variable	18
	`bsp_pop_reg(*variable);`	Deregister variable	19
	`bsp_put(pid, *source, *dest, offset, nbytes);`	Write into remote memory	17
	`bsp_hpput(pid, *source, *dest, offset, nbytes);`	Unbuffered put	132
	`bsp_get(pid, *source, offset, *dest, nbytes);`	Read from remote memory	19
	`bsp_hpget(pid, *source, offset, *dest, nbytes);`	Unbuffered get	133
	`bsp_direct_get(pid, *source, offset, *dest, nbytes);`	Blocking get	363
BSMP	`bsp_set_tagsize(*tagsz);`	Set new tag size	48
	`bsp_send(pid, *tag, *source, nbytes);`	Send a message	47
	`bsp_hpsend(pid, *tag, *source, nbytes);`	Unbuffered send	363
	`bsp_qsize(*nmessages, *nbytes);`	Number, total size of received messages	48
	`bsp_get_tag(*status, *tag);`	Get tag of received message	48
	`bsp_move(*dest, maxnbytes);`	Store payload locally	48
	`bsp_hpmove(**tagptr, **payloadptr);`	Store tag, payload by setting pointers	363

REFERENCES

[1] Acer, S., Selvitopi, O., and Aykanat, C. (2018). Optimizing nonzero-based sparse matrix partitioning models via reducing latency. *Journal of Parallel and Distributed Computing* **122**, 145–158.

[2] Agarwal, R. C., Balle, S. M., Gustavson, F. G., Joshi, M., and Palkar, P. (1995). A three-dimensional approach to parallel matrix multiplication. *IBM Journal of Research and Development* **39**(5), 575–582.

[3] Aggarwal, A., Chandra, A. K., and Snir, M. (1990). Communication complexity of PRAMs. *Theoretical Computer Science* **71**(1), 3–28.

[4] Agullo, E., Demmel, J., Dongarra, J., Hadri, B., Kurzak, J., Langou, J., Ltaief, H., Luszczek, P., and Tomov, S. (2009). Numerical linear algebra on emerging architectures: the PLASMA and MAGMA projects. *Journal of Physics: Conference Series* **180**, 012037.

[5] Allombert, V., Gava, F., and Tesson, J. (2017). Multi-ML: Programming multi-BSP algorithms in ML. *International Journal of Parallel Programming* **45**(2), 340–361.

[6] Alpert, R. D. and Philbin, J. F. (1997, February). cBSP: Zero-cost synchronization in a modified BSP model. Technical Report 97-054, NEC Research Institute, Princeton, NJ.

[7] Anderson, E., Bai, Z., Bischof, C., Blackford, L. S., Demmel, J., Dongarra, J., Du Croz, J., Greenbaum, A., Hammarling, S., McKenney, A., and Sorensen, D. (1999). *LAPACK Users' Guide* (Third edn). SIAM, Philadelphia, PA.

[8] Anthonisse, J. M. (1971, October). The rush in a directed graph. Technical Report BN 9/71, Stichting Mathematisch Centrum, Amsterdam, the Netherlands.

[9] Arlazarov, V. L., Dinic, E. A., Kronrod, M. A., and Faradžev, I. A. (1970). On economical construction of the transitive closure of a directed graph. *Soviet Mathematics—Doklady* **11**(5), 1209–1210.

[10] Ashcraft, C. (1991, March). A taxonomy of distributed dense LU factorization methods. Technical Report ECA-TR-161, Boeing Computer Services, Seattle, WA.

[11] Avis, D. (1983). A survey of heuristics for the weighted matching problem. *Networks* **13**(4), 475–493.

[12] Axtmann, M., Bingmann, T., Sanders, P., and Schulz, C. (2015). Practical massively parallel sorting. In *Proceedings 27th ACM Symposium on Parallelism in Algorithms and Architectures (SPAA 2015)*, pp. 13–23. ACM, New York.

[13] Azad, A. and Buluç, A. (2016). A matrix-algebraic formulation of distributed-memory maximal cardinality matching algorithms in bipartite graphs. *Parallel Computing* **58**, 117–130.

[14] Azad, A., Buluç, A., and Pothen, A. (2017). Computing maximum cardinality matchings in parallel on bipartite graphs via tree-grafting. *IEEE Transactions on Parallel and Distributed Systems* **28**(1), 44–59.

[15] Bai, Z., Demmel, J., Dongarra, J., Ruhe, A., and van der Vorst, H. (ed.) (2000). *Templates for the Solution of Algebraic Eigenvalue Problems: A Practical Guide.* SIAM, Philadelphia, PA.

[16] Ballard, G., Demmel, J., Holtz, O., and Schwartz, O. (2011). Minimizing communication in numerical linear algebra. *SIAM Journal on Matrix Analysis and Applications* 32(3), 866–901.

[17] Barnett, M., Gupta, S., Payne, D. G., Shuler, L., van de Geijn, R., and Watts, J. (1994*a*). Building a high-performance collective communication library. In *Proceedings of the 1994 ACM/IEEE Conference on Supercomputing*, pp. 107–116. IEEE Press, Los Alamitos, CA.

[18] Barnett, M., Gupta, S., Payne, D. G., Shuler, L., van de Geijn, R., and Watts, J. (1994*b*). Interprocessor collective communication library (Intercom). In *Proceedings of IEEE Scalable High Performance Computing Conference*, pp. 357–364.

[19] Barrett, R., Berry, M., Chan, T. F., Demmel, J., Donato, J., Dongarra, J., Eijkhout, V., Pozo, R., Romine, C., and van der Vorst, H. (1994). *Templates for the Solution of Linear Systems: Building Blocks for Iterative Methods* (Second edn). SIAM, Philadelphia, PA.

[20] Barros, S. R. M., Dent, D., Isaksen, L., Robinson, G., Mozdzynski, G., and Wollenweber, F. (1995). The IFS model: A parallel production weather code. *Parallel Computing* 21(10), 1621–1638.

[21] Bastian, M., Heymann, S., and Jacomy, M. (2009). Gephi: An open source software for exploring and manipulating networks. In *Proceedings Third International AAAI Conference on Weblogs and Social Media*.

[22] Batcher, K. E. (1968). Sorting networks and their applications. In *Proceedings AFIPS Spring Joint Computer Conference*, Volume 32 of *AFIPS Conference Proceedings*, pp. 307–314. Thomson Book Company, Washington D.C.

[23] Bauer, F. L. (2007). *Decrypted Secrets: Methods and Maxims of Cryptology* (Fourth edn). Springer-Verlag, Berlin.

[24] Bäumker, A., Dittrich, W., and Meyer auf der Heide, F. (1998). Truly efficient parallel algorithms: 1-optimal multisearch for an extension of the BSP model. *Theoretical Computer Science* 203(2), 175–203.

[25] Berge, C. (1957). Two theorems in graph theory. *Proceedings National Academy of Sciences* 43(9), 842–844.

[26] Bienz, A., Gropp, W. D., and Olson, L. N. (2019). Node aware sparse matrix-vector multiplication. *Journal of Parallel and Distributed Computing* **130**, 166–178.

[27] Bilardi, G., Herley, K. T., Pietracaprina, A., Pucci, G., and Spirakis, P. (1996). BSP vs LogP. In *Eighth Annual ACM Symposium on Parallel Algorithms and Architectures*, pp. 25–32. ACM, New York.

[28] Bisseling, R. H. (1993). Parallel iterative solution of sparse linear systems on a transputer network. In *Parallel Computation* (ed. A. E. Fincham and B. Ford), Volume 46 of *The Institute of Mathematics and its Applications Conference Series*, pp. 253–271. Oxford University Press, Oxford, UK.

[29] Bisseling, R. H. (1997). Basic techniques for numerical linear algebra on bulk synchronous parallel computers. In *Numerical Analysis and Its Applications* (ed. L. Vulkov, J. Waśniewski, and P. Yalamov), Volume 1196 of *Lecture Notes in Computer Science*, pp. 46–57. Springer.

[30] Bisseling, R. H., Fagginger Auer, B. O., Yzelman, A. N., van Leeuwen, T., and Çatalyürek, Ü. V. (2012). Two-dimensional approaches to sparse matrix partitioning. In *Combinatorial Scientific Computing* (ed. U. Naumann and O. Schenk), Computational Science Series, pp. 321–349. CRC Press, Boca Raton, FL.

[31] Bisseling, R. H. and McColl, W. F. (1993, December). Scientific computing on bulk synchronous parallel architectures. Preprint 836, Department of Mathematics, Utrecht University, Utrecht, the Netherlands.

[32] Bisseling, R. H. and McColl, W. F. (1994). Scientific computing on bulk synchronous parallel architectures. In *Technology and Foundations: Information Processing '94, Vol. I* (ed. B. Pehrson and I. Simon), Volume 51 of *IFIP Transactions A*, pp. 509–514. Elsevier, Amsterdam.

[33] Bisseling, R. H. and Meesen, W. (2005). Communication balancing in parallel sparse matrix-vector multiplication. *Electronic Transactions on Numerical Analysis* **21**, 47–65.

[34] Bisseling, R. H. and van de Vorst, J. G. G. (1989). Parallel LU decomposition on a transputer network. In *Parallel Computing 1988* (ed. G. A. van Zee and J. G. G. van de Vorst), Volume 384 of *Lecture Notes in Computer Science*, pp. 61–77. Springer.

[35] Blackford, L. S., Choi, J., Cleary, A., D'Azevedo, E., Demmel, J., Dhillon, I., Dongarra, J., Hammarling, S., Henry, G., Petitet, A., Stanley, K., Walker, D., and Whaley, R. C. (1997). *ScaLAPACK User's Guide*. SIAM, Philadelphia, PA.

[36] Blake, A. M., Witten, I. H., and Cree, M. J. (2013). The fastest Fourier transform in the South. *IEEE Transactions on Signal Processing* **61**(19), 4707–4716.

[37] Boisvert, R. F., Pozo, R., Remington, K., Barrett, R. F., and Dongarra, J. J. (1997). Matrix Market: a web resource for test matrix collections. In *Quality of Numerical Software: Assessment and Enhancement* (ed. R. F. Boisvert), pp. 125–137. Springer, Boston, MA.

[38] Boman, E. G., Çatalyürek, Ü. V., Chevalier, C., and Devine, K. D. (2012). The Zoltan and Isorropia parallel toolkits for combinatorial scientific computing: Partitioning, ordering and coloring. *Scientific Programming* **20**(2), 129–150.

[39] Boman, E. G., Devine, K. D., and Rajamanickam, S. (2013). Scalable matrix computations on large scale-free graphs using 2D graph partitioning. In *Proceedings of the International Conference on High Performance Computing, Networking, Storage and Analysis (SC 2013)*, pp. 50:1–50:12. ACM, New York.

[40] Bonorden, O., Juurlink, B., von Otte, I., and Rieping, I. (2003). The Paderborn University BSP (PUB) library. *Parallel Computing* **29**(2), 187–207.

[41] Borowski, S. and Klüner, T. (2004). Massively parallel Hamiltonian action in pseudospectral algorithms applied to quantum dynamics of laser induced desorption. *Chemical Physics* **304**(1–2), 51–58.

[42] Bracewell, R. N. (1999). *The Fourier Transform and its Applications* (3rd edn). McGraw-Hill Series in Electrical Engineering. McGraw-Hill, New York.

[43] Bradley, J. T., de Jager, D. V., Knottenbelt, W. J., and Trifunović, A. (2005). Hypergraph partitioning for faster parallel PageRank computation. In *Proceedings Formal Techniques for Computer Systems and Business Processes, European Performance Engineering Workshop (EPEW 2005) and International Workshop on Web Services and Formal Methods (WS-FM 2005)* (ed. M. Bravetti, L. Kloul, and G. Zavattaro), Volume 3670 of *Lecture Notes in Computer Science*, pp. 155–171. Springer.

[44] Brandes, U. (2001). A faster algorithm for betweenness centrality. *The Journal of Mathematical Sociology* **25**(2), 163–177.

[45] Brent, R. P. (1976). Fast multiple-precision evaluation of elementary functions. *Journal of the ACM* **23**(2), 242–251.

[46] Briggs, W. L. and Henson, V. E. (1995). *The DFT: An Owner's Manual for the Discrete Fourier Transform*. SIAM, Philadelphia, PA.

[47] Brin, S. and Page, L. (1998). The anatomy of a large-scale hypertextual Web search engine. *Computer Networks and ISDN Systems* **30**(1–7), 107–117.

[48] Bui, T. N. and Jones, C. (1993). A heuristic for reducing fill-in in sparse matrix factorization. In *Proceedings Sixth SIAM Conference on Parallel Processing for Scientific Computing* (ed. R. F. Sincovec, D. E. Keyes, M. R. Leuze, L. R. Petzold, and D. A. Reed), pp. 445–452. SIAM, Philadelphia, PA.

[49] Buluç, A., Meyerhenke, H., Safro, I., Sanders, P., and Schulz, C. (2016). Recent advances in graph partitioning. In *Algorithm Engineering: Selected Results and Surveys* (ed. L. Kliemann and P. Sanders), Volume 9220 of *Lecture Notes in Computer Science*, pp. 117–158. Springer.

[50] Buluç, A. and Gilbert, J. R. (2011). The Combinatorial BLAS: Design, implementation, and applications. *International Journal of High Performance Computing Applications* 25(4), 496–509.

[51] Buttari, A., Langou, J., Kurzak, J., and Dongarra, J. (2009). A class of parallel tiled linear algebra algorithms for multicore architectures. *Parallel Computing* 35(1), 38–53.

[52] Buurlage, J., Bannink, T., and Bisseling, R. H. (2018). Bulk: a modern C++ interface for bulk-synchronous parallel programs. In *Euro-Par 2018: Parallel Processing* (ed. M. Aldinucci, L. Padovani, and M. Torquati), Volume 11014 of *Lecture Notes in Computer Science*, pp. 519–532. Springer.

[53] Buurlage, J., Bannink, T., and Wits, A. (2016, August). Bulk-synchronous pseudo-streaming algorithms for many-core accelerators. `arXiv:1608.07200 [cs.DC]`.

[54] Caldwell, A. E., Kahng, A. B., and Markov, I. L. (2000). Improved algorithms for hypergraph bipartitioning. In *Proceedings Asia and South Pacific Design Automation Conference*, pp. 661–666. ACM Press, New York.

[55] Cannon, L. E. (1969, August). *A Cellular Computer to Implement the Kalman Filter Algorithm*. Ph. D. thesis, Montana State University, Bozeman, MT.

[56] Çatalyürek, Ü. V. and Aykanat, C. (1996). Decomposing irregularly sparse matrices for parallel matrix-vector multiplications. In *Proceedings Third International Workshop on Solving Irregularly Structured Problems in Parallel (Irregular 1996)* (ed. A. Ferreira, J. Rolim, Y. Saad, and T. Yang), Volume 1117 of *Lecture Notes in Computer Science*, pp. 75–86. Springer.

[57] Çatalyürek, Ü. V. and Aykanat, C. (1999). Hypergraph-partitioning-based decomposition for parallel sparse-matrix vector multiplication. *IEEE Transactions on Parallel and Distributed Systems* 10(7), 673–693.

[58] Çatalyürek, Ü V. and Aykanat, C. (2001). A fine-grain hypergraph model for 2D decomposition of sparse matrices. In *Proceedings Eighth International Workshop on Solving Irregularly Structured Problems in Parallel (Irregular 2001)*, pp. 118. IEEE Press, Los Alamitos, CA.

[59] Catalyurek, Ü. V., Boman, E. G., Devine, K. D., Bozdağ, D., Heaphy, R. T., and Riesen, L. A. (2009). A repartitioning hypergraph model for dynamic load balancing. *Journal of Parallel and Distributed Computing* 69(8), 711–724.

[60] Çatalyürek, Ü. V., Aykanat, C., and Uçar, B. (2010). On two-dimensional sparse matrix partitioning: Models, methods, and a recipe. *SIAM Journal on Scientific Computing* 32(2), 656–683.

[61] Chan, E., Heimlich, M., Purkayastha, A., and van de Geijn, R. (2007). Collective communication: theory, practice, and experience. *Concurrency and Computation: Practice and Experience* 19(13), 1749–1783.

[62] Chapman, B., Jost, G., and van der Pas, R. (2007). *Using OpenMP: Portable Shared Memory Parallel Programming*. MIT Press, Cambridge, MA.

[63] Chernoff, H. (1952). A measure of asymptotic efficiency for tests of a hypothesis based on the sum of observations. *Annals of Mathematical Statistics* 23(4), 493–507.

[64] Chevalier, C. and Pellegrini, F. (2008). PT-Scotch: A tool for efficient parallel graph ordering. *Parallel Computing* 34(6-8), 318–331.

[65] Ching, A., Edunov, S., Kabiljo, M., Logothetis, D., and Muthukrishnan, S. (2015). One trillion edges: Graph processing at Facebook-scale. *Proceedings of the VLDB Endowment* 8(12), 1804–1815.

[66] Choi, J., Dongarra, J. J., Ostrouchov, L. S., Petitet, A. P., Walker, D. W., and Whaley, R. C. (1996). Design and implementation of the ScaLAPACK LU, QR, and Cholesky factorization routines. *Scientific Programming* 5(3), 173–184.

[67] Chu, E. and George, A. (1987). Gaussian elimination with partial pivoting and load balancing on a multiprocessor. *Parallel Computing* 5(1-2), 65–74.

[68] Chudnovsky, D. V. and Chudnovsky, G. V. (1989). The computation of classical constants. *Proceedings National Academy of Sciences* 86(21), 8178–8182.

[69] Cole, R. (1988). Parallel merge sort. *SIAM Journal on Computing* 17(4), 770–785.

[70] Cooley, J. W. (1990). How the FFT gained acceptance. In *A History of Scientific Computing* (ed. S. G. Nash), pp. 133–140. ACM, New York.

[71] Cooley, J. W. and Tukey, J. W. (1965). An algorithm for the machine calculation of complex Fourier series. *Mathematics of Computation* 19(90), 297–301.

[72] Cormen, T. H., Leiserson, C. E., Rivest, R. L., and Stein, C. (2009). *Introduction to algorithms* (Third edn). MIT Press, Cambridge, MA.

[73] Culler, D., Karp, R., Patterson, D., Sahay, A., Schauser, K. E., Santos, E., Subramonian, R., and von Eicken, T. (1993). LogP: Towards a realistic model of parallel computation. *ACM SIGPLAN Notices* 28(7), 1–12.

[74] Culler, D., Karp, R. M., Patterson, D., Sahay, A., Santos, E. E., Schauser, K. E., Subramonian, R., and von Eicken, T. (1996). LogP: A practical model of parallel computation. *Communications of the ACM* 39(11), 78–85.

[75] Czarnul, P. (2018). *Parallel Programming for Modern High Performance Computing Systems.* CRC Press, Boca Raton, FL.

[76] Danielson, G. C. and Lanczos, C. (1942). Some improvements in practical Fourier analysis and their application to X-ray scattering from liquids. *Journal of the Franklin Institute* 233(4/5), 365–380, 435–452.

[77] Daubechies, I. (1988). Orthonormal bases of compactly supported wavelets. *Communications on Pure and Applied Mathematics* 41(7), 909–996.

[78] Davis, T. A. (2019). Algorithm 1000: SuiteSparse:GraphBLAS: graph algorithms in the language of sparse linear algebra. *ACM Transactions on Mathematical Software* 45(4) 44: 1–44:25.

[79] Davis, T. A. and Hu, Y. (2011). The University of Florida sparse matrix collection. *ACM Transactions on Mathematical Software* 38(1), 1:1–1:25.

[80] Davis, T. A., Rajamanickam, S., and Sid-Lakhdar, W. M. (2016). A survey of direct methods for sparse linear systems. *Acta Numerica* 25, 383–566.

[81] de la Torre, P. and Kruskal, C. P. (1996). Submachine locality in the bulk synchronous setting. In *Euro-Par'96 Parallel Processing. Vol. II* (ed. L. Bougé, P. Fraigniaud, A. Mignotte, and Y. Robert), Volume 1124 of *Lecture Notes in Computer Science*, pp. 352–358. Springer.

[82] Demmel, J., Grigori, L., Hoemmen, M., and Langou, J. (2012). Communication-optimal parallel and sequential QR and LU factorizations. *SIAM Journal on Scientific Computing* 34(1), A206–A239.

[83] Deveci, M., Kaya, K., Uçar, B., and Çatalyürek, Ü. V. (2015). Hypergraph partitioning for multiple communication cost metrics: Model and methods. *Journal of Parallel and Distributed Computing* 77, 69–83.

[84] Devine, K., Boman, E., Heaphy, R., Hendrickson, B., and Vaughan, C. (2002). Zoltan data management services for parallel dynamic applications. *Computing in Science and Engineering* 4(2), 90–97.

[85] Devine, K. D., Boman, E. G., Heaphy, R. T., Bisseling, R. H., and Catalyurek, U. V. (2006). Parallel hypergraph partitioning for scientific computing. In *Proceedings 20th International Parallel and Distributed Processing Symposium (IPDPS 2006)*, pp. 102. IEEE Press, Los Alamitos, CA.

[86] Dijkstra, E. W. (1968). Go to statement considered harmful. *Communications of the ACM* 11(3), 147–148.

[87] Dion, C. M., Hashemloo, A., and Rahali, G. (2014). Program for quantum wave-packet dynamics with time-dependent potentials. *Computer Physics Communications* 185(1), 407–414.

[88] Dolan, E. D. and Moré, J. J. (2002). Benchmarking optimization software with performance profiles. *Mathematical Programming* 91(2), 201–213.

[89] Dongarra, J., Heroux, M. A., and Luszczek, P. (2016). High-performance conjugate-gradient benchmark: A new metric for ranking high-performance computing systems. *The International Journal of High Performance Computing Applications* 30(1), 3–10.

[90] Dongarra, J. J., Luszczek, P., and Petitet, A. (2003). The LINPACK benchmark: past, present and future. *Concurrency and Computation: Practice and Experience* 15(9), 803–820.

[91] Dongarra, J. and Sullivan, F. (2000). Guest editors' introduction to the top 10 algorithms. *Computing in Science and Engineering* 2(1), 22–23.

[92] Dongarra, J. J. (1992). Performance of various computers using standard linear equations software. *SIGARCH Computer Architecture News* 20(3), 22–44. Updated at https://www.netlib.org/benchmark/performance.pdf, accessed December 14, 2019.

[93] Dongarra, J. J., Du Croz, J., Hammarling, S., and Duff, I. (1990). A set of level 3 Basic Linear Algebra Subprograms. *ACM Transactions on Mathematical Software* 16(1), 1–17.

[94] Dongarra, J. J., Du Croz, J., Hammarling, S., and Hanson, R. J. (1988). An extended set of FORTRAN Basic Linear Algebra Subprograms. *ACM Transactions on Mathematical Software* 14(1), 1–17.

[95] Dongarra, J. J., Duff, I. S., Sorensen, D. C., and van der Vorst, H. A. (1998). *Numerical Linear Algebra for High-Performance Computers*. Software, Environments, Tools. SIAM, Philadelphia, PA.

[96] Drake, D. E. and Hougardy, S. (2003a). Linear time local improvements for weighted matchings in graphs. In *Experimental and Efficient Algorithms (WEA 2003)* (ed. K. Jansen, M. Margraf, M. Mastrolilli, and J. D. P. Rolim), Volume 2647 of *Lecture Notes in Computer Science*, pp. 107–119. Springer.

[97] Drake, D. E. and Hougardy, S. (2003b). A simple approximation algorithm for the weighted matching problem. *Information Processing Letters* 85(4), 211–213.

[98] Dubey, A., Zubair, M., and Grosch, C. E. (1994). A general purpose subroutine for Fast Fourier Transform on a distributed memory parallel machine. *Parallel Computing* 20(12), 1697–1710.

[99] Duff, I. S., Erisman, A. M., and Reid, J. K. (2017). *Direct Methods for Sparse Matrices* (Second edn). Oxford University Press, Oxford, UK.

[100] Duff, I. S., Grimes, R. G., and Lewis, J. G. (1989). Sparse matrix test problems. *ACM Transactions on Mathematical Software* 15(1), 1–14.

[101] Duff, I. S., Grimes, R. G., and Lewis, J. G. (1997, September). The Rutherford–Boeing sparse matrix collection. Technical Report RAL-TR-97-031, Rutherford Appleton Laboratory, Oxon, UK.

[102] Duff, I. S. and Koster, J. (2000). On algorithms for permuting large entries to the diagonal of a sparse matrix. *SIAM Journal on Matrix Analysis and Applications* 22(4), 973–996.

[103] Eijkhout, V. (2017). *Parallel Programming in MPI and OpenMP*. Lulu.com.

[104] El-Ghazawi, T., Carlson, W., Sterling, T., and Yelick, K. (2005). *UPC: Distributed Shared Memory Programming*. Wiley Series on Parallel and Distributed Computing. Wiley, Hoboken, NJ.

[105] Feng, W. and Cameron, K. W. (2007). The Green500 list: Encouraging sustainable supercomputing. *IEEE Computer* 40(12), 38–43.

[106] Feng, W. and Scogland, T. (2007–2018). Green500. https://www.top500.org/green500/. Accessed December 14, 2019.

[107] Ferdous, S. M., Khan, A., and Pothen, A. (2018). Parallel algorithms through approximation: B-edge cover. In *Proceedings 32nd International Parallel and Distributed Processing Symposium (IPDPS 2018)*, pp. 22–33.

[108] Fiduccia, C. M. and Mattheyses, R. M. (1982). A linear-time heuristic for improving network partitions. In *Proceedings 19th Design Automation Conference (DAC 1982)*, pp. 175–181. IEEE Press, Piscataway, NJ.

[109] Fleming, P. J. and Wallace, J. J. (1986). How not to lie with statistics: The correct way to summarize benchmark results. *Communications of the ACM 29*(3), 218–221.

[110] Fortmeier, O., Bücker, H. M., Fagginger Auer, B. O., and Bisseling, R. H. (2013). A new metric enabling an exact hypergraph model for the communication volume in distributed-memory parallel applications. *Parallel Computing 39*(8), 319–335.

[111] Fortune, S. and Wyllie, J. (1978). Parallelism in random access machines. In *Proceedings Tenth Annual ACM Symposium on Theory of Computing (STOC 1978)*, pp. 114–118. ACM, New York.

[112] Foster, I. T. and Worley, P. H. (1997). Parallel algorithms for the spectral transform method. *SIAM Journal on Scientific Computing 18*(3), 806–837.

[113] Fox, G. C., Johnson, M. A., Lyzenga, G. A., Otto, S. W., Salmon, J. K., and Walker, D. W. (1988). *Solving Problems on Concurrent Processors: Vol. I, General Techniques and Regular Problems.* Prentice Hall, Englewood Cliffs, NJ.

[114] Freeman, L. C. (1977). A set of measures of centrality based upon betweenness. *Sociometry 40*(1), 35–41.

[115] Frigo, M. and Johnson, S. G. (1998). FFTW: An adaptive software architecture for the FFT. In *Proceedings IEEE International Conference on Acoustics, Speech, and Signal Processing*, Volume 3, pp. 1381–1384. IEEE Press, Los Alamitos, CA.

[116] Frigo, M. and Johnson, S. G. (2005). The design and implementation of FFTW3. *Proceedings IEEE 93*(2), 216–231.

[117] Gabow, H. N. (2018). Data structures for weighted matching and extensions to b-matching and f-factors. *ACM Transactions on Algorithms 14*(3), 39:1–39:80.

[118] Gale, D. and Shapley, L. S. (1962). College admissions and the stability of marriage. *American Mathematical Monthly 69*(1), 9–15.

[119] Gauss, C. F. (1866). Theoria interpolationis methodo nova tractata. In *Carl Friedrich Gauss Werke*, Volume 3, pp. 265–327. Königlichen Gesellschaft der Wissenschaften, Göttingen, Germany.

[120] Geist, A., Beguelin, A., Dongarra, J., Jiang, W., Mancheck, R., and Sunderam, V. S. (1994). *PVM: Parallel Virtual Machine. A Users' Guide and Tutorial for Networked Parallel Computing.* Scientific and Engineering Computation Series. MIT Press, Cambridge, MA.

[121] Gerbessiotis, A. V. (2015). Extending the BSP model for multi-core and out-of-core computing: MBSP. *Parallel Computing 41*, 90–102.

[122] Gerbessiotis, A. V. and Valiant, L. G. (1994). Direct bulk-synchronous parallel algorithms. *Journal of Parallel and Distributed Computing 22*(2), 251–267.

[123] Ghosh, S., Halappanavar, M., Kalyanaraman, A., Khan, A., and Gebremedhin, A. H. (2019). Exploring MPI communication models for graph applications using graph matching as a case study. In *Proceedings 33th International Parallel and Distributed Processing Symposium (IPDPS 2019)*, pp. 761–770. IEEE Press, Los Alamitos, CA.

[124] Golub, G. H. and Van Loan, C. F. (2013). *Matrix Computations* (Fourth edn). Johns Hopkins Studies in the Mathematical Sciences. Johns Hopkins University Press, Baltimore, MD.

[125] Gorlatch, S. (2001). Send-recv considered harmful? Myths and truths about parallel programming. In *Parallel Computing Technologies* (ed. V. Malyshkin), Volume 2127 of *Lecture Notes in Computer Science*, pp. 243–257. Springer.

[126] Goudreau, M. W., Lang, K., Rao, S. B., Suel, T., and Tsantilas, T. (1999). Portable and efficient parallel computing using the BSP model. *IEEE Transactions on Computers 48*(7), 670–689.

[127] Goudreau, M. W., Lang, K., Rao, S. B., and Tsantilas, T. (1995, June). The Green BSP library. Technical Report CS-TR-95-11, Department of Computer Science, University of Central Florida, Orlando, FL.

[128] Graham, R. L., Knuth, D. E., and Patashnik, O. (1994). *Concrete Mathematics: A Foundation for Computer Science* (Second edn). Addison Wesley, Upper Saddle River, NJ.

[129] Grama, A., Gupta, A., Karypis, G., and Kumar, V. (2003). *Introduction to Parallel Computing.* (Second edn) Addison-Wesley, Harlow, UK.

[130] Grigori, L., Demmel, J. W., and Xiang, H. (2011). CALU: A communication optimal LU factorization algorithm. *SIAM Journal on Matrix Analysis and Applications 32*(4), 1317–1350.

[131] Gropp, W., Hoefler, T., Thakur, R., and Lusk, E. (2014a). *Using Advanced MPI: Modern Features of the Message-Passing Interface.* MIT Press, Cambridge, MA.

[132] Gropp, W., Lusk, E., and Skjellum, A. (2014b). *Using MPI: Portable Parallel Programming with the Message-Passing Interface* (Third edn). MIT Press, Cambridge, MA.

[133] Gupta, A. and Kumar, V. (1993). The scalability of FFT on parallel computers. *IEEE Transactions on Parallel and Distributed Systems 4*(8), 922–932.

[134] Gustafson, J. L. (1988). Reevaluating Amdahl's law. *Communications of the ACM 31*(5), 532–533.

[135] Gustavson, F. G. (1972). Some basic techniques for solving sparse systems of linear equations. In *Sparse Matrices and Their Applications* (ed. D. J. Rose and R. A. Willoughby), pp. 41–52. Plenum Press.

[136] Hains, G. (2018). *Algorithmes et programmation parallèles: Théorie avec BSP et pratique avec OCaml.* Ellipses, Paris, France.

[137] Halappanavar, M., Pothen, A., Azad, A., Manne, F., Langguth, J., and Khan, A. (2015). Codesign lessons learned from implementing graph matching on multithreaded architectures. *IEEE Computer 48*(8), 46–55.

[138] Hamidouche, K., Falcou, J., and Etiemble, D. (2010). Hybrid bulk synchronous parallelism library for clustered SMP architectures. In *Proceedings 4th International Workshop on High-Level Parallel Programming and applications (HLPP 2010)*, pp. 55–62. ACM, New York.

[139] Hamidouche, K., Mendonca, F. M., Falcou, J., de Melo, A. C. M. A., and Etiemble, D. (2013). Parallel Smith–Waterman comparison on multicore and manycore computing platforms with BSP++. *International Journal of Parallel Programming 41*(1), 111–136.

[140] Hamming, R. W. (1973). *Numerical Methods for Scientists and Engineers* (Second edn). Dover.

[141] Hart, M. (1971). Project Gutenberg. https://www.gutenberg.org. Accessed December 14, 2019.

[142] Heideman, M. T., Johnson, D. H., and Burrus, C. S. (1985). Gauss and the history of the fast Fourier transform. *Archive for History of Exact Sciences 34*(3), 265–277.

[143] Hendrickson, B. (1998). Graph partitioning and parallel solvers: Has the emperor no clothes? In *Proceedings Fifth International Workshop on Solving Irregularly Structured Problems in Parallel (Irregular 1998)* (ed. A. Ferreira, J. Rolim, H. Simon, and S.-H. Teng), Volume 1457 of *Lecture Notes in Computer Science*, pp. 218–225. Springer.

[144] Hendrickson, B., Jessup, E., and Smith, C. (1999). Toward an efficient parallel eigensolver for dense symmetric matrices. *SIAM Journal on Scientific Computing 20*(3), 1132–1154.

[145] Hendrickson, B. and Leland, R. (1995). A multi-level algorithm for partitioning graphs. In *Proceedings of the 1995 ACM/IEEE Conference on Supercomputing.* IEEE Press, Los Alamitos, CA.

[146] Hendrickson, B., Leland, R., and Plimpton, S. (1995). An efficient parallel algorithm for matrix-vector multiplication. *International Journal of High Speed Computing* 7(1), 73–88.

[147] Hendrickson, B. and Plimpton, S. (1995). Parallel many-body simulations without all-to-all communication. *Journal of Parallel and Distributed Computing* 27(1), 15–25.

[148] Hendrickson, B. A. and Womble, D. E. (1994). The torus-wrap mapping for dense matrix calculations on massively parallel computers. *SIAM Journal on Scientific Computing* 15(5), 1201–1226.

[149] Hestenes, M. R. and Stiefel, E. (1952). Methods of conjugate gradients for solving linear systems. *Journal of Research of the National Bureau of Standards* 49(6), 409–436.

[150] Higham, D. J. and Higham, N. J. (2017). *MATLAB Guide* (Third edn). SIAM, Philadelphia, PA.

[151] Hill, J. M. D., Donaldson, S. R., and McEwan, A. (1998, September). Installation and user guide for the Oxford BSP toolset (v1.4) implementation of BSPlib. Technical report, Oxford University Computing Laboratory, Oxford, UK.

[152] Hill, J. M. D., Donaldson, S. R., and Skillicorn, D. B. (1997). Portability of performance with the BSPLib communications library. In *Proceedings Third Working Conference on Massively Parallel Programming Models (MPPM 1997)*, Washington, DC, pp. 33–42. IEEE Press.

[153] Hill, J. M. D., McColl, B., Stefanescu, D. C., Goudreau, M. W., Lang, K., Rao, S. B., Suel, T., Tsantilas, T., and Bisseling, R. H. (1998). BSPlib: The BSP programming library. *Parallel Computing* 24(14), 1947–1980.

[154] Hill, J. M. D. and Skillicorn, D. B. (1997/1998a). Lessons learned from implementing BSP. *Future Generation Computer Systems* 13(4–5), 327–335.

[155] Hill, J. M. D. and Skillicorn, D. B. (1998b). Practical barrier synchronisation. In *Proceedings Sixth EuroMicro Workshop on Parallel and Distributed Processing (PDP 1998)*, pp. 438–444. IEEE Press, Los Alamitos, CA.

[156] Hinsen, K. (2007). Parallel scripting with Python. *Computing in Science and Engineering* 9(6), 82–89.

[157] Hoare, C. A. R. (1961). Algorithm 64: Quicksort. *Communications of the ACM* 4(7), 321.

[158] Hoare, C. A. R. (1985). *Communicating Sequential Processes*. Prentice-Hall, Englewood Cliffs, NJ.

[159] Hockney, R. W. (1996). *The Science of Computer Benchmarking*. SIAM, Philadelphia, PA.

[160] Hoefler, T., Dinan, J., Thakur, R., Barrett, B., Balaji, P., Gropp, W., and Underwood, K. (2015). Remote memory access programming in MPI-3. *ACM Transactions on Parallel Computing* 2(2), 9:1–9:26.

[161] Hoepman, J.-H. (2004, October). Simple distributed weighted matchings. arXiv: 0410047 [cs.DC].

[162] Hopcroft, J. E. and Karp, R. M (1973). An $n^{5/2}$ algorithm for maximum matchings in bipartite graphs. *SIAM Journal on Computing* 2(4), 225–231.

[163] Horvitz, G. and Bisseling, R. H. (1999). Designing a BSP version of ScaLAPACK. In *Proceedings Ninth SIAM Conference on Parallel Processing for Scientific Computing* (ed. B. Hendrickson et al.). SIAM, Philadelphia, PA.

[164] Inda, M. A. and Bisseling, R. H. (2001). A simple and efficient parallel FFT algorithm using the BSP model. *Parallel Computing* 27(14), 1847–1878.

[165] Inda, M. A., Bisseling, R. H., and Maslen, D. K. (2001). On the efficient parallel computation of Legendre transforms. *SIAM Journal on Scientific Computing* 23(1), 271–303.

[166] Irony, D., Toledo, S., and Tiskin, A. (2004). Communication lower bounds for distributed-memory matrix multiplication. *Journal of Parallel and Distributed Computing* 64(9), 1017–1026.

[167] JáJá, J. (1992). *An Introduction to Parallel Algorithms*. Addison-Wesley, Reading, MA.

[168] Janse van Rensburg, E. J. (2015). *The Statistical Mechanics of Interacting Walks, Polygons, Animals and Vesicles* (Second edn). Oxford University Press, Oxford, UK.

[169] Johnsson, S. L. (1987). Communication efficient basic linear algebra computations on hypercube architectures. *Journal of Parallel and Distributed Computing* 4(2), 133–172.

[170] Juurlink, B. H. H. and Wijshoff, H. A. G. (1996). Communication primitives for BSP computers. *Information Processing Letters* 58(6), 303–310.

[171] Karp, A. H. (1996). Bit reversal on uniprocessors. *SIAM Review* 38(1), 1–26.

[172] Karypis, G. and Kumar, V. (1998). A fast and high quality multilevel scheme for partitioning irregular graphs. *SIAM Journal on Scientific Computing* 20(1), 359–392.

[173] Karypis, G. and Kumar, V. (1999a). Multilevel *k*-way hypergraph partitioning. In *Proceedings 36th ACM/IEEE Conference on Design Automation*, pp. 343–348. ACM Press, New York.

[174] Karypis, G. and Kumar, V. (1999b). Parallel multilevel *k*-way partitioning scheme for irregular graphs. *SIAM Review* 41(2), 278–300.

[175] Keller, J., Keßler, C. W., and Träff, J. L. (2001). *Practical PRAM programming*. Wiley series on parallel and distributed computing. Wiley, Hoboken, NJ.

[176] Kepner, J., Aaltonen, P., Bader, D. A., Buluç, A., Franchetti, F., Gilbert, J. R., Hutchison, D., Kumar, M., Lumsdaine, A., Meyerhenke, H., McMillan, S., Moreira, J. E., Owens, J. D., Yang, C., Zalewski, M., and Mattson, T. G. (2016). Mathematical foundations of the GraphBLAS. In *Proceedings IEEE High Performance Extreme Computing Conference (HPEC 2016)*, pp. 1–9.

[177] Kepner, J. and Gilbert, J. (ed.) (2011). *Graph Algorithms in the Language of Linear Algebra*. SIAM, Philadelphia, PA.

[178] Kepner, J., Kumar, M., Moreira, J., Pattnaik, P., Serrano, M., and Tufo, H. (2017). Enabling massive deep neural networks with the GraphBLAS. In *Proceedings IEEE High Performance Extreme Computing Conference (HPEC 2017)*, pp. 1–10.

[179] Kernighan, B. W. and Lin, S. (1970). An efficient heuristic procedure for partitioning graphs. *Bell System Technical Journal* 49(2), 291–307.

[180] Keßler, C. W. (2000). NestStep: Nested parallelism and virtual shared memory for the BSP model. *Journal of Supercomputing* 17(3), 245–262.

[181] Khan, A., Pothen, A., Patwary, M. M. A., Halappanavar, M., Satish, N. R., Sundaram, N., and Dubey, P. (2016). Designing scalable *b*-MATCHING algorithms on distributed memory multiprocessors by approximation. In *Proceedings of the International Conference for High Performance Computing, Networking, Storage and Analysis (SC 2016)*, pp. 773–783.

[182] Kirkpatrick, S., C. D. Gelatt, Jr., and Vecchi, M. P. (1983). Optimization by simulated annealing. *Science* 220(4598), 671–680.

[183] Kleinberg, J. M. (1999). Authoritative sources in a hyperlinked environment. *Journal of the ACM* 46(5), 604–632.

[184] Kleinjung, T., Aoki, K., Franke, J., Lenstra, A. K., Thomé, E., Bos, J. W., Gaudry, P., Kruppa, A., Montgomery, P. L., Osvik, D. A., te Riele, H., Timofeev, A., and Zimmermann, P. (2010). Factorization of a 768-bit RSA modulus. In *Advances in Cryptology – CRYPTO 2010* (ed. T. Rabin), Volume 6223 of *Lecture Notes in Computer Science*, pp. 333–350. Springer.

[185] Knigge, T. E. and Bisseling, R. H. (2020). An improved exact algorithm and an NP-completeness proof for sparse matrix bipartitioning. *Parallel Computing* **96**, p.102640.

[186] Knuth, D. E. (1997). *The Art of Computer Programming, Volume 1, Fundamental algorithms* (Third edn). Addison Wesley, Upper Saddle River, NJ.

[187] Knuth, D. E. (1998). *The Art of Computer Programming, Volume 3, Sorting and Searching* (Second edn). Addison Wesley, Upper Saddle River, NJ.

[188] Koblitz, N. (1994). *A Course in Number Theory and Cryptography* (Second edn). Springer-Verlag, Berlin.

[189] Kosloff, R. (1988). Time-dependent quantum-mechanical methods for molecular dynamics. *The Journal of Physical Chemistry* 92(8), 2087–2100.

[190] Koster, J. H. H. (2002, July). Parallel templates for numerical linear algebra, a high-performance computation library. Master's thesis, Department of Mathematics, Utrecht University, Utrecht, the Netherlands.

[191] Langr, D. and Tvrdík, P. (2016). Evaluation criteria for sparse matrix storage formats. *IEEE Transactions on Parallel and Distributed Systems* 27(2), 428–440.

[192] Langville, A. N. and Meyer, C. D. (2006). *Google's PageRank and Beyond: The Science of Search Engine Rankings*. Princeton University Press, Princeton, NJ.

[193] Lawson, C. L., Hanson, R. J., Kincaid, D. R., and Krogh, F. T. (1979). Basic Linear Algebra Subprograms for Fortran usage. *ACM Transactions on Mathematical Software* 5(3), 308–323.

[194] Le Gall, F. (2014). Powers of tensors and fast matrix multiplication. In *Proceedings 39th International Symposium on Symbolic and Algebraic Computation (ISSAC 2014)*, pp. 296–303. ACM, New York.

[195] Leforestier, C., Bisseling, R. H., Cerjan, C., Feit, M. D., Friesner, R., Guldberg, A., Hammerich, A., Jolicard, G., Karrlein, W., Meyer, H.-D., Lipkin, N., Roncero, O., and Kosloff, R. (1991). A comparison of different propagation schemes for the time dependent Schrödinger equation. *Journal of Computational Physics* 94(1), 59–80.

[196] Leskovec, J. and Sosič, R. (2016). SNAP: A general-purpose network analysis and graph-mining library. *ACM Transactions on Intelligent Systems and Technology* 8(1), 1:1–1:20.

[197] Lewis, J. G. and van de Geijn, R. A. (1993). Distributed memory matrix-vector multiplication and conjugate gradient algorithms. In *Proceedings of the 1993 ACM/IEEE Conference on Supercomputing*, pp. 484–492. ACM, New York.

[198] Li, X., Lu, P., Schaeffer, J., Shillington, J., Wong, P. S., and Shi, H. (1993). On the versatility of parallel sorting by regular sampling. *Parallel Computing* 19(10), 1079–1103.

[199] Loulergue, F. (2017). A BSPlib-style API for bulk synchronous parallel ML. *Scalable Computing: Practice and Experience* 18(3), 261–274.

[200] Loulergue, F., Gava, F., and Billiet, D. (2005). Bulk synchronous parallel ML: modular implementation and performance prediction. In *Proceedings 5th International Conference on Computational Science (ICCS 2005)* (ed. V. S. Sunderam, G. D. van Albada, P. M. A. Sloot, and J. J. Dongarra), Volume 3515 of *Lecture Notes in Computer Science*, pp. 1046–1054. Springer.

[201] Loulergue, F., Hains, G., and Foisy, C. (2000). A calculus of functional BSP programs. *Science of Computer Programming* 37(1–3), 253–277.

[202] Loyens, L. D. J. C. and Moonen, J. R. (1994). ILIAS, a sequential language for parallel matrix computations. In *PARLE'94 Parallel Architectures and Languages Europe* (ed. C. Halatsis, D. Maritsas, G. Philokyprou, and S. Theodoridis), Volume 817 of *Lecture Notes in Computer Science*, pp. 250–261. Springer.

[203] Luby, M. (1986). A simple parallel algorithm for the maximal independent set problem. *SIAM Journal on Computing* 15(4), 1036–1053.

[204] Lusseau, D., Schneider, K., Boisseau, O. J., Haase, P., Slooten, E., and Dawson, S. M. (2003). The bottlenose dolphin community of Doubtful Sound features a large proportion of long-lasting associations. *Behavioral Ecology and Sociobiology* 54(4), 396–405.

[205] Malewicz, G., Austern, M. H., Bik, A. J. C, Dehnert, J. C., Horn, I., Leiser, N., and Czajkowski, G. (2010). Pregel: A system for large-scale graph processing. In *Proceedings 2010 ACM SIGMOD International Conference on Management of Data*, pp. 135–145. ACM, New York.

[206] Manlove, D. F. (2013). *Algorithmics of Matching Under Preferences*, Volume 2 of *Series on Theoretical Computer Science*. World Scientific.

[207] Manne, F. and Bisseling, R. H. (2008). A parallel approximation algorithm for the weighted maximum matching problem. In *Proceedings Seventh International Conference on Parallel Processing and Applied Mathematics (PPAM 2007)*, Volume 4967 of *Lecture Notes in Computer Science*, pp. 708–717. Springer.

[208] Manne, F. and Halappanavar, M. (2014). New effective multithreaded matching algorithms. In *Proceedings 28th International Parallel and Distributed Processing Symposium (IPDPS 2014)*, pp. 519–528. IEEE Press, Los Alamitos, CA.

[209] Manne, F., Naim, Md., Lerring, H., and Halappanavar, M. (2016). On stable marriages and greedy matchings. In *Proceedings 7th SIAM Workshop on Combinatorial Scientific Computing*, pp. 92–101. SIAM, Philadelphia, PA.

[210] Marek, A., Blum, V., Johanni, R., Havu, V., Lang, B., Auckenthaler, T., Heinecke, A., Bungartz, H.-J., and Lederer, H. (2014). The ELPA library: scalable parallel eigenvalue solutions for electronic structure theory and computational science. *Journal of Physics: Condensed Matter* 26(21), 213201.

[211] Martella, C., Logothetis, D., and Shaposhnik, R. (2015). *Practical Graph Analytics with Apache Giraph*. Apress, CA.

[212] McColl, W. F. (1993). General purpose parallel computing. In *Lectures on Parallel Computation* (ed. A. Gibbons and P. Spirakis), Volume 4 of *Cambridge International Series on Parallel Computation*, pp. 337–391. Cambridge University Press, Cambridge, UK.

[213] McColl, W. F. (1995). Scalable computing. In *Computer Science Today: Recent Trends and Developments* (ed. J. van Leeuwen), Volume 1000 of *Lecture Notes in Computer Science*, pp. 46–61. Springer.

[214] McColl, W. F. (1996a). A BSP realisation of Strassen's algorithm. In *Abstract Machine Models for Parallel and Distributed Computing* (ed. M. Kara, J. R. Davy, D. Goodeve, and J. Nash), pp. 43–46. IOS Press, Amsterdam, The Netherlands.

[215] McColl, W. F. (1996b). Scalability, portability and predictability: The BSP approach to parallel programming. *Future Generation Computer Systems* 12(4), 265–272.

[216] McColl, W. F. and Tiskin, A. (1999). Memory-efficient matrix multiplication in the BSP model. *Algorithmica* 24(3-4), 287–297.

[217] McVitie, D. G. and Wilson, L. B. (1971). The stable marriage problem. *Communications of the ACM* 14(7), 486–490.

[218] Message-Passing Interface Forum (2015). *MPI: A Message-Passing Interface Standard, Version 3.1*. High Performance Computing Center Stuttgart (HLRS), Germany.

[219] Metcalf, M., Reid, J., and Cohen, M. (2018). *Modern Fortran Explained* (Fifth edn). Oxford University Press, Oxford, UK.

[220] Métivier, Y., Robson, J. M., Saheb-Djahromi, N., and Zemmari, A. (2011). An optimal bit complexity randomized distributed MIS algorithm. *Distributed Computing* 23(5), 331–340.

[221] Metropolis, N., Rosenbluth, A. W., Rosenbluth, M. N., Teller, A. H., and Teller, E. (1953). Equation of state calculations by fast computing machines. *The Journal of Chemical Physics* 21(6), 1087–1092.

[222] Miller, Q. (2002). BSP in a lazy functional context. In *Trends in Functional Programming* (ed. K. Hammond and S. Curtis), Volume 3, pp. 37–50. Intellect Books, Bristol, UK.

[223] Miller, R. (1993). A library for bulk synchronous parallel programming. In *General Purpose Parallel Computing*, pp. 100–108. British Computer Society Parallel Processing Specialist Group, London.

[224] Miller, R. and Reed, J. (1993). The Oxford BSP library users' guide, version 1.0. Technical report, Oxford Parallel, Oxford, UK.

[225] Mitzenmacher, M. and Upfal, E. (2017). *Probability and Computing: Randomization and Probabilistic Techniques in Algorithms and Data Analysis* (Second edn). Cambridge University Press, Cambridge, UK.

[226] Moler, C. (2011). *Experiments with MATLAB*. Mathworks, Inc.

[227] Narasimha, M. J. and Peterson, A. M. (1978). On the computation of the discrete cosine transform. *IEEE Transactions on Communications* 26(6), 934–936.

[228] Naumann, U. and Schenk, O. (ed.) (2012). *Combinatorial Scientific Computing*. Computational Science Series. CRC Press, Taylor & Francis Group, Boca Raton, FL.

[229] Newman, M. (2018). *Networks* (Second edn). Oxford University Press, Oxford, UK.

[230] Newman, M. E. J. and Barkema, G. T. (1999). *Monte Carlo Methods in Statistical Physics*. Oxford University Press, Oxford, UK.

[231] Nishtala, R., Zheng, Y., Hargrove, P. H., and Yelick, K. A. (2011). Tuning collective communication for Partitioned Global Address Space programming models. *Parallel Computing* 37(9), 576–591.

[232] Numrich, R. W. and Reid, J. K. (1998). Co-array Fortran for parallel programming. *ACM SIGPLAN Fortran Forum* 17(2), 1–31.

[233] Ogielski, A. T. and Aiello, W. (1993). Sparse matrix computations on parallel processor arrays. *SIAM Journal on Scientific Computing* 14(3), 519–530.

[234] O'Leary, D. P. and Stewart, G. W. (1985). Data-flow algorithms for parallel matrix computations. *Communications of the ACM* 28(8), 840–853.

[235] O'Leary, D. P. and Stewart, G. W. (1986). Assignment and scheduling in parallel matrix factorization. *Linear Algebra and Its Applications* 77, 275–299.

[236] Onnela, J-P., Saramäki, J., Kertész, J., and Kaski, K. (2005). Intensity and coherence of motifs in weighted complex networks. *Physical Review E* 71(6) 065103.

[237] Open MPI Development Team (2018). Open MPI v3.1. https://www.open-mpi.org/doc/. Accessed December 14, 2019.

[238] OpenMP Team (2018). OpenMP v4.5. https://www.openmp.org. Accessed December 14, 2019.

[239] Orr, W. J. C. (1947). Statistical treatment of polymer solutions at infinite dilution. *Transactions Faraday Society* 43, 12–27.

[240] Pacheco, P. S. (1996). *Parallel Programming with MPI*. Morgan Kaufmann, San Francisco, CA.

[241] Parlett, B. N. (1971). Analysis of algorithms for reflections in bisectors. *SIAM Review* 13(2), 197–208.

[242] Patwary, M. M. A., Bisseling, R. H., and Manne, F. (2010). Parallel greedy graph matching using an edge partitioning approach. In *Proceedings 4th international workshop on High-Level Parallel Programming and applications (HLPP 2010)*, pp. 45–54. ACM, New York.

[243] Pease, M. C. (1968). An adaptation of the fast Fourier transform for parallel processing. *Journal of the ACM* 15(2), 252–264.

[244] Pellegrini, F. and Roman, J. (1996). SCOTCH: A software package for static mapping by dual recursive bipartitioning of process and architecture graphs. In *Proceedings High-Performance Computing and Networking (HPCN Europe 1996)*, Volume 1067 of *Lecture Notes in Computer Science*, pp. 493–498. Springer.

[245] Pelt, D. M. and Bisseling, R. H. (2014). A medium-grain method for fast 2D bipartitioning of sparse matrices. In *Proceedings 28th International Parallel and Distributed Processing Symposium (IPDPS 2014)*, pp. 529–539. IEEE Press, Los Alamitos, CA.

[246] Pelt, D. M. and Bisseling, R. H. (2015). An exact algorithm for sparse matrix bipartitioning. *Journal of Parallel and Distributed Computing* 85, 79–90.

[247] Petersen, T., Mitschker, J., and Klüner, T. (2018). High-dimensional wave packet dynamics from first principles: Photodissociation of water on TiO_2-rutile (110). *Journal of Photochemistry and Photobiology A: Chemistry* **366**, 3–11.

[248] Pooch, U. W. and Nieder, A. (1973). A survey of indexing techniques for sparse matrices. *ACM Computing Surveys* 5(2), 109–133.

[249] Poole, S. W., Hernandez, O., Kuehn, J. A., Shipman, G. M., Curtis, A., and Feind, K. (2011). OpenSHMEM - toward a unified RMA model. In *Encyclopedia of Parallel Computing* (ed. D. Padua), Boston, MA, pp. 1379–1391. Springer.

[250] Pothen, A., Ferdous, S. M., and Manne, F. (2019). Approximation algorithms in combinatorial scientific computing. *Acta Numerica* **28**, 541–633.

[251] Poulson, J., Marker, B., van de Geijn, R. A., Hammond, J. R., and Romero, N. A. (2013). Elemental: A new framework for distributed memory dense matrix computations. *ACM Transactions on Mathematical Software* 39(2), 13:1–13:24.

[252] Preis, R. (1999). Linear time 1/2-approximation algorithm for maximum weighted matching in general graphs. In *Proceedings 1999 Symposium on Theoretical Aspects of Computer Science (STACS 1999)*, Volume 1563 of *Lecture Notes in Computer Science*, pp. 259–269. Springer.

[253] Press, W. H., Teukolsky, S. A., Vetterling, W. T., and Flannery, B. P. (2007). *Numerical Recipes: The Art of Scientific Computing* (Third edn). Cambridge University Press, Cambridge, UK.

[254] Primate Labs (2016). Geekbench. https://primatelabs.com. Accessed December 14, 2019.

[255] Püschel, M., Franchetti, F., and Voronenko, Y. (2011). Spiral. In *Encyclopedia of Parallel Computing* (ed. D. Padua), Boston, MA, pp. 1920–1933. Springer.

[256] Püschel, M., Moura, J. M. F., Johnson, J. R., Padua, D., Veloso, M. M., Singer, B. W., Xiong, J., Franchetti, F., Gačić, A., Voronenko, Y., Chen, K., Johnson, R. W., and Rizzolo, N. (2005). SPIRAL: Code generation for DSP transforms. *Proceedings of the IEEE* 93(2), 232–275.

[257] Quinn, M. J. (2003). *Parallel Programming in C with MPI and OpenMP*. McGraw-Hill, New York.

[258] Rajamanickam, S. and Boman, E. G. (2013). Parallel partitioning with Zoltan: Is hypergraph partitioning worth it? In *Graph Partitioning and Graph Clustering* (ed. D. A. Bader, H. Meyerhenke, P. Sanders, and D. Wagner), Volume 588 of *Contemporary Mathematics*, pp. 37–52. AMS, Providence, RI.

[259] Reed, J., Parrott, K., and Lanfear, T. (1996). Portability, predictability and performance for parallel computing: BSP in practice. *Concurrency: Practice and Experience* 8(10), 799–812.

[260] Roth, A. E. (1984). The evolution of the labor market for medical interns and residents: A case study in game theory. *Journal of Political Economy* 92(6), 991–1016.

[261] Saad, Y. (1989). Krylov subspace methods on supercomputers. *SIAM Journal on Scientific and Statistical Computing* 10(6), 1200–1232.

[262] Saad, Y. (2003). *Iterative Methods for Sparse Linear Systems* (Second edn). SIAM, Philadelphia, PA.

[263] Saad, Y. and Schultz, M. H. (1986). GMRES: A generalized minimal residual algorithm for solving nonsymmetric linear systems. *SIAM Journal on Scientific and Statistical Computing* 7(3), 856–869.

[264] Salamin, E. (1976). Computation of π using arithmetic-geometric mean. *Mathematics of Computation* 30(135), 565–570.

[265] Schlag, S., Henne, V., Heuer, T., Meyerhenke, H., Sanders, P., and Schulz, C. (2016). k-way hypergraph partitioning via n-level recursive bisection. In *Proceedings 18th Workshop on Algorithm Engineering and Experiments (ALENEX 2016)*, pp. 53–67. SIAM, Philadelphia, PA.

[266] Shi, H. and Schaeffer, J. (1992). Parallel sorting by regular sampling. *Journal of Parallel and Distributed Computing* 14(4), 361–372.

[267] Shingu, S., Takahara, H., Fuchigami, H., Yamada, M., Tsuda, Y., Ohfuchi, W., Sasaki, Y., Kobayashi, K., Hagiwara, T., Habata, S., Yokokawa, M., Itoh, H., and Otsuka, K. (2002). A 26.58 Tflops global atmospheric simulation with the spectral transform method on the Earth Simulator. In *Proceedings of the 2002 ACM/IEEE Conference on Supercomputing*, pp. 1–19. IEEE Press, Los Alamitos, CA.

[268] Shoup, V. (1990–). NTL: A library for doing number theory. https://www.shoup.net/ntl/. Accessed December 14, 2019.

[269] Siddique, K., Akhtar, Z., Yoon, E. J., Jeong, Y.-S., Dasgupta, D., and Kim, Y. (2016). Apache Hama: An emerging bulk synchronous parallel computing framework for big data applications. *IEEE Access* **4**, 8879–8887.

[270] Skillicorn, D. B., Hill, J. M. D., and McColl, W. F. (1997). Questions and answers about BSP. *Scientific Programming* 6(3), 249–274.

[271] Slatkevičius, R., Vogel, L., and Blazek, J. (2005–). PrimeGrid. http://primegrid.com. Accessed December 14, 2019.

[272] Sloane, N. J. A. (1964–). The On-line Encyclopedia of Integer Sequences. https://oeis.org. Accessed December 14, 2019.

[273] Solomonik, E. and Demmel, J. (2011). Communication-optimal parallel 2.5D matrix multiplication and LU factorization algorithms. In *Euro-Par 2011 Parallel Processing* (ed. E. Jeannot, R. Namyst, and J. Roman), pp. 90–109. Springer.

[274] Solomonik, E. and Kalé, L. V. (2010). Highly scalable parallel sorting. In *Proceedings 24th IEEE International Symposium on Parallel and Distributed Processing (IPDPS 2010)*, pp. 1–12.

[275] Sonneveld, P. and van Gijzen, M. B. (2008). IDR(s): A family of simple and fast algorithms for solving large nonsymmetric systems of linear equations. *SIAM Journal on Scientific Computing* 31(2), 1035–1062.

[276] Stewart, G. W. (1998). *Matrix Algorithms: Volume 1: Basic Decompositions*. SIAM, Philadelphia, PA.

[277] Stijnman, M. A., Bisseling, R. H., and Barkema, G. T. (2003). Partitioning 3D space for parallel many-particle simulations. *Computer Physics Communications* 149(3), 121–134.

[278] Strassen, V. (1969). Gaussian elimination is not optimal. *Numerische Mathematik* 13(4), 354–356.

[279] Strohmaier, E., Dongarra, J., Simon, H., Meuer, M., and Meuer, H. (1993–2019). TOP500. https://www.top500.org. Accessed December 14, 2019.

[280] Suijlen, W. (2017). Mock BSPlib for testing and debugging bulk synchronous parallel software. *Parallel Processing Letters* 27(1), 1740001.

[281] Suijlen, W. (2019). BSPonMPI v1.1. https://github.com/wijnand-suijlen/bsponmpi/ releases. Accessed December 14, 2019.

[282] Sunderam, V. S. (1990). PVM: A framework for parallel distributed computing. *Concurrency: Practice and Experience* 2(4), 315–339.

[283] Symul, T., Assad, S. M., and Lam, P. K. (2011). ANU quantum random numbers server. https://qrng.anu.edu.au. Accessed December 14, 2019.

[284] Takahashi, D., Uno, A., and Yokokawa, M. (2012). An implementation of parallel 1-d FFT on the K computer. In *Proceedings 14th IEEE International Conference on High Performance Computing and Communication*, pp. 344–350.

[285] Thakur, R., Rabenseifner, R., and Gropp, W. (2005). Optimization of collective communication operations in MPICH. *The International Journal of High Performance Computing Applications* 19(1), 49–66.

[286] Tiskin, A. (1998). The bulk-synchronous parallel random access machine. *Theoretical Computer Science* 196(1-2), 109–130.

[287] Trifunović, A. and Knottenbelt, W. J. (2008). Parallel multilevel algorithms for hypergraph partitioning. *Journal of Parallel and Distributed Computing* 68(5), 563–581.

[288] Valiant, L. G. (1982). A scheme for fast parallel communication. *SIAM Journal on Computing* 11(2), 350–361.

[289] Valiant, L. G. (1989). Bulk-synchronous parallel computers. In *Parallel Processing and Artificial Intelligence* (ed. M. Reeve and S. E. Zenith), pp. 15–22. Wiley, Hoboken, NJ.

[290] Valiant, L. G. (1990a). A bridging model for parallel computation. *Communications of the ACM* 33(8), 103–111.

[291] Valiant, L. G. (1990b). General purpose parallel architectures. In *Handbook of Theoretical Computer Science: Vol. A, Algorithms and Complexity* (ed. J. van Leeuwen), pp. 943–971. Elsevier, Amsterdam.

[292] Valiant, L. G. (2011). A bridging model for multi-core computing. *Journal of Computer and System Sciences* 77(1), 154–166.

[293] van de Geijn, R. A. (1997). *Using PLAPACK: Parallel Linear Algebra Package*. MIT Press, Cambridge, MA.

[294] Van de Velde, E. F. (1990). Experiments with multicomputer LU-decomposition. *Concurrency: Practice and Experience* 2(1), 1–26.

[295] van de Vorst, J. G. G. (1988). The formal development of a parallel program performing LU-decomposition. *Acta Informatica* 26(1-2), 1–17.

[296] van der Pas, R., Stotzer, E., and Terboven, C. (2017). *Using OpenMP: The Next Step*. MIT Press, Cambridge, MA.

[297] van der Stappen, A. F., Bisseling, R. H., and van de Vorst, J. G. G. (1993). Parallel sparse LU decomposition on a mesh network of transputers. *SIAM Journal on Matrix Analysis and Applications* 14(3), 853–879.

[298] van der Vorst, H. A. (2003). *Iterative Krylov Methods for Large Linear Systems*, Volume 13 of *Cambridge Monographs on Applied and Computational Mathematics*. Cambridge University Press, Cambridge, UK.

[299] van der Vorst, H. A. (1992). Bi-CGSTAB: A fast and smoothly converging variant of Bi-CG for the solution of nonsymmetric linear systems. *SIAM Journal on Scientific and Statistical Computing* 13(2), 631–644.

[300] van Duijn, M., Visscher, K. M., and Visscher, P. E. (2016). BSPLib: a fast, and easy to use C++ implementation of the Bulk Synchronous Parallel (BSP) threading model. https://bsplib.eu. Accessed December 14, 2019.

[301] van Duijn, M., Visscher, K. M., and Visscher, P. E. (2018). SyncLib. https://zenodo.org/record/1285745. Accessed December 14, 2019.

[302] van Heukelum, A., Barkema, G. T., and Bisseling, R. H. (2002). DNA electrophoresis studied with the cage model. *Journal of Computational Physics* 180(1), 313–326.

[303] Van Loan, C. (1992). *Computational Frameworks for the Fast Fourier Transform*, Volume 10 of *Frontiers in Applied Mathematics*. SIAM, Philadelphia, PA.

[304] Vastenhouw, B. and Bisseling, R. H. (2005). A two-dimensional data distribution method for parallel sparse matrix-vector multiplication. *SIAM Review* 47(1), 67–95.

[305] Vishkin, U. (1993). Structural parallel algorithmics. In *Lectures on Parallel Computation* (ed. A. Gibbons and P. Spirakis), Volume 4 of *Cambridge International Series on Parallel Computation*, pp. 1–18. Cambridge University Press, Cambridge, UK.

[306] Vishkin, U. (2011). Using simple abstraction to reinvent computing for parallelism. *Communications of the ACM* 54(1), 75–85.

[307] W. Gropp *et al.* (2018). MPICH v3.3. https://www.mpich.org. Accessed December 14, 2019.

[308] Watts, D. J. and Strogatz, S. H. (1998). Collective dynamics of 'small-world' networks. *Nature* 393(6684) 440–442.

[309] Wedi, N. P., Bauer, P., Deconinck, W., Diamantakis, M., Hamrud, M., Kühnlein, C., Malardel, S., Mogensen, K., Mozdzynski, G., and Smolarkiewicz, P. K. (2015, November). The modelling infrastructure of the Integrated Forecasting System: Recent advances and future challenges. Technical Memorandum 760, ECMWF, Reading, UK.

[310] Wedi, N. P., Hamrud, M., and Mozdzynski, G. (2013). A fast spherical harmonics transform for global NWP and climate models. *Monthly Weather Review 141*(10), 3450–3461.

[311] Whaley, R. C., Petitet, A., and Dongarra, J. J. (2001). Automated empirical optimizations of software and the ATLAS project. *Parallel Computing 27*(1–2), 3–35.

[312] Wilkinson, B. and Allen, M. (2004). *Parallel Programming: Techniques and Applications Using Networked Workstations and Parallel Computers* (Second edn). Pearson.

[313] Xiong, J., Johnson, J., Johnson, R., and Padua, D. (2001). SPL: A language and compiler for DSP algorithms. *ACM SIGPLAN Notices 36*(5), 298–308.

[314] YarKhan, A., Kurzak, J., Luszczek, P., and Dongarra, J. (2017). Porting the PLASMA numerical library to the OpenMP standard. *International Journal of Parallel Programming 45*(3), 612–633.

[315] Yzelman, A. N (2014). MulticoreBSP for C: a quick-start guide. http://www.multicorebsp.com/documentation/quickC/. Accessed December 14, 2019.

[316] Yzelman, A. N. and Bisseling, R. H. (2009). Cache-oblivious sparse matrix–vector multiplication by using sparse matrix partitioning methods. *SIAM Journal on Scientific Computing 31*(4), 3128–3154.

[317] Yzelman, A. N. and Bisseling, R. H. (2012). An object-oriented bulk synchronous parallel library for multicore programming. *Concurrency and Computation: Practice and Experience 24*(5), 533–553.

[318] Yzelman, A. N., Bisseling, R. H., Roose, D., and Meerbergen, K. (2014). MulticoreBSP for C: a high-performance library for shared-memory parallel programming. *International Journal of Parallel Programming 42*(5), 619–642.

[319] Yzelman, A. N. and Roose, D. (2014). High-level strategies for parallel shared-memory sparse matrix-vector multiplication. *IEEE Transactions on Parallel and Distributed Systems 25*(1), 116–125.

[320] Zhang, Y. (2014). Bounded gaps between primes. *Annals of Mathematics 179*(3), 1121–1174.

[321] Zheng, Y., Kamil, A., Driscoll, M. B., Shan, H., and Yelick, K. (2014). UPC++: A PGAS extension for C++. In *Proceedings 28th International Parallel and Distributed Processing Symposium (IPDPS 2014)*, pp. 1105–1114. IEEE Press, Los Alamitos, CA.

[322] Ziv, J. and Lempel, A. (1977). A universal algorithm for sequential data compression. *IEEE Transactions on Information Theory 23*(3), 337–343.

INDEX

accidental zero 197–198, 205
adjacency list 300, 305
adjacency matrix 319, 350
adjacency set 296, 300
all-to-all 64, 157, 179, 208,
    282, 283
allocation
    of a matrix 360
    of a vector 360
    of memory 360
API, *see* application programming
    interface
application programming
    interface 1, 13, 58–60,
    62, 66
approximation algorithm
    293–296, 312, 346–348
argmax 80
arithmetic mean 189
artificial intelligence 74
ASCII 71
augmentation 348
augmenting path 346, 358
authority 194

b-matching 347, 348
backwards design 82
bandwidth of a matrix
    lower 119, 284
    upper 119, 284
barrier, *see* synchronization
basic linear algebra subprograms,
    see BLAS
benchmark
    HPCG 279, 285, 293
    HPL 36, 67, 96, 98–99, 117,
    120, 279
benchmarking vii, 7, 24
    MPI 64
    program 27–32, 66, 69, 114
    results of 32–38, 56, 118
Bernoulli trial 239
betweenness centrality 357–358
BFS, *see* breadth-first search

Bi-CGSTAB 276
Big Data v, 2, 60, 74, 201, 293, 350
binary matrix 319, 341
bipartite graph 292, 293,
    347–349, 358
bipartitioning 218, 221, 225, 229
    of a graph 223
    of a hypergraph 222, 223, 228
    recursive 260
bisection, *see* bipartitioning
bit reversal 143–146, 151–152,
    158–159, 177–178
bit-reversal matrix 143
bitonic sequence 68
BLAS 25, 67, 117, 121, 132
block distribution, *see* distribution,
    block
block size, algorithmic 97, 102,
    113, 117, 132
block-tridiagonal matrix 245
blocking of an algorithm 96, 98,
    100, 115, 120
body-centred cubic (BCC)
    lattice 253
branch-and-bound method 288
breadth-first search 193, 358
breadth-first traversal 139
breakdown rule 176
broadcast 11, 64, 83, 90, 91,
    101–102
    one-phase 91, 113–115,
    117, 123
    tree-based 121
    two-phase 91, 113–115, 120,
    121, 123, 213
BSML 61
BSMP 363
BSP
    algorithm 3–4, 176, 177
    computer vii, 2–3, 6, 9, 24, 57,
    114, 284
    cost 4–7, 207, 280
    decomposable 58, 256
    hybrid- 256–261, 290

model v–vii, xi, 2–9, 26, 47, 49,
    57, 113, 115, 118–119,
    247, 280
    parameters 6–7, 24, 27, 34, 36,
    64, 114, 130, 167
    variants of 8, 57, 256
BSP Worldwide vi, xv
bsp_abort 19, 354, 364
bsp_begin 14, 364
bsp_broadcast 101
bsp_direct_get 279,
    363–364
bsp_end 14, 364
bsp_get 19, 49, 262, 364
bsp_get_tag 48, 49, 263, 364
bsp_hpget 133, 364
bsp_hpmove 363, 364
bsp_hpput 132, 133, 364
bsp_hpsend 279, 363, 364
bsp_init 14, 364
bsp_move 48, 364
bsp_nprocs 15, 364
bsp_pid 15, 364
bsp_pop_reg 19, 364
bsp_push_reg 18, 157, 364
bsp_put 17, 46, 49, 132, 133,
    262, 326, 364
bsp_qsize 48–49, 263, 364
bsp_send 46–49, 262–263,
    342, 364
bsp_set_tagsize 48, 49,
    364
bsp_sync 15, 114, 364
bsp_time 15, 114, 364
bspcc 20
BSPedupack ix, x, 65, 127, 262,
    263, 359–362
BSPlib vi, vii, xi, 2, 13, 63, 64, 66,
    102, 121, 177, 363, 364
    implementation of x, 59
    primitives 13–19, 46–49
    programs
        compiling of 20
        running of 20

BSPlib vs. MPI 64–66
BSPonMPI x, 2, 13, 59, 65, 114, 115, 167–168, 273, 342
bsprun 20
buffer memory 48, 49
Bulk x, 61, 65, 66, 177, 290
bulk synchronous message passing 363
bulk synchronous parallel, see BSP
Bullx supercomputer 36, 37, 53, 166
butterfly
    block 148, 150, 152, 155
    matrix 141, 147, 157
    operation 142, 148, 150, 151, 156

C vii, x, 10, 13–14, 21, 59, 64, 124, 132, 158
    compiler x, 20
    mathematics library 20
    standard library 56
C++ x, 13, 60, 61, 66, 69, 276, 290
cache 25
    effects 54, 169, 273
    hit 101, 158
    line 101
    miss 54, 97, 158, 201
    primary 25
    secondary 25
    tertiary 25
cache-friendly 101, 173, 178, 242
cache-oblivious 179, 242, 279
Cannon's algorithm 125
cardinality matching 292, 314, 324, 346–349, 358
carry-add operation 188
Cartesian distribution 83, 119, 350
Cartesius xii, 36, 53–56, 166–173, 269–275, 340–346
CCS, see compressed column storage
centrality, betweenness 357–358
Chernoff bound 239–240
Cholesky factorization 120, 123
    sparse 275
circular list 326
climate simulation 179
clustering coefficient 356
Coarray Fortran 62
coarsening 223, 224, 280

codelet 174
collective communication 20, 60, 64, 66, 101, 120–121
column-net model 225
combinatorial scientific computing xi, xv, 276
combining, two-phase 213
communicating sequential processes 62
communication volume 90, 207, 215
communication-avoiding algorithm 98–99
communicator 64
commutativity 126
compare-and-swap 67, 68
compiler, parallelizing 201
compressed column storage 199, 277
compressed row storage 198–199, 204, 277, 300, 325
    incremental 199–200, 204, 261, 263, 325
    bidirectional 279
compressed sparse columns, see compressed column storage
compressed sparse rows, see compressed row storage
compression 71–72, 186
conformal partitioning 283
conjugate gradient method 192, 276, 278, 284–286
connected components 286
connective constant 355
connectivity of a net 225
consistency constraint 231, 236, 237
convolution 174, 187, 188
    theorem 187
Cooley–Tukey FFT 139, 142, 146, 147
cooling schedule 290
coordinate scheme 198
Cori xii, 113–119, 349
correctness 76, 307, 310–314
cosine transform, fast (FCT) 174, 184
    inverse 184, 185
counting sort 67, 261, 300
CRCW PRAM 57, 68
CRS, see compressed row storage
cryptanalysis 70, 188

cryptology 70
CSC, see compressed column storage
CSR, see compressed row storage
curse of dimensionality 271
cut edge 306
cut-off radius 286
cyclic distribution, see distribution, cyclic

DAG, see directed acyclic graph
data analytics 291
data compression 71
data structure 194, 277, 298
    dynamic 198
    sparse 196, 198–201, 204
    static 198
DAXPY 25, 27, 67, 172, 173, 202, 232
DCT, see discrete cosine transform
dead edge 298–300
deadlock 11, 64, 65
deallocation of memory 360
decimation in frequency 147, 177
decimation in time 142
decomposable BSP 58
decompression 72
deep learning 215
degree of a vertex 235–236, 245
delta-indexing 199
density of a sparse matrix 190, 196, 207, 237, 240, 242
depth, parallel 344
depth-first search 296, 354
depth-first traversal 139
deregistration 19, 264
determinism 314, 316
DFS, see depth-first search
DFT, see discrete Fourier transform
DGEMM 25, 33, 67, 132
diagonal dominance 285
diagonal matrix 128, 276
diagonal processor 212, 213
DIF, see decimation in frequency
differentiation, by Fourier transform 181
digital diamond 247–253, 278
    three-dimensional 252
direct remote memory access 60–61, 363, 364
direct solution method 192

directed acyclic graph viii, 63, 121
discrete convolution 187
discrete cosine transform 184
  inverse 184
discrete Fourier transform 135, 138, 174
  inverse 135
  three-dimensional 182
  two-dimensional 181–182
discrete Legendre transform 179
discrete wavelet transform 186–187
  inverse 187
  two-dimensional 187
distributed memory 8, 113, 167
distributed/shared-memory ratio 260
distribution
  alternative block 45
  block 9–10, 149
  block with bit-reversed processor numbering, 152
  block-cyclic 62, 99, 120, 122, 150, 176
  Cartesian 83, 119, 202, 208–213
  cyclic 9, 45, 88, 149, 182
  cyclic row 119
  diamond 254–255
  geometric 287
  group-cyclic 149–152, 159, 177
  matrix 83, 209, 215
  $M \times N$ block 283
  $M \times N$ cyclic 88, 116, 120, 123, 182
  Mondriaan 215–224, 228
  non-Cartesian 119, 122, 202, 208
  row 242, 246
  square 89
  square cyclic 89
  vector 209, 231–237, 260, 282
  zig-zag cyclic 183
DIT, see decimation in time
div operator 9
DLT, see discrete Legendre transform
DNA 62, 191, 229, 341

domain view 245, 246
dominant edge 294–296, 310, 312, 315, 351
dot product, see inner product
double-precision arithmetic 25
DRMA, see direct remote memory access
DWT, see discrete wavelet transform
dynamic programming 62, 175, 346

edge 234–236, 279–280, 292
  cut 279
  dead 298–300
  directed 236
  dominant 294–296, 310, 312, 315, 351
  external 306, 315, 325
  internal 306, 315, 325, 342
  parallel 235
  undirected 221, 236
edge covering 348
edge cut 318, 322
edge partitioning 305, 324, 352
efficiency 55, 170, 173, 207, 242
efficient computation 44
eigensystem 128, 191, 192, 202, 276, 280
elapsed time 15
encryption 70
energy consumption 20, 33, 67, 293, 317, 349
enumeration 288
Eratosthenes 72–73
EREW PRAM 57, 68
error handling ix, 19, 104
error, roundoff 156
Euclidean norm 128
even–odd sort 140
exact algorithm 287
external edge 306, 315, 325

fanin 205
  global 259
  local 259
fanout 205, 260
  global 259
  local 259
FFT, see Fourier, transform, fast
FFTW 160, 174–175, 177, 180, 181
fill-in 192

fine-grain model 225, 228, 281, 282
finite differences 245
flop 3, 96, 98, 155, 196
'for all'-statement 194
forest 286
Fortran 13, 63, 132, 276
Four-Russians method 125
four-step framework 178
Fourier
  coefficient 134, 135, 181
  matrix 136, 139, 147, 176
  series 134, 135
  transform
    continuous 174
    differentiation by 181
    discrete 135, 138, 174, 182
    fast vii, viii, xiii, 134–189
    inverse fast 151, 158, 181
    radix-2 fast 174, 180
    radix-4 fast 174, 180
    real 174, 182–184
    three-dimensional 182
    two-dimensional 174, 181–182
    unordered fast 146, 156
  transform, continuous 174
free nonzeros 244

g (communication cost) 5–6, 25
  optimistic value of 70, 118, 159, 172
  pessimistic value of 70, 118, 120, 159, 172
gain of a vertex move 223–224
gap 5
gap-to-optimality 348
Gauss–Jordan elimination 121
Gaussian elimination 75, 275
Gaussian function 181
gcc compiler 20, 185, 271, 273, 342
geometric mean 189, 229–230, 356
get 11, 66, 204
Gflop 7
ghost vertices, see halo
Giraph 2, 318
global view 21, 217, 231, 242
GMRES 276, 278
GNU General Public License ix, x
Goldbach conjecture 73

goto-statement 64
GPU v, 36, 66, 256
graph
    bipartite 292, 293, 347–349,
        358
    directed 236
    directed acyclic viii, 63, 121
    edge-weighted 292
    undirected 221, 234–236, 279
graph colouring 280, 281
graph Laplacian 245
graph matching vii, 291–358
Graph500 349
GraphBLAS 349–351
graphics processing unit, *see* GPU
greedy matching 296, 346,
        347, 351
Green500 67
grid 179–180, 244–255, 269, 278,
        284, 287
Gustavson's data structure 201

h-relation 4–6, 8, 26, 90, 257
    balanced 90, 91, 241
    full 5, 25, 90
halo 287, 305–306, 319, 325
halo edge 306, 325
Harwell–Boeing collection 199,
        237, 276–277
header overhead 118
heapsort 67
heat equation 190, 244
heuristic algorithm 294
heuristic method 218
high-performance primitives 14,
        17, 46, 66, 132
high-precision arithmetic 187
HITS algorithm 194, 203
hMetis 281
Householder reflection 128, 130
Householder tridiagonalization
        120, 128–130
HPCG benchmark 279, 285, 293
HPL benchmark 36, 67, 96,
        98–99, 117, 120, 279
hub 194
Hubble Space Telescope 134
hybrid architecture 8, 58, 66, 256
hybrid-BSP vi, x, 58, 69, 256–261,
        290
    algorithm 256
    computer 256
    cost 257

hypercube 57, 119, 176, 278
hyperedge 221
hypergraph 221–223, 225–226,
        282, 283, 288, 324
    directed 283
    fine-grain 288
    partitioning 225, 280–282, 287
hypersparse matrix 350
hyperthreading 15

I/O 15, 63
identity matrix 74, 226, 227,
        245, 319
identity permutation 80
image
    compression 186
    processing 184
    reconstruction 134, 174, 201
imbalance
    of communication 90, 213
    of computation 90, 216–219,
        239
    parameter 216–217, 219
        for hybrid-BSP 260
incidence matrix 288, 350, 351
increment 199, 261
independent set 352
index set 203–205
indirect addressing 200
inefficiency 170
initial partitioning 223, 224, 280
inner product 9–12, 202,
        223, 285
internal edge 306, 315, 325, 342
invariant 40, 76
inverse FFT 151, 158, 181
invertible matrix 74
irregular algorithm viii, 3, 46,
        159, 348
Ising model 244
isoefficiency 176
iterative refinement 228
iterative solution method 192,
        202, 232, 276, 278, 284

jagged diagonal storage
        (JDS) 200–201
Java 13

KaHyPar 281–282
kernelization 352
Kernighan–Lin
        algorithm 223–224

boundary 224, 280
Kronecker product 140, 141,
        174, 176
    property of 141, 175
Krylov subspace 276

l (synchronization cost) 5, 7, 25
Lanczos method 192
Laplacian matrix 244–255, 260,
        269, 271, 280
Laplacian operator 211, 244–245,
        278, 284, 287
large-integer multiplication 188
latency 5
lattice 248, 249
    body-centred cubic 253
least-squares fit 26, 27, 33, 35, 36
Legendre transform 179
linear programming 278
linear system 74, 75, 192, 202,
        275–276, 278
linked list 201
    two-dimensional 201
LINPACK 66, 67
Lisp 175
list, circular 326
load balancing 206, 207, 213, 223,
        316–318, 344
local domination algorithm 296,
        298, 299, 305, 306
local preference 315–316, 342,
        345, 346
local view 21, 220, 221
local-bound heuristic 234
LogP model 57, 177
loop invariant 40, 76
LU decomposition vii, viii, 36,
        74–133, 202, 212
    high-performance xii
    sparse 192, 201, 275, 293
Luby's algorithm 353
LZ77 71–72

machine learning viii, 74, 213
Manhattan distance 248
matching 292
    cardinality 292
    greedy 296, 346, 347, 351
    maximal 292, 294, 350
    maximum 292, 294, 295, 346
    stable 347
MATLAB 77, 276
matrix

adjacency 319
banded 119, 284
binary 319, 341
bit-reversal 143
block-diagonal 129, 186
block-tridiagonal 245
boolean 124
butterfly 141, 147, 157
dense 84, 190, 212–215, 240, 242
diagonal 128, 276
diagonally dominant 285
Fourier 136, 139, 147, 176
hypersparse 350
identity 74, 226, 227, 245, 319
incidence 288, 350, 351
invertible 74
Laplacian 244–255, 260, 269, 271, 280
lower triangular 74, 123, 130
nonsingular 74
orthogonal 128, 187, 276
pentadiagonal 245
permutation 78–79, 140, 143, 175, 200
positive definite 123, 285
random sparse 237–244, 269, 278, 285
sparse 84, 139, 141, 187, 190–290
stochastic 191
symmetric 123, 128, 220
tall-and-skinny 97, 100, 101, 104, 115, 284
tridiagonal 128, 211, 284
twiddle 175
unit lower triangular 74
unstructured sparse 237, 278
unsymmetric 191
upper triangular 74
matrix allocation 360
matrix density 190, 196, 207, 237, 240, 242
Matrix Market 198, 277
matrix update 84
matrix view 245
matrix–matrix multiplication 97, 98, 101, 123–124, 126
boolean 124–125
sparse 284
Strassen 125–128
three-dimensional 122–124

traditional 126–127
two-dimensional 122, 123
matrix–vector multiplication 136
dense 212, 213, 277, 283
hybrid sparse 257–261
sparse vii, viii, 190–290, 293, 319–321, 324
node-aware 258
matrix-free storage 201, 246
matrix/vector notation 77
maximal independent
set 352–353
maximal matching 292, 294, 350
maximal set 286
maximum matching 292, 294, 295, 346
medium-grain method 225–228, 282
memory
allocation 359, 360
deallocation 359, 360
overflow 360
use 156–158
mergesort 41, 43, 49, 56, 67
message count 208–209
message net 283
message passing 3, 11, 46, 62–64, 121
bulk synchronous 46, 262, 326, 363
message payload, see payload
message tag, see tag
Message-Passing Interface, see MPI
Metropolis algorithm 289
mod operator 9
mod-m sort 175
molecular dynamics 194, 278, 286–287
quantum xiii, 179, 180
Mondriaan
distribution 215–224, 228
partitioner x, 217, 220, 244, 270, 282, 320, 341
MondriaanOpt 282, 287
Monte Carlo simulation 237
MPI x, 1, 2, 63–66, 120, 121, 167, 168, 175, 180, 290, 349
taming 168
MPI+X v, 66
MPI-2 x, 60, 63, 66
MPI-3 x, 2, 60–61, 65, 114, 349
MPI_Alltoallv 64, 167

MPI_Bcast 64
MPI_COMM_WORLD 64
MPI_Recv 64
MPI_Send 64
MPIedupack 65
multi-BSP model vi, 2, 58
multicast 101
multicore revolution v
MulticoreBSP
for C vi, x, 2, 13–14, 33, 34, 36, 53, 59, 167, 177, 271
for Java 13
multilevel method 222, 224, 279–282, 293

n-queens puzzle 353–354
need-to-know principle 83–84, 130
nested dissection 275, 282
net 221
cut 222
neural network
artificial viii, 215, 351
Newton–Raphson method 189
nondeterminism 314, 316
nonsingular matrix 74
nonzero-based partitioning 283
norm 128
normalized cost 170–171, 239–240, 289
noticeboard 264
number-theoretic
transform 185–186
Nyquist frequency 181

one-sided communication 2, 11, 60–61, 63, 307
OpenMP 1, 66, 175
OpenMPI 273
orthogonal matrix 128, 187, 276
orthogonal recursive
bisection 219
overflow of memory 360
overhead 96, 169, 171, 217, 260, 262, 271–273
overlap of computation and
communication 17
Oxford BSP toolset vi, 2, 13, 20, 59, 66

p (number of processors) 6
packet 160
packing 159, 264

padding with zeros 188
Paderborn University BSP
	library 2, 9, 60
PageRank 192–194, 201, 281
parallel computer 1
	solar-powered 275
parallel depth 344
parallel prefix 69
parallel programming v, ix, x, 1
parallel random access machine,
	see PRAM model
parallelizing compiler 201
partial differential equation
	278
partial row pivoting 79,
	99, 100
partitioning 202, 215, 218,
	279–283
	conformal 283
	edge 305, 324, 352
	geometric 286
	graph 279, 280
	nonzero-based 283
	p-way 215, 216, 218–220
	symmetric 220
	vertex 305, 319, 341, 352
path 235–236
path-growing algorithm (PGA),
	346–347
PaToH 228, 281, 283
payload 47–48, 263
peer-to-peer file sharing 91
pentadiagonal matrix 245
perfect shuffle 176
performance profile 230
periodic boundaries 286
periodic function 134, 135, 181
permutation matrix 78–79, 140,
	143, 175, 200
Pflop 36
PGAS 62, 121
π, decimals of 187, 189
piecewise 134
pivot 80, 84, 92, 99, 103, 104,
	201, 275, 293
pivoting
	partial row 79, 99, 100
	tournament 99–100, 121, 122
pivots, independent 293
pixel 135
plan for computation 174–175
pointer arithmetic 263
polymer 191

portability 83
	layer 1–2
	of algorithms 3
POSIX threads 66, 175
postcondition 76
power method 191
power-law network 324
PRAM model 57, 68
precondition 76
preconditioner 276
prediction 7, 55–56, 115, 118,
	171–172
	ab initio 56
Pregel 2, 318
prime 72, 73
primes, twin 72
privacy 348
processor
	column 83, 208
	row 83, 208
	view 220
proposal 297, 306, 307,
	315, 347
	mutual 311
protein 341
Pthreads 66, 175
put 11, 66, 204, 205
PVM 63
Python 61

QR decomposition 120
quantum molecular dynamics xiii,
	179, 180
queue 48, 61, 300, 326, 347
quicksort 38–41, 53–55, 67,
	302, 303

r (computing rate) 6, 25
radix sort 262
radix-2 FFT 174, 180
radix-4 FFT 174, 180
radix-m splitting 175
random number
	generator 237–238,
		240, 255
	pseudo- 237, 238
	quantum 237
random sparse matrix 237–244,
	269, 278, 285
RDMA, see direct remote memory
	access
recursion tree 139
recursive

computation 126–127,
	136–139, 179, 218
	level of 126, 219
	doubling 120
	function 38
recursive bisection, see
	bipartitioning, recursive
redistribution 149, 151–154,
	159, 177
reduction operation 120
redundant computation 12, 41,
	44, 85, 89
registration 18–19, 101, 103, 157
	of a two-dimensional array
		101
regular algorithm 159, 160
ReLU function 214
repartitioning 281
reproducibility 34, 167, 344
residual 276
ring 185
RMA, see direct remote memory
	access
road network 229, 271
root of unity 136
	primitive 185
round-robin distribution, see
	distribution, cyclic
roundoff error 156
row-net model 222, 225, 226, 281
RSA 188
Rutherford–Boeing collection
	199, 237, 277

sampled storage 201
samplesort 38, 40–46, 49–56, 68,
	70–71
SBD 242
scalability
	strong 54, 55
	weak 55
scalable memory use 46,
	156–158, 262
ScaLAPACK 63, 120–121
Schrödinger equation,
	time-dependent 179
self-avoiding walk 354–356
self-edge 292, 341
semiring 349–351
separated block diagonal 242
separation of concerns 7, 17,
	261, 275
serialization 311–314

shared memory 113, 167
SHMEM 58
shuffle, perfect 176
sieve of Eratosthenes 72–73
simple graph 235, 292, 355
simulated annealing 289–290
sine transform, fast 174
single program multiple data, *see* SPMD
singular value decomposition 276
six-step framework 178
slowdown 55
smooth function 134, 181
SMP 36
social network 291, 349, 356, 357
  of dolphins 319, 357
sorting vii, 38–56, 261–262
  by counting 300
  partial 300, 303, 305, 343, 349, 351
  stable 261
sparse matrix 190–290
sparse matrix algorithm 195, 196, 198
spectral transform 179
speedup 53–55, 170, 173, 273, 275
  superlinear 54, 273, 289, 354
Spiral 175–177
splitter 38–40, 300–303
SPMD 10, 14–15, 21, 62, 157, 363
SpMSpV 349
SpMV 192, *see also* matrix—vector multiplication, sparse
stable marriage problem 291, 347
stable matching 347
stable roommate problem 347
stable sorting 261
stack 19, 300, 347
startup cost 26, 59, 63, 280
Strassen matrix—matrix multiplication 125–128
stride 10, 77, 101, 178
strip 246–247
strong scalability 54, 55

subtractive cancellation 128
SuiteSparse library 351
SuiteSparse Matrix Collection 191, 198, 228, 269, 277, 282, 287, 341
suitor 298–299, 326, 347, 348
Summit 67, 279, 293
supercomputer vi, 35, 67, 255, 275
superlinear speedup 54, 273, 289, 354
superstep vi, xiii, 3, 15
  communication 3, 87, 307
  computation 3, 87, 307
  global 257
  local 257
  mixed 3, 102, 307
  program 15, 16
surface-to-volume ratio 247, 252
symmetric multiprocessor 36
Sync-statement 307, 311
synchronization 3–4
  bulk 3
  global vi
  pairwise 3
  subset 9, 60
  zero-cost 60
synchronization-avoiding algorithm 98–100, 102

tag 47–49, 263
tall-and-skinny matrix 97, 100, 101, 104, 115, 284
Templates 200, 276
tensor 350
tensor product 140
Tflop 117
think like a vertex 318
thread 8, 60, 61, 66, 290
tie-breaking 41, 45–46, 250, 253, 283, 296, 302, 312, 314–316, 342, 345
tomography 134, 201, 286
TOP500 36, 67, 96, 117, 179, 279, 293
total exchange 64
tournament pivoting 99–100, 121, 122

transpose algorithm 177, 178
transposition 9, 128, 132, 136, 178
trapezoidal rule 135, 181
tree 288
triangle counting 356–357
triangular system 75, 80, 96, 130–131
tridiagonal matrix 128, 211, 284
triple scheme 198
truncated octahedron 253, 287
twiddle matrix 175
two-sided communication 307

UFFT 146, 158
uncoarsening 223, 224, 280
unordered FFT 146, 158
unpacking 159, 160
UPC 62

variability 34
vector addition, sparse 196–197
vector allocation 360
vectorization 33
vertex 121, 221–224, 234–236, 279–280, 292
  adjacent 224
  degree 235–236, 245
  think like a 318
vertex partitioning 305, 319, 341, 352
  p-way 305
video compression 186
volume, *see* communication volume
volume net 283
Voronoi cell 250, 253
voxel 135, 201, 286

wall-clock time 15
wavefront 130
wavelet 186–187
  Daubechies 186
weak scalability 55
weather prediction 179
web search 192
weight
  of an edge 292
  trigonometric 148, 155–158
World Wide Web 192, 201, 291